A STUDY OF ORGANIZATIONAL LEADERSHIP

A STUDY OF ORGANIZATIONAL LEADERSHIP

**Edited by
the Associates,
Office of
Military Leadership,
United States Military Academy**

Stackpole Books

A STUDY OF ORGANIZATIONAL LEADERSHIP

Copyright © 1976 by the Associates,
Office of Military Leadership, United States Military Academy

Published by
STACKPOLE BOOKS
Cameron and Kelker Streets
P.O. Box 1831
Harrisburg, Pa. 17105

Printed in the U.S.A.

Library of Congress Cataloging in Publication Data
Main entry under title:

A Study of organizational leadership.

Includes bibliographical references and index.
1. Leadership. 2. Sociology, Military. I. United States Military Academy, West Point. Office of Military Leadership.
UB210.S75   301.15'5   76-25242
ISBN 0-8117-2059-4

Contents

Applications

Part III—The Individual as Leader

Leader Behavior

Leader Style

Applications

Part IV—Transactions

Communications—Organizational and Interpersonal

Civil–Military Relations

The Military: A Professional Organization

The Professional Military Ethic: A Rationale

Index

Preface

A Study of Organizational Leadership is the product of the faculty of the Office of Military Leadership past and present. It represents a continuing effort to synthesize and organize a field that has roots in many disciplines and strong moral and emotional overtones. Many officers drawing upon a wide range of leadership experiences and on studies at a number of graduate schools have contributed to this evolving course of study. Constant revision has led to the development of a text that weaves the relevant theories and concepts into a coherent unit. The text is organized in support of a pedagogical model; a model that prescribes viewing the leadership process from the perspective of the individual, both as group member and leader, that focuses attention on the requirements and constraints of the group and the organization, and that insures consideration of situational factors. It is important to note that this study is focused on organizational leadership as opposed to the broad, imprecise web of ideas related to leadership in general

Effective leaders in civil, governmental, and military organizations are the product of selection and development. Leadership development is a multifaceted, long term process and includes: (1) the acquisition of the resources for effective leadership—knowledge, skills, a professional orientation, and (2) the improvement of leadership performance through practice, evaluation and feedback. The course that this text was designed to support is part of a developmental program for military leaders; it is a capstone course providing a degree of sophistication in terminology, heightened awareness of the issues and improved understanding of the crucial factors involved in the influence act—it is a course that draws on the student's leadership experience

11

and builds a base for continued development. In spite of its military orientation, this study of organizational leadership is totally relevant to students in many fields.

It is presumed that a student entering this course has an understanding of the language of basic psychology; in addition, some acquaintance with sociology, social psychology and organizational behavior will enhance an appreciation of the factors involved in individual and group behavior.

This text is intended as source material and as a stimulant to classroom discussion. When readings are combined with student involvement in a thoughtful exchange of ideas and experiences, the end result will be a more thorough understanding of leadership in formal organizations.

HARRY A. BUCKLEY, PhD
Colonel, Infantry
United States Military Academy

An Organizational Approach to the Study of Leadership

by .
*Paul M. Bons**

An approach to the study of leadership that focuses directly on the require-ments of the undergraduate student of military science is long overdue. In many ways these students face a unique set of leadership problems. As with other students who anticipate entry into formal and highly structured organiza-tions, they must learn those special aspects of the leadership process that sur-face when leadership begins by fiat rather than by group choice. In addition, however, students of military science face a leadership situation where the di-vision of subordinate loyalties between the organization and outside indi-viduals and agencies can impact heavily on organizational effectiveness and where the complex interface with society strongly influences the manner in which leadership is exercised. Because this unique combination of problems is not covered adequately by any single approach to leadership, military science students are forced into a hit-or-miss review of existing literature that often leaves them with more questions than answers.

It is the purpose of this introductory section to set the stage for the study of leadership in such a way as to help meet the need cited above. To accom-plish this, first of all a brief historical examination of the major approaches to the study of leadership will be presented. Upon this foundation will be based a

*Paul M. Bons, (Lieutenant Colonel, U.S. Army) is on the faculty of the Office of Military Leadership at the United States Military Academy, West Point, New York. He received his BS from the United States Military Academy (1958), his MA in Psychology (Social) from Wayne State University (1967), and his PhD in Social Psychology (Organi-zational Research) from the University of Washington (1974). He is also a graduate of the US Army Command and General Staff College (1972).

functional definition of leadership with emphasis on its organizational context. Finally, a model of organizational leadership will be presented. The purpose of this model is to act as a conceptual guide to the student of military science as he or she begins to study the subject of leadership.

Prior to beginning this historical perspective, however, it is important to note that the study of leadership has developed considerably over the past few years. Not quite two decades ago, Browne and Cohn (1958) felt compelled to conclude that although mankind had long recognized the significance of leadership as an essential aspect of human activity and that great masses of literature had been assembled, leadership literature could be classified as "a mass of content without any coagulating substance to bring it together or to produce coordination and point out interrelations." (p. iii)

In the time since this rather discouraging conclusion, the scientific process has led to much refinement of theory and has caused the body of knowledge about the leadership process to take many giant strides forward. Unfortunately, we have not yet reached the point where we can cite a single, generally acceptable "theory of leadership." Nor are we likely to be able to do so in the near future. Nevertheless, we are at a point of academic sophistication where certain concepts and theories of leadership taken together are beginning to bear fruit in terms of understanding and usefulness to the practitioner.

AN HISTORICAL PERSPECTIVE TO THE STUDY OF LEADERSHIP

A question that students of leadership often ask is: "How can we best understand the leadership process and thereby make better leaders of ourselves and others?" Not long ago by historical standards, this question would have been considered quite presumptuous. It was reasoned at that time that if leadership had not been predisposed by deity or by blood line, there was no need for one to concern himself with such thoughts. This approach, spawned by the traditional view of society and perpetuated by the feudal system, found its way into government, the military, the economics of family business, and most other aspects of human social existence. Even after these conclusions began to be questioned and people began to aspire to positions of leadership by their own talents, the study of leadership through analyzing the lives and actions of historically great leaders persisted. One need only look at the earliest photographs and paintings of aspiring military leaders to note the resemblance in gesture, posture and decorum to the military heros of an earlier day.

As late as 1841, Carlyle formally proposed the theory that "great men" with dynamic and charismatic qualities shaped the events of history. This thesis was accepted for many years in lay circles and had a strong impact on the initial academic study of leadership. Some systematic observation of leaders, mixed with a great deal of intuitive feeling on the part of lay persons and practitioners in the field of leadership generated lists of characteristics, special talents, traits and interpersonal skills which seemed to characterize a person as a "leader." After the fashion of the earlier "great man" theory, it

was felt that if such characteristics could be clearly isolated, adopted and practiced, individuals could be developed into leaders in multiple, if not all situations. This *trait approach* to the study of leadership dominated the literature
during the early formal study of leadership.

The events of World War II were instrumental in bringing the trait approach into academic focus. Several attempts were made to determine the
validity of such an approach to the study of leadership. Stogdill (1948), for
instance, conducted an exhaustive review of the academic literature from the
turn of the century to that date in an effort to determine if there was any
substance to the trait approach. His review almost put an end to the serious
study of trait theory when he was forced to conclude that there was no evidence of a single trait or characteristic that identified a person as a leader.
Furthermore, he could find no constellation of traits which could be used to
describe the leader in all situations. Many possible explanations were proposed
for this finding. Personality theorists, for example, continue to point out that
we do not yet have adequate measures of leadership and personality traits.
However, by far the most accepted explanation for the failure to identify
universal traits is simply that there are no such traits.

One problem with the trait approach stems from the way in which it came
into being. It is easy for persons to recall leaders they have known who do have
specific traits. It is just as easy to recall non-leaders who do not. However,
these same persons tend to ignore or make excuses for the leaders they have
known who seem to *lack* some or most of the "leadership traits" as well as for
the non-leaders who appear to possess many of the same traits. .

In a more recent effort, Stogdill (1974) reviewed an additional 163 studies
of leadership characteristics. He analyzed studies that differentiated leaders
from followers, effective leaders from ineffective leaders, and higher-echelon
from lower-echelon leaders. He concluded the following:

"The leader is characterized by a strong desire for responsibility and task
completion, vigor and persistence in pursuit of goals, venturesomeness and
originality in problem solving, drive to exercise initiative in social situations, self-confidence and a sense of personal identity, willingness to
accept consequences for decision and action, readiness to absorb interpersonal stress, willingness to tolerate frustration and delay, ability to influence other persons' behavior, and capacity to structure social interaction systems to the purpose at hand." (p. 81)

Stogdill is careful to point out, however, that this new "list" does not
constitute a return to the trait approach. He merely sees it as a "sensible
moderation of the extreme situationist point of view" (p. 82)—a view which
tends to ignore the impact of the leader altogether.

He also notes, however, the apparent absence in the literature of trait
studies with negative results. Perhaps this is due to the fact that the trait approach, no longer a serious avenue of study among leadership theorists, would

not be of sufficient interest among theorists to generate any serious effort to dispute its existence.

The major problem with the trait approach, however, is not the existence or absence of lists of admirable traits, but rather the answer to the question: "What can be done with them even if they could be verified?" As Fiedler (1967) points out, it takes several years of intensive psychotherapy to change the personality (traits) of a person. If this is true, how can a knowledge about traits alone be useful to us in developing effective leaders? Certainly, the drill of memorizing lists of traits does not appear to produce more effective leaders.

Suffice it to conclude that it would probably be an improved society if all people could acquire the traits usually attributed to the leader. However, to attempt to study leadership and, further, to develop leadership ability through the study of traits is perhaps not very fruitful at our present level of understanding.

As an historical counterpoint to Carlyle, in the late 1800s Marx and Engles proposed that it is not dynamic and charismatic persons who turn the course of history, rather, it is history which thrusts certain people into power. Max Weber (1947) proposed in the early 1900s an impersonal, bureaucratic type of leadership—not leadership by attribute, characteristic or loyalty to a particular leader, but, leadership by legal authority based on established rule. The implication of this philosophy for the study of leadership is that leaders may be viewed as changeable parts within the organizational structure without regard to personal characteristics (except necessary expertise). Such a philosophy is perhaps the historical forerunner of the *situationist approach* to the study of leadership. In essence, this approach asserts that aspects of the situation determine the effectiveness of leaders and the organizations which they lead.

There does appear in the literature considerable evidence to support the hypothesis that groups tend not only to accept, but demand leaders who exhibit abilities and characteristics that lend themselves to the accomplishment of group purposes and goals (Korten, 1968; Stogdill, 1974). Further, it is generally known that given the opportunity, groups will discard leaders who do not fulfill their expectations (Hamblin, 1958). However, more contemporary situationists are presently looking at such unique aspects of the situation as leadership climate (House and Rizzo, 1972), communications processes (Leavitt, 1951), situational uncertainty and ambiguity (Lawrence and Lorsch, 1969), conflict and control (Taylor and Bowers, 1970), and social exchange (Jacobs, 1971). Like trait theory, the purely situationist approach has not produced a generally accepted theory of leadership. One must conclude, however, that situational factors must be taken into consideration in the study of the leadership process.

Notwithstanding the apparent demise of trait theory, there are currently those in the academic field who concern themselves with the observation probably best expressed by Fiedler (1963): "And yet, we know of men who consistently manage to build up ineffective groups and sick organizations, while there are others 'who could not lead a troop of hungry girl scouts to a hamburger stand'. . . . Unless we close our eyes to these cases, we are forced to the conclusion—long held by laymen—that there must be some abilities or personal attributes which distinguish good leaders from bad ones."

These theorists conclude that perhaps it is not sufficient to consider either the leader *or* the situation in isolation—that only by taking into consideration the interaction between the two can we really understand the true nature of leader effectiveness. In summary, their argument is as follows: If we can identify leaders who are effective in *all* situations then we must seriously consider the trait approach to leadership. However, this has clearly not been the case. On the other hand, if any person can be an effective leader in a given situation, then we must consider the situationist approach more seriously. This has also received little support. Therefore, they conclude, it is more reasonable to assert that some leaders are effective in some situations and less so in others.

This *interactionist* view of the leadership process is the most current (and perhaps most productive) approach to the study of leadership—one which presently has the attention of several major theorists in the leadership area (Fiedler, 1967; Fiedler and Chemers, 1974; Kerr, Schriesheim, Murphy and Stogdill, 1974; Evans, 1970; House, 1971). The chapters to follow will consider both the situationist and interactionist point of view in some detail. It will be left up to the student to judge the merits and usefulness of each approach.

LEADERSHIP DEFINED

Much confusion in the study of leadership is generated by the multiplicity of definitions. Stogdill (1974) in his massive review of the leadership literature devotes ten pages to categorizing the various definitions of leadership. Among others he includes categories which focus on the group process, the personality or behavior of the leader, the exercise of influence and power, the attainment of group goals, the differentiation of roles, and the effects of interaction. Because each definition is defensible when viewed in the context in which its author presents it, it is difficult to justify a preference for a certain definition. Conversely, to present a definition of leadership that will satisfy all those who study the subject of leadership is equally as presumptuous.

However, when considering the unique purpose of this chapter—the presentation of an approach for studying leadership in an organizational context—it appears that the category most adequately conveying this purpose is that of considering leadership as an influence process. As Stogdill (1974) points out, influence implies a reciprocal relationship between the leader and his followers. At the same time, however, it also leaves room for influence of significant others with whom the leader must concern himself, e.g., peers and seniors. As will be explained later in greater detail, such influence processes are essential to the functioning of leadership within organizations.

In its simplest form, leadership may be defined as the process of influencing human behavior. However, this simplistic definition does not appear to be sufficient to express the true function of the leader within an organizational context. Organizations, in their most basic sense are goal-oriented and purposeful. It would seem, therefore, that in an organizational context an appropriate definition might be: the process of influencing human behavior so as to accomplish the goals of the organization. From our point of view, however, this puts the leader in the position of merely transmitting goals and ensuring fulfillment of the desires of his seniors (representing the organization). Although such a definition may be adequate for most organizations, it is felt that in the military organization, where the goals may involve destruction of life and property on a broad scale, the relegation of the leader at any level to a function of goal transmission and accomplishment may not be totally appropriate. Consequently, we would prefer to include the element of ultimate responsibility for actions as an integral part of the definition. Accordingly, we shall define organizational leadership as:

> The process of influencing human behavior so as to accomplish the goals prescribed by the organizationally appointed leader.[1]

Perhaps some amplification of this definition is needed to more clearly express the concept intended. Katz and Kahn (1966) have indicated that the essence of organizational leadership is the "influential increment over and above mechanical compliance with routine directives of the organization." This is best illustrated in Figure 1.

Given that the larger organization has certain demands of productivity, it is generally found that the goals of the organization can be expressed in terms of an optimum performance criteria, bracketed by a minimum and sometimes a maximum acceptable performance level. That is, although the organization sets certain optimum goals which it expects its members to meet, it also sets a minimum acceptable level of performance below which it cannot operate. At the same time, too much "efficiency" might also be counter-productive and therefore an upper limit to performance might be in order (e.g., if the section in charge of producing automobile left front fenders over-produces, this can be just as inefficient to the organization as too few fenders). In some organizations this maximum performance level may be open-ended or even undefined (think-tanks, etc).

Given this demand level of the organization, however, the individual subordinate is willing to accomplish a portion of the goal by virtue of his being a member of the organization and society in general. (see "a," Fig. 1) The amount of this goal that the individual is willing to accomplish, of course, varies with the individual.

Certain subordinates will accomplish the demands of the organization *without* influence. In this case, no leadership is required. However, when individuals will not on their own accomplish tasks of which they are aware, it becomes a function of the leader to influence them in such a way so as to achieve task accomplishment—that is, to close the gap (see "b," Fig. 1). If the leader is successful, he is said to be an efficient leader; if not, then he is ineffective.

Another implication of this model, however, is that the leader may also

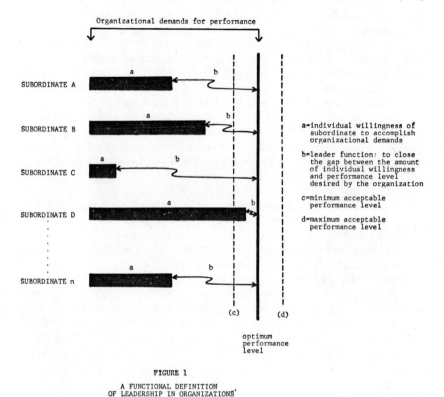

FIGURE 1

A FUNCTIONAL DEFINITION
OF LEADERSHIP IN ORGANIZATIONS'

close the gap between organizational demands and individual willingness by convincing the organization (his seniors) that its demands may not be reasonably accomplished (thereby causing the demands to be reduced). Herein lies an equally viable process of influence—albeit, one with certain organizational risks. Halpin (1954) described this dual responsibility of the leader as the "dilemma of leadership"—meeting the demands of both the organization and subordinates (mission and men). Organizationally, the resolution of this dilemma becomes a most critical part of the leadership process. It is the leader's responsibility to resolve the dilemma so that both the organization and the subordinates receive the optimum benefit.

The functional model presented in Figure 1 also presents another aspect of the definition of leadership—one which is often ignored when considering the problems of the leader. As previously indicated, the level of willingness to meet the organization's demands varies from subordinate to subordinate (see subordinate "A" thru "n," Fig. 1). Consequently, it is apparent that a specific influence attempt cannot be viewed as generally applicable. Rather, it must be considered as one that takes the variation of subordinate willingness into account. That is, the leader's influence attempts must be tailored to account for the individual willingness of each subordinate to meet the demands of the organization (know your men).

The reader is cautioned that other terms used in the military (and to a lesser extent in other organizations) sometimes become used almost interchangeably with the concept of leadership. Although such terms as management and command have specific connotations and are uniquely defined in the Army Dictionary (AR310-25), we often find them used indiscriminately in conversations concerning the topic of leadership. Perhaps the best analysis of the distinction between these terms is contained in a paper by Colonel H. A. Buckley (PhD), Director, Office of Military Leadership, West Point, New York and Major Norman Grunstad (PhD) (TRADOC Leadership Conference, 1974):

> "The business of influencing men to accomplish a mission almost invariably involves the application of a wide range of skills, and that certainly includes the managerial skills—planning, organizing, coordinating, directing, and controlling resources of all kinds. It generally requires the use of authority and an acceptance of responsibility and that is commandership. It seems to me that to teach leadership as if the ability to influence was derived entirely from good interpersonal communications or empathy or an understanding of human and organizational behavior is deceptive. An effective leader must be an effective manager and in military situations he must deal with a fact that he is an organizationally imposed leader, a commander, with authority and direction externally derived." (p. 26).

By this argument, therefore, the definitions of managership and commandership may be subsumed under the general classification of military leadership.

A working definition is critical to the development of any model of leadership. It is felt that the definition described herein (with its qualifications) can now permit us to move on to the development of an organizational approach to the study of leadership.

A MODEL OF ORGANIZATIONAL LEADERSHIP

To guide us in the study of leadership it is sometimes helpful to visualize relationships by means of a diagram or model. Such a model should adequately describe the essential elements and relationships peculiar to the particular context in which the leadership process is taking place. The military organization is by no means unique in its structure. It involves such familiar aspects of a hierarchial relationship as lines-of-responsibility, span-of-control for leaders, homogeneity of tasks within subgroups, and the delegation of authority. Furthermore, communications (both formal and informal) travel up, down and laterally across the organization. To attempt to include all of these organizational elements, however, would generate a model of extreme complexity. As with any model, therefore, its builders must make a determination of which attributes of the real-world situation they want to include and which they choose to ignore for the sake of clarity and understanding. A model of a ship, for instance, may not need to float in order to describe the real ship in the way the model builder would like us to see it. And, even if it does float, the propulsion system would probably not be identical to that of the real ship. The inconsistencies could go on and on. Perhaps the best criterion for a model's usefulness is not its completeness, but the extent to which the authors and the reader can jointly "hang" all parts of the real world on it—a goodness of fit, so to speak. The Model of Organizational Leadership shown in Figure 2 is designed to do just that.

Leaders at all levels of military organizations are influenced in their behavior and actions by many aspects of the organizational environment—both within the organization and from the outside. It is our primary intent by using

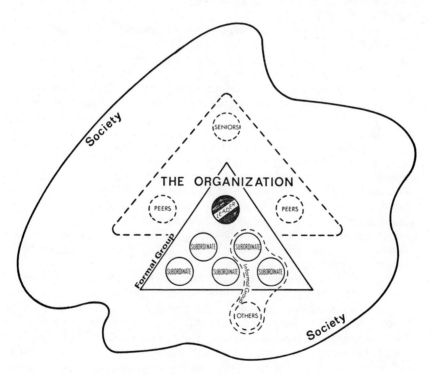

A Model Of Organizational Leadership

Figure 2

this model to show these relationships, and clearly indicate their impact on the leadership process at any level. In order to accomplish this, the primary focus of the model must be on the LEADER within the organization being led. The leader must be able to locate him or herself within the organizational framework and clearly see relationships with significant others, both within and outside the organization. Organizational leadership, of course, implies a position-oriented, linking function for the leader. That is, the leader in effect serves as a link for communications between his subordinates and those higher in the organization (Likert, 1967). This unique position of the leader emphasizes potential sources of conflict which are implicit in the "dilemma of leadership" previously discussed. At the same time, however, this linking function implies a need to associate with, coordinate with, and be influenced by individuals and formal groups adjacent to the leader's own work group.

Of course, the leader cannot be examined without simultaneously focusing attention on the FORMAL GROUP being led. These are the individuals which form the work group for which the leader has ultimate organizational responsibility. The model must clearly show that the interaction between the leader and these individual subordinates demands consideration of their individual differences.[2]

Also depicted by the model must be those aspects of the leadership situation which directly impact upon the influence process between leader and subordinates. Certainly, such inter-organizational relationships as those with SENIORS at all levels in the hierarchy as well as with PEERS within the organization have a significant impact on the leader's ability to influence his subordinates. As previously mentioned, the leader may spend a good deal of his available time attempting to influence these elements of the organization for the good of his own group.

Additionally, extra-organizational persons and groups are of great concern to the leader. These are represented in the model as OTHERS. They are persons over whom the leader has little or no control, yet whose associations with subordinates in the form of INFORMAL GROUPS (and sometimes formal groups) may have a significant impact on the leadership process. Included herein are such people as the subordinate's family, his friends, and political, religious, cultural and social affiliations. At a minimum, such affiliations can cause subordinates to share loyalties and allegiances which the leader might believe belong to the formal group.

Another extra-organizational influence which the military leader must consider is the SOCIETY itself. In this model, an amorphous society is depicted with ubiquitous, constantly changing and sometimes fickle characteristics. Yet, within this society, and constitutionally designed to be responsive to it, is a formal and relatively inflexible military ORGANIZATION. The problem presented here is that at one point in time the society in general might hold the military hierarchy in lowest esteem for participating in an "undesirable" armed conflict. Shortly after, however, this same society might classify the same military hierarchy among its most respected citizenry (reference: Rogers, Bachman and Johnston, 1974).

Such rapid changes present two major sources of conflict for the military leader at any echelon. First of all, the view of society concerning the military organization cannot help but have an impact within the organization in terms of policy, control, goals and morale. Secondly, however, the input to the military organization at the lowest level (and at the lowest leadership levels as well) is composed of members of this changing society. Only recently the military has gone through a radical adjustment period in response to changes in society that affected the willingness of entrants to comply with traditional organizational values (reference the complicated matter of hair length). A would-be leader in the military organization must understand the unique impact that society has on the leadership functions within that organization.

The elements discussed in the preceding paragraphs are considered to be of such import to the understanding of the leadership process within the military organization so as to be explicitly included in the model. However, other aspects of the leader's relationships are not shown and must be implied. For instance, the SITUATION in which the leadership process takes place certainly has an impact on that process. Why then is it not explicitly represented in the model? The answer is that with the possible exception of "acts-of-God" there are no situations that are not contained within the confines of the group (formal and informal), or the organization, or the society. Therefore, situational aspects of the leadership process are considered in the model and will be discussed in this context throughout the text.

Second, the reader might wonder about the dynamics of the model. Perhaps arrows, representing significant interactions could have been explicitly shown. It is believed that these interactive processes are sufficiently implied by the organizational and hierarchial boundaries. As it becomes necessary to discuss specific interactions (as will be done subsequently in this text), critical elements will be clearly identified.

In addition to the above, one criticism of the model which is certain to surface concerns the purist view of the term "leadership." Such criticism will insist that this model is really addressing what Gibb (1969) refers to as "headship" rather than leadership. Headship, according to Gibb is an influence process characterized by positional dominance, designated goals, fear relationships and authority derived by position rather than spontaneously accorded by the membership. The argument is sound and as previously stated, definitional problems such as these can become insurmountable. However, it is considered appropriate that this potential source of conflict be specifically addressed. It is our feeling that a person placed by authority in a position within an organization and charged with the responsibility of accomplishing specified tasks, by necessity, must engage in the process of influencing other human beings. Our definition of leadership within organizations makes no inference of "popularity." Nevertheless, for the organizationally designated leader to eventually become the accepted (popular) leader of the group is certainly a desirable end—one which will be discussed in some detail in later articles. Therefore, we do not ignore the topic of emergent leadership—we merely approach it from a "real-world" viewpoint. Generally, in organizations, leaders do not enter their job possessing personal charisma. Initially, recognition of societally granted authority is the major criterion on which the leader can rely in order to gain acceptance of subordinates. Leaders eventually may, and usually do, gain the attributes that the purist would classify as "real leadership." But, in the beginning we must focus the model on the problem that exists—and not on what could be.

In summary, the study of leadership has progressed considerably since the day when would-be leaders would mimic the gestures, speech and decorum of historically great leaders in order to portray their own leadership potential. Although to some degree this activity still persists among lay-leaders, the academic study of leadership is better served by understanding that a knowledge of the capabilities and peculiarities of the leader *within* a given situational context is perhaps more beneficial. The processes of influencing human behavior so as to accomplish the goals of the leader become complex when viewed in an organizational context. The influence process is much broader in scope than the mere transference of goals from higher to lower groups and the assurance that such goals are performed properly. The influence process involves relations with seniors, peers and significant others who may be outside the direct control of the leader.

The model of leadership presented herein describes the potential conflicts in which leaders may find themselves. By focusing on the leader's unique position within the organization, the student can better understand those elements of the organizational environment which have potential impact on his or her attempts to influence human behavior.

The chapters to follow will examine in considerable detail the various aspects of the Model of Organizational Leadership. Specifically, the text is divided into six parts. Initially, attention will be directed to THE INDIVIDUAL. Special concern will be given to individual differences among people. Next, attention will be directed toward examining THE GROUP, both formal and informal, and its impact on the leadership process. Third, there will be a closer examination of the INDIVIDUAL AS LEADER, attempting to answer the question: What aspects of the leader's behavior and style impact on the leadership process? Fourth, attention will be turned to the interaction process itself. TRANSACTIONS between significant individuals and the leader will be considered in terms of interpersonal and organizational communication processes as well as the various aspects of counseling. Fifth, we will concentrate on the higher and larger ORGANIZATION and attempt to assess how it impacts on the leadership process. Finally, the INTERFACE WITH SOCIETY and its impact upon the leadership process within the military organization which will be studied.

At the beginning of each Part, the student will find a transition article. This article will briefly review where the student has been and where the articles in that Part fit into the Model of Organizational Leadership. At the conclusion of each transition article will be a list of terms with which the student should be throughly familiar after reading the articles.

END NOTES

1. The definition contained in this section is a modified version of the definition originally authored by Henderson and Campbell (1972).

2. Throughout this discussion it should be understood that the leader is also an individual. Accordingly, the leader, too, is subject to environmental constraints, cultural and societal heritages, and the impact of those around him (seniors, peers and subordinates). That is, the leader is not merely a "stimulator"—he is also being "stimulated."

REFERENCES

Browne, C.G., & Cohn, T.S. *The study of leadership.* Danville, Ill.: Interstate Printers and Publishers, 1958.

Buckley, H.A., & Grunstad, N. Concepts of Leadership. In *TRADOC Leadership Conference Report,* United States Army Infantry School, Ft. Benning, Georgia, 20–24 May 1974.

Carlyle, T. *Heroes and hero worship.* Boston: Adams, 1907 (original 1841).

Evans, M.G. The effects of supervisory behavior on the path-goal relationship. *Organizational Behavior and Human Performance,* 1970, 5, 277–298.

Fiedler, F.E. Leadership and leadership effectiveness traits: a reconceptualization of the leadership trait problem. In E.P. Hollander & R.G. Hunt (Eds.), *Current perspectives in social psychology.* New York: Oxford University Press, 1963. P. 480–485.

Fiedler, F.E. *A theory of leadership effectiveness.* New York: McGraw-Hill, 1967.

Fiedler, F.E., & Chemers, M.M. *Leadership and effective management.* Ill: Scott, Foresman & Co., 1974.

Gibb, C.A. Leadership. In G. Lindzey & E. Aronson. *The handbook of social psychology,* 2nd ed., vol. 4. Reading, Mass.: Addison-Wesley, 1969.

Halpin, A.W. The leadership behavior and combat performance of airplane commanders. *Journal of Abnormal and Social Psychology,* 1954, 49, 19–22.

Hamblin, R.L. Group integration during a crisis. *Human Relations,* 1958, 11, 67–76.

Henderson, W. & Campbell, J.G. Leadership: Quo Vadis? In Office of Military Leadership, *Reading in The Study of Leadership,* United States Military Academy, West Point, New York, 1972.

House, R.J. A path goal theory of leader effectiveness. *Administrative Science Quarterly,* 1971, 16, 321–338.

House, R.J. & Rizzo, J.R. Role conflict and ambiguity as critical variables in a model of organizational behavior. *Organizational Behavior and Human Performance,* 1972, 7, 467–505.

Jacobs, T.O. *Leadership and exchange in formal organizations.* Alexandria, Va.: Human Resources Research Organization, 1971.

Katz, D., & Kahn, R.L. *The social psychology organizations.* New York: Wiley, 1966.

Kerr, S., Schriescheim, C.A. Murphy, C.J., & Stogdill, R.M. Toward a contingency theory of leadership based upon the consideration and initiating structure literature. *Organizational Behavior and Human Performance,* Vol. 12, No. 1, Aug. 1974.

Korten, D.C. Situational Determinants of Leadership Structure. In D. Cartwright and A. Zander (Eds.), *Group Dynamics* (3rd Ed) New York: Harper & Row Publishers, 1968, 351–361.

Lawrence, P.R. & Lorsch, J.W. *Organization and Environment.* Homewood, Ill: Richard D. Irwin, Inc., 1969.

Leavitt, H.J. Some effects of certain communications patterns on group performance. *J. Abnormal Social Psychology.,* 1951, 40, 38–50.

Likert, R. *The Human Organization: Its Management and Value*. New York: McGraw-Hill Book Co., 1967.

Rodgers, W., Bachman, J., & Johnston, L. IRS Newsletter. Institute for Social Research, University of Michigan, Ann Arbor; 1974.

Taylor, J.C. and Bowers, D.G. *The Survey of Organizations*. Ann Arbor, Mich: Institute for Social Research, 1970.

Stogdill, R.M. Personal factors associated with leadership: a survey of the literature. *Journal of Psychology*, 1948, 25, 35–71.

Stogdill, R.M. *Handbook of Leadership: a survey of theory and research*. New York: Free Press, 1974.

U.S. Department of the Army, *Dictionary of United States Army Terms*, Army Regulations 310–25, Washington, D.C.: U.S. Government Printing Office, March 1969.

Weber, M. *The theory of social and economic organizations*. New York: Oxford University Press, 1947.

Part I

The Individual

by
*Robert N. Seigle**

In this part of the study of an organizational approach to leadership, the examination will focus on one of the model's most readily identifiable, yet highly complex elements—the INDIVIDUAL. It is necessary to examine the distinctively human peculiarities of this individual whether he is studied as a leader, a peer, a superior, a subordinate, or a significant other in order to better understand his uniquely pervasive impact on the model of organizational leadership. Regardless of the specific focus on an individual's position, it will be necessary to examine the differential influence created through that position by its human occupant.

Yet, the entire scope of individual differences is much too broad to cover in sufficient detail to assure understanding. Entire introductory courses and programs in psychology are often devoted to this subject alone. Consequently, it is assumed that most students will have completed at least an initial course in individual psychology prior to initiating their study of leadership. Only those salient features of the individual that are relevant to the organizational approach to leadership will be reviewed briefly in this part in order to reinforce the student's prior learning. For those students who have not received such an introductory psychology course, and for those students who would like to

*Robert N. Seigle (Captain, U.S. Army) is a member of the faculty of the Office of Military Leadership at the United States Military Academy, West Point, New York. He received his B.S. from the United States Military Academy (1966) and his M.S. in Business Administration (Human Resource Management) from the University of Utah, Salt Lake City (1974).

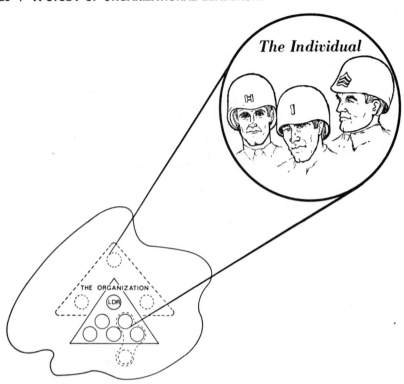

The Individual

review the psychology of the individual in more depth, it is strongly suggested that they examine one of the following introductory psychology texts: Krech and Crutchfield (1974), Morgan and King (1975), or Zimbardo and Ruch (1975).

The review in this part will cover some of the significant factors that help to define how people are motivated. While there is some disagreement as to what constitutes motivated behavior, it is known that certain factors affect the motivation process. People are driven by a particular set of needs to act in such a manner as to satisfy those needs. As individuals engage in specific behavioral acts aimed at satisfying their needs, society judges the appropriateness of their actions. Thus, the individual learns which types of need-fulfilling behaviors are acceptable to the society, and this continual learning pattern constitutes the socialization process. As the socialization process continues, the individual even learns what attitudes are most acceptable to specific segments of society. These attitudes, in turn, have the ability to shape a person's tendency to act in a particular manner. Therefore, motivation is influenced by learning, socialization, and attitudes.

In "Why Psychology for Leaders?" by Witherspoon, a social learning process will be examined to provide a better understanding of how an individual's experiences combine to produce a patterned or learned response to certain occurrences. It is through such a process that the complexities of human behavior can be studied by categorizing wide ranges of individual experiences and attempting to describe broad classifications of expected responses elicited by those experiences. In this manner it is possible to understand how certain punishing consequences serve to eliminate specific undesirable behaviors while at the same time the prolonged use of the punishing consequences may serve to generate an entirely new set of undesirable behaviors. An example of this case is illustrated by the soldier who is given extra work details for failure to shine his shoes properly. The soldier may eventually learn to shine his shoes and avoid the work details, but he might also resign from the Army.

A critical factor in how an individual interprets his experiences and learns to respond to them is his perception of the events surrounding the experience. It is entirely possible for a leader to think that he is rewarding a soldier with a particular incentive when in fact the soldier perceives the reward as a punishment. For instance, a leader might feel that he is rewarding a soldier's outstanding performance by arranging a congratulatory meeting with the commanding general. However, the soldier might perceive this opportunity for recognition as a punishment because of the extra time and effort required to get ready for his meeting with the general when he would rather spend his available time with his own reference group—his friends. In such a case, the leader would expect a continued high performance level from the soldier, but the soldier, having perceived a punishment, would be influenced to avoid the behavior that he felt led to the incentive. Some fundamental principles of applying incentives will be reviewed in the article, "Rewards and Punishment" by OML.

It has been proposed that an individual's potential to perceive the events surrounding his experience is affected by what society taught him to perceive in those events. This societal learning process is known as socialization, a lifelong, continuous process of learning and adaption. While socialization should be understood on a long-term, sociological basis, Schein's, "Organizational Socialization and the Profession of Management", addresses the more applicable concept of "learning the ropes" in large organizations. As individuals become members of organizations, they must learn how to live and operate within the guidelines of their particular organization and position. By dealing with the elements of the social learning process, perception, and socialization on a general basis, the student should be able to describe their collective impact on the individual.

Once the general processes described above are understood, it becomes necessary to examine the influence of those processes over the individual's desire to engage in specific behaviors in order to become familiar with the concept of individual motivation. The article, "Individual Motivation" by Seigle deals with the individual's goal-directed behavior toward the satisfaction of certain predetermined and learned needs. Maslow proposes a specific set of those needs in his article, "The Study of Man at His Best." Again, the range of behaviors available to any one individual in satisfying his needs is affected by the nature and degree of his socialization process. That is, an individual learns from his society an acceptable range of behaviors that he can expect to perform in order to satisfy his needs. However, in reviewing the processes which affect the individual, one presupposes the condition that individuals will often be working toward goals which are not their own. Therefore, external influences which have the potential to induce the behavior necessary to meet the imposed goal must be examined. These external influences will be reviewed in terms of the previously cited "Rewards and Punishments" article. It should be remembered, however, that rewards and punishments themselves are open to perceptual differences, which are, in turn, influenced by the socialization process.

Also included in this part is the concept of attitudes. This concept is reviewed in terms of its relationship to behavior and how that relationship impinges on the motivation process. Mager's, "Where's Your Attitude" helps one understand the difference between the abstract concept of attitude and the overt reality of behavior. Kelman, in his article entitled, "The Study of Social Influence" reveals a three-step process of attitude formation where the importance of the socialization process in forming attitudes is presented. Then, Freedman, Carlsmith, and Sears describe several elements which have the potential to influence attitude changes in their article, "Factors Affecting Attitude Change."

The student should be aware of the tenuous causal relationship of attitudes and behavior. There are those authors, generally influenced by Allport (1935), who feel that attitudes represent predispositions to respond, favorably or unfavorably, toward an object or class of objects. This group represents the attitudes-lead-to-behavior concept. Opposed to this concept are a number of authors headed by Campbell (1950), who believe that attitudes are rationalizations for reinforced behaviors. Thus, this group feels that behavior influences attitude formation and change.

For the purposes of this part, it is generally felt that the stronger causal relationship exists from behavior to attitudes. That is, a stronger influence can be exerted on an individual in an organization by first changing his behavior with the understanding that an appropriate and consistent attitude will follow. An excellent clarification of the research and evidence relative to attitudes and behavior is contained in King and McGinnes (1972) for the interested student.

By this time, the interdependencies of learning, perception, socialization, needs, motivation, rewards and punishments, and attitudes ought to be apparent. The enormous complexity of attempting to understand the many diverse processes which affect individuals should not be mistaken. The individual is truly a complex being. Freudian psychology, according to Hall and Lindzey (1970), attempted to describe the myriad of relationships embodied in an individual and resulted in the following conclusion concerning Freudian theory:

". . . it tries to envisage a full-bodied individual living partly in a world of reality and partly in a world of make-believe, beset by conflicts and inner contradictions, yet capable of rational thought and action, moved by forces of which he has little knowledge and by aspirations which are beyond his reach, by turn confused and clearheaded, frustrated and satisfied, hopeful and despairing, selfish and altruistic; in short, a complex human being." (p. 72)

It is anticipated that the articles which follow will provide some insight to the student's understanding of this complex human being.

Terms you should be able to discuss when you finish this part:

Perception	Worthwhileness
Needs	Motivation
Attitudes	Socialization
Instrumental Behavior	Rewards
Goals	Punishment
Incentives	Compliance
Subjective Probability	Identification
Availability	Internalization
Expectancy	Prepotency

REFERENCES

Allport, G.W. Attitudes. In C. Murchinson (Ed.), *Handbook of Social Psychology.* Worcester, Massachusetts: Clark University Press, pp. 798–884, 1935.

Campbell, D.T. "The Indirect Assessment of Social Attitudes," in *Psychological Bulletin,* Vol. 47, pp. 15–38, 1950.

Hall, C.S. and Lindzey, G. *Theories of Personality* (Second Edition): New York: John Wiley and Sons, Inc., 1970.

King, B.T., and McGinnes, E. (Eds.), *Attitudes, Conflict, and Social Change.* New York: Academic Press, 1972.

Krech, D., Crutchfield, R.S., Livson, N., and Wilson, W.A. Jr. *Elements of Psychology.* (Third Edition) New York: Alfred A. Knopf, 1974.

Morgan, C.T. and King, R.A. *Introduction to Psychology.* (Fifth Edition) New York: McGraw-Hill Book Company, 1975.

Zimbardo, P.G. and Ruch, F.L. *Psychology and Life* (Ninth Edition) Glenview, Illinois: Scott, Foresman and Company, 1975.

Psychology and the Individual

Why Psychology for Leaders?

by
Jerry W. Witherspoon*

Leadership has previously been defined as "the process of influencing human behavior so as to accomplish the goals prescribed by the organizationally appointed leader" (Bons, 1976). At the same time, psychology has been described, in part, as the scientific study of human behavior (Zimbardo & Ruch, 1975; Morgan & King, 1975; Kendler, 1974). Clearly, there exists some common ground between these two definitions. However, sometimes it is difficult for the leadership practitioner to visualize the exact nature of this commonality. It is the purpose of this paper to attempt to clarify the relationship between these two disciplines and to help the would-be leader to appreciate the value to be gained from understanding certain basic psychological principles.

All of us, as we interact with others (particularly in a leadership capacity) become "psychologists" of sorts. We interact with others; we watch their response to our action; and then, we adjust our subsequent interaction attempts appropriately. Some of us have become pretty good at this over the years and we speak in terms of "common sense" behaviors. Trial-and-error, however, has never been a very efficient method of dealing with complicated interpersonal matters. Occasionally, it leads to awkward situations, un-

*Jerry W. Witherspoon, (Lieutenant Colonel, US Army), is a former member of the faculty of the Office of Military Leadership at the United States Military Academy, West Point, New York. He received his BS from the United States Military Academy (1960), his M.A.C.T. in Psychology from the University of North Carolina, Chapel Hill (1973), and his M.B.A. in Management from Long Island University (1975). He is also a graduate of the Armed Forces Staff College (1971).

necessarily strained relationships, and sometimes even embarrassment on the part of one party or the other. Leader/subordinate relationships are certainly made unnecessarily complicated by such trial-and-error methods.

Consider, now, the stated goals of psychology—to describe, explain, predict and influence behavior (Zimbardo & Ruch, 1975). If we examine these goals closely, the rationale for a leader becoming interested in psychological principles comes into sharper focus. For example, if we are to be able to *influence* effectively the behavior of others, as the definition of leadership implies, shouldn't we be able to *predict* the outcomes of our influence attempts? Extending this question even further, can we really predict the outcomes of our influence attempts if we cannot *explain* or *describe* for ourselves what it is that is going on within the individual we are trying to influence? The logical conclusion to this line of questioning appears to be obvious. If the understanding of some basic psychological principles will help us to be more effective leaders, then it would appear to be prudent for us to set out to become aware of these principles.

MODELS OF HUMAN BEHAVIOR

There are a number of possible explanations or models of behavior which one could accept in the study of human behavior. The models are based on the theories of various types of psychologists including:

a. Behaviorists (Skinner, 1938) who tend to ignore the effects on behavior of such mentalistic processes as motivation, attitudes, or personality.

b. Cognitive psychologists (Neisser, 1967) who concern themselves with the mental events involved in the processing of information to include such concepts as sensation, perception, imagery, memory, and thinking.

c. Psychoanalysts (Hjelle & Ziegler, 1976) who base their ideas of motivation, personality, and psychotherapy on the works and theory of Sigmund Freud.

d. Humanists (Maslow, 1954) who postulate a human tendency toward growth, health, excellence, identity, autonomy, and self-actualization.

However, since we are approaching the study of the behavior of individuals from a standpoint of applying our knowledge in the leadership process, we need a model of behavior that is specific enough to be useful in actual situations and simple enough to be easily understood, yet general enough to have widespread application.

The behaviorist model meets the requirements for simplicity and specificity in that it is concerned only with observable stimuli and responses. It is referred to as the Stimulus-Response Model. When you touch a hot stove, your hand automatically pulls away from the painful stimulus. As you drive down the street and the traffic light turns red, you apply the brakes to stop your automobile. In each case, there is an observable stimulus which evokes an observable response. A strict behavioristic psychologist such as B.F. Skinner would contend that this model is sufficient since it includes all of the observable, measurable variables in the behavior and does not postulate any variables internal to the individual which cannot be measured or observed. However, the Stimulus-Response (S-R) Model is not general enough to have the wide applications needed to meet our purposes. For example, the S-R Model does not account for the variation in behavior between two drivers approaching a traffic light which turns from green to yellow. One driver speeds up to "beat" the light, and the other slows down to stop for the red. In this case, there is one stimulus which results in two different responses. One is almost forced to the conclusion that there are variables which are unaccounted for in the S-R Model. Although they would probably postulate different specific variables to explain the different behavior in the two drivers, cognitive, psychoanalytic, and humanistic psychologists would all indicate that the missing variable lies within the characteristics of the individual in question. Therefore, in order to account for this other set of variables affecting human behavior, we shall use the following model:

STIMULUS — ORGANISM — RESPONSE

and call it the S-O-R Model. Simply stated, it says that behavior (R) is a function of environmental variables (S) and of individual characteristics (O). In some instances, the situation or environment will be the dominating factor and in others it will be the characteristics of the individual, but in all cases the exact behavior which is observed will result from an interaction of the two sets of variables. A stimulus variable (S) is anything, element, characteristic, or change in the physical or social environment. Organismic variables (O) which we will consider are learning (prior experience, ability), motivation, emotions, attitudes, perception, personality, and the social factors to do with attribution and social motives. It should be emphasized at this point that these individual characteristics or variables are not directly measurable or observable. They are abstract notions which go by many titles such as mediating variable, hypothetical construct, intervening variable, or theoretical construct. Regardless of the name, their purpose is the same. They are inferred from observable events and are used to help understand, explain, and predict behavior. For consistency, the general title of mediating variable will be used here to indicate individual characteristics. In the SOR Model, the O mediates the effects of S on R.

   With this expanded model of behavior, we can look again at the two motorists approaching the traffic light as it turns yellow. The first driver is in a hurry because he is late for work so he speeds on through the intersection. The second driver, however, slows down because he received a traffic ticket yesterday for "running a red light" and does not desire to repeat the incident. We say the first driver was *motivated* to arrive on time at work in order to complete an important task. We might assume the second driver *learned* through prior experience the negative consequences of not stopping. Motivation and learning are two possible explanations for the different behaviors which are observed in response to the same stimulus. However, neither explanation would be possible without some prior knowledge about the individuals. This means that anyone who intends to lead others, that is, to influence their behavior, must know the specific individuals concerned well enough to be able to apply the general concepts of psychology in specific situations.

The information on organismic variables which follows in this and subsequent pages will be of little use to the leader who does not take the time to learn the specific backgrounds, problems, abilities, and goals of the people he intends to lead. In addition, we must always keep in mind that the description of behavior in terms of each variable is of necessity oversimplified. In each case, all other variables are more or less held constant while a single concept is examined. In actuality, of course, virtually all variables will be operating simultaneously to interact and determine the observed behavior. Nevertheless, to understand the mediating nature of these variables in isolation is fundamental to predicting and subsequently influencing behavioral outcomes—the primary function of leaders. Once we have examined each variable separately, an example of how they act simultaneously to affect behavior will be presented.

LEARNING

Learning can be defined as a relatively permanent change in behavior which occurs as a result of practice or experience (Morgan & King, p. 97). "Relatively permanent" means that it does not include behavior changes caused by drugs, alcohol, fatigue, motivation, or sensitivity of the individual while "practice or experience" rules out changes resulting from injury, growth, or maturation. There are three basic types of learning or conditioning: classical, operant (or instrumental), and cognitive. (The terms "learning" and "conditioning" are basically interchangeable).

Classical conditioning is also referred to as Pavlovian (after the Russian scientist Ivan R. Pavlov), respondent, or reflexive conditioning. This method of learning is very limited in its applications to human beings in that only those behaviors which occur naturally in the organism such as the knee-jerk, eyeblink or salivation can be conditioned (learned) in this manner.

A more useful method of learning is operant conditioning. The key to understanding this type of conditioning is the term *reinforcement*. A reinforcer (or reinforcing stimulus) is defined as any stimulus that follows a response and increases the probability of its occurrence (Zimbardo & Ruch, p. 111). A reinforcer is basically a reward. It can be candy for a child, praise from the boss, or escape from an unpleasant situation. The individual learns, either through experience or verbal instruction, which stimulus conditions serve as cues to tell him that a given behavior will be reinforced, i.e., rewarded. For example, an individual who is learning to shoot a rifle receives instruction on sight picture, position, breathing, and other aspects of the exercise, but it is not until he actually begins to practice that he learns. If he fires the weapon (behavior) with the proper sight picture (stimulus condition), he will hit the target (reinforcement). If he misses, he will continue to adjust his behavior until he does hit his target and thereby "learn" to shoot.

Operant conditioning can be used to teach desired behavior through reinforcement or it can be used to eliminate undesired behavior through *punishment* or *extinction*. When a behavior is followed by a reward (reinforcer), that behavior will be learned and the probability of its occurrence in the future will be increased. If a behavior is followed by some sort of punishment, the probability of its occurrence in the future will be reduced, and under the proper conditions the behavior will be eliminated. In order to be effective, punishment must be timely, response and situationally specific, at the highest reasonable level of intensity, but not of prolonged duration. It must allow for alternative acceptable responses but not for any escape, avoidance, or displays of sympathy or affection. The negative side effects of punishment include: (a) the arousal of strong negative emotions in both the punisher and the punished, (b) severity and intensity of the punishment is too easily underestimated by the punisher, (c) immediate and consistent punishment is difficult to apply, and (d) punishment suppresses undesired behavior only during surveillance. All told, punishment is usually quick and easy to apply for immediate results, but in the long run, extinction is probably more effective with fewer ill effects. Extinction is the process by which undesired behavior "dies out" for lack of reinforcement. If a given behavior is not rewarded in some way, then there is no incentive for the individual to continue it. For example, if someone irritates you by seeking your favor or attention through obvious flattering behavior, you can eliminate the undesired behavior by not giving the favor or attention. Although slower in operation than punishment, extinction does not have the many negative side effects of punishment and is more effective in permanently eliminating undesired behavior. A leader who understands operant conditioning will be more effective in applying rewards and punishment to influence the behavior of his followers.

Cognitive learning is the type of learning with which most people are familiar. It is what you are doing now. You are storing new information as you read, and old information is taking on new meanings. This type of learning occurs as you watch a newscast on television or listen to a briefing by your company commander. Earlier we defined learning as a relatively permanent behavior change resulting from experience. Cognitive learning then is a change in the way one processes information because of the experience he has had. For additional discussion of cognitive learning, see Morgan & King, pp. 120–125 or Zimbardo & Ruch, Chapter 5.

MOTIVATION

An organismic process tangentially related to learning is the concept of motivation. Motivation is an energizing process which serves to direct the individual toward a certain learned goal as illustrated by the Motivational Cycle (Morgan & King, p. 225).

In Figure 1, the term "Driving State" refers to needs, drives, or motives which might lead a person to perform some instrumental behavior to obtain a goal and thereby relieve the drive state.

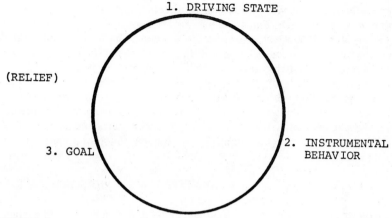

FIGURE 1. MOTIVATIONAL CYCLE

Using the most basic example, an individual becomes affected by the motive of hunger (driving state) so he performs some instrumental (learned) behavior such as going to the refrigerator, obtains his goal of food, eats it, and attains relief from his need (the hunger pangs go away). It is fairly easy to follow the cycle in such a familiar situation, but the cycle is no less applicable in more complex social situations such as interacting with buddies, training, and work. The basic idea behind the Motivational Cycle is the concept of homoestasis, the tendency of the human organism to maintain internal stability or equilibrium. As long as our needs are met, we remain in balance, but when we are pushed out of balance, a form of internal tension results which we are motivated to relieve. According to Maslow (1954), this internal tension may result from *deficit* needs or from *growth* needs. The former include physiological needs, safety needs, need for belongingness and love, and need for esteem. The only growth need Maslow posited is the need for *self-actualization* which does not come into play until deficit needs are satisfied. The need for self-actualization motivates an individual so that he feels he *must* act to become whatever he *can* become, a sort of "ideal self." Since very few people ever reach the level of fulfillment associated with Maslow's concept of self-actualization, the military leader will be concerned for the most part with the deficit needs of his men. Usually the basic physical needs for food, shelter, and security are provided for by the organization, so the leader's interactions with his men will be primarily concerned with the needs for belongingness and esteem.

The leader using the concept of the Motivational Cycle should recognize that there are three basic variables to consider: motive, instrumental behavior, and goal. If the leader wishes to influence behavior, he must affect one or more of the three variables. He can influence instrumental behavior by offering or withholding desired goals (called incentives). In some situations he might be more effective in changing behavior if he directs his attention toward changing the motives of his men. Finally he may find himself in the situation where his men are properly motivated to work for the goals he offers, but they do not have the ability (learned behavior) to do as he wishes. Then the leader must work directly on the behavior to change it through coaching and training.

Motivation is closely associated with the concept of learning. Whereas learning is the ability or potential for performing some particular act, motivation is the energizer which gives life and direction to the potential. The relationship between motivation and learning can be conceptualized mathematically by saying that they combine multiplicatively to determine performance (Logan, 1970, p. 152):

$$\text{MOTIVATION} \quad \times \quad \text{LEARNING} \quad = \quad \text{PERFORMANCE}$$

By this illustration, we can see that if either motivation or learning (ability) is low, then performance will be low. It is important to be able to determine which factor is deficient when attempting to improve performance in others. Supposing a platoon leader has two men in his unit who make failing scores on the physical fitness test. If he considers only their performance, he may make a mistake by taking inappropriate action to improve their scores. If one man is perfectly capable physically of passing the test but does not care to do a good job, he should not be treated in the same way as the other man who has tried as hard as he could but is in poor condition. The first man is obviously a motivational problem while the second is an ability (learning) failure. Again, in order for the leader to use the concepts of individual characteristics discussed here, he must know his men well enough to know which process is in operation.

EMOTIONS

Even though the military atmosphere is often perceived as devoid of emotion, the leader must have a basic understanding of the effects of emotions on individual behavior. When a person becomes aroused by such emotions as love, hate, anger, or fear, he is affected both psychologically and physically. The initial effects of increased arousal are usually beneficial to performance in that the individual is more alert and less sensitive to pain. He is also able to exert maximum strength for short periods of time and to sustain general activity over longer time than is ordinarily possible. What happens is that when an individual is emotionally aroused, say by fear, his body reacts to prepare itself for "fight" or flight." Adrenalin production is increased, the heart rate increases and pumps more blood to the muscles, and the digestive system slows down.

These physiological reactions give the body temporarily increased ability to fight if necessary or to flee if advisable. However, if this state of arousal is sustained for too long a period, or is too intense, then the individual may begin to break down physically or psychologically and become unable to function. Unfortunately, there is no easy way to determine how much arousal is too much in any particular person and it varies from individual to individual. What this means to the leader is that he can probably increase the performance of his troops if he can find some way to increase emotional arousal in them through esprit de corps, competition, or even hate or fear. He must be careful, though, not to take them beyond their optimum level, and he should be careful not to sustain the arousal too long. In addition, the leader must realize that emotions can interfere with the proper performance of his men if the emotions become too intense and that he may have to take action to "relieve the tension" at times. The man who is too fearful may need reassurance or the man who hates the enemy so much as to be a menace to himself or others may need to be reasoned with or calmed. Each case is going to be different, and the leader must know his men as individuals so that he can take advantage of the positive effects of emotional arousal and avoid the negative ones.

ATTITUDES

An attitude is defined as "a relatively stable, emotionalized predisposition to respond in some consistent way toward some person or group of people or situations." (Zimbardo & Ruch, p. 586) In examining this definition, one notes three basic components of an attitude: (a) a belief, (b) an emotional aspect, and (c) a tendency to act. Anyone interested in influencing the behavior of others needs a good understanding of the concept of attitudes and their effect on behaviors.

Attitudes for the most part are *learned* through observation of models (significant others), absorption of information, or as a result of rewards and punishment. Most of our attitudes, such as prejudice or religious faith, are adopted very early in life from our parents and are thus very difficult to change. As with the other mediating variables discussed thus far, attitudes tend to focus or distort stimulus data so as to result in differential behavior among individuals. Although a leader is primarily interested in influencing observable behavior, personal desires or organizational goals may require that he also attempt to change an undesirable attitude such as racial prejudice. He could present new information which is designed to change the belief (cognitive) component of the attitude, but it is very likely that the emotional (affective) component will tend to distort the information and make it less effective. Another possible way to change attitudes is to work directly on behavior by creating situations which will lead others to act in a manner counter to their attitude: in debates, in plays, because of job requirements, for personal gain, or to avoid trouble. For these situations to be effective, though, the individuals must see their behavior as being of their own choosing. If they are forced to act in a given manner, they will not be motivated to change their attitude and even though their behavior is in accordance with your desires, when you are not present the behavior will probably change. However, if they see their behavior to be of their own choice and that it is discrepant with their attitude, they will experience "cognitive dissonance" (Festinger, 1957) which will motivate them either to: (a) separate the attitude and the act psychologically, (b) accept that their behavior is irrational, or (c) change their attitude to be in accord with their behavior. An example is the situation in which a leader is having problems in his unit because of discrimination (behavior) resulting from racial prejudice (attitude). If he can create situations leading to "voluntary" nondiscriminatory behavior on the part of the prejudiced members of his unit, the leader may be able to reduce the prejudice and alleviate the underlying cause of the problems. However, if the leader attempts to force compliance, the prejudiced person will probably see the coercion as the cause of his discrepant behavior, and therefore will not be motivated to change his attitude. Consequently, when the leader is not present to enforce his orders, discriminatory behavior may resume.

PERCEPTION

Perception is the process by which an individual organizes and interprets the data received through the sensory system of the body. When you read the words on this page, your eyes are sensing the form and contrast of the ink on the paper and relaying data to your mind. Your mind processes and organizes this stimulation so that you can interpret the incoming data.

Perception is readily demonstrated with the S-O-R Model. An individual's response (R) to any stimulus event (S) is mediated or affected by that individual's perception (O) of the event. One good way of visualizing the concept of perception is that of a filter having certain characteristics which affect the way an individual "views" incoming stimulus data and which thereby affect the individual's response to it. The characteristics of the "filter" are primarily determined by the prior experience (learning), motivation, emotions, and attitudes of the individual. For example, you receive an order from your commander to "push your platoon harder in training next week." The way you perceive and thereby carry out the order will be affected by your emotional condition when you hear it. Your perception will be much different if you are upset because he just chewed you out than if he had just told you that you had been doing a good job. By the same token, your perception would be one thing if you are motivated to have the best platoon around and something else if you really do not care much. And finally, your perception of the order would be affected by what you have learned about the commander from previous encounters with him. Remember that your orders to your men will be perceived and interpreted through the same processes just described.

SOCIAL FACTORS

Thus far the topics addressed have been concerned with the characteristics of a single individual. However, very few of us operate alone. We are almost always interacting and working with other people. This section will be devoted to some of the individual characteristics which are based on these interactions.

Attribution. This is the cognitive process by which we perceive the behavior of other people. We make inferences about their motivation, ability, emotions, and personality to explain their behavior. We *attribute* to the person underlying characteristics which we cannot see but only infer. Referring again to the S-O-R Model, we say that behavior is a function of situational variables and dispositional or "personality" variables. There is a tendency in most of us to perceive more consistency in the behavior of others than is really there. Because of this, when we observe other people, we tend to make dispositional attributions concerning the cause of their behavior. In other words, when one of your men is late to formation or slovenly dressed, you will probably attribute his behavior to lack of motivation or ability with little or no consideration for situational variables over which he may have had no control. It is interesting to note, however, that when viewing one's own behavior, we often overemphasize the other side and make situational attributions. Looking again at the man who was late and in a sloppy condition, he probably sees his own behavior more a function of external causes. "I would have been on time in a clean uniform if the motor sergeant had released me five minutes earlier." The main point here is that behavior is a function of *both* situational and dispositional variables. Remember that your men have external constraints over which they have no control and that you should not always overlook the contribution of your own personal characteristics to your performance.

Social Motives. In the earlier discussion of individual motives, social motives were mentioned but not fully addressed. Social motives are associated with such needs as love, affection, esteem, and self-esteem. Their effect on behavior is basically the same as indicated earlier with the Motivational Cycle. The *need for achievement* leads to a general tendency to approach success. Its strength is dependent upon expectation of success, the incentive value of the particular kind of success involved, and perception of personal responsibility for success (Atkinson, 1964; Feather, 1967). In the United States and particularly in the military, competition is continually stressed at work, at play, and in education. Whether the competition results from the need for achievement or fear of failure is subject to controversy, but in either case the leader must be aware of it and use it to influence his men. Give them the opportunity to compete and achieve success, and they will normally perform better.

The need for social approval is also strong in our society. We need to know that others approve of us and our behavior. Little children work hard for the approval of their parents. We all work hard for the approval of people important to us. Social approval confers identity, legitimates existence, provides security, and is one criterion for control over your environment.

The need for affiliation or to be with others was long thought to be an instinct. It certainly serves survival needs in time of danger. However, there are great differences among individuals in the strengths of their need for affiliation which would eliminate the instinct hypothesis. Regardless of the source of the need, though, almost all people want to be with other people in varying degrees. Research has shown that increased anxiety tends to increase the need for affiliation (Schacter, 1959). The leader should be aware of this tendency and in times of stress take action to allow his men increased contact with one another.

PERSONALITY

Personality is "the sum total of the ways in which an individual characteristically reacts and interacts with others and objects" (Zimbardo & Ruch, p. 409). When we interact with another person, we do so on the basis of our perception of that person's personality. There are a number of theories of how personality develops in an individual (see Hjelle & Ziegler, 1976; Zimbardo & Ruch, 1975; or Morgan & King, 1975), but the common thread running through all of the theories is that each individual has developed into the person he is over a long period of time. It is unlikely that a leader will be able to change anyone's personality significantly, so he must basically work with his men *as they are* and try to influence their behavior through the other variables discussed here such as motivation and training.

PUTTING IT ALL TOGETHER

Now that we have addressed a number of mediating variables individually it is time to look at them in simultaneous operation as they interact to affect human behavior. This interaction will be illustrated using an example of a platoon leader who desires to influence the behavior of two different members of his unit.

On a recent field exercise, the platoon leader was rather pleased with the performance of all but two of his men. Neither of them took good care of his individual weapon and equipment. They both made numerous mistakes in carrying out directions and managed to get lost in different areas during a night cross-country movement. On the surface, it might appear that these two men are very much alike and that the platoon leader should treat them the same in trying to influence them to perform better. However, this platoon leader has taken the time and effort to get to know his men as individuals, and he knows that giving them "equal" treatment does not necessarily mean treating each of them in the same manner. The platoon leader knows that one man is highly motivated to do well, to gain the approval of his superiors, and to be considered a member of the group. The source of his poor performance lies in his slowness to learn and in certain emotional problems he has with his family. In attempting to help this individual to improve, the platoon leader must focus his attention on training the man and, if possible, helping him with his personal problems. It may well be that he cannot help with them directly, but he might be able to refer the man to an agency whose mission is to take care of such problems.

With regard to the other poor performer, the platoon leader knows that the man has the capability of doing well so there must be some other source of difficulty. In talking to the man and his squad leader, the platoon leader learns that the man feels that what he and the platoon are doing are unimportant so he is not motivated to "put out." He has the perception that his talents and abilities are not being properly used and that he is wasting his time. In dealing with this individual, the platoon leader will probably want to take action to affect his motivation. Ideally, it should be possible to show him the importance of his contribution to the success of the platoon and thereby motivate him to use the abilities he possesses. However, in some cases it may be necessary to use some form of implied punishment to cause him to change his motivation to comply in order to avoid some undesirable stimulus—a substitute goal which generates the desired instrumental behavior.

Needless to say, these examples are somewhat simplistic, but the idea is to realize first that people are not the same, even if they seem to act that way, and second that the basic principles of human behavior presented here can be useful as a tool to help the leader *describe* and thereby *predict* the outcomes of his *influence* attempts. The leader in this example must take into account the different factors at work in the subordinates because to do otherwise would probably result in poorer performance on the part of both. Treating both "alike" may salvage one but essentially make the other a permanent liability to the organization.

SUMMARY

Psychology, as the study of the behavior of individuals, seeks to describe and explain behavior so as to be able to predict and influence it. Of course, the influencing of human behavior is the leadership process with which we are concerned. In briefly describing and explaining behavior, we have addressed the various characteristics of the individual which one must understand to be an effective leader. Although the complexity of human behavior requires that the characteristics be examined separately, we have shown that behavior is not so complex it cannot be put together and understood by such "practicing psychologists" as platoon leaders and company commanders. These leaders should also realize that they, too, are individuals with the same types of characteristics as other people. They have certain needs and drives which affect their behavior as individuals, but they are also subject to certain environmental pressures not felt by others which may make their behavior even more complex. However, if the leader will keep the concept of the S-O-R Model in mind and remember that behavior is a function of *both* situational variables and individual characteristics, he should be able to avoid overemphasizing the effects of either to the detriment of the other.

REFERENCES

Atkinson, J.W. *An Introduction to Motivation*. Princeton: Van Nostrand, 1964.

Bandura, A.L. *Social Learning Theory*. New York: General Learning Press, 1971.

Dollard, J. and Miller, N.E. *Personality and Psychotherapy*. New York: McGraw-Hill, 1950.

Feather, N. "Valence of outcome and expectation of success in relation to task difficulty and perceived locus of control" in *Journal of Personality and Social Psychology*, Vol. 7, pp. 372–386, 1967.

Festinger, L. *A Theory of Cognitive Dissonance*. Stanford: Stanford University Press, 1957.

Hjelle, L.A. and Ziegler, D.J. *Personality: Basic Assumptions, Research, and Applications*. New York: McGraw-Hill, 1976.

Kendler, H.H. *Basic Psychology*. Menlo Park: W.A. Benjamin, Inc, 1974.

Logan, F.A. *Fundamentals of Learning and Motivation*. Dubuque, Iowa: Wm. C. Brown Company, 1970.

Maslow, A.H. *Motivation and Personality*. New York: Harper and Row, 1954.

Morgan, C.T. and King, R.A. *Introduction to Psychology*, Fifth Edition. New York: McGraw-Hill, 1975.

Neisser, U. *Cognitive Psychology*. New York: Appleton Century-Crofts, 1967.

Schachter, S. *The Psychology of Affiliation*. Stanford: Stanford University Press, 1959.

Skinner, B.F. *The Behavior of Organisms*. New York: Appleton-Century-Crofts, 1938.

Zimbardo, P.G. and Ruch, F.L. *Psychology and Life*, Ninth Edition. Glenview, Illinois: Scott, Foresman, and Company, 1975.

Motivation

The Study of Man at His Best

concepts of
Abraham H. Maslow

If someone had surveyed businessmen ten years ago to find out which behavioral science theories or behavioral scientists had influenced them, it is unlikely the name Abraham Maslow would appear on the list. Yet the influence of Maslow on the whole behavioral science movement in industry is profound. There are at least two reasons, however, why Maslow wouldn't have been listed a decade ago: (1) much of the behavioral and humanistic principles that have been incorporated into the movement were predicated on Maslow's theories without an awareness of their relationship to his research or philosophy; and (2) Maslow himself evidenced no particular awareness of the relevance of his research or theorizing to the world of work. In fact, not until 1962 did Maslow begin to study industrial organizations or show any interest in the psychology of organizations.

In the summer of 1962, he was invited to be a "visiting fellow" at Non-Linear Systems, Inc. in Del Mar, California. While he was there, Maslow produced a journal of his experiences and impressions as a theoretical psychologist having his initial first-hand exposure to the rapidly developing field of organization psychology and the attempts of a functioning industrial firm to apply behavioral research findings to the everyday operation of a business. Maslow's reactions and impressions, which he recorded in his personal

Reprinted from "Behavioral Science—Concepts and Management Application", *The Conference Board, Inc.*, Research Report No. 216, 1969, with permission.

journal, were later edited and published under the title, *Eupsychian Management*.[1]

The word "eupsychian" is a coinage of Maslow's. He defines Eupsychian Management as "the culture that would be generated by 1,000 self-actualizing people on some sheltered island where they would not be interfered with . . ."

EUPSYCHIAN SOCIETY

Maslow also characterizes a eupsychian society as a society inhabited by superior human beings—superior physically, emotionally, mentally, and spiritually—and having an ideal mental and social environment. In his preface to *Eupsychian Management,* he acknowledges the utopian implications of his theorizing about the future, but the conditions he sets forth are to him not just idle dreams, but within the realm of possibility. He says, "I am quite aware of the possibility that all mankind may be wiped out. But it is also possible that it *won't* be wiped out. Thinking about the future and even trying to bring it about is, therefore, still a good idea. In an age of rapid automation, it is even a necessary task."

Maslow's interest in human striving and in man's need for personal superiority led him to develop a systematic theory of human motivation.[2] In this work he published his now famous "Hierarchy of Needs," which is the core of his theory of personality and its relation to motivation. Because of this work, Maslow became known as a personality theorist with an abiding interest in the study of "man at his best." To describe the condition of man at his best, Maslow chose Kurt Goldstein's term "self-actualization," but he used it in a very different sense. Goldstein's self-actualization, described any gratification or self-fulfillment, whether it be a hungry person's eating or an ignorant person's acquiring knowledge. Maslow used self-actualization in a very specialized sense to describe a rarely obtained state of perfect human achievement. He further postulated that self-actualization isn't possible to achieve—that, indeed, a person isn't even concerned with it—until he has satisfied a complex set of lower level needs.

NATURE OF MOTIVATION

Before considering the nature of man's upward striving for self-actualization, it is necessary to examine some of the assumptions that Maslow makes about the nature of motivation itself. There has been widespread acceptance of the belief that motivation is something one person does for or to someone else. Nevertheless, while external forces or incentives are seen as having an effect on motivation, according to many theories real motivation is not something externally produced or imposed. Quite the contrary, motivation is defined as the state of having an *internal* motive that incites the individual to some kind of action. By its very nature, motivation comes from within the individual and *cannot* be imposed on him. Man is viewed as goal-seeking from the beginning of life to its end. The ubiquitous nature of his goals serves as a measure of man's nature and the form his behavior takes. Any action a person takes to reach a goal is commonly called a drive. The acting out of a drive is seen as evidence of his motivation to reach a goal.

Maslow's theory of personality and motivation converts these goals to a set of needs; man is motivated to reach a certain goal because he has an internationally generated *need* to reach it.[3] Maslow chose to categorize and rank these sets of human needs into a conceptual hierarchy, beginning with the most primitive and urgent human needs and ranging upward to the apex of the hierarchy, self-actualization. While there may be nuances and graduations within any given level of need, Maslow identified the primary breakdown as follows in his *Hierarchy of Needs.*

- Need for self-actualization
- Need for esteem
- Need for belongingness and love
- Safety needs
- Physiological needs

The *physiological needs* refer to food, warmth, shelter, elimination, water, sleep, sexual fulfillment, and other bodily needs.

The *safety needs* include actual physical safety, as well as a *feeling* of being safe from injury, both physical and emotional; therefore a feeling of emotional security as well as a feeling of freedom from illness would be included under safety needs.

The *need for belongingness and love* represents the first social need. Physiological and safety needs are centered around the individual's own person. The need to have love and belongingness is the need for other people. It is the need to feel a part of a group or the need to belong to and with someone else. It implies the need both to give and to receive love.

The *need for esteem* is based on the belief that a person has a basic need for self-respect and the esteem of others (except in extreme pathology). The need for esteem is divided into two subsets: first, there is the need for feeling a personal worth, adequacy, and competence; and secondly, there is the need for respect, admiration, recognition, and status in the eyes of others.

The *need for self-actualization* is a more difficult concept to describe. Self-actualization is the process whereby one realizes the real self and works toward the expression of the self by becoming what one is capable of becoming. In other words, self-actualization is the process of making actual the person's perception of his "self."

Maslow posits that these needs occur in a hierarchy of preeminence throughout a person's development and maturation. The graphic model of steps is used to underscore the ascending occurrence of each need. Of more significance, the hierarchy underscores the fundamental point that until one need is fulfilled, a person's behavior is not motivated by the next higher level need. For example, if his physiological needs are not taken care of, a person isn't concerned with his safety. And until his physiological and safety needs are both fulfilled, he isn't particularly interested in fulfilling his need for love.

A person isn't concerned with a higher level need until the lower level needs are satisifed and form a base for the next higher level. By the same token, once a need is satisified, it no longer motivates (a hungry man is motivated toward food, but once he is well fed, he is no longer motivated to strive for food). The implications of the maxim, *"a satisfied need is no longer a motivator of behavior,"* are probably among the most intriguing outgrowths of the need/motivation theory.

Maslow assumes that just as the needs appear in sequence as a person grows from infancy to adulthood, the pattern may be repeated as he encounters new experiences at various times in his life. For example, he normally first seeks companionship, affection, and love through his identification with his parents and his immediate family. But the pattern is repeated throughout his lifetime in a myriad of experiences. From the standpoint of motivation, however, Maslow's theory assumes that individuals can be characterized as being primarily at an observable level at a given time or in a given set of circumstances.

NOT STATIC, BUT SITUATIONAL

The matter of time and circumstances is a crucial variable in understanding the hierarchical nature of need and motivation. Since the lower-level needs are the most urgent ones, they must continually be satisfied in order for a person to be motivated toward higher level needs. But even when the lower level needs are satisfied, if they are threatened, they again become the stimulus for motivation. A man who is safe may risk his safety, even his life, if he becomes hungry enough. Or a person whose prime motivation has been esteem may drop down a level to seek belongingness if the sense of belongingness is threatened.

"In the study of the outward manifestation of motivations, clearly some consideration must be paid to the inner motive. A "clotheshorse" isn't building up an elaborate wardrobe, for example, because he has a physiological need to protect the body from heat or cold. Rather he may be seeking to satisfy his need for esteem or admiration—or it may represent his need for group acceptance or belongingness, if his friends are all concerned with style.

The fulfillment of the human needs as outlined in Maslow's hierarchy are held to be universal and applicable, at least in the lower levels, to all persons. Maslow's need theory postulates that all human beings have the *capacity* to climb up the motivational hierarchy, and the ever-upward reaching of a person is seen as evidence of his emotional maturity. However, Maslow cautions that there are persons who never grow beyond certain levels and whose total life style is geared to the satisfaction of lower level needs. To him, such cases represent immaturity, stunted growth, or neurosis.[4] In fact, he calls the first four needs *deficit* needs because their fulfillment, he holds, is so much a part of the natural development of a normal personality that they are stimulated only in their absence or deficit. That is, one strives for fulfillment of each successive level of the first four steps of the hierarchy because of *lack* of food, *lack* of safety, *lack* of love, and *lack* of esteem.

THE ONLY "GROWTH" NEED

Self-actualization, however, far from being a deficit need, is labeled a *growth* need. This implies that the person who has reached this summit has already taken care of the deficit needs and is in that state of psychological health where he begins the process of self-realization or becoming what he is capable of becoming. Not only is this mature individual driven to become what he *can* become, he has an inner compulsion to integrate his interests, talents, and abilities to the point that he works toward becoming what he *must* become.[5] The determinants here are the individual's own peculiar set of potentialities and the internally defined goals he sets for himself.

The self-actualizing person, as Maslow sees him, freed from the externally imposed deficit needs, is now ready to explore the heretofore untried possibilities of the true self.[6] With his freedom, the self-actualizing person is characterized as spontaneous, creative, and capable of achieving immense satisfaction from doing the thing or things that represent the realization of his capabilities.[7]

Because of the uniqueness of each person, the form or content of self-actualization is a highly individual proposition. Self-actualizing satisfactions are seen as almost entirely internal. The *self-actualizing* artist *must* paint; his gratification, and the thing that motivates him, is the act of creating through painting rather than the end product. In contrast, the person who says "I don't like writing, but I like being an author," may be motivated toward esteem, since he is primarily concerned with what he can create through his writing; the self-actualizing author would get his sense of fulfillment through the actual process of creating the work or writing.

SUPERIOR PEOPLE

For Maslow, self-actualizing people are motivated to involve themselves in creative expression that they themselves find gratifying. To Maslow, some of the more easily observable examples of self-actualization are found among the artistic or aesthetic professions. But given the highly individual nature of self-actualization, truly self-actualizing persons may be found almost anywhere. What motivates one person may be of no interest to another person. While Maslow considers self-actualizing people superior beings, the individual's frame of reference is an important determinant. A dedicated musician maybe a self-actualizing person, but so may a dedicated architect, or manager, or mother.

By its very essence, self-actualization is a self-perpetuating, ongoing, and never finished process. It implies that each new involvement of the self begets further involvement. Therefore a person is never "self-actualized" but is always in the process of finding new goals and new means of expression. Or to paraphrase Shakespeare, self-actualization is ". . . as if increase of appetite grows by what it feeds on."

END NOTES

1. Richard D. Irwin, Inc., Homewood, Illinois, 1965.

2. *Motivation and Personality,* Harper & Row, Inc., New York, 1954.

3. Maslow acknowledges that there are some relatively unmotivated actions, but it would appear that the difference is a matter of intensity of motivation rather than whether motivation is at work or not.

4. An example of this kind of pathology is consistent with Karen Horney's study of the neurotic need for love. In the neurotic personality the need for love is so great that there can never be enough; each reassurance of love merely requires more. In Maslow's theory, this kind of person would never reach the need for esteem.

5. This process may be likened to the implications of Nietzche's admonition, "Be what thou art!"

6. "Self" is used here in a special sense, as it is in several theories of personality. For example, Carl Rogers, the American psychotherapist who has been active in the group dynamics movements, speaks of a "self" as being something that is more than a synonym for the organism, man; rather it is "awareness of being, of functioning," and behavior is seen as being dependent upon how the person perceives himself—his self-concept. C.G. Jung viewed the "self" as the real essence of a person and a part of the personality that transcends the finite limits of the individual's experience of observed self. Maslow's concept of the self has some common characteristics with the self of both Rogers and Jung. In fact, self-actualization, in the Maslow sense, is roughly analogous to Jung's "individualization process," which represents attainment of the true self and wholeness of personality.

7. For a discussion of the nature of growth needs and their implications in the world of work, see pp. 20–25 on the work of Herzberg.

Individual Motivation—A Human Systems Approach

by
*Robert N. Seigle**

Individual motivation is a topic which has been researched thoroughly over the past several decades, yet it remains a topic with many more questions than answers. Why is one man motivated to lead while others are content to follow? Why do some people consistently do top quality work while others consistently do sloppy work? Why do some people perform very poorly in certain situations and then do very well in other situations? Finally, what is it that causes some people to do well in every endeavor they undertake? These, and many other questions have been examined in detail by motivational theorists and multiple explanations have been offered.

Early theories of motivation (1910–1940) concentrated on the innate drive states of man. Freud, Hall, and Murray (Teevan & Birney, 1964), and McDougall and Allport (Madsen, 1968) all postulated theories of motivation which attempted to capture the essence of man's instinctual, goal-directed behavior, albeit they differed drastically in their basic philosophies. More contemporary theories of motivation expressed by McClelland, Atkinson, and Maslow (Teevan & Birney, 1964), Vroom (1964), Lawler (1973), and Herzberg (1966) have attempted to expand the applicability of the early theories. Unfortunately, there is little agreement among these motivational theorists as to what constitutes motivated behavior and how it should be measured. There does appear to be one consistent thread in all motivation theories, however, and that is that man's behavior is goal-directed.

---

*See also earlier article *The Individual,* by same author.

At the risk of oversimplification of the theories involved, motivation theorists may be separated into two camps. In one camp there is a significant belief that motivation is a uniquely internal phenomenon where a particular set of needs or factors arouses a desire to act or behave in such a manner as to satisfy the aroused need. From this camp, then, one learns that the stimulus for motivated behavior is internal to the organism. In the other camp, the fundamental belief is that forces external to the organism engender appropriate behavior which is aimed at satisfying the externally derived condition. Scientifically, neither camp has been able to prove its own claims conclusively while disproving the others. Consequently, a student of motivation must consider both arguments.

Because of the enormous complexity involved in explaining man's behavior, a comprehensive method of analyzing both internal and external forces acting on man must be followed. Such a comprehensive method is the systems concept.

The systems concept represents a convenient way of thinking about the interdependencies of the several forces acting on man to influence his behavior. This concept can help one understand the multiple influences impinging on an individual at a given time and it can aid in learning how an individual attempts to balance those influences. Viewing man as a system—a capable, functioning, autonomous element—it is not difficult to accept the nearly automatic balancing functions that man's internal organs (sub-systems) perform. The respiratory sub-system is balanced with the cardiovascular sub-system. The digestive sub-system is balanced with the structural sub-system, and so on. This internal balancing, termed homeostasis, is so scientifically obvious that its significance is often overlooked as we isolate individual sub-systems to study them in detail.

But, just as the internal organs are sub-systems of man, so is man a sub-system of another larger system, the environment. Therefore, if we assume man's skin to be a boundary around his internal system, it should become more obvious why man's external system must be balanced across that boundary. Everything that man, the system, does has an effect on, and in turn, is affected by the society in which he lives. The means by which man transfers energy across the boundary is through his senses. He feels, sees, smells, hears, and tastes the events going on around him. The energy from those events is transmitted to the brain for storage and later use. Exactly how and why all of the sources of energy combine to produce specific behavioral responses from an individual is a matter for personality theorists and is presently open to conjecture.

The enormous complexity of man then demands that some systematic procedure be followed in attempting to understand the internal and external forces which motivate individuals to act the way they do.

Similarly, a leader who wants to understand the implications of his actions on the motivation of his subordinates should consider both the internal and external stimuli of motivation using the systems concept. To aid in the understanding of the complexities of human motivation, a simple descriptive model known as the motivation cycle will be used. (Adapted from Morgan and King, 1971, p. 188.) Hopefully, through the use of this learning device, the student will be able to gain an appreciation for the many forces acting on man and how those forces combine to produce motivated behavior.

From the basic diagram in Figure 1, one can see that motivation is a continuous and cyclical process which follows three specific steps. In step one, the human organism experiences an arousal of need either externally or internally derived. In step two, appropriate behavior is engendered by the need, and is directed toward the ultimate goal (step 3) of satisfying the aroused need. Thus one completes the cycle only to find that another need is aroused or perhaps the same need is aroused again and the process continues.

A simplistic example of how this model describes motivated behavior will clarify the process. Suppose that a basic physiological need of hunger is aroused in an individual. That individual will engage in the exploratory behavior of searching for food in an attempt to satisfy his hunger need. Generally, the exploratory behavior is successful in locating some food and the consuma-

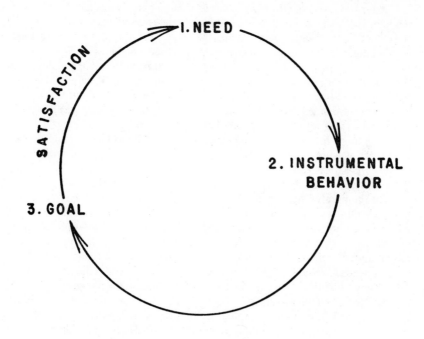

FIGURE 1.

BASIC MOTIVATION CYCLE

tory behavior of eating ensues. While it is recognized that these behaviors are instrumental in leading toward the goal, they are merely the means through which the goal of satisfaction of the hunger is reached. It is important to understand that through normal associative learning, individuals tend to confuse eating behavior as a goal because it invariably leads to a reduction of the hunger pangs. It is necessary to follow this reasoning to be able to explain why some people eat more food than others. Humans continue to engage in the individually aroused consumatory behavior of eating until their own level of satisfaction is reached.

This individually-based physiological arousal and satisfaction is best illustrated by a hospital case reported by Wilkins and Richter (1940). A three-year old boy was admitted to the hospital because of physical abnormalities. He was placed on a routine hospital diet where, after seven days he died. An autopsy revealed that his adrenal glands had malfunctioned, causing him to lose valuable body salt through his urine faster than his hospital diet could replace it. Apparently, the boy died of a salt deficiency.

After the boy's death, it was learned that he had always had peculiar eating habits. While most children loved sweets, he avoided them in favor of any salty food like crackers and bacon. He would eat the salt off those foods without ingesting the cracker or the bacon and then ask for more. When he was 18 months old, he inadvertently got the salt shaker from the table and devoured the available salt. Once he learned where the pure salt was, he would go into the kitchen and scream until someone gave him the salt. At about this time, it was reported that the boy would eat reasonably well if his food was doused in salt and if he was permitted a spoonful of table salt a day.

This tragic incident clearly illustrates the three steps of motivation. In step one, there was an almost insatiable craving for salt. In step two, specific behaviors were observed that led directly to obtaining and eating the salt. In step three, the goal of satisfying the craving for salt was temporarily reached.

On the purely physiological cycle, motivation of human behavior is relatively easy to see and understand. A more difficult concept to grasp is that of all the other motives or needs which engender some form of internal arousal in the human organism. Needs, drives, and motives, while generally differentiated in scientific terminology, are considered interchangeable here. Also, a need is considered to be some state of internal arousal that a person can "feel" and "identify." Such is the case as one "feels" the pangs of hunger, or as one "feels" the drowsiness of sleep. Again, these physiological needs are commonly understood and accepted but they are only a portion of the factors which have the capability to create an internal arousal in the individual.

From Figure 2, one is able to gain a limited perspective for how the needs get activated or energized. Any of the conditions listed in the figure have the capability of creating an internal arousal in the individual. It should be recognized that this list is representative only, and not exhaustive. As an example, a student readily comprehends the sweating palms and jittery feelings which accompany the last hurried moments of cramming before a major exam.

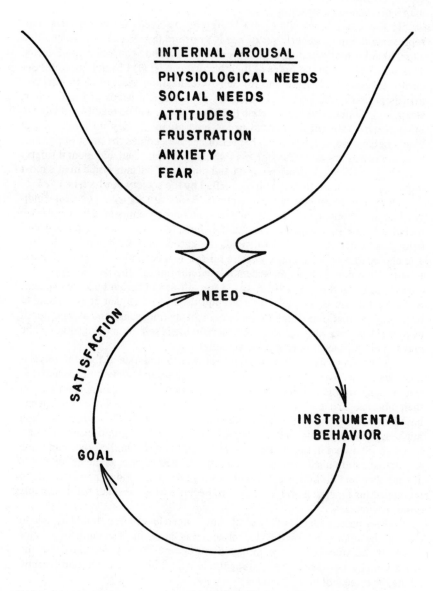

INTERNAL AROUSAL

PHYSIOLOGICAL NEEDS
SOCIAL NEEDS
ATTITUDES
FRUSTRATION
ANXIETY
FEAR

NEED

SATISFACTION

INSTRUMENTAL
BEHAVIOR

GOAL

FIGURE 2.

INTERNAL AROUSAL OF NEEDS

However, the cause of the pre-test anxiety is understood only by examining man's peculiar need structure.

In this case, Maslow's (1943) Hierarchy of Needs is chosen because it represents the most generic set of needs in use today. Maslow suggested that all mankind is motivated through a predetermined and sequential set of needs. This set of needs, in the order of their occurrence is: (1) Physiological, (2) Security, (3) Social, (4) Ego, and (5) Self-Actualization. According to Maslow, man is primarily motivated to attain the physiological needs of food, water, sleep, and shelter until he is certain that those needs will be readily available in his society. Once these survival needs are satisified, they no longer direct man's behavior and the next higher set of needs becomes the most important. Security needs are manifested in man's search for physical and mental safety. The feeling of freedom from physical and emotional harm become man's most important needs until they too, are satisified by the society in which he lives.

Once the physiological and security needs are satisifed to some individually acceptable level, the social needs become preeminent. This need level includes man's striving for social relationships, love, affection, and a sense of belonging. Once this need is satisfied, the ego need directs man's behavior. The ego need is based on man's desire for self-respect and esteem from others. Finally, as one maintains an acceptable equilibrium in the physiological, security, social, and ego needs, the need for self-actualization becomes salient. Self-actualization is seen as man's attempt to become all that he is capable of becoming, a condition which exists only in an abstract sense and as a matter of degree. Thus, one who has found his place in life is self-actualizing although he may never become completely self-actualized.

It is germane to Maslow's theory for one to understand that the physiological, security, social, and ego needs are all considered deficit needs and that self-actualization is the only growth need. Deficit needs are important only in their absence. That is, man moves through the sequential lower four needs based on an expected lack of fulfillment of each need. Therefore, a person might join several fraternal organizations and a church group in order to attempt to fill a void in the social or belongingness need. On the other hand, the self-actualization need is considered a growth need in that, as the deficit needs are satisfied and no longer provide the energy for motivation, man attempts to recognize his inner self and he strives to become what his inner self is capable of becoming.

With a basic understanding of Maslow's need levels, one should be able to explain the anxiety felt by the student who was hurriedly cramming for a major exam. If the student was operating in the ego need level, the cause for the anxiety might be traced to the student's fear of failing the exam and thereby losing the esteem of his classmates.

In this example, illustrated in Figure 3, the ego need is threatened by an impending loss of esteem which engenders the internal arousal felt as anxiety. This internal arousal causes the student to study in order to pass the exam and ultimately to attain the goal of satisfying the ego need.

This example of the ego need fulfillment brings up another critical dif-

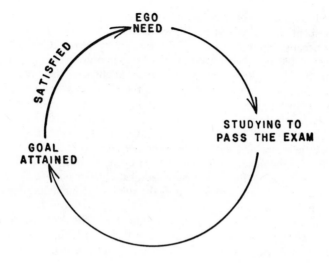

FIGURE 3.

ANXIOUS STUDENT MOTIVATION CYCLE

ference between the lower order physiological and security needs and the higher order social, ego, and self-actualization needs. The main difference in the two orders of needs is the number of alternate behaviors that one may choose to fulfill a need. The lower order needs are rather simple to fulfill—the thirst need will cause one to ingest water in some form or other. However, in the higher order needs, multiple behaviors are available to satisfy the need. Therefore, one who is at the ego need level might gain esteem by writing a book, buying a flashy car, becoming a scratch golfer, throwing the best parties in town, or any other individually derived behavior that leads to the personal fulfillment of the ego need. Consequently, by using this simple motivation cycle model, one is able to predict that a thirsty person will be motivated to search for water and to drink it, but one is not able to predict with any degree of assurance what specific behavior this person might employ to satisfy a social, ego, or self-actualization need.

Because the satisfying behaviors for the higher order needs are not easily predicted, the knowledge of the particular need level being activated is a necessary but not sufficient condition for a leader to understand in his attempt to motivate his followers toward a particular task. Take the case of a teacher who wants to motivate a class to study so that all members of the class can achieve a maximum score on a standardized exam. If the teacher knew that all of the students were operating from the ego need level, and if he or she attempted to capitalize on that fact by offering recognition for superior academic achievement, it still would not be sufficient to predict diligent studying behavior because alternate esteem behaviors are available. It is likely that some students would study very hard for the exam in order to satisfy their need for recognition and esteem. Others, however, might gain their recognition and esteem by applying their efforts outside the classroom toward some athletic endeavor. In both cases, the ego need might be satisified while the teacher would have failed to get the class achievement to the desired level. Therefore, in order to entice all students to perform very highly in the classroom and not to apply their available time to an alternate endeavor, the teacher must add some outside influence to the motivation cycle. In this example, the teacher might offer a special free time award for all students who reach a certain level of achievement, in hopes of permitting the students to maximize their ego satisfaction in their own way.

This example helps to point out the necessity for understanding an external model of the motivation cycle. In this model, shown as Figure 4, the GOAL is replaced by an INCENTIVE in hopes of engendering a specific

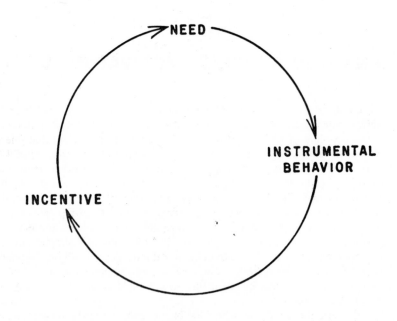

FIGURE 4.

EXTERNAL MOTIVATION CYCLE

instrumental behavior which, ideally, would also permit the individual to reach the goal of need satisfaction.

The external nature of this model is emphasized because, by definition, the individual probably would not have chosen the one instrumental behavior desired by the leader without the external influence of the incentive. Remembering the student example from above, it is obvious that all students would not choose to perform the necessary amount of studying to assure a maximum score. Therefore, the externally imposed incentive was applied by the teacher in an attempt to influence the necessary studying behavior.

It should be recognized at this point that the leader's influence on the motivation cycle is limited to observing the instrumental behavior, to setting the particular incentives, and in a limited sense, to teaching the preferred method of dealing with an excited need. The last case is the most difficult operation to implement because it involves a detailed analysis of the socialization process and will not be covered in this article. The leader can also observe and make spot corrections on instrumental behavior but this influence requires the leader's presence for every correction. The more practical situation is for the leader to develop incentives with sufficent attractiveness to draw out the desired behavior and cause individuals to work on their own toward the achievement of the incentive.

Selecting incentives with sufficient attractiveness is, however, a complex problem. Incentives come in two packages—punishment and reward. What appears to be attractive to one individual in a group may not seem to be as attractive to another. Therefore, the leader is met again with the responsibility of understanding the individual need levels of his followers and, in addition, understanding how well-received certain incentives would be for each individual. To help understand the attractiveness of incentives, the concept of subjective probability will be useful (Mosel, 1964). *Subjective probability* refers to the potential value one might ascribe to any one incentive and it is defined by three terms. These terms are (1) availability, (2) expectancy, and (3) worthwhileness. *Availability* is a leader characteristic and refers to an individual's perception that the leader has the authority and/or the resources to apply the incentive. *Expectancy* is a follower characteristic and refers to an individual's perception that it is within his repertoire of behaviors to perform the necessary instrumental behavior that will assure the attainment or avoidance of the incentive. *Worthwhileness* is a value judgment by the individual and refers to the trade-off of what must be sacrificed in order to obtain the reward or avoid the punishment.

These three terms, which can be assigned numerical values form 0 to 1 (no chance to complete assurance), must be multiplied together to arrive at the relative strength of any stated incentive. This dynamic characteristic is similar to the technique of expectancy theory (Lawler, 1973) represented in its most elemental form. The numerical values assigned to each term are dependent on an individual's perception of their significance. But, because the perception is based on an individual's belief in the existence of each term, it is difficult, if not impossible, to know their value before the fact.

For instance, take the case of a leader who offers a reward that is not available to him but one which his troops believe he has the ability to award. As long as they perceive that the leader can provide the reward (availability), that they have the behavioral capability to perform the tasks required to get the reward (expectancy), and that the reward is considered valuable to them (worthwhileness), then the subjective probability of that incentive would be high. If, over time, however, the leader promises rewards that he either cannot or will not deliver, the troops' perception of the availability of that reward, and possibly most other rewards offered by that particular leader will diminish. Since the three terms must be multiplied together to arrive at the strength of an incentive, if any of the terms is perceived as having a value of zero, then the incentive becomes essentially meaningless to the concerned individual. It is critical to understand that an individual's perception of the values applied to each element of subjective probability is the determining factor for the strength of each incentive.

The leader should be aware of some fundamental principles concerning incentives and their expected effectiveness. It is safe to assume that most people equate rewards with positive feelings and punishment with negative feelings and thereby conclude that rewards are better. A more accurate conclusion drawn from behavioral research indicates that there are appropriate times for both types of incentives. As Hays and Thomas (1967) have reported, it is appropriate to reward particularly outstanding behavior which serves as a positive example because rewards tend to result in better retention and learning in the long run. However, rewards can also foster dishonesty in overzealous attempts to gain their positive benefits, and they can be mistaken as a bribe to tolerate unethical manipulation of behavior.

Recently, Green and Lepper (1974) reported another disadvantage of rewards. It was found that in cases where task performance was intrinsically motivating, but where external rewards were applied to induce better performance, that lower performance resulted when the external rewards were no longer available. Therefore, a person who likes to work for the sheer enjoyment of doing a good job, but who is offered a reward for continuing to do what he likes to do anyway, might learn to dislike his work unless some external reward is continually offered. This means that a leader must be able to identify particularly outstanding accomplishments because rewards have the potential to lose their incentive value if awarded too often or for normal accomplishments.

Also, according to Hays and Thomas (1967), punishment incentives have similar advantages and disadvantages. It is considered appropriate to use punishment when there is a need to maintain minimum standards in all members and minimum standards are acceptable. It is also appropriate to use punishment when an individual fails, over time, to respond to other incentives. In any event, prior to punishing an individual, it must be determined that the failure of the individual was based on his lack of motivation and not his lack of ability. It is unacceptable to punish a soldier for getting lost in the woods if he was never trained in land navigation nor issued a compass.

There are two main disadvantages to the use of punishment as an incentive. Punishing people for undesirable behavior merely illustrates what not to do instead of concentrating on the range of acceptable behaviors. Also, punishment tends to motivate behavior to meeting only the minimum level of performance.

It should be remembered that while rewards and punishments are established by the leader, their effectiveness is judged through the perceptions of the followers. Several incentive programs have failed to engender the desired behavior because what the leader thought to be a reward was perceived by his unit as a punishment. Time off is generally regarded as a reward except in those circumstances where, because of location or lack of facilities, the free time results in long, boring hours with nothing to do.

With the emphasis on incentives and their applicability to individual perception, it should now be possible to superimpose the internal and external motivation cycle and to work with a situation involving the composite motivation cycle (see Figure 5).

For example, consider the situation where a platoon leader is interested in motivating increased physical fitness performance from his troops. It would be assumed that the platoon's mission demanded a specific physical fitness level from each member and that the platoon leader was interested in assuring that everyone met that condition. In designing his motivation plan, the platoon leader would know from past experience which members of his platoon had or had not internalized the value of staying in good physical condition and which ones did not have the basic ability. Also, it would be appropriate to assume that most platoon members were operating at Maslow's social or ego need levels and that the platoon leader should develop his motivation plan with those needs in mind.

For those individuals who had internalized the value of physical fitness because of the intrinsic benefits of remaining physically fit, perhaps no external incentive would be necessary to continue to elicit their motivated performance. However, if a reward incentive is offered to induce higher performance from others, that same reward should be offered to the internally-committed troops so that a relative deprivation condition would not exist.

For those individuals who had the basic ability but had not internalized the value of physical fitness, it would be necessary to influence better performance through incentives. The platoon leader would plan his incentives to support the internal needs of the individuals. By so doing, he would be attempting to link the externally-derived incentives to the positive internal valuation process of worthwhileness, and thereby, to the ultimate satisfaction of the individual's aroused need.

It is hoped that the platoon leader would endeavor to provide a sufficient number of reward incentives to cover all of his platoon's ability levels. However, it must be recognized that it remains the platoon leader's responsibility to insure minimum performance level attainment from those for whom the subjective probability value of the reward is low or zero. Punishment incentives should perhaps be considered to insure these minimum standards.

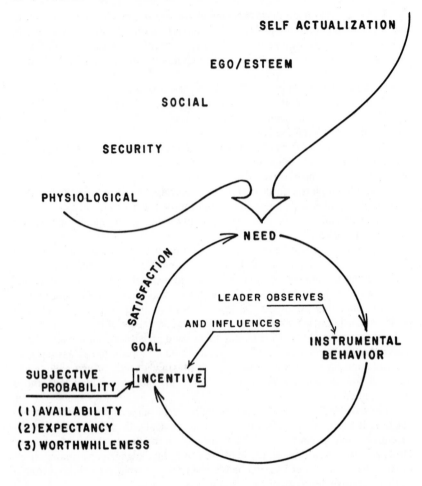

FIGURE 5.

COMPOSITE MOTIVATION CYCLE

By now it should be apparent that in order to be successful at motivating individuals to higher levels of performance, a leader must understand the fundamental concepts and relationships of the composite motivation cycle. To influence the behavior of others toward the accomplishment of organizational tasks will demand a working knowledge of the needs, capabilities, and goals of individuals working in groups. However, because of the size of most groups that a leader will influence and the requirement to attend to other organizational matters, it will be a rare occasion when the leader can plan for and implement a completely individual motivation program—one which will touch everyone. One should not forget, however, that the essence of individuality must be understood by each potential leader, for it is to this uniquely complex quality that motivation applies.[1]

END NOTE

1. The student should recall the functional definition of leadership in organizations referred to in the introductory article of this text (see the Model of Organizational Leadership). Many of the concepts discussed in that definitional model apply to the motivational aspects discussed in the present article.

REFERENCES

Green, D. and Lepper, M.R. "How to Turn Play into Work", *Psychology Today*. Vol. 8, No. 4, September, 1974, pp. 49–54.

Hays, S.H. and Thomas, W.N. (Eds.) *Taking Command*. Harrisburg, Pennsylvania: Stackpole Company, 1967.

Herzberg, F. *Work and the Nature of Man*. New York: World Publishing Company, 1966.

Lawler, E.E. *Motivation in Work Organizations*. Monterey: Brooks/Cole Publishing Company, 1973.

Madsen, K.B. *Theories of Motivation*. Kent State University Press, 1968.

Maslow, A.H. "A Theory of Human Motivation" in *Psychological Review*, Vol. 50, pp. 370–396, 1943.

Morgan, C.T. and King, R.A. *Introduction to Psychology* (Fourth Edition) New York: McGraw-Hill Book Company, 1971.

Mosel, J.N. "Motivation" in *Management Views; Selected Speeches,* Vol IX, Part 3, pp. 95–119, 1964.

Teevan, R.C. and Birney, R.C. (Eds.) *Theories of Motivation in Personality and Social Psychology*. New York: Van Nostrand Reinhold Company, 1964.

Vroom, V.H. *Work and Motivation*. New York: John Wiley and Sons, 1964.

Wilkins, L. and Richter, C.P. "A great craving for salt by a child with cortico-adrenal insufficiency," in *Journal of American Medical Association,* Vol. 114, pp. 866–868, 1940.

Rewards and Punishments

by
Office of Military Leadership

REWARDS

Basically a reward consists of something of value that the learner or performer may obtain as a result of his performance. There are a large number of specific rewards that are available to leaders, including verbal approval, training holidays and passes, monetary rewards, trophies, badges, and combat decorations. For the reward to be of value, it must be something that either satisfies a basic motive or can be used to gain some satisfaction. For example, a decoration for valor is of direct value because it increases the status of the recipient. On the other hand, a training holiday has value only in that the time may be used to satisfy some other need, such as rest.

In comparison with punishment, reward has certain advantages. Psychological research indicates that as a general rule, reward results in better learning, both in that it occurs more rapidly and is more lasting (Sarason, 1957). Reward shows specifically what to do by reinforcing exactly that behavior which is to be learned. As a motivational device, it has the advantage of having a positive attraction. If the soldier really wants the reward, he will be willing to expend a great deal of effort to get it. Further, the use of reward usually results in higher morale and a desire to continue to do well in the future.

Reproduced from text *Taking Command,* Stackpole Company 1967, pp. 181–189 by permission of the publisher and the Director of OML.

There are disadvantages inherent in the rewarding process, however. It may foster the use of dishonest methods in order to gain the reward without meeting the required standard of performance. Cheating in school is one example. In this case, the dishonest person is attempting to gain the reward—a passing grade—without meeting the standard of performance, knowing the subject. In the Army the falsification of range scores constitutes another example. Again, the overuse of rewards can take on the aspects of a bribe. "If you reward me, I will do as you ask." This unhealthy situation may well lead to reduced effort when no further rewarding takes place. The concept of periodic reinforcement is particularly applicable here. Psychological studies show that learning is extinguished more slowly if the learner is rewarded only occasionally during the learning process rather than every time he performs satisfactorily (Jenkins and Stanley, 1950). In practical terms, this would seem to indicate that only exceptional behavior should be rewarded consistently. Behavior that just meets the standard deserves only occasional reward.

Promised Reward

The technique of promising a reward for good performance can be an effective means of achieving increased effort on that task. But, it may have little if any effect on performance in the future.

If overdone, it can actually result in poor performance in the future when no such promise is made. Before making such a promise, the leader must know that he can deliver. If a promise is made and the performance meets that standard, but the promise cannot be fulfilled, the result is a loss of faith in the leader. His followers will tend to place less faith in his promises. In this respect, it is not even wise to promise to "try to get" a reward for good performance. In spite of the qualifying nature of such statements, they are perceived as actual promises by the subordinates; and the same loss of faith occurs if the reward cannot be obtained. The leader must have a realistic concept of his power to produce on his promises. He undermines his influence whenever he attempts to do more for his men than he can reasonably hope to accomplish (Pelz, 1952).

Unpromised Rewards

It is not necessary to promise a reward before giving one. Good work deserves recognition. When an individual or unit has performed in an exceptional manner, they have earned some reward. The purpose of a reward of this nature is to motivate future good performance both by the person rewarded and by others who observe that he has been rewarded. Actually, the leader has a great deal more flexibility in a reward of this nature. A pat on the back, a word of praise or an expression of thanks is often an excellent form of reward in a case of this nature; yet, surprisingly, a promise of such a reward may be looked upon as hardly worth striving for. Decorations fall in this category. It is doubtful that more than a tiny fraction of Americans ever fought well in combat simply to earn a decoration, yet, most men deeply appreciate recognition of their acts. Contrary to the situation in which a reward is promised before performance, it is not inappropriate to promise to "try to get" a reward for performance after it has occurred.

Except in the case of a private word of thanks or praise, a reward granted after performance must be for performance which is clearly exceptional. Since no previous standards are established, it becomes increasingly necessary that the performance is perceived as clearly deserving of recognition by all who do not achieve the reward. Otherwise, the commander may be accused of playing favorites. Because of the halo effect, there is a tendency to perceive good performance on the part of those men who have performed well in the past, when in fact their current performance is not so deserving.

Presentation of Rewards

As a general rule, when a reward is rendered, it deserves public recognition. In this way, it not only adds to the status of the individual being rewarded, but it also aids in the teaching and motivation of others by showing what behaviors are worthy of reward. Public recognition may be accomplished by presenting the reward at a ceremony, by publishing it in the newspaper or in official orders, or by merely praising the individual in front of the group. The word "public", however, probably requires some clarification. The reward should be public to those who perceive it as worthy. A combat decoration for valor deserves the widest public recognition, but commendations for good work in other fields may prove embarrassing to the individual recipient if public recognition is made before a group that does not appreciate the work. For example, if a rifle company commander should publicly praise his orderly room clerk in front of a company formation, he may find that he has done considerably more harm than good. The combat troops in the company may subject the clerk to considerable ridicule. Yet, if the clerk's work has been clearly deserving of reward, it should at least be so recognized by the commander and the others in the orderly room who can appreciate the reward.

Group rewards build solidarity and esprit providing that the group works together as a team to achieve the reward. Group reward is normally more effective than individual awards in competitions between groups. It is interesting to note that competitions of this nature can build solidarity even in groups that do not receive the reward, although there is a danger in group rewards that some members may be singled out as scapegoats if the group fails to achieve the reward.

An example of an activity that may be applicable for group reward would be a squad Army Training Test. The success of the entire group depends on the degree to which each member performs his own duty, as well as on the way they interact in the group performance. Since the group is relatively small, each member knows what the other member is doing. Therefore, there can be some control of individual behavior by the group.

PUNISHMENT

Normally punishment is considered as the diametric opposite of reward. It consists of some unpleasant penalty imposed upon the learner or performer because of behavior that fails to meet the desired standard. Training involves the correction of errors.

Punishment is one method of achieving discipline, because it indicates errors to avoid and provides motivation to avoid them.

In the use of punishment for either learning or motivational purposes, the basic guiding concept is that of justice. There are some serious disadvantages to punishment. If it is to accomplish its purpose and avoid unsatisfactory consequences, the followers must perceive the punishment as basically just. Consequently, the first principle in the administration of punishment is that the standards of punishable behavior are known beforehand. That is, not only should the soldier know what the standard is, but he should also know that behavior that fails to meet the standard will probably be punished. Although, legally, ignorance of the law is no excuse, it certainly is considered unjust by the soldier to be punished for an act that he did not know was wrong.

Behaviors that may be punishable are set forth by law and regulation and in the policies and direct orders of the commander. To ensure that the soldier is aware of those that are set forth by law, the Articles of the Uniform Code of Military Justice are read periodically to all troops. The leader also has a responsibility to bring other regulations and policies to the soldier's attention. This does not necessarily mean that each unit must prepare a detailed set of instructions outlining punishable behaviors. Many standards are learned in basic training, and the soldier should be aware thereafter that violation of these standards can lead to punishment. For example, the soldier learns in training that a failure to salute may lead to a verbal reprimand. He need not be periodically reminded of this. Nor is it necessary to point out that behavior that is generally socially disapproved, such as fighting, will be punished. In any case wherein there is a possibility that the soldier does not know that a particular act will be punished, however, he should be informed of this fact.

At times, it is appropriate for the leader to promise before a particular performance that those who fail in that performance will be punished. The purpose of such an act is to motivate to a minimum acceptable level, but it will seldom lead to performance much above this minimum level. An example of such a threatened use of punishment might be the warning that all who fail to pass a particular inspection will have to stand a second inspection on Saturday afternoon. Since such a punishment would occur at a specific time during which the soldier may have made previous plans, it is more just to announce this ahead of time than to wait until after the failure occurs. But, the constant use of threat every time a new task arises is an unhealthy device. As a general rule, it is better to establish general standards of punishable behavior and to ensure periodically that these standards are understood. As in the use of rewards, the extent of promised punishment should not exceed the leader's authority. For example, his ability to lead effectively is jeopardized if he threatens to reduce a man in rank and the reducing authority does not concur in the punishment.

When an act occurs that may lead to punishment, it is important that the leader make a thorough and impartial investigation to determine the cause of the individual's failure.

Research by the Human Resources Research Organization (HumRRO) reports that one characteristic of the effective platoon leader is his ability to differentiate between motivational failures and ability failures (Lange et al., 1958 and 1960). Motivational failures should be punished, but ability failures should not. In other words, if the soldier fails because he simply does not try enough or just does not care, the men perceive his punishment as just. But, if he fails because he lacks ability or because of other factors beyond his control, his punishment appears unjust. Thus, some form of investigation into the cause is essential. In the conduct of this investigation, if there is a possibility that the offense may lead to a court-martial, it is important to remember the rights of the accused and to protect these rights from the very beginning.

There is a certain danger in the term "disciplinary action" because it leads to the thought that discipline is gained solely through the use of punishment. Basically, good discipline is the product of good overall leadership in an organization. When a commander must resort to a great deal of punishment, this is an indication that discipline has already broken down. The further use of punishment may be the least appropriate method of restoring it.

Because of the basic American values of the freedom of the individual and the rule of law, the exact nature and authorized limits of punishments that a leader may impose are much more closely spelled out by law and regulation than is true of rewards. There are still a very large number and variety of punishments that he can impose. At the least severe level, the failure to achieve a reward is "punishing" to the individual who fails. With increasing severity, punishments range up to verbal disapproval, reprimand, loss of privileges, extra duty, restriction, or reduction in rank. They continue on to those that may only be imposed by court-martial—loss of pay and allowance, confinement, dishonorable discharge, and even death. Although court-martial offenses may occur with any group of soldiers, the small unit commander is primarily interested in those less severe punishments that increase learning and motivate performance.

In comparison with rewards, punishments also have certain advantages. Generally, they are easier to administer in the sense that it is easier to discriminate behaviors that are worthy of punishment than those that are worthy of reward. It is easier to select a punishment that most men would wish to avoid than a reward that most would seek to achieve. It is probably for these reasons that punishment tends to be used more frequently than reward as a motivating device in the Army. Punishment does show behaviors to be avoided, and at times this may be highly important. For example, careless behavior that could lead to a safety violation must be avoided, and punishment can teach avoidance of such acts. Punishment is considered just and necessary when behavior is substantially out of line with expected standards. A failure to punish in such cases may well lead to considerable dissatisfaction on the part of the other members of the group who are complying with the standards. Further, both the potential to administer and the occasional use of some form of punishment is often necessary if the unit is to function at all. Otherwise, some persons may easily divert the group from the task.

Punishment does, however, have some serious inherent disadvantages. It is a poor learning technique in that it is based on fear, and the emotion may well interfere with learning. Although it shows what not to do, it does not show what to do. Thus, it is a highly inefficient method of learning because mistakes of a completely different nature may still occur after punishment. Many will search for loopholes—and find them—so that the leader finds himself constantly refining his rules until the discriminations become so minute that no one can understand them. In some cases punishment backfires, resulting in a stereotyped repetition of the same error. This occurs either because the anxiety associated with the punishment prevents logical thinking, or because the punishment has angered the recipient to the extent that he stubbornly refuses to comply.

Because of its unpleasant nature, punishment can lead to a dislike of everything connected with it, to include both the activity and the punishing person. For example, a soldier punished for some action taking place on the firing range may grow to dislike all aspects of weapons firing. He may actively seek to avoid future firing and make little effort to do well on the range. The punishing person is usually resented, even when the punishment is just. This resentment may lead to derogatory remarks about the leader and possibly to displaced aggression upon some innocent party. In a unit that leans heavily on punishment, there is often much bickering and fighting among members, which destroys esprit. Finally, punishment is somewhat unpleasant for the leader to administer. In spite of its unpleasantness and its possible bad effects, the leader should not hesitate to punish when the situation calls for it. If he is wise and just in his use of punishment, he can avoid many of the disadvantages of this form of motivation.

Rendering Punishment

In punishing offenses the leader must take into consideration the effect of the punishment on the offender, as well as on the group as a whole. Its purpose is threefold—to prevent a repetition of the offense by the offender, to deter a similar offense by another individual, and to maintain group standards of discipline.

Any punishment must, of course, be within the authority of the leader to administer. It should be appropriate to the offense and to the individual being punished. Although the general rule is that the commander should be consistent in his punishment, there are factors that militate against the assignment of the exact same penalty every time the same offense is committed. For one thing, the standards upon which punishment is based shift upward as the soldier becomes better trained. For example, the soldier who fails to salute during his first few days in basic training probably receives a correction. But, if he has been in the service for several months and still fails to salute, he deserves more severe punishment. The number of the soldier's previous offenses has an effect on the severity of the punishment meted out by the commander. The commander also considers extenuating circumstances or matters in mitigation in deciding on the exact punishment. Basically, he must be consistent in that all failures to meet the required standards are noted, investigated, and some action taken to correct them. Whether this action involves mere correction, retraining, or some degree of punishment, are all matters which depend on the facts uncovered in the investigation.

If punishment is to be of any value, it must be informative. The soldier punished must know what he is being punished for so he will know what to avoid in the future. Punishment in the form of censure of the individual is normally administered in private so as to avoid embarrassing the soldier in front of others. It may on occasions be necessary to make a public, on-the-spot correction. This is embarrassing and thus a punishment in the eyes of the soldier. Also, the announcement of other punishments to the individual is usually private. Even punishment in private aids learning on the part of others. Troops usually know when a soldier commits an offense that results in his being called into the commander's presence. Further, when the punishment involves more than mere reprimand, the serving of the punishment is public.

It is especially important that the leader administers punishment with dignity and that he respects the dignity of the soldier. The leader must avoid displays of anger or personal animosity toward the punished person. He should convey the impression that the soldier is being punished because of improper behavior and not because the soldier is basically bad. The soldier should leave the interview with the impression that he can, and is expected to, perform better in the future.

One of the hardest things for a leader to learn and practice is that when a man has undergone punishment, he then becomes a member in good standing in the organization. One may have lingering or lasting doubts as to the man's judgment or attitude, but the leader must scrupulously avoid further penalty for an atoned offense. Other members of the organization perceiving any extension of a punishment may become incensed and resentful, even to the point of condoning or minimizing the offense that led to the punishment.

As a general rule, punishment should be meted out to specific violators rather than the entire group. It can be extremely discouraging to a soldier to strive hard personally but still get punished because someone else did not. Such a situation is equivalent to punishing a man for an ability failure. Although adequately motivated, he is punished because of his inability to control the behavior of the others in the group. Thus, unless rarely used, group punishment may lead to a "what's-the-use" attitude on the part of the initially motivated soldier. There are times, however, when group punishment may be in order to increase the sense of responsibility among group members for each other's behavior.

The authors of The American Soldier studies, noting the strong American tradition of team sports, wondered that the Army used group reward so seldom as a motivating device during World War II. They noted also that very little experimental research had been done in the areas of both group reward and group punishment. Based on the results of several questionnaires administered to Army samples, they were able to draw up certain conditions that appear necessary for either group reward or group punishment to be effective motivating devices. Two key points are particularly applicable to both group reward and group punishment. These are: the men must know that all members of the group will win the reward or receive the punishment, and the group must be able to identify the potential violators and control their behavior (Stouffer et al., 1949).

A barracks inspection may be an appropriate situation for group punishment. Of course, it is necessary to announce ahead of time that the whole barracks will be restricted or receive some other punishment if it fails to pass. In this case, definite group pressure can be placed upon those individuals who do not take action to prepare for the inspection. The delinquency report rate of an organization is an example of a situation that would not be appropriate for either group reward or group punishment. The men have little if any control over the off-duty behavior of the other men in the group. This illustrates the point that group rewards and punishments are most effective in accomplishing their purposes of learning, motivation, and group solidarity when they are based on duty performances rather than any off-duty activity. Esprit, expressed in group norms and group sanctions, can often act to influence off-duty activity. This is a manifestation of the interaction between discipline and esprit.

Where's Your Attitude?†

by
Robert F. Mager

What does your doctor do when you ask him, Am I healthy? How does he determine your state of health? What does it take to cause him to use that abstract term in relation to your condition? He looks at specifics. He takes your blood pressure, counts your pulse—checks your reflexes and kicks your tires. He looks for a great number of specific indicators that, taken collectively, are the basis for statements about health. If most of these indicators are positive (no sign of trouble), he is willing to say you are healthy. The point is, when you want to find out if you are healthy, a doctor doesn't check your health; he checks specific physiological indicators and uses them as his basis for judgments about health. The specifics collectively define the abstract.

Now let's consider abstractions in general—and attitudes in particular. The main reason we don't succeed too well with attitudes is that we just don't know what we are talking about when we use the term. One hears teachers saying things like, "Today I'm teaching a cognitive lesson; tomorrow I'm going to do an affective one,"* as though they believed they had some control over whether they influenced someone's attitude, as though they didn't know that they influence attitude whether they like it or not. One also hears comments such as, "We've got to teach them to have the right attitude," implying that attitudes are mainly influenced by cognitive lessons, by teaching someone to know something he didn't know before. It is as though they have forgotten that

---

†From the book, *Goal Analysis* by Robert Mager, copyright © 1972 by Fearon Publishers. Reprinted by permission of Fearon Publishers, Inc.

*If words like "cognitive" and "affective" disturb you, do what I do. When you see cognitive, think "knowing"; when you see affective, think "feeling"; and when you see psychomotor, think "doing." This oversimplifies things, it is true; but at least you don't lose out when someone uses special words when ordinary ones will do.

the cognitive and psychomotor have to do with what a person can do, and the affective with what he will do.

But think about it for a moment. Just what do we mean when we use the word "attitude"? Is attitude a thing?

Well, no. Not a thing like a meringue or a mukluk. Things are what you can poke with your fingers or beat with a stick. Attitudes are not that sort of thing. You can't dissect someone and take out his attitude any more than you can dissect him and take out his laugh. That doesn't mean that attitudes and laughter don't exist; it's just that they aren't directly available for physical examination—or for poking or punching. So if attitude isn't a thing, what is it?

Attitude is a word, that's what it is. And words mean whatever their users want them to mean. (This one seems to have more misusers than users.)

By attitude, we generally mean to describe an abstraction, some sort of general state or condition existing inside ourselves or others. When someone says, "He has a favorable attitude toward mukluks," he is suggesting that the person will behave in one way when faced with a mukluk rather than in another. He is suggesting that the mukluk-lover will tend to say favorable things about the object, that he will tend to move toward the object when he sees one rather than away from it, and that he will tend to seek out ways to come into contact with the object. Similarly, a person who is said to have a favorable attitude toward music would be expected to say favorable things about the activity, to respond favorably when in the presence of the activity, and to seek out ways of increasing the amount of time that he is in the presence of the activity.

An interesting thing about attitudes is that every statement about attitude is a statement of prediction. No matter what someone says about the attitude of someone else, he is making a prediction about how that person is likely to behave in the future. Based on what he has seen someone do or heard him say in the past, he predicts how he will perform in the future. If you see me turn a bowl of fish soup over the cook's head, you might be urged to comment: "He has a negative attitude toward fish soup." Such a comment is based on what you saw me do, and is intended to predict that putting me in the presence of fish soup will be followed by some sort of negative act or comment on my part (toward the soup). You might be right or wrong, but the statement about attitude is a statement of prediction, a statement that intends to suggest how I might behave in some future time.

Since an attitude is not directly visible, it follows that all statements about attitude are based on circumstantial evidence that takes the form of visible behavior. If you hadn't seen me dump the fish soup on the cook, or heard or read an account of the fish story, you would have had no basis whatever for making a statement about how I am likely to behave in the presence of fish soup. You might be wrong in your attitude statement (your prediction); it might be the cook I dislike and not the fish soup. No problem; lots of people make incorrect predictions from the information available to them. The point is simply that, right or wrong, a statement about attitude is a statement of prediction based on what somebody says or what somebody does.

The behaviors on which attitude statements are made can properly be called indicator behaviors, for they are used as indicators of attitude. Indicators are a common item of our existence. We use thermometers to indicate temperature, speedometers to indicate speed, and voltmeters to indicate voltage. In each case, we use some sort of device to tell us the state or condition of something we cannot see or measure directly.

Some indicators are better than others. A voltmeter is a better indicator of the amount of voltage present in a circuit than the sensation you feel when you grab the wire. The loudness of the "ouch" is not directly related to the amount of the voltage; if you hired a wire-grabbing Ouchman and tried to measure the amount of voltage from the loudness of his ouches, you would have less success than if you employed a voltmeter.

The same holds true for attitudes and their indicator behaviors. Some behaviors are better indicators (predictors) of attitude than others, and it isn't always easy to tell which is better. To make it more difficult, any particular behavior might well be an indicator of any number of attitudes. When I poured the fish soup on the cook, he couldn't tell whether that behavior was indicating a distaste for fish soup, his version of fish soup, fat cooks, fur-lined soup bowls, or dirty aprons. In the absence of some other indicators (behaviors) on my part, he could predict pretty well that I found something distinctly not to my liking, but not what. He would need more behavior on my part if he wanted to be sure. If, while carrying out the deed, I spoke thusly: "Sir, my distaste for fish soup is exceeded only by my distaste for fish stew," he would have a better clue as to how to interpret my soup-pouring behavior.

So, for example, instead of merely noting that someone chews gum when he enters a classroom and then predicting, "He has a poor attitude about my course," it is more prudent to try to find at least several of the indicators that are predictive of the attitude in which you are interested. If you know which performances you will accept as your meaning of an attitude or other goal, you will also know how to assess whether the attitude (tendency to perform one way rather than another) is in the condition you would like. You will also have clues about which performances to change in order to improve that condition; when someone changes what he does, others are likely to change the words they use to describe him. As an example, if a person has been labeled "hostile" because of his tendency to throw pies in the faces of his colleagues and then gives up this performance, others are likely to stop calling him hostile and begin referring to him as reformed, or mellowed, or as having had a change of heart.

Notice that nothing in this discussion has had anything to do with behaviorism . . . or any sort of ism. The concern with what people do and what they say does not stem from any sort of philosophical base. We are concerned with behavior because we have no other choice, no other route into the heart or mind of a person. It is the only sound basis we have for judgments about what is happening inside another human being. No matter how deeply we may desire that someone "internalize his growing awareness" or "feel a deep appreciation for the value of trees," the only evidence we have of the existence of such conditions is the person's behavior—what he says and what he does.

To make a goal more achievable, it is useful to know the meaning of the goal in terms of the performances that would cause you to agree the goal has been achieved. This is the purpose of the goal analysis, one tool to use toward derivation of meaningful outcomes of instruction. Since knowing when to use a tool is a significant part of knowing how to use it, we will begin with some practice in recognizing situations in which it will pay you to rummage through your toolbox for the goal analysis.

Attitude Change*

by
Jonathan L. Freedman, J. Merrill Carlsmith, and David O. Sears

FACTORS AFFECTING ATTITUDE CHANGE

Although there are many variables that affect attitude change, they can all be described in terms of two general factors—trust in the persuasive message and the strength of the message itself. If the target does not trust the message or its source, he will not accept the communication nor change his attitude. Similarly, if the message is not strong enough to convince him or discrepant enough to attack his own position, there will be no pressure on him to change. Thus, in order to effect an attitude change, a message must be both trusted and powerful.

Since a persuasive communication presents a position that is discrepant from the one held by the target, there is always some tendency for him to disbelieve or mistrust it. This lack of trust usually centers around the source of the communication—he is dishonest, stupid, misinformed, etc.—but can be produced by the communication itself—it is so extreme or biased that it loses credibility. To the extent that mistrust is aroused, the individual is unlikely to be influenced. As we have said, rejection of the source and of the message are two alternatives to attitude change, and the less trust he feels, the more likely the target is to use these alternatives. Conversely, the more trustworthy the source and the message, the more likely the target is to accept what the communication says and to change his attitude.

Largely independent of the trust factor is the power of the communication

---

itself. How much pressure does it put on the individual to change his attitude? A perfectly trusted, clearly heard, and clearly understood communication would still produce little change if its arguments were weak and presented in a faltering, unimpressive manner. The same message presented twice—or fifty times, as in television advertising—has more power than if shown only once. The discrepancy between the position of the individual and that of the message is also a determinant of power—the larger the discrepancy, the more stress the message produces.

The power of the persuasive communication is especially related to the target's ability to refute, distort, or ignore its arguments. The weaker the message, the more likely he is to use these alternatives rather than changing his attitude. Thus, assuming a communication is heard and is perfectly trusted, the amount of attitude change it can produce still varies, and this variance is due largely to what may be called its power or force.

It is not always possible to say that a particular variable involves only trust or only power, but most factors do seem to affect one more than the other. In any case, keeping these two dimensions in mind will help in understanding how each factor determines the effectiveness of a persuasive attempt.

With this background, we can turn to a consideration of the specific factors that increase or decrease the amount of attitude change produced by a persuasive communication after it has reached its target. These factors are divided into several classes: factors involving the source of the communication, factors concerning the communication itself, factors in the surrounding environment that are extraneous to the communication and the participants, and factors that involve characteristics of the individual who is the target of the persuasive attempt.

THE SOURCE OF THE COMMUNICATION
Prestige of the Communicator

One of the most straightforward and reliable findings is that the greater the prestige of the communicator, the more attitude change is produced. By *prestige* we refer primarily to how expert the communicator is perceived to be in the area of concern and how much he is respected by the individual receiving the communication. For example, when evaluations of a new medicine are attributed to a noted doctor, they are more persuasive than when they are attributed to a housewife. If T.S. Eliot says that a certain poem is good, he should have more influence than a barber saying it is good. This effect of prestige was demonstrated in a study by Hovland and Weiss (1952).

Subjects heard communications concerned with four issues: the advisability of selling antihistamines without a prescription, whether the steel industry was to blame for the then-current steel shortage, the future of the movie industry in the context of the growing popularity of television, and the practicality of building an atomic-powered submarine. Each communication came from either a high or low-prestige source. For example, the communication on atomic submarines was supposedly either by J. Robert Oppenheimer, a noted, high-prestige physicist, or from Pravda. The results indicated that communications attributed to high-prestige sources produced more change than those from low-prestige sources.

In another study (Aronson, Turner, and Carlsmith, 1963), subjects were told they were in an experiment on aesthetics and were asked to evaluate nine stanzas from obscure modern poems. They then read someone else's evaluation of one of the stanzas they had not liked very much. The communication argued that the poem was better than the subject had indicated. It was described as being either somewhat better, much better, or very much better than the subject had thought. The crucial variable was that the communication was supposedly from either T.S. Eliot or Agnes Stearns, who was described as a student at Mississippi State Teachers College. After reading the communication, the subjects reevaluated the poems. Regardless of the level of discrepancy between the communication and the subject's initial position, there was more change with the high-prestige communicator than there was with the low-prestige one.

The evidence shows that we give more weight to a communication from someone we respect—someone who has high status, who is renowned in his field—than to a communication from someone who has less prestige. If we disagree with a communicator, it is more difficult to reject him if he has high prestige than if he has low prestige. This does not mean that a communication from a high-prestige source automatically or universally produces a huge amount of attitude change. But it does mean that, other things being equal, a high-prestige communicator effects more attitude change than a low-prestige communicator, because people have more faith or trust in his knowledge and opinions.

An interesting question, not yet answered, is whether an expert in one field can transfer the influence of his expertise to another field. If T.S. Eliot, who is highly respected in the field of poetry, took a stand on politics or education, would his opinion carry more weight and produce more attitude change than someone less well-known? Although there is little evidence on this question, it seems likely that an expert may be able to transfer some of his influence to *related* fields. For example, T.S. Eliot would probably be quite influential if he discussed the teaching of English or even of music. However, as the area of concern became more different from his own area, the fact that he was an expert would matter less and he would be less able to transfer his power of persuasion. His comments on the teaching of English would probably be quite persuasive even though teaching is not his major field; his comments on the teaching of music or on contemporary theater would also be quite persuasive; his comments on politics or ethics would be less persuasive; and his comments on space technology or submarine warfare would probably be no more persuasive than anybody else's. However, for the moment this is just speculation. The question of the transferability of prestige is an open question, which should be more fully investigated in the future.

Politicians often try to transfer their own popularity and prestige to another politician. An outgoing President tries to campaign for his party's candidate. A popular senator may campaign for local candidates in his home state. Although the popular figures do attract large crowds, there is little evidence that their popularity is transferred to the other person. At the end of his Presidential term, Eisenhower was one of the most popular men who ever held public office, and yet his endorsement of Nixon seemed to have done little good. Although this is not exactly the same thing as transferring prestige from one area of concern to another, it does suggest the difficulty of any such transfer.

It might be noted that many advertisements involve famous athletes or movie stars endorsing a product. Obviously the advertising companies believe that this helps sales. Whether or not it does is not known for certain, but if it does, it might be due to a somewhat different phenomenon than the one we have been discussing. The football star who shaves with a particular razor blade may help sales of that blade by associating his popularity with it. He is not convincing anyone that he knows much about blades or that they are better blades but is lending the glamor of his name to the blade and thereby making it seem more attractive. He is not the source of the message in the usual sense but is part of it.

Intentions

Regardless of the expertise of the communicator, it is extremely important for the listener to trust his intentions. Even though someone may be the world's greatest expert on poetry, we would not be influenced by his writing reviews of his own poetry or of poetry written by a friend of his. We would not be concerned about his inherent ability to write accurately; we would be concerned about his objectivity and, therefore, his trustworthiness. To the extent that a communicator is not a disinterested observer, his trustworthiness may be in doubt and what he says will have less effect. If he is perceived as having something to gain from the position he is advocating or if he is taking that position for any other personal reasons, he would be less persuasive than someone perceived as advocating the position for entirely objective reasons.

A major problem is how to convince an audience that one is a disinterested observer. How does the communicator increase his credibility? One way is for him to argue for a position that appears to be counter to his self-interest. A district attorney, whose main role is supposed to be procuring convictions, would be expected to argue in favor of greater power for law-enforcement agencies. But if he does so, his credibility would be lessened, because he clearly has something to gain from this position. On the other hand, if he argues for greater protection of the rights of individuals and against strengthening law-enforcement agencies—that is, if he argues against his self-interest—his credibility should be enhanced. We would expect that a district attorney would be more persuasive and produce more attitude change when he takes the latter rather than the former position. A study by Walster, Aronson, and Abrahams (1966) concerned the effect of a communication from a convicted criminal. When the criminal argued in favor of more individual freedom and against greater powers for the police, he produced virtually no attitude change. When he argued in favor of a stronger police force, he produced a great deal of attitude change. Thus, even a low-prestige and highly doubtful communicator appears to have a considerable amount of influence when he argues in favor of a position that would hurt rather than benefit him.

A similar effect is produced when the target thinks the communicator does not intend for him to hear the communication. People tend to be more influenced when they "accidentally" overhear a persuasive communication than when it is directed at them (Walster and Festinger 1962; Brock and Becker, 1965). This effect also seems to be due to the perceived credibility of the communicator. If he knows people are listening, he may try to convince them and may not be entirely honest. If he does not even know anyone is within earshot, it is less likely that he is being dishonest. People are more likely to believe the message in the latter case and are therefore more likely to be convinced.

Given these findings, it might be thought that perception of intent to influence would have a major impact on attitude change. If the target thinks the communicator is trying to change his opinion, presumably the target should be more suspicious and change his attitude less. The research on this variable, however, has produced mixed results. The target's perception of the source's intent to persuade sometimes decreases the effect of the communication, but sometimes increases it.

Apparently, there are two different processes involved. On the one hand, the communicator is seen as more trustworthy and more credible when he is not deliberately trying to change the target's opinion. This should make his message more effective. On the other hand, there are many times when the communicator tries to disguise his intent to persuade by making the communication very subtle, using the soft sell, or presenting his message in some disguised form. When this is done, the content often loses impact. The position the communicator is trying to advocate is not as clear to the subject, the arguments are less forceful, and the message in general does not get through as successfully. Whenever this happens, the effect of the communication is decreased. The two processes, suspiciousness and impact, often seem to cancel each other out and produce a net effect of zero. A message with a clear intent to persuade gains as much in impact as it loses because of suspiciousness; it therefore produces as much attitude change as the message that is not clearly intended to persuade.

There is also evidence that when the communicator has extremely high prestige or is well liked, perceived intent to persuade produces more change. Under these circumstances, the individual generally would do whatever he could do to please the communicator. When he knows exactly what the communicator would like him to do, he is more likely to do it than when the communicator's intent is disguised. This is particularly true in experimental situations, when most subjects are trying to do what the experimenter wants them to. It should also be true when the souce of the communication is a liked authority figure, whom the target wants to please and has no particular reason to distrust. Thus, although at first glance it seems that intent to persuade would always decrease the effect of the communication, there are many times when it has the opposite effect.

This should not be interpreted to mean that the trustworthiness of the communicator is sometimes unimportant. What it does mean is that when the communicator is essentially unassailable, his trustworthiness will not suffer simply because he is trying to persuade. And even if he does become somewhat less trustworthy, the greater forcefulness of a direct message often makes up for the loss of credibility.

In general, any characteristic of the communicator that implies that he either knows what he is talking about (is an expert) or is being honest (has no ulterior motive) increases the effectiveness of the communication. Since derogation of the source of the communication is one of the major ways of avoiding attitude change, these variables relating to the communicator are extremely important. Any lack of trust in the competence or credibility of the communicator makes it relatively easy to reject the message by attacking him; in this way, the target frees himself from the pressure of worrying about the message itself. Therefore, preventing this particular mode of resolution by emphasizing the honesty and expertise of the source of the communication is a major concern in the attempt to influence. In most cases, it is clear that the communicator is trying to change one's attitude, and he is therefore already somewhat suspect. It is usually quite difficult to convince an audience that he is a disinterested commentator, and thus, at least in politics and advertising there is great emphasis on the sincerity of the speaker and on his basic integrity and honesty.

Liking

A communicator who is trusted is more difficult to reject, and his message should produce more attitude change. A somewhat different process underlies the effect of liking for the source of the communication. As we discussed in detail in the chapter on liking, there is a strong tendency for people to like others who have views similar to theirs. This follows from any of the cognitive-consistency models and is clearly supported by the available evidence. The consistency models also predict that there is a tendency for people to agree with others whom they like. If one thinks that marijuana is terrible but his friend says it is great, the system is imbalanced. One way of reducing the imbalance is to change his attitude toward marijuana and agree with his friend. In contrast, if someone he dislikes has an attitude different from his, there is no imbalance and no pressure to change his attitude. Thus, the more that people like the source of a discrepant communication, the more likely they would be to change their attitude.

Similarity

People tend to be influenced more by people who are similar to them than by people who are different. This is partly because of the tendency to like people who are similar and, as just noted, to be more influenced by people we like. But similarity also increases influence for another reason. Suppose someone is similar to us in terms of national, economic, racial, and religious background, and we also share many ideological values. If he then says that he thinks drugs are bad, we would probably assume that he made this judgment on the same bases that we would. He is not using irrelevant or incorrect (in our eyes) criteria. Accordingly, his judgment tends to carry considerable weight. If he were different from us in terms of background and values, his attitude toward drugs would be less meaningful, because we would assume it was based on criteria different from those we would apply. Thus, in terms of both increased liking and shared values, the greater the similarity between the source and recipient of a discrepant communication, the more attitude change is produced.

The balance model would suggest the same effect of similarity. If someone is similar to us on many dimensions and agrees with us on most things but disagrees with us on one issue, some imbalance is produced by the disagreement. We can resolve this imbalance by changing either all the things on which we already agree and thereby making us disagree on everything or our stand on the one source of disagreement. Obviously it is easier to change our attitude on the one issue, and that is what would be expected.

Reference Groups

One of the strongest sources of persuasive pressure is a group to which an individual belongs. The group could be as large and inclusive as all American citizens or the middle class or a labor union or college students or all liberals or all blacks. It can also be a much smaller, more specialized group, such as a college fraternity, social psychologists, the Young Republicans, or the Elks Club. And it can be extremely small, such as a group of friends or a bridge club or a discussion group or just five people who happen to be in a room together.

As we saw in the chapter on conformity, there is a strong tendency for individuals to go along with the group, particularly when everyone else in the group holds the same opinion or makes the same response. In those cases, however, there was little actual change in the individual's opinions—he conformed to the group overtly but did not change his internal attitude. Nevertheless, the opinion of the group can also be an extremely persuasive force and can cause the individual to change his internal attitude on an issue. If the Young Republicans endorse a particular candidate, there is a tendency for all the members of the club to feel he is a good candidate. If a group of friends tell us they are in favor of student activism or like a particular movie, we probably are convinced by them. If most of the members of a fraternity think initiations are a good idea, the rest of the members may agree with them.

There are two important reasons why reference groups are so effective at producing attitude change and creating attitudes. If people value a group, it is a high-prestige, highly credible, highly esteemed source of communication. When the group says something, each member tends to trust it and believe the message. In addition, because they consider themselves of the group, they tend to evaluate themselves in comparison with it. In essence, the group serves as the standard for their own behavior and attitudes. They evaluate the group highly and want to be similar to the other members. When the other members express a particular opinion, each member thinks his own opinion wrong if it is different. Only when their opinion is the same as the group's would it be correct or "normal." Therefore they tend to change their opinion so as to make it agree.

Attachment to the group can also serve to prevent somebody from being influenced by a communication from an outside source. If the group agrees with the individual's opinion, they provide him with strong support. Consider a fraternity member whose fraternity believes strongly in initiations. He may occasionally be exposed to an attack on initiations from someone outside the fraternity. Whenever he is so exposed, knowledge that his group agrees with him provides strong support and makes it easier for him to resist persuasion.

This dual effect of groups—changing a member's opinion to make it coincide with the rest of the group and supporting a member's opinion so he can resist persuasion from without—depends to some extent on how strong the individual's ties are to the group. The more he wants to be a member of it and the more highly he evaluates it, the more he would be influenced by the group's beliefs (Gerard 1954). Kelley and Volkart (1952) demonstrated the effect of attachment to the group on members' resistance to outside influence. A communicator attempted to change some Boy Scouts' opinion on various issues that were closely related to their troop's norms. The more the Scouts valued their membership in the troop, the less effect the communicator had on their opinions.

Reference groups are thus important in both attitude formation and change. Individuals tend to form their attitudes or change them so as to make them agree with attitudes held by the group. In addition, when the individual agrees with his group, his attitude is more resistant to outside influence.

The Sleeper Effect

An interesting and important phenomenon connected with the source variables we have been discussing is the so-called sleeper effect. It appears that the effect of the source of a communication is strongest immediately after exposure to the communication and is much less important some time later.

Kelman and Hovland (1953) conducted an experiment in which high school students heard a communication that argued for lenient treatment of juvenile delinquents. The communicator was made to appear either competent, fair, and generally positive or biased, uninformed, and generally negative. Immediately after hearing the communication, the students indicated their attitudes on the issue. Three weeks later, the subjects again gave their attitudes on the same issue, but just before doing so, half the subjects were reminded of the source of the communication, that is, whether it was positive or negative.

The results are shown in Figure 1. It can be seen that the immediate effect of the positive communicator is greater than that of the negative communicator. After three weeks, however, when the subjects are not reminded of the source of the communications, the effect of the positive communicator has declined while that of the negative communicator has increased. This is called the sleeper effect because the influence of the negative communicator is greater than it appears at first.

The explanation usually given for this effect is that individuals forget the source of a communication quicker than the content. Although they remember the message, they do not spontaneously connect it with the person from whom it came. Thus, the effect of the communicator disappears or declines with time, whereas the effect of the message remains relatively constant.

Originally, the subjects' attitudes were changed more by the communication from the positive source than by the one from the negative source. The former increased the effectiveness of the message by lending it his prestige and trustworthiness; the latter decreased the message's effectiveness by associating it with his own low prestige and untrustworthiness. When the source was forgotten or was no longer spontaneously associated with the message, both effects declined. The positive communicator no longer helped the message; the negative communicator no longer hurt it. Thus, forgetting the source should decrease the effect of a message from a positive source and increase the effect of one from a negative source.

The results of the reinstatement condition in the Kelman and Hovland experiment supported this interpretation. When the students were reminded of

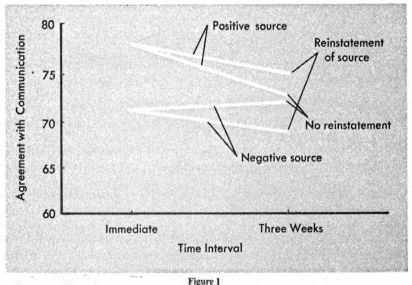

Figure 1

The effects of the prestige of the communicator, time, and reinstatement of the source on attitude change. The high-prestige communicator produces more immediate change but loses strength over time; the low-prestige source is less effective immediately but gains strength. Reinstatement of the source minimizes the effect of time, thus indicating that the effect of time is primarily due to forgetting the source.

the sources of the communications, the sleeper effect disappeared. Those who had heard the positive communicator and were reminded of this showed more change even after three weeks than did those who were reminded that they had heard the message from a negative communicator.

These results highlight the difference between getting a message through and getting people to accept it. Presumably, people hear a message and learn its content regardless of how they feel about the communicator. Although they accept the message less if they hear a negative communicator, they still retain it. Then, when they forget the source of the communication, the message begins to have more effect, because it is no longer damaged by being connected with a negative source.

THE COMMUNICATION

Social psychologists tend to concentrate on factors that increase the effectiveness of a persuasive message rather than on the content of the message itself. This is because we are looking for general laws that determine the effectiveness of all messages. We do not mean to give the impression, however, that the content of the message is unimportant. Naturally it is easier to sell something good than something less good. Crest toothpaste was successful in part because it offered protection against cavities; the automobile became popular because it was a great product; and some political candidates are more qualified than others. A good campaign does better than a poor one, but a really terrible product would be difficult to sell even with great advertising. Given a particular product or opinion to sell, however, a number of variables in the communication itself have important effects on the amount of attitude change that is produced.

Discrepancy

As mentioned earlier, the major source of stress in any influence situation comes from the discrepancy between the target's initial position and the position advocated by the communication. The greater the discrepancy, the greater the stress. If a smoker is told that smoking may cause his teeth to turn yellow (a mildly negative statement), there is less stress than if he is told that smoking causes cancer (an extremely negative statement). If someone who thinks John Kennedy was a great President hears a communication arguing that he was only moderately successful, the individual's attitude is under pressure; if the communication argues that Kennedy was a terrible President, there is much more pressure. The more pressure, the more the individual must do to reduce it. If he chooses to change his attitude, he will change more with more pressure. Thus, the greater the discrepancy, the greater the stress, and to the extent that attitude change occurs, the more occurs.

Another way of conceptualizing this effect of discrepancy is that greater discrepancy requires the individual to change his attitude more in order to reduce it. If on a scale there are 2 points of discrepancy, 2 points of attitude change would eliminate it. If there are 5 points of discrepancy, 5 points of change are necessary. An individual who changes his attitude under the pressure of a discrepant message must, accordingly, change it more with greater discrepancy. Therefore, within a wide range, there is more attitude change with greater discrepancy (Fisher and Lubin, 1958; Hovland and Pritzker, 1957).

However, the relationship between discrepancy and amount of change is not always this simple. There is more stress with greater discrepancy, but this does not always produce more change. The complicating factors are that as discrepancy becomes quite large, the individual finds it more difficult to change his attitude enough to eliminate the discrepancy and that extremely discrepant statements tend to make the individual doubt the credibility of their source. Suppose someone thinks Kennedy was a very great President and is faced with a discrepant opinion from a teacher of political science. What happens as the discrepancy between his and the teacher's opinions increases? This is diagramed in Figure 2.

We shall consider this situation in terms of two modes of resolution—at-

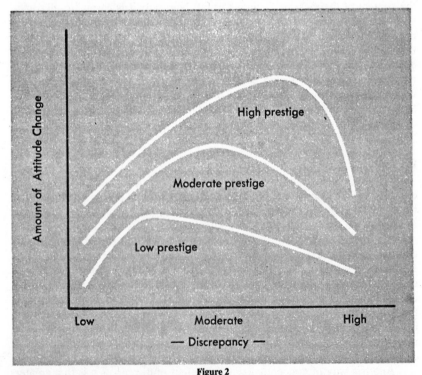

Figure 2
Discrepancy, prestige of the communicator, and attitude change. Maximum change is always produced by intermediate levels of discrepancy, but the point at which it occurs is determined by prestige. The higher the prestige, the greater the discrepancy that produces the maximum change.

titude change and rejection of the communicator—and, for the moment, shall ignore other modes.

If one can reject the communicator, he need not change his opinion; if he cannot reject the communicator, he must change his opinion. At low discrepancy, when the teacher says he thinks Kennedy was not a great President but still a pretty good one, the individual is likely to be somewhat influenced. There would be some pressure on him to change his opinion in the direction of the teacher's, and if the teacher presented a fairly persuasive argument, the individual would probably do so. In this situation, it is difficult to reject the moderately prestigeful communicator but is easy to change one's opinion the little bit required to reduce the discrepancy. It is fairly easy to decide that Kennedy was not a great President but only a good one; it is considerably more difficult to decide that a teacher in political science is not a valid source of information about politics. Since attitude change is easier than rejection of the communicator, the individual would tend to resolve the situation by changing his attitude. He would, however, change his attitude only slightly, because that is all that is necessary to reduce the discrepancy.

With somewhat greater degrees of discrepancy (e.g., the teacher thinks Kennedy was a mediocre President), it becomes harder to reduce the discrepancy by changing one's attitude. It is one thing to change from thinking Kennedy was great to thinking he was only good; it is more difficult to change from great to mediocre. Nevertheless, it may still be easier to change his opinion than to reject the communicator, and the research indicates that this is what happens. With moderate discrepancy, subjects still resolve the situation primarily by changing their attitudes rather than by rejecting the communicator. Note that moderate discrepancy results in more attitude change than small discrepancy because greater change is necessary in order to reduce the discrepancy. Thus, as discrepancy increases from slight to moderate, the amount of attitude change also increases.

As the discrepancy becomes extreme, however, it becomes still harder for the individual to reduce the stress by changing his opinion. A greater change in his opinion is necessary in order to reduce the discrepancy, and the greater the change that is necessary, the more difficult it is for the person to make it. It is certainly extremely difficult for someone who thought Kennedy was great to decide that he was terrible.

As discrepancy increases, something else important happens. Congruity theory points out that a communicator who makes an extremely discrepant statement tends to lose credibility. If one thinks Kennedy was great and someone says he thinks Kennedy was terrible, there is a tendency to decide that this communicator does not know much about government or men. The extremity of his statement compared to the individual's initial belief tends to cast doubt on his credibility. Thus, as discrepancy becomes quite large, it becomes relatively easy to reject the source of the communication. One decides he is dumb, ignorant, or biased.

There are thus two factors operating as discrepancy increases—attitude change gets more difficult and rejection of the communicator gets easier. At some point, rejection becomes easier than attitude change as a means of removing the stress. Perhaps it is when the teacher says he thinks Kennedy was a poor President; perhaps it is when he says he thinks Kennedy was a very bad President. When this degree of discrepancy is passed, people begin to reject the communicator rather than change their attitudes and the amount of attitude change decreases. Thus, as discrepancy increases, the amount of attitude change produced increases up to a point and decreases beyond that point. Conversely, rejection of the communicator is relatively slight until the maximum point of discrepancy is reached, and then rejection becomes the primary mode of resolution.

This effect is heightened by the tendency to assimilate or contrast the position advocated in the discrepant communication. As mentioned earlier, discrepant positions that are close to the individual's are often seen as closer than they actually are, whereas those that are far away are seen as farther away than they are. Exaggerating the closeness of a discrepant position makes it easy to change enough to reduce the small discrepancy, or it may eliminate change by making the two positions essentially identical. Exaggerating the remoteness of a position makes it easier to attack the credibility of the person advocating it, by making his position even more extreme and less reasonable. Thus, it is easier to reject the source and not change the attitude.

Thus far we have been considering situations in which the communication comes from a person of moderate prestige. Higher prestige makes it more difficult to reject the source and causes the point at which rejection is easier than attitude change to occur at higher levels of discrepancy. If one's most respected teacher says that Kennedy was a poor President, it is harder to decide that he does not know what he is talking about. Only extreme statements from him could make the individual come to this conclusion. Therefore, the greater the prestige of the communicator, the higher the level of discrepancy at which rejection, rather than attitude change, starts at which the maximum of change occurs. Similarly, a lower-prestige source makes rejection relatively easy and the maximum point occurs at lower levels of discrepancy. The study by Aronson, Turner, and Carlsmith (1963) described earlier demonstrated this effect. Subjects read opinions about poetry that were slightly, moderately or greatly discrepant from their own. When the discrepant opinion was attributed to T.S. Eliot, maximum attitude change occurred with the highest discrepancy. When another student was the source, maximum change was produced by the moderately discrepant message. Presumably, even T.S. Eliot's prestige has some limits, and if discrepancy became great enough, attitude change would begin to decline.

Thus, the level of prestige does not change the basic relationship between discrepancy and attitude change, but it does change the point at which maximum change occurs. A similar effect is produced by any other factor that affects the difficulty of rejection or the difficulty of changing. The more difficult it is to reject the communicator, the greater the discrepancy at which maximum change occurs; the more difficult it is to change one's attitude, the lower the discrepancy producing maximum change. This example illustrates how an interplay of forces determines which mode of resolution is adopted in a given situation, and how the use of one mode implies that there is less use of another.

One-Sided Versus Two-Sided Communications

To produce the maximum effect, should a communication argue entirely on one side of the issue or should it contain some arguments on the other side? Should a man trying to sell a Chevrolet tell a customer that a Ford is a good car and rides smoothly before launching into his arguments in favor of the Chevrolet? Or should he never say anything nice about competitive cars and concentrate entirely on the virtues of the Chevrolet? These approaches can be seen in political campaigning. Some candidates make a point of occasionally saying nice things about their opponent. Others are extremely careful not to say favorable things about their opponent and sometimes not even to mention their opponent's name in public. What is the effect of these two tactics?

It appears that under most circumstances, the two-sided communication is more effective. This approach produces more attitude change when the listener initially disagrees with the position advocated by the communication and when the listener is relatively well informed and intelligent. One likely, though as yet unproven explanation, is that including some arguments on the other side tends to make the speaker seem less biased, better informed, and, in general, more credible. A speaker who is willing to concede some point to the opposition probably seems more objective than one who denies that there are arguments other than those favoring his position. By demonstrating that he is familiar with these other arguments, he suggests that he has arrived at his own position after considering both sides of the issue. This would make him seem not only well informed but also careful and thoughtful.

The two-sided communication has another advantage. As mentioned above, when someone thinks a speaker is trying to make him change his mind, he tends to be influenced less. It seems likely that the intent to persuade is somewhat more disguised when the communication contains both sides of an issue. Other things being equal, it sounds less like a propaganda message and more like a dispassionate talk. Thus, the two-sided communication makes the speaker appear more dispassionate, better informed, more objective, and less obviously attempting to persuade the listener. All these factors increase the credibility of the communication and tend to produce greater attitude change.

However, there appear to be certain times when a one-sided communication is preferable. Although the evidence on this point is somewhat weak, there is reason to believe that a one-sided communication is more effective when it is directed mainly at poorly informed, relatively unintelligent individuals who already generally agree with the position advocated in the communication. Under these circumstances, presenting arguments on both sides of an issue seems merely to confuse the listeners, to give them counter-arguments they had not thought of before, and to result in a weakened effect. Moreover, because the listeners generally agree with the communication already, it does not arouse suspicion and its main effect is to strengthen their existing attitudes.

Factors that increase the credibility of the communicator or communication increase its effectiveness only when the audience has some reason to doubt the credibility of the message. When there is no such doubt the relatively subtle factors, such as using two-sided communications, disguising the fact that the speech is intended to persuade, and pretending that the speech is not directed at the individual, may have the effect of diverting the audience from the main content of the speech and therefore lessening its power. Thus, a teacher who is trying to instruct his class on how to solve a problem in algebra or on the chronology of the Kings of England should be as direct as possible. Since the class has no reason to doubt his credibility, he should simply present his arguments as clearly and forcibly as possible, and he should make it explicit that he is trying to convince the class of the correctness of his position. On the other hand, if an instructor in English is trying to change the political attitudes of his class, the situation is different. Politics is not his area of expertise, and the class might well doubt his credibility on the issue. In order to have maximum effect, he should use all the techniques described to increase his crediblity and to disguise the fact that he is trying to change their opinions.

Stating A Conclusion

When presenting arguments to support a particular position, the communication can either state the conclusion explicitly or leave it unstated. Stating the conclusion has the advantage of making the speaker's position clear and thus avoids the possibility that anyone in the audience could misinterpret it. On the other hand, leaving it unstated has two advantages: the speaker may appear less intent on convincing the audience of a particular position and therefore may seem more credible; and the audience is encouraged to reach the conclusion without aid, which may increase its effectiveness. In much the same way we discussed above, it is a question of whether enough is gained from the greater clarity to make up for the trust that may be lost by the low credibility of the explicitly stated conclusion.

The data indicate that the relative effectiveness of the two procedures depends on the conditions of the situation. Although the findings are somewhat inconsistent, it appears that the effect of stating the conclusion is similar to that of using a one-sided communication. It is more effective when the audience is composed primarily of less intelligent people or when the communication contains complex arguments with which the audience is unfamiliar and that concern an issue that is not highly involved. In one study (Hovland and Mandell, 1952), a talk concerning current economic theory, the financial status of the United States, and the possibility of devaluating American currency was presented under two conditions. In one case, the conclusion that the currency should be devalued was clearly stated; in the other, it was not. Although the same conclusion could logically be drawn from the arguments that were presented, a large percentage of the audience that did not hear it stated explicitly was probably unable to deduce it themselves, and more attitude change occurred when the conclusion was stated.

With a relatively intelligent, well-informed audience and familiar arguments and issues, the effect appears to be different. Under these conditions, stating the conclusion does not produce an increase in attitude change and, in fact, may actually produce less change than leaving it unstated. Once again, the clarity that is gained by the explicit statement may be balanced or perhaps outweighed by the loss of credibility. The findings on this problem are inconclusive. What does seem to be clear is that stating the conclusion is not always more effective and that the intelligence, sophistication, and involvement of the audience, plus the complexity of the issues, appear to be important determinants of the relative effectiveness of the two methods.

Order Of Presentation

The question of whether first impressions tend to be dominant has been of considerable interest to psychologists studying attitude formation. There are plausible reasons why either the first or the last impression would be dominant. A primacy effect, that is, the first impression dominant, could be caused by the person's becoming committed to his first position and thus, as cognitive consistency would lead us to expect, rejecting subsequent, discrepant information. On the other hand, a recency effect, that is, last dominant, might be caused by the last piece of information being more vivid and salient.

The results of research on this problem have been inconsistent. Whether primacy or recency occurs seems to depend on the particular situation. One of the critical factors appears to be the length of time between the two communications and between the second communication and the measurement of the attitude. To some extent, a person's attitude depends on how well he has learned and how well he remembers the information in the communication. If he remembers the first communication better than the second, a primacy effect tends to appear. If he remembers the second better, there is a recency effect. And memory of the two communications depends in large part on time.

Miller and Campbell analyzed the situation in terms of traditional learning principles. According to their analysis, when the two communications occur together and the attitude is measured immediately afterward, retention of the material in the two communications should be approximately equal. The same is true if the individual hears one communication, there is a long delay, he hears a second communication, and there is another long delay before the attitude is measured. Virtually all memory loss occurs after the first long delay, and the additional delay does not appreciably reduce memory for the first communication. Under either of these circumstances, there should be no difference in memory and, therefore, no difference in the effect of the two communications. Neither a primacy nor a recency effect should appear.

In two other possibilities, however, there should be differences in memory for the two communications. When an individual hears one communication that is followed by a substantial time interval and then hears a second communication that is immediately followed by the attitude measure, his memory for the second communication should be better than for the first. He has just heard the second communication, whereas he has already forgotten a considerable amount of the first communication. Under these circumstances, he should remember the second communication better and should be more influenced by it, thereby producing a recency effect. When the two communications are heard with no pause between them and there is a time interval before the attitude is measured, the opposite effect should occur. This is based on the assumption that ordinarily the first message has a slight advantage—it is learned and accepted somewhat more. The advantage does not appear immediately, but, as memory declines, it becomes increasingly important. In other words, the slight advantage of being first shows up more in terms of remembering better than in producing an initially greater effect. Although there is no difference in the attitude when it is measured immediately after the two communications, when it is measured a week later, the first communication is remembered somewhat better, and we therefore get a primacy effect.

In a study (Miller and Campbell, 1959) to test these predictions, college students listened to a trial involving a suit for damages. Some students heard the defense first; some heard the plaintiff first. After both sides of the case were presented, the students were asked to give their opinion.

The time intervals between the presentations of the two sides and between the communications and the opinions were varied. The two communications either followed each other immediately or were separated by one week; the students gave their opinions either immediately after hearing the second argument or one week later.

As shown in Table 1, the second argument was more effective when it came a week after the first and when the students' opinions were taken immediately after hearing the argument. In contrast, the first argument was more effective when the two arguments were not separated in time and when the students' opinions were expressed a week later. In other words, as Miller and Campbell hypothesized, which effect occurred depended on the exact temporal sequence and seemed to be produced by the relative strength of the memories of the two communications.

It also appears that primacy is maximized when the issue and situation tend to produce feelings of commitment and when subjects are given the opportunity to become committed to their first position. Such conditions prevail when, for example, subjects listen to one communication and are then forced or induced to take a public stand on the issue. Presumably they take the stand favored by the first communication and become publicly committed to it. When the second communication is presented, they tend to reject it and maintain their initial position.

Novelty Of The Information

Throughout this discussion, we have been assuming that the stronger the communication in terms of the quality and quantity of its arguments, the more

TABLE 1
PRIMACY AND RECENCY IN ATTITUDE FORMATION

CONDITION	EFFECT[a]	DIRECTION
Communication 1, communication 2, test	−.06	None
Communication 1, communication 2, one week, test	2.11	Primacy
Communication 1, one week, communication 2, test	−1.67	Recency
Communication 1, one week, communication 2, one week, test	.11	None

[a]A positive figure indicates that the first communication had more effect; a negative figure indicates that the second communication had more effect.

Source: Adapted from Miller and Campbell (1959).

effective it is. The more arguments there are, the more logical they are, the more evidence presented to support them, the more important the implications of the arguments are, and so on, the more influence they should have. There is little solid evidence to support this, because, in a sense, we define the quality of the arguments by how effective they are. But from any theoretical and even practical consideration, it must be assumed that, other things being equal, four pieces of evidence to support an argument make the argument more convincing than only two pieces of evidence supporting it. In other words, the stronger the arguments on purely logical grounds, the more attitude change should be produced.

Much of our discussion has been dealing with ways in which to make the arguments more trustworthy. There are probably also a number of factors that directly affect how strong the arguments appear to be. The clarity of the presentation, the forcefulness with which the arguments are pressed, and other such rhetorical considerations have a great effect on the strength of the arguments themselves. A clear presentation may, however, reveal the weakness of arguments that are not very strong to begin with. Thus someone who is on weak ground may want to present his arguments unclearly so the audience cannot realize how poor they are. If a handsome, attractive, liked, and trusted speaker says nothing, he has more impact than if he utters clear but weak statements. This does not contradict the idea that a better presentation in rhetorical terms strengthens the arguments that do exist. But it does mean that sometimes speakers want to rely not on the arguments but on the effect of the communication.

One factor that probably always affects the strength of the arguments is the novelty of the information being presented. A communication that contains new information on an issue should be more effective than one that simply contains information with which the audience is already familiar. Presumably, the audience has not taken into account the new information when they took the position they presently hold, and therefore, when they receive new information, they should be more willing to change than when they receive old. Thus, in presenting an argument, the more new information included, the more attitude change should be produced.

One implication of this effect is that regardless of the actual novelty of the information, it is desirable to make it seem new. Even if the information is quite familiar, the speaker may be able to convince the audience he is presenting something new and may therefore increase the effectiveness of his argument. In a study of this problem (Sears and Freedman, 1965), all subjects were presented with an identical persuasive communication, but some were told that it contained novel arguments and information whereas the others were told that all the information was material with which they were already familiar. Those who were expecting novel information were significantly more influenced by the communication than those who were expecting familiar information. Simply being told that the information was new made it more effective.

SITUATIONAL FACTORS

The factors described thus far affect attitude change primarily by increasing the trust in the communication, by strengthening the persuasive message, and, in general, by determining how much the individual believes what is being said. An attempt to influence someone's opinion need not, however, be done in an entirely logical, unemotional, cognitive situation. The situation may, and often does, involve strong motivations, appeals to deep-seated needs, and a great many factors that are extraneous to the logical arguments contained in the message itself. An entirely rational, cognitive man would be influenced only to the extent that the arguments presented were logically sound. But since there are few, if any, entirely rational beings motivational and emotional factors are also important in determining the effectiveness of a persuasive communication.

The Effect Of Reinforcement—"Things Go Better With Coke"

Much of our discussion has been influenced by the reinforcement or incentive approach to attitude change. One of the basic ideas of this approach is that an attitude-change situation consists of an interplay of forces—some pushing the individual to change his attitude and some pulling him back to his initial position. All the arguments in the persuasive communication are, in a sense, a motivation for changing his opinion or approaching the new position. On the other hand, all the reasons he initially had for maintaining his own position are reasons for continuing to maintain it and for avoiding the new position. Under these circumstances, anything that associates additional incentive with either position should affect the outcome.

This argument suggests that associating the persuasive message with some reinforcing stimulus increases the effectiveness of the message. A simpler line of reasoning is that the more positive the persuasive message is seen to be, the more effect it has, and reinforcement simply makes the message more positive. Whatever the rationale for the prediction, conceptualizing the situation in terms of approach-avoidance and positive and negative reinforcements does suggest this effect.

The advertising industry and political campaigners have been acting on this assumption for some time. Television commercials are one example. They have recently been referred to as "one-minute movies," because they are so elaborate and so much care goes into making them as attractive and even enjoyable as possible. We are not simply shown a sleek car and told how powerful, quiet, and comfortable it is. Rather, while the message is being delivered, we are shown beautiful women, handsome men, and lovely children, with perhaps a couple of graceful horses or cute dogs cavorting around. And, as mentioned earlier, the car may be endorsed by a famous athlete or movie star. Presumably, all this beauty, fame, and popularity are reinforcing; and the reinforcement becomes associated with the message, which is asking us to buy the car, and with the car itself. The hope is that the reinforcement will increase our positive feelings toward the car and thus increase the likelihood that we will buy it.

Research has provided some support for this widespread idea. Subjects were presented with a persuasive communication in the usual manner, but some subjects were given an extraneous reward whereas others were not given the reward. For example, while reading a persuasive communication on foreign aid, some objects were given a Pepsi Cola to drink and others were not given anything (Jan et al., 1965). In this study, the reward, or positive stimulus, had nothing to do with the content of the persuasive message or the issue itself. Nevertheless, the subjects receiving a reward tended to be influenced more than those who did not receive a reward.

One possible alternative interpretation of this finding is that the reward acted primarily to make the subjects feel more positive toward the experimenter and the experimental situation as a whole. Or, it may simply have put them in a better mood, which would probably have had the effect of making the subjects feel positive toward everything and therefore less likely to disagree with the persuasive communication—particularly when that communication came directly or indirectly from the experimenter. In other words, it may have been simply a halo effect. This explanation is considerably less interesting than that involving the reinforcement theory, which implies that the subject is actually more influenced, but at the moment it is difficult to choose between the two. We do know that giving a reward increases the amount of agreement with the persuasive communication, but the specific mechanism behind this effect is as yet somewhat unclear.

Fear Arousal

How the individual feels or is made to feel during the persuasive attempts is an important factor in the attitude-change situation. His motivational state makes him more or less susceptible to influence and determines the effectiveness of particular messages. Sometimes high arousal of a motive decreases the amount of change produced; sometimes it increases it. As we shall see, the effect of arousal depends on the motive involved and the appeal of the communication.

Arousing fear is one of the most natural ways of trying to convince someone of something. A mother tells her young son that he will be run over if he crosses the street without her. Religious leaders frighten their followers with threats of eternal damnation and suffering. Political philosophers and candidates warn that if their opponents are elected, the country will be ruined, and people will starve, civilization will collapse. And opponents of fluoridation tell us that fluorides cause cancer, heart disease, hardening of the arteries, calcification of the brain, etc., while supporters of fluoridation warn that without it, children's teeth will decay.

All these arguments are frightening. If they are true, they are sound reasons for agreeing with the persuasive communication. We are interested in the effect of this fear arousal. In order to produce the most attitude change, should a communication be presented to maximize fear arousal or in such a way that less fear is aroused? Given a particular argument in favor of a position, how does the amount of fear aroused affect the success of the argument?

The original study in this area was conducted by Janis and Feshbach in 1953. They showed high school students a film that emphasized the importance of brushing one's teeth three times a day, after every meal. The film described the dangers of not doing this and explained the advantages of good dental care. High fear was aroused by showing pictures of badly decayed teeth and gums, close-ups of diseased teeth, mouths in which the gums had pulled away from the teeth, etc. They were extremely vivid and dramatic. In the mild-fear condition, subjects saw less dramatic and less frightening pictures. And in the no-fear, or control, condition, the subjects saw no pictures of diseased teeth. The subjects in the high-fear condition reported being more impressed by the presentation and agreeing with it more. However, when, a week later, they were all questioned again, it was found that the subjects in the no-fear condition had changed their behavior more than the subjects in either of the fear conditions. The authors concluded that the maximum effect was produced by the persuasive arguments without the fear-arousing slides.

This result has generally failed to replicate in later experiments. Much of the work done in recent years has produced the opposite result. For example, a series of experiments conducted by Howard Leventhal at Yale University have shown that the arousal of fear tends to facilitate both attitude and behavioral change. In one study (Dabbs and Leventhal, 1966), college students were urged to get inoculations for tetanus. The disease was described in detail—it was pointed out how serious it was, that it was often fatal, and this it was easy to catch. In addition, the students were told that the inoculation was extremely effective and that it gave almost complete protection against the disease.

The message was delivered under several different conditions of fear arousal. In the high-fear condition, the descriptions of the disease were extremely vivid, the symptoms were made very explicit, and everything was done to make the situation as frightening as possible. In the second condition, a moderate amount of fear was aroused; and in the third, very little. Students were then asked how important they thought it was to get the inoculation and whether or not they intended to get one. In addition, the university health service, which was nearby, recorded how many of the students went for inoculations during the next month.

The findings (Table 2), are straightforward and impressive. The greater the fear aroused, the more strongly the subjects intended to get shots. Perhaps more important, higher fear induced more subjects actually to go to the health service and receive inoculations. Thus, fear arousal not only produced more attitude change but also had a greater effect on the relevant behavior.

Various other studies have used a wide range of issues, including automotive safety, atom bomb testing, fallout shelters, and dental hygiene, to study the effects of fear. Table 3 presents a summary of this work, dividing the studies into those that showed more effect with higher fear and those that showed more effect with less fear. There is an overwhelming weight of evidence favoring the positive effect of fear. There were only a few studies that clearly showed low fear having more effect, whereas many experiments, conducted by a number of different experimenters, have shown fear facilitating attitude change. Some studies also indicated that high fear had a greater effect on relevant action, although the evidence for this is somewhat less consistent. It seems clear that under most circumstances fear arousal increases the effectiveness of a persuasive communication. Occasionally, the level of fear aroused had no effect; once or twice higher fear produced less effect; but in most experiments and on most measures, the highest fear condition had the greatest effect.

There may be some situations, however, in which fear does reduce the effectiveness of a communication. Janis has recently suggested that the relationship between fear and attitude change depends on the level of fear involved. He argued that at low levels, greater fear produces more attitude change but that at some point, the fear becomes too intense, arouses defensive mechanisms, and thereby produces less change. This would explain the seemingly contradictory

TABLE 2
EFFECTS OF FEAR AROUSAL ON ATTITUDES AND BEHAVIOR

CONDITION	INTENTION TO TAKE SHOTS[a]	PERCENTAGE TAKING SHOTS
High fear	5.17	22
Low fear	4.73	13
Control	4.12	6

[a]The figures are ratings on a scale from 1 (lowest) to 7 (highest).
Source: Adapted from Dabbs and Leventhal (1966).

TABLE 3
RESULTS OF STUDIES ON EFFECTS OF FEAR AROUSAL

STUDIES SHOWING GREATER EFFECT WITH HIGHER FEAR	STUDIES SHOWING GREATER EFFECT WITH LOWER FEAR
Berkowitz and Cottingham (1960)	Janis and Feshbach (1953)
Dabbs and Leventhal (1966)	Janis and Terwilliger
DeWolfe and Governale (1964)	(1962)
Haefner (1964)	
Hewgill and Miller (1965)	
Inski, Arkoff, and Insko (1965)	
Leventhal, Jones, and Trembly (1966)	
Leventhal and Singer (1966)	
Leventhal, Singer, and Jones (1965)	
Singer (1965)	

results that have been found, because the studies have involved different amounts of fear. Janis has reanalyzed a number of experiments in these terms, and although not all the data fit this model, most of the results appear to be consistent with it.

To sum up, the evidence strongly indicates that under most circumstances arousing fear increases the effectiveness of persuasive communications. But arousing too much fear may be disruptive. Causing a person to be too frightened can make him either so paralyzed that he is unable to act or so threatened that he tends to deny the danger and reject the persuasive communication. Aside from such extreme cases, however, it appears that fear-arousing arguments are more effective in producing attitude change than are arguments that arouse little or no fear.

The Arousal Of Aggression

One general theory dealing with the effect of motivational arousal on attitude change concerns the appropriateness of the motive aroused. In most of the studies on fear arousal, the persuasive communication contains information about a real danger such as cancer, tetanus, or reckless driving. When fear of cancer is aroused by vivid pictures, the fear is appropriate, because it is realistic to be afraid of cancer, with or without pictures. Perhaps more important, the messages are urging the subjects to take steps that would reduce the danger and the fear. If one takes a tetanus inoculation, one is, in fact, less liable to get tetanus and should no longer fear the disease. In situations such as these, the arousal of fear is appropriate to the attitude-change situation, and therefore the arousal should increase susceptibility to the message.

A study by Weiss and Fine (1956) on the arousal of aggression is relevant to this explanation of the effect of motivation. Some subjects were put through an annoying, frustrating experience designed to make them feel aggressive. Other subjects had the opposite experience—they went through a pleasant, satisfying, experience. Then, both groups of subjects were exposed to a persuasive communication that took either a lenient or a punitive attitude toward juvenile delinquency. Thus, the experiment exposed aggressive and nonagressive subjects to lenient or punitive persuasive communications.

The experimenters hypothesized that the subjects who had been made to feel aggressive would be more likely to accept the punitive communication than the lenient one and that the nonaggressive subjects would be more likely to accept the lenient communication. The rationale was that the punitive message would satisfy the motivational needs of the aggressive subjects by providing them with a way of displacing their aggression and that the lenient message would be more likely to satisfy the relatively nonaggressive needs of the other subjects. The results were in line with these expectations—the aggressive subjects were more influenced by the punitive communication, and the nonaggressive subjects were more influenced by the lenient one.

Another demonstration of this effect came in a study by Cohen (1957), in which the order of the arousal and the message was varied. In one condition, subjects were made nervous about their grades and were then given a communication describing how the new system of grading on a curve would solve some of their problems. In another condition, the communication about grading on a curve was given first, and then the subjects' concerns about their grades were aroused. The study found that when the need was aroused before the communication was presented, there was significantly more attitude change than when the communication was presented before the need was aroused. Thus this work indicated that arousing strong motivations increases the effect of a communication that is directly relevant to that motivation but may actually decrease the effect of nonrelevant communications.

Distraction

In parts of our discussion, we have described the individual as actively fighting the persuasive message. Although he may sometimes be quite passive, the person whose opinions are attached usually tries to resist changing. He counterargues, derogates the communicator, and generally marshals all his forces to defend his own position. One important implication of this is that the ability to resist persuasion is weakened by anything that makes it harder for the individual to fight the discrepant communication. In particular, distracting his attention from the battle may enable the persuasive message to get through without being fought.

A study by Festinger and Maccoby (1964) demonstrated this effect of distraction. Subjects listened to a speech against fraternities while watching a film. For some of the subjects, the film showed the person making the speech. For others, the film was "The Day of the Painter," a funny, somewhat zany satire on modern art. Presumably, those watching the irrelevant film were more distracted from the antifraternity speech than were those watching the person speak. Subjects who initially disagreed with the speech (who were in favor of fraternities) were more influenced in the distraction than the nondistraction condition. Taking the subjects' minds off the speech increased its effectiveness.

The evidence in favor of the distraction effect is somewhat equivocal at the moment. Two other studies (Allyn and Festinger, 1961; Freedman and Sears, 1965) provided only marginal support for it. If distraction does increase persuasion, the effect is generally weak. In any case, the effect logically must depend on the right amount of distraction. As usual, there is a conflict between getting the message through and getting it accepted. Obviously, too much distraction prevents the persuasive message from being heard at all and reduces its effectiveness to zero. Advertisers may want to distract television viewers from the main point of commercials by having irrelevant pictures and action going on during the speech. They do not, however, want to have the irrelevancies so fascinating or interfering that the message is lost. Having a beautiful girl in the background during a soap commercial may help to sell soap; having her in the foreground may even help; but having her in the foreground singing so loud that the commercial can barely be heard would certainly reduce the effectiveness of the ad. Thus, the effect of distraction may work under limited conditions, but it is important that the distraction be not too great or the effect will be reversed.

CHARACTERISTICS OF THE TARGET

Even after a message from a particular source has reached the target, the problems of attitude change are not over. Various characteristics of the individual's personality and factors in his immediate and past experience are important determinants of his reaction to the message. These factors affect primarily his tendency to trust the message or its source, his ability to argue against the message, his motivation not to change his opinion, and his confidence in his own position.

Personality Factors

All the factors we have discussed are variations, in one way or another, of the persuasive appeal. They are all external to the individual who is the target of the persuasive attempt. Although these external factors are important determinants of how much attitude change is produced, characteristics that the individual himself brings to the situation are also important. One such characteristic is his personality.

Some people are generally more persuasible than others, regardless of the issue involved or the type of influence being attempted. Experiments (Hovland and Janis, 1959) have been conducted in which subjects were exposed to persuasive communications on a variety of issues with different types of appeals and arguments and in different attitude-change situations. They indicated that the subjects who were highly persuasible under one set of conditions tended to be relatively highly persuasible under others. The effect is not very strong; it explains only a small percentage of the total variance. But considering the diversity of the situations and issues studied, the consistency found offers convincing support for the existence of the trait of general persuasibility. However, relatively little is known about the specific sources of this trait. Quite a number of personality characteristics have been suggested as affecting persuasibility, but only a few of these suggestions have been supported by the data.

Self-Esteem.   One fairly consistent finding has been that subjects with low self-esteem tend to be more persuasible than those with high self-esteem. The variable has been defined in various ways by different experimenters. Low self-esteem has been considered to entail feelings of inadequacy, social inhibitions, social anxiety, and test anxiety. Self-esteem has also been defined as the discrepancy between the ideal and the actual self, with greater discrepancies indicating lower self-esteem. Although the actual measures have varied somewhat, the basic notion has been similar. Self-esteem is defined implicitly or explicitly as the worth the person places on himself or how much the person esteems himself.

Cohen (1959) gave subjects a chance to influence one another and found that high-self-esteem subjects tended to make more attempts to influence others than did low-self-esteem subjects and that low-self-esteem subjects were more easily persuaded than were high-self-esteem subjects. Another study (Janis and Field, 1959) found low but significant correlations between feelings of inadequacy and persuasibility for men but not for women. Sears (1966) found that making subjects socially anxious by threatening them with criticism for their views increased their susceptibility to persuasion. Other work has generally confirmed the relationship between self-esteem and persuasibility, although the correlations tend to be rather small.

Cohen explains the effect of self-esteem in terms of the kinds and effectiveness of the defenses used by high- and low-self-esteem people. He proposed that high-self-esteem people tend to be better able to deny or forget information that attacks them or their ideas. Low-self-esteem people, on the other hand, tend to be relatively sensitive to negative information and are therefore more affected it.

The more traditional explanation of the relationship between self-esteem and persuasibility is that low-self-esteem people place a low value on their opinions just as they do on everything else about themselves. Since they do not value their own opinions, they are less reluctant to give them up and, accordingly, are more likely to change them when they are attacked.

A slightly different explanation would be in terms of the prestige of the source of the persuasive message. We have seen how important prestige is in determining the amount of attitude change, and anything that tended to increase it would certainly increase the amount of change. A person who has high-self-esteem is less impressed by a given source than is someone with low-self-esteem. To some extent, prestige is determined by the difference between one's own and the other's position, and this difference is always greater for someone of low-self-esteem. Thus, a given source is considered of higher prestige by a low-self-esteem person than by a high-self-esteem person and the former is accordingly more influenced by it than the latter.

Intelligence. One factor that has often been said to affect persuasibility is intelligence. It has seemed likely to many people that individuals with high intelligence would be less persuasible than those with lower intelligence. Research has not, however, supported this assumption; there is no evidence that level of intelligence is consistently related to degree of persuasibility. On the average, people of high intelligence are persuaded just as much as people of low intelligence.

Although intelligence has no overall effect on persuasibility, there is reason to believe that it does have some effect on the kinds of persuasive appeals that are more effective. People of high intelligence are influenced less by inconsistent and illogical arguments than are people of lower intelligence, and the latter may be influenced less by complex, difficult arguments. Some evidence for this was provided in the work, described above, on the relative effectiveness of stating or not stating a conclusion. The research suggested that stating the conclusion was more effective for relatively uninformed and less intelligent audiences and not stating the conclusion was more effective for relatively informed and intelligent audiences. It is important to note that the lack of an overall correlation between intelligence and persuasibility does not necessarily mean that intelligence is entirely unrelated to the influence process. Rather, it indicates that the relationship is complex and that level of intelligence affects how much the individual is influenced in any given situation.

Sex Differences. There is a considerable amount of evidence that women are generally more persuasible than men. Women change their attitudes more (Janis and Field, 1959) and also conform more to others' opinions. The usual explanation is that, at least in our society, men are supposed to be independent and dominant, whereas women are allowed or perhaps encouraged to be submissive and dependent. Most men are taught that they should make up their own minds and should not be influenced by other people. This may not necessarily make them able to do so, but it should certainly make them more determined to resist influence and more resistant to admitting they have been influenced. An additional piece of evidence that fits the role explanation is that the difference between the sexes is present in high school students but not in first-grade students (Abelson and Lesser, 1959). Presumably, six-year-old children have not yet learned their sex roles clearly enough for the difference to appear.

If this explanation of the difference in persuasibility between men and women is correct, we would expect that within each sex, the more independent and dominant members would be less persuasible than those who are relatively dependent and submissive. At the moment, however, there is little evidence to support this, and it should certainly be followed up. The question is: Do people who are relatively persuasible behave submissively in other ways also?

Defensive Styles. One of the explanations offered for the effect of self-esteem on persuasibility was in terms of the types of defenses used by different people, specifically, that people of high self-esteem tend to deny or forget unpleasant information, whereas people of lower self-esteem do this to a lesser extent. Whether or not this is a sufficient explanation of the effect of self-esteem, the kind of defensive process an individual uses to protect himself from negative information, does determine to some extent how much he is influenced by a particular persuasive attempt.

Defenses can be divided broadly into two types—those that are relatively cognitive and logical and those that are relatively noncognitive and illogical. The former have been discussed at length. They include refuting the arguments; producing counterarguments; attacking the credibility of the source; and, in general, responding directly to the content, meaning, and reliability of the persuasive message. The illogical defenses correspond more or less to what Freud called the *defense mechanisms*. These include denial of the conflict between the persuasive message and the original position; distortion of the message; repression of or forgetting the message; reaction formation, which is moving in the direction opposite from that advocated by the message; and projection, which in this case would be attributing to the source of the message some of one's own characteristics or beliefs. These defenses do not attempt to attack or weaken the content of the communication but, rather, protect the individual's opinion in less logical but nevertheless often extremely effective ways.

People differ considerably in the extent to which they rely on cognitive and noncognitive defenses. Katz, Sarnoff, and McClintock (1956) investigated the effect of the two types of defenses on reactions to persuasive communications. They divided the subjects into those who relied heavily and those who relied less heavily on defense mechanisms (high-and low-defense users). They then presented two kinds of persuasive communications dealing with prejudice against Negroes. One message, which they called an information appeal, contained a variety of facts about Negroes and whites, all of which were designed to show that prejudice was not based on sound reasoning. The other message, which they called the insight appeal, described the psychodynamic relationship between defense mechanisms and prejudice.

The results showed that the high- and low-defense users responded quite differently to the two appeals. The highly defensive subjects were hardly affected by the insight appeal and were more influenced by the information appeal; those who used defense mechanisms relatively little were more influenced by the insight appeal. The authors explained these results by saying that the high-defense subjects strongly resisted the attack on their defensive mechanisms, whereas the low-defense subjects were relatively open to this kind of attack.

Other experiments, principally by Sarnoff, have shown that the specific defense mechanism a person tends to use may determine to some extent how much he is influenced by a given appeal. In order to be maximally effective, an appeal should attack a weak defense and should be designed not to arouse the defenses that are favored and strong. If someone tends to deny or ignore negative information, the appeal should attempt to introduce the information in a subtle way so that the target is exposed to it before he can put the mechanism of denial into operation. On the other hand, if he does not use denial but tends to argue against persuasive messages, it is important to concentrate on the strength of the attack and not to worry too much about how it is presented. Knowledge of the kinds of defense mechanisms a person tends to use should enable the communicator to concentrate on avoiding the target's strongest defenses and attacking his weakest.

Summary

Relatively little is known about the effect of personality on persuasibility. We know that some people are generally more persuasible than others, and we are fairly sure of a number of personality traits that affect this trait. Other than the evidence for the few factors that have been mentioned, however, there is little to support hypotheses about how other aspects of personality affect persuasibility. There have been many suggestions (e.g., authoritarianism, richness of fantasy), but the evidence for any of these is rather weak at the moment. We are therefore left with few solid findings except consistent evidence that personality does affect persuasibility. A detailed specification of which dimensions of personality are most important is not yet possible.

Commitment

One of the important aspects of the attitude-change situation is the power or force of the persuasive communication. The corresponding factor in the target is the strength of his commitment to his own attitude, that is, the extent to which he feels reluctant to give up his initial position. Thus, commitment is largely a motivational variable. If one has just bought a house, he is more committed to the belief that it is a fine house than if he had not yet bought it. Changing his opinion of the house has broader implications for him if he owns it than if he is only thinking about buying it. Someone who has just stated on television that he thinks smoking is bad for health and is an evil, dirty habit is more committed to this attitude than if he had made these statements only to his wife or had kept them to himself. Changing his attitude is harder if he expressed it on television, because then the change would involve publicly admitting he was wrong. Anything that means that changing an attitude would cause the individual to give up more, suffer more, or change more of his other attitudes or behaviors increases his commitment to his initial attitude and makes it more difficult for him to change it.

Two factors that affect the strength of commitment are action taken on the basis of the attitude and public statement of the attitude. In addition, it appears that freely choosing a position produces a greater feeling of commitment than being forced. In a study on this problem (Freedman and Steinbruner, 1964), subjects were given information about a candidate for graduate school and asked to rate him, under circumstances of either high or low choice. That is, the subjects were made to feel either that they had made up their own minds and freely selected the particular rating or that they had virtually nothing to do with the decision and had been forced to select the rating. The subjects were then exposed to information that strongly contradicted their initial rating and were allowed to change their rating if they desired. Those who had made the first rating with a feeling of free choice changed less than did those in the low-choice condition.

A fourth factor affecting commitment is the extent to which the attitude is imbedded in other behaviors and attitudes. Someone in favor of fluoridation of drinking water may feel very strongly about it, but this attitude probably stands by itself to a large extent. Most people have taken no action related to fluoridation and have few attitudes related directly to it. Changing their attitude toward it from favorable to unfavorable would involve relatively few other changes in their cognitive systems. This is not so for a dentist who has been fighting tooth decay for years, who has been coating teeth with fluorides, who has donated money to fluoridation campaigns, and who has read extensive literature supporting fluoridation. Changing his opinion about it would involve many contradictions, inconsistencies, and eventually, changes in his cognitive and behavioral system. Thus, he is more committed to his attitude and would find it harder to change.

The effect of commitment of this kind is to reduce the amount of attitude change produced by a persuasive communication. Greater commitment makes it harder for the individual to change his attitude and means that he is more likely to use other modes of resolution instead. Thus, the greater the commitment to the initial position, the less attitude change occurs.

The relationship between commitment, discrepancy, and attitude change is similar to that of prestige. The prestige of the source does not change the relationship between discrepancy and attitude change but does affect the point at which maximum change occurs—the higher the prestige, the greater the discrepancy at which there is maximum attitude change. Commitment to one's initial position also shifts the maximum point but in the opposite direction. The harder it is to change his position, the lower the discrepancy at which rejection of the source is easier than change. Therefore, the greater the commitment, the lower the discrepancy at which maximum attitude change occurs.

Inoculation and Support

William McGuire and his associates conducted a series of experiments on the effects of giving people experiences designed to increase their ability to resist persuasion. McGuire has used a medical analogy to describe the influence situation. He pictured the individual faced with a discrepant communication as being similar to somebody being attacked by a virus or a disease. The stronger the persuasive message (virus), the more damage it would do; and, of course, the stronger the person's defenses, the better able he is to resist persuasion (disease). There are two different ways of strengthening someone's defense against a disease. We can strengthen his body generally, by giving him vitamins, exercise, and so on; and we can strengthen his defenses against that particular disease by building up antibodies. McGuire argued that these two approaches are also applicable to the influence situation.

To begin with, he identified a number of *cultural truisms*—opinions that are so universally held in our society that they are almost never subjected to any kind of attack. One example is the belief that it is good to brush one's teeth three times a day. Probably almost everybody in the United States believes that this is basically a good idea in terms of dental health. And also, most people have never heard anything to the contrary. Thus, someone holding this opinion is analogous to an individual who has never been exposed to the smallpox germ. He has never been forced to defend himself from attack so has never built up any defenses against attack.

One procedure that strengthens resistance is to build up the person's opinion directly, by giving the individual additional arguments supporting his original position. If he believes that it is good to brush his teeth three times a day he is shown a study by the United States Public Health Service that shows that people who do so have fewer cavities than those who brush their teeth less often or not at all. Giving individuals this kind of support for their position does, in fact, increase their resistance to a subsequent persuasive communication. Thus, one way of increasing somebody's resistance to persuasion is simply to give him more reasons for believing what he already does. This gives him more ammunition to use in the coming argument and he therefore changes his opinion less.

A different approach is to strengthen the individual's defenses against persuasion rather than strengthening his opinion. McGuire has argued that, as with diseases, the most effective way of increasing resistance is to build up defenses. If a person is given a mild case of smallpox that he is able to fight off, his body produces antibodies, which in the future provide an effective and strong defense against more powerful attacks of small pox. Similarly, if a particular opinion has never been attacked, it is extremely vulnerable because no defenses have been built up around it. When such an opinion is suddenly and surprisingly subjected to persuasive pressure, the individual does not have a set of defenses immediately available, and the opinion tends to be relatively easy to change. However, if the opinion has been attacked and the individual has successfully defended himself, he should be better able to resist subsequent attacks because he has built up a relatively strong defensive system around that opinion. In other words, McGuire argued that it is possible to inoculate individuals against persuasive attacks just as we can inoculate them against diseases.

This is accomplished by weakly attacking the individual's attitude. The attack must be weak or it would change his attitude and the battle to maintain his attitude would be lost. To be certain that this does not occur, the target is helped to defend himself against the mild attack. He is given an argument directed specifically at the attack or is told that the attack is not very good and he should be able to refute it.

One study by McGuire and Papageorgis (1961) used both the supportive and inoculation methods to build up defenses. There were three groups of subjects: one group received support for their position; one group had their position attacked weakly and the attack refuted (the inoculation condition); and the third group received neither of these procedures. Afterward, all groups were subjected to a strong attack on their initial position. Table 4 shows how much each group changed as a result of the attack. It is clear that the supportive method helped subjects resist persuasion—the group receiving support changed less than the group that had no preparation. But the inoculation method helped even more—subjects receiving this preparation changed least of all.

Later research has shown that support tends to be particularly effective when the subsequent attack contains arguments similar to the content of the supporting arguments, but it is relatively ineffective when new arguments are used. In contrast, inoculation is effective even when the attack includes new arguments.

The specific mechanism by which inoculation operates is not yet clear. It may be that in refuting the mild attack, the individual uses and therefore exercises all his defenses—by preparing arguments supporting his own position, constructing counterarguments against the opposing position, derogating the possible sources of opposing views, etc. This would make each of these defensive mechanisms stronger and would provide the individual with a generally more effective defensive position.

Another explanation is that giving the target a counterargument or telling him that the original argument is not good strikes at the reliability and credibility of the source of the discrepant communication. Showing an individual an argument against his position and then telling him that this argument is all wrong is the standard technique of setting up a straw man and then knocking it down. This probably serves to make anyone who takes the other side seem somewhat foolish, miguided, and ignorant. The person is told, in effect, that these are the stupid kinds of arguments that some people have put forth against a commonly held idea. Then, when he comes across another argument against

---

TABLE 4
SUPPORT, INOCULATION, AND RESISTANCE TO PERSUASION

CONDITION	AMOUNT OF ATTITUDE CHANGE
Support	5.87
Inoculation	2.94
Neither	6.62

Source: Adapted from McGuire and Papageorgis (1961).

the position, even if he is not capable of refuting it himself, he may assume that it is just as stupid as the first argument and therefore may not be influenced by it. Thus, the refutation serves as an attack on the source of any discrepant message and is effective even when subsequent messages have different content. The opposition has been made to look unreliable; anything they say is suspect and unpersuasive.

Forewarned Is Forearmed

If someone is told ahead of time that he is going to be exposed to a persuasive communication, he is better able to resist persuasion by that message. In a study by Freedman and Sears (1965), teen-agers were told ten minutes beforehand that they were going to hear a talk titled "Why Teen-agers Should Not Be Allowed to Drive." Other teen-agers were not told about the talk until just before the speaker began. Thus, one group had a ten-minute warning and the other group had no warning at all. Under these circumstances, those who had the warning were less influenced by the talk than were the others. In some way, the warning enabled the teen-agers to resist better.

This is certainly a plausible finding, and it seems to be believed by many people in the business of persuasion. For example, we often find an advertisement on radio or television introduced with no warning that this is going to be an advertisement. Instead, the station sneaks in the ad before we are fully aware of what it is. Thus, a hit tune ends and immediately another "hit tune" begins—but it turns out to be an ad for Coca Cola. A similar, although more altruistic example is the dentist who warns us that something is going to hurt. He seems to feel that we will be better able to withstand the pain if we are warned. In fact, there is some experimental evidence that subjects who are warned ahead of time that they are going to receive an electric shock report that it hurts less than subjects who are not warned. All this sounds plausible and reasonable, but why does it occur? Why does a ten-minute warning help people resist persuasion more than a two-second warning?

It is important to keep in mind that all the subjects know as soon as the talk or the discrepant message begins is that it is, in fact, discrepant. In these studies, there is no attempt to fool the subjects. Thus, the explanation cannot be in terms of greater acceptance of the message simply because the subjects do not know that the speaker is against them. Everybody knows that the speaker disagrees with them—the only difference is that some people know it ten minutes ahead of time and others know it only just before the speech. The greater resistance shown by those with the longer warning is due to some process, some mechanism that goes on during those ten minutes between the warning and the speech.

It seems likely that this process resembles that which is produced by the inoculation procedure. In some way, the individual's defenses are exercised or strengthened. In the inoculation situation they are strengthened by the person actually using them to refute an argument; in the forewarning situation they are strengthened by the person preparing to refute an argument. The net results, however, are quite similar.

Although there is little evidence that directly demonstrates the kinds of processes that go on during this period, we can cite those that the individual *probably* indulges in. He tries to marshal and strengthen his defenses, and in doing this, he employs all the defensive maneuvers and tactics we discussed previously. He constructs arguments supporting his own position and attempts to refute the arguments that will possibly come from the opponent. In the inoculation situation, he is provided with some of the opponent's arguments and works at refuting them. At the same time, he thinks about other arguments that might be presented and tries to refute them. In the warning experiment, the teen-agers probably say to themselves, "The message is going to present arguments against teen-age driving. It will probably say that teen-agers don't drive as well as adults. Well, that's not true. I know teen-agers drive better, so that's a bad argument." The teen-agers would also think about arguments in favor of teen-age driving, such as "Old enough to fight, old enough to vote and drive." They would also employ derogation of the discrepant source. As discussed above, the person who has been through the inoculation procedure has ample opportunity to derogate the opponent. Similarly, the forewarned person has ten minutes to convince himself that the communicator is unreliable, prejudiced, and misinformed. In other words, the individual who is warned or who has just experienced a mild attack is like a fighter who has prepared for a match. He has been through training, so when the fight comes, he is in better shape and better able to meet his opponent. He also spends time convincing himself that his opponent is not very good and that he, himself, is great. This makes him more confident and better able to fight his best.

We do not mean to give the impression that this is all done deliberately. Especially in the forewarned situation, most people probably do not decide to strengthen their defenses. There is no evidence that they worry about the coming attack, feverishly preparing themselves for it. Rather, they tend to think about the issue a little, go over some of the points in their minds, and in this way build up their defenses. As far as we know, the process is all quite casual and almost accidental. But the effect is clear—their defenses get strengthened and their resistance increases.

CHAPTER REVIEW

1. Large-scale attempts to change attitudes tend to be unsuccessful.
2. Attitude change conceptualized in terms of a communicator, a communication, a target, and a surrounding situation.
3. Exposure to information as low and selective.
4. Do people deliberately avoid nonsupportive information?
5. Alternatives to attitude change.
6. Individuals distort communications.
7. The prestige and trustworthiness of the communicator as important variables in attitude change.

8. Prestige of the communicator and the passage of time—the sleeper effect.
9. Discrepancy and attitude change—complex relationship.
10. Two-sided communications and stating a conclusion.
11. Primacy-recency.
12. "Things go better with Coke."
13. Fear arousal increases effectiveness.
14. Motives other than fear reduction as important determinants of attitude change.
15. Distraction and resistance to persuasion.
16. Individual differences in persuasibility.
17. Commitment to a position results in less attitude change.
18. Inoculation, forewarning, and resistance to influence.

APPLICATIONS AND SPECULATIONS

1. Innovation of new ideas and values is a crucially important ingredient in society. Since people tend to be quite resistant to anything new, only people of high prestige and credibility are generally able to introduce new ideas. However, such a person risks losing his credibility if he tries to be innovative. What are the implications of this conflict between the need to have high prestige in order to be innovative and the danger of losing that prestige by being innovative?
2. Intentionally or otherwise, the advertising industry uses many of the principles we have discussed. Reinforcement, prestige sources, familiarity, distractions, warnings, and so on all appear in television commercials and other forms of advertising. Think of specific examples of their use and try to estimate their effects.
3. Arguments have been made for and against allowing speakers to present unpopular views on college campuses. What do you think the effects are of allowing such speeches to be made? Can you think of arguments for and against allowing them?
4. The intensive antismoking campaign has tried to arouse people's fear of lung cancer, tuberculosis, and other diseases. Do you think this is an effective tactic, and how might you improve it?
5. What do you think is the effect of humor in persuasive communications? Some of the factors that might be relevant are exposure level, memory, distraction, and reinforcement.
6. We have concentrated on the positive effects of persuasive attempts. That is, we have talked about how much attitude change was produced in the direction of the communication. It is also possible that an attempt to persuade would have a reverse effect, would cause the target to move in the opposite direction. This is usually referred to as a "boomerang" effect. Do you think it ever occurs? (Note that this is a tricky, complicated issue, which has not been fully resolved.)
7. As one way of organizing the material on attitude change, you might try to apply everything you know to a persuasive campaign on some topic. For

example, if you were trying to convince a town to vote in favor of fluoridation, what would you do?

SUGGESTIONS FOR ADDITIONAL READING

ARTICLES

*Aronson, E., Turner, J., and Carlsmith, J.M. Communicator credibility and communi-
cation discrepancy. *Journal of Abnormal and Social Psychology*, 1963, 67, 31–36.

*Dabbs, J.M., Jr., and Leventhal, H. Effects of varying the recommendations in a fear-
ousing communication. *Journal of Personality and Social Psychology*, 1966, 4 (5), 525–
531.

*Janis, I.L., Kaye, D., and Kirschner, P. Facilitating effects of "eating-while-reading"
on responsivness to persuasive communications. *Journal of Personality and Social
Psychology*, 1965, 1, 181–186.

*Janis, I.L., and Mann, L. Effectiveness of emotional role-playing in modifying smoking
habits and attitudes. *Journal of Experimental Research in Personality*, 1965, 1, 84–90.

*McGuire, W.J., and Papageorgis, D. The relative efficacy of various types of prior
belief-defense in producing immunity against persuasion. *Journal of Abnormal and
Social Psychology*, 1961, 62, 327–337.

*Schein, E.H. The Chinese indoctrination program for prisoners of war. *Psychiatry*,
1956, 19, 149–172.

*Sears, D.O. The paradox of de facto selective exposure without preferences for sup-
portive information. In R.P. Abelson et al. (Eds.), *Theories of cognitive consistency*.
Chicago: Rand McNally, 1968, Pp. 777–787.

BOOKS AND LONGER DISCUSSIONS

Cohen, A. *Attitude change and social influence*. New York: Basic Books, 1964.

Hovland, C.I., Janis, I.L, and Kelley, H.H. *Communication and persuasion*. New
Haven Conn.: Yale, 1953.

Lane, R.E., and Sears, D.O. *Public opinion*. Englewood Cliffs, N.J.: Prentice-Hall,
1964.

---

*Starred items are reprinted in Freedman, J.L., Carlsmith, J.M., and Sears, D.O. (Eds.),
Readings in social psychology. Englewood Cliffs, N.J.: Prentice-Hall, 1970.

REFERENCES

Abelson, R.P., and Lesser, G.S., 1959. The measurement of persuasibility in children. In
C.I. Hovland and I.L. Janis (Eds.), *Personality and persuasibility*. New Haven, Conn.:
Yale. Pp. 141–166.

Allyn, J., and Festinger, L., 1961. The effectiveness of unanticipated persuasive communications. *Journal of Abnormal and Social Psychology*, 62, 35–40.

Aronson, E., Turner, J., and Carlsmith, J.M., 1963. Communicator credibility and communication discrepancy. *Journal of Abnormal and Social Psychology*, 67, 31–36.

Berkowitz, L., and Cottingham, D.R., 1960. The interest value and relevance of fear-
arousing communications. *Journal of Abnormal and Social Psychology*, 60, 37–43.

Brock, T.C., and Becker, L.A., 1965. Ineffectiveness of "overheard" counter-
propagagnda. *Journal of Personality and Social Psychology*, 2, 654–660.

Cohen, A.R., 1957. Need for cognition and order of communication as determinants of
opinion change. In C.I. Hovland (Ed.), *The order of presentation in persuasion*. New
Haven, Conn.: Yale. Pp. 79–97.

Cohen, A.R., 1959. Some implications of self-esteem for social influence. In C.I. Hovland and I.L. Janis (Eds.) *Personality and persuasibility*. New Haven, Conn.: Yale. Pp. 102–120.

Dabbs, J.M., Jr., and Leventhal, H., 1966. Effects of varying the recommendations in a fear-arousing communication. *Journal of Personality and Social Psychology*, 4 (5), 525–531.

DeWolfe, A.S., and Governale, C. N., 1964. Fear and attitude change. *Journal of Abnormal and Social Psychology*, 69, 119–123.

Festinger, L., and Maccoby, N., 1964. On resistance to persuasive communications. *Journal of Abnormal and Social Psychology*, 68, 359–366.

Fisher, S., and Lubin, A., 1958. Distance as a determinant of influence in a two-person serial interaction situation. *Journal of Abnormal and Social Psychology*, 56, 230–238.

Freedman, J.L., and Sears, D.O., 1965. Selective exposure. In L. Berkowitz (Ed.), *Advances in Experimental Social Psychology*. Vol. II. New York: Academic.

Freedman, J.L., and Steinbruner, J.D., 1964. Perceived choice and resistance to persuasion. *Journal of Abnormal and Social Psychology*, 68, 678–681.

Gerard, H.B., 1954. The anchorage of opinions in face-to-face groups. *Human Relations*, 7, 313–326.

Haefner, D.P., 1964. The use of fear arousal in dental health education. Paper presented at the meeting of the American Public Health Association, October 7.

Hewgill, M.A., and Miller, G.R., 1965. Source credibility and response to fear-arousing communication. *Speech Monograph*, 32, 95–101.

Hovland, C.I., and Janis, I.L. (Eds.), 1959. *Personality and persuasibility*. New Haven, Conn.: Yale.

Hovland, C.I., and Mandell, W., 1952. An experimental comparison of conclusion-drawing by the communicator and by the audience. *Journal of Abnormal and Social Psychology*, 47, 581–588.

Hovland, C.I., and Pritzker, H. A., 1957. Extent of opinion change as a function of amount of change advocated. *Journal of Abnormal and Social Psychology*, 54, 257–261.

Hovland, C.I., and Weiss, W., 1952. The influence of course credibility on communication effectiveness. *Public Opinion Quarterly*, 15, 635–650.

Insko, C.A., Arkoff, A., and Insko, V.M., 1965. Effects of high and low fear arousing communications upon opinions toward smoking. *Journal of Experimental Social Psychology*, 1, 256–266.

Janis, I.L., and Feshbach, S., 1953. Effects of fear-arousing communications. *Journal of Abnormal and Social Psychology*, 48, 78–92.

Janis, I.L., and Field, P.B., 1959. *Sex differences in personality factors related to persuasibility*. New Haven, Conn.: Yale. Pp. 55–68.

Janis, I.L., Keye, D., and Kirschner, P., 1965. Facilitating effects of "eating-while-reading" on responsiveness to persuasive communications. *Journal of Personality and Social Psychology*, 1, 181–186.

Janis, I.L., and Terwilliger, R.F., 1962. An experimental study of psychological resistances to fear-arousing communications. *Journal of Abnormal and Social Psychology*, 65, 403–410.

Katz, D., Sarnoff, I., and McClintock, C.G., 1956. Ego-defense and attitude change. *Human Relations*, 9, 27–46.

Kelley, H.H., and Volkart, E.H., 1952. The resistance to change of group-anchored attitudes. *American Sociological Review*, 17, 453–456.

Kelman, H.C., and Hovland, C.I., 1953. "Reinstatement" of the communicator in delayed measurement of opinion change. *Journal of Abnormal and Social Psychology*, 48, 327–335.

Leventhal, H., Jones, S., and Trembly, G., 1966. Sex differences in attitude and behavior change under conditions of fear and specific instructions. *Journal of Experimental and Social Psychology*, 2 (4), 387–399.

Leventhal, H., Singer, R.P., and Jones, S., 1965. Effects of fear and specificity of recommendation upon attitudes and behavior. *Journal of Personality and Social Psychology*, 2 (1), 20–29.

Leventhal, H., and Singer, R.P., 1966. Effect arousal and positioning of recommendations in persuasive communication. *Journal of Personality and Social Psychology*, 4, 137–146.

McGuire, W.J., and Papageorgis, D., 1961. The relative efficacy of various types of prior belief-defense in producing immunity against persuasion. *Journal of Abnormal and Social Psychology*, 62, 327–337.

Miller, N., and Campbell, D.T., 1959. Recency and primary in persuasion as a function of the timing of speeches and measurements. *Journal of Abnormal and Social Psychology*, 59, 1–9.

Sears, D.O., 1966. Opinion formation and information preferences in an adversary situation. *Journal of Experimental Social Psychology*, 2, 130–142.

Sears, D.O., and Freedman, J.L., 1965. Effects of expected familiarity of arguments upon opinion change and selective exposure. *Journal of Personality and Social Psychology*, 2, 420–425.

Walster, E., Aronson, E., and Abrahams, D., 1966. On increasing the persuasiveness of a low prestige communicator. *Journal of Experimental Social Psychology*, 2, 325–342.

Walster, E., and Festinger, L., 1962. The effectiveness of "overheard" persuasive communications. *Journal of Abnormal and Social Psychology*, 65, 395–402.

Weiss, W.A., and Fine, B.J., 1956. The effect of induced aggressiveness on opinion change. *Journal of Abnormal and Social Psychology*, 52, 109–114.

Processes of Opinion Change*

by
Herbert C. Kelman

THE STUDY OF SOCIAL INFLUENCE

Social influence has been a central area of concern for experimental social psychology almost since its beginnings. Three general research traditions in this area can be distinguished: (1) the study of social influences on judgments, stemming from the earlier work on prestige suggestion,[1] (2) the study of social influences arising from small-group interaction,[2] and (3) the study of social influences arising from persuasive communications.[3] In recent years, there has been a considerable convergence between these three traditions, going hand in hand with an increased interest in developing general principles of social influence and socially induced behavior change.

One result of these developments has been that many investigators found it necessary to make qualitative distinctions between different types of influence. In some cases, these distinctions arose primarily out of the observation that social influence may have qualitatively different effects, that it may produce different kinds of change. For example, under some conditions it may result in mere public conformity—in superficial changes on a verbal or overt level without accompanying changes in belief; in other situations it may result in private acceptance—in a change that is more general, more durable, more integrated with the person's own values.[4] Other investigators found it necessary

Abridged from *Public Opinion Quarterly*, 1961, 25, pages 57–78, by permission of the author and publisher, Princeton University.

*This paper is based on a research program on social influence and behavior change, supported by grant M-2516 from the National Institute of Mental Health.

to make distinctions because they observed that influence may occur for different reasons, that it may arise out of different motivations and orientations. For example, under some conditions influence may be primarily informational—the subject may conform to the influencing person or group because he views him as a source of valid information; in other situations influence may be primarily normative—the subject may conform in order to meet the positive expectations of the influencing person or group.[5]

My own work can be viewed in the general context that I have outlined here. I started out with the distinction between public conformity and private acceptance, and tried to establish some of the distinct determinants of each. I became dissatisfied with this dichotomy as I began to look at important examples of social influence that could not be encompassed by it. I was especially impressed with the accounts of ideological conversion of the "true believer" variety and with the recent accounts of "brainwashing," particularly the Chinese Communist methods of "thought reform."[6] It is apparent that these experiences do not simply involve public conformity, but that indeed they produce a change in underlying beliefs. But it is equally apparent that they do not produce what we would usually consider private acceptance—changes that are in some sense integrated with the person's own value system and that have become independent of the external source. Rather, they seem to produce new beliefs that are isolated from the rest of the person's values and that are highly dependent on external support.

These considerations eventually led me to distinguish three processes of social influence, each characterized by a distinct set of antecedent and a distinct set of consequent conditions. I have called these processes *compliance, identification,* and *internalization.*[7]

THREE PROCESSES OF SOCIAL INFLUENCE

Compliance can be said to occur when an individual accepts influence from another person or from a group because he hopes to achieve a favorable reaction from the other. He may be interested in attaining certain specific rewards or in avoiding certain specific punishments that the influencing agent controls. For example, an individual may make a special effort to express only "correct" opinions in order to gain admission into a particular group or social set, or in order to avoid being fired from his government job. Or, the individual may be concerned with gaining approval or avoiding disapproval from the influencing agent in a more general way. For example, some individuals may compulsively try to say the expected thing in all situations and please everyone with whom they come in contact, out of a disproportionate need for favorable responses from others of a direct and immediate kind. In any event, when the individual complies, he does what the agent wants him to do—or what he thinks the agent wants him to do—because he sees this as a way of achieving a desired response from him. He does not adopt the induced behavior—for example, a particular opinion response—because he believes in its content, but because it is instrumental in the production of a satisfying social effect. What the individual learns, essentially, is to say or do the expected thing in special situations, regardless of what his private beliefs may be. Opinions adopted through compliance should be expressed only when the person's behavior is observable by the influencing agent.

Identification can be said to occur when an individual adopts behavior derived from another person or a group because this behavior is associated with a satisfying self-defining relationship to this person or group. By a self-defining relationship I mean a role relationship that forms a part of the person's self-image. Accepting influence through identification, then, is a way of establishing or maintaining the desired relationship to the other, and the self-definition that is anchored in this relationship.

The relationship that an individual tries to establish or maintain through identification may take different forms. It may take the form of classical identification, that is, of a relationship in which the individual takes over all or part of the role of the influencing agent. To the extent to which such a relationship exists, the individual defines his own role in terms of the role of the other. He attempts to be like or actually to be the other person. By saying what the other says, doing what he does, believing what he believes, the individual maintains this relationship and the satisfying self-definition that it provides him. An influencing agent who is likely to be an attractive object for such a relationship is one who occupies a role desired by the individual—who possesses those characteristics that the individual himself lacks—such as control in a situation in which the individual is helpless, direction in a situation in which he is disoriented, or belongingness in a situation in which he is isolated.

The behavior of the brainwashed prisoner in Communist China provides one example of this type of identification. By adopting the attitudes and beliefs of the prison authorities—including *their* evaluation of *him*—he attempts to regain his identity, which has been subjected to severe threats. But this kind of identification does not occur only in such severe crisis situations. It can also be observed, for example, in the context of socialization of children, where the taking over of parental attitudes and actions is a normal, and probably essential, part of personality development. The more or less conscious efforts involved when an individual learns to play a desired occupational role and imitates an appropriate role model would also exemplify this process. Here, of course, the individual is much more selective in the attitudes and actions he takes over from the other person. What is at stake is not his basic sense of identity or the stability of his self-concept, but rather his more limited "professional identity."

The self-defining relationship that an individual tries to establish or maintain through identification may also take the form of a reciprocal role relationship—that is, of a relationship in which the roles of the two parties are defined with reference to one another. An individual may be involved in a reciprocal relationship with another specific individual, as in a friendship relationship between two people. Or he may enact a social role which is defined with reference to another (reciprocal) role, as in the relationship between patient and doctor. A reciprocal-role relationship can be maintained only if the participants have mutually shared expectations of one another's behavior. Thus, if an individual finds a particular relationship satisfying, he will tend to behave in such a way as to meet the expectations of the other. In other words, he will tend to behave in line with the requirements of this particular relationship. This should be true regardless of whether the other is watching or not: quite apart from the reactions of the other, it is important to the individual's own self-concept to meet the expectations of his friendship role, for example, or those of his occupational role.

Thus, the acceptance of influence through identification should take place when the person sees the induced behavior as relevant to and required by a reciprocal-role relationship in which he is a participant. Acceptance of influence based on a reciprocal-role relationship is similar to that involved in classical identification in that it is a way of establishing or maintaining a satisfying self-defining relationship to another. The nature of the relationship differs, of course. In one case it is a relationship of identity; in the other, one of reciprocity. In the case of reciprocal-role relationships, the individual is not identifying with the other in the sense of taking over *his* identity, but in the sense of empathically reacting in terms of the other person's expectations, feelings, or needs.

Identification may also serve to maintain an individual's relationship to a group in which his self-definition is anchored. Such a relationship may have elements of classical identification as well as of reciprocal roles: to maintain his self-definition as a group member an individual, typically, has to model his behavior along particular lines and has to meet the expectations of his fellow members. An example of identification with a group would be the member of the Communist Party who derives strength and a sense of identity from his self-definition as part of the vanguard of the proletarian revolution and as an agent of historical destiny. A similar process, but at a low degree of intensity, is probably involved in many of the conventions that people acquire as part of their socialization into a particular group.

Identification is similar to compliance in that the individual does not adopt the induced behavior because its content per se is intrinsically satisfying. Identification differs from compliance, however, in that the individual actually believes in the opinions and actions that he adopts. The behavior is accepted both publicly and privately, and its manifestation does not depend on observability by the influencing agent. It does depend, however, on the role that an individual takes at any given moment in time. Only when the appropriate role is activated—only when the individual is acting within the relationship upon which the identification is based—will the induced opinions be expressed. The individual is not primarily concerned with pleasing the other, with giving him what he wants (as in compliance), but he is concerned with meeting the other's expectations for his own role performance. Thus, opinions adopted through identification do remain tied to the external source and dependent on social support. They are not integrated with the individual's value system, but rather tend to be isolated from the rest of his values—to remain encapsulated.

Finally, *internalization* can be said to occur when an individual accepts influence because the induced behavior is congruent with his value system. It is the content of the induced behavior that is intrinsically rewarding here. The individual adopts it because he finds it useful for the solution of a problem, or because it is congenial to his own orientation, or because it is demanded by his own values—in short, because he perceives it as inherently conducive to the maximization of his values. The characteristics of the influencing agent do play an important role in internalization, but the crucial dimension here—as we shall see below—is the agent's credibility, that is, his relation to the content.

The most obvious examples of internalization are those that involve the evaluation and acceptance of induced behavior on rational grounds. A person may adopt the recommendations of an expert, for example, because he finds them relevant to his own problems and congruent with his own values. Typically, when internalization is involved, he will not accept these recommendations *in toto* but modify them to some degree so that they will fit his own unique situation. Or a visitor to a foreign country may be challenged by the different patterns of behavior to which he is exposed, and he may decide to adopt them (again, selectively and in modified form) because he finds them more in keeping with his own values than the patterns in his home country. I am not implying, of course, that internalization is always involved in the situations mentioned. One would speak of internalization only if acceptance of influence took the particular form that I described.

Internalization, however, does not necessarily involve the adoption of induced behavior on rational grounds. I would not want to equate internalization with rationality, even though the description of the process has decidedly rationalist overtones. For example, I would characterize as internalization the adoption of beliefs because of their congruence with a value system that is basically irrational. Thus, an authoritarian individual may adopt certain racist attitudes because they fit into his paranoid, irrational view of the world. Presumably, what is involved here is internalization, since it is the content of the induced behavior and its relation to the person's value system that is satisfying. Similarly, it should be noted that congruence with a person's value system does not necessarily imply logical consistency. Behavior would be congruent if, in some way or other, it fit into the person's value system, if it seemed to belong there and be demanded by it.

It follows from this conception that behavior adopted through internalization is in some way—rational or otherwise—integrated with the individual's existing values. It becomes part of a personal system, as distinguished from a system of social-role expectations. Such behavior gradually becomes independent of the external source. Its manifestation depends neither on observability by the influencing agent nor on the activation of the relevant role, but on the extent to which the underlying values have been made relevant by the issues under consideration. This does not mean that the individual will invariably express internalized opinions, regardless of the social situation. In any specific situation, he has to choose among competing values in the face of a variety of situational requirements. It does mean, however, that these opinions will at least enter into competition with other alternatives whenever they are relevant in content.

It should be stressed that the three processes are not mutually exclusive. While they have been defined in terms of pure cases, they do not generally occur in pure form in real-life situations. The examples that have been given are, at best, situations in which a particular process predominates and determines the central features of the interaction.

END NOTES

1. See, for example, S.E. Asch, *Social Psychology*, New York, Prentice-Hall, 1952.

2. See, for example, D. Cartwright and A. Zander, editors, *Group Dynamics*, Evanston, Ill., Row, Peterson, 1953.

3. See, for example, C.I. Hovland, I.L. Janis, and H.H. Kelley, *Communication and Persuasion*, New Haven, Yale University Press, 1953.

4. See, for example, L. Festinger, "An Analysis of Compliant Behavior," in M. Sherif and M.O. Wilson, editors, *Group Relations at the Crossroads*, New York, Harper, 1953, pp. 232–256; H.C. Kelman, "Attitude Change as a Function of Response Restriction," *Human Relations*, Vol. 6, 1953, pp. 185–214; J.R.P. French, Jr., and B. Raven, "The Bases of Social Power," in D. Cartwright, editor, *Studies in Social Power*, Ann Arbor, Mich., Institute for Social Research, 1959, pp. 150–167; and Marie Jahoda, "Conformity and Independence," *Human Relations*, Vol. 12, 1959, pp. 99–120.

5. See, for example, M. Deutsch and H.B. Gerard, "A Study of Normative and Informational Social Influence upon Individual Judgment", *Journal of Abnormal and Social Psychology*, Vol. 51, 1955, pp. 629–636; J.W. Thibaut and L. Strickland, "Psychological Set and Social Conformity," *Journal of Personality*, Vol. 25, 1956, pp. 115–129; and J.M. Jackson and H.D. Saltzstein, "The Effect of Person-Group Relationships on Conformity Processes," *Journal of Abnormal and Social Psychology*, Vol. 57, 1958, pp. 17–24.

6. For instance, R.J. Lifton, "Thought Reform of Western Civilians in Chinese Communist Prisons," *Psychiatry*, Vol. 19, 1956, pp. 173–195.

7. A detailed description of these processes and the experimental work based on them will be contained in a forthcoming book, *Social Influence and Personal Belief: A Theoretical and Experimental Approach to the Study of Behavior Change* to be published by John Wiley & Sons.

Socialization

Organizational Socialization and the Profession of Management*

by
Edgar H. Schein

INTRODUCTION

Ladies and gentlemen, colleagues and friends. There are few times in one's professional life when one has an opportunity, indeed something of a mandate, to pull together one's thoughts about an area of study and to communicate these to others.

I can define my topic of concern best by reviewing very briefly the kinds of issues upon which I have focused my research over the last several years. In one way or another I have been trying to understand what happens to an individual when he enters and accepts membership in an organization. My interest was originally kindled by studies of the civilian and military prisoners of the Communists during the Korean War. I thought I could discern parallels between the kind of indoctrination to which these prisoners were subjected, and some of the indoctrination which goes on in American corporations when college and business school graduates first go to work for them. My research efforts came to be devoted to learning what sorts of attitudes and values students had when they left school, and what happened to these attitudes and values in the first few years of work. To this end I followed several panels of graduates of the Sloan School into their early career.

When these studies were well under way, it suddenly became quite apparent to me that if I wanted to study the impact of an organization on the at-

*From Edgar Schein, "Organizational Socialization and the Profession of Management," *Industrial Management Review*, Vol. 9, No. 2, Winter, 1968. Reprinted by permission.

titudes and values of its members, I might as well start closer to home. We have a school through which we put some 200 men per year—undergraduates, regular Master's students, Sloan Fellows, and Senior Executives. Studies of our own students and faculty revealed that not only did the student groups differ from each other in various attitude areas, but that they also differed from the faculty.

For example, if one takes a scale built up of items which deal with the relations of government and business, one finds that the Senior Executives in our program are consistently against any form of government intervention, the Sloans are not as extreme, the Master's students are roughly in the middle, and the faculty are in favor of such intervention. A similar line-up of attitudes can be found with respect to labor-management relations, and with respect to cynicism about how one gets ahead in industry. In case you did not guess, the Senior Executives are least cynical and the faculty are most cynical.

We also found that student attitudes change in many areas during school, and that they change away from business attitudes toward the faculty position. However, a recent study of Sloan Fellows, conducted after their graduation, indicated that most of the changes toward the faculty had reversed themselves to a considerable degree within one year, a finding which is not unfamiliar to us in studies of training programs of all sorts.

The different positions of different groups at different stages of their managerial career and the observed changes during school clearly indicate that attitudes and values change several times during the managerial career. It is the process which brings about these changes which I would like to focus on today—a process which the sociologists would call "occupational socialization," but which I would prefer to call "organizational socialization" in order to keep our focus clearly on the setting in which the process occurs.

Organizational socialization is the process of "learning the ropes," the process of being indoctrinated and trained, the process of being taught what is important in an organization or some subunit thereof. This process occurs in school. It occurs again, and perhaps most dramatically, when the graduate enters an organization on his first job. It occurs again when he switches within the organization from one department to another, or from one rank level to another. It occurs all over again if he leaves one organization and enters another. And it occurs again when he goes back to school, and again when he returns to the organization after school.

Indeed, the process is so ubiquitous and we go through it so often during our total career, that it is all too easy to overlook it. Yet it is a process which can make or break a career, and which can make or break organizational systems of manpower planning. The speed and effectiveness of socialization determine employee loyalty, commitment, productivity, and turnover. The basic stability and effectiveness of organizations therefore depends upon their ability to socialize new members.

Let us see whether we can bring the process of socialization to life by describing how it occurs. I hope to show you the power of this process, particularly as it occurs within industrial organizations. Having done this, I would like to explore a major dilemma which I see at the interface between organizations and graduate management schools. Schools socialize their students toward a concept of a profession; organizations socialize their new members to be effective members. Do the two processes of socialization supplement each other or conflict? If they conflict, what can we do about it in organizations and in the schools?

SOME BASIC ELEMENTS OF ORGANIZATIONAL SOCIALIZATION

The term socialization has a fairly clear meaning in sociology, but it has been a difficult one to assimilate in the behavioral sciences and in management. To many of my colleagues it implies unnecessary jargon, and to many of my business acquaintances it implies the teaching of socialism—a kiss of death for the concept right there. Yet the concept is most useful because it focuses clearly on the interaction between a stable social system and the new members who enter it. The concept refers to the process by which a new member learns the value system, the norms, and the required behavior patterns of the society, organization, or group which he is entering. It does not include all learning. It includes only the learning of those values, norms, and behavior patterns which, from the organization's point of view or group's point of view, it is necessary for any new member to learn. This is defined as the price of membership.

What are such values, norms, and behavior patterns all about? Usually they involve:

1. The basic goals of the organization.

2. The preferred means by which these goals should be attained.

3. The basic responsibilities of the member in the role which is being granted to him by the organization.

4. The behavior patterns which are required for effective performance in the role.

5. A set of rules or principles which pertain to the maintenance of the identity and integrity of the organization.

The new member must learn not to drive Chevrolets if he is working for Ford, not to criticize the organization in public, not to wear the wrong kind of clothes or be seen in the wrong kinds of places. If the organization is a school, beyond learning the content of what is taught, the student must accept the value of education, he must try to learn without cheating, he must accept the authority of the faculty and behave appropriately to the student role. He must not be rude in the classroom or openly disrespectful to the professor.

By what processes does the novice learn the required values and norms? The answer to this question depends in part upon the degree of prior socialization. If the novice has correctly anticipated the norms of the organization he is joining, the socialization process merely involves a reaffirmation of these norms through various communication channels, the personal example of key people in the organization, and direct instructions from supervisors, trainers, and informal coaches.

If, however, the novice comes to the organization with values and behavior patterns which are in varying degrees out of line with those expected by the organization, then the socialization process first involves a destructive or unfreezing phase. This phase serves the function of detaching the person from his former values, of proving to him that his present self is worthless from the point of view of the organization and that he must redefine himself in terms of the new roles which he is to be granted.

The extremes of this process can be seen in initiation rites or novitiates for religious orders. When the novice enters his training period, his old self is symbolically destroyed by loss of clothing, name, often his hair, titles and other self-defining equipment. These are replaced with uniforms, new names and titles, and other self-defining equipment consonant with the new role he is being trained for.

It may be comforting to think of activities like this as being characteristic only of primitive tribes or total institutions like military basic training camps, academies, and religious orders. But even a little examination of areas closer to home will reveal the same processes both in our graduate schools and in the business organizations to which our graduates go.

Perhaps the commonest version of the process in school is the imposition of a tight schedule, of an impossibly heavy reading program, and of the assignment of problems which are likely to be too difficult for the student to solve. Whether these techniques are deliberate or not, they serve effectively to remind the student that he is not as smart or capable as he may have thought he was, and therefore, that there are still things to be learned. As our Sloan Fellows tell us every year, the first summer in the program pretty well destroys many aspects of their self-image. Homework in statistics appears to enjoy a unique status comparable to having one's head shaved and clothes burned.

Studies of medical schools and our own observations of the Sloan program suggest that the work overload on the students leads to the development of a peer culture, a kind of banding together of the students as a defense against the threatening faculty and as a problem-solving device to develop norms of what and how to study. If the group solutions which are developed support the organizational norms, the peer group becomes an effective instrument of socialization. However, from the school's point of view, there is the risk that peer group norms will set up counter-socializing forces and sow the seeds of sabotage, rebellion, or revolution. The positive gains of a supportive peer group generally make it worthwhile to run the risks of rebellion, however, which usually motivates the organization to encourage or actually to facilitate peer group formation.

Many of our Sloan Fellow alumni tell us that one of the most powerful features of the Sloan program is the fact that a group of some 40 men share the same fate of being put through a very tough educational regimen. The peer group ties formed during the year have proven to be one of the most durable end-results of the educational program and, of course, are one of the key supports to the maintaining of some of the values and attitudes learned in school. The power of this kind of socializing force can be appreciated best by pondering a further statement which many alumni have made. They stated that prior to the program they identified themselves primarily with their company. Following the program they identified themselves primarily with the other Sloan Fellows, and such identification has lasted, as far as we can tell, for the rest of their career.

Let me next illustrate the industrial counterpart of these processes. Many of my panel members, when interviewed about the first six months in their new jobs, told stories of what we finally labeled as "upending experiences." Upending experiences are deliberately planned or accidentally created circumstances which dramatically and unequivocally upset or disconfirm some of the major assumptions which the new man holds about himself, his company, or his job.

One class of such experiences is to receive assignments which are so easy or so trivial that they carry the clear message that the new man is not worthy of being given anything important to do. Another class of such experiences is at the other extreme—assignments which are so difficult that failure is a certainty, thus proving unequivocally to the new man that he may not be as smart as he thought he was. Giving work which is clearly for practice only, asking for reports which are then unread or not acted upon, protracted periods of training during which the person observes others work, all have the same upending effect.

The most vivid example came from an engineering company where a supervisor has a conscious and deliberate strategy for dealing with what he considered to be unwarranted arrogance on the part of engineers whom they hired. He asked each new man to examine and diagnose a particular complex circuit, which happened to violate a number of textbook principles but actually worked very well. The new man would usually announce with confidence, even after an invitation to double-check, that the circuit could not possibly work. At this point the manager would demonstrate the circuit, tell the new man that they had been selling it for several years without customer complaint, and demand that the new man figure out why it did work. None of the men so far tested were able to do it, but all of them were thoroughly chastened and came to the manager anxious to learn where their knowledge was inadequate and needed supplementing. According to this manager, it was much easier from this point on to establish a good give-and-take relationship with his new man.

It should be noted that the success of such socializing techniques depends upon two factors which are not always under the control of the organization. The first factor is the initial motivation of the entrant to join the organization. If his motivation is high, as in the case of a fraternity pledge, he will tolerate all kinds of uncomfortable socialization experiences, even to the extremes of hell week. If his motivation for membership is low, he may well decide to leave the organization rather than tolerate uncomfortable initiation rites. If he leaves, the socialization process has obviously failed.

The second factor is the degree to which the organization can hold the new member captive during the period of socialization. His motivation is obviously one element here, but one finds organizations using other forces as well. In the case of basic training there are legal forces to remain. In the case of many schools one must pay one's tuition in advance, in other words, invest one's self materially so that leaving the system becomes expensive. In the case of religious orders one must make strong initial psychological commitments in the form of vows and the severing of relationships outside the religious order. The situation is defined as one in which one will lose face or be humiliated if one leaves the organization.

In the case of business organizations the pressures are more subtle but nevertheless identifiable. New members are encouraged to get financially committed by joining pension plans, stock option plans, and/or house purchasing plans which would mean material loss if the person decided to leave. Even more subtle is the reminder by the boss that it takes a year or so to learn any new business; therefore, if you leave, you will have to start all over again. Why not suffer it out with the hope that things will look more rosy once the initiation period is over.

Several of my panel members told me at the end of one year at work that they were quite dissatisfied, but were not sure they should leave because they had invested a year of learning in that company. Usually their boss encouraged them to think about staying. Whether or not such pressures will work depends, of course, on the labor market and other factors not under the control of the organization.

Let me summarize thus far. Organizations socialize their new members by creating a series of events which serve the function of undoing old values so that the person will be prepared to learn the new values. This process of undoing or unfreezing is often unpleasant and therefore requires either strong motivation to endure it or strong organizational forces to make the person endure it. The formation of a peer group of novices is often a solution to the problem of defense against the powerful organization, and, at the same time, can strongly enhance the socialization process if peer group norms support organizational norms.

Let us look next at the positive side of the socialization process. Given some readiness to learn, how does the novice acquire his new learning? The answer is that he acquires it from multiple sources—the official literature of the organization; the example set by key models in the organization; the instructions given to him directly by his trainer, coach, or boss; the example of peers who have been in the organization longer and thus serve as big brothers; the rewards and punishments which result from his own efforts at problem solving and experimenting with new values and new behavior.

The instructions and guidelines given by senior members of the organization are probably one of the most potent sources. I can illustrate this point best by recalling several incidents from my own socialization into the Sloan School back in 1956. I came here at the invitation of Doug McGregor from a research job. I had no prior teaching experience or knowledge of organizational or managerial matters. Contrary to my expectations, I was told by Doug that knowledge of organizational psychology and management was not important, but that some interest in learning about these matters was.

The first socializing incident occurred in an initial interview with Elting Morison, who was then on our faculty. He said in a completely blunt manner that if I knew what I wanted to do and could go ahead on my own, the Sloan School would be a great place to be. If I wasn't sure and would look to others for guidance, not to bother to come.

The second incident occurred in a conversation with our then Dean, Penn Brooks, a few weeks before the opening of the semester. We were discussing what and how I might teach. Penn said to me that he basically wanted each of his faculty members to find his own approach to management education. I could do whatever I wanted—so long as I did not imitate our sister school up the river. Case discussion leaders need not apply, was the clear message.

The third incident (you see I was a slow learner) occurred a few days later when I was planning my subject in social psychology for our Master's students. I was quite nervous about it and unsure of how to decide what to include in the subject. I went to Doug and innocently asked him to lend me outlines of previous versions of the subject, which had been taught by Alex Bavelas, or at least to give me some advice on what to include and exclude. Doug was very nice and very patient, but also quite firm in his refusal to give me either outlines or advice. He thought there was really no need to rely on history, and expressed confidence that I could probably make up my own mind. I suffered that term but learned a good deal about the value system of the Sloan School, as well as how to organize a subject. I was, in fact, so well socialized by these early experiences that nowadays no one can get me to coordinate anything with anybody else.

Similar kinds of lessons can be learned during the course of training programs, in orientation sessions, and through company literature. But the more subtle kinds of values which the organization holds, which indeed may not even be well understood by the senior people, are often communicated through peers operating as helpful big brothers. They can communicate the subtleties of how the boss wants things done, how higher management feels about things, the kinds of things which are considered heroic in the organization, the kinds of things which are taboo.

Of course, sometimes the values of the immediate group into which a new person is hired are partially out of line with the value system of the organization as a whole; if this is the case, the new person will learn the immediate group's values much more quickly than those of the total organization, often to the chagrin of the higher levels of management. This is best exemplified at the level of hourly workers where fellow employees will have much more socializing power than the boss.

An interesting managerial example of this conflict was provided by one recent graduate who was hired into a group whose purpose was to develop cost reduction systems for a large manufacturing operation. His colleagues on the job, however, showed him how to pad his expense account whenever they traveled together. The end result of this kind of conflict was to accept neither the cost reduction values of the company nor the cost inflation values of the peer group. The man left the company in disgust to start up some businesses of his own.

One of the important functions of organizational socialization is to build commitment and loyalty to the organization. How is this accomplished? One mechanism is to invest much effort and time in the new member and thereby build up expectations of being repaid by loyalty, hard work, and rapid learning. Another mechanism is to get the new member to make a series of small behavioral commitments which can only be justified by him through the acceptance and incorporation of company values. He then becomes his own agent of socialization. Both mechanisms involve the subtle manipulation of guilt.

To illustrate the first mechanism, one of our graduates went to a public relations firm which made it clear to him that he had sufficient knowledge and skill to advance, but that his values and attitudes would have to be evaluated for a couple of years before he would be fully accepted. During the first several months he was frequently invited to join high ranking members of the organization at their luncheon meetings in order to learn more about how they thought about things. He was so flattered by the amount of time they spent on him, that he worked extra hard to learn their values and became highly committed to the organization. He said that he would have felt guilty at the thought of not learning or of leaving the company. Sending people to expensive training programs, giving them extra perquisites, indeed the whole philosophy of paternalism, is built on the assumption that if you invest in the employee he will repay the company with loyalty and hard work. He would feel guilty if he did not.

The second mechanism, that of getting behavioral commitments, was most beautifully illustrated in Communist techniques of coercive persuasion. The Communists made tremendous efforts to elicit a public confession from a prisoner. One of the key functions of such a public confession, even if the prisoner knew he was making a false confession, was that it committed him publicly. Once he made this commitment, he found himself under strong internal and external pressure to justify why he had confessed. For many people it proved easier to justify the confession by coming to believe in their own crimes than to have to face the fact that they were too weak to withstand the captor's pressure.

In organizations, a similar effect can be achieved by promoting a rebellious person into a position of responsibility. The same values which the new member may have criticized and jeered at from his position at the bottom of the hierarchy suddenly look different when he has subordinates of his own whose commitment he must obtain.

Many of my panel members had very strong moral and ethical standards when they first went to work, and these stood up quite well during their first year at work even in the face of less ethical practices by their peers and superiors. But they reported with considerable shock that some of the practices they had condemned in their bosses were quickly adopted by them once they had themselves been promoted and faced the pressures of the new position. As one man put it very poignantly—"my ethical standards changed so gradually over the first five years of work that I hardly noticed it, but it was a great shock to suddenly realize what my feelings had been five years ago and how much they had changed."

Another version of obtaining commitment is to gain the new member's acceptance of very general ideals like "one must work for the good of the company," or "one must meet the competition." Whenever any counter-organizational behavior occurs one can then point out that the ideal is being violated. The engineer who does not come to work on time is reminded that his behavior indicates lack of concern for the good of the company. The employee who wears the wrong kind of clothes, lives in the wrong neighborhood, or associates with the wrong people can be reminded that he is hurting the company image.

One of my panel members on a product research assignment discovered that an additive which was approved by the Food and Drug Administration might, in fact, be harmful to consumers. He was strongly encouraged to forget about it. His boss told him that it was the F.D.A.'s problem. If the company worried about things like that it might force prices up and thus make it tough to meet the competition.

Many of the upending experiences which new members of organizations endure are justified to them by the unarguable ideal that they should learn how the company really works before expecting a position of real responsibility. Once the new man accepts this ideal it serves to justify all kinds of training and quantities of menial work which others who have been around longer are unwilling to do themselves. This practice is known as "learning the business from the ground up," or "I had to do it when I first joined the company, now it's someone else's turn." There are clear elements of hazing involved not too different from those associated with fraternity initiations and other rites of passage.

The final mechanism to be noted in a socialization process is the transition to full-fledged member. The purpose of such transitional events is to help the new member incorporate his new values, attitudes, and norms into his identity so that they become part of him, not merely something to which he pays lip-service. Initiation rites which involve severe tests of the novice serve to prove to him that he is capable of fulfilling the new role—that he now is a man, no longer merely a boy.

Organizations usually signal this transition by giving the new man some important responsibility or a position of power which, if mishandled or misused, could genuinely hurt the organization. With this transition often come titles, symbols of status, extra rights or prerogatives, sharing of confidential information or other things which in one way or another indicate that the new member has earned the trust of the organization. Although such events may not always be visible to the outside observer, they are felt strongly by the new member. He knows when he has finally "been accepted," and feels it when he becomes "identified with the company."

So much for examples of the process of socialization. Let us now look at some of the dilemmas and conflicts which arise within it.

FAILURES OF SOCIALIZATION—NON-CONFORMITY AND OVER-CONFORMITY

Most organizations attach differing amounts of importance to different norms and values. Some are pivotal. Any member of a business organization who does not believe in the value of getting a job done will not survive long. Other pivotal values in most business organizations might be belief in a reasonable profit, belief in the free enterprise system and competition, belief in a hierarchy of authority as a good way to get things done, and so on.

Other values or norms are what may be called relevant. These are norms which it is not absolutely necessary to accept as the price of membership, but which are considered desirable and good to accept. Many of these norms pertain to standards of dress and decorum, not being publicly disloyal to the company, living in the right neighborhood and belonging to the right political party and clubs. In some organizations some of these norms may be pivotal. Organizations vary in this regard. You all know the stereotype of IBM as a company that requires the wearing of white shirts and hats. In some parts of IBM such values are indeed pivotal; in other parts they are only relevant, and in some parts they are quite peripheral. The point is that not all norms to which the new member is exposed are equally important for the organization.

The socialization process operates across the whole range of norms, but the amount of reward and punishment for compliance or non-compliance will vary with the importance of the norm. This variation allows the new member some degrees of freedom in terms of how far to conform and allows the organization some degrees of freedom in how much conformity to demand. The new man can accept none of the values, he can accept only the pivotal values, but carefully remain independent on all those areas not seen as pivotal, or he can accept the whole range of values and norms. He can tune in so completely on what he sees to be the way others are handling themselves that he becomes a carbon-copy and sometimes a caricature of them.

These basic responses to socialization can be labeled as follows:

Type 1. Rebellion: Rejection of all values and norms

Type 2. Creation individualism: Acceptance only of pivotal values and norms; rejection of all others

Type 3. Conformity: Acceptance of all values and norms

Most analyses of conformity deal only with the type 1 and 3 cases, failing to note that both can be viewed as socialization failures. The rebellious individual either is expelled from the organization or turns his energies toward defeating its goals. The conforming individual curbs his creativity and thereby moves the organization toward a sterile form of bureaucracy. The trick for most organizations is to create the type of 2 response—acceptance of pivotal values and norms, but rejection of all others, a response which I would like to call "creative individualism."

To remain creatively individualistic in an organization is particularly difficult because of the constant resocialization pressures which come with promotion or lateral transfer. Every time the employee learns part of the value system of the particular group to which he is assigned, he may be laying the groundwork for conflict when he is transferred. The engineer has difficulty accepting the values of the sales department, the staff man has difficulty accepting the high pressure ways of the production department, and the line manager has difficulties accepting the service and helping ethic of a staff group. With each transfer, the forces are great toward either conforming or rebelling. It is difficult to keep focused on what is pivotal and retain one's basic individualism.

PROFESSIONAL SOCIALIZATION AND ORGANIZATIONAL SOCIALIZATION

The issue of how to maintain individualism in the face of organizational socialization pressures brings us to the final and most problematical area of concern. In the traditional professions like medicine, law, and teaching, individualism is supported by a set of professional attitudes which serve to immunize the person against some of the forces of the organization. The questions now to be considered are (1) Is management a profession? (2) If so, do professional attitudes develop in managers? and (3) If so, do these support or conflict with organizational norms and values?

Professionalism can be defined by a number of characteristics:

1. Professional decisions are made by means of general principles, theories, or propositions which are independent of the particular case under consideration. For management this would mean that there are certain principles of how to handle people, money, information, etc., independent of any particular company. The fact that we can and do teach general subjects in these areas would support management's claim as a profession.

2. Professional decisions imply knowledge in a specific area in which the person is expert, not a generalized body of wisdom. The professional is an expert only in his profession, not an expert at everything. He has to have license to be a "wise man." Does management fit by this criterion? I will let you decide.

3. The professional's relations with his clients are objective and independent of particular sentiments about them. The doctor or lawyer makes his decisions independent of his liking or disliking of his patients or clients. On this criterion we have a real difficulty since, in the first place, it is very difficult to specify an appropriate single client for a manager, and, in the second place, it is not at all clear that decisions can or should be made independent of sentiments. What is objectively best for the stockholder may conflict with what is best for the enterprise, which, in turn may conflict with what is best for the customer.

4. A professional achieves his status by accomplishment, not by inherent qualities such as birth order, his relationship to people in power, his race, religion, or color. Industry is increasingly moving toward an acceptance of this principle for managerial selection, but in practice the process of organizational socialization may undermine it by rewarding the conformist and rejecting the individualist whose professional orientation may make him look disloyal to the organization.

5. A professional's decisions are assumed to be on behalf of the client and to be independent of self-interest. Clearly this principle is at best equivocal in manager-customer relations, though again one senses that industry is moving closer to accepting the idea.

6. The professional typically relates to a voluntary association of fellow professionals, and accepts only the authority of these colleagues as a sanction on his own behavior. The manager is least like the professional in this regard, in that he is expected to accept a principle of hierarchical authority. The dilemma is best illustrated by the previous example which I gave of our Sloan Fellow alumni who, after the program, related themselves more to other Sloans than to their company hierarchy. By this criterion they had become truly professionalized.

7. A professional has sometimes been called someone who knows better what is good for his client than the client. The professional's expertness puts the client into a very vulnerable position. This vulnerability has necessitated the development of strong professional codes and ethics which serve to protect the client. Such codes are enforced through the colleague peer group. One sees relatively few attempts to develop codes of ethics for managers or systems of enforcement.

On several bases, then, management is a profession, but on several others it is clearly not yet a profession.

This long description of what is a profession was motivated by the need to make a very crucial point. I believe that management education, particularly in a graduate school like the Sloan School, is increasingly attempting to train professionals, and in this process is socializing the students to a set of professional values which are, in fact, in severe and direct conflict with typical organizational values.

For example, I see us teaching general principies in the behavioral sciences, economics, and quantitative methods. Our applied subjects like marketing, operations management, and finance are also taught as bodies of knowledge governed by general principles which are applicable to a wide variety of situations. Our students are given very broad concepts which apply to the corporation as a whole, and are taught to see the relationship between the corporation, the community, and the society. They are taught to value the long-range health and survival of economic institutions, not the short-range profit of a particular company. They come to appreciate the necessary interrelationships between government, labor, and management rather than to define these as mutually warring camps. They are taught to look at organizations from the perspective of high ranking management, to solve the basic problems of the enterprise rather than the day-to-day practical problems of staff or line management. Finally, they are taught an ethic of pure rationality and emotional neutrality—analyze the problem and make the decisions independent of feelings about people, the product, the company, or the community. All of these are essentially professional values.

Organizations value many of the same things, in principle. But what is valued in principle by the higher ranking and senior people in the organization often is neither supported by their own behavior, nor even valued lower down in the organization. In fact, the value system which the graduates encounter on their first job is in many respects diametrically opposed to the professional values taught in school. The graduate is immediately expected to develop loyalty and concern for a particular company with all of its particular idiosyncrasies. He is expected to recognize the limitation of his general knowledge and to develop the sort of ad hoc wisdom which the school has taught him to avoid. He is expected to look to his boss for evaluation rather than to some group of colleagues outside the company.

Whereas the professional training tells him that knowledge is power, the graduate now must learn that knowledge by itself is nothing. It is the ability to sell knowledge to other people which is power. Only by being able to sell an application of knowledge to a highly specific, local situation, can the graduate obtain respect for what he knows. Where his education has taught the graduate principles of how to manage others and to take the corporate point of view, his organizational socialization tries to teach him how to be a good subordinate, how to be influenced, and how to sell ideas from a position of low power.

On the one hand, the organization via its recruiters and senior people tells the graduate that it is counting on him to bring fresh points of view and new techniques to bear on its problems. On the other hand, the man's first boss and peers try to socialize him into their traditional mold.

A man is hired to introduce linear programming into a production department, but once he is there he is told to lay off because if he succeeds he will make the old supervisors and engineers look bad. Another man is hired for his financial analysis skills but is not permitted access to data worth analyzing because the company does not trust him to keep them confidential. A third man is hired into a large group responsible for developing cost reduction programs in a large defense industry, and is told to ignore the fact that the group is overstaffed, inefficient, and willing to pad its expense accounts. A fourth man, hired for his energy and capability, put it this way as an explanation of why he quit to go into private consulting: "They were quite pleased with work that required only two hours per day; I wasn't."

In my panel of 1962 graduates, 73 percent have already left their first job and many are on their third or fourth. In the class of 1963, the percentage is 67, and in the class of 1964, the percentage is 50. Apparently, most of our graduates are unwilling to be socialized into organizations whose values are incompatible with the ones we teach. Yet these organizations are precisely the ones who may need creative individualists most.

What seems to happen in the early stages of the managerial career is either a kind of postponement of professional socialization while organizational socialization takes precedence, or a rebelling by the graduate against organizational socialization. The young man who submits must first learn to be a good apprentice, a good staff man, a good junior analyst, and perhaps a good low level administrator. He must prove his loyalty to the company by accepting this career path with good graces, before he is trusted enough to be given a position of power. If he has not lost his education by then, he can begin to apply some general principles when he achieves such a position of power.

The businessman wants the school to provide both the professional education and the humility which would make organizational socialization smoother. He is not aware that teaching management concepts of the future precludes justifying the practices of today. Some professional schools clearly do set out to train for the needs of the profession as it is designed today. The Sloan School appears to me to reject this concept.

Instead we have a faculty which is looking at the professional manager of five, ten, or twenty years from now, and is training its graduates in management techniques which we believe are coming in the future.

Symptomatic of this approach is the fact that in many of our subjects we are highly critical of the management practices of today, and highly committed to re-educating those managers like Sloan Fellows and Senior Executives who come back to study at M.I.T. We get across in a dozen different ways the belief that most organizations of today are obsolete, conservative, constipated, and ignorant of their own problems. Furthermore, I believe that this point of view is what society and the business community demands of a good professional school.

It would be no solution to abandon our own vision of the manager of the future, and I doubt that those of you in the audience from business and industry would really want us to do this. What you probably want is to have your cake and eat it too—you want us to teach our students the management concepts of tomorrow, and you want us to teach them how to put these concepts into deep freeze while they learn the business of today. Then when they have proven themselves worthy of advancement and have achieved a position of some influence, they should magically resurrect their education and put it to work.

Unfortunately, socialization processes are usually too powerful to permit that solution. If you succeed in socializing your young graduates to your organizations, you will probably also succeed in proving to them that their education was pretty worthless and might as well be put on a permanent rather than temporary shelf. We have research evidence that many well educated graduates do learn to be complacent and to play the organizational game. It is not at all clear whether they later ever resurrect their educational arsenal.

What Is To Be Done About This Situation?

I think we need to accept, at the outset, the reality of organizational socialization phenomena. As my colleague, Leo Moore, so aptly put it, organizations like to put their fingerprints on people, and they have every right to do so. By the same token, graduate schools of business have a right and an obligation to pursue professional socialization to the best of their ability. We must find a way to ameliorate the conflicts at the interface, without, however, concluding that either schools or organizations are to blame and should stop what they are doing.

What The Schools Can Do

The schools, our school in particular, can do several concrete things which would help the situation. First, we can insert into our total curriculum more apprenticeship experience which would bring the realities of organizational life home to the student earlier. But such apprenticeship experiences will not become educational unless we combine them with a second idea, that of providing a practicum on how to change organizations. Such a practicum should draw on each of the course specialties and should be specifically designed to teach a student how to translate his professional knowledge into viable action programs at whatever level of the organization he is working.

Ten years ago we would not have known how to do this. Today there is no excuse for not doing it. Whether the field is operations research, sophisticated quantitative marketing, industrial dynamics, organizational psychology or whatever, we must give our students experience in trying to implement their new ideas, and we must teach them how to make the implementation effective. In effect, we must teach our students to become change-agents, whatever their disciplinary speciality turns out to be. We must teach them how to influence their organizations from low positions of power without sacrificing their professional values in the process. We must teach them how to remain creative individualists in the face of strong organizational socialization pressures.

Combined with these two things, we need to do a third thing. We need to become more involved in the student's efforts at career planning and we need to coordinate our activities more closely with the company recruiters and the university placement officers. At the present I suspect that most of our faculty is quite indifferent to the student's struggles to find the right kind of a job. I suspect that this indifference leaves the door wide open to faulty selection on the part of the student, which can only lead, in the end, to an undermining of the education into which we pour so much effort. We need to work harder to insure that our graduates get jobs in which they can further the values and methods we inculcate.

What The Companies Can Do

Companies can do at least two things. First, they can make a genuine effort to become aware of and understand their own organizational socialization practices. I fear very few higher level executives know what is going on at the bottom of their organization where all the high priced talent they call for is actually employed. At the same time, I suspect that it is their own value system which ultimately determines the socialization activities which occur throughout all segments of the organization. Greater awareness and understanding of these practices should make possible more rational choices as to which practices to encourage and which to de-emphasize. The focus should be on pivotal values only, not on peripheral or irrelevant ones.

Second, companies must come to appreciate the delicate problems which exist both for the graduate and for his first boss in the early years of the career when socialization pressures are at the maximum. If more companies appreciated the nature of this dilemma they would recognize the necessity of giving some training to the men who will be the first bosses of the graduates.

I have argued for such training for many years, but still find that most company effort goes into training the graduate rather than his boss. Yet it is the boss who really has the power to create the climate which will lead to rebellion, conformity, or creative individualism. If the companies care whether their new hires use one or the other of these adaptation strategies, they had better start looking at the behavior of the first boss and training him for what the company wants and hopes for. Too many bosses concentrate on teaching too many peripheral values and thus undermine the possibilities for creative individualism and organization improvement.

CONCLUSION

The essence of management is to understand the forces acting in a situation and to gain control over them. It is high time that some of our managerial knowledge and skill be focused on those forces in the organizational environment which derive from the fact that organizations are social systems who do socialize their new members. If we do not learn to analyze and control the forces of organizational socialization, we are abdicating one of our primary managerial responsibilities. Let us not shrink away from a little bit of social engineering and management in this most important area of the human side of the enterprise.

REFERENCES

1. Blau, P.M. and Scott, R.W. *Formal Organizations*. San Francisco: Chandler, 1962.

2. Goffman, E. *Asylums*. Garden City, N.Y. Doubleday Anchor, 1961.

3. Schein, E.H., Schneier, Inge and Barker, C.H. *Coercive Persuasion*. New York: W.W. Norton, 1961.

4. Schein, E.H. "Management Development as a Process of Influence," *Industrial Management Review*, II (1961), 59–77.

5. Schein, E.H. "Forces Which Undermine Management Development," *California Management Review*, Vol. V, Summer, 1963.

6. Schein, E.H. "How to Break in the College Graduate," *Harvard Business Review*, Vol. XLII (1964).

7. Schein, E.H. "Training in Industry: Education or Indoctrination," *Industrial Medicine and Surgery*, Vol. XXXIII (1964).

8. Schein, E.H. *Organizational Psychology*. Englewood Cliffs, N.J.: Prentice-Hall, 1965.

9. Schein, E.H. "The Problem of Moral Education for the Business Manager," *Industrial Management Review*, VIII (1966), 3–14.

10. Schein, E.H. "Attitude Change During Management Education," *Administrative Science Quarterly*, XI (1967), 601–628.

11. Schein, E.H. "The Wall of Misunderstanding on the first Job," *Journal of College Placement*, February/March, 1967.

Part II

The Group

by
*William A. Bachman**

Since almost all human activity takes places in groups, and since most complicated and important organizational tasks are achieved as a result of individual
effort coordinated through group interactions, it is important that the student of
leadership understand the dynamics of group processes. It is especially important for the military leader to be aware of these dynamics, because his
particular style of leadership (Part III) will affect them; and he, in turn, will be
affected by them, for he is also a member of the group.

In this part, four major questions will be considered: (1) what are groups?
(2) why do individuals join and remain in them? (3) what are the processes and
products of individual and group interaction? and (4) what are the aspects of
group dynamics to which the military leader must pay particular attention? The
articles in this part address these questions from various perspectives. Certain
concepts of group dynamics theory have been emphasized because an understanding of how they relate to the leader is essential to an integrated approach
to leadership. These concepts are included at the end of this introduction to
groups.

What is a group? A group may be defined as "a collection of individuals
among whom a set of interdependent relationships exist." (Bobbitt, 1974, p.
110) Implied in this definition are (1) members with some degree of interdependent status and role relationships, (2) a collective goal, and (3) a set of

---

*William A. Bachman (Captain, U.S. Army) is on the faculty of the Office of Military
Leadership at the United States Military Academy, West Point, New York. He received
his BS from the United States Military Academy (1968) and his MS in Administration
(Organizational Behavior) from the University of California at Irvine (1974).

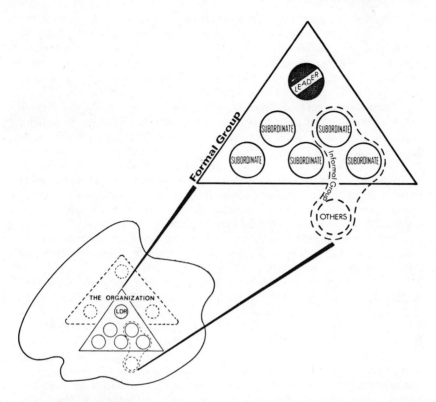

norms that regulate the behavior of members, at least in those areas of consequence to the members.

What prompts individuals to join groups? Coleman and Hammen's article
describes these reasons in detail. Briefly, as seen in the first article and in Part
I, individuals have a need for human interaction, for affiliation and social support. They need to be valued members of groups that they value. Also, individuals join groups to achieve goals that they cannot achieve by themselves.
Through the socialization process, as described in Part I, individuals learn to
appreciate and desire many goals that require group effort to attain. In the
military context, survival itself can be considered a goal achievable primarily
through group action.

Despite the motivation to join groups, there exists an inescapable dilemma
for individuals concerning group membership. The dilemma, simply stated, is
that although persons need to feel accepted as members of groups that satisfy
their needs and support their values, membership costs them their autonomy of
behavior and thus, to varying degrees, their individuality. This dilemma must
be resolved if an individual is to remain in the group. Several coping
mechanisms arise out of the dynamics of group interaction and individual
psychological processes to help resolve this dilemma. The articles included
touch on many of these mechanisms.

What are the processes and products of group interaction? Several key concepts are addressed by Coleman and Hammen in their article, from the perspective of the individual. Obviously, groups can be structured into organizations, and within organizations many groups may operate. Keeping in mind that both informal and formal groups exist, the focus in this part will be on informal groups. Formal organizations will be discussed in Part V.

The need to direct the individual's efforts toward group goals, and the individual's perception of the degree to which group member behavior is being regulated, combine to create pressures for conformity. These pressures can be intense, as described by Leavitt in his article on independence and conformity. A comprehensive discussion of the direct effects of groups on member behavior is included in the section by Porter, et al. The sets of expected behaviors through which group members agree to regulate their activities are called norms. Communicating group norms to members is accomplished through the norm-sending process, as described in the included Porter, et al, article.

As the group performs its various tasks, certain needs of the group for successful accomplishment of its goal become recognizable. These needs produce different functions and, in turn, these different functions produce roles for members to fulfill. This process of role differentiation is mentioned in Coleman & Hammen and explained in detail in Secord and Backman's section on leadership.

Obviously, for students of leadership, the most significant role to emerge is that of the leader. One of the most important findings of group dynamics research is that leadership usually emerges to meet two different sets of group needs. These needs are (1) to achieve the group goal and (2) to satisfy individual relationships within the group. These needs lead to what are described as task and maintenance functions. They are explained in the article by Secord and Backman. This has become known in the military as the "white hat-black hat" phenomenon, wherein one commander, due to personality or circumstance, may adopt one role and his assistant, the other. For the long term effectiveness of the group, these roles should be mutually supportive and mutually appreciated by both task and maintenance leaders.

The concept of social power is a useful way to explain the influence process that provides a dynamic to group relationships. Power can be considered the potential to influence behavior. Secord and Backman explain the parameters and bases of social power. Positional power, or authority, derives from the organization, and will be discussed in Part V. It should be stressed that power relationships ultimately depend upon the perceptions of those in the relationship, and that the different bases of power of each participant cause complex interdependencies. This explains why, for example, a commander may wield influence over his unit due to coercive, legitimate or referent power, yet be influenced by his clerk, who has expert power based on his knowledge of regulations. An understanding of power relationships as they are manipulated by those without formal power in an organization is provided by the Mechanic article.

Social exchange theory addresses the individual motivation for entering these interdependent relationships and the reciprocity implicit in group processes. Social exchange is explained in the excerpt by T.O. Jacobs. The basic assumption is that individuals enter into social relationships because they expect them to be rewarding, based upon a subjective determination of benefits and costs. Often these rewards are intangible; for the leader, they could be respect, esteem, or a sense of service. In Part III, social exchange theory will form the basis for a discussion of the "informal contract" that exists between the organization and its members.

The concept of social power complements social exchange theory in that the amount and type of power an individual possesses in a particular relationship provides him with resources or potential benefits to exchange. Power acts as the "coinage" in the psycho-economic theory of social exchange, and as such, can also be the result of the exchange process. That is, power differentials both cause social exchanges and are the results of exchanges.

The related concept of idiosyncracy credits is explained by Jacobs as a supplementary part of social exchange. Idiosyncracy credits are the balance of favorable impressions an individual accumulates that allows him to deviate from group norms. For the leader, an understanding of the dynamics of idiosyncracy credits is important for it allows him to guide the group toward new behaviors if he desires. Contributing to the group goal increases an individual's credits, deviating from group norms decreases them.

From this general discussion of the concepts of group dynamics, we can proceed to the final major question: What aspects of group interaction have special consequences for the military leader? Obstacles to the accomplishment of the group goal, or the difficulty of the goal itself, often cause strains on the routine functioning of the group. In particular, the nature and environment of military operations can serve to place unique and, at times, severely dysfunctional strains upon group processes. The impact of stress, that is, group reactions to perceived threats, can cause alterations in the leadership desired by the group, as explained in the Korten article. Uncertainty in the environment, vague or ambiguous goals, or anxiety of the individual members, among other factors, can contribute to deviancy from the existing group norms. Several articles in this part discuss various aspects of deviancy and their impact on group processes. Pronounced deviancy is of concern to military leaders because it can destroy the cohesiveness and effectiveness of the group, as noted in the George article.

If combat operations produce severe stress on groups, what keeps groups intact and functioning in the face of these threats? George states that the reasons lie in allegiance to face-to-face or primary groups. Moskos, citing personal surveys from Vietnam, disagrees, offering the combined explanations of self-interest and latent belief in the superiority of American cultural materialism. Hatred of the enemy seems to have a very low priority; the cohesive potential of group processes appears to be strong enough to withstand disintegration, provided the leader develops the necessary intragroup relationships and interdependencies.

For the military leader, who will spend his career intimately involved in focusing individual efforts to accomplish group tasks, often under trying conditions, an appreciation for and understanding of group dynamics is essential for effective leadership. Part III will explain the unique impact that the leader has upon these group processes.

Terms you should be able to discuss when you finish this part:

Coercive Power	Norm-sending Process
Cohesiveness	Primary Group
Deviancy	Referent Power
Emergent Leader	Reward Power
Expert Power	Roles
Group	Role Differentiation
Group Processes	Social Exchange
Idiosyncracy Credit	Social Power
Legitimate Power	Status
Maintenance Function	Stress
Norm	Task Function

REFERENCE

Bobbitt, H. Randolph, Jr., Breinholt, Robert H., Doktor, Robert H., and McNaul, James P. *Organizational Behavior: Understanding and Prediction.* Englewood Cliffs, New Jersey: Prentice-Hall, Inc. 1974.

Group Processes

The Individual and the Group*

by
Coleman and Hammen

"If it were possible for the overworked hypothetical man from Mars to take a fresh view of the people of Earth, he would probably be impressed by the amount of time they spend doing things together in groups. He would note that most people cluster into relatively small groups, with the members residing together in the same dwelling, satisfying their basic biological needs within the group, depending upon the same source for economic support, rearing children, and mutually caring for the health of one another. He would observe that the education and socialization of children tend to occur in other, usually larger groups in churches, schools, and other social institutions. He would see that much of the work of the world is carried out by people who perform their activities in close interdependence within relatively enduring associations. He would perhaps be saddened to find groups of men engaged in warfare, gaining courage and morale from pride in their unit and a knowledge that they can depend on their buddies. He might be gladdened to see groups of people enjoying themselves in recreations and sports of various kinds. Finally he might be puzzled why so many people spend so much time in little groups talking, planning, and being 'in conference.' Surely he would conclude that if he wanted to understand much about what is happening on Earth he would have to examine rather carefully the ways in which groups form, function, and dissolve." (Cartwright & Zander, 1968, p. 3)

---

*From *Contemporary Psychology and Effective Behavior* by James C. Coleman and Constance L. Hammen. Copyright © 1974 by Scott, Foresman and Company. Reprinted by permission of the Publisher.

In our discussion of interpersonal relations, marriage, and the family, we have seen the extent to which we are "group creatures." Only recently, however, have psychologists systematically studied the structure and behavior of groups and the ways in which individuals and groups mutually influence each other. Yet, simply placing the individual in his "social habitat," in terms of the groups to which he belongs and his position in these groups, takes us a long step forward in understanding his behavior. And as we probe into interactions between a group and its members, we add indispensable information to our understanding of human behavior.

"The groups that I belong to, I belong to for a purpose."

"I'm not a joiner; I guess that's one group I'm in—nonjoiners."

"I can't describe myself in terms of my affiliations and identifications—I've always felt like such an outsider that I don't feel I belong."

In this chapter, then, we shall concern ourselves with the social setting of behavior. Specifically, we shall study: (1) why we have groups, (2) the group as a living system, and (3) special problems in individual-group interaction, including conformity and nonconformity.

WHY WE HAVE GROUPS

To observe people, even casually, is to see that much of their time is spent in groups. And if we take a closer look at any individual we will find that he or she is a member of a large number of groups.

Let us take a fictitious man named Mr. Smith. In describing him, or identifying him, those who know him will tell us he is a human being (species identification), he is a man (sexual identification), he is a Smith (family identification), he is a teacher (occupational identification), he is a Christian (religious identification), he is an American (national identification), he is Irish (ethnic identification), and he is a Democrat (political identification). Besides being all these, we might be told he is a veteran, a golfer, a beer drinker, a lover of popular music and impressionist art, a football fan, a regular viewer of detective stories on television, and a user of a particular deodorant. All these adjectives indicate his membership in groups.

During the course of the day, Mr. Smith will move in and out of numerous groups, many of which will demonstrate his membership in the groups we have named. But many of the groups to which he belongs meet only infrequently, and some not at all. And at times, during the day, he will be part of groups which are so transient as to have little meaning for him: the group eating in a restaurant at one time, the group in the elevator, the group on the bus, or the group stuck in a traffic jam. Sometimes these transient groups are suddenly transformed into much more meaningful groups, as when the elevator stalls, or there is a fire in the restaurant.

"I'm a woman, and being a member of that group sometimes has its drawbacks. When I encounter discrimination against women, it makes me wish *not* that I wasn't a woman, but it makes me wish that things were a little more equal between those two groups—men and women."

THE VARIETY OF GROUPS TO WHICH WE BELONG

In seeking to understand the impact of groups on the behavior of individuals, we must take into account the variety of groups to which people belong, as in the hypothetical case of Mr. Smith. In looking more closely at these groups, we can see several different kinds.

1. We are involuntary members of some groups. It is difficult, if not impossible, to get out of these. Many we are born into, like our family, our race, our ethnic group (which sometimes decides our religious affiliation). Our membership in our nation and our social and economic class is also largely a matter of birth, though with difficulty we may do something to change these. Such involuntary membership, due to birth, can be a source of pride or can be experienced as a burden; it can confer great privilege (as it does for members of high-status families) or it can saddle us with heavy difficulties (as many members of ethnic and racial minorities know).

2. We must, of necessity, belong to some *types* of groups, though we may have some choice about which particular group of this type we will belong to. For example, most of us must live in *some* community, work in *some* group, go to *some* school (usually determined by where we choose to live), associate with *some* people. Besides these, if we want to work at some jobs, we may have to join unions or other work-related associations; if we want to practice our religious faith, we will probably have to be part of some religious community; if we want to participate in political processes, we will have to be part of some political party or organization.

3. There are many other groups to which we choose to belong, where membership is strictly voluntary. We join these groups in order to enjoy sharing interests with others of like mind, to work with others for common goals, to increase our social status, or because joining promises to be profitable in some other way. When membership in any of these groups costs more than we feel it is worth, we can usually get out without much conflict.

4. We belong to other groups not because we have joined them but because we have the trait or characteristic on the basis of which certain people have been grouped. Mr. Smith is forty years old, so he is in the forty-year-old age group. He watches TV detective stories, so he is in the group of detective-story fans, and so on. These groups usually have little influence on the individuals who comprise them and cause them few problems. Only if there develops some move to identify people on the basis of one of these characteristics and to do something to them would there be a problem. If a movement develops to make everyone retire at age 60, then all in this group would likely be far more conscious of their membership in this group. The same would be true if there develops a movement to outlaw the reading of *Playboy Magazine*

or the playing of golf on Sunday or the televising of football games. Then all the people who belong to the group characterized by the interest or activity in question would be more aware of their membership in this group, and we might see this group become organized.

WHY PEOPLE JOIN GROUPS

1. *Attraction to the members of the group.* The prospective member may find the present group members appealing. General attractiveness has been found to be strongly affected not only by physical attractiveness, but also by proximity and contact. In at least a general way, we tend to love our neighbors and form groups with them. Factors known to be related to interpersonal attraction have been shown to affect voluntary group membership.

2. *Attraction to the activities of the group.* The prospective member may be drawn to the things the group members do—skiing, playing bridge, public service, task accomplishment in business.

3. *Attraction to the goals of the group.* This category is often difficult to separate from the one above. Individuals may be drawn to the group's objectives, such as community service, recreation, pollution control, the election of a political candidate.

4. *Desire for group membership per se.* Some theorists have proposed that simply being in a group may be rewarding for many; affiliation may be especially likely to occur under conditions of stress or anxiety and, of course, loneliness. Group membership may also be valued as a way of attaining rewarding by-products, such as access to desirable people or increased social status.

---

5. We also belong to many transient groups, which form and dissolve leaving no traces that they have ever been. We mentioned Mr. Smith's elevator companions and the group in the restaurant. While ordinarily these groups have little importance in themselves, they constitute one of the important arenas of social action. They make up what we call *the public,* and, as Goffman (1967, 1972) has pointed out, our behavior in these situations is as carefully regulated as our behavior in the most tightly controlled groups.

Thus, like it or not, we are involved in groups. What are the rewards and costs of this involvement? How do the rewards and costs balance out?

THE REWARDS OF GROUP MEMBERSHIP

Groups evolve and continue to exist because important needs of individuals are best met in this way. Basic here are the meeting of food and other visceral needs, security, and belongingness. But as we have seen, group membership also strongly influences our identity and opportunities for self-fulfillment.

Security and Related Benefits

For human beings, the protection of the group is vital, because of a long period of helplessness after birth and because of a physical make-up that leaves them defenseless against many kinds of attack. Because it is easier to see this need for group protection in primitive societies, we may be tempted to think that we are no longer so desperately dependent on the group. A little thought, however, should make us aware that life in our "advanced civilizations" is, if anything, even more group dependent. It is simply that the group's methods for protecting us generally work so well that we are not aware of them. But when the systems break down, as in inability to control violence, runaway inflation, or mob rule, we recognize how dependent we have been all along. The Preamble to the Constitution of our nation shows the concern of the founding fathers that the security-related needs of individuals be met by the group:

"We the People of the United States, in Order to form a more perfect Union, establish Justice, insure domestic Tranquility, provide for the common defense, promote the general Welfare, and secure the Blessings of Liberty to ourselves and our Posterity, do ordain and establish this Constitution for the United States Of America."

But we do not belong to most groups for protection from enemies. More often it is to benefit from various kinds of mutual help. No less pressing than the need for protection are the needs for food, shelter, and companionship. While it may not be impossible for an individual adult to provide his own food and shelter and care for himself in other respects, it is not easy even in reasonably favorable circumstances. For most residents of large cities in today's America, this kind of self-sufficiency would be not only difficult but impossible. As societies have become more complex, there have been greater role differentiation and specialization, with the result that today people are more interdependent than ever. And so we live and work in groups through which we cooperate for the maintenance and enrichment of our lives.

"I belong to a lot of professional organizations, because they do interesting things and because I enjoy talking with other people who are involved in the same kinds of problems I am. In fact, I think I have a real need to talk about these things with others who have the same kinds of interests and goals I do—who work with the same ingredients I do all day long."

So deep is our inherited social nature and so pervasive is the social conditioning we experience that few human fears are as strong as the fear of being alone. We can learn to be alone, and some few individuals seek solitude as a way of life. But most of us panic at the thought of having to make it on our own, and the threat of ostracism is still one of the most potent of persuaders.

Identity and Fulfillment

N̲ot as old as our security needs, but still very old and linked to them, are our needs for identity and self-esteem. People's identity and sense of self-worth have long been provided by the group. To return to our hypothetical Mr. Smith his sense of self-identity is strongly influenced by his membership and status in various groups—and by the roles he plays in these groups.

There is a curious paradox attached to membership in a given group. Often it is the person who has an identity apart from the group who is most valued by the group, while the person whose identity is dependent upon the group—and thus desperately needs the group—may be valued much less by the group and thus be given a less important place. Frequently, the individual who is chosen as leader of a group will be someone with a broad range of interests and activities outside the group.

Many of our finest possibilities as human beings can be fulfilled only in a group. A sense of achievement, the joys of loving and being loved, the feeling of being needed, and some of the greatest opportunities for growth are found only in a community.

Without the group there is no opportunity for leadership and there is no fellowship. Without the community there is no continuity of values that we call *heritage,* no shared vision to live and die for, no sowing of seeds that only others can harvest. Without ties to certain special others there is no enlargement of the self to include a family, a nation, a people. All of these supraindividual identities may become—and at times have become—destructive. Yet it remains true that it is through such communities that people have often fulfilled their greatest potentials.

THE COSTS OF GROUP MEMBERSHIP

Even as we have described the rewards of group membership we have hinted at some of the costs. There always are costs, and all of us have experienced them.

"I don't feel any obligations to society. Society let me down when they sent me off to fight in Vietnam. Some of my friends died. Others rot away in veterans' hospitals. I struggle to survive in a society that does not care if I live or die so long as I do not interrupt their affluent lives. A piece of paper says I served honorably. It should read that I was used dishonorably."

Limitations

The first cost of group membership is the experience of limitations. A word heard often by young children is the word "No." Those who protect us and care for us have the power to restrict us. The price of dependency is to be controlled. Even as adults, we still find that membership in a group bring limitations with it. To be a member of a particular church we must limit our behavior and even our professed beliefs. Many of the commandments are "Thou shalt nots." If we are active in a political party there are boundaries that we must not cross. Even informal groups have limits. Though they may not be so clearly defined, we know when we have "gone too far."

Demands

Not only does the group set limits; it also makes demands of us, and sometimes these demands can be very heavy. There is, first of all, and perhaps most important, the demand that we be loyal to the group. "Are you with us or against us?" No words are more loaded with negative feelings than *traitor* and *renegade*. Much deviant behavior will be tolerated if there is no question about loyalty, while scrupulous conformity will be of no avail if there is a strong suspicion that one's loyalties are with "the other side."

There are also demands for conformity, especially in public. In some areas the public gesture is the important thing, while at other times (as with loyalty) it is what is in the heart that matters. The sensitive areas in which conformity may be required can be quite changeable, depending on who has power and what is decreed to be important. The demand to conform or take the "correct" stand on issues which have been made tests of one's soundness, whether religious or political, can be one of the most onerous costs of group membership. This was the theme of the powerful story, *A Man for All Seasons*. There are times when it is precisely those with integrity and conscience (like Sir Thomas More) who are sacrificed in the name of group ideals while unethical and opportunistic persons ride high.

Then there are the demands for responsible participation—for assuming specified roles, paying dues (taxes), voting or backing leadership. Sometimes the demand is to fight in battles the group is involved in, and this can cost a person his life. To refuse to fight, when chosen for this role by the group, can result in imprisonment and dishonor. As we have noted, groups cannot survive and function unless certain needs of the group are met. Few groups will allow members to benefit from the rewards of group membership without sharing in the cost of group maintenance. One of the perennial questions faced by groups is how these costs should be distributed. Should each pay the same? Should each pay as he can? Or, should each pay in proportion to the benefits he receives? This is, of course, the issue involved in tax policies.

Threats to Integrity

The real issue in meeting both the limitations and the demands of the groups is the threat these can pose to an individual's integrity. It is, of course, the more sensitive and conscientious person who feels this threat most keenly. All group life calls for compromise. But how far can a person compromise before he loses his soul? When is silence discreet and when is it cowardly? When is dissent irresponsible and when is it courageous? There are no easy answers here, and the struggle for integrity by persons who love the group but have misgivings about the direction it is going can be intensely painful. It is this price of group membership that makes many persons reluctant to join groups.

THE BALANCE SHEET

We have noted some of the rewards and some of the costs of group membership. If we weight one against the other, how do they balance out? Undoubtedly each individual will find a different answer. For some the costs are greater than the rewards, and for others the rewards are greater than the costs. And the balance may be different for each group to which we belong.

But once we have balanced costs against reward, what can we do? In the case of groups to which we belong voluntarily, if the costs are greater than the rewards, we can get out—but sometimes the cost of doing so is greater than the cost of staying in the unrewarding group. For this reason, many people remain in communities where they are not happy, stay on jobs they do not enjoy, or retain membership in unions with which they disagree.

For all practical purposes, we cannot withdraw or resign from the many groups in which we have involuntary membership. Thus when our life in these groups is unrewarding there may be no easy solution. Sometimes we can learn skills with which to change the group or improve our position in it. We can seek as much satisfaction as possible outside the group. Or we can seek to change the image or evaluation of the group. This has been seen in recent years in the case of black Americans who have refused to accept a derogatory self-image but have found a new pride and self-identity in their assertion that "Black is beautiful."

> "In college I belonged to a sorority, because I was afraid that if I didn't join as soon as I was eligible, that maybe I wouldn't get a chance to join anything, and I would be an outsider. So I joined this group of girls and went through the initiations procedures and everything, and found that I really disliked it. It seemed to me that it was silly and shallow. So I withdrew more and more from the group and went on and did my own thing. They were kind of upset, and after about a year of this, they asked me to resign. I did resign and felt much the better for it after it was all over."

THE GROUP AS A LIVING SYSTEM

Groups come into being and continue because they have survival value. The individual members of systems pay a price for inclusion but are rewarded with greater probability of survival and with the opportunity for participation in a kind of life not available outside the system.

The study of groups has shown that there are many parallels between individual and group functioning—that groups must meet certain needs if they are to maintain themselves and achieve the purposes for which they were formed, and they face stresses and attempt to cope with them in ways that closely resemble the behavior of individuals. Of course, the needs and purposes of groups may often conflict with the needs and purposes of the individuals who constitute them.

For this reason, it is important that we understand how groups are structured, how they function, and how the group as a system interacts with its environment.

Structure

Every system has a structure. By this we mean that its parts are put together in such a way that they function as a system. The same parts can be put together in a way that will not form a system, as may be seen if all the parts of a watch are thrown into a box. Continuing groups, as distinguished from the transient ones mentioned earlier, are made up of individual persons held together by goals, values, and mutual needs and attractions, working together in assigned places within a communication network. They perform their roles according to rules enforced by leaders using power generated within the system from input by individual members and from the system's interaction with the environment.

Not all groups need the same kind of structure to be effective; each one needs the type of structure appropriate to its tasks. Some tasks require complex and fairly rigid organization, whereas others can be accomplished by a relatively unstructured group. Overorganization can be as detrimental to successful group functioning as can be underorganization. Yet all groups will to some degree and in some form have the following structural elements:

1. *Members.* Sometimes membership is clearly defined, sometimes not.

2. *Differentiation of parts.* There must be some differences in positions and roles which are distributed among the members. Sometimes these assignments are relatively permanent; at other times there is a fluid exchange of positions and roles.

3. *Communication.* Different members of the group must be in touch with one another to some extent. At times this can be minimal, at other times it must be continual.

4. *Rules.* There must be some regularity or dependability in the behavior of individual members if there is to be a group. Again, the amount of this regularity varies greatly from group to group.

5. *Regulation.* Regularity results from some kind of organization which involves power or influence directed by some agency. In groups leaders direct power.

In addition to these structural elements, groups may also be characterized by the degree of commonality of purpose shared by members, and by cohesiveness. The degree of cohesiveness, the "group spirit" that develops among members, appears to be an important determinant of the success and productivity of the group, and affects and is affected by the various structural features of the group.

Function

Group structure and function are so interdependent that it is difficult to separate them even for discussion. In this section, however, we are less concerned with the organization of the group and more concerned with its functioning, including its goals, the means it uses, and the results of its efforts in terms of effectiveness or ineffectiveness.

Task and Maintenance Goals. It is apparent that group goals may vary widely. For a football team, the winning of games may be the primary goal; in a planning group, the key objective may be to formulate strategies for dealing with a specific problem such as air pollution; in a "brainstorming" group, the goal may be the generating of new ideas; in a therapy group, the goal is the personal growth and more effective adjustment of the individual members.

The primary objectives of the group—for example, the winning of games by a football team—are referred to as *task goals*. But whatever its primary goals, the group must also take measures to maintain its organization and integration if it is to function effectively or even survive. Thus the group must also be concerned with *maintenance goals*. Usually maintenance goals center around resolving conflicts among group members and meeting their emotional-social needs; for conflict, dissension, and dissatisfaction among group members are major sources of disorganization in groups. The replacement of group members lost as a result of death or other causes is also a major maintenance goal of many groups; if such members cannot be replaced, the group may work out a new organizational equilibrium, based on different relationships and responsibilities for the members who are left.

This tendency to restore organizational equilibrium can be seen in dramatic form when a military leader is killed during an enemy attack and a new leader emerges to head the unit as it strives to regain its functional effectiveness. Similarly, the loss of the mother or father in a family may lead to changed roles and responsibilities as the family attempts to regain its organizational equilibrium.

Thus group goals and strivings are roughly analogous to those of individuals. Like individuals, too, some groups are highly task-oriented with the predominance of their effort directed toward their task goals, while other groups are more concerned with maintaining themselves as an organized entity—for example, by making the group attractive to the members or to possible new members.

Group pressures toward conformity are often decried today; yet they develop inevitably as a group tries to maintain itself and achieve its goals. In fact, no group could long function as a unit without some uniformity and discipline of its members. A football team without training rules or an established practice time would probably not win many games, and a political party would suffer if its candidates openly supported greatly differing positions. Uniformity of opinion also can increase efficiency when a group must act quickly. A group with one voice can determine its direction and reach its goal faster than a group with many voices urging different actions.

Group pressures toward uniformity thus serve basic needs of the group. If the pressure to conform is too strong, however, it can stifle individual creativity and lead to rigid, unadaptive behavior on the part of the group as a whole—for part of a group's basic resources are the initiative and enthusiasm of its individual members. The special problem of maintaining the opportunity for variation and dissent—for the society's benefit as well as the individual's—will be discussed later in this chapter.

Solving Problems and Making Decisions. Groups process problems in much the same way that individuals do. The problem is assessed, alternative solutions are formulated, and a given alternative is chosen on the basis of such factors as probable outcome, risk, and satisfaction of needs.

In comparisons of the performance of groups and of individuals working alone on problem-solving tasks, it has been found that groups have advantages and disadvantages. Groups can often assess a problem more accurately because several perceivers are able to compare their impressions; the pooling of individual resources may lead to the formulation of a wider range of alternative choices; and the varied past experiences of group members may lead to a more accurate prediction of probable outcome, risk, and satisfaction in selecting a given alternative. In one study dealing with problems in which a high degree of inference and judgment were called for, group solutions were found to be better than the average individual solution but not better than the best individual solution (Hall, Mouton, Blake, 1963). Thus though the less able members may reap benefits they could not earn by themselves, the more able members may be held back or inhibited by the requirement of functioning in a group.

A group's ability to solve a problem is heavily dependent upon its composition—upon the abilities and characteristics of its individual members. Where no one in the group is qualified to deal with the problems at hand, group action is not likely to have the advantages mentioned above. Sometimes, too, the members of a group are operating on the basis of different information or assumptions; in such cases, they may have serious difficulties in communicating with each other and may work at cross-purposes. Members may also have conflicting needs or belong to other groups which pull them in opposing directions.

Sometimes group members irritate each other, and emotional conflicts and tensions arise which distract attention from the task at hand and interfere with objective consideration of the problem. And, of course, as in the case of individuals, groups may become more concerned with the safety and prestige of the group than with carrying out their original goals.

Group Action and Feedback. As in individual action, action taken by groups may be primarily task-oriented or defense-oriented. A football team trying to perfect new plays for an important game is task-oriented in its behavior; the same team trying to explain a defeat erroneously as due to "poor refereeing" would be defense-oriented.

Like an individual, a defense-oriented group may rationalize, project blame, indulge in "scapegoating," or utilize other defense mechanisms. Such defensive patterns are commonly initiated by group leaders and communicated to members through established communication channels; their intent is to maintain the adequacy and worth of the group in the eyes of its members—and hence to maintain or improve group cohesiveness and morale.

As in individual behavior, task-oriented action by the group varies greatly in strength and persistence. For the big game, a football team may outdo itself, showing great effort and determination; for a less important game, the players may neither try as hard nor perform as well. In general, the amount and persistence of group effort depend heavily on the degree to which group goals are perceived as relevant to the members' needs and accepted, as their own. One of the key problems faced by leaders—from football coaches to presidents to companies or countries—is that of mobilizing group effort toward key group goals.

Like individuals, groups also utilize feedback concerning the outcome of their actions as a basis for making possible changes—whether in a task-oriented or a defense-oriented way. When feedback is used in a task-oriented way, the group becomes a "self-correcting" energy system. When not, it may become so concerned with its "image" or its good name that its efforts go into defensive maneuvers instead of into more effective efforts toward its goals.

Thus group action appears to follow the same basic principles as individual coping behavior. Groups have certain potential advantages, such as the potential for specialization of function of individual members, the ability to handle multiple tasks at the same time, and the capacity to deal with problems that are beyond the range of any one individual. At the same time, groups are often at a disadvantage compared to the individual with respect to such factors as communication, decision time, and coordination of action.

Factors in Group Effectiveness

In recent years there has been extensive research on the variables that are related to group effectiveness—the success of the group in achieving its goals and meeting the need of its members. Three sets of factors play a role in determining how effective a group will be: (1) characteristics of the group members, (2) the group organization and manner of functioning, and (3) the setting in which the group functions. Some of the most important conditions in each of these three general categories are summarized above. These conditions contribute not only to the level of group effectiveness but also to the level of stress tolerance of the group—to the difficulty of adjustive demands with which the group can cope without undergoing serious disorganization—and hence to the quality of the group's performance under sustained stress and in crisis situations.

FACTORS IN GROUP EFFECTIVENESS

Group members

A group's effectiveness depends heavily upon the individuals within it since ultimately it is individuals who actually make and implement group decisions. Members with serious personality weaknesses, immaturities, or lack of essential skills may disrupt or prevent group progress just as mature, competent, and dedicated members help to ensure group effectiveness and success. Characteristics of members—especially in terms of the possession of essential competencies and commitment to group goals—are especially important when the group is under severe stress. A group's loss of dedicated and capable members, particularly those with outstanding leadership skill or other key abilities needed by the group, can be seriously disruptive to group performance and effectiveness.

Group organization and performance

Group effectiveness is influenced by each of the major elements of group structure. Effectiveness is enhanced by a type of power and leadership structure appropriate to the group's tasks; clear-cut, realistic and agreed-upon goals; clear and appropriate social roles compatible with the self-concepts and values of group members; sound group values and an accurate frame of reference; and efficient communication.

The group's record of past successes and failures, its level of cohesiveness and morale, the efficiency with which it uses its human and material resources, and its ability to meet the needs of group members also play key roles in group effectiveness.

Environmental (field) conditions

Group effectiveness is fostered by a reasonable correspondence between the group and its environment—between what it is trying to accomplish and the resources and possibilities provided by its setting. In many underdeveloped countries, the lack of material resources, made more acute by overpopulation, makes it well-nigh impossible for individual and group needs to be met effectively.

Intergroup relationships are also often of great importance. Where groups cooperate in the interests of common goals, their effectiveness may be enhanced. Even intense competition among groups may lead to greater group effectiveness. However, if the relations go beyond competition to hostility and conflict, the achievement of group goals may be made more difficult, and group effectiveness may be reduced.

THE GROUP AND ITS ENVIRONMENT

The environment of a group includes the spacetime it occupies, comprised of the physical environment, historical setting, and cultural milieu, and the other groups with which it interacts. Just as a group exists to meet the needs of its constituent members, it also comes into being and exists partly to meet the needs of other systems of which it is a part. The environment is the content in which groups function, providing resources and limitations for the group and often making demands of its own.

> "Global travel should be made more economical and instead of national service, young people should be encouraged to travel abroad for a few years, to observe other cultures and traditions—and not be coerced into conforming to our own society just through ignorance, when they could become, through exposure to other cultures, better members of our own society."

It is difficult to investigate scientifically the way in which a physical environment shapes the behavior of people, but some relationships are obvious. Groups who live in mountainous areas like Switzerland act differently from groups who live on tropical islands like Samoa. It is not surprising that rural groups differ from city groups, that groups of fishermen differ from groups of miners, or that Eskimos differ from Tahitians. Many theorists have speculated that there is a connection between the Mediterranean climate and the Latin temperament, between the English climate and the British temperament, between German geography and Germanic culture.

The historical setting, too, determines what a group can do and is likely to do. The German term *Zeitgeist* (spirit of the time) is used to denote the historical climate. Both individuals and groups find, as Shakespeare said, that "there is a tide in the affairs of men," and that actions have very different effects at different times.

The effect the larger culture has on the nature and functioning of groups within it is so obvious that we need hardly be reminded of it. The effects of the cultural setting on the development of political institutions, religion, family life, and economic enterprises are especially noteworthy.

Finally, there is the effect of other groups which make up the environment of a group. Just as individuals react to other individuals, so groups react to other groups. Groups may compete with one another, cooperate, seek to destroy each other, or merge. Many times the behavior of a group changes radically because of what it perceives to be the intentions of another group.

There is no more pressing problem for all national groups than to find ways of reducing conflict between themselves. The cost of war and related ills is incalculable, and with modern nuclear weapons we all know that we might not survive another world war. Yet many of us have mixed feelings about group conflict. On the one hand we love peace and hate the bitterness of strife, but on the other hand we may love the excitement and a heightened sense of self-importance that can come with conflict. This fact may be a serious barrier to peace. Someone has said, in fact, that we will have no peace until we can find a peaceful substitute for war. His point is that many of us may need the meaningful commitment, the sense of urgency, the excitement, and the simplification of life that comes when we have an enemy on whom we can blame all our troubles.

Less pressing, but surely important to us all, is the reduction of tensions generated by conflict between management groups and labor groups, between majority and minority ethnic groups, and between privileged groups and underprivileged groups. To the extent that such groups are interdependent parts of a functioning system, destructive conflict harms all concerned.

PATTERNING OF GROUP CHANGE

With time, group structure and functioning may undergo marked changes. Changes may take place in group goals, leadership, roles, values, membership, and other aspects of the group's structure. Similarly, the group may show improvement or deterioration in its level of performance and in its ability to achieve its goals. Such changes result from a combination of inner and outer determinants, including changes in the composition of the group.

Life-cycle Changes

Many groups appear to follow a pattern of change somewhat comparable to the life cycle of the individual—with an early period of growth, a middle period of maturity, and a later period of deterioration or atrophy. The historian Toynbee (1947) has described the characteristic stages of this pattern as: (1) a formative, youthful period, during which the group is vigorous, dedicated to its aims, and highly productive; (2) a period of conservative middle-age, during which initiative and dedication are reduced and the group rests on its laurels, content with the progress it has made; and (3) a period of old age and disintegration, during which internal conflicts and inconsistencies within the group gradually lead to its decline and fall. Rome, for example, had its period of youth and vigor, during which it conquered most of the known world and made remarkable technological and cultural advances, its period of middle-age, during which it tended to maintain its gains rather than to implement them or show further creativity, and its period of old age, during which it suffered corruption, decline, and eventual fall to the barbarians some five hundred years after its founding.

But group change does not always follow this pattern. Many conditions within the group or in its environment can influence the direction and rate of change—or even keep the group from changing appreciably. Many groups remain small and ineffectual for the entire period of their existence; others have a sudden spurt in growth and effectiveness because of favorable changes in their environment. Certain types of groups also appear to follow their own characteristic patterns. For example, the family group follows a typical pattern from its inception with marriage, through the rearing of children and their eventual leaving of the family, to the dissolution of the marriage with the death of the marital partners. But here too the pattern is not always followed, as when a family is prematurely disrupted by divorce or the early death of family members.

As we have noted, rapid change in group customs, beliefs, and values may pose a threat to group integration. If old anchorages are torn away before the foundations for new ones can be laid, group members tend to become confused, uncertain of their roles, and "alienated" from the group. Thus the rate as well as the patterning and quality of social change may have far-reaching effects on individuals as well as on the survival and effectiveness of the group.

Group Decompensations

Groups generally try to change in ways that will further the attainment of their goals and improve their effectiveness, but they are not always successful. In some cases, under severe and sustained stress, a group shows changes in the direction of disorganization of decompensation rather than increased effectiveness.

"We started out as a fairly cohesive group. What we wanted was a place to practice our crafts and arts, a place where people could come to see our work, and a place where we could teach grownups and youngsters both. Eventually, it was to be a money-making venture. That is, eventually we each hoped to make a living or part-living from it. So at first we all worked very hard, and we made a little money here and there, and we enjoyed ourselves tremendously. I don't know at what point it occurred to me that the thing was going off in another direction. But it is, and that's not the kind of atmosphere, not the kind of situation I want. A couple of members have dropped out and there's a general downer feeling about the group now. My wife and I will probably drop out too."

The course of group decompensation follows stages comparable to those we traced for individuals: (1) alarm and mobilization, (2) resistance, and (3) exhaustion—the end of the group as a unit. The sequence of group decompensation is vividly illustrated in the case of the Xetas (see accompanying boxed-in text).

Sometimes a group undergoes some measure of decompensation but manages to stabilize itself during the stage of resistance. Thus a threatened marriage may be stabilized sufficient to continue, though without adequately meeting the needs of the marital partners or fulfilling its initial promise. On the other hand, a failing marriage may recompensate as a result of the determined efforts of the marital partners to make the necessary readjustments.

GROUP DECOMPENSATION

The Xetas were an Indian tribe discovered in southwestern Brazil in the 1950s and believed to be among the most primitive humans in existence.

"They have no agriculture, know no metal, make no pottery. They sleep on the ground instead of in hammocks as most Brazilian primitives do. Their weapons are bows and arrows and stone axes. Their knives are sharp flakes of stone. They eat everything that they can find or kill in the jungle: fruit, insects, snakes, roots too fibrous for white men's stomachs." (Time, Jan. 5, 1959, p. 62)

The alarm and mobilization period had evidently begun for this tribe when it was driven back into rugged mountain country by stronger tribes and the white man. This pattern of resistance was successful to the extent that the Xetas managed to hide from the civilized world for several hundred years, but the weaknesses within the group and its inhospitable environment doomed it to eventual exhaustion. Eventually they were flushed out of hiding by starvation and the wooings of an anthropologist—who hoped the surviving members of the tribe would be given government protection in a jungle preserve.

By 1959 only about 250 remained, and for a time they lived in small bands, shifting camp every few days. Ten years later, they had left their forest retreats and the survivors had scattered, working on the farms of the area. As a tribe, they no longer exist (Croker, 1968).

INTERACTION OF THE INDIVIDUAL AND THE GROUP

In the previous section we considered some of the structural characteristics of groups—the somewhat formal properties that help us to detect similarities among quite unlike collections of people, and which help us to predict aspects of group functioning. In this section we will look more directly at some of the effects that groups have on individual behavior. Although it is impossible to specify all of the conditions under which behavior is facilitated or inhibited in groups, we do know that on the whole groups cause people to behave differently than they would as individuals—and some of the differences are quite intriguing.

Group-individual interaction is not a one-way street, however. What about the effects of the individual on the group? In particular, we will focus on the leader. What factors both within the situation and within the person are conducive to leadership behavior?

One of the most problematical effects of the group on the individual is the exertion of certain pressures toward uniformity of perception, thought, and behavior. Even the most rugged individualists among us are susceptible to various conformity pressures. In this section, we will attempt to examine the issue—the origins and extent of conformity, and its repercussions, including the effects of deviation.

HOW THE GROUP AFFECTS THE INDIVIDUAL

As noted earlier, collections of people become "groups" when they perceive that some common purposes will be met by their continued affiliation. A hoped-for effect of the group will be meeting of the needs which led the individual to join the group. Beyond that, however, we find instances in which the presence of others will facilitate individual performance on tasks and others in which it will impede performance; we find cases in which "too many cooks spoil the broth" and others in which the produce generated by a group is superior to the product of any single member; and we find situations in which individuals do things in groups that they might never do singly, perhaps taking greater risks, or even violating their principles of proper conduct. Although the effects of groups on individuals could comprise a lengthy list, in this section we will limit our discussion to several of the more widely researched topics.

Social Facilitation

One of the earliest topics of research in social psychology, which intrigued investigators in the early part of this century and was then temporarily abandoned, is the study of social facilitation—the study of the effects of the sheer presence of others on individual behavior. Observations and controlled studies reviewed by Zajonc (1968) indicated that in the presence of a passive "audience," humans would perform simple motor tasks more accurately, compared with performance while unobserved. And in the presence of "co-actors" performing the same behavior, chickens and rats would eat more, ants would work harder in nest-building, and cyclists would ride faster. Such effects are termed *social facilitation*. In other situations, performance appeared to be inhibited: cockroaches were poorer in learning mazes, and human subjects made more errors on certain tasks in the presence of others. Zajonc has proposed that, for a wide variety of tasks, performance in the presence of other organisms causes greater arousal. In well-learned skills or ingrained habits, such increased activation enhances performance, but with tasks that involved new learning, the increased arousal and distractions are likely to be detrimental to performance.

> "How it works in my profession, at our conferences each of us is a specialist—mechanical, electrical, architectural. We each present an opinion in our particular sphere, and essentially that's the governing decision. It's kind of a group decision, and not a group decision, all at the same time."

In a dramatic way, social facilitation can be seen in the mutual stimulation and "social contagion" of crowd behavior, as in a riot or in the panic reactions of individuals attempting to escape from some serious situation, such as a burning building. Apparently, especially in emotion-arousing situations, individuals respond to and, in turn, further contribute to heightened emotionality in those around them. This phenomenon of "social contagion" helps to account for both the tremendous force and the irrationality of much crowd behavior (Mc-

David & Harari, 1968). Social facilitation and contagion can also be observed in smaller groups, such as a football team whose high morale helps the members buoy each other up and exert greater effort in competitive play.

Groups vs. Individual Task Performance

Some tasks clearly require joint action, where the labor is divided, and the achievement of the final goal could not be accomplished without the group, such as playing a Beethoven string quartet, mass-producing automobiles, or providing mental-health services for a large community. In such instances, the group product clearly represents an improvement over the individual performance. On the other hand, it has long been debated whether individual or group efforts are superior in areas of intellectual or creative activity.

Obviously, the nature of the task is a major factor. But in general, there is research evidence which suggests that groups produce more and better solutions to problems than do individuals (Shaw, 1971). There are many factors which may account for this result: The summation or coordination of individual strengths; rejection of incorrect suggestions and the checking of errors; social stimulation and the arousal of greater interest in the task; and others. On the other hand, when time is a factor, the number of man-hours per solution is lower for the individual than for the group. Although groups may provide superior solutions in many instances, efficiency is the price that must be paid. Shaw has summarized the findings as follows:

"Groups are more effective than individuals on tasks which require a variety of information, which can be solved by adding individual contributions, and which require a number of steps that must be correctly completed in a definite order; individuals are better on tasks that call for centralized organization of parts. Groups perform better than individuals when the process is learning or problem solving, but not necessarily when the process investigated is judgment. These conclusions are based upon measures of outcome; when the measure of effectiveness is the amount of investment per man, individuals are generally shown to be more efficient." (1971, pp. 7071)

In Groups, Individuals Do The Darndest Things

Picture the usually stern, self-contained, emotionless man who finds himself weeping unashamedly in front of other people—something he never did until he was persuaded to attend a weekend marathon encounter group. Or imagine a conscientious, well-groomed college student, nonviolent in both ideology and demeanor, who finds herself throwing tomatoes at a politician she dislikes. Clearly, these people are engaged in behavior that they might never have expected of themselves; yet, in a group situation, such "discontinuities" seem to be quite common.

A much more dramatic and serious example is that of sadistic mob violence, such as occurred in lynch mobs in the South of the 1920s and '30s. Jones and Gerard cite an account originally reported by psychologists Dollard and Miller in the 1940s:

> "The victim in the case they describe was systematically tortured for some 10 hours; castrated compelled to eat his own genitals, burned by hot irons plunged into his body at various points, hung several times almost to the point of death and then revived, sliced with knives, and finally killed. There is every reason to doubt that any single member of the mob could have engaged in such sustained sadism as an isolated individual. Whereas the victim was actually tortured and killed by those who were most directly involved in vengeance, the body was later delivered to a large crowd of bystanders who drove knives into the corpse, kicked it, and drove automobiles over it. Children came and drove sharpened sticks into the body. Clearly such a frenzy is not the product of some accidental collection of sadists trying to outdo each other. Many of the most prominent citizens of the community were actually involved in the planning and execution of the lynching." (1967, pp. 623-24).

One attempt to account for such behavior is the idea of "responsibility diffusion" which may occur in some groups. The individual feels submerged in the group and loses his feelings of accountability for the consequences of his own actions. A kind of deindividuation may occur among groups of strangers, or among large crowds, or among groups where individuals abdicate personal responsibility in the name of following orders or some higher principle.

Not only may the individual feel anonymous and therefore not accountable, but he may not question at the time the morality of his actions. One major standard that we use for defining what is right is what everybody else seems to be doing (Jones & Gerard, 1967). Similar principles have been used to explain the "unresponsive bystander" phenomenon in which witnesses stand and watch victims being robbed or beaten to death and later justify their behavior on the grounds that they "didn't want to become involved." In simulated situations, individuals by themselves are much more likely to go to the aid of a "victim" than are individuals in groups, presumably due to "responsibility diffusion" (Darley & Latane, 1969). Principles of group contagion and social facilitation and conformity also help to account for differences between group and individual behavior.

> "Last night we had gone out to get an ice-cream bar at that little market, and this gal had fallen . . . it looked like she could be dead or passed out . . . she was curled up in a fetal position against the wall, and the men in the store said they had called the police. And I felt like, 'Well, it's cold, why doesn't somebody put a blanket over?' I didn't say, 'Why don't I?' So we sat down . . . they said they'd call the ambulance, and we wanted to see what was going to happen. I could have done something to help her, I suppose—or at least find out was wrong—I guess. I felt like if nobody else had done anything, why should I?"

Another interesting area of research has suggested that group participation results in individuals making higher-risk decisions than they do without group contact. Contrary to the view voiced by White in *The Organization Man* (1956), who contended that the process of group discussion invariably leads to conservatism and drags the creative innovator down into mediocrity, researchers have found opposite effects (Wallach, Kogan, & Bem, 1962, 1964). In these and subsequent studies, responsibility diffusion has been supported as an explanatory principle. Group members appear to feel that the responsibility for failure in a high-risk situation will not be attributed to any single member. Although it has generated much activity and questions remain unanswered, the "risky-shift" phenomenon, as it is called, has been repeated frequently. It is worth contemplating possible implications of the finding; perhaps in military or high-level business situations, or other conditions which bear on the fate of many, groups will be more prone to high-risk decisions than would individuals. On the other hand, it must be noted that risky-shift experiments have typically involved homogeneous groups without leadership structure, and have employed decisions whose magnitude of importance is far less than issues of national security. These and other factors may mitigate the more harrowing possibilities of risk-taking in groups.

LEADERSHIP: THE INFLUENCE OF THE INDIVIDUAL ON THE GROUP

Groups differ greatly in their leadership structure. In formal or loosely organized groups, especially where there is unanimity of purpose, leadership may be virtually nonexistent or constantly shifting. In highly organized groups, on the other hand, leadership becomes an important characteristic of group structure. Such groups may be led by an individual or by a committee or other subgroup. Sometimes it is quite difficult to determine who is the group "leader" because the one designated by formal role may seem less influential than other members of the group. Sometimes two leaders will emerge—a task specialist who directs the group toward its primary goals, and a social specialist who helps maintain the functional harmony of the group itself (Bales, 1958).

Leadership is a highly complex phenomenon and is strongly influenced by other aspects of the group. It is a rather widespread but naive view that a high level of group effectiveness will automatically follow from the provision of "good" leadership.

A further issue in leadership stems from the age-old controversy about men making history or history making men. Early concepts of leadership invariably stressed characteristics of individuals which made them unique and successful in their prominent and influential roles. A more modern viewpoint stresses the "emergence" of leaders according to situational factors operative in a given group at a given time. Many leadership situations appear to involve varying combinations of both factors.

Leadership as a Personal Quality

The search for qualities within a person that distinguish him as a leader from the followers has been hampered by methodological problems such as difficulty in identifying leaders (especially "good" leaders) and problems in measurement of traits. Depending upon one's biases, the results have been called "disappointing" and support for the trait conception "not satisfactory" (Cartwright & Zander, 1968) or small but consistent (Shaw, 1971).

> "Some years ago, in a sensitivity group, we originally started out with a therapist as leader. Subsequently the time for separation arrived and we wanted to keep going. The therapist did leave, and said he thought we needed a leader, and that I should be the leader because I had the ability to establish relationships and also, looking at it now I should say, a certain amount of courage to follow my inclination in certain situations—to follow wherever the path went. I enjoyed leading the group. It was hard work, but pleasurable. It felt natural doing it."

It has, in fact, been shown that in certain instances leaders tend to be bigger but not too much bigger, brighter but not too much brighter, show greater knowledge and skills related to the task to be accomplished, display sociability factors such as greater activity and participation, popularity, and cooperativeness, have higher initiative and persistence, and to be older than other members of the group. These findings have been disputed in many instances, and simply indicate a slight preponderance of positive instances over negative ones. A somewhat more fruitful approach to leadership comes from the study of the needs and characteristics of the group and their effect upon the emergence of certain leaders.

Leadership as a Function of the Situation

As mentioned earlier, there are numerous situations which favor the development of inequities in the distribution of influence in groups, a condition we call leadership. Among them are complexity of decisions that have to be made or goals to be reached, the size of a group, and the urgency of a situation or the importance of taking decisive and effective action. Given certain of these elements, several factors may influence the rise to influence of particular people.

1. *Chance.* Jones and Gerard note that:

> ". . . it is important to recognize the potential role of chance in the emergence of particular leaders. In the early stages of group formation it may happen that a particular person quite accidentally makes a correct suggestion or two and as a consequence finds himself thenceforth in the leadership role." (1967, p. 670)

Chance may determine that the first person who speaks up at a meeting is assumed by the others to have leadership qualities. Or, in a group that includes one man and several women, traditional assumptions about the male role may lead to his selection as committee chairman, jury foreman, or the like. Similarly, the oldest member of a group may be thought to have greater knowledge or skill, and members may react to the person as if he or she is the group leader. In situations like these, the actual personality and skill characteristics of the individual may have little to do with his or her selection as leader.

2. *Participation rate.* Especially in the earlier stages of group formation, the rate of participation among members is likely to be related to members' evaluation of contributions to the group. A high contributor is very likely to be selected as leader. Studies have shown that high participators are frequently identified as leaders of the group. In one interesting study (Riecken, 1958), rate of participation appeared to influence members' judgments of each other more than did actual skill. Following two problem-solving discussions in four-man groups, high and low participators were identified by the researcher. For the third problem-solving task, the solution was subtle and not likely to appear freely in the discussion. For half of the groups, a hint about the solution was given to a high participator; for the other half of the groups, the hint was given to a low participator. If the solution was offered by the high participator, it was much more likely to be accepted by the group (11 of 16 acceptances) than if offered by the low participator (5 of 16 acceptances). In another study (Bavelas, Hastorf, Gross, & Kite, 1965), rate of participation in groups was induced artificially through signals from the experimenters; when subjects were asked to nominate the person making the greatest contribution to the group and to respond to questions about leadership, they uniformly chose the high participators. In both studies, rate of participation, regardless of the quality or content, is an important index of leadership in the eyes of the other members.

3. *Other factors conducive to leadership.* Communication networks have been shown to affect leadership. Studies have shown that persons central in the communication network, through whom a great deal of information is passed, are most frequently identified as leaders, even though they have not been formally specified as such in the experiment (Bavelas, 1968). Certainly in real life, to maintain leadership, the leader must have access to all relevant information affecting the group.

Time, feedback, and actual competence are also important factors. Over time, and if there is feedback about the adequacy of the leader's decisions, then actual competence is likely to emerge as the key ingredient in leadership.

Types or Styles of Leadership

The methods used by leaders in exerting their influence and control appear to depend upon the characteristics of the leader, group, and situation. Some leaders are prone to autocratic, others to democratic, and still others to laissez-faire methods of leadership. Similarly, some groups will respond favorably to one kind of leadership and not another, often depending upon what they are used to or what the larger culture expects. For example, individuals may accept autocratic leadership in a military setting which they would not countenance in a civilian setting; or they may accept laissez-faire leadership in a neighborhood group which they would not countenance in a business organization. The general nature and effects of autocratic, democratic, and laissez-faire methods of leadership were demonstrated in the classic study by Lewin, Lippitt, and White (1939) (see accompanying boxed-in text).

In assessing the effects of different styles of leadership on group members, it is now realized that past socialization experiences also play an important role: Individuals with different past social experience may respond differently to the same kind of leadership. In general, Americans and western Europeans are reared under conditions which lead to a preference for democratic methods of leadership—whether in the family or in a larger group setting. But in a society where leaders are expected to be autocratic, a democratic leader may be perceived as weak and inept and may elicit noncooperation instead of better member participation. Thus it is risky to predict the effects of a given method of leadership without knowing something of the experiences and expectations of the particular group.

EFFECTS OF THREE TYPES OF LEADERSHIP

In a classic study of the effects of different kinds of leadership, clubs were formed of 10-year-old boys matched as to age, intelligence, economic background, and so on, and three different types of adult leadership were practiced in the various groups. In the *authoritarian* groups the leader set the group goals, controlled all activity with step-by-step directions, and evaluated the boys' work. In the *laissez-faire* groups the leader simply stood by and answered when spoken to: the groups were entirely on their own in planning and assigning work. In the *democratic* groups members and leader discussed and determined policies and assignments together. The factor of possible personality differences was controlled by having each leader and all the boys operate in at least two different climates.

Differences in performance and other reactions were striking. In the autocratic groups performance was fairly good, but motivation was low and the boys worked only when the leader was present to direct them. The laissez-faire groups did less work and work of a poorer quality. The boys in the democratic groups showed more interest in their work and more originality and kept on working whether the leader was present or not. There was more destruction of property and more aggressiveness and hostility in the autocratic groups, but the hostility tended to be channeled toward a scapegoat member or toward the working materials rather than toward the leader. Members of the autocratic groups were also more dependent and more submissive, showed less individuality, and gave less friendly praise to each other. Morale and cohesiveness were lowest in the laissez-faire groups, highest in the democratic groups. The democratic leaders were liked best by the boys (Lewin, Lippitt, & White, 1939).

In general, it can probably be said that autocratic leadership may be efficient for meeting immediate and temporary crisis situations—as in the fighting of wars—but will tend to defeat its own purposes if maintained over a long period of time or used in situations that do not require it. For it usually reduces the initiative and creativity of individual members and subgroups, thus eventually reducing the adaptive potentiality of the group.

On the other hand, democratic leadership appears to have greater long-range survival value for a group because it elicits member involvement and places minimum restraints on their initiative and creativity, thus tending to promote the adaptability so necessary for meeting changing conditions and demands. Democratic leadership is often more difficult to achieve, however, because it demands more of the leader as well as of the group members.

The Influence of Leaders

The actual role of leaders in shaping human affairs is a subject of some dispute. Many social psychologists and sociologists attribute great powers to leaders and consider them key influences in shaping history. Others believe that the leaders merely symbolize what their followers want and exert influence over the group only insofar as they go in the direction that the group desires. They point out that the leader who tries to guide his followers in a direction they oppose will either lose his position of leadership, be unsuccessful, or cause the group to disintegrate.

History gives examples which seem to support both these contentions. A particular social situation must usually exist before a particular kind of leader can emerge and be accepted; a leader like Mao, for example, could come to power only during a period of great social unrest and change. Yet often a group could be led in any of several directions by a strong leader—for example, toward innovation and experiment with new ways of solving the group's problems, or toward efforts to maintain the status quo, or toward preoccupation with problems of secondary importance and denial of the reality of a major demand to be met. Also the leader can deploy the group's resources wisely or inefficiently; he can inspire dedication and enthusiasm or dissension and discontent; and he can raise or lower members' sights in terms of their collective goals and purposes. Different leaders can move the same group toward reasoned action, emotionalism, apathy, or violence. Thus individual leaders may have a potent influence on the group.

But what the group achieves depends on the quality of "followership" as well as on the leader. As we have seen, the motives, capabilities, attitudes, and commitment of individual members are of key importance in determining how a group functions. In fact, in an interesting study of men working in small groups during a twelve-month period of isolation in Antarctic scientific stations, several of the same personality traits were consistently found to be characteristic of both effective leaders and effective followers; these included a high degree of satisfaction with work assignments, acceptance of authority, and motivation to be part of the group and work as a team (Nelson, 1964).

LEVELS OF POWER

A "hierarchy of power" involving five distinct types of authority can be delineated.

1. *Force*. Authority exercised through the use of any kind of force. It is the most primitive kind of authority, seen among animals as well as man. He who is strongest has the most authority.

2. *Law*. Authority of the community. Legal codes may be based on the will of the majority or they may represent the will of the strong or influential. Compliance is compelled by force when necessary.

3. *Role*. Authority of custom and tradition. Right to act is based on playing designated role. Compliance is achieved mostly by application of pressures within the primary groups.

4. *Ability*. Authority based on respect. Power is based on knowing how to do things valued by others. Once established, tends to function through prestige. Most important in leadership.

5. *Spirit*. Authority that appeals to the minds or souls of those who follow. It is the authority of truth, justice, and inspiration. This is the power of the poet, the prophet, the friend, the loving person.

It would seem to be ideal to rely most on the authority of the spirit, then ability, then role, then law, and to use a minimum of force.

"When I took on this project for the group I realized I would have to be the chairman, but I expected other members to help me out. I found that other members were not interested in helping, and they expected me to know how to organize the project and I didn't, and I felt that the whole thing was a big failure, and there was a great deal of criticism. The other members weren't living up to my expectations, really, and I certainly wasn't living up to theirs. It was disastrous."

Again it becomes apparent that we must have adequate knowledge of group members as well as of the leadership, and of the situation in which the group is functioning—and the interaction among these three sets of factors—if we are to understand the behavior of the group and of individuals in it.

THE SPECIAL PROBLEM OF CONFORMITY

As we have seen, group pressures toward conformity serve a basic need of the group for self-maintenance. Thus they develop to some extent in any organized group, although the strength of such pressures—and the degree of conformity actually needed for a group's maintenance—vary greatly from one situation to another. For example, the conformity demanded and actually needed in a military organization during wartime is much greater than the conformity sought or needed in a sensitivity-training group or a college classroom. Even in the latter two cases, however, certain ground rules are established and members are under some pressure to conform to them.

We have termed conformity a special problem because of its potential for both harm and good, both for the individual and the group. Pressures toward conformity on the one hand may produce a uniformity which is stifling and unproductive, and which violates individual autonomy. On the other hand, individual behavior would be chaotic and unpredictable if it were not affected by

---

EFFECTS OF CONFORMITY PRESSURES

In the classic experiment by Asch (1952, 1955), groups of seven to nine college students were asked to say which of three lines on a card (*right*) matched the length of a standard line on a second card (*left*). One of the three lines they could choose from was actually the same length as the standard line; the other differed from the standard by anywhere from three–fourths of an inch to an inch and three–fourths. It had been determined in advance that these differences were clearly distinguishable.

In each group all but one of the "subjects" were actually stooges, previously instructed to make a *unanimous wrong* choice on most of the trials after the first two. The actual subject was always in such a position that he would not announce his own judgment until after most or all of the others had announced theirs. Thus, after hearing the false judgment given by the planted majority, the minority subject had to choose between denying the evidence of his senses and contradicting the judgment of the group.

Under such pressure, minority subjects accepted the majority's wrong selections in 36.8 percent of the trials. Some individuals, however, were able to stand up to such pressure better than others: about a fourth of the 123 naive subjects clung consistently to their minority judgments, while a few subjects yielded to the majority decision on almost every trial.

When the test subjects were interviewed after the experiment, it was found that some had yielded out of fear of "seeming different," even though they continued to believe in the correctness of their own judgments. Others assumed that, although their own perceptions clearly *seemed* correct, the majority could not be wrong. In a few cases perception itself had apparently been distorted: the subject was apparently unaware of having yielded to group pressure.

Even subjects who consistently maintained their independent judgments tended to be considerably disturbed by their disagreement with the majority and reported that they had been seriously tempted to go along with the group in order to avoid seeming inferior or absurd. In fact, in a later study utilizing the same experimental setup, Bogdonoff et al. (1961) found that students who "called them as they saw them" suffered more anxiety, as evidenced by psyiological changes. One subject who consistently disagreed with the group was dripping with perspiration by the end of the session even though his judgments were right in each instance.

group norms. We shall attempt to note some of the consequences, both positive and negative, of conformity.

"When my sister was in high school she was a member of the top elite social group. And I was a little envious, maybe, but I felt they were all hypocrites and that my sister was a hypocrite. Many years later I found out that my sister didn't particularly like the social whirl, that she didn't really like those people that much, that she was just conforming. She happened to be able to conform in that fashion, and she didn't have the personal security at all—it would have been much too painful to her—to be able to be an individual, so she just had to go along with the crowd."

Why Do People Conform?

Both in the laboratory and in natural settings, researchers and others have been intrigued with the relative ease with which people can be induced to behave similarly to others. A rather dramatic example is provided in the conformity studies by Asch, described earlier.

Conforming behaviors have been found to result from several classes of causes.

1. *Personality factors.* Although many have attempted to link conformity to characteristics of the individual, on the whole this approach has proven of little value. There is a tendency for more intelligent persons to be less conforming than less intelligent persons (Nakamura, 1958), but correlations between intelligence and conformity are only moderately strong. Females tend to conform to majority opinion more than males (Costanzo & Shaw, 1966; Reitan & Shaw, 1964). Personality traits have been found to be generally unpredictive of conformity behaviors.

2. *Stimulus factors.* The nature of the situation is probably the most potent determinant of whether or not conformity occurs. In general, it has been shown that more ambiguous tasks produce greater conformity than tasks with unambiguous stimuli. It seems likely that when the individual has little objective evidence about reality or what is expected, he must rely upon others to provide cues or validate his opinions.

3. *Situational factors.* This includes all aspects of the group context such as size of the group, unanimity of the majority, group structure, and the like. Research evidence generally supports the idea that conformity increases with the increasing size of the majority, up to a certain point. Some studies have shown that a majority of three produced maximum conformity (Asch, 1951), while others have found increases in conformity beyond that size (Gerard, Wilhelmy, & Conolley, 1968). However, there appears to be a point beyond which increasing the size of the group majority does not make a difference in the amount of conformity behavior.

Also, as common sense suggests, a group member is more likely to conform to group judgments when other members are in unanimous agreement than when they are not.

4. *Intragroup factors.* This term refers to the relations among the

members of the group, such as amount of conformity pressure exerted, the group composition, the group's success in achieving past goals, the individual's identification with the group, and so on. All of these variables have been shown to be related to conformity. Conformity tends to be higher in cohesive groups. Also, Costanzo, Reitan, and Shaw (1968) found that persons who perceive their own competence relative to the task to be high, conform less than those with low perceived competence, regardless of their perception of the majority's competence. However, an individual conforms more when the perceived competence of the majority is high than when it is low, regardless of his own level of competence.

Techniques for Inducing Conformity

The techniques and pressures that groups exert to achieve conformity take many forms. Often there are role definitions that set limits to permissible behavior and thus tend to induce conformity. Group members may be subjected to a continual barrage of factual information and/or propaganda in an effort to convince them of the validity of group goals and values—and hence to elicit their cooperation and support. In small groups, the participation of members in setting goals and making decisions helps to create and maintain the involvement of group members and some measure of conformity. In special cases, extreme measures such as "brainwashing" may be utilized in an attempt to change basic thought patterns.

"No one should be able to say one kind of life is the only way for all 'normal' people. If a person can live in the world he chooses without being overwhelmed by it, and he can find a degree of happiness, then he has successfully reacted with his environment and is of sound mind, and has even been useful to society by taking care of himself well. I don't think that people should be considered capable of judging others. People will always condemn that which is different, even though the unfamiliar actions may, in the long run, be much more beneficial to everyone."

Usually group pressures toward conformity rest heavily upon the manipulation of rewards and punishments. The recognition and approval of other group members, advancement to a higher position in the group, and chances for awards and honors are common incentives for inducing conformity behavior, whereas members who create difficulties for the group by their deviant behavior may suffer social disapproval, loss of position, expulsion from the group, or a wide range of other punishments.

"Most people will give almost anything, even their lives if necessary, to retain the approval and comforting feelings of belonging to the group. It is this overwhelming need for group approval and response that makes the primary group the most powerful controlling agency known to man." (Horton & Hunt, 1968, p. 131).

In larger groups, sanctions may follow codes of law, in which norm violations and their attendant penalities are formally prescribed. In small face-to-face groups, sanctions are usually informal but may be even more influential in controlling the behavior of group members since so many personal psychological needs are normally met through close social interaction.

Not all nonconforming behavior meets with group sanctions. Sometimes nothing happens to the nonconformist—for example, if the norm he breaks is unimportant or if he is considered an important member of the group. In some cases group leaders are allowed more latitude in behavior than are other members of the group (McDavid & Harari, 1968). The immediate situation of the group is also important. If the group is not under threat and is generally performing effectively, it is likely to permit more latitude on the part of its members than if it is struggling to establish itself or survive.

The Group's Need for Nonconformists

In discussing the group as a system, we mentioned that groups have needs of their own that may differ from the needs of individual members. Paradoxically, one of these needs is for members who have integrity and enough commitment to values beyond the group to challenge the group when it makes mistakes.

Although some measure of conformity appears essential for coordinating group effort, some measure of nonconformity also appears essential for maintenance of the group's adaptability. If a group is to adapt effectively to changing conditions, it must be capable of making needed changes within its own structure and functioning. This means that someone in the group must recognize the new conditions, propose new approaches, and make other group members aware of the need for change.

> "I feel nonconformity is essential to society. Because without that there's no art, no literature, no anything of value in society. All of that comes from nonconformity—all things of any interest are created by nonconformity. I think everybody really is a nonconformist; it's just a matter of degree.
>
> "Nonconformity only means that you've got the guts to be yourself. And I don't care what you are, if you're yourself, you're happy. Not continuously, but certainly far more than other people."

Slavish loyalty to the group at the price of individual integrity is usually characteristic of insecure persons who are overly dependent on the group. Exploitative individuals may play the loyalty game, but they are not really loyal. And both overdependent members and the exploitative are likely to desert the group when it no longer meets their needs. Fanatically loyal members, too, can be more of a liability than an asset to a group if they are unable or unwilling to recognize weaknesses in the group that need correcting.

Groups that have no room for individuals of integrity—individuals who think for themselves and are loyal to what they value—will in time suffer from the loss of contributions that may be vital to the life of the group. This point has been well elaborated by Buckley in his concept of requisite deviation:

> "A requisite of sociocultural systems is the development and maintenance of a significant level of nonpathological deviance manifest as a pool of alternative ideas and behaviors with respect to the traditional, institutionalized ideologies and role behaviors. Rigidification of any given institutional structure must eventually lead to disruption or dissolution of the society by way of internal upheaval or ineffectiveness against external change" (1968, p. 495).

In spite of pressures toward conformity, every large group has its share of people who do not conform. Some of these deviants—like our criminals—are emotionally immature or have learned distorted values that make them unable or unwilling to conform to the norms of society—though they may be conforming to the norms of their own deviant subgroup and be reaping the usual rewards of conformity from it. But many nonconformists in man's history have been men and women of maturity and vision—individuals like Columbus, Galileo, Roger Bacon, Jane Addams, and Joan of Arc. Nonconformists like these perform lasting services to their society by initiating necessary or desirable changes in group norms, even at the cost of great personal sacrifice. Albert Einstein once said:

> "I gang my own gait and have never belonged to my country, my home, my friends, or even my immediate family, with my whole heart, in the face of all ties, I have never lost an obstinate sense of detachment, of the need for solitude—a feeling which increases with the years" (1949, p. 3).

Unfortunately, it is often difficult for society to evaluate its nonconformists accurately. Even when there is an honest attempt to weigh historical and scientific evidence in judging new ideas, our perspective is always limited and the decision of contemporaries may be different from that of later generations. Thus it will be interesting to see how today's nonconformists are assessed 20 or 50 years from now. Sometimes history shows that nonconforming behavior has been divisive and detrimental to the groups; in other instances, nonconformists who were roundly condemned in their time, like Jesus, were the prophets and founders of new ideas and movements and the instigators of needed social change.

The problem for any group is how to maintain a necessary measure of conformity, while also maintaining the degree of deviance essential for flexibility and adaptability of the group. In the long run, individual and group interests appear to be best served when conformity pressures are limited to those areas where unanimity is essential for coordinated group functioning and effectiveness. Ideally, a group concerns itself explicitly with setting up ways of fostering requisite deviation and identifying it when it occurs.

Direct Effects of Groups on Member Behavior: Group Norms*

by
Lyman W. Porter, Edward E. Lawler, and J. Richard Hackman

In the previous sections, we have examined how group-supplied discretionary stimuli can affect various psychological and informational states of group members. Change in the actual behavior of group members was viewed as a typical (but indirect) consequence of changes in the beliefs members hold and in their attitudes and skills. It also is true, of course, that a member's behavior can be affected *directly* by the discretionary stimuli controlled by his fellows; indeed, one of the most generally accepted principles of psychology is that the behavior of a person can be shaped effectively by someone who is in control of stimuli which are valued (or disvalued) by the target person.

Since most groups do, in fact, have many resources which are valued by group members, member behavior can be directly affected by the rewards (and punishments) which are administered by the group contingent upon the actions of the individual. Such effects must, however, take place on a highly individualistic basis. That is, when other group members wish a particular person to engage in some behavior, they must use their control of discretionary stimuli in such a way that the individual comes to realize that it is in his personal best interest to comply with the behavioral demands of his peers.

Such a process, while powerful, can consume a great deal of time and energy of group members and thus is not a very efficient means of coordinating their activities—especially if the group is moderately large. Therefore, most of

---

the regulating of group member behavior typically takes place through behavioral *norms* which are created and enforced by group members. Indeed, norms are so pervasive and powerful in groups that it has been suggested that "it is only in imagination that we can talk about a human group apart from norms" (Davis, 1950, p. 53).

This section focuses on the nature of group norms and their effects on member behavior. In particular, we will examine (1) the structural characteristics of norms, (2) what happens when someone deviates from a norm, and (3) the conditions under which individuals are and are not likely to comply with group norms. In the paragraphs which follow immediately below, we specify several of the major characteristics of group norms which guide the subsequent discussion.

1. *Norms are structural characteristics of groups, which summarize and simplify group influence processes.* Although numerous definitions and conceptualizations of norms have been proposed, there is general agreement that a norm is a *structural* characteristic of a group, which summarizes and highlights those processes within the group which are intended to regulate and regularize group member behavior. Thus, norms represent an important means of short-cutting the need to use discretionary stimuli on a continuous basis to control the behavior of individual group members.

2. *Norms apply only to behavior—not to private thoughts and feelings.* Although some writers speak of the effects of group norms on member attitudes and beliefs, norms are treated here as being exclusively relevant to the actual behavior of group members. This usage does include verbal behavior, and so what a member *says* he believes or what he says his attitude is can be very much under the normative control of the group. It should be emphasized, however, that such behavioral compliance does not necessarily reflect the true private attitudes and beliefs of group members. Group-supplied discretionary stimuli can indeed affect one's private attitudes and beliefs—but the process is considerably more complex and subtle than merely coercing a member to *say* he agrees with the stance of the group on some matter.

3. *Norms generally are developed only for behaviors which are viewed as important by most group members.* Norms generally develop only for behaviors which otherwise would have to be controlled by direct and continuous social influence (Thibaut & Kelley, 1959). While this implies that only those behaviors viewed as most important in the eyes of group members will be brought under normative control, it does not mean that normatively controlled behaviors are necessarily *objectively* the most important to the group. Some businesses, for example, even today have a norm that one should wear a hat when he leaves the building; it is doubtful that hat-wearing behavior is objectively important to the group, but the fact that most members *believe* it to be important is sufficient cause for the norm to be developed and enforced.

4. *Norms usually develop gradually, but the process can be short-cut if members wish.* Norms about behavior typically develop gradually and informally as members learn what behaviors are, in fact, important for the group to control and what discretionary stimuli seem most effective in regulating the oc-

currence of those behaviors. It is possible, nevertheless, for groups to consciously short-cut the process of norm development. If for some reason group members decide that a particular norm would be desirable or helpful, they may simply agree to institute such a norm suddenly by declaring that "from now on" the norm exists. Someone might say, for example, "We seem to interrupt each other a lot in this group; let's agree (i.e., have a norm) that nobody talks until the other person is finished." If the group as a whole agrees with this proposal, then one might observe marked differences in the social interaction within that group thereafter.

5. *Not all norms apply to everyone.* Finally, it should be noted that norms often do not apply uniformly to all group members. For example, as is discussed in detail later, high-status members often have more freedom to deviate from the letter of the norm than do other people—that is, they build up so-called idiosyncrasy credits. Also, groups will at times form a norm which applies only to one person (or to a small subset of persons) within a group. In such cases, we may speak of the norms as representing the *roles* of the person(s) to whom the norms apply (Thibaut & Kelley, 1959, pp. 142-147).

A MODEL OF GROUP BEHAVIORAL NORMS

An elegant conception of the structure of group norms has been proposed by Jackson (1960, 1965, 1966). The model, which focuses on the distribution of potential approval and disapproval others feel for various behaviors which might be exhibited in a given situation, can be represented in two-dimensional space: the ordinate is the amount of approval and disapproval felt, and the abscissa is the amount of the given behavior exhibited. A "return potential curve" can be drawn in this space, indicating the *pattern and intensity* of approval and disapproval associated with various possible behaviors. An example of a return potential curve is shown in Figure 1.

The "return potential model" (RPM) can be used to describe any situation in which a group norm serves to regulate the behavior of group members. To apply the model, one would obtain from group members (or infer from observations of behavior in the group) the amount of approval or disapproval associated with various behaviors and, from this data, plot a return potential curve. The curve in Figure 1 for example, might reflect the norms of a group regarding the amount of talking an individual member does during a group meeting. Both too little and too much talking, in this case, would be disapproved—but the intensity of the disapproval is stronger for someone who talks too much than for someone who talks too little. (The units of behavior in the example in Figure 1 are arbitrary; in practice, the abscissa would be scaled using units appropriate to the behavior in question.)

A return potential curve can, theoretically, assume any shape. In a formulation similar to that of Jackson, March (1954) suggests three basic types of norms: the unattainable-ideal norm, the preferred-value norm, and the attainable-ideal norm. The unattainable-ideal and attainable-ideal norms are depicted as return potential curves in Figure 2, the preferred-value norm is of

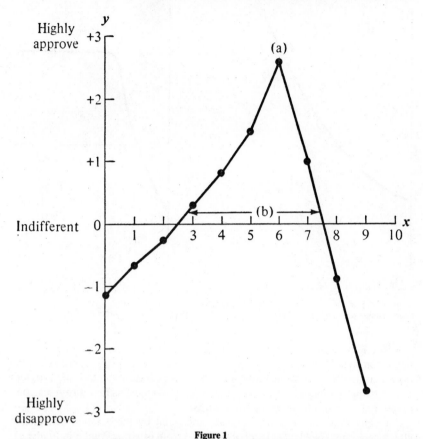

Figure 1
Schematic representation of the return potential model (RPM) of normative structure. The ordinate is an axis of evaluation; the abscissa is an axis of behavior. (Adapted from Jackson, 1965, p. 303)

the general type shown in Figure 1. In essence, the unattainable ideal norm connotes "the more the better"; thus, among a group of scholars, the more insightful one's contributions are the better; or on a football team, the more tackles made the better. The preferred-value norm is often characteristic of the approval and disapproval felt by members of a work group regarding the productivity of individual members: too little output is disapproved—but so is too *much* output. An example (from March, 1954) of the attainable-ideal norm might involve a football team in possession of the ball on the opponents' 20-yard line. A halfback will earn increasing approval as he carries the ball increasing distances—up to 20 yards. After that, he will have made a touch-down and can gain no further approval: 25 yards are no better than 21. There are, of course, many other possible curves which would be descriptive of other types of group norms.

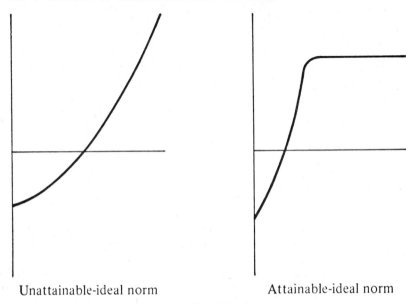

Unattainable-ideal norm   Attainable-ideal norm

Figure 2
Unattainable—ideal and attainable—Ideal Norms (March 1954) shown as return potential curves

The RPM is a useful device for thinking about norms and can be especially helpful in making systematic one's observations of normative behavior in an organization. It is possible, for example, to generate objective measures of norms using the model, and Jackson (1965, 1966) suggests (and provides computational formulas for) five such measures:

1. The Point of Maximum Return: the point on the behavior dimension which generates the highest level of approval from others. (Point *a* in Figure 1)

2. The Range of Tolerable Behavior: the segment of the behavior dimension which is *approved* by others. (Indicated by *b* in Figure 1)

3. The Potential Return Difference: the amount of approval versus disapproval associated with norm-regulated behaviors—indicating the relative emphasis on rewards versus punishments in regulating member behavior.

4. Intensity: the overall strength of approval and disapproval associated with norm-regulated behavior—indicating the amount of affect associated with the norm, regardless of whether that affect is predominately positive or negative in direction.

5. Crystallization: the degree of consensus among group members regarding the amount of approval or disapproval associated with each point or the behavioral dimension.

The RPM has been utilized in research in a number of group and organizational settings, both for understanding the internal dynamics of ongoing groups and organizations and for making comparative studies of different social systems (Jackson, in press). In addition to its obvious uses for research on the effects of various organizational practices aimed at changing the social climate of work groups, the RPM has considerable potential for making *diagnoses* of the normative state of affairs within a given group—as a first step in a change program involving diagnosis, feedback, and action. Through the RPM it should be possible to help group members see, objectively and in simple terms, what the group norms actually are and how they may be guiding behavior in ways that are unrealized or unintended—which should provide an impetus for group-generated changes.

DEVIANCE FROM GROUP NORMS

In an analysis of the reasons for the Bay of Pigs fiasco undertaken by President Kennedy and his advisers in 1961, Janis (1972, Ch. 2) quotes Arthur Schlesinger explaining why he had not pressed more urgently his objections to the developing plans:

"In the months after the Bay of Pigs I bitterly reproached myself for having kept so silent during those crucial discussions in the Cabinet room, though my feelings of guilt were tempered by the knowledge that a course of objection would have accomplished little save to *gain me a name as a nuisance*. I can only explain my failure to do more than raise a few timid questions by reporting that one's impulse to blow the whistle on this nonsense was simply undone by the circumstances of the discussion." (Schlesinger, 1965, p. 255, italics added)

It is not difficult to understand how Schlesinger might have come to hold the above views, given the following event:

At a large birthday party for Mrs. Robert Kennedy, the Attorney General, who had been constantly informed about the Cuban invasion plan, took Schlesinger aside and asked him why he was opposed. The President's brother listened coldly and then said, "You may be right or you may be wrong, but the President has his mind made up. Don't push it any further. Now is the time for everyone to help him all they can." (Janis, 1972, Ch. 2)

Communicating with the Deviant

The "treatment" given Schlesinger illustrates how groups can use their control of discretionary stimuli to bring into line members who are behaving contrary to group norms. A number of research studies document that when a group member expresses a view which deviates from that of the group, his fellow members do increasingly direct communications toward him (e.g. Schachter, 1951; Emerson, 1954, Berkowitz & Howard, 1959).

The researchers interpret this communication as reflecting attempts to move the member back into congruence with the group norm. Sometimes the stimuli provided may be material or physical rather than verbal. For example, the practice of "binging" (i.e., hitting someone forcefully on the upper arm) has been described as an effective means used by work group members to correct the behavior of a worker who is violating the group norms about production quantity (cf. Homans, 1950).

It may be recalled from earlier in the Chapter that a *role* in a group can be described in terms of special behavioral norms which apply specifically to the role occupant(s). Thus, it is not surprising to find that a member who deviates from his role in the group (e.g., a leader who quits leading) encounters reactions which are. similar to those observed when someone violates a general group norm. Unfortunately, experimental research which focuses on the reactions of groups to this type of deviance is scarce.

The literature on role conflict, however, offers some relevant insights. For example, research on interrole conflict suggests that when a person deviates from his role (even if the reason is to fulfill another equally legitimate role), discretionary stimuli may be applied swiftly by his peers to enforce the expectations associated with the first role. A similar process often ensues when an individual encounters intersender conflict—i.e., when conflicting expectations are sent from different sources regarding appropriate behavior for the occupant of a single role. The essence of role conflict (and the crux of the problem for the role occupant) in either case is that the individual is confronted with discretionary stimuli aimed at changing his behavior *regardless* of how he actually behaves. Because he cannot please all role senders at once, the individual experiences conflict. (The effects of such conflict and the ways individuals react to it are discussed by Kahn et al., 1964, and by Sarbin & Allen, 1968).

Rejection of the Deviant

When a member persistently deviates from what is acceptable to his fellow group members (either by his expressions of attitudes and beliefs or by his overt behavior), he becomes vulnerable to rejection by the group. In other words, the application of discretionary stimuli intended to persuade or pressure the deviant to change will persist for only so long, whereupon the other members may "change the composition of the psychological group" (Festinger, 1950). A number of studies provide support for the hypothesis that a persistently deviant member tends to be rejected. In general, however, research results suggest—and informal observation of groups in operation provide some confirmation—that rejection of a member is viewed as a fairly serious step for a group to take, and may be administered by a group only when all else has failed or when the deviant is seen as completely incorrigible (e.g., Sampson & Brandon, 1964).

Yet there may be another reason why groups apparently are so hesitant to cease communicating with a deviant and to reject him with finality. It has been argued that the group *needs* the deviant—and therefore cannot really afford to eliminate him completely (Dentler & Erikson, 1959). Group norms, for example, may become more explicit and more clearly understood by group members as a result of their observation of various deviant behaviors and the consequences which ensue. In addition, because deviants are observed to receive negative outcomes from the group, the incentive value of conformity may be enhanced as a result. Moreover, the process of dealing with deviant members may help the group clarify its own boundaries and gain a better sense of what is distinctive about the group and central to its identity—and what is not.

In a number of ways, then, deviant members can contribute positively to the stability of the group and to the maintenance of its identity. As a consequence, the role of the deviant often becomes institutionalized within the group, and group members will strongly resist any trend toward complete elimination of a deviant member (Dentler & Erikson, 1959, p. 102). While this particular perspective does not purport to handle all the dynamics of a group's response to deviance, it does suggest one important and frequently overlooked set of reasons why groups may be reluctant to respond to deviance by immediately rejecting the member who deviates.

SOME DETERMINANTS OF MEMBER COMPLIANCE WITH GROUP NORMS

Group members tend to behave in accord with the norms of the group in two general cases:

Case 1. The norm-specified behaviors are congruent with the personal attitudes, beliefs, and prior behavioral dispositions of the group members. In this case, there is no conflict between the individual and the group; the member would tend to behave in norm-congruent ways anyway. It should be noted, however, that the reason group members are predisposed toward compliance with the norm in such cases may be that the group has long ago done an effective job of inculcating in the individual attitudes and beliefs which are consistent with the norm.

Consider, for example, a work group that enforces a norm of not communicating very much or very openly with members of management. A member who has been in that group for some time may have come to genuinely believe that "managers can't be trusted—they'll use what you tell them to exploit you whenever they can." The group would not need to pressure this member into compliance with the norm; the more subtle and continuing influences of the group on his attitudes and beliefs over time would have rendered such direct pressure unnecessary.

Case 2. It is frequently the case, however, that the behaviors specified by a group norm are *not* consistent with the personal attitudes or beliefs of one or more members. In the example described above, a recent college graduate just joining the work group would be unlikely to hold an antimanagement set of beliefs and attitudes—and therefore would not be likely to comply with the group norm if left entirely to his own devices. Whether or not the member does in fact comply with the group norm in such cases depends upon two conditions:

1. Pressures to comply must be sent from the group and sent strongly enough to be experienced and understood by the target individual.

2. The target individual must value the rewards (or devalue the sanctions) controlled by the group sufficiently that he is willing to be guided by the wishes of the group, rather than by his own predispositions or by pressures he may experience from other groups.

In the paragraphs to follow, we will list several factors which affect the degree to which these two conditions are met.

Noticeable pressures to comply must be sent by the group. The degree to which discretionary cues will be sent to the target individual strongly enough to attract his attention depends both upon (1) who the target individual is and what his role is in the group (2) the characteristics of the group and the nature of the deviant behavior in question.

1. Some members can get away with deviance more readily than others. It has been suggested (Hollander, 1958, 1964) that group members can earn "idiosyncrasy credits" during the course of their experience in a group. When held in sufficient numbers, these credits permit a member to exhibit some deviant behaviors without incurring the pressures or sanctions usually applied to members who violate a group norm. Group members generate "idiosyncrasy credits" mainly by being "good group citizens"—that is, by generally conforming to the expectations of the group and by contributing effectively to the attainment of group goals. Thus, new group members should not have a balance of "idiosyncrasy credits" to draw upon and therefore should not have much freedom to deviate early in their tenure. Consistent with this prediction, it has been found that new members of a work group were expected to conform more closely to group production norms than were workers who had been group members for some time (Hughes, 1946). Members who have attained high status in the group also would be expected to have a substantial balance of "idiosyncrasy credits" (Hollander, 1961). And, as would be predicted, research evidence suggests that higher-status members are able to be more resistive to conformity pressures than are their lower-status peers (e.g., Harvey & Consalvi, 1960).

2. Some groups send more pressures to comply than do others—and even in the same group, some deviant members will be sanctioned more severely than others. In general, research literature suggests that a group will tend to send more pressures to conform to group norms when (a) group members are strongly motivated to achieve uniformity within the group (Festinger, 1950); (b) the norm in question is of high importance or relevance to the group; and (c) the behavior in question is deviant from the norm to an especially noticeable extent (Mudd, 1968).

Alternatively, in terms of the Jackson RPM of norms, it might be predicted that pressures sent to group members to comply with norms should be especially strong (a) when the norm is of *high intensity*—i.e., when group members hold strong feelings of approval or disapproval contingent upon norm-congruent behavior; and (b) when the norm is *highly crystallized*—i.e., when there is substantial agreement among members about the amount of approval or disapproval associated with each possible behavior relevant to the norm.

The stimuli used to enforce the norm must be valued by the target member(s). The second general condition which must be met by an initially recalcitrant member to comply with group norms is for the rewards of compliance (or sanctions for noncompliance) to be sufficiently potent that the individual comes to *want* to change his behavior. Thus, the more a member personally needs or desires those resources over which the group has control, the more likely he is to go along with group norms.

As noted throughout this chapter, groups generally have control over many affectively powerful stimuli. Therefore, a group typically has a variety of means to add considerable "punch" to the pressures it places on group members for compliance to group norms. It should be noted, however, that the group need not always actually use the stimuli under its control to obtain member compliance; merely having the member know that the group has the potential to administer such stimuli often is quite sufficient. One does not need to be struck down by a bolt of lightning to know the fear of God. It also is true, on the other hand, that when a group is not present in a given situation (or when responses of group members are made in private), behavioral compliance decreases—presumably in part because the capability of the group to apply rewarding or punishing stimuli to the members in such circumstances is lessened (Kiesler, 1969, Ch. 11; Allen, 1965, pp. 145-146).

Previous research has focused on the use of *interpersonal* rewards and punishments as a means of gaining member compliance to group norms. Little attention has been given to the use of material rewards, the provision of information as a reward, or the provision of access to external rewards. The emphasis on interpersonal rewards and sanctions should not restrict the generality of research findings in the area substantially, however, since interpersonal stimuli are probably the most widely used means of obtaining norm compliance in groups and interpersonal rewards and punishments are highly potent for most people.

The not-surprising conclusion from such research is that, in general, the more an individual is attracted to a group (or the more he has a personal need for the social rewards controlled by the group), the more he conforms. Thus, as would be expected, compliance tends to be very high in highly cohesive groups—where members presumably care a great deal about being together and about continuing their mutually satisfying social interaction. Further, there is evidence that group members who do not much need or care about the social rewards which can be provided by their fellows (for example, very high-status members, or very low-status members who are not committed to remaining in the group) often conform less than other group members.

It should be emphasized, however, that the relationship between a member's need for rewards controlled by the group and his conformity to the group assumes that "other things" are constant. Other things never are. By and large, it has been found that when the individual has a high *personal* stake in the task situation—i.e., he has something else he may value as much or more than the potential rewards or punishments he may receive or forgo in the group—he shows less conformity to group norms.

CONCLUSION

Most broadly viewed, this has been a chapter about social influence processes which take place in organizations—and especially how those processes affect what employees think, feel, and do at work. We have elected to discuss these processes in terms of the stimuli which are provided by the groups of which individuals are members—using the concept of "group" very loosely to refer to all those people with whom a person has meaningful and continuing contact in the organization.

Our general conclusion is that the people with whom one works in an organization can—and often do—have rather substantial effects not only on behavior but on how one think and feels as well.

REFERENCES

Allen, V.L. Situational factors in conformity. In L. Berkowitz (ed.). *Advances in experimental social psychology* (Vol. II). New York: Academic Press, 1965.

Berkowitz, L., & Howard, R.C. Reactions to opinion deviates as affected by affiliation need (n) and group member interdependence. *Sociometry*, 1959, 22, 81–91.

Davis, K. *Human society.* New York: Macmillan, 1950.

Dentler, R.A., & Erikson, K.T. The functions of deviance in groups. *Social Problems,* 1959, 7, 98–107.

Emerson, R.M. Deviation and rejection: An experimental replication. *American Sociological Review,* 1954, 19, 688–693.

Festinger, L. Informal social communication. *Psychological Review,* 1950, 57. 271–282.

Harvey, O.J., & Consalvi, C. Status and conformity to pressures in informal groups. *Journal of Abnormal and Social Psychology,* 1960, 60, 182–187.

Homas, G.C. *The human group.* New York: Harcourt, Brace & World, 1950.

Hollander, E.P. Conformity, status, and idiosyncracy credit. *Psychological Review,* 1958, 65, 117–127.

Hollander, E.P. *Leaders, groups and influence.* New York: Oxford University Press, 1964.

Hollander, E.P. Some effects of perceived status on responses to innovactive behavior. *Journal of Abnormal and Social Psychology,* 1961, 63, 247–250.

Hughes, E.C. The knitting of racial groups in industry. *American Sociological Review,* 1946, 11, 512–519.

Jackson, J. A conceptual and measurement model for norms and roles. *Pacific Sociological Review,* 1966, 9, 35–47.

Jackson, J. *Norms and roles: Studies in systematic social psychology.* New York: Holt, Rinehart & Winston, in press.

Jackson, J. Structural characteristics of norms. In I.D. Steiner and M. Fishbein (Eds.), *Current studies in social psychology.* New York: Holt, Rinehart & Winston, 1965.

Jackson, J. Structural characteristics of norms. In N.B. Henry (Ed.), *Dynamics of instructional groups* (The fifty-ninth yearbook of the National Society for the Study of Education). Chicago: University of Chicago Press, 1960.

Janis, I.L. *Victims of groupthink: A psychological study of foreign-policy decisions and fiascos.* Boston: Houghton Mifflin, 1972.

Kahn, R.L., Wolfe, D.M., Quinn, R.P., Snoek, J.D., & Rosenthal, R.A. *Organizational stress: Studies in role conflict and ambiguity.* New York: Wiley, 1964.

Kiesler, C.A. Group pressure and conformity. In J. Mills (ed.), *Experimental social psychology.* New York: Macmillan, 1969.

March, J.G. Group Norms and the active minority. *American Sociological Review,* 1954, *19,* 733–741.

Mudd, S.A. Group sanction severity as a function of degree of behavior deviation and relevance of norm. *Journal of Personality and Social Psychology,* 1968, 8, 258–260.

Sampson, E.E., & Brandon, A.C. The effects of role and opinion deviation on small group behavior. *Sociometry,* 1964, 27, 261–281.

Sarbin, T.R., & Allen, V.L. Increasing participation in a natural group setting: A preliminary report. *The Psychological Record,* 1968, 18, 1–7. (a)

Schacter, S. Deviation, rejection and communication. *Journal of Abnormal and Social Psychology,* 1951, 46, 190–207.

Schlesinger, Arthur M. *A Thousand Days: John F. Kennedy in the White House.* Boston: Houghton Mifflin Company, 1965.

Thibaut, J.W., & Kelley, H.H. *The social psychology of groups.* New York: Wiley, 1959.

Leadership*

by
Paul F. Secord and Carl W. Backman

Leadership has played a vital role in the affairs of men since earliest recorded history. Historians give considerable attention to the role of politicians and statesmen in the development of empires, territories, and nations. In modern society, organizational and informal activities alike are characterized by a difference in the contributions of the participants. Some individuals contribute more of their energies or skills than others, and they vary in the extent to which they exert influence over each other. Business organizations, government, political parties, and nonprofit institutions illustrate this emphasis on leadership by providing unusually high rewards for their leaders, by conducting a continual search for men with leadership ability, and by stressing human relations or leadership training.

This widespread interest in leadership documents the point that it is of considerable concern. But both the popular view of leadership and the early research of behavioral scientists overestimate the importance of the contribution of the individual leader. Current formulations of the problem take a quite different form, focusing on the nature of leadership behavior and its relation to individual personality, to the composition and function of the group, to the situation, and to the group structure.

The history of research on leadership reflects in capsule form the gradual evolution of social psychology into an increasingly complex and sophisticated structure. Like much early research in the behavioral sciences, the initial approach to leadership was to compare individuals, in this case to explore how leaders differ from nonleaders. This tactic is generally acknowledged to have been premature: Few stable differences were found. A later approach focused on leadership *behavior,* emphasizing those acts leading either to goal achievement or to the maintenance and strengthening of the group. In this approach all members of the group were seen as performing leadership acts in varying degrees. Subsequently, the identification of different kinds of leader behaviors made it possible to identify some individual characteristics associated with these behaviors.

The focus on leadership behavior was accompanied by an interest in the effects of the situation and of the composition of the group on leadership behavior. Also of concern were the effects of various kinds or styles of leadership behavior on the productivity and satisfaction of group members. Out of this line of investigation, interest turned toward the structural determinants of leadership: It was believed that relatively permanent patternings of group interaction developed and provided a context within which leadership was exercised. An evolving view of leadership placed stress on the *leader-follower relation,* recognizing that the behavior of the leader depends upon the complementary behavior of followers. Also, it has become increasingly apparent that a type or style of leader behavior that is effective in one situation may not be effective in another. Finally, many present-day students of the topic regard leadership as the allocation of leadership roles to certain individual members of a group. Such role allocation may be readily interpreted by exchange theory, which analyzes the leadership process in terms of the reward-cost outcomes to leadership, placing emphasis upon the more current research strategies.

NATURE OF LEADERSHIP

Early research on leadership shared with the average man a fundamental bias: the tendency to see persons as origins of actions. Leadership behavior was believed to originate from the personal qualities of the leader, and insufficient attention was given to the contribution of the group structure and situation to such behavior. The extreme form of this bias is reflected in such statements as "A military officer is a leader of men," which implies that his personal qualities enable him to lead enlisted men in any and all situations.

Empirical studies compared leaders with nonleaders, focusing on personality traits in the hope of uncovering the bases of leadership. Unfortunately, the relation between personality traits and leadership proved more complex than originally assumed. After a review of the research on this topic conducted before 1952, Gibb concluded that attempts to find a consistent pattern of traits that characterize leaders had failed.[1] He pointed out that the attributes of leadership are any or all of those personality characteristics that, in any *particular situation,* make it possible for a person either to contribute to achievement of a group goal or to be seen as doing so by other group members.

As Cartwright and Zander noted, dissatisfaction with the trait approach led to a new tactic focusing on leadership *behavior:*

"Dissatisfaction with the trait approach has, then, given rise to a view of leadership which stresses the characteristics of the group and the situation in which it exists. Research conducted within this orientation does not attempt to find certain invariant traits of leaders. Rather, it seeks to discover what actions are required by groups under various conditions if they are to achieve their goals or other valued states, and how different group members take part in these group actions: Leadership is viewed as the performance of those acts which help the group achieve its preferred outcomes. Such acts may be termed *group functions*. More specifically, leadership consists of such actions by group members as those which aid in setting group goals, moving the group towards its goals, improving the quality of the interactions among the members, building the cohesiveness of the group, or making resources available to the group. In principle, leadership may be performed by one or many members of the group."[2]

As the above quotation suggests, a wide variety of acts, depending on the situation and the character of the group, could be classified as leadership behavior. There is growing empirical[3] and theoretical convergence[4] on considering as leadership behavior those acts that are functionally related either to goal achievement or to the maintenance and strengthening of the group. Acts in the former category, instrumental to achieving the goals of the group, include making suggestions for action, evaluating movement toward the goal, preventing activities irrelevant to the goal, and offering solutions for goal achievement. Acts serving to maintain the group through meeting the social-emotional needs of the group members include encouraging other members, releasing tension that builds up, and giving everyone a chance to express himself.

In short, the attributes of leadership are any or all of those personality characteristics that, in any particular situation, make it possible for a person to contribute to achievement of a group goal, to help hold the group together, or to be *seen as doing so by other members*. The latter qualification concerning the perceptions of group members should be underscored. Certain characteristics of an individual or his behavior may not in fact be functionally related either to goal achievement or to the maintenance and strengthening of the group. But to the degree that they are perceived as related, other members will accord leadership status to persons possessing the characteristics or performing the behavior. The emphasis, then, is placed on leadership behavior: those actions that actually are or perceived to be functionally related either to goal achievement or to the maintenance and strengthening of the group. Such behavior is engaged in to varying degree by all group members. At the same time, some individual personality or other characteristics are associated with those persons who take the lead in performing these functions, but these characteristics will vary depending upon the type of group and the task situation.

ROLE DIFFERENTIATION

The behavioral or functional approach to leadership emphasizes that leadership behavior may be performed by any group member; yet relatively early in the life of a group, certain persons engage in such behavior to a much greater degree than others. This specialization has been conceptualized as *role differentiation.*[5] Since role differentiation is most readily observed in groups with a minimum of structure, most of the relevant research has been done on newly formed laboratory groups. While many of the findings have implications for leadership behavior in well-established groups, some caution should be exercised in generalizing to such groups.

Nature of Role Differentiation

At a relatively early point in the development of newly formed, initially leaderless groups, the frequency, direction, and content of communication became established at different levels for different members. The individual who talked the most also received the most communication from others. He directed a larger proportion of his comments to the group as a whole rather than to individual members, and these comments were more often in the positive task-oriented categories—giving suggestions, information, and opinion. Other group members were more apt to consider the person most frequently initiating actions as having the best ideas and as doing the most to guide the discussion effectively. Such specialization of behavior and the development of consensus in recognition of the specialization are the substance of role differentiation.

Heinicke and Bales, who observed the development of such consensus in groups over a series of sessions, describe it in terms of an early struggle between men with top status from which the victor ultimately emerges as the agreed-upon leader.[6] Although the groups studied had developed a high degree of status consensus by the end of the first session, during the second session this consensus declined, and a somewhat different hierarchy emerged. The second session was characterized by a status struggle, particularly between the two top men. Subsequently, however, the struggle was resolved, and consensus on the old structure reappeared, along with a more positive social-emotional atmosphere.

The roles of the two top-status individuals were critical. During the first two sessions, the number one man played a very active part, apparently in order to establish his position and defend it. He initiated many suggestions, and received many agreements and disagreements. His activity in the second session appeared to be a defense of his top position, challenged by the number two man. Since he was secure by the third and fourth sessions, however, he was able to permit other persons to play more active roles. Although he continued to receive the most responses, especially agreement, he no longer had to exert himself unduly to win his point

Some of the groups studied by these investigators, however, did not show this trend toward consensus. For these groups, member agreement on the statuses of other members fluctuated in an erratic fashion. This appeared to be a function of the extent to which agreement was reached at the end of the first session. The high-consensus groups were characterized by high agreement among members on their relative ranking at the end of the first session. Those groups who failed to obtain any stability in agreement even in later sessions were characterized by low agreement from the beginning. This suggests the underlying reason for their failure to reach consensus: the groups reaching agreement early were high in initial value consensus, and the groups failing to agree contained members holding divergent values. Bales and Slater suggest that this initial agreement made it possible for members to agree on who was producing the best ideas for solving the group task, and that these individuals were allowed and encouraged to specialize in this task actively.

Recently, differentiation in rates of participation has been shown to occur immediately in some groups.[7] In about half of the discussion groups studied, the rates of participation for members gradually diverged during the forty-five-minute session, as in the groups studied in successive sessions by Heinicke and Bales, with a similar type of explanation. For the remainder, however, such differentiation appeared full-blown as early as the first minute of interaction. A possible explanation for both initial consensus and early differentiation is that members were similar in background and personality characteristics, as well as in shared interpersonal perceptions.

Task and Social-Emotional Specialization

Role differentiation between leader and nonleader is not the only kind of differentiation that may occur. Under certain circumstances, both a task leader and a social-emotional leader may emerge. The *task leader* is a person who supplies ideas and guides the group toward a solution. The *social-emotional leader* helps to boost group morale and to release tension when things are difficult. Such a differentiation was observed in the groups studied by Bales and Slater.[8] In their investigation, the task specialist was ranked high on initiation, receiving, and guidance, but was not ranked high on liking. The social-emotional leader was usually the best liked among the members. Increasing specialization in these two functions appeared in successive sessions. In the first session, in slightly over half the groups, the man who ranked first on ideas was liked best, but by the fourth session this held true for only 9 percent of the groups.

Role Differentiation and Equilibrium

Such role differentiation has been related theoretically and empirically to certain basic tendencies toward a state of equilibrium in groups.[9] It may be briefly noted here that movement toward task accomplishment in groups frustrates needs and incurs other costs. These diversionary activities, since they interfere with task accomplishment, eventually in turn give rise to forces directing the group back to task activities.

The effect of the two sets of forces is to maintain a balance or equilibrium between meeting both the task and the social-emotional functions of groups. One manifestation of the forces toward equilibrium is the development of hostility toward the task leader, who is pushing the group toward task accomplishment. Bales and Slater describe this process for groups high on status consensus which have a clear-cut differentiation between task and social-emotional roles.[10] According to these investigators, the task leader initially generates liking because he satisfies needs of members for completing the task. But he arouses hostility because of his prestige, because he talks a large proportion of the time, and because he requires other members to focus on the task. The more he talks, the more ambivalent other members become toward him. Eventually they transfer some liking from him to another person who is less active and who contributes to the release of tensions in the group by joking or by diverting the group momentarily at peak tensions. This social-emotional leader reasserts the desirable values and attitudes that have been disturbed, deemphasized, threatened, or repressed by the requirements of the task.

Apparently, to the degree that hostility toward the task leader occurs, differentiation between the two roles takes place. There are two grounds for this expectation. First, such hostility makes performance of both roles incompatible, and second, the personalities of the members attracted to and capable of playing the two roles are likely to be different.[11] The social-emotional specialist must like and be liked if he is to meet the social-emotional needs of others. In contrast, the task specialist must be emotionally detached. If he is to lead the group to accomplish its goals, he cannot become so emotionally dependent upon other members that he is unable to exercise power over them.

Data on differences between the idea specialist and the best-liked person are consistent with this supposition.[12] Best-liked persons like other group members strongly and about equally. The idea specialist differentiates his liking to a much greater extent: He likes some members much more than others. Other research indicates that effective leaders differentiate between followers to a greater extent than ineffective leaders: They see the personalities of the members they like best and least as more dissimilar.[13] Bales and Slater suggest that these differences reflect personality differences between those persons who become social-emotional specialists and those who function as task leaders. Liking everyone strongly and to an equal degree may reflect a strong need to be liked on the part of those who become social-emotional leaders. Because of this need, they may have developed considerable skill in making other people like them. The task leader, on the other hand, may well be one who is able to accept negative reactions from others.

Conditions Favoring Maximum Role Differentiation

The reasoning to this point suggests that the degree of role differentiation varies directly with the extent to which task functions are unrewarding or costly. The less satisfaction experienced in working toward a goal and the more costs incurred, the more likely task and social-emotional functions are to be centered in different persons. Rewards are low where task success is unrelated to member needs. Costs are high where members disagree on both the importance of the task and how it is to be accomplished. Similarly, costs are apt to be high to the degree that influence attempts among group members must be largely personal in nature. These conditions prevail in groups where the affect, status, power, and communication structures are relatively undeveloped and where there is little consensus on values, on the appropriateness of activities, or on the facts of the situation and how facts are to be assessed. Where members agree on the appeal to norms, conformity is attained without the high costs incurred through the use of personal influence.

These suppositions may be tested by examining cases both where role differentiation has occurred to the greatest degree and where it has not. Verba has argued that the temporary small experimental groups studied by Bales and his colleagues provided conditions especially conducive to role differentiation.[14] Having to arrive at a joint solution to a hypothetical problem in human relations could be expected to stimulate differences of opinion because of value differences. At the same time, the patently experimental atmosphere would not prompt high involvement in the task, and thus task efforts by a leader would not be well appreciated. Moreover, these initially leaderless groups were composed of university undergraduates who, with few exceptions, were strangers whose status characteristics (age, sex, etc.) provided little basis for differentiation, and hence attempts to assume leadership had little support from established status characteristics or from an established group structure. Experimental studies of emergent leaders and of leaders in groups with an established structure suggest that established leaders are less directive and evoke less resistance on the part of followers than emergent leaders. Verba draws the following conclusions:

> "In the experiments, therefore, individuals who do not value highly interpersonal control by others are brought together in groups where the exercise of such control has no external backing from some extra-group hierarchy. The members are unknown to each other and have no apparent status differences such that one member would be expected to exert more influence in the group than another. Under these circumstances it is no wonder that the most active group member, even if he contributes the most to group performance, will tend to be rejected by the group on socioemotional criteria. His control attempts are viewed as arbitrary and as direct personal challenges. And such directives are likely to arouse negative reactions. As Frank has put it,' "Resistance to an activity is readily aroused if it involves submitting to an arbitrary personal demand of someone else, and it is thereby equivalent to a personal defeat.' "[15]

These comments should not be interpreted to mean that role differentiation will not occur in established groups outside the peculiar culture of the laboratory. Everyday experience, as well as empirical studies, shows that role differentiation does occur in some established groups under many circumstances.[16] Evidence of such differentiation in the structure of families in many societies has been found,[17] but other studies arouse some doubt about whether such differentiation occurs uniformly in family interaction in American society.[18] In established groups in natural settings, bifurcation of roles might be expected where the leader and other group members differ sharply in task involvement and in their views or orientation to the task. In industrial groups, by virtue of his position in the managerial hierarchy, the supervisor is likely to be more involved in task accomplishment than the worker, and to see the work situation differently from him. Under these circumstances it is not surprising that informal leaders emerge to perform a social-emotional function. In fact, a wide range of circumstances can create differences in attitudes and values between a task leader and his followers, thus encouraging the emergence of a social-emotional leader.

On the other hand, any set of circumstances that reduces these differences increases the probability that one person will be able to carry on both functions, and this seems to be the general case. Several studies indicate that where conditions make either task accomplishment or solving emotional problems highly salient for all members of the group, the person who leads the way in solving the salient problem will be liked, and bifurcation of the two roles will be minimized.[19] It would seem that the task leader is especially apt also to perform a social-emotional function where highly skilled, closely coordinated teamwork is required, in a situation involving risk. Such conditions rouse much tension that must be repeatedly dissipated if the group is to function well as a team. Goffman discusses this function of the chief surgeon supervising his team during an operation. Some tension-relieving examples are:

(Intern holds retractor at wrong end of incision and goes "away", being uninterested in the operation.) Chief Surgeon (in mock English accent): "You don't have to hold that up there, old chap, perhaps down here. Going to sleep, old boy?"

Chief Surgeon (on being accidentally stabbed in the finger by the assistant surgeon, who is using the electric scalpel): "If I get syphilis (sic) I'll know where I got it from, and I'll have witnesses."[20]

Hostility toward the leader and role differentiation are also reduced where the style of leadership encourages a wide distribution of directive acts so that no one person becomes the sole target of hostility for reward-cost outcomes reduced by such acts. Thus, the democratic leader who encourages division of responsibility and participation in decisions may well be able, as Thibaut and Kelley suggest, to carry on both a social-emotional and a task role.[21] Hostility generated by the activities of a task leader may also be expressed by scapegoating, or by the displacement of hostility toward the low-status member of a group. In groups where task motivation and interest were low, a moderately strong relationship was observed between the degree to which the task leader stood out above the others in task-related activity and the amount of hostility directed toward the person with the lowest score in task participation.[22] Where the legitimacy of task activity was high, as measured by the members' task motivation and interest, there was little relation between these indicators of role differentiation and scapegoating.

Legitimacy of Leadership

The laboratory groups in which the bifurcation of leadership was first studied differed in another respect which is important to an understanding of why this phenomenon is less evident in groups that have existed over a period of time. As previously noted, where costs incurred by group members are perceived to be due to the personal acts of the task leader, hostility is likely to be directed toward him. Thibaut and Kelley point out, however, that where group members perceive the directive attempts of the leader as *legitimate,* hostile reactions are not apt to occur. Verba makes the following comment on this point:

> "One of the most effective ways in which the instrumental directives of a group leader acquire legitimacy and avoid being received as personal, arbitrary challenges to the group members is for the leader to be perceived as acting not as an individual but as the agent of some impersonal force, such as the "demands of the situation" or the group traditions and norms. The invocation of some external authority by the group leader relieves the follower of the burden of accepting the control of another individual. Thibaut and Kelley, in a study of power relations in the dyad, conclude that group norms have the effect of reducing the tension between the more powerful and the less powerful member of the group. The impersonalization of expectations of behavior through the adoption of norms makes the influence relationship between the more and the less powerful group member more stable and palatable for both of them. For the less powerful member, the use of controls without a normative base would make those controls arbitrary and unpredictable, and lead to resistance on his part. For the more powerful member of a dyad, the use of purely personal power would also be unpleasant. He must either reduce his attempted control (and thereby perhaps endanger the accomplishment of the group goal) or risk the negative reactions of the other member. Thus the exercise of control in the name of a set of norms that legitimizes the control is to the advantage of both leader and follower."[23]

One way in which the leader's actions acquire legitimacy is through formal recognition of his leadership role. This is demonstrated in an experiment where one supervisor was elected and the other was assigned by the experimenter.[24] Under these circumstances, the elected supervisor, who is likely to be perceived as having more legitimate power, was shown to exert a greater influence over his work group than the nonelected supervisor.

Another investigation, conducted in a classroom situation, indicated that the arousal of hostility toward the instructor was a direct function of the extent to which he violated the legitimate expectations of the student by following his own inclinations rather than the student's desires.[25] In ROTC classes, instructions for making paper objects were given somewhat too rapidly to be grasped thoroughly. Votes were then taken to determine whether the procedure should be repeated or not, under the following two conditions: In the *teacher-centered condition,* students were led to expect that the instructor's vote would have twice the weight of the group. In the *student-centered condition,* students were led to expect that the instructor's vote would be weighted only one-fourth as heavily as that of the group.

Actual votes, which took the form of ratings of the desire for continuing or for going back over the instructions, were disregarded. Votes were announced by arrangement so that the instructor moderately favored going on to the next topic, but the group moderately favored repeating the instructions for making the paper objects. With these ratings, continuing was legitimate in the teacher-centered group because of the extra weight given to the instructor's rating. In the student-centered group, however, going on meant that the instructor was arbitrarily reducing the weight given to the students' desires relative to the weight given his own, and this action was perceived as illegitimate. Considerably more hostility toward the instructor was expressed in this condition, as determined by student evaluations of him collected by the experimenter.

Another type of social norm protects the task leader from the damaging psychological effects of withdrawal of positive affect. In time, norms develop to encourage a degree of social distance between the leader and most of his followers, preventing the development of emotional dependence of the leader on all but a few of his followers. This allows him to carry out his task functions without experiencing too painfully the emotional rejections that he encounters.

As Homans notes, a distinction should be made between liking and esteem.[26] Leaders are often respected, particularly if they have earned respect through skillful leadership; but they are less often liked. To the degree that a task leader is successful in providing the group with many rewards, he may be liked. In the long run, however, his control over the rewards and costs received by the members of the group and his superior status are likely to produce ambivalent feelings toward him. Thus, in most groups outside the special conditions of the laboratory, a full-blown distinction between task and social-emotional leadership does not occur. The tendency for these functions to be incompatible when lodged in the same person results in a certain ambivalence toward the leader, and undoubtedly contributes to the costs that a leader experiences.

Summary: Role Differentiation

Under certain circumstances, a task leader and a social-emotional leader emerge to lead the group. The task specialist organizes and directs the activities of members so that they are focused on achieving group goals with maximum efficiency. The social-emotional specialist boosts morale and releases tensions arising from the group's work activities. These two specialists help to maintain the group in a state of equilibrium. Movement toward task accomplishment in groups frustrates needs and incurs other costs, so that forces arise to direct group activities away from the task and toward dealing with the needs and reducing or compensating for the costs. The social-emotional specialist, through joking or encouragement, or through generating esprit de corps, helps to dissipate these diversionary forces.

The task specialist is seldom the best-liked member of the group. His role in focusing the efforts of other members on achievement precludes this and occasionally generates some hostility toward him. For adequate functioning, moreover, he cannot become so emotionally dependent on other members that he is unable to exercise power over them. This is reflected in his highly selective linking for other members, as compared with the social-emotional leader, who likes others strongly and equally well.

Role differentiation varies directly with the extent to which task functions are unrewarding or costly. It is likely to be maximized in groups where the affect, status, power, and communication structures are relatively undeveloped and where there is little consensus on values, on the appropriateness of activities, or on the facts of the situation and how these facts are to be assessed. In established groups, where the power of the leader has mainly a legitimate basis, hostile feelings and reactions toward him are somewhat reduced. His requests are seen not as stemming from some personal or arbitrary need, but from the demands of the situation or from the group norms. In most groups outside the laboratory, a full-blown distinction between task and social-emotional leadership does not occur. These functions, when lodged in the same person, generate feelings of ambivalence toward him, and contribute to the costs he experiences.

Leadership is also less likely to be divided when, for all members of the group, conditions make either task accomplishment or solving emotional problems dominant and the other function becomes minimal. In that case the one person contributing to the salient function will probably be liked. Another factor reducing hostility toward the task leader is the distribution of responsibility for and participation in decisions, so that no one person becomes the sole target of hostility.

ROLE ALLOCATION AND EXCHANGE THEORY

Exchange theory suggests that whether a person assumes a leadership function depends upon the reward-cost outcomes experienced by him and his followers. The rewards and costs would be a function of the requirements of the situation, such as the nature of the task confronting the group, the characteristics, needs, and skills of the person and his followers; his position in the power and communication structures; and in some instances, his position in the affect structure. These rewards and costs are considered in more detail below.

Rewards and Costs of the Leader

The rewards of leadership are twofold: first the satisfactions to be gained from successful task accomplishment, and second, the rewards gained from leadership activity in itself. These include satisfaction of needs for achievement and dominance, as well as other social-emotional needs.

Persons who assume leadership incur a number of costs. In addition to the effort directly expended in goal-related activities, the leader experiences costs in the form of strains stemming from the necessity of serving as a model for group behavior. Other costs include anxiety imposed by the ever-present possibility of failure, rebuffs in his attempts to lead, with consequent loss of status; and blame as well as guilt when his direction is accepted but results in group failure. Finally, since his behavior is apt to affect adversely the reward-cost outcomes of other members, he faces the costs of losing their friendship. He risks not only his status but also his popularity. Closely related is the cost of loneliness. The leader is often avoided, not only because he may have incurred hostility, but also because of his power: others regard interaction with him as risky in terms of possible adverse reward-cost outcomes.

Rewards and Costs of Followers

Following a leader has several rewards. First among these is goal achieve-ment. Often followers are willing to be led because they recognize that without leadership, the goals of the group would not be achieved. Second, just as certain personality needs are met by leadership behavior, others are met by followership. Dependency needs are directly met by following a leader. If the leader has highly valued characteristics, other needs may be met vicariously through identification with him. Similarly, through identification with the leader, followers may be provided with a sense of shared outlook that provides support for their view of social reality.[27] Both of these consequences of iden-tification with the leader may underlie the phenomenon of leader charisma, a special quality thought to characterize many leaders.[28] The suggestion, in other words, is that charisma is a function of the extent to which followers can identify with a leader—can take him as a model to which they aspire either in fantasy or in reality. Finally, one of the rewards gained by the follower is a cost foregone. By accepting a follower role he escapes anxiety over the risk of failure in a leadership role and also escapes blame when failure occurs.

Among the costs of being a follower is low status. In some groups—for example, work groups—the worker-follower receives less pay as well. The follower also has less control over the activities of the group and of specific other members. Thus these activities may be less rewarding and more costly to him than they would be if he had a greater degree of control. He also foregoes the intrinsic satisfaction that might be gained from engaging in leadership tasks: He is more likely to be assigned the duller routine jobs.

Situational Determinants of Leadership

Rewards and costs associated with various leader and follower behaviors are in part a function of situationally imposed requirements. A number of studies suggest that if the costs of inaction in the face of situational demands are great enough, group members will respond with appropriate behavior. Thus, in initially leaderless groups studied in the laboratory, or in groups studied in a natural setting where established leaders fail to carry out leadership functions, certain members will rise to the occasion.[29] What kinds of behavior will occur and who will perform them are in part dictated by the demands of the situation. One investigator finds that the social-emotional specialist in a mental hospital group is more apt to exercise leadership when conflict develops between patients.[30] Others have shown that as a group proceeds through the problem-solving process, members respond with behavior appropriate to the problem that the group faces at that particular phase of the process.[31]

Who will respond depends on the rewards and costs arising out of the interplay between the demands of the situation and the characteristics of individuals. The distribution of skills affects the costs of members; those who have the required skills to a high degree can respond at less cost to themselves than those less skilled. Studies that show a shift in leadership with a change in the nature of the task document this point. For example, in one study, the same group was observed while performing six different tasks, and leadership ratings for each member in each task situation were obtained.[32] These were statistically analyzed to determine the basic task functions underlying the specific tasks. The analysis suggested that there were two families of tasks underlying leadership in the group. One was characterized by ability to lead in task situations that call for *intellectual* solutions and the other by ability to lead in task situations that call for *manipulation of objects*.

Situations calling for different interests also yield varying reward-cost outcomes for members assuming leadership. Persons other than the designated leader emerge to perform a leadership function in connection with a specific problem in which they are especially interested.[33]

END NOTES

1. Gibb, C.A. Leadership. In G. Lindzey (Ed.), *Handbook of social psychology*. Vol 2. Cambridge, Mass.: Addison-Wesley Press, Inc., 1954.

2. Cartwright, D. & A. Zander (Eds.). *Group dynamics: Research and theory*. (2nd ed.) Evanston, Ill.: Row Peterson, 1960.

3. Halpin, A.W. & B.J. Winer. *The leadership behavior of the airplane commander.* Columbus: Ohio State University Research Foundation, 1952.

4. Parsons, T. & R.F. Bales. *Family socialization and interaction process.* Chicago: The Free Press of Glencoe, Ill., 1955.

   Thiabaut, J.W., & H.H. Kelley, *The social psychology of groups,* New York: John Wiley & Sons, Inc., 1959.

   Cartwright, D., & A. Zander (Eds.). *Group dynamics: Research and theory.* (2nd ed.) Evanston, Ill.: Row Peterson, 1960.

5. Bales, R.F. & P.E. Slater. Role differentiation in small decision-making groups. In T. Parsons & R.F. Bales (Eds.), *Family, socialization and interaction process.* Chicago: The Free Press of Glencoe, Ill., 1955. P. 259–306.

6. Heinicke, C. & R.F. Bales. Developmental trends in the structure of small groups. *Sociometry*, 1953, 16, 35, 36.

7. Fisek, M.H. & R. Oeshe. The process of status evolution. *Sociometry*, 1970. 33, 327–346.

8. Bales, R.F. & P.E. Slater. Role differentiation in small decision-making groups. In T. Parsons & R.F. Bales (Eds.), *Family, socialization and interaction process*. Chicago: The Free Press of Glencoe, Ill., 1955. Pp. 259–306.

9. Parsons, T. & R.F. Bales. *Family socialization and interaction process*. Chicago: The Free Press of Glencoe, Ill., 1955.

Lewin, K.R. Lippitt, & R.K. White. Patterns of aggressive behavior in experimentally created social climates. *Journal of Social Psychology*, 1939, 10, 271–299.

Coch, L. & J.R.P. French, Jr. Overcoming resistance to change. In E.E. Maccoby, T.M. Newcomb, & E.L. Hartley (Eds.) *Readings in social psychology*. (3rd Ed) New York: Holt, Rinehart and Winston, Inc., 1958. Pp. 233–250.

10. Bales, R.F. & P.E. Slater. Role differentiation in small decision-making groups. In T. Parsons & R.F. Bales (Eds.) *Family, socialization and interaction process*. Chicago: The Free Press of Glencoe, Ill., 1955. Pp. 259–306.

11. Bales, R.F. & P.E. Slater. Role differentation in small decision-making groups. In T. Parsons & R.F. Bales (Eds.), *Family socialization and interaction process*. Chicago: The Free Press of Glencoe, Ill., 1955. Pp. 259–306.

12. Fiedler, R.E. The leader's psychological distance and group effectiveness. In D. Cartwright & A. Zander (Eds.) *Group dynamics: Research and theory*. Second edition. Evanston, Ill.: Row, Peterson & Company, 1960. Pp. 586–606.

13. Bales, R.F. & P.E. Slater. Role differentiation in small decision-making groups. In T. Parsons & R.F. Bales (Eds.), *Family, socialization and interaction process*. Chicago: The Free Press of Glencoe, Ill., 1955. Pp. 259–306.

14. Verba, S. *Small groups and political behavior: A study of leadership*, Princeton, N.J.: Princeton University Press, 1961.

15. Verba S. *Small groups and political behavior: A study of leadership*, Princeton, J.J.: Princeton University Press, 1961.

16. Zelditch, M., Jr. Role differentiation in the nuclear family: A comparative study. In T. Parsons & R.R. Bales (Eds.) *Family socialization and interaction process*. Chicago: The Free Press of Glencoe, Ill., 1955. Pp. 307–351.

Grusky, O. A case for the theory of familial role differentiation in small groups. *Social Forces*, 1957, 15, 209–217.

17. Zelditch, M., Jr. Role differentiation in the nuclear family: A comparative study. In T. Parsons & R.F. Bales (Eds.), *Family socialization and interaction process*. Chicago: The Free Press of Glencoe, Ill., 1955. Pp. 307–351.

18. Leik, R.K. Instrumentality and emotionality in family interaction. *Sociometry*, 1963, 26, 131 145.

Levinger, G. Task and social behavior in marriage. *Sociometry*, 1964, 27, 433–448. (b)

19. Marcus, P.M. Expressive and instrumental groups: Toward a theory of group structure. *American Journal of Sociology*, 1960, 66, 54–59.

Turk, H. Instrumental and expressive ratings reconsidered. *Sociometry*, 1961, 24, 76–81.

Meile, R.L. Perceptions of threat and group leadership. Paper presented at the annual meeting of the American Sociological Association, Washington, D.C., 1962.

Burke, P.J. The development of task and social-emotional role differentiation. *Sociometry*, 1967, 30, 379–392.

Burke P.J. Role differentiation and the legitimation of task activity. *Sociometry*, 1968, 31, 404–411.

20. Goffman, E. *Encounters: Two studies in the sociology of interaction*, Indianapolis: The Bobbs-Merrill Company, Inc. 1961.

21. Thibaut, J.W. & H.H. Kelley, *The social psychology of groups*, New York: John Wiley & Sons, Inc., 1959.

22. Burke, P.J. Scapegoating: An alternative to role differentiation, *Sociometry,* 1969, 32, 159–168.

23. Verba, S. *Small groups and political behavior: A study of leadership,* Princeton, N.J.: Princeton University Press, 1961.

24. Raven, B.H., & J.R.P. French, Jr. Group support, legitimate power, and social influence. *Journal of Personality,* 1958, 26, 400–409.

25. Horwitz, M. Hostility and its management in classroom groups. In W.W. Charters, Jr. & N. J. Gage, (Eds.) *Readings in the social psychology of education,* Boston: Allyn and Bacon, Inc., 1963. Pp. 196–211.

26. Homans, G.C. *Social behavior: Its elementary forms.* New York: Harcourt, Brace & World, Inc., 1961.

27. Hollander, E.P. & J.W. Julian. Contemporary trends in the analysis of leadership processes. *Psychological Bulletin,* 1969, 71, 387–397.

28. Weber, M. (Collected writings) in S.N. Eisenstadt (Ed.) *Max Weber on charisma and institution building: Selected papers.* Chicago: The University of Chicago Press, 1968.

29. Bales, R.F. & P.E. Slater. Role differentiation in small decision-making groups. In T. Parsons & R.F. Bales (Eds.), *Family, socialization and interaction process.* Chicago: The Free Press of Glencoe, Ill., 1955. Pp. 259–306.

30. Parker, S. Leadership patterns in a psychiatric ward. *Human Relations,* 1958, 11, 287–301.

31. Bales, R.F. & F.L. Strodtbeck. Phases in group problem solving. *Journal of Abnormal and Social Psychology,* 1951, 46, 485–495.

32. Carter, I.F. W.W. Haythorn, & M. Howell. A further investigation of the criteria of leadership. *Journal of Abnormal and Social Psychology,* 1950, 45, 350–358.

33. Crockett, W.H. Emergent leadership in small, decision-making groups. *Journal of Abnormal and Social Psychology,* 1955, 51, 378–383.

Independence and Conformity: The Problem of Truth in the Face of Pressure*

by
Harold J. Leavitt

Here is a problem:

You are a member of a committee. It doesn't matter what sort of a committee; you may be trying to select new products, or working out a strategy for up-coming negotiations with the union, or allocating space in the new laboratory, or deciding which of several men to promote to a new job. It is a committee made up mostly of people at about your level, chaired by a man who is intelligent and reasonable and rather well liked by all of you. He has circulated an agenda in advance of your next meeting, and you have thought a good deal about it and arrived at a position on the very first item—a position you feel rather strongly about.

When you arrive at the meeting room, a few of the eight members have not yet shown up, so you and four or five others chat about this and that until things get under way. After the late arrivals show up and you exchange a few pleasantries, the chairman gets things started and gradually one member after another begins to express his views about the first item on the agenda. By the time you get into the act, it has become pretty clear that most members seem to share one opinion—*an opinion very different from yours*. Most people seem to be nodding their heads and saying, "Yes, method X suggested by Joe Blow looks like a pretty good solution."

Then you come in rather strongly for method Y. Nobody seems very upset. Everybody listens politely. Some of the fellows ask you questions and make comments that are partially supportive and partially in disagreement. And the discussion goes on.

After a while the chairman says, "Well, we've been at this for awhile; let's see where we stand." And he tries to summarize the two positions that have been taken, essentially Joe Blow's position X and your position Y. It's all done informally, but one after another, each in his own style, the members go along with X rather than Y. As one after another of the members goes this way, you begin to feel some discomfort. People seem to be turning toward you, psychologically if not physically; and the chairman casts an inquiring look your way. This is a committee that likes to operate informally, and you approve of this informality. You know that the chairman doesn't want to have to put this issue up to a formal vote and say, "We have decided seven to one in favor of X over Y." On the other hand, in your opinion, Y is right and X is wrong.

So the pressure begins to build and the spotlight begins to focus on you. The chairman says, "Well look, gentlemen, we've got a little time. Why don't we talk a little longer." And turning to you, he says, "Why don't you give us a rundown on the reasons for your position?" So you do. You lay it out in a way that sounds (to you) forceful and reasonable and correct.

The rest of the committee, which is now focusing rather intently on you, asks questions. It's as though you are the center of a star communication net. Everybody is turning toward you and talking to you. They are not shouting at you; they are not angry at you; they are simply asking you "rationally" to prove your position.

This goes on for a while and then people begin to get a little fidgety. Finally, one of the members turns to you and says, "Perhaps our differences aren't as big as they look. Perhaps it's all really just a matter of words. Sometimes differences that are really small begin to blow up to look like something bigger than they are." And the chairman adds, "Well, gentlemen, it is getting rather late and in the interests of getting this job done, I think we have to arrive at some kind of conclusion." Then somebody laughs, turns to you, and says, "Why don't you just come along for the ride, and then we can all go out and have a cup of coffee?"

You are no dope. You can really feel the pressure now. You know that what these people are really saying is, "You are one of us. We want to get going. Don't hold us up any longer."

But you're a tough and rugged individualist. You're a man of principle. Position Y is right, by golly, and you say so again rather forcefully. There is a long silence. Then one of the members says something forceful in reply: "Oh for Chrissakes! You've been riding that horse for about three-quarters of an hour now, and you haven't come up with a single new reason. Why the hell are you being so stubborn?" As though this first opening is a signal, others join in on the attack. People go at you from all sides. They point out that you've been wrong before when you've held out in situations like this. They attack your loyalty to the group. After all you know this group likes to operate by consensus, and that it is important to all the rest of them that you all agree. They hit you with everything they've got. Even the chairman seems to be joining in.

But still you hold out. You just can't bring yourself to accept position X when it is so patently clear to you that Y is the only reasonable answer. So there you sit thinking that this is a little like how it must feel to be interrogated by the Gestapo. Your mouth is dry and you seem to be all alone inside your own thin skin. But you've been raised right! You also think of individuality and honor. And so you grit your teeth and fight back. And the clock ticks along.

What comes next?

Pretty far down inside you, you know damn well what will come next. The floodlights will be turned off; but not to give you relief. Finally (and rather suddenly), one of the members turns to the chairman and says, "We've been at this for almost an hour and half. We have other business at hand. I think we should adopt position X, and then go on about our business." And other people turn their chairs, facing one another and the chairman; and no longer facing you. They summarize the arguments for position X and someone says, "Okay, we've decided to do X; now let's go on with the next item."

You've been quiet for the last few minutes because people haven't been talking to you. You have listened to the summary of the reasons for accepting position X, and since one of them is clearly absurd, you open your mouth to say something about it. A couple of people in the group turn and look at you as you talk, but they don't say anything in return. The others don't even look, and the chairman finally says, "Let's get on to the next problem on the agenda." And the group goes ahead.

You know what's happened. You have been psychologically amputated. As far as the group is concerned, you are no longer there. When you say things, you are no longer heard. Your influence is now zero. This is the last stage in the process by which groups deal with deviating, nonconforming members. You have been sealed off.

The story we have just told is probably reasonably familiar to almost every adult. It is not limited to committees of executives in industry. We encountered the same pressures when we were kids in the family, in street corner gangs, and in school groups. We met it again as teen-agers, when we were pressed to conform to group standards of dress and deportment—standards we often tried to resist. And we keep hitting it.

THE STAGES OF GROUP PRESSURE

But the fact that we have encountered it often doesn't make the pain and the pressure any less. In fact, our experience has taught this so well that we can foretell early in the process what we will be in for if we buck the group. We know they are likely to start out being reasonable and rational, discussing the pros and cons of the issue. But even at that stage, it is implicitly quite clear that the deviant, not the group, is expected to change.

We can sense what comes next, too. We know the seductive pat-on-the-back routine. We know that some members of the group will be friendly and smile and joke with us. They will, in effect, tell us how much they love us and remind us of how valuable the group is to us. They will behave like a woman who wants a mink coat from a man, chucking us under the chin and making up to us.

And we also know what is likely to happen if we don't come across.

Groups, like (some) women, are likely to get tired of playing games rather quickly. At some point, they will decide that they have wasted enough time on that tactic. Then the silken glove will come off to expose the iron fist. If reason won't work, and seduction won't work, then the group moves to stage 3, attack. Now they try to beat us into submission. They pull out all stops; the mask is off.

But even that isn't the last stage in the process of exerting pressure on the deviating individual. The last stage is amputation. It's as though the members of the group were saying, "Let's reason with him; if that doesn't work, let's try to tease him by emotional seduction; and if even that doesn't work, let's beat him over the head until he has to give up. Failing that, we'll excommunicate him; we'll amputate him from the group; we'll disown him."

This last and final stage is for most of us a very serious and frightening possibility; the more frightening, the more we value the group. The threat of isolation, physical or psychological, is a very grave threat indeed. We don't want to be abandoned by our families, nor by our friends, nor by our business associates.

Perhaps it is because we can foresee this ultimate stage that even mild and early pressures can often cause us to change positions or beliefs or attitudes. Most of us don't get all the way through meetings like the one we described at the beginning of this chapter. We are apt to give in a good deal earlier in the game. We "work things out" when we are still at the reasoning level or at the emotional seduction level. For the paradox in this process is that the greater the pressure the group exerts on the deviant through these steps, the more difficult it is for the deviant to give in. The state at which we can give in most easily (and still save face) is the first stage; the reasonable, rational stage. If we say "yes" in response to the chucking under the chin and the love-making, we are apt to feel a little sheepish, but that isn't terribly embarrassing. To give in under a beating is a lot more painful, and a lot weaker and more shameful. And to give in after we have been amputated is darn near impossible because nobody is there to accept our surrender.

IS THE GROUP BEING CRUEL AND CAPRICIOUS?

So far we have been viewing the group's pressures on the deviant from the deviant's perspective. For most of us the individual who holds out is the hero, whether he wins or loses. For we value individuality and nonconformity in our society, or at least we say we do. We identify with the underdog, with the deer attacked by wolves. But it is useful to view this same problem from the other perspective, that of the group. We may ask: Why are these people doing this? Why are they reasoning, seducing, attacking, amputating? Is it just a malicious, devilish kind of behavior to satisfy some sadistic needs of the group members? Not usually. If we think of the times we ourselves have been members of the majority, we can begin to see the other side of the picture.

Here is a group that is trying to get a job done. To get the job done well depends in large part on getting wholehearted agreement and cooperation from all members of the group. But there is a clock, and there are other constraints imposed by the world.

We go about the problem in good spirit, trying to cooperate, trying to understand, trying to work out a solution that we can all accept and to do it in a reasonable time. And we get very close to an answer. Everybody seems to be in perfect agreement except for that one character there.

Then what shall we do? As reasonable men, we do not steam-roller a person because he thinks differently from us. We listen to him and we ask him to listen to us. So we go through that ritual. We reason with him. But that doesn't work; he just doesn't seem to be able to see it our way. The clock is ticking away.

What next? Why then we try to appeal to him on emotional grounds, on grounds of loyalty or decency. We almost beg him to agree. This is a difficult thing for us to do, but we want to get the job done and we don't want to hurt him. We appeal to him to join up, to go along, to maintain a solid front. But he stubbornly refuses even to go with that one.

Now what? So now we hit him. Now we really are mad at him, so we let him have it. Maybe if we all jump up and down on him, he will have sense enough to come around. And the clock ticks on. But the stupid, stubborn s.o.b still holds out.

What then? Well, then we must take a step that is as painful for us as it is for him. We must dismember our group. We must amputate one of our own members, leaving us less than whole, less than intact, but at least capable of coming to a conclusion. With this recalcitrant, stubborn, impossible member, this group cannot remain a group. To preserve it, we have no choice but to cut him out.

Viewed this way, the deviant individual is not such a hero. Much of the world's complex work is done by groups. When a group exerts pressure on an individual, it may thus not constitute an arbitrary imposition of power, but rather a set of increasingly desperate efforts to try to hold the group together in order to get the work done.

DOES THE DEVIANT DO ANYBODY ANY GOOD?

Besides the argument that it is good and wholesome and healthy for individuals to be independent thinkers—an argument that is not always as sensible as it sounds—is there any other good argument for encouraging individuals to take deviant positions if they believe in them, and for encouraging groups not to clobber people who deviate?

The answer, of course, is that there is at least one very good practical reason, in addition to all the moral reasons. It is the fact that deviants stimulate groups to think about what they are working on. Deviants, whether they are themselves creative or not, generate creativity in groups.

The process is simple enough and understandable enough. When like-minded people get together to talk over an issue, they are likely to come to agreement pretty quickly and then to pat one another on the back and go out and drink beer. When the same people get together in the presence of a person with quite different ideas, they are forced to reexamine their own beliefs, to go over them in detail, to consider sides and aspects of the problem which they never had to consider before. They must do this in order to argue effectively with the deviant, in order to attack him, in order to reason with him. As a consequence, they end up knowing more about their own problem than they would have if the deviant hadn't been there. It costs the group time and sweat. But what they earn is greater understanding, broader search, more knowledge of their own subject matter.

CAN THE DEVIANT EVER WIN?

We now come to the next question in this logical sequence: Suppose the deviant is right? Does he have a chance? Or will his presence simply cause the group that is already wrong to believe more strongly but more sophisticatedly in its wrong position?

The answer to this one is rather complicated. There is rather good research evidence that people can and will distinguish better answers from worse ones. And a deviant who comes up with a clearly better answer, even in the face of a large group that has agreed upon another answer, has a very good chance of getting his answer accepted. Such is the case at least for problems with a clear logical structure. If I can demonstrate to you a clearly easier way to add a column of figures than the way all of you are now adding them, it will not be hard for me to swing you over to my method. So the deviant who comes up with a new solution—one that other people had not even thought of, but clearly a good solution—is likely to have little trouble getting it through.

Unfortunately, many problems, probably *most* problems, tackled by groups aren't quite of that nature. They are fuzzily outlined judgmental problems, in which ordering the quality of solutions is not so easy. The "normal" problems are problems like selecting or promoting personnel, or allocating funds among several departments, or deciding on a promotion. On those kinds of issues the deviant doesn't have much of a chance in most groups.

And here we encounter another paradox. The guy with the different ideas, the deviant, is apt to have a better chance of getting his ideas accepted by a group that isn't very solid, isn't very cohesive, hasn't worked together very much, than by a group that is solid, whose members do know and like one another. So the executive may find himself faced with what looks like a strange dilemma. On the one hand he wants solidity, loyalty, high morale in his group. On the other hand, he may want the creativity he can get from the deviant. And yet it is precisely the high-morale, cohesive group that will go after the deviant hard and fast; that will clobber him even more quickly than the new group or the unsure group.

But the paradox may be more apparent than real. In a way all we are saying is that the guy with different ideas may be able to pull a snow job on a bunch of people who feel shy and uncertain with one another. He has a chance of influencing them, of getting his ideas through more readily than he could in a solid group. But he is likely to get his ideas through, not because a pick-up group will examine and consider those ideas more rationally or more seriously than a solid group; but rather because they are constrained, uncertain, unwilling to open up themselves for fear of attack by others. So the aggressive deviant, the one who talks loud and fast, may be able to get to them.

On the other hand, when faced with a solid, self-assured group, the snow job is almost impossible. The deviant will have to prove his case and prove it rather thoroughly. But, of course, the probability of his being able to prove it to a group that is solid and self-assured is not very great. For they are not likely to break ranks unless the logic of the case is so clear, so rational, so obviously better than their own solutions, that only a fool could reject it.

WHAT KIND OF DEVIANT CAN SURVIVE?

Interestingly enough, even powerful deviants don't seem to have much chance against a strong and solid group. As all of us know, a member of the group who is already peripheral and uninfluential—the new, young member of a street corner gang, for example—is in a poor position to try to push a new idea through. But we are apt to think that if a man is strong and central in the group—the leader of the street corner gang—then he should be omnipotent, and capable of getting the group to accept even extremely different ideas. The fact of the matter seems to be, however, that even strong men in groups, men with authority or with personal influence and power, have a very tough time pushing a group very far from its own standards. Even the kingpin has to move slowly, by bits and pieces, to get the gang to stop stealing apples and start playing basketball. If he doesn't move slowly, he will get the same treatment as any other deviant and eventually find himself amputated.

The same thing seems to be true in industry. Even the powerful boss will meet a good deal of trouble in pushing a very different idea through a solid group of subordinates. If he is a real Machiavellian manipulator, he will work first on individuals when he is trying to bring about a radical change, rather than on the face-to-face group.

THE LONELY EXECUTIVE

It may seem a shockingly soft thing to say, but one can interpret most of the research and common-sense analysis of conformity as essentially a problem of loneliness. Group pressures can be exerted on individuals—lone individuals—much more effectively than they can be exerted on pairs or subgroups. It is when the deviant finds himself alone, without a twig of support, without even another deviant (even one who deviates in quite different directions), that the pressures of the group are apt to become overpowering. It may be this fear of isolation, of singleness, that permits a group to press the individual to conform, even if the individual has authority or other kinds of power. Even the president seems to want and need some sources of support, some assurance of psychological backing from his people. He may need very little, but he needs not to be all alone. In fact, much of the effect of group pressure can be washed out in the sort of case we talked about at the start of this chapter, by the simple expedient of having just one other member of the group back up the deviant.

Thus again we encounter a paradox. For now we are saying that it is loneliness that will force a man to conform to the group. Which implies that he will feel less pressure to conform (and therefore feel more independent) if he is in the group—a member of it—and thus not at all lonely. So how now are we to answer the earlier question: Does the group force the individual to fit into its mold, thereby reducing his individuality, thereby brainwashing him? Or is it only when he is a psychologically secure member of the group that he can express his individuality without feeling pressure and restraint?

The answer begins to become a little clearer. It seems to be true that people need psychological support, an environment free from the fear of loneliness. But if that support is bought at the price of constricting conformity, the individual loses his individuality no matter which way he goes. So the critical issue becomes the nature of the group. To what extent does it demand conformity, and on what dimensions of behavior? Does it demand, as the price of support, that he dress as they dress, that he believe as they believe? Or does it set more open standards, requiring conformity in fewer dimensions and perhaps less critical ones, requiring, perhaps, that everyone conform to certain time demands and certain demands of procedure, but consciously avoiding requirements of conformity in opinion or belief?

Since the individual needs the group, the group can exploit the individual, forcing him to bend to its demands. But individuals make groups, and it is possible to make groups that can work while exerting tolerable pressures on procedure without constraining beliefs and ideas.

IN SUMMARY

Groups put pressure on members who deviate. Usually the pressure moves through several stages, from rational argument through emotional seduction, to attack, and finally to amputation of the deviant member. But the process is not usually capricious or sadistic. From the group's side, they exert pressure in an effort to survive intact and to get the job done.

Group pressures work mostly when the deviant feels all alone. Given any kind of minimal support, he can hold out much more effectively. And though a powerful deviant has a better chance than a weak one, no deviant can try to push a solid group very far very fast and expect to get away with it.

Clearly, deviants make groups think, even when they don't change the groups' mind. But we need to temper two prevalent notions about deviation: The first is the notion that nonconformity is somehow always better than conformity. We must remember that much of the world's work can only be done by conforming to agreed-upon standards. The second is the notion that groups kill individuality by exerting pressures to conform. We need to remember that most of us feel freer to be ourselves in groups where our position and membership are secure, than in settings in which we feel alone and unsupported.

Social Power and Exchange

Social Power*

by
Paul F. Secord and Carl W. Backman

It has been shown that one can look at the totality of social interaction and select some particular attribute, such as affect or feeling. In this chapter the focus is on *social power*. Consider the relations between the following dyads: supervisor and employee, officer and soldier, parent and child, politician and voter, doctor and patient, teacher and student. All these dyads have a common feature: One member has more social power than the other. The same can be said for members of almost any group, for social power is rarely distributed evenly among members. One can also speak of the relative social power of two groups; however, this discussion will deal primarily with social power as it is manifested in interaction between two persons or among the members of small groups, because the focus of social psychology is at this level, and because research on larger units in terms of social power is scarce.

Social power is a property of a relationship between two or more persons, and is best understood in terms of exchange theory. A tentative definition of social power is that the power of person P over person O is a joint function of his capacity for affecting the outcomes of person O relative to his own outcomes. Thus, the more control P has over O's outcomes and the less adverse the effects of such control on his own outcomes, the more power he has over O. Put more simply, if P can give O a great deal at minimum cost to himself, or can use strong coercion with little cost, he is apt to have considerable power

*From *Social Psychology* (2d Edition) by Paul F. Secord and Carl W. Backman. Copyright 1974 by McGraw-Hill Book Company, Inc. Reprinted by permission of the publisher.

over O. This is a tentative and partial statement, for social power is a complex function of certain additional factors.

Social power is most often used to influence the behavior of other persons, but is conceptually distinct from influence. A person might have considerable social power but rarely exercise it. Social power does not arise directly from the personal characteristics of the individual wielding power, but is dependent on the relation between individuals and the place of that relation in the context of the larger social structure. The power of a corporation president, for example, stems primarily from the authority vested in his position which enables him to make decisions that radically affect the employees of the corporation and its functioning.

But even at a less formal level, say in interaction between two friends, the social power of each stems from certain properties of the relation between them and their relation to other persons. In a continuing relationship, each exercise of power involves an expenditure of rewards and costs by both parties, and results in specific outcomes for each. A child who gets his way with his parents by throwing a temper tantrum receives the reward he wants, but only at the cost of an emotional upheaval. The parents are relieved at resolving the emotional crisis, but incur some cost in letting the child do something they oppose. Underlying this transaction is the mutual dependency of the child on the parents (who control rewards and punishments), and the parents on the child (who want him to behave according to certain standards). This mutual dependency is at the base of the power that each has over the other. Each exercise of power involves an exchange. The more powerful person may exact compliance from the less powerful, but in return he is expected to give his good will, his approval, or some other resource.

DETERMINANTS OF SOCIAL POWER

Either explicitly or implicitly, most contemporary discussions of social power recognize three interdependent properties of a relation that determine the amount of power that individuals are able to exert in a given situation: resources, dependencies, and alternatives. A *resource* is a property or conditional state of an individual—a possession, an attribute of appearance or personality, a position he holds, or a certain way of behaving—which enables him to modify the rewards and costs experienced by another person. The value of such resources is determined primarily by the *dependency* of the other person on him. For example, the beauty of a woman is a resource only in relation to those men who are attracted by feminine beauty. The value of a resource also varies with the situation; beauty is more likely to be a resource on a date than in work as a laboratory technician where competence is at a premium. Some situations create temporary dependencies; in an emergency a group may desperately need an expert to solve a problem.

The potentialities for influence in a relation between two persons are, however, dependent on more than just the characteristics of each person and the situation. They extend beyond the dyad itself and are a function of the availability of *alternative sources* of reward and alternative means of reducing costs outside the dyad. The power of an expert, for example, depends upon the scarcity of persons with his expertise and the scarcity of sources of expert knowledge. This simple description does not exhaust the determinants of resources, dependencies, and alternatives. The following discussion identifies them in more detail.

Resources

French and Raven have delineated types of social powers, mainly according to the resources on which they are based.[1] Each type has associated with it certain rewards and costs. In addition, these investigators have shown how types of powers vary in such matters as the range of behavior subject to influence and the degree to which the exercise of power changes the balance of power between persons. These types of powers are not entirely independent and are rarely found in pure form in actual situations. Most acts of influence involve a combination of several types. Nevertheless, identifying those pure forms is a useful aid to understanding power in social relations.

Reward and Coercive Power

The first type of power is *reward power*. This type, exerted by person P on another person O, is based on the perception by O that P has the ability to provide rewards for him. A supervisor has power over an employee because the worker knows that his supervisor can recommend wage increases or perhaps even get him promoted. Similarly, a second type of power is called *coercive power*, and is based on O's perception that P has the ability to punish him. A supervisor is perceived as capable of withholding a raise or getting a worker fired.

These two types of power are similar in a number of respects. In both, the power is limited to that range of behaviors for which P can reward or punish O. The strength of both appears to be a joint function of the magnitude of the rewards or punishments involved and the perceived probabilities that these will be incurred, if one yields or does not yield to P's influence attempts. These perceived probabilities are a function of two factors. One is the extent to which O thinks he is being observed by P. The greater the surveillance by P, the more likely O is to believe that his behavior will be rewarded or punished. The other is the past history of O's relation to P. If a supervisor has seldom rewarded or punished an employee, either directly or indirectly, his reward and coercive power is likely to be weak. The effectiveness of rewards and punishments will also depend on how accurately P gauges what behaviors are rewarding or costly to O.[2] Finally, one difference between reward and coercive power should be mentioned. Thibaut and Kelley have suggested that surveillance is apt to be more difficult in the case of coercive power. Whereas persons display behavior that is apt to be rewarded, they hide behavior that leads to punishment.[3] Thus, the use of coercion by P will be more costly to him than the use of reward, since he must divert his energies from other activities to carry on the necessary surveillance.

Referent Power

Reward power has a property which coercive power lacks: It may gradually be transformed into *referent power*. Referent power is based on identification. To the degree that O is attracted to P, he will model himself after P and in that way be influenced by P's behavior. A possible explanation of this transformation of reward into referent power is that, first, the exercise of reward power by P makes him attractive to O, and second, P's attractiveness makes him an object for identification. That reward power makes P attractive is suggested by an experiment demonstrating that individuals whose power was based solely on reward were rated more favorably than those having no power or those whose power was based solely on punishment.[4] French and Raven suggest that the strength of the referent power of P over O, as well as the range of behaviors to which it applies, will vary with the attractiveness of P to O.

Another determinant of identification is the need for consensual validation. It has been previously noted that in the absence of some physical basis for assessing the validity of his opinions and feelings, a person compares his experiences with those of other persons, particularly persons similar to himself. Thus, P may influence O by providing him with a model on which to pattern his behavior and interpret his experiences. This form of power appears to be particularly effective to the degree that P is similar to O and the situation is ambiguous. Under these conditions O is especially apt to find identification with P rewarding.

While behaviors that O adopts as a result of P's referent power are initially dependent on O's relation to P, some of them may in time become independent of P. Unlike the case of reward or coercive power, the persistence of such behavior is not dependent on P's ability to observe it. In fact, unlike reward or coercive power, O may be influenced by referent power even when neither he nor P is aware of the influence, or even when they are aware and opposed to any exertion of influence. Herein lies a distinction between the powers of parents and police officers: Parental power is largely referent power, but police power is based mainly on coercion. Thus, children eventually behave well in the absence of their parents, but traffic laws are frequently broken when no policemen are around.

The comments so far have been relevant to positive referent power. P may influence O to behave oppositely to P. This phenomenon has been termed *negative referent power*.[5] Although evidence suggests that the strength of this type of power varies with the degree to which P is unattractive to O;[6] whether this form of power is analogous in other respects to its positive form is yet to be adequately demonstrated.

Expert Power

Expert power is based on O's perception that P has some special knowledge in a given situation, as in the case of a patient who is influenced by his physician to follow a particular regimen. (A more extended discussion of the determinants of expert power is given by Thibaut and Kelley.[7]) The rewards obtained by O from recognition of P's expert power involve feelings of confidence and assurance that the course of action is a correct one. Costs that can be avoided by consulting an expert are feelings of uncertainty and fear of doing the wrong thing. The strength of this type of power varies with the degree of expertness attributed by O to P. Though the power of the expert is usually limited to behavior relevant to his area of expertise, expertise in one area may give rise to expectations of proficiency in other areas as well.[8] Whether behavior induced in O by his perception of P's proficiency will persist depends upon its continued association with the advice of the expert. Continuation of P's expert power over O is not dependent, however, on the degree to which O's behavior is subject to surveillance by P. Expert power may also be lost if the expert transmits his knowledge or skill.

Legitimate Power

Legitimate power is based on the acceptance by O of internalized norms and values which prescribe behaving in a particular fashion. This may include accepting the authority of P by virtue of certain characteristics such as age, social class, or caste; by virtue of his position in some recognized hierarchy; or because he has been designated by some authority as having a legitimate right to prescribe O's behavior in one or more areas. The nature of the exchange in the exercise of legitimate power is that individuals feel satisfied when their behavior conforms to their values and norms; when their behavior does not conform, they incur costs in the form of guilt feelings. Both parties may receive rewards or punishments from outside sources.

Examples of legitimate power abound. The power held by military officers, corporation executives, governmental officials, and parents rests, in part, on legitimate power. Somewhat surprising, however, is the extent of legitimate power that resides in the experimenter-subject relation. Though it has been known for some time that college students would perform extremely boring and seemingly irrelevant tasks at the request of an experimenter, the strength of the power stemming from the experimenter's institutionalized position has been dramatically demonstrated by Milgram.[9] In his experiments, each participant administered electric shocks to another person at the request of the experimenter. Participants willingly increased the level of shocks to levels that apparently were dangerously high, even though the victim, a confederate of the experimenter, convincingly portrayed severe and increasing discomfort. The legitimacy in this situation stemmed from the position of the experimenter as a scientist from a high-prestige university, from the voluntary status of both the participant and his victim, and from various comments of the experimenter made whenever the shock giver objected to continuing, such as: "Please go on." "The experiment must go on." "It is absolutely essential that you continue."

The exercise of legitimate power may also include evoking norms which, while not explicitly requiring O to accept the influence of P, nevertheless require O to behave in a manner that favors P. A powerful norm governing the exchange process among persons is the *norm of reciprocity*.[10] This is the generally accepted idea that when a person does a favor for you, you are obligated to return it in some fashion. Where P evokes this norm requiring O to repay some past social debt, he exerts influence on O. Also widely held is the *norm of social responsibility,* which dictates that one should help other persons in need. A series of investigations has demonstrated the force of this norm.[11] To the degree that O is seen to be dependent on P, P is motivated to exert himself on O's behalf.

The continuation of behavior induced by the exercise of legitimate power depends not on its observability but on the persistence of the underlying values and norms involved. The strength of legitimate power depends upon the degree of O's adherence to the underlying norms and values. Although legitimate power may on occasion cover a broad area of behavior, more frequently it is narrow in scope. For example, while a mother may exert legitimate power over a wide range of her child's behavior, a department head in a business firm must restrict his legitimate power to job-related behavior.

Not much studied, but obviously important, is the extent to which these various powers are associated in everyday situations. Parents, for example, typically possess all five types of power over their young children. But as the children grow older, the expert, reward, and coercive powers of the parents dwindle. Ultimately, especially in adolescence, their referent power may disappear or even become negative, and their legitimate power may be vigorously challenged. Teachers have legitimate power only with respect to classroom discipline and school requirements, and are narrowly limited in their use of reward and coercive power. (As an exercise, the student might work out for himself the types of power held by policemen, judges, babysitters, and corporation executives.)

Continued Exercise of Power

An important contribution from exchange theory is that in a continuing relationship a person uses his resources to influence another only at some cost.[12] Thus, the strength of his power over another person is a function not only of his resources, but also of the cost of using them. A parent who spanks his child to get him to behave incurs the emotional cost of inflicting pain on his child. The more costly the resource is, the less net strength of P's power over O. A lover who threatens to commit suicide if his loved one deserts him is using a very costly resource, his own life, and is not likely to be effective. A legislator may have a number of favors owed to him by various other legislators, and these debts provide him with some power over their votes. But use of this power is costly; once the favors are returned, his power is lost. Thus he is likely to use them only for issues very important to him on which he expects a close vote.

The types of power differ in the extent to which they may be continually exercised and still remain effective. A change in the power relation resulting from exercise of it may occur in two ways: (1) through its effects on rewards and costs, and (2) through creation of conditions that alter the bases of power.

The first of these changes occurs because continued use of power by P over O directly affects the rewards or costs experienced. Repeated use of the same rewards by P may make them less satisfying to O as his needs become satiated. For example, as an executive's salary continues to rise, his major needs become relatively satiated, and other costs in terms of responsibility and demands upon his time continue to rise. The promise of a further salary increase is likely to be less effective as a means of control over his behavior. In contrast are other rewards which increase dependency and thus increase power. The executive may develop a strong personal tie to his superior as well as a deep involvement in the company's success.

It was noted earlier that reward power may be transformed into referent power; this transformation is an example of a change in power base resulting from the continued exercise of power. Similarly, the continued use of coercive power is likely to diminish O's feeling for P and decrease identification with him, thereby reducing P's positive referent power, or perhaps engendering negative referent power. In the latter, O would be motivated to do the opposite of what P wants. In contrast to reward and coercive power, the continued exercise of legitimate power is not apt to lead to an increase or diminution of power except where it might lead to further affirmation or to questioning of norms and values.

Blau has emphasized that the exchange of resources for compliance is governed by norms of justice which discourage exploitation on the part of the more powerful person.[13] Only when legitimate power is justly exercised does it maintain its strength or become enhanced. Expert power is not apt to be affected by continued use except where its continuation increases or decreases P's stature as an expert or results in O's picking up the knowledge upon which P's expert power is based. The use of reward or coercive power to extract public compliance without initial changes in private attitudes may, in time, bring about change of private attitudes independently of future reward or punishment contingencies.[14]

Status as a Resource

Though the preceding discussion of resources suggests that the power of P over O always rests on some attribute of P which is objectively related to O's satisfaction, this is not always the case. Resources that make P powerful in one situation may maintain his power even in another situation where they are irrelevant.[15] Thus, a wealthy businessman or a distinguished statesman may find that people accede readily to his requests in nonbusiness or nonpolitical situations. Similarly, a person may acquire superior power because of such characteristics as age or beauty, which manifestly are unrelated to performance in many situations.

Summary: Resources

A resource is a property or conditional state of an individual—a possession, an aspect of his behavior, or merely his presence—which enables him to affect the rewards and costs experienced by another person. The value of a resource is not determined by the individual alone, but also by the dependency of the other person on him.

Five types of powers have been distinguished, each based on somewhat different resources. The first is *reward power,* based upon the perception by O that P can directly or indirectly reward him. The second, *coercive power,* is the counterpart of reward power and is based on O's perception that P can directly or indirectly punish him. Both of these kinds of power apply only to the behavior that P can reward or punish, and their strength is a joint function of the strength of the reward or punishment and the probability that it will be incurred. Reward power, however, has a property which coercive power lacks: It may gradually be transformed into a third type of power, referent power. *Referent power* is based on the mechanism of identification. Unlike reward and coercive power, it does not require continued surveillance of O by P in order to ensure conformity of O's behavior to P's wishes. A fourth type of power, *expert power,* stems from special knowledge P has which O needs. Fifth, *legitimate power* is based on the acceptance by O of internalized norms and values which dictate that he accept influence from P.

These types of power differ in the extent to which they may be continually exercised and still remain effective. They also interact in their effects; one form may augment or reduce the effects of another. A change in the power relation resulting from continued exercise may occur in two ways: (1) through its direct effects on rewards and costs and (2) through creation of conditions that alter the bases of power. Thus, the continual use of certain kinds of rewards may lead to satiation or, conversely, to increased dependency. The continued exercise of power may produce changes in identification, in norms and values, or in expert knowledge, similarly altering the power bases.

From the viewpoint of exchange theory, each exercise of power is an exchange of rewards and costs. Resources may be interpreted in such terms, and exchange theory will be useful in the treatment of power processes later in the chapter.

Dependencies

The behavior or other characteristics of a person constitute a resource only if they satisfy another person. An understanding of why person P is able to influence O requires as much knowledge of O's dependencies as of P's resources. Such dependencies may have their source in characteristics of the individual or the situation, or in some combination of both. Characteristics of a person take the form of social needs or other attributes that make the resources of P especially valuable to him. For example, a person with a strong need for approval and emotional support will be dependent on those persons who can provide it.

Children are apparently dependent on the friendliness and helpfulness of other children. A study of power in children's groups suggests that children whose behavior facilitates the gratification of the social-emotional needs of other children have high power in a group. The investigator summarizes his results as follows:

> "The data show that the higher power children are in fact more friendly as a group, more likely to be helpful to their peers, and more able in terms of their psychological adjustments to be outgoing in social relationships, while the low power children as a group are quite different, and are, for example, more likely to use physical force as a method of attempting to influence their peers and more likely to manifest behavior symptoms of deeper lying disturbances."[16]

That this principle is not restricted to children's groups is suggested by another study.[17] The investigators found that characteristics associated with high power in a group of boys aged twelve to fourteen were also generally found among adult women. For boys, the order in which characteristics were associated with high power was: helpfulness, fairness, sociability, expertness, fearlessness, and physical strength. For the women, the order of the items was the same except that fairness was placed before helpfulness.

The more frequently situations call for a particular resource, the more dependent on that resource an individual is apt to be. The finding that fearlessness and physical strength were not attributed to power figures by boys or women was explained by the fact that relatively few situations call for these resources. Ability to satisfy social-emotional needs is a much more important resource, as noted in the previous chapter in the discussion of characteristics of individuals with high sociometric choice status. The discussion revealed a high correlation between popularity and social power, particularly in small, informal groups, where satisfaction of social-emotional needs is dominant.

Alternatives

Power is determined not only by the resources of P and the dependency of O on P, but also by the consequence of not complying. O compares his reward-cost outcome for compliance with that for noncompliance. The greater the disparity between these outcomes, the greater P's power over O. Essentially this disparity is a function of the alternatives available to O. If O has a resource in sufficient quantity himself, or if he may gain the resource at lower cost in relations with persons other than P, it will be relatively ineffective as a source of P's power over O. This is most obvious in the case of expert power: The expert influences others by his possession of scarce knowledge. If everyone were an expert (a contradiction in terms), the expert would be powerless.

The consequences of not complying have a special significance when P's influence attempt is based upon threats. One possibility is that P will not carry out his threat anyhow. Thus, the extent to which P's threat is convincing affects the power that P has over O. One of the most interesting forms of threats, that which is based on the promise of mutual harm, has been analyzed intensively by Schelling.[18] A union may threaten a strike costly to itself if management does not raise wages a few cents. A furious driver may threaten to smash another car with his own if the right of way is not yielded. The mutual dependence of each person on the other's actions is nicely illustrated in the game of "chicken," shown in matrix form in the Figure. Such matrices are very useful in clarifying exchange-theory application. Schelling notes that in these instances P really does not have much incentive to carry out the threat, because of its cost to himself. In the case of such threats, power appears to vary with the extent to which P can make O believe that he is committed to carry out the threat. A driver may speed up so that a collision cannot be avoided unless the other party yields the right of way. Any means by which P gives up his control over the exercise of the threat is a strategy likely to secure his power. A favorite of crime writers is the blackmailer who deposits a damaging secret paper

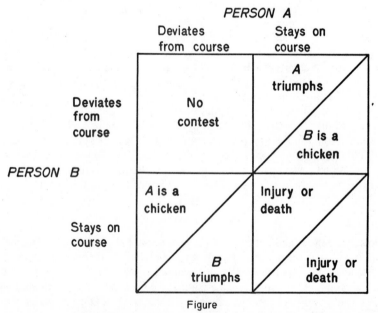

Figure

Exchange outcomes of two persons playing the game of "chicken." The four possible outcomes for A and B are shown to be a joint function of their choices.

with another person unknown to O, with instructions to release it in the event of his death.

POWER PROCESSES

The previous discussion emphasized that we must not think of power as an attribute of a person. The exercise of power is a function of characteristics of both the influencer and the influencee, as well as of other people in the situation. But the analysis must be carried still further: power must be examined in the context of ongoing interaction processes.

From the point of view of exchange theory, a conception of power as a process whereby one person causes changes in the behavior of another is inadequate because it ignores the symmetry implied by the notion of exchange. Not one but both persons are influencing and being influenced. They are exchanging behaviors that result in their experiencing certain costs and certain rewards. What is exchanged differs depending upon the type of power exercised. When an employee complies with his supervisor's legitimate requests, he receives continued approval in exchange. Behind this approval, of course, lies the power of the supervisor to facilitate or retard the employee's advancement. If power is based upon identification, the identifier obtains psychic satisfaction in modeling his behavior after that of the model.

If it is true that each person is influencing the other, why do we view one person as more powerful? The answer lies in the nature of the *bargain* made between the two persons. That person is more powerful who receives rather valuable behavior from the other in exchange for behavior that he is able to produce at low cost. A nod of approval for an arduous task well done illustrates the disparity in what each person gives. Another way of stating it is that the higher-power person can affect the outcomes experienced by the lower-power person to a greater extent.

Elements of Power Processes

Emerson has delineated a number of power processes. He defines power as follows: "Power (PAB), the power of actor B, is the amount of resistance on the part of B which can be potentially overcome by A." This power lies in B's dependency on A, which is determined by the variables in the following proposition: "Dependency (DBA), the dependency of actor B upon actor A is (a) directly proportional to B's *motivational investment* in goals mediated by A, and (b) inversely proportional to the *availability* of these goals to B outside of the A-B relation."[19] Thus, as previously emphasized, power is a function not only of A's resources, but also of B's dependencies and alternatives.

Since both parties in a relation have varying degrees of power over the other, Emerson demonstrates that a power-dependence relation between A and B can be described as a pair of equations:

$$PAB = DBA$$
$$PBA = DAB$$

These may be translated as follows: The power that A has over B is equal to the dependency of B on A. Similarly, the power that B is capable of exercising over A is equal to A's dependency on B.

Power relations described in this manner may vary in two independent ways. First, they may vary in the degree to which each person is capable of exercising power relative to the other. This depends on the strength of the dependencies that exist between the two persons. They may be relatively independent, as in the case of two casual acquaintances neither of whom has much influence over the other, or highly dependent, as in the case of lovers each of whom has the power to strongly affect the outcomes of the other. A second manner in which power relations may vary is in the degree of equality that exists between the two persons. Emerson characterizes a relation as balanced where, regardless of the degree or level of dependency, the parties hold equal power over each other. In terms of his equations this is represented as follows:

$$PAB = DBA$$
$$\|\qquad\|$$
$$PBA = DAB$$

A relation is described as unbalanced when one actor has greater power than the other. Symbolically this could be represented as:

$$PAB = DBA$$
$$\lor\qquad\lor$$
$$PBA = DAB$$

In this instance, the power of A over B (PAB) is greater than the power of B over A (PBA) because the dependency of B on A (DBA) is greater than A's dependency on B (DAB).

Consequences of High but Equal Power: Balanced Relations

Where both members of a pair have high power over each other, each person's power might appear to be balanced by the counterpower of the other, thereby producing a minimum of mutual influence. It would seem that each person, being highly dependent on the other, would be reluctant to make demands, since the other could impose equally costly counter-demands or interfere with his gratification by breaking off the relation. One might further suppose that the potentiality for conflict in such a situation would be great. Yet everyday observation, as well as more systematic evidence, suggests that persons who are close friends exercise considerable influence on each other and at the same time maintain amicable relations.[20] This occurs because certain arrangements emerge to facilitate influence without conflict.

In one such arrangement, the two parties assign different values to various activities. Norms are established dictating that in one situation, one party will give way, and in another situation, the other will give way. For example, a pair of friends whose preferences differ may agree to go ice-skating one week and to play tennis the next. In a second type of arrangement, norms dictate some alternation of advantage, as when two children equally powerful and equally motivated to play with a particular toy agree to take turns. Many of the rules of "fairness" have as their function the avoidance of costs arising out of power struggles. Third, since two persons are unlikely to be precisely equal in power, conflict may be avoided by the regular acquiescence of the less powerful member. The parties themselves may not be aware of a condition of slight inequality, and hence the stronger of the two is unlikely to get his way all the time.

Modes of Resolving Imbalance

Emerson has argued that an unbalanced relation is unstable since it encourages the use of power, which in turn sets into motion processes that he has called cost-reduction and balancing operations.[21] These are illustrated in the following hypothetical example.

Consider a man and a woman who have been having a love affair. Suppose that, in its current stage, the interest of one party (designated P) has lessened somewhat, while the interest of the other party (O) remains sustained. In that case, the power of P over O is greater than that of O over P. If P uses this power differential, P may be less punctual for appointments, may have more conflicting engagements and more unaccounted-for weekends, and may occasionally see someone else.

These actions greatly raise the psychological costs of O. But O may reduce these costs somewhat by making excuses for P's behavior or by attributing the causes of it to inadvertent failings in O's own actions. This resolution does not reduce O's power disadvantage. A second solution helps to restore balance: O may redefine the relation as a nonserious, temporary one, and occasionally date other persons. This *partial withdrawal* from the relation reduces O's dependency on P, possibly to the point where it is equal to that of P on O.

Complete withdrawal from a relation occurs when the costs incurred by the less powerful member result in a reward-cost outcome that is below some alternative, including the alternative of no relation at all. In a voluntary relation, this places a limit on the degree to which the more powerful member of a party may exploit the less powerful.

The process of partial withdrawal is one of four balancing operations in which inequality can be corrected. In the second balancing operation, *forming alternative relations* (termed by Emerson *extending the power network*), the dependency of one party is also decreased so that it is equal to that of the other.

In the case cited above, for example, O might develop a satisfying relation with someone other than P.

The third and fourth balancing operations require more discussion, since they are related to a number of features of process and structure in interaction. Emerson derives the phenomenon of *status* or *differential evaluation* from the third balancing operation. The status given to the more powerful member is a source of satisfaction to him *which is provided by the less powerful person.* As the more powerful member becomes increasingly motivated to achieve positive evaluation from the less powerful, his dependency on the latter is increased and the power discrepancy between the two is decreased. Abuse of power on the part of the more powerful is discouraged by the prospect that such behavior will lead to loss of status.

The fourth balancing operation involves a process that has received considerable attention: *coalition formation.*[22] Ever since the observations of Georg Simmel in this regard, investigators have been intrigued with the tendency in three-person groups for a pattern to emerge which consists of a pair and a third party.[23] Emerson views this as a model of the process leading to the emergence of norms which ensure group functioning against the disruptive effects of abuse of power. The power of each member is restricted by the potential combination of other members that constrains him to behave in conformity to a norm.

It is difficult to illustrate this point, since such norms are an integral part of every group situation. They only become visible when they are violated. Even in newly formed groups, members are guided by norms (such as those of courtesy) which control unrestricted use of power and which have been developed in other group contexts. Yet during a crisis created by an overuse of power, this process of coalition formation may be readily observed, as when workers combine and demand that a boss agree to rules restricting the requests that he can make of them. Perhaps a clearer illustration is the instance where two children threaten not to play with a third unless he stops being so bossy. In situations where the male has a dominant role in relation to subordinate females, and where he might thereby exploit the relation for sexual purposes, norms placing limits on his power hold him in check. This is illustrated by norms against dating and other forms of association between a male supervisor and a female worker or between a male teacher and a female student.

One final point not made by Emerson might be included. In general, continued interaction between two persons will increase the motivational investment of each in the goals mediated by the other *in the direction of greater equality* unless there are certain safeguards against this process. This might occur for a number of reasons. Outcomes of each member of a dyad increase with continued interaction because each person becomes increasingly adept at providing and motivated to provide rewards to the other, and they provide them with less cost. But because the higher-power member is able to exact more from the relation, his dependency increases at a more rapid rate. The lower-power member provides rewards at greater cost, and ultimately may feel the burden too onerous. Accordingly, the balance of power moves toward equality. In addition, increased interaction between members of a pair decreases both the degree of dependency on and the availability of relations with other persons. These processes, together with the inertia inherent in human relations, go far to explain the continuation of a relation which appears, to the outsider at least, to be an exploitative one.

Maintenance of Power Differences

Where it is essential for power differences to be maintained, various features of the social structure operate to discourage the development of mutual dependency. In the military, officers and enlisted men are segregated to some extent and a degree of formality is maintained in their relations, as illustrated by the salute and the use of titles and last names. Similarly, in business organizations, high executives erect a variety of barriers between themselves and their underlings, such as separate lunchrooms and rest rooms. The most common form of dependency that threatens to develop between superiors and subordinates is friendship, which would upset the power differential required if the organization is to function properly. Other mechanisms with a similar function arise in other relations requiring a power differential, such as the teacher-student relation and the officer-soldier relation. In all these situations it is essential for the achievement of organizational goals that the more powerful person retain the power of decision and control of the relation.

Perception of Power

Power is such a pervasive and vital aspect of interaction that most persons seem to be quite sensitive to the facts about power. There is some systematic evidence that most people perceive fairly accurately the power structure in a group and their own relative position in the structure, and further, that their behavior toward other persons is consistent with such perceptions. In a study of power in two boys' camps, boys were found to perceive accurately the relative power of group members, including their own.[24] Furthermore, the frequency and character of the attempts of each boy to influence another person were consistent with these perceptions. Boys who perceived themselves as high in power made more attempts to influence others and in one camp were more directive in these attempts. A study of Air Force enlisted men solving laboratory problems provides similar evidence.[25] The amount of influence attempted by an airman was proportional to the extent that he was liked and accepted by the person he influenced.

Perhaps more striking are the results of another study.[26] The perception of the relative power of partners working together on a task was experimentally varied over a series of joint decision-making trials. Individuals were given different initial perceptions of their own resources and of their task ability relative to the partner, and the partner (who actually was the experimenter's assistant) varied the degree to which he accepted or rejected the naive participant's attempts to influence him. Variations in initial information and in the feedback of information from the partner were expected to produce corresponding variations in the participant's perceived power, and he was expected to behave in accordance with his perceived power. For example, if he believed his power was low, he was expected to reduce his influence attempts, to decrease his refusals to concede to his partner, and to reveal less confidence when speaking to him. These hypotheses were confirmed. In particular, whether the partner acquiesced to or resisted influence attempts appeared to be the most important determinant of the perception of power and of power-relevant behavior.

Summary: Power Processes

When the exercise of power is examined in the context of interaction, a number of features are seen to be associated with it. Each exercise is an exchange between persons, often an asymmetrical exchange of behavior varying in value to each party. Power is seen to be a direct function of the dependency of O upon P. The greater O's dependency, the stronger P's power over O. Dependencies may be mutual or balanced, or they may be disparate and unbalanced, with one member of the pair being considerably more dependent. This type of imbalanced situation often leads to efforts to redress the balance. Such balancing operations include withdrawing from the relation, forming an alternative relation, increasing the status and resultant dependency of the higher-power person, and forming a coalition. Balancing does not always occur: Elements of the social structure operate to maintain differences in power.

END NOTES

1. French, J.R.P., Jr., & B.H. Raven. The basis of social power. In D. Carlwright (Ed.), *Studies in social power*. Ann Arbor, Mich.: University of Michigan Press, 1959.

2. Collins, B.E., & B.H. Raven. Psychological aspects of structure in small groups: Interpersonal attraction, coalitions, communication and power. In G. Lindsey & E. Aronson (Eds.) *Handbook of Social Psychology*. Vol. 4. Reading, Mass., Addison-Wesley Publishing Company, Inc., 1969, 102–204.

3. Thibaut, J.W., & H.H. Kelley. *The social psychology of groups*. New York: John Wiley & Sons, Inc., 1959.

4. Brigante, T.R. Adolescent evaluations of rewarding, neutral, and punishing power figures. *Journal of Personality* 1958, 26, 435–450.

5. Collins, B.E., & B.H. Raven. Psychological aspects of structure in small groups: Interpersonal attraction, coalitions, communication and power. In G. Lindsey & E. Aronson (Eds.) *Handbook of Social Psychology*. Vol. 4. Reading, Mass., Addison-Wesley Publishing Company, Inc., 1969, 102–204.

6. Osgood, C.E., & P.H. Tannenbaum. The principle of congruity in the prediction of attitude change. Psychological Review, 1955, 62, 42–55. Also in E.E. Sampson (Ed.), *Approaches, contexts, and problems of social psychology*. Englewood Cliffs, N.J.: Prentice-Hall, Inc., 1964, Pp. 237–248.

7. Thibaut, J.W., & H.H. Kelley. *The social psychology of groups*. New York: John Wiley & Sons, Inc., 1959.

8. Allen, V.L., & R.S. Crutchfield. Generalization of experimentally reinforced conformity. *Journal of Abnormal and Social Psychology*, 1963, 67, 326–333.

9. Milgram, S. Behavioral study of obedience. *Journal of Abnormal and Social Psychology*, 1963, 67, 371–378.

Mixon, D. Instead of deception. *Journal for the Theory of Social Behaviour,* October 1972, 2, 145–177.

10. Couldner, A.W. The norm of reciprocity: A preliminary statement. *American Sociological Review,* 1960, 25, 161–178.

Blau, P.M. Justice in social exchange. *Sociological Inquiry,* 1964, 34, 193–206. (b)

11. Berkowitz, L., & L.R. Daniels. Responsibility and dependency. *Journal of Abnormal and Social Psychology,* 1963, 66, 429, 436.

Berkowitz, L., & L.R. Daniels. Affecting the salience of the social responsibility norm: Effects of past help on the response to dependency relationships. *Journal of Abnormal and Social Psychology,* 1964, 68, 275–281.

Berkowitz, L., S.B. Klanderman, & R. Harris. Effects of experimenter awareness and sex of subject and experimenter on reactions to dependency relationship. *Sociometry,* 1964, 27, 327–337.

Schopler, J., & N. Bateson. The power of dependence. *Journal of Personality and Social Psychology,* 1965, 2, 247–254.

Goranson, R.E., & L. Berkowitz. Reciprocity and Responsibility reactions to prior help. *Journal of Personality and Social Psychology,* 1966, 3(2), 227–232.

12. Harsanyi, J.C. Measurement of social power, opportunity costs, and the theory of two-person bargaining games. *Behavioral Science,* 1962, 7, 67–80.

13. Blau, P.M. *Exchange and power in social life.* New York: John Wiley & Sons, Inc., 1964. (a)

14. Collins, B.E., & B.H. Raven. Psychological aspects of structure in small groups: Interpersonal attraction, coalitions, communication and power. In G. Lindsey & E. Aronson (Eds.) *Handbook of Social Psychology.* Vol 4. Reading, Mass., Addison-Wesley Publishing Company, Inc., 1969, 102–204.

15. Berger, J.B., P. Cohen, & M. Zelditch, Jr. Status characteristics and expectation states. In J. Berger, M. Zelditch, & B. Anderson (Eds.), *Sociological theories in progress.* Vol. 1. Boston: Houghton Mifflin Company, 1966.

16. Gold, M. Power in the classroom. *Sociometry,* 1958, 21, 50–60.

17. Rosen, S., G. Levinger, & R. Lippitt. Perceived sources of social power. *Journal of Abnormal and Social Psychology,* 1961, 62, 439–441.

18. Schelling, T.C. *The strategy of conflict.* Cambridge, Mass.: Harvard University Press, 1960.

19. Emerson, R.M. Power-dependence relations. *American Sociological Review,* 1962, 27, 31–41.

20. Back, K.W. Influence through social communication. *Journal of Abnormal and Social Psychology,* 1951, 46, 9–23.

21. Emerson, R. M. Power-dependence relations. *American Sociological Review,* 1962, 27, 31–41.

22. Mills, T.M. Power relations in three-person groups. *American Sociological Review,* 1953, 18, 351–357.

Mills, T.M. The coalition pattern in three-person groups. *American Sociological Review,* 1954, 19, 657–667.

Mills, T.M. Developmental processes in three-person groups. *Human Relations,* 1956, 9, 343–354.

Caplow, T. A theory of coalitions in the triad. *American Sociological Review,* 1956, 21, 489–493.

Vinacke, W.E., & A. Arkoss. An experimental study of coalitions in the triad. *American Sociological Review,* 1957, 22, 406–414.

Gamson, W.A. Experimental studies of coalition formation. In L. Berkowitz (Ed.), *Advances in experimental social psychology.* Vol. 1, New York: Academic Press, Inc., 1964, Pp. 81–110.

23. Simmel, G. *The sociology of Georg Simmel*. Translated by Kurt H. Wolff. Glencoe, Ill.: The Free Press, 1950.

24. Lippitt, R., N. Polansky, F. Redl, & S. Rosen. The dynamics of power. *Human Relations*, 1952, 5, 37–64.

25. French, J.R.P., Jr., & R. Snyder. Leadership and interpersonal power. In D. Cartwright (Ed.), *Studies in Social Power*. Ann Arbor: The University of Michigan Press, 1959, Pp. 150–165.

26. Levinger, G. The development of perceptions and behavior in newly formed social power relationships. In D. Cartwright (Ed.), *Studies in Social Power*. Ann Arbor: The University of Michigan Press, 1959, Pp. 83–98.

Sources of Power of Lower
Participants in Complex Organizations*

by
David Mechanic

It is not unusual for lower participants[1] in complex organizations to assume and wield considerable power and influence not associated with their formally defined positions within these organizations. In sociological terms they have considerable personal power but no authority. Such personal power is often attained, for example, by executive secretaries and accountants in business firms, by attendants in mental hospitals, and even by inmates in prisons. The personal power achieved by these lower participants does not necessarily result from unique personal characteristics, although these may be relevant, but results rather from particular aspects of their location within their organizations.

INFORMAL VERSUS FORMAL POWER

Within organizations the distribution of authority (institutionalized power) is closely if not perfectly correlated with the prestige of positions. Those who have argued for the independence of these variables[2] have taken their examples from diverse organizations and do not deal with situations where power is clearly comparable.[3] Thus when Bierstedt argues that Einstein had prestige but no power, and the policeman power but no prestige, it is apparent that he is comparing categories that are not comparable. Generally persons occupying high-ranking positions within organizations have more authority than those holding low-ranking positions.

One might ask what characterizes high-ranking positions within organizations. What is most evident, perhaps, is that lower participants recognize the

---

*From *Administrative Science Quarterly*, Vol. 7, No. 3 (December, 1962), pp. 349–64. Reprinted by permission of the publisher.

right of higher-ranking participants to exercise power, and yield without difficulty to demands they regard as legitimate. Moreover, persons in high-ranking positions tend to have considerable access and control over information and persons both within and outside the organization, and to instrumentalities or resources. Although higher supervisory personnel may be isolated from the task activities of lower participants, they maintain access to them through formally established intermediary positions and exercise control through intermediary participants. There appears, therefore, to be a clear correlation between the prestige of positions within organizations and the extent to which they offer access to information, persons, and instrumentalities.

Since formal organizations tend to structure lines of access and communication, access should be a clue to institutional prestige. Yet access depends on variables other than those controlled by the formal structure of an organization, and this often makes the informal power structure that develops within organizations somewhat incongruent with the formally intended plan. It is these variables that allow work groups to limit production through norms that contravene the goals of the larger organization, that allow hospital attendants to thwart changes in the structure of a hospital, and that allow prison inmates to exercise some control over prison guards. Organizations, in a sense, are continuously at the mercy of their lower participants, and it is this fact that makes organizational power structure especially interesting to the sociologist and social psychologist.

Clarification of Definitions

The purpose of this paper is to present some hypotheses explaining why lower participants in organizations can often assume and wield considerable power which is not associated with their positions as formally defined within these organizations. For the purposes of this analysis the concepts "influence," "power," and "control" will be used synonymously. Moreover, we shall not be concerned with type of power, that is, whether the power is based on reward, punishment, identification, power to veto, or whatever.[4] Power will be defined as any force that results in behavior that would not have occurred if the force had not been present. We have defined power as a force rather than a relationship because it appears that much of what we mean by power is encompassed by the normative framework of an organization, and thus any analysis of power must take into consideration the power of norms as well as persons.

I shall also argue, following Thibaut and Kelley,[5] that power is closely related to dependence. To the extent that a person is dependent on another, he is potentially subject to the other person's power. Within organizations one makes others dependent upon him by controlling access to information, persons, and instrumentalities, which I shall define as follows:

a. Information includes knowledge of the organization, knowledge about persons, knowledge of the norms, procedures, techniques, and so forth.

b. Persons include anyone within the organization or anyone outside the organization upon whom the organization is in some way dependent.

c. Instrumentalities include any aspect of the physical plant of the organization or its resources (equipment, machines, money, and so on).

Power is a function not only of the extent to which a person controls information, persons, and instrumentalities, but also of the importance of the various attributes he controls.[6]

Finally, following Dahl,[7] we shall agree that comparisons of power among persons should, as far as possible, utilize comparable units. Thus we shall strive for clarification by attempting to oversimplify organizational processes; the goal is to set up a number of hypothetical statements of the relationship between variables taken two at a time, "all other factors being assumed to remain constant."

A Classic Example

Like many other aspects of organizational theory, one can find a classic statement of our problem in Weber's discussion of the political bureaucracy. Weber indicated the extent to which bureaucrats may have considerable power over political incumbents, as a result, in part, of their permanence within the political bureaucracy, as contrasted to public officials, who are replaced rather frequently.[8] Weber noted how the low-ranking bureaucrat becomes familiar with the organization—its rules and operations, the work flow, and so on, which gives him considerable power over the new political incumbent, who might have higher rank but is not as familiar with the organization. While Weber does not directly state the point, his analysis suggests that bureaucratic performance has some relationship to increased access to persons, information, and instrumentalities. To state the hypothesis suggested somewhat more formally:

H1 Other factors remaining constant, organizational power is related to access to persons, information, and instrumentalities.

H2 Other factors remaining constant, as a participant's length of time in an organization increases, he has increased access to persons, information, and instrumentalities.

While these hypotheses are obvious, they do suggest that a careful scrutiny of the organizational literature, especially that dealing with the power or counterpower of lower participants, might lead to further formalized statements, some considerably less obvious than the ones stated. This kind of hypothesis formation is treated later in the paper, but at this point I would like to place the discussion of power within a larger theoretical context and discuss the relevance of role theory to the study of power processes.

IMPLICATIONS OF ROLE THEORY FOR THE STUDY OF POWER

There are many points of departure for the study of power processes within organizations. An investigator might view influence in terms of its sources and strategies; he might undertake a study of the flow of influence; he might concentrate on the structure of organizations, seeing to what extent regularities in behavior might be explained through the study of norms, roles, and traditions; and, finally, more psychological oriented investigators might concentrate on the recipients of influence and the factors affecting susceptibility to influence attempts. Each of these points of departure leads to different theoretical emphases. For our purposes the most important emphasis is that presented by role theorists.

Role theorists approach the question of influence and power in terms of the behavioral regularities which result from established identities within specific social contexts like families, hospitals, and business firms. The underlying premise of most role theorists is that a large proportion of all behavior is brought about through socialization within specific organizations, and much behavior is routine and established through learning the traditional modes of adaptation in dealing with specific tasks. Thus the positions persons occupy in an organization account for much of their behavior. Norms and roles serve as mediating forces in influence processes.

While role theorists have argued much about vocabulary, the basic premises underlying their thought have been rather consistent. The argument is essentially that knowledge of one's identity or social position is a powerful index of the expectations such a person is likely to face in various social situations. Since behavior tends to be highly correlated with expectations, prediction of behavior is therefore possible. The approach of role theorists to the study of behavior within organizations is of particular merit in that it provides a consistent set of concepts which is useful analytically in describing recruitment, socialization, interaction, and personality, as well as the formal structure of organizations. Thus the concept of role is one of the few concepts clearly linking social structure, social process, and social character.

Many problems pertaining to role theory have been raised. At times it is not clear whether role is regarded as a real entity, a theoretical construct, or both. Moreover, Gross has raised the issue of role consensus, that is, the extent to which the expectations impinging upon a position are held in common by persons occupying reciprocal positions to the one in question.[9] Merton has attempted to deal with inevitable inconsistencies in expectations of role occupants by introducing the concept of role-set which treats differences in expectations as resulting, in part, from the fact that any position is differently related to a number of reciprocal positions.[10] Furthermore, Goffman has criticized role theory for its failure to deal adequately with commitment to roles[11]—a factor which Etzioni has found to be related intimately to the kind of power exercised in organizations.[12] Perhaps these various criticisms directed at role theory reflect its importance as well as its deficiencies, and despite the difficulties involved in role analysis, the concept of role may prove useful in various ways.

Role theory is useful in emphasizing the extent to which influence and power can be exercised without conflict. This occurs when power is integrated with a legitimate order, when sentiments are held in common, and when there are adequate mechanisms for introducing persons into the system and training them to recognize, accept, and value the legitimacy of control within the organization. By providing the conditions whereby participants within an organization may internalize the norms, these generalized rules, values, and sentiments serve as substitutes for interpersonal influence and make the workings of the organization more agreeable and pleasant for all.

It should be clear that lower participants will be more likely to circumvent higher authority, other factors remaining constant, when the mandates of those in power, if not the authority itself, are regarded as illegitimate. Thus as Etzioni points out, when lower participants become alienated from the organization, coercive power is likely to be required if its formal mandates are to be fulfilled.[13]

Moreover, all organizations must maintain control over lower participants. To the extent that lower participants fail to recognize the legitimacy of power, or believe that sanctions cannot or will not be exercised when violations occur, the organization loses, to some extent, its ability to control their behavior. Moreover, insofar as higher participants can create the impression that they can or will exert sanctions above their actual willingness to use such sanctions, control over lower participants will increase. It is usually to the advantage of an organization to externalize and impersonalize controls, however, and if possible to develop positive sentiments toward its rules.

In other words, an effective organization can control its participants in such a way as to make it hardly perceivable that it exercises the control that it does. It seeks commitment from lower participants, and when commitment is obtained, surveillance can be relaxed. On the other hand, when the power of lower participants in organizations is considered, it often appears to be clearly divorced from the traditions, norms, and goals and sentiments of the organization as a whole. Lower participants do not usually achieve control by using the role structure of the organization, but rather by circumventing, sabotaging, and manipulating it.

SOURCES OF POWER OF LOWER PARTICIPANTS

The most effective way for lower participants to achieve power is to obtain, maintain, and control access to persons, information, and instrumentalities. To the extent that this can be accomplished, lower participants make higher-ranking participants dependent upon them. Thus dependence together with the manipulation of the dependency relationship is the key to the power of lower participants.

A number of examples can be cited which illustrate the preceding point. Scheff, for example, reports on the failure of a state mental hospital to bring about intended reform because of the opposition of hospital attendants.[14] He noted that the power of hospital attendants was largely a result of the dependence of ward physicians on attendants. This dependence resulted from the physician's short tenure, his lack of interest in administration, and the large amount of administrative responsibility he had to assume. An implicit trading agreement developed between physicians and attendants, whereby attendants would take on some of the responsibilities and obligations of the ward physician in return for increased power in decision-making processes concerning patients. Failure of the ward physician to honor his part of the agreement resulted in information being withheld, disobedience, lack of cooperation, and unwillingness of the attendants to serve as a barrier between the physician and a ward full of patients demanding attention and recognition. When the attendant withheld cooperation, the physician had difficulty in making a graceful entrance and departure from the ward, in handling necessary paper work (officially his responsibility), and in obtaining information needed to deal adequately with daily treatment and behavior problems. When attendants opposed change, they could wield influence by refusing to assume responsibilities officially assigned to the physician.

Similarly, Sykes describes the dependence of prison guards on inmates and the power obtained by inmates over guards.[15] He suggests that although guards could report inmates for disobedience, frequent reports would give prison officials the impression that the guard was unable to command obedience. The guard, therefore, had some stake in ensuring the good behavior of prisoners without use of formal sanctions against them. The result was a trading agreement whereby the guard allowed violations of certain rules in return for cooperative behavior. A similar situation is found in respect to officers in the Armed Services or foremen in industry. To the extent that they require formal sanctions to bring about cooperation, they are usually perceived by their superiors as less valuable to the organization. For a good leader is expected to command obedience, at least, if not commitment.

FACTORS AFFECTING POWER

Expertise

Increasing specialization and organizational growth has made the expert or staff person important. The expert maintains power because high-ranking persons in the organization are dependent upon him for his special skills and access to certain kinds of information. One possible reason for lawyers obtaining many high governmental offices is that they are likely to have access to rather specialized but highly important means to organizational goals.[16]

We can state these ideas in hypotheses, as follows:

H3 Other factors remaining constant, to the extent that a low-ranking participant has important expert knowledge not available to high-ranking participants, he is likely to have power over them.

Power stemming from expertise, however, is likely to be limited unless it is difficult to replace the expert. This leads to two further hypotheses:

H4 Other factors remaining constant, a person difficult to replace will have greater power than a person easily replaceable.

H5 Other factors remaining constant, experts will be more difficult to replace than nonexperts.

While persons having expertise are likely to be fairly high-ranking participants in an organization, the same hypotheses that explain the power of lower participants are relevant in explaining the comparative power positions of intermediate- and high-ranking persons.

The application of our hypothesis about expertise is clearly relevant if we look at certain organizational issues. For example, the merits of medical versus lay hospital administrators are often debated. It should be clear, however, that all other factors remaining unchanged, the medical administrator has clear advantage over the lay administrator. Where lay administrators receive preference, there is an implicit assumption that the lay person is better at administrative duties. This may be empirically valid but is not necessarily so. The special expert knowledge of the medical administrator stems from his ability legitimately to oppose a physician who contests an administrative decision on the basis of medical necessity. Usually hospitals are viewed primarily as universalistic in orientation both by the general public and most of their participants. Thus medical necessity usually takes precedence over management policies, a factor contributing to the poor financial position of most hospitals. The lay administrator is not in a position to contest such claims independently, since he usually lacks the basis for evaluation of the medical problems involved and also lacks official recognition of his competence to make such decisions. If the lay administrator is to evaluate these claims adequately on the basis of professional necessity, he must have a group of medical consultants or a committee of medical men to serve as a buffer between medical staff and the lay administration.

As a result of growing specialization, expertise is increasingly important in organizations. As the complexity of organizational tasks increases, and as organizations grow in size, there is a limit to responsibility that can be efficiently exercised by one person. Delegation of responsibility occurs, experts and specialists are brought in to provide information and research, and the higher participants become dependent upon them. Experts have tremendous potentialities for power by withholding information, providing incorrect information, and so on, and to the extent that experts are dissatisfied, the probability of organizational sabotage increases.

Effort and Interest

The extent to which lower participants may exercise power depends in part on their willingness to exert effort in areas where higher-ranking participants are often reluctant to participate. Effort exerted is directly related to the degree of interest one has in an area.

  H6 Other factors remaining constant, there is a direct relationship between the amount of effort a person is willing to exert in an area and the power he can command.

For example, secretarial staffs in universities often have power to make decisions about the purchase and allocation of supplies, the allocation of their services, the scheduling of classes, and, at times, the disposition of student complaints. Such control may in some instances lead to sanctions against a professor by polite reluctance to furnish supplies, ignoring his preferences for the scheduling of classes, and giving others preference in the allocation of services. While the power to make such decisions may easily be removed from the jurisdiction of the lower participant, it can only be accomplished at a cost—the willingness to allocate time and effort to the decisions dealing with these matters. To the extent that responsibilities are delegated to lower participants, a certain degree of power is likely to accompany the responsibility. Also, should the lower participant see his perceived rights in jeopardy, he may sabotage the system in various ways.

Let us visualize a hypothetical situation where a department concludes that secretarial services are being allocated on a prejudicial basis as a result of complaints to the chairman of the department by several of the younger faculty. Let us also assume that, when the complaint is investigated, it is found to be substantially correct; that is, some of the younger faculty have difficulty obtaining secretarial services because of preferences among the secretarial staff. If in attempting to eliminate discretion by the secretarial staff, the chairman establishes a rule ordering the allocation of services on the basis of the order in which work appears, the rule can easily be made ineffective by complete conformity to it. Deadlines for papers, examinations, and the like will occur, and flexibility in the allocation of services is required if these deadlines are to be met. Thus the need for flexibility can be made to conflict with the rule by a staff usually not untalented in such operations.

When an organization gives discretion to lower participants, it is usually trading the power of discretion for needed flexibility. The cost of constant surveillance is too high, and the effort required too great; it is very often much easier for all concerned to allow the secretary discretion in return for cooperation and not too great an abuse of power.

H7 Other factors remaining constant, the less effort and interest higher-ranking participants are willing to devote to a task, the more likely are lower participants to obtain power relevant to this task.

Attractiveness

Another personal attribute associated with the power of low-ranking persons in an organization is attractiveness or what some call "personality." People who are viewed as attractive are more likely to obtain access to persons, and, once such access is gained, they may be more likely to succeed in promoting a cause. But once again dependence is the key to the power of attractiveness, for whether a person is dependent upon another for a service he provides, or for approval or affection, what is most relevant is the relational bond which is highly valued.

H8 Other factors remaining constant, the more attractive a person, the more likely he is to obtain access to persons and control over these persons.

Location and Position

In any organization the person's location in physical space and position in social space are important factors influencing access to persons, information, and instrumentalities.[17] Propinquity affects the opportunities for interaction, as well as one's position within a communication network. Although these are somewhat separate factors, we shall refer to their combined effect as centrality[18] within the organization.

H9 Other factors remaining constant, the more central a person is in an organization, the greater is his access to persons, information, and instrumentalities.

Some low participants may have great centrality within an organization. An executive's or university president's secretary not only has access, but often controls access in making appointments and scheduling events. Although she may have no great formal authority, she may have considerable power.

Coalitions

It should be clear that the variables we are considering are at different levels of analysis; some of them define attributes of persons, while others define attributes of communication and organization. Power processes within organizations are particularly interesting in that there are many channels of power and ways of achieving it.

In complex organizations different occupational groups attend to different functions, each group often maintaining its own power structure within the organization. Thus hospitals have administrators, medical personnel, nursing personnel, attendants, maintenance personnel, laboratory personnel, and so on. Universities, similarly, have teaching personnel, research personnel, administrative personnel, maintenance personnel, and so on. Each of these functional tasks within organizations often becomes the sphere of a particular group that controls activities relating to the task. While these tasks usually are coordinated at the highest levels of the organization, they often are not coordinated at intermediate and lower levels. It is not unusual, however, for coalitions to form among lower participants in these multiple structures. A secretary may know the man who manages the supply of stores, or the person assigning parking stickers. Such acquaintances may give her the ability to handle informally certain needs that would be more time-consuming and difficult to handle formally. Her ability to provide services informally makes higher-ranking participants in some degree dependent upon her, thereby giving her power, which increases her ability to bargain on issues important to her.

Rules

In organizations with complex power structures lower participants can use their knowledge of the norms of the organization to thwart attempted change. In discussing the various functions of bureaucratic rules, Gouldner maintains that such rules serve as excellent substitutes for surveillance, since surveillance in addition to being expensive in time and effort arouses considerable hostility and antagonism.[19] Moreover, he argues, rules are a functional equivalent for direct, personally given orders, since they specify the obligations of workers to do things in specific ways. Standardized rules, in addition, allow simple screening of violations, facilitate remote control, and to some extent legitimize punishment when the rule is violated. The worker who violates a bureaucratic rule has little recourse to the excuse that he did not know what was expected, as he might claim for a direct order. Finally, Gouldner argues that rules are "the 'chips' to which the company staked the supervisors and which they could use to play the game";[20] that is, rules established a punishment which could be withheld, and this facilitated the supervisors' bargaining power with lower participants.

While Gouldner emphasizes the functional characteristics of rules within an organization, it should be clear that full compliance to all the rules at all times will probably be dysfunctional for the organization. Complete and apathetic compliance may do everything but facilitate achievement of organizational goals. Lower participants who are familiar with an organization and its rules can often find rules to support their contention that they not do what they have been asked to do, and rules are also often a rationalization for inaction on their part. The following of rules becomes especially complex when associations and unions become involved, for there are then two sets of rules to which the participant can appeal.

What is suggested is that rules may be chips for everyone concerned in the game. Rules become the "chips" through which the bargaining process is maintained. Scheff, as noted earlier, observed that attendants in mental hospitals often took on responsibilities assigned legally to the ward physician, and when attendants refused to share these responsibilities the physician's position became extremely difficult.[21]

The ward physician is legally responsible for the care and treatment of each ward patient. This responsibility requires attention to a host of details. Medicine, seclusion, sedation and transfer orders, for example, require the doctor's signature. Tranquilizers are particularly troublesome in this regard since they require frequent adjustment of dosage in order to get the desired effects. The physician's order is required to each change in dosage. With 150 patients under his care on tranquilizers, and several changes of dosages a week desirable, the physician could spend a major portion of his ward time in dealing with this single detail.

Given the time-consuming formal chores of the physician, and his many other duties, he usually worked out an arrangement with the ward personnel, particularly the charge (supervisory attendant), to handle these duties. On several wards, the charge called specific problems to the doctor's attention, and the two of them, in effect, would have a consultation. The charge actually made most of the decisions concerning dosage change in the back wards. Since the doctor delegated portions of his formal responsibilities to the charge, he was dependent on her good will toward him. If she withheld her cooperation, the physician had absolutely no recourse but to do all the work himself.[22]

In a sense such delegation of responsibility involves a consideration of reward and cost, whereby the decision to be made involves a question of what is more valuable—to retain control over an area, or to delegate one's work to lower participants.

There are occasions, of course, when rules are regarded as illegitimate by lower participants, and they may disregard them. Gouldner observed that, in the mine, men felt they could resist authority in a situation involving danger to themselves.[23] They did not feel that they could legitimately be ordered to do anything that would endanger their lives. It is probably significant that in extremely dangerous situations organizations are more likely to rely on commitment to work than on authority. Even within non-voluntary groups dangerous tasks are regarded usually as requiring task commitment, and it is likely that commitment is a much more powerful organizational force than coercive authority.

SUMMARY

The preceding remarks are general ones, and they are assumed to be in part true of all types of organizations. But power relationships in organizations are likely to be molded by the type of organization being considered, the nature of organizational goals, the ideology of organizational decision making, the kind of commitment participants have to the organization, the formal structure of the organization, and so on. In short, we have attempted to discuss power processes within organizations in a manner somewhat divorced from other major organizational processes. We have emphasized variables affecting control of access to persons, information, and facilities within organizations. Normative definitions, perception of legitimacy, exchange, and coalitions have all been viewed in relation to power processes. Moreover, we have dealt with some attributes of persons related to power; commitment, effort, interest, willingness to use power, skills, attractiveness, and so on. And we have discussed some other variables: time, centrality, complexity of power structure, and replaceability of persons. It appears that these variables help to account in part for power exercised by lower participants in organizations.

END NOTES AND REFERENCES

1. The term "lower participants" comes from Amitai Etzioni, *A Comparative Analysis of Complex Organizations* (New York, 1961) and is used by him to designate persons in positions of lower rank: employees, rank-and-file, members, clients, customers, and inmates. We shall use the term in this paper in a relative sense denoting position vis-a-vis a higher-ranking participant.

2. Robert Bierstedt, An Analysis of Social Power, *American Sociological Review*, 15 (1950), 730–738.

3. Robert A. Dahl, The Concept of Power, *Behavioral Science*, 2 (1957), 201–215.

4. One might observe, for example, that the power of lower participants is based primarily on the ability to "veto" or punish. For a discussion of bases of power, see John R.P. French, Jr., and Bertram Raven, "The Bases of Social Power," in D. Cartwright and A. Zander, eds., *Group Dynamics* (Evanston, Ill., 1960), pp. 607–623.

5. John Thibaut and Harold H. Kelley, *The Social Psychology of Groups* (New York, 1959). For a similar emphasis on dependence, see Richard M. Emerson, Power-Dependence Relationships, *American Sociological Review*, 27 (1962), 31–41.

6. Although this paper will not attempt to explain how access may be measured, the author feels confident that the hypotheses concerned with access are clearly testable.

7. *Op. cit.*

8. Max Weber, "The Essentials of Bureaucratic Organization: An Ideal-Type Construction," in Robert Merton et al., *Reader in Bureaucracy* (Glencoe, Ill., 1952), pp. 18–27.

9. Neal Gross, Ward S. Mason, and Alexander W. McEachern, *Explorations in Role Analysis* (New York, 1958).

10. Robert Merton, The Role-Set: Problems in Sociological Theory, *British Journal of Sociology,* 8 (1957), 106–120.

11. Erving Goffman, *Encounters* (Indianapolis, Ind., 1961), pp. 85–152.

12. Etzioni, *op. cit.*

13. *Ibid.*

14. Thomas J. Scheff, Control over Policy by Attendants in a Mental Hospital, *Journal of Health and Human Behavior,* 2 (1961), 93–105.

15. Gresham M. Sykes, "The Corruption of Authority and Rehabilitation," in A. Etzioni, ed., *Company Organizations* (New York, 1961), pp. 191–197.

16. As an example, it appears that 6 members of the cabinet, 30 important sub-cabinet officials, 63 senators, and 230 congressmen are lawyers (*New Yorker,* April 14, 1962, p. 62). Although one can cite many reasons for lawyers holding political posts, an important one appears to be their legal expertise.

17. There is considerable data showing the powerful effect of propinquity on communication. For summary, see Thibaut and Kelley, *op. cit.,* pp. 39–42.

18. The concept of centrality is generally used in a more technical sense in the work of Bavelas, Shaw, Gilchrist, and others. For example, Bavelas defines the central region of a structure as the class of all cells with the smallest distance between one cell and any other cell in the structure, with distance measured in link units. Thus the most central position in a pattern is the position closest to all others. Cf. Harold Leavitt, "Some Effects of Certain Communication Patterns on Group Performance," in E. Maccoby, T.N. Newcomb, and E.L. Hartley, eds., *Readings in Social Psychology* (New York, 1958), p. 559.

19. Alvin W. Gouldner, *Patterns of Industrial Bureaucracy* (Glencoe, Ill, 1954).

20. *Ibid.,* p. 173.

21. Scheff, *op. cit.*

22. *Ibid.,* p. 97.

23. Gouldner, *op. cit.*

A Transactional Approach to Leadership*

by
Dr. T.O. Jacobs

One of the persistent themes that characterized the trait approach to leadership was the belief that leaders and followers were basically different in some way. Viewed in perspective, it really makes little difference whether the basic nature of these differences resides in personality characteristics (traits) or in behavior styles. When leadership research moved from a study of leader behavior, it moved only a little in terms of advancing leadership theory. The one major advantage in studying behavior was that behavior could be observed, whereas traits could not be. However, there still was a basic assumption that leaders and followers were different, though this assumption had not been clearly demonstrated to be true.

The importance of this assumption is demonstrated by an examination of how a group would look if it were true. Figure 1 shows two possible ways of looking at group composition. The first assumes a dichotomy between leaders and followers, where members of the group are able to differentiate among themselves as to who the leaders are. Since leaders are considerably less numerous than followers, a pyramid results, with the followers constituting the base of the pyramid.

There is evidence that this is not a correct model (Hollander, 1959). One study (Hollander and Webb, 1955) dealt with peer nominations on three topics: friendship, perceived value as follower, and perceived value as leader. This study was specifically designed to test whether followership and

*Extracted from Jacobs, T.O. *Leadership and Exchange in Formal Organizations,* (pp. 96–122), Alexandria: HumRRO, 1971.

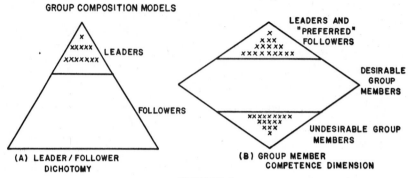

FIGURE 1

leadership are actually opposites. Subjects were naval cadets in their last week of training. Each cadet was asked to assume that he was assigned to a special unit with an undisclosed mission. He was then asked to name the three persons, in order, from his unit whom he considered best qualified to lead the unit, and, similarly, the three least qualified. On the followership form, he was asked to assume that he was the leader of the unit, and to select the three men from his section whom he would most like to have in his unit, and the three whom he would least want. Each cadet was asked to name three other cadets from his section whom he considered his best friends.

Analysis of the data from this study yielded the correlations shown in Table 1. Two features of this table are noteworthy. First, there is a very high relationship between leadership and followership, almost the maximum strength such a relationship can have. This means that a cadet who was nominated as a leader was also very likely to be nominated as a follower. Further, the strength of the relationship indicates that, with few exceptions, it is probable that the same cadets were chosen on both questions in approximately the same order. However, the relationship between friendship and either followership or leadership is not nearly as strong.

These findings show clearly that the more desired followers tend to be at the upper end of the distribution of desired leaders. Leaders and highly preferred followers are the same people. Further, the choice of leader or follower

Table 1

RELATIONSHIPS BETWEEN LEADERSHIP,
FOLLOWERSHIP, AND FRIENDSHIP[a]

Role	Followership	Friendship
Leadership	.92	.47
Followership		.55

[a]After Hollander and Webb (1955)

is not determined by friendship choice. This, of course, suggests that the pyramid model is not correct. In contrast, some other model, perhaps like the diamond shown as Part B of Figure 1, is more realistic.

The interpretation of these findings (Hollander, 1959) is that the underlying basis for choice as either leader or follower is individual competence at group tasks. When group members perceive that a given member has competence, he is esteemed by them and, other things being equal, acquires status in the group. These and similar findings have led to the development of an important theoretical approach to understanding how status develops within group structures (Hollander, 1956). (For present purposes, status can be regarded as synonymous with leadership status.)[1]

Figure 2 illustrates how status develops within a group. Motivation to belong to a group, in the first place, is thought to be of two kinds; to satisfy needs external to the group itself (e.g., status satisfaction from fraternity membership) or intrinsic (e.g., association and social approval of other group members, or participation in group's focal activity). To the extent that one or the other of these two is stronger for a person, his choice of group may be governed by the emphasis of available groups. Some groups may emphasize social interaction to a greater extent, while other groups may emphasize a specific kind of activity. As an example, one might contrast an informal group that regularly engages in a variety of social activities with a group that is focused toward a type of activity where task competence is a variable, such as a bridge club or a work group in a formal organization. The individual's motivation to belong to the group depends largely on the group's attractiveness, which is termed idiosyncrasy credit (Hollander, 1956). This produces a certain and the prospective member's needs.

A member's behavior while in the group is determined partly by his competence at the kind of activity on which the group is concentrating, and

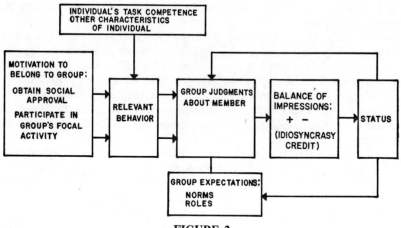

FIGURE 2

partly by his other characteristics, such as personality. The key element of this model is that other group members continually make evaluative judgments about the adequacy of his behavior. These judgments of adequacy are based, to a major extent, on whether his behavior has conformed to their expectations of what it should have been.

Two kinds of expectations exist. One consists of norms, which are expectations held by each group member for all other group members. For example, most groups have a norm (set of general expectations) which limits the amount of negative emotional behavior that will be tolerated between group members; a group member who exceeds this limit is likely to be punished. The second kind of expectation consists of roles, specific either to individuals or to defined positions in the group. For example, the group leader is expected, among other things, to represent his group well to other groups. Group members need to feel proud of their leader, and therefore expect him to behave in a way that will justify their pride. If he does not, he will be less well accepted and respected as a leader.

To the extent that a group member conforms to expectations, and contributes toward the accomplishment of the group's goal, the group's judgments about him will be positive. To the extent this is not true, they will be negative. According to this theory, each group member accumulates a balance, which is termed idiosyncrasy credit (Hollander, 1956). This produces a certain status within the group for that member, which is quite similar to a summary evaluation of his judged worth to the group in comparison with other members. Knowledge of the member's status, in turn, influences subsequent judgments the group makes about him and, in addition, may influence the expectations they have of him and the role he should play in the group. For example, a group member who demonstrates a substantial level of skill in a group task will, other things being equal, rise in status within the group. This may modify expectations, in that group members may then expect that he will continue to make noteworthy contributions toward goal attainment, and may be disappointed if he does not—although they would not have been disappointed before the rise in status occurred.

Idiosyncrasy credit, according to this theory, is very much like a bank balance. A group member who has accumulated a substantial positive "balance" is valued by other group members, has high status within the group, and is generally free to vary his behavior from the group's expectations to some degree, without apparent penalty. This is particularly true when his deviations violate relatively noncritical norms rather than, as in the case of the leader, role expectations that are considered by group members to be an important part of his job.

If this model of leadership status is correct, it would be predicted that a newcomer to an established group or a member of a new group would not initially have a "credit balance," but would need to develop one over a period of time. This has been found to be true (Hollander, 1959). This study tested the prediction that in problem solving groups, a task-competent member who deviates from procedural norms of the group early in the life of the group will have lower influence, while a task-competent member who initially conforms, and then deviates at a later time, will not have diminished influence. This, of course, is a graphic illustration of the meaning of idiosyncrasy credit. An individual who has accumulated a positive "balance" then has freedom to deviate because of that balance.

The group task in this study was to maximize the value of a series of 15 choices. For each one, the decision as to the nature of the choice was to be announced by the group after a three-minute discussion. Unknown to the other subjects, one of the group was a confederate of the experimenter and provided two effects. First, he knew the correct answer and announced it on all but four of the 15 choices. If the group had always followed his suggestions, it would have received a maximum payoff on all but those four choices.

The second effect introduced by the confederate was nonconformity to some of the rules by which the group operated. This nonconformity occurred either throughout the experimental session, in some of the trials but not all of them, or in none of them. It consisted of violating rules, such as majority rule would hold, group members would speak in turn, or winnings would be shared equally. When the confederate was scheduled to nonconform, he would speak out of turn, challenge the choice of another group member, or comment that majority rule was perhaps not working too well. The measure of influence was how many times the group accepted his suggestion as to what the choice should be for the group as a whole.

The findings indicated that early nonconformity had a significant effect on the number of times the confederate's suggestion was accepted, though nonconformity at a later time did not. An accumulated credit balance apparently was effective in protecting the confederate against loss of influence as a consequence of violation of procedural norms. However, just being correct did not lead to the development of influence potential when accompanied from the outset by deviation.

At the end of the problem, all subjects were asked to rate each other on overall contributions to the group activity. On this rating, 44 of the 48 subjects rated the confederate first and 45 of the 48 rated him first on an item relating to influence over the group's decision. This strong unanimity of opinion existed despite significant differences in the acceptance of his suggestions during the experiment itself. Observations of the behavior of subjects during the experiment supported these findings. In groups in which the confederate's nonconforming behavior appeared late, his behavior was accepted without question. For example, when he suggested, as he sometimes did, that majority rule was faulty, this suggestion was often rubber-stamped. However, when he had failed to conform from the beginning, such suggestions more often led to his being censured by other group members.

These findings provide clear support for the idiosyncrasy credit view of how leadership status develops, and underscore the essentially transactional basis for such status. If this theory is correct, a member's position in the group is determined by the extent of the contribution he can make to the group's success in achieving goals. The more capability he can bring to the group, the more effectively the group can accomplish its purposes. Since all members then benefit, all share in the results of his efforts. He therefore is of unique value to the group as a whole, and is esteemed by them as a valuable resource. This is the source of his idiosyncrasy credit balance, and his status within the group.

This analysis produces an interesting corollary, which is also important in its relationship to the emphasis of organizational psychologists, and others, on the importance of group goals as a determiner of properties of the group itself. Idiosyncrasy credit theory probably applies much more strongly to task-oriented groups than to socially oriented groups. In groups characterized as primarily "socially minded," a member probably will be more likely to achieve status through being well liked.

However, results in accordance with idiosyncrasy credit theory have not always been obtained. In one such study (Wiggins, Dill, and Schwartz, 1965), groups of undergraduate students were told that they were in competition with another group for a $50 prize. The task was one in which each of its four members was working on five tasks which were to be graded. "Cheating" was punished by subtracting a certain number of points from the group total. The experimental treatment was the report that one of the group's members had cheated, causing the group to lose a certain number of points. In one condition, a large number of points was subtracted, in another a medium number of points, and in a third condition only a few points. The status of the offending group member was manipulated by reporting that his score (contribution to the group's overall success) was either high, intermediate, or low. Thus, high, medium, and low status members caused their respective groups to lose a high, medium, and low number of points.

At the end of the experiment, the members were asked to rank every other person in the group on a scale from 1 to 5 indicating strong "like" to strong "dislike." Key findings from this study are shown in Table 2.

A high status subject who caused a high point loss for his group was disliked considerably more than high status subjects who caused medium or low point losses to their group, and were also disliked more than medium status subjects who had caused an equally high point loss. In contrast, medium status subjects were disliked more than high status subjects when they had caused

Table 2
AVERAGE LIKE—DISLIKE SCORES[a]

Status of Fictitious Subject	Point Loss to Group		
	High	Medium	Low
High	4.8	2.6	2.0
Medium	3.8	3.7	2.9

[a]High scores indicate less liking. From Wiggins, Dill, and Schwartz (1965).

medium and low point losses. (Low status subjects were omitted from the analysis by the original authors.)

Disregarding the high status subject who caused a high point loss to his group, these results conform to what would have been predicted from idiosyncrasy credit theory. High status subjects, who achieved their status by contributing more to the overall success of the group, were more likely to be excused by their groups for having transgressed than were medium status subjects who had contributed less. However, the very substantial reduction in liking for high status subjects with high point losses to their groups is not in conformity with idiosyncrasy status theory.

Another study (Alvarez, 1968) produced a similar conclusion. In this study, groups of 10 persons were used, one of whom was a confederate of the experimenter. These groups met for one-hour work sessions on each of four consecutive days. The confederate was assigned as an intermediate supervisor in some groups and as a worker in others. The task was to generate creative ideas for the manufacture of greeting cards.

The confederate was instructed to make a certain proportion of his task-relevant behaviors violate specific task instructions and general social standards in the work setting. He was instructed to direct aggression first toward higher officials in the synthetic organization, and then toward both them and his fellow workers. Some groups were told they were successful while others were told they were not doing well. The criterion consisted of ratings made by other group members of one another, at the end of each daily meeting.

Table 3 shows ratings by other group members of the experimenter's confederate on each of the four trials of the experiment. While the experimenter did not perform statistical tests on his data, it appears that two predictions from idiosyncrasy credit theory are not borne out. First, the higher status confederate, who occupied the intermediate supervisory position, theoretically should not have incurred as much loss in esteem as the lower status worker. However, the average loss for the confederates acting as supervisors was about the same as that for the two groups of worker confederates. Second, the confederate in the supervisor's role in an unsuccessful group appears to have lost more esteem than that of the confederate in a supervisor's role in successful groups. Idiosyncrasy credit theory does not seem to provide for this finding either.[2]

Taken together, these studies, and others conducted by Hollander, seem to confirm most of the provisions of idiosyncrasy credit theory, but at the same time indicate that the theory may not be quite sufficient as it presently stands. Apparently, a leader's peculiarities, or idiosyncrasies, are tolerated by his followers only as long as they themselves do not incur a resulting cost. This is shown by the experiments in which leaders did not suffer a loss of group member esteem when the groups were successful despite the leader's behavior. On the other hand, when group members do incur a cost, they may react in a disapproving or punishing manner, that may appear almost excessive in degree. It is almost as though the leader is being measured against a standard of what leaders in general should do, and then is punished for failure to meet

Table 3

EFFECTS OF CONFEDERATE STATUS AND GROUP SUCCESS ON
GROUP REACTIONS TO CONFEDERATES NONCONFORMING

	Group Success			
	Successful Confederate Status		Unsuccessful Confederate Status	
	Supervisor	Worker	Supervisor	Worker
1	210	218	237	212
2	212	180	195	222
3	151	174	206	217
4	163	150	170	177
1–4	47[a]	68[a]	67[a]	35[a]

[a]Number of points difference between fourth trial rating—less favorable in all cases—and first trial rating.

this standard in proportion to the status of the position in the group he occupies. In this view, the position of the leader is one that brings high rewards if he is successful, and high costs if he is not, with the criterion in both cases being, to a large extent, whether the group as a whole is successful.

This set of conclusions clearly supports the idiosyncrasy model when groups are successful, but apparently does not under conditions of group failure. They consequently indicate a need for a more comprehensive approach that will deal adequately with both sets of conditions, or a modification in idiosyncrasy theory that will enable it to deal with group failure conditions more adequately.

SOCIAL EXCHANGE THEORY

In exchange theory, a central question is why a group member subordinates himself to someone of higher status, the leader. If this occurred only in formal organizations with appointed leaders, it might not be necessary to have more than a superficial answer. However, it is commonly observed that informal groups almost inevitably also have status hierarchies with leaders, provided, of course, the members of these groups have shared goals (as will be seen later, this is a necessary condition).

Homans (1958) has been given credit for having first conceptualized communication and interaction within groups as an exchange process, suggesting adoption of the view that interaction between persons constitutes an exchange of goods, both material and nonmaterial.[3] In its simplest form, social behavior requires at least two persons. In Homans' view, assuming the interaction is regarded as desirable by both, the behavior each produces toward the other is rewarding in some way. At its most basic level, such behavior might consist of a compliment, an expression of agreement, or even assistance in performing some task of mutual interest.

Some social exchange behaviors are produced at a cost, and some are essentially cost-free. For example, a compliment usually "costs" little or nothing, especially if it is an accurate compliment and does not tacitly admit that the giver of the compliment could not have earned an equal one. To compliment someone's choice of a tie, or pair of shoes, is an example. There are other behaviors that may produce a real, and sometimes substantial "cost." For example, the behavior involved in a game may be viewed as social exchange. Assuming the game is of mutual pleasure to the players, each player rewards the others by participating in the game with them. However, for some players a substantial "cost" comes from playing the game—they lose, and losing is a "cost."

One important aspect of social exchange theory is that it proposes to regard social behavior in terms of the relative costs and benefits to participants, under the assumption that each individual seeks to maximize his benefits and to reduce his costs. Thus, in a game situation, some players might find the "cost" too great. This would occur when one player or one team is sufficiently strong that he, or the team, will always win. Since there is a "cost" associated with losing, it would be expected that the player or team which always loses would eventually decide to stop playing. This does, indeed, conform to common-sense observation.

Leadership can be viewed in exactly the same frame of reference. As Hollander and Julian (1969) note, the person in the role of leader fulfills certain expectations that his group members have, in general, for leaders. Examples of these expectations are that the leader represent the group in relation to other groups, facilitate the accomplishment of group goals, coordinate group effort, and so on. These activities usually require an unusual level of competence and a balance of skills of different types, so outstanding leaders are almost always in demand and are highly valued by their groups. Because they can provide unique services for their groups, it becomes worthwhile for the groups to provide them with unique and large rewards in the form of status, esteem, and influence. The more valuable the leaders are to their groups, the larger their rewards may be.

As long as the leader is successful—defined by the fact that under his direction his group is successful—group members may have little reason to protest, regardless of what his non-task relevant behavior is. Even though his behavior may be "unusual" or in violation of a goal, and the leader's direction results in the attainment of the goal, the group members are getting a "fair bargain." That is, they do what the leader says and, as a result, the group succeeds. The exchange is more efficient and/or effective attainment of group goals is exchanged for compliance with the leader's directives.

When the group fails to achieve its objectives, quite a different situation prevails. Under conditions of failure, if the leader has conformed well to what was expected of him, and the group's failure can be attributed to chance or uncontrollable circumstances, he apparently is not particularly blamed for the group's failure, and may retain his influence within the group. In contrast, when the leader has behaved at variance with group member expectations or with "the rules of the game," and group members can reasonably blame the group's failure on his particular failure to conform, then there apparently is a substantial negative reaction toward him. It probably is in proportion to the benefits they gave him, such as esteem and status, which he did not fairly reciprocate in guiding the group toward success.

The extent of this negative reaction is probably in proportion to either (a) the group's judgment of inequity in the exchange—the value of the status they accorded the leader in comparison with the returns he provided the group, or (b) their estimate of the value of the benefits they would have achieved had the leader not violated norms or role expectations. If it is the latter, then a ready explanation exists for the extreme reaction that can exist against a leader who through nonconformity, has cost the group members a highly desired benefit or reward.

In all probability, as will be seen later, both processes are operative, the question of which is the more important in a given situation being based on group members' judgments as to the effort expended by the leader for the group. If this judgment is high, reactions toward the unsuccessful leader probably are based more on an evaluation of the degree of inequity in the exchange, and will not tend to be extreme, though replacement of the leader (or non-support) may eventually occur.

Nonconformity, however, is a different matter. It tends to be seen as behavior that serves selfish motives. Group members may therefore judge that a nonconforming leader has put his own interests ahead of those of the group. When this results in group failure, with attendant costs to themselves, reactions against the leader can become extreme. They will not be nearly as extreme, and may not even be negative, when the leader continues to produce success, because in this case the group members continue to receive the rewards of group success—that is, the leader has still kept his part of the "bargain."

This suggests the need for a small (but crucial) change in, or departure from, idiosyncrasy theory. The implication is that the judgments of group members about their leaders—and one another—are made in terms of the criterion of successful accomplishment of group goals, weighted by their estimate of the value of those goals to themselves, and perhaps secondarily by the degree of status the leader actually presumed for himself in relation to other members of the group. In conformity to idiosyncrasy theory, these evaluations are presumed to be based at least in part on social learning that has occurred at a prior time, which has led to the development of general expectations not only for what leaders can and should do, but also for what is fair exchange for that behavior.

If these implications are correct, it follows that a comprehensive theory of leadership should take into account this early learning, the kinds of expectations that arise from it, and basic social exchange processes that lead to their development.

The Development of Social Exchange

According to current sociological thought,[4] it is possible to understand social structure and events that occur within social structures, such as leadership, by looking first at individual processes that occur between people, and building on them. Social exchange theory attempts to do just that: use individual interaction processes between persons as a basis for understanding more complex social behavior within group structures.

The most fundamental interaction between people, according to this orientation, is interaction that tends to be reciprocated and leads to mutual attraction as a consequence of the mutually satisfying nature of the exchange. This satisfaction can take quite simple forms, and, with many persons, can consist of the mere presence of an agreeable or attractive other person.

The need for association with others is a fundamental need in normal humans, probably in all cultures, though some have the need to a greater degree than others. In all probability it is a learning need, derived from early experiences, such as that of the infant experiencing satisfaction of his own physical needs in association with the presence of other humans. Indeed, there is evidence that the comfort derived from being held by others, such as a parent holding a baby, or other close physical contact, may be necessary for normal development (Harlow, 1958; Harlow and Suomi, 1970). Further, it may be this need that produces the learned need for the presence of others in contrast to the physiological basis for satisfaction of needs such as hunger.

It is probable that the ability to engage in successful social exchange at later ages is developed from the learned need for the presence of others. As physical needs are satisfied, always in the presence of others, the mere presence of others becomes rewarding. However, other learning is made possible by the learned need for the presence of others. As a consequence of this need, the infant learns to discriminate times when he is not in the presence of others from those times when he is. When others are absent, and the derived need for their presence becomes strong enough, the infant will engage in behavior of various types (e.g., crying, "cooing," etc.), some of which will eventually be found to attract the attention of adults (or others), and result in their presence. This behavior will then have been learned, through the process of instrumental learning.

As further learning occurs, the infant, and later the child, learns to discriminate between behavior that both attracts and results in approval, as opposed to attracting and resulting in disapproval. Another stage in the child's life is marked by these behaviors that serve the function of both attracting favorable attention and obtaining approval. (Approval is discriminated from disapproval because the parent typically does especially "nice" things for or to the infant/child when the infant/child has done something that is "approved," and often just the reverse for disapproved behaviors.)

It is probably in this way that the child learns to seek approval by others, and this, in turn, becomes one of the individual's basic goals in the social exchange process. It also serves as one of the motivating forces that bring individuals together in social groups, and one of the types of satisfactions that members of groups in formal organizations derive from their group membership. It is one of the "rewards" that make worthwhile those performances that earn the privilege of group membership.

There is more learning that occurs at an early age as the child learns to compete with other children for the presence/approval of another child, and also learns how to dominate, or establish primitive power relationships. These also are essential to the development of mature social exchange skills.

As a child first engages in social behavior with other children, he continues the basically selfish (self-oriented) behavior that had become his pattern with adults. However, he finds that other children are engaging in the same types of behaviors toward him. The result is that neither he nor the others approve, though each is seeking approval, and additional learning of a trial-and-error sort is necessary. This consists, in the main, of learning that he can do things that will attract other children to him, and win their approval as well. Of course, these things consist of behaviors that reward others in some way. Once a child has learned the principle of rewarding others in order to win their approval and, better still, to elicit specific desired behaviors from them, he has mastered the basics of social exchange.

Such behaviors are so elementary and commonplace that they almost escape notice as significant elements of social learning. Examples might consist of allowing another child to play with a favorite toy for a short while, sharing some candy, or even just smiling at the other child. The most difficult part of this learning is for the first few instances to occur and be associated with a stable attraction/approval response from the other child. When this has occurred, the child will have learned to exchange "favors" for needed approval and association with other children.

The discussion of social exchange behavior is begun at the level of the infant and the small child for two reasons. First, it is at this level that the simplest forms of social exchange occur. Second, it is at this level that the social learning underlying the development of more mature social exchange behavior occurs. In all probability an understanding of the learning processes itself is important for the leader who must understand not only what he is doing, but also why he is doing it.

Several important principles may be derived that are fundamental and worthy of emphasis.

(1) Social exchange behavior is derived from the fundamental learned need to experience the presence of others, and to obtain their approval.

(2) The most basic form of social exchange behavior consists of behaviors that reward others in some way, and the most elementary of these are behaviors that indicate approval.

(3) Derived from the exchange process, at an early time, is the expectation that rewards will accrue from benefits provided, that is, that benefits or "favors" will be reciprocated.

(4) There is a principle of marginal return in which a little of a scarce

benefit will offset a lot of a benefit that is not scarce, and in which providing more of a type of benefit of which a lot already exists is not very rewarding.

(5) There is a strong tendency to get the most one can for the benefits he provides in return, that is, to maximize the benefits/cost ratio.

(6) A superior bargaining position, particularly stemming from the ability to command scarce or uniquely desirable resources, is fundamental to the concept of power and the ability to influence others.

During the learning that occurs later in childhood, resulting in maturing of social exchange skills, it is probable that the emphasis is on establishing the values of various benefits that can be provided by various persons, and on seeking to develop greater skill in maximizing returns while minimizing costs. Remembering that the child is undergoing a socialization process (which teaches him the values and beliefs of adult society), it is axiomatic that at the time he is not yet completely socialized. His lack of a mature social conscience enables him to attempt techniques for minimizing his costs that are not available to more highly socialized adults—for example, the use of physical forces, or direct verbal assault and insult.

The child who has the capability of using physical force, or invective, for securing the benefits he desires will have found a low-cost way of obtaining them. This is another source of learning about power, which takes the form of inflicting costs (pain, loss of self-esteem, etc.) on someone else if they do not provide desired benefits.

As the socialization process continues, these behaviors[5] may, and usually do, become tempered by the finding that "approval" obtained by coercion is not lasting, and may indeed backfire, when someone of superior physical ability is able to meet the challenge successfully and enable those previously intimidated to obtain revenge. Maturity, then, brings awareness that such assets can be used to obtain positive approval only when they are used to the benefit of someone other than oneself.

For example at an intermediate age, the child who is physically capable of successful aggression may find a friend being the subject of aggression by still another child. By protecting his friend—or even someone who was not initially his friend—from the aggression of the other child, he earns the gratitude of the child who was "protected." Thus, his physical assets become of high value to his friend, and he is then able to obtain the rewards of social presence and approval in a positive and enduring way, and often without additional major costs to himself. This may also extend to other friends. When he finds that he does not need to give orders coupled with threats, but rather that he need only make suggestions to them, which they will accept in exchange for his continued willingness to protect them, he will then have learned an important basis for influence (leadership, power) within a group context. This is, simply stated, that the individual who can and does make a unique contribution to the attainment of some shared objective will acquire unique influence within that group.

It is, of course, not necessary that this contribution be based on physical assets. The assets that are important are simply those required for the attainment of the shared objective. For the leaderless discussion group responsible for hammering out and writing a group consensus on a specified topic, the required assets may consist of verbal fluency, that is, the ability to talk and write well, and to express the group's thoughts in a desirable manner. For a football team, it might be the ability to call plays in a sequence that keeps the other team off balance. For a small work group in a formal organization, it might be planning ability, together with the effort required to look beyond the immediate task at hand and anticipate the next problem that may occur, or lay out the next job. Whatever it is, the key is that it will be an asset that is needed by the group for successful and efficient accomplishment of goals and objectives. Further, it will be a scarce asset, and the individual who has it must consider that it is worthwhile for him to offer that asset in exchange for the position of status and esteem that will then be available for him within the group. (It is worth noting that if the individual does not desire these rewards, which are the main ones the group can give him, then he may not be a leader because he is not willing to provide his assets for the accomplishment of group goals. Also, he may naively offer the assets to the advantage of the group without requiring status in return. In this case as well, he probably will not be accorded leadership status.)

Two phenomena of group process are explained by the preceding paragraphs. One is how an individual group member gains the willing compliance of others to his influence attempts as a leader, and the other is why the group reacts so negatively to a leader who causes his group to fail either through a lack of effort or through deliberate violation of "the rules of the game."

As a group member contributes in a unique manner to the accomplishment of goals, the other group members because of their prior social learning, feel constrained to provide benefits in return, if they are demanded by the contributor. As was noted, among these benefits are status and esteem. As the contributor's status and esteem grow, he becomes increasingly "visible" to other members of the group, and they increasingly defer to him (if this is seen to be what he wants) because of the belief that if they do not, he will then remove the scarce assets which the group needs. This offers him the opportunity to make influence attempts of an ever more general nature, to include decisions about group goals, ways they should be attained, who should do what, and so on. If these decisions are good ones, he will continue to accumulate status and esteem, and group members are likely to defer even more to him.

Put another way, this person is in the process of emerging as a recognized, or the recognized leader of the group. When the members of the group eventually reach the point of believing that his decisions are likely to be right, and the best ones for the group, he will then have cemented his position of influence and leadership within the group, and it is likely that his suggestions, or influence attempts, will then be successful in producing the desired behavior in group members. This is not only because they fear he will otherwise deprive them of scarce resources, but also because they may trust his judgment in task-relevant areas more than they trust their own.

It should be recognized that, in many respects, social exchange theory is similar to idiosyncrasy credit theory. A review of the findings of the study by Wiggins, et al. illustrates how influence develops within the group to a point at which the leader can deviate successfully from the rules, but only so long as the group as a whole continues to be successful. The probable determining factor is that the group initially trusts the judgment of the influential member who has provided the means for the group to be successful, or lacks the resources to offer immediate resistance to the deviation. (This may be seen as only reasonable, anyway, because this member had previously demonstrated the ability to provide correct answers in a situation in which the basis for these answers was not clearly apparent. They may well have been willing at least to test the hypothesis that he was still just demonstrating the superior "whatever-it-is" that he apparently had.)

The point is that the group probably was not willing immediately to superimpose its judgment on the judgment of the leader who had been right so many times before. When the group continues to be successful, despite the apparently malappropriate behavior of the leader, he has then proved his point. It is possible that his influence might even increase as a result.

But there is a substantial difference when the group is not successful. When the leader leads, he exercises influence, they implicitly, attribute higher status, greater wisdom, and more competence to him. The attribution of status, wisdom, competence, and so forth, is "payment" given by the group members in return for the resources and assets of the leader which they need in order to attain their own objectives. When the group does not succeed, they will still have paid him his "leader pay" but will not have received the expected return benefit. The reaction to this is not so great if the group believes that the leader actually tried as hard as he could, and that the failure to achieve goals was the result of factors beyond his or their control. On the other hand, when they judge that the leader did not try hard enough, or that he caused the group to fail because he engaged in behavior that satisfied his own personal needs at the sacrifice of the needs of the group members, then the reaction can be predicted to be strongly negative. It amounts to "breaking the faith." For this, the group punishes severely, in part because the leader took his benefits without proper reciprocation, and in part because they cannot trust him not to do it again.

This is shown again by examination of the Wiggins et al. study. It will be recalled that the status of the offending subject in that experiment was manipulated through his alleged contribution to the group's performance, and that high status and medium status subjects were the focus of interest. A subject of intermediate status loses no more (.1 of a point is an immaterial difference) in esteem for a high point loss to the group, which virtually put the group out of contention, than for a medium point loss. In contrast, the high status subject lost much more for a high point loss. One possible interpretation is that the medium status subject was never held in sufficient esteem that his behavior constituted a violation of their expectations for a return obligation to the group.

Additional important principles have been illustrated by this discussion, which can be added to those previously listed.

(7) While power over others can be obtained by coercion, it is not stable

and does not satisfy the same needs as that obtained by positive means, and this fact tends to be learned during the socialization process.

(8) Stable group leadership consists of an established social exchange process between leader and group members, in which the leader makes unique and valuable contributions to the attainment of group goals, and, in turn, is accorded unique status and esteem by the group members. This is an exchange that is viewed by both sides as equitable, that is, a "fair exchange." However, in order for these unique assets to produce leadership status (a position of influence or power within the group), four conditions must be met:

(a) The group members cannot easily do without the benefit the leader provides.

(b) They cannot obtain it elsewhere, or from someone else.

(c) They cannot force the leader to provide the benefit.

(d) They cannot reciprocate equally, "in kind."

(9) Stable group leadership probably cannot exist in the absence of agreed-upon group goals, because, lacking such goals, it is difficult to conceive how a group member could contribute uniquely to the group. Note, however, that popularity and leadership are not the same thing, as was shown earlier (Hollander and Webb, 1955).

(10) Group success is a crucial factor in determining whether the leader will retain his influence within the group, because facilitating attainment of group goals is the leader's main reason for existing, and the main benefit he can offer the group in exchange for the status they give him. Under conditions of group failure, leader rejection is highly likely when he is seen either as not having tried to satisfy his responsibility to the group, or as having tried to use his position to satisfy his own personal needs at the cost of satisfaction of the group's needs.

It should again be emphasized that this view of leadership as a social exchange process is quite similar to idiosyncrasy credit theory. In fact, it may well be that minor elaboration of idiosyncrasy credit theory, as suggested earlier, might satisfy its apparent failure to account for a few of the experimental findings. The principal value of exchange theory is that it appears somewhat more general. For example, it is possible to discuss such phenomena as motivation and group cohesion (Homans, 1958) in terms of exchange theory, while idiosyncrasy credit theory was not designed to handle such variables. This probably does not do great violence to idiosyncrasy theory, since Hollander, who formulated idiosyncrasy credit theory, has since suggested that the leadership role is legitimated by a social exchange process (Hollander and Julian).

END NOTES

1. The material on idiosyncratic behavior and status is a liberal interpretation of the original model; some aspects have been omitted for clarity of presentation.

2. It can be debated whether this actually is a reasonable test of idiosyncrasy credit theory. In the theory itself, the accumulation of credit occurs as a result of perceptions of members, and resulting judgments. The installation of a subject in a supervisory position is not the same thing. However, as will be seen, the purpose of this section is not to reject idiosyncrasy theory, but rather to suggest a minor modification of it. This study is at least illustrative of the need for that modification.

3. Of course, this was not the first use of the concepts important to exchange theory, such as reciprocation (e.g., of gifts), distributive justice, and so forth. However, it is the first attempt known by this writer to deal with social interaction in the same terms as those used by economists (e.g., the law of supply and demand, marginal utility).

4. This discussion is based principally on Blau (1964).

5. For a discussion of such early behaviors, which lead to role development, see Longabaugh (1966).

REFERENCES

1. Alvarez, Rodolfo. "Informal Reactions to Deviance in Similated Work Organizations: A Laboratory Experiment," *American Sociological Review*, vol. 33, 1968, pp. 895–912.

2. Blau, Peter M. *Exchange and Power in Social Life*, John Wiley and Sons Inc., New York, 1964.

3. Fiedler, Fred E. *Personality, Motivational Systems and Behavior of High and Low LPC Persons*, Technical Report 70–12, University of Washington, Seattle, September 1970.

4. Graen, George, Alvares, Kenneth, Orris, James B., and Martella, Joseph A. "Contingency Model of Leadership Effectiveness: Antecedent and Evidential Results," *Psychological Bulletin*, vol. 74, 1970, pp. 285–296.

5. Harlow, H.F. "The Nature of Love," *American Psychologist*, vol. 13, 1958, pp. 673–685.

6. Harlow, H.F., and Suomi, Stephen J. "Nature of Love-Simplified," *American Psychologist*, vol. 25 no. 2, 1970, pp. 161–168.

7. Hollander, E.P. *Variables Underlying Sociometric Status: 1. A Theoretical Model of Idiosyncratic Behavior and Status*, Navy Technical Report 4–56, Carnegie Institute of Technology, Pittsburgh, July 1956.

8. Hollander, E.P. *Emergent Leadership and Social Influence*, Washington University, St. Louis, December 1959.

9. Hollander, Edwin P., and Julian, James W. "Contemporary Trends in the Analysis of Leadership Processes," *Psychological Bulletin*, vol. 71, 1969, pp. 387–397.

10. Hollander, E.P., and Webb, W.B. "Leadership, Followership, and Friendship: An Analysis of Peer Nominations," *Journal of Abnormal and Social Psychology*, vol. 50, 1955, pp. 163–167.

11. Homans, George C. "Social Behavior as Exchange," *American Journal of Sociology*, vol. 63, 1958, pp. 587–606.

12. Janda, Kenneth F. "Towards the Explication of the Concept of Leadership in Terms of the Concept of Power," *Human Relations*, vol. 13, no. 4, 1960, pp. 345–363.

13. Korman, A.K. "Consideration, Initiating Structure, and Organizational Criteria: A Review, *Personnel Psychology*, vol. 19, 1966, pp. 349–361.

14. Longabaugh, Richard. "The Structure of Interpersonal Behavior," *Sociometry*, vol. 29. 1966, pp. 441–460.

15. Stogdill, R.M. *Individual Behavior and Group Achievement*. Oxford University Press, New York, 1959.

16. Stogdill, R.M. *Individual Behavior and Group Achievement: A Behavioral Model of Organization*. Paper presented at Annual Meeting of American Psychological Association Washington, September 1969.

17. Wiggins, James A., Dill, Forrest, and Schwartz, Richard D. "On 'Status-Liability'," *Sociometry*, vol. 28, no. 2, 1965, pp. 197–209.

Applications

Primary Groups, Organization and Military Performance

by
Alexander L. George

Soldiers can be made to accept the hardships of military service and the dangers of combat in different ways. They may come to believe that it is necessary to endure them, a feeling created when military service is accepted as legitimate and its requirements are internalized; or they may anticipate even worse deprivations if they seek to avoid these demands. An army fights best when discipline and the performance of military duties rest at least in part on genuinely voluntaristic motives and are not extracted solely through fear of punishment for disobedience. All modern armies recognize, therefore, the desirability of blending coercion with persuasion in some way in order to obtain discipline and obedience. While the methods they employ vary, all modern armies seek to minimize reliance on coercion by subjecting soldiers to indoctrination, by resocializing men taken from civilian life and attempting to assimilate them into the social organization of the army, and by bringing to bear material inducements as well as symbolic rewards and deprivations.

I. *Rediscovery of Primary Groups in Military Organizations*

Studies of military morale during and since World War II have underscored the central importance of comradely ties among individuals in small combat groups. This has been established for national armies of quite different

"Primary Groups, Organization, and Military Performance," by Alexander L. George is reprinted from *Handbook of Military Institutions,* Roger W. Little, Editor © 1971, pp. 293–318 by permission of the Publisher, Sage Publications, Inc.

social-political origins and for different service branches of the armed forces. Those who conducted these studies were by no means oblivious of the complexity and diversity of motivational structure among combat soldiers. They were cognizant, too, of the variety of factors and circumstances that can affect combat performance. Notwithstanding this, they were impressed with the evidence of the relative importance of comradely ties in small military groups. Thus, for example, two eminent psychiatrists, Roy R. Grinker and John P. Siegel (1945), summarized their work with the U.S. Air Force in World War II with the following, often-quoted observation: "The men seem to be fighting more for someone than against somebody."

That cohesion in the small combat unit is to be understood in part as a collective response to an external threat is a common theme that runs through detailed studies of combat behavior by Samuel Stouffer and his associates, S.L.A. Marshall, Edward Shils and Morris Janowitz, Roger Little, Charles Moskos and others. Investigators have called attention again and again to the fact that the most significant persons for the combat soldier are the men who fight by his side and share with him the ordeal of trying to survive. The point has been made authoritatively more than once by S.L.A. Marshall, a military historian and trained observer of combat in many different kinds of wars, perhaps most succinctly in his classic study, *Men Under Fire* (1947);

> "I hold it to be one of the simplest truths of war that the thing which enables an infantry soldier to keep going with his weapons is the near presence or the presumed presence of a comrade."

It is indeed ancient wisdom that groups often become integrated more closely when faced by an external threat. And it is also true that over the ages military leaders have attempted to incorporate this theorem into military doctrine and practice, and to operationalize it in organizational and morale-building practices.

Modern weapons have only exacerbated a long-standing problem of warfare—the task of getting everyone to engage effectively in combat and the related task of maintaining the cohesion and performance of the combat unit under the shock, danger, and cumulative stress of battle. As early as 1880, Colonel Ardant du Picq, a French combat officer and military theorist, noted that the problem of troop morale had worsened with the increase in the destructive power of weapons. As a result the courage to face these new weapons was becoming more rare. No longer could soldiers comprising the company mass their fire by standing shoulder to shoulder, firing volley after volley at the company commander's orders. In this classic formation they were now too vulnerable before the new infantry weapons and suffered high casualties. The shoulder-to-shoulder tactic clearly had to be extended; but when this was done new problems arose. Thus, in dispersed formations the company commander could no longer control his men's fire. Fire control was also lost if each man was allowed to act independently. There was need, clearly, for devolution of the company commander's leadership, direction, and control of combat to lower levels of authority. Thus was set into motion a long period of experimentation and combat tactics employing smaller groups—platoons, squads, and fire teams of three or four soldiers. (Holmes, 1952)

Du Picq thought that the solution to problems created by more destructive weapons lay in "mutual aid," in strengthening the comradely ties and informal organization within combat units. His views in this respect foreshadowed in a remarkable way some of the sophisticated innovations in organizational doctrine that were to come many years later. Du Picq summarized his views in a pithy observation:

"Four brave men who do not know each other will not dare to attack a lion. Four less brave men, but knowing each other well, sure of their reliability and consequently of mutual aid, will attack resolutely. There is the science of the organization of armies in a nutshell." (1958)

What is noteworthy here is the explicit recognition that individual bravery will not suffice, and that the morale and performance of the individual soldier depends on membership in a cohesive small group. Elsewhere in his *Battle Studies,* long since a classic, du Picq noted that to base military discipline on formal sanctions alone was of limited effectiveness. Foreshadowing modern sociological research once again, du Picq argued that a special system of social and organizational relationships would be needed to sustain the individual combat soldier under the changed conditions of modern warfare:

"But to order discipline is not enough. . . . Discipline itself depends on moral pressure which actuates men to advance from sentiments of fear or pride. But it depends also on surveillance, the mutual supervision of groups of men who know each other well.

"A wise organization insures that the personnel of combat groups changes as little as possible, so that comrades in peace time maneuvers shall be comrades in war. From living together, and obeying the same chiefs, from commanding the same men from sharing fatigue and rest, from cooperation among men who quickly understand each other in the execution of war-like movements, may be bred brotherhood, professional knowledge, sentiment, above all unity. The duty of obedience, the right of imposing discipline and the impossibility of escaping from it, would naturally follow." (1958)

In the modern era du Picq's views and similar ones advanced by Lt. C.B. Mayne of the Royal Engineers and Lt. D.H. Mahan, USN, were either forgotten or overlooked. (Holmes, 1952). Perhaps du Picq's stature as a military theorist suffered, too, because those strategists of World War I who, like Foch, had drawn upon du Picq in developing their infantry tactics, fell into disrepute when their insistence upon "l 'offensive a l'ottrance" led to calamitous casualties and occasional mutinies within the ranks.

Following World War II, new empirical findings on matters of military morale and combat performance led to rediscovery and sharper formulation of some of the ideas du Picq had advanced sixty years earlier. The sociological perspective on these matters has steadily broadened since World War II. Mature reflection on cumulative research findings has led investigators to conclude that the concept of "morale" is too limited and needs to be replaced by a more inclusive *theory of organizational behavior*. In a comprehensive review of trends in theory in this research area, Morris Janowitz (1964) has emphasized that morale can no longer be regarded as "a vague dimension of organizational behavior grounded in personal attitudes. Even in the smallest unit there is an 'iron framework' of organization which serves as a basis of social control." The single concept of military "morale" must give way, therefore, to "a theory of organizational behavior in which an array of sociological concepts is employed: authority, communications, hierarchy, sanctions, status, social role, allocation, and integration." (Janowitz & Little, 1965)

It may be noted, too, that *policy* questions concerning military morale that were of major interest in World War II forced investigators to view the performance of combat groups from a sociological perspective. U.S. authorities had encountered severe difficulties in their efforts to develop effective political warfare against German and Japanese armed forces. The peculiar invulnerability of Axis armed forces to many kinds of psychological warfare led two separate groups of social scientists working for the U.S. government independently to recast operational and strategic intelligence into sociological models. (Leighton, 1949; Shills and Janowitz, 1948). The social system perspective they applied to these problems helped focus attention on the fact that it was the ability of combat leaders to maintain primary group functions in small fighting units rather than adherence to Nazi ideology that lay at the root of the stubborn resistance put up by hard pressed units of the Wehrmacht. Let us look more closely, therefore, at what sociologists mean by "primary group" and how it has been applied to the study of military organizations and, in particular, to combat behavior.

II. *"Primary Group" As a Variable*

By "primary groups" sociologists mean those small groups in which social behavior is governed by intimate face-to-face relations. The term was employed initially sixty years ago by Charles H. Cooley in his book, *Social Organization* (1909). A similar concept had emerged earlier in European sociological theory with Ferdinand Toennies' distinction between *Gemeinschaft* (small, intimate communal relationships) and *Gesellschaft* (organized, impersonal relationships). Cooley defined primary groups in the following terms:

> "By primary groups I mean those characterized by intimate face-to-face association and cooperation. They are primary in several senses, but chiefly in that they are fundamental in forming the social natures and ideals of the individual. The result of intimate association . . . is a certain fusion of individualities in a common whole, so that one's very self, for many purposes at least, is the common life and purpose of the

group. Perhaps the simplest way of describing this wholeness is by saying it is a 'we'; it involves the sort of sympathy and mutual identification for which 'we' is the natural expression." (1909)

The most explicit and detailed application of the primary group concept to the study of small military groups appears in the study of the cohesion and disintegration of the German army in World War II by Shils and Janowitz (1948). These investigators made ingenious use of a rich body of theory to illuminate some of the complexities and puzzles surrounding the combat performance of German soldiers, and to account for the ability of German units to stand up in the face of severe, prolonged stress. Shils and Janowitz saw the small military unit as maintaining itself insofar as it was able to fulfill a number of the essential needs of the individual soldier:

"For the ordinary German soldier the decisive fact was that he was a member of a squad or section which maintained its structural integrity and which coincided roughly with the *social* unit which satisfied some of his major primary needs. He was likely to go on fighting, provided he had the necessary weapons, as long as the group possessed leadership with which he could identify himself, and as long as he gave affection to and received affection from the other members of his squad and platoon. In other words, as long as he felt himself to be a member of his primary group and therefore bound by the expectations and demands of its other members, his soldierly achievement was likely to be good. . . . In the army, when isolated from civilian primary groups, the individual soldier comes to depend more and more on his military primary group. His spontaneous loyalties are to its immediate members whom he sees daily and with whom he develops a high degree of intimacy."

Some disagreement exists among investigators as to the *scope* and *quality* of primary group ties within small military units. Earlier studies (*The American Soldier, Cohesion and Disintegration of the Wehrmacht*) postulated or seemed to imply the existence of a rather rich cluster of primary group ties shared by many members of units as large as squads or even platoons. In the more recent literature, however, a new conception of primary group ties under conditions of military stress has emerged. They are now described as being more molecular or grandular in structure, often taking the form of a series of two-person relationships rather than affiliations among larger numbers of men. Several investigations have noted a more elementary, less developed type of primary group structure. (Marlowe, 1959; Little, 1964; Seaton, 1964)

This changed conception of primary group ties may be a result of more precise and more direct observation than was possible in the earlier studies. Or, as seems more likely, it may reflect the fact that *considerable variation in scope and content of primary group ties is to be expected, depending on the conditions and circumstances surrounding small military groups.* Thus, in Korea spatial dispersion and personnel rotation may have inhibited the development of more extensive interpersonal systems of a comradely character. The "buddy" relationship between two soldiers was built around mutual interest in minimization of risk; a buddy was a fellow soldier on whom one could rely in situations of danger. But the buddy relationship was maintained as private knowledge. (Little, 1964; see also discussion in Janowitz and Little, 1965.) Similar observations were made by Seaton (1964) in a study of military work groups under severe environmental stress in arctic Greenland. Support relations were developed by the individual with just one or two others; resources and opportunities for interaction with larger numbers in the unit were limited by circumstances. As a result, the form of social organization that emerged in these small groups was "primitive and immature, and unable to sustain extended or sustained friendships."

The instrumental aspect of "buddyship" and primary group ties is given particular emphasis by Marlowe (1959) and Moskos (1968). In a study of social adjustment during the course of basic training. Marlowe concluded that "buddyship" and friendship were not coterminous; rather, "buddyship" appears to be "an operational concept designed to take the place of friendship and serve as the initial stage in the foundation of a friendship." The instrumental importance of "buddyship," he found, was at times expressed forthrightly and with vehemence: "Everybody has to have a buddy. Without a buddy you could never make it here." The use of a two-man buddy system has also been reported for the British commandos in World War II.

In his recent study of U.S. soldiers in Vietnam, Moskos, too, found it necessary to challenge the earlier hypothesis that primary group ties are based on deep identifications and solidarity with fellow squad and platoon members, with the result that individuals value the maintenance of the group and its goals for their own sake. As against this, the data obtained in Vietnam pointed to the greater importance of "the instrumental and self-serving aspects of primary relations in combat units." Even the buddy relationship was at its core "a mutually pragmatic effort to minimize personal risk." Hence, rather than viewing primary group relations in combat units as "some kind of semi-mystical bond of comradeship," Moskos argues they can be better understood as essentially "pragmatic and situational responses." (Moskos, 1968)

It seems reasonable to conclude from available empirical studies, therefore, that the *scope* and *content* of primary group ties within small military units are both subject to variations. While the general character of primary group ties is suggested by the traditional definition of the concept and in sociological theory, care must be taken by the investigator not to reify the term or, a more likely danger, to utilize one or two indicators of the existence of primary group ties (such as evidence of "buddyship") as a basis for inferring that a richer, more pervasive form of primary group relationships necessarily exists within the military groups that are being studied.

Thus, the scope and content of primary groups should be regarded as an open question to be settled in each case by empirical observation. We can now turn to a broader discussion of the emergence and significance of primary groups in different military organizations.

III. *Primary Groups in Different Types of Military Organizations*

While the phenomenon of primary groups is ubiquitous, the context in which it occurs varies depending on the type of military organization in question and the attitude higher authorities take toward close informal relations within small military groups. Thus, the study of primary group ties takes a greater significance if it is an integral part of a broader study of any given army. A more comprehensive study of this kind should describe (a) *the kind of social organization that is officially fostered and/or tolerated within the army in question:* (b) *the major policies regulating service conditions:* and (c) *the practices employed to mold and shape civilian recruits* (or conscripts) into the kinds of soldiers and cadres wanted within the framework of the preferred disciplinary and social system.

The fact that armies differ in these three respects is sometimes passed over in calling attention to features common to all military organizations. Military sociology will be enriched, however, if the way in which armies differ from each other is also systematically examined. In this section we shall indicate some of the directions in which comparative military sociology might move by contrasting as best we can on the basis of available data the origins and nature of comradely relations in small units in several different armies. (A more detailed comparison is presented in George, 1967.)

In the U.S. Armed Forces the development of comradely ties is not officially sponsored as it is, for example, in the Chinese Communist army. Rather, comradely ties in small U.S. units are a consequence of the men's recognition that they are working together on a common job, that each is dependent on the other, and that teamwork is to everyone's advantage. It is expected that most soldiers have the capacity, derived from earlier experiences in civilian society, to develop comradely ties within their units that will reinforce the workings of formal authority.

In contrast, Chinese Communist authorities make explicit provision for creating and maintaining small social groups. What is even more intriguing about the Chinese People's Liberation Army (PLA) is that its leaders insist that the social system within the army should have the explicit political-ethical content of their revolutionary ideals. The purpose of basic training and indoctrination in the PLA is not simply to produce "good soldiers." Rather, Chinese Communist leaders have been engaged in an ambitious pedagogical enterprise which attempts to alter important aspects of the individual's personality, attitudes, and behavior in order to make a "good Communist soldier" out of him. It is not an exaggeration to say that PLA leaders attempt to socialize raw conscripts not only for service in the army but also for their subsequent role as citizens of a revolutionary communist society. The PLA organizational model, that is to say, sprang from its revolutionary origins. The political-ethical goals of the Chinese Communist revolution have been infused into the social organization sponsored within the army.

A comparison of the PLA and Soviet models for small group life reveals important differences. Many of the strikingly egalitarian features of social political organization that were still visible in the PLA at the time of the Korean War were either altogether lacking or much muted in the history of the Soviet army, or have survived only in a much attenuated form. The Bolshevik leaders recognized the importance of military professionalism at the outset of their successful revolution; and they gave professional values and forms priority over the revolutionary-egalitarian model in creating the Soviet Red Army. Moreover, professionalism has continued to grow in scope and emphasis within the Red Army and this is evident in many aspects of its social organization. For example, higher authority in the Red Army attempts to keep relations between officers and men on a formal, hierarchical basis while units are in training or in garrison. In contrast, within the framework of a revolutionary-egalitarian model in which formal ranks were abolished, PLA authorities have actively encouraged friendly comradely relations between leaders and men in periods of indoctrination and training, and under garrison conditions.[1]

Though comradely ties between officers and men in the Soviet Red Army were officially discouraged during peacetime, they developed spontaneously in combat during World War II. A detailed study of the bases of Soviet military morale, based on detailed interviews with defectors, reported as follows:

> Comradely solidarity in small informal groups plays an important part and enters significantly into the motivations of the Soviet soldier in battle. . . . Under combat conditions the formalization of relationships among officers and men is greatly reduced. The genuinely personal qualities of the men become more apparent; the organization comes to rest more upon its informal bases, upon the spontaneously worked out human relations which have, in a sense, been held in check by the formal organization. . . . A change takes place in combat. The danger and the tremendous piling up of acute discomforts creates a sort of community and solidarity among the men which hardly existed in the garrison. (Dicks, Shils, and Dinerstein, 1951)

These comradely ties, it is further reported, were often grounded in patriotism; but what the Russian soldier typically expressed thereby was a nationalism that was largely divorced from communist ideology. Early in World War II Soviet leaders realized that the large reserve of patriotism in the Russian people could be utilized for purposes of military as well as civilian morale. In contrast, the PLA system prior to and during the Korean conflict had very little tolerance for comradely ties that were not cemented, at least on the surface, by mutually shared communist convictions or orientation.

We noted earlier that PLA authorities (unlike both their Soviet and U.S. counterparts) took an active interest in developing and controlling the character of small group ties. Comradely ties were not permitted to have an autonomous basis for evidently PLA authorities felt threatened by informal group ties and loyalties that were essentially apolitical in character. From the standpoint of the PLA political organization, interpersonal ties within combat units that rested largely on human considerations and to which the men gave priority over political values were potentially dangerous, being thought of as too vulnerable to subversion and transformation into oppositional activity.

In contrast, the informal ties that cement small groups within the U.S. Army are extraordinarily spontaneous, overtly apolitical or even anti-political, and largely unregulated by higher authorities. Higher leadership does not feel its control threatened by these autonomous comradely ties. Rather, it regards the personal loyalties felt by the men towards each other as contributing to good military discipline; and it builds upon small group loyalties to create larger loyalties that reinforce the formal authority structure and its goals.

We note that in more systematic analyses of primary groups in military organizations, "primary group" can be employed either as a dependent variable and/or as an independent variable, depending upon what aspect of military organization is singled out for attention. Thus,

> "Primary group" is a *dependent* variable when the investigator seeks to ascertain the preconditions and variables that contribute to or impede the formation of social cohesion in small unit.
>
> "Primary group" is an *independent* variable (one among many) when the investigator seeks to determine the conditions and variables that determine the level (a) of combat motivation and (b) of combat performance.

Let us consider, first, primary group cohesion as a dependent variable and ask what antecedent conditions and independent variables determine the formation and degree of social cohesion in small military units.

IV. *Factors Affecting Formation of Primary Group Ties in Small Units*

Some dozen pre-conditions and variables have been identified as contributing to formation and maintenance of primary group ties in small military units. Since they have been discussed in some detail by a number of investigators (Janowitz and Little, 1965; Dicks, Shils, and Dinerstein, 1951; Lang, 1965; Mandlebaum, 1952; Coates and Pellegrin, 1965; George, 1967; Moskos, 1968), we need summarize them only very briefly here without attempting to order them or to consider their interrelationships:

1. *Social background of unit members:* A number of investigators have noted that a common social background assists soldiers in a unit to develop intimate interpersonal relations; similarities in previous social experience—such as social class, regional origin, or age—appear to contribute in this way. Conversely, heterogeneous ethnic and national origins among soldiers within a unit tend to inhibit formation of primary group relations. (Janowitz and Little, 1965; Shils and Janowitz, 1948; George, 1967)

2. *Personality of unit members:* Among the characteristics mentioned as facilitating an individual's participation in the primary group life of his unit is the ability to offer and receive affection in an all-male society. Attention has been called also to the importance of family stability, especially satisfactory

identification with one's father, as affecting the individual soldier's capacity to enter into informal group relationships. (Shils, 1950; Janowitz and Little, 1965)

3. *Protectiveness of immediate leaders:* The individual soldier's need for a protective, exemplary authority whose qualities permit identification is well documented. (Shils, 1950; Shils and Janowitz, 1948; George, 1967). In the U.S. Army in World War II, companies with high morale were characterized by a far higher frequency of belief that the officers were "interested" in their men, "understood" them, were "helpful," would "back them up"—all of which are qualities of primary group leaders. (Stouffer *et al,* II, 1949)

4. *Performance of immediate leaders:* Tactical leadership based on example and demonstrated competence promotes social cohesion and reduces the need to rely on commands based on the threat of sanctions. (Dollard, 1943; Shils and Janowitz, 1948; Homans, 1946; George, 1967; Stouffer et al, 1949)

5. *Military discipline, professionalism, and role of soldierly honor:* A political motivation of the order of "getting the job done," being "a good soldier who does his duty" and not letting comrades down, were found to be dominant in several armies that have been studied. (Shils and Janowitz, 1948; Stouffer *et al,* 1949; Moskos, 1968) Subjugation to military discipline supports those young soldiers who experience the need for asserting manliness and toughness, a need which regression to an adolescent condition in military life reactivates. Coincidence of these personal needs with group norms and military codes reinforces group cohesion.

6. *Commitment to one's social-political system, ideology, and patriotism:* There is substantial agreement among those who have studied different military organizations that a soldier's patriotism and attachment to related secondary symbols generally can provide, at the very least, "the rudiments of one of the most important preconditions for the formation of primary groups which (in turn) have a more positive and immediate function in strengthening the soldier's will to exert himself under dangerous conditions." This formulation, which Shils (1950) provided in his commentary on *The American Soldier,* did much to clarify seeming ambiguities of data and conflicting interpretations, and has generally been accepted as being a probable application to other armies as well. (See also George, 1967; Moskos, 1968; Dicks, Shils and Dinerstein, 1951.)

Political ideals are of greater significance in strengthening solidarity in those armies in which the cadre structure is highly politicized. Thus, the Nazi "hard core" within the Wehrmacht played an important role in strengthening the stability and effectiveness of the military primary groups. (Shils and Janowitz, 1948) A similar function is performed by communist adherents within the cadre structure of communist armies, particularly in the Chinese Communist army at the time of the Korean War, in which politicization of the cadre structure extended to the squad and sub-squad level. (George, 1967; Dicks, Shils and Dinerstein, 1951)

7. *War indoctrination:* This is related to the tacit patriotism and the attachment to other secondary symbols, and plays a similar indirect role as a pre-condition for formation of primary groups. War indoctrination typically stresses two themes: (a) the legitimacy and/or justification of the war, which is based

upon an account of the origin of the war, the nature of the enemy, and the character of the war aims; and (b) the wisdom and/or necessity for fighting it (which includes an estimate of expectations of success and a prediction of the probable consequences of defeat). (Dollard, 1943; Speier, 1950; George, 1967)

8. *Exigencies of military life and of the combat situation:* These will often suffice in themselves to create a sense of elementary social cohesion, a mutually-shared recognition of the necessity for "buddyship" and coopera-tion, if not also comradeliness.

9. *Technical aspects of weapons systems:* It has been postulated that "weapons systems which maintain close physical proximity of team members and enhance the process of communication contribute most to primary group cohesion." (Janowitz and Little, 1965)

10. *Replacement system and rotation policy:* The replenishment of understrength units by *individual* replacements has been thought to exacerbate the problem of maintaining group cohesion. An alternative replacement practice of *packets of small groups* has also been tried, but this appears to bring with it a different set of problems. (Janowitz and Little, 1965) In the Vietnam War there has been a rapid turnover of personnel in the U.S. Army units, occasioned by the unusually benign rotation policy followed in this con-flict. As a result, the development of closer primary group ties appears to have been limited even while, paradoxically, the rotation policy has contributed to the usually high morale of the individual combat soldier. (Moskos, 1968)

11. *Social prestige of soldierly profession:* There is some indication that raising the social prestige of the soldierly profession and improving civil-military relations in countries such as China where soldiers have been held in traditional disrepute by the civilian population helps to enhance the self-respect of soldiers and thereby contributes to the formation of social cohesion in small military units. (George, 1967)

12. *Egalitarian practices within the military organization:* There is some indication, once again, that favorable results have been achieved with the in-troduction of egalitarian practices into the armies of countries such as China, in which military service has been traditionally associated with highly coercive, arbitrary, and discriminatory practices. There is evidence that practices within the PLA which served to "democratize" respect, equalize and rationalize service conditions, encourage mass participation in official ideology, rituals and group decision-making have been successful in encouraging the individual soldier to identify with, and participate in the prescribed type of small group life. (George, 1967)

V. *Primary Group Cohesion as an Independent Variable Affecting Combat Motivation and Combat Performance*

Linkage of Primary Group Cohesion to Formal Military Organization

A number of investigators have emphasized that primary group solidarity in small military groups can work either to reinforce or to impede the goals of the formal military organization. As is the case in other kinds of organizations, peer group cohesion among soldiers in small units may take a direction that is positive or negative from the standpoint of higher military authority. (Etzioni, 1961, chpt. 8)

Clearly, therefore, social cohesion that is generated in small groups has to be extended to larger units and higher levels of the military organization. "Cohesive primary groups contribute to organizational effectiveness only when the standards of behavior they enforce are articulated with the requirements of formal authority." (Janowitz and Little, 1965)

How, then, is this linkage established? Two factors are of particular importance here. First, the leaders of small military groups are often the vehicle through which the formal demands and sanctions of higher military authority are linked with the norms and sanctions of the small group itself. The primary group member's identification with the leaders of his unit often results in commitment to the norms of the formal organization which these leaders represent. In this fashion "hierarchical cohesion" is established along with peer cohesion at the lowest working level.

In the Wehrmacht, Nazi soldiers and the apolitical but tough professionalized NCOs constituted the nucleus or "hard core" of the primary group. "The presence of a few such men in the group, zealous, energetic, and unsparing of themselves, provided models for the weaker men, and facilitated the process of identification. For those for whom their charisma did not suffice and who were accordingly difficult to incorporate fully into the intimate primary group, frowns, harsh words, and threats served as a check on divisive tendencies." (Shils and Janowitz, 1948)

An even more systematic application of the "hard core" organizational principle was evident in the Chinese Communist army at the time of the Korean War. The PLA organizational model called for merging the entire military cadre structure, even down to the squad level, with membership in the Party; moreover, a separate political organization was created within the army that straddled its military command structure from top to bottom. In addition to installing political co-commanders alongside military commanders at every organizational level, the PLA attempted to place communist personnel, insofar as possible, as leaders of platoons, squads and subsquad groups of three. This was a particularly useful device for shaping group life along desired lines. By this means, PLA authorities tried to ensure that comradeliness and peer cohesion in the small units would take on a communist hue and be responsive to the demands and goals of the higher organization. (George, 1967)

A political hard core type of organization has also been employed in the Soviet Army with some variations over the years; but it does not ever seem to have been extended to the squad level or applied as thoroughly as in the PLA. (Dicks, Shils and Dinerstein, 1951; Kolkowicz, 1967; George, 1967) On the other hand, this and other features of the PLA military model were evidently taken over by Vo Nguyen Giap in organizing the View Minh People's Army, which fought and finally defeated the French Army in Indochina. (Roy, 1965) The Viet Cong in South Vietnam has also been using a military model closely patterned on that of the PLA. (George, 1967; Zasloff, 1968)

A second means by which peer group cohesion is linked with the higher organization is the soldier's acceptance of the legitimacy of its demands. As noted earlier, an hypothesis along these lines has emerged from the work of several investigators and was stated most recently by Moskos (1968): "Primary groups serve to maintain the soldier in his combat role only when there is an underlying commitment to the worthwhileness of the larger social system for which he is fighting. This commitment need not be formally articulated, nor even perhaps consciously recognized. But at some level there must be an acceptance, if not of the specific purposes of the war, then at least of the broader rectitude of the social system of which the soldier is a member." This states, as it were, the "minimal" role of ideology and war indoctrination. But it is clear that these factors are also capable of playing a far more important role in combat motivation. Of three hundred veterans of the Abraham Lincoln Brigade who had fought in the Spanish Civil War, 77% stated that "belief in war aims" had been among the most important things that had helped to overcome fear in battle. This factor was mentioned more frequently than other factors such as leadership (49%), military training (45%), material (42%). (Dollard, 1943)

Such is the ubiquity of primary groups in military organizations, however, that we must not be surprised to find that under special circumstances they can promote compliance with the goals of the organization even when members of the small group are highly dissatisfied with, and even alienated from formal military authorities. In a Chinese Nationalist Air Police company, studied by Wen-Lung Chang (1968), the dissatisfaction of ordinary soldiers with their military lives and with the rigid and harsh system of rule enforcement by military authorities was the most important basis for formation of primary group cohesion. The men needed each other's friendship for psychological support in order to be able to meet better the hardships of military service inflicted on them by higher authorities. The informal primary groups that spring up in this oppressive milieu, though composed of dissidents, nonetheless promoted compliance by members with the organization's goals and demands. For primary group norms enjoined the individual member to "play it safe," to obey rather than subject himself to the likelihood of harsh punishment by higher authorities.

Finally, we should take note of the fact that primary group norms that support the goals of the organization under one set of circumstances may have the opposite effect when combat stress is intensified and prolonged. Thus Little (1964) noted that the longer a platoon was on the line in Korea, the more intensive the relationship of its members became, "and the more their behavior deviated from the norms of the organization. Even the officers who lived with their platoons tended to think like their men. . . . Relations between the company commander and the platoon leaders became increasingly contentious. The probable response of the latter in executing orders in situations involving great risk was accordingly uncertain. When an organization reached this stage, it was described as having 'low morale' and withdrawn into reserve for 'retraining'."

Other Independent Variables Affecting Level of Combat Motivation and Combat Performance

While the present chapter focuses on the nature and significance of primary group cohesion in military organizations, it would be grossly misleading to discuss as we have been doing its role in combat motivation and performance without some brief mention of the many other variables that are also relevant in this respect. For this purpose it is useful to separate "combat motivation" from "combat performance," since the latter depends on a variety of factors in addition to the level of motivation for combat within fighting units.

Functions of Primary Group in Combat

It is widely recognized by military leaders that informal comradely ties that often develop in small groups can contribute greatly to morale and performance of combat duties. This is particularly true in guerrilla warfare and special warfare action which require highly motivated, closely knit small groups.

The special motivational impetus provided combat soldiers by their membership in primary groups is all the more critical insofar as the formal coercive powers at the disposal of military authorities tend to lose some of their efficacy and force in the battle situation and with increased duration of combat experience. (Shils, 1950; Stouffer *et al.*, II, 1949)

What then, do primary group ties contribute to combat motivation? The authors of *The American Soldier* (II) concluded that the primary or informal group "served two principle functions in combat motivation: it *set and emphasized group standards* of behavior and it *supported and sustained the individual* in stresses he would otherwise not have been able to withstand." Thus, a primary group generates norms of its own and joins or withholds its own informal sanctions to enforce organizational commands and expectations. (See also Stouffer *et al.*, I, 1949)

It is striking in this respect that even after the end of the war ninety percent of U.S. enlisted men interviewed by Research Branch in one survey expressed the belief that soldiers are greatly concerned with the opinion in which they are held by other enlisted men in their units. Other surveys indicated that the desire to avoid "letting the other fellow down" was one of the most important reasons given by soldiers in their assessment of factors which caused them "to keep going." (Stouffer *et al.*, I and II, 1949) This consideration was given even broader recognition by the 300 veterans of the Abraham Lincoln Brigade who had fought in Spain. Ninety-four percent stated that the wish not to let fellow soldiers down had made better soldiers of them. Moreover, some said that the thought of their comrades and of the outfit as a whole had helped them to overcome fear in battle. (Dollard, 1943)

In this connection, Janowitz and Little (1965) note that research efforts to establish the thresholds at which combat psychiatric breakdowns occur have shifted emphasis from efforts to ascertain individual tolerance for stress to an understanding of the positive sustaining effects of the primary groups.

Organizational Controls as an Alternative to Primary Group Support for Combat

When primary group motivations wither or are nonexistent, military authorities must rely increasingly on combat surveillance and enforcement. The implied or immediate threat of official coercive sanctions must then assume the burden of motivation that concepts of duty and legitimacy no longer provide and that the informal norms and sanctions of the small group can no longer reinforce.

The efficacy of combat enforcement under these circumstances depends on the *numbers* and *quality* of combat leaders. The same "hard core" cadres who in more favorable circumstances provide the models with which the men can identify, thus facilitating the critical linkage of primary groups with the goals of the formal organization we noted earlier, must now exact and enforce combat on the part of reluctant soldiers. The integrity of the combat unit now depends critically on the efficacy of the organizational control structure.

Such a trend was noted within the Chinese Communist armies in Korea during the late winter and spring of 1950. (George, 1967) What is remarkable is not that morale within PLA combat units should sag under the adverse conditions encountered in Korea, but that the PLA's organizational controls should succeed as well as they did in preventing the disintegration of demoralized combat units and in extracting performance of combat duties. Increasingly strong emphasis was placed upon mutual supervision and surveillance during combat. Depending on the numbers and quality of personnel filling the cadre positions in fighting units, tendencies toward unit disintegration could be more or less effectively controlled. So long as reasonably well-motivated Party adherents straddled the cadre structure of a unit down to the squad and sub-squad level, as was called for in PLA organizational doctrine, each group leader had only two or three non-Party rank-and-file soldiers to watch over and control.

PLA prisoners taken during this period frequently noted that the surveillance and control system within their units had been quite effective in combat. Disaffected soldiers were afforded few opportunities to desert to the rear or to voluntarily surrender to the enemy. The effectiveness of the surveillance network in preventing desertion or surrender was indirectly conveyed by the answers 86 PLA prisoners (63 privates, 23 cadres) gave to the question: "What made you follow the PLA to the last, undergoing so many hardships in this war?" Eighty-three percent of the privates and over forty percent of the cadres referred to the deterrent effect of the surveillance system in their units.

Moreover, so long as surveillance remained pervasive it operated to isolate the individual soldier and to prevent him from coming together with like-minded members of his unit to discuss and plan desertion or surrender. At this level of efficiency, it may be noted, surveillance effectively prevented the development of informal peer cohesion within small groups that would have been directed against the goals of the organization.

It is sobering to recognize the considerable extent to which the erosion of morale within PLA combat units and the disruption of the officially-sponsored primary groups was compensated for by the strength of the PLA's organizational controls. In this respect, it may be noted, the experience of the PLA differed from that of the German Wehrmacht in World War II. Primacy groups evidently survived longer under severe pressure in the Wehrmacht than in the PLA, and this enabled the German combat units to keep fighting without having to rely as much as the PLA on coercive sanctions applied by hard core cadres. (Shils and Janowitz, 1948)

A more serious development from the standpoint of higher PLA leaders was the general demoralization and attrition of the all-important junior cadres who manned the control structure of their combat units. As the war dragged on during the spring of 1950, the caliber of combat leadership declined markedly as the PLA began to run out of skilled and well-motivated junior cadres. Party adherents who had formed the hard core cadre in their units suffered heavy casualties, particularly at company and lower echelons, and many of them lost their ideological fervor and became demoralized. That the Achilles Heel of the PLA was not the erosion of morale in its combat units, but rather, the erosion of organizational controls became evident in late May when the Eighth Army's counteroffensive hit the Chinese armies before they could carry out their usual practice of withdrawing after an offensive to rest, reorganize, resupply, and replenish the cadre structure. The Eighth Army's heavy blows on the ground and from the air imposed a severe strain on the ability of the already weakened and demoralized cadres to maintain control over their units. The remaining cadres were unable in many units to prevent the PLA withdrawal from taking on the character of a precipitous, disorderly flight. For the first time in the war surrender was no longer confined to single individuals or small groups. Remnants of platoons, companies, and even battalions were now giving up.

VI. *Some Research Difficulties*

A number of practical difficulties arise in attempts to employ the primary group concept as a variable in rigorous research. In the first place, it is important but often difficult to develop a research model that employs the small group rather than the individual soldier as the *unit of analysis*. In the second place, it is far easier to obtain data on the *individual soldier's attitudes* than on the *behavior of the small group* to which he belongs or belonged.

These difficulties are accentuated when, as is often the case, the investigator obtains his data largely through interviews with individual soldiers (or prisoners of war) who have been selected through a sampling procedure, whether fortuitous or purposive, that cuts across the natural small units within the military organization. Insofar as few soldiers interviewed in a study of this kind belong to the same small military group, the information they provide tends to be sparse and highly fragmented when the investigator attempts to use it as data bearing on the behavior of small groups.

While interview data of this kind is useful at the level of microanalysis and while it is also capable of being aggregated to study some general preconditions and effects of membership in primary groups, it has important limitations. Information about discrete individual soldiers who have no relationship to each other cannot be combined very well for studying the etiology and dynamic processes of primary group behavior. The problem of bridging the gap between micro and macro analysis is, therefore, particularly severe.

This problem was evident in *The American Soldier,* truly a monumental and pioneering study, but one based essentially on studies of attitudes of individuals with no direct observation of groups in action and only occasional indirect observations of group performance. In consequence, the actual operation of primary group life was not described in this study and indeed was seldom referred to. The result was that many important problems having to do with primary groups could not be studied at all. (Stouffer, I, 1949; Shils, 1950) Extending this point to a discussion of the limitations of attitude research more generally for sociological study of military organizations, Janowitz and Little (1965) warn that "attitude research fails to describe the underlying social system—the realities of bureaucratic organization—of the armed forces."

Still another kind of research model, one employing sociometric techniques of analysis, was utilized in a recent study of "Cohesion of Marine Recruit Platoons" (Nelson and Berry, 1968). The investigators developed a "cohesiveness measure" for each of 24 recruit training platoons by asking each soldier to nominate the five men in his platoon whom he liked best. The linkages established by reciprocal nominations were the basis for postulating, by definition, the existence of "cliques." The study suffers, however, from the fact that findings regarding both "cohesion" and "cliques" are too much an artifact of the special mode of analysis. The operational definitions of "cohesion" and "clique" are at best only loosely relevant to the richer concepts and hypotheses of primary group theory. For what it is worth, "cohesiveness" as measured in this study did not correlate very significantly with other variables, nor was there much indication of change in cohesion over a two-month period.

The complex social organization and social processes within an army can be more advantageously studied by methods which rely at least in part on participant observation. Ideally, a group of investigators might be assigned the task of observing many small military units directly, employing a variety of data acquisition techniques. Longitudinal studies are needed, moreover, in which the same unit is observed over a period of time, in a variety of situations and circumstances. In this connection, Janowitz (1964) persuasively argues that the dynamics of small comradely groups can best be studied when the organization is under pressure. But prolonged and systematic participant observation of this kind is not easily arranged. One of the few examples thus far of research which employed this preferred approach is the study by Roger Little (1964) who directly observed a single U.S. army combat unit in Korea from November 1952 through February 1953.

Also interesting from the standpoint of research methodology is a study of socialization of two types of officer candidates in the Royal Netherlands Navy. (Lammers, 1963) This study illustrates the value of combining several methods; the investigator employed intensive, prolonged participant observation initially for hypothesis formation and then undertook systematic surveys for more rigorous assessment of hypotheses.

When direct observation of individual military units is not possible and only individual soldiers or prisoners-of-war are available for interview, the investigator may nonetheless attempt to utilize the subjects as providing an opportunity for *indirect* participant observation. Thus, each subject who is interviewed can be cast into the role of *informant* on matters affecting the character, development, and significance of small group ties within his old unit.[2]

The investigator attempts in this fashion to bridge as best he can analysis at the micro and macro levels. This kind of improvised research model was employed by George (1967) in his study of the Chinese Communist army in Korea. It may be noted that while individuals are interviewed in this approach too, as in a Gallup Poll type survey, nonetheless the research model differs in important respects. It is not the individual soldier but rather the small military formation (company, platoon, squad, or sub-squad—depending on the nature of the specific problem being investigated) which constitutes the *unit of analysis*. This research approach requires, typically, a more flexible mode of interviewing to take advantage of the varying utility of different respondents as informants about their units. When possible the investigator employs multiple informants on each unit; in principle, this could extend to the entire membership of the unit. Finally, if the investigator wishes to generalize about the state of affairs in the total order of battle, he must "sample" an appropriately broad and representative number of the individual military formations comprising the whole.

Still another approach for partly bridging the gap between micro-analysis of individual behavior and macro-analysis of groups based on variables common to political sociology has been suggested by Moskos (1968). He develops a concept of combat motivation that draws on the recent emphasis in social science writings on the nature of underlying aspects of a group's belief systems—such as political culture, basic value orientations, political ideology, etc.—which may set the context for political behavior. It is from this standpoint, Moskos argues, that one can best examine the dynamics of attitude formation on the part of American combat soldiers in the Vietnam war. He singles out several sets of attitudes or underlying value orientations that comprise the "latent ideology" of many American soldiers in the present conflict. These he calls "anti-ideology," "Americanism," "materialism," and "manly honor." The "latent ideology" of American soldiers in Vietnam, he argues further, is generally supportive and contributes indirectly to good combat performance.

END NOTES

1. After the conclusion of the Korean War, Chinese Communist leaders attempted to graft important features of military professionalism on to their revolutionary-egalitarian type of army. Ranks and a professional officer class were introduced into the PLA for the

first time in 1955. Following Soviet practice, PLA authorities tried to allow greater scope for military professionalism by permitting the role of the political apparatus within the army to be curtailed, particularly at the all-important company level. But the consequences of this innovation frightened top-level Chinese leaders and this led to reimposition of political controls in 1959–60. (Joffe, 1965; George, 1967) This abortive effort to introduce professionalism into the PLA may be contrasted with the successful experience of the leaders of the new Israeli state in combining features of their egalitarian underground army with the model of a professional army such as the British army in which many Israeli soldiers had earlier served. (Etzioni, 1959, 1960)

2. Generally, research efforts of this kind place the respondent in the position of serving as a retrospective informant on events which occurred some time ago; but in principle at least it is possible to arrange for informants to report on more recent events.

BIBLIOGRAPHY

Biderman, Albert D. *March to Calumny*. New York: Macmillan, 1963.

Chang, Wen-lung. "A Study of a Nationalist Chinese Air Police Company; Leadership and Primary Groups" Unpublished M.A. Thesis, Department of Sociology and Anthropology, Kansas State University, 1968.

Coates, Charles H. and Pelligrin, Roland. *Military Sociology*. University Park, Maryland: The Social Science Press, 1965.

Cooley, Charles H. *Social Organization*. New York: Charles Scribner's Sons, 1909.

Dicks, H.V.; Shils, Edward A.; and Dinerstein, Herbert S. *Service Conditions and Morale in the Soviet* Armed Forces. Santa Monica: The RAND Corporation, 1951.

Dicks, H.V. "Observations on Contemporary Russian Behavior" *Human Relations*, 5 (1952).

Dicks, H.V., Lt. Col., R.A.M.C. *The Psychological Foundations of the Wehrmacht*, London: Directorate of Army Psychiatry, War Office, (D.A.R.), February, 1944.

Dollard, John. *Fear in Battle*. New Haven: The Institute of Human Relations, Yale University, 1943.

du Picq, Ardant, Co. *Battle Studies: Ancient and Modern*. Translated by Col. John N. Greeley and Major Robert C. Cotton from the eighth edition in French. Harrisburg, Pa.: The Military Service Publishing Co., 1958. (Original edition, 1880)

Etzioni, Amitai. "The Israeli Army: The Human Factor: In two parts, *Jewish Frontier*, 26 (November 1959) and 27 (January 1960).

Etzioni, Amitai. *A Comparative Analysis of Complex Organizations*. New York: Free Press, 1961.

George, Alexander L. *The Chinese Communist Army in Action: The Korean War and Its Aftermath*. New York: Columbia University Press, 1967.

Ginzberg, E. et. al. *The Ineffective Soldier*. 3 vols. New York: Columbia University Press, 1959.

Grinker, R.R. and Spiegel, J.P. *Men Under Stress*. Philadelphia, Pa.: Blakiston, 1945.

Holmes, L.M., 2nd Lt. "Birth of the Fire Team" *Marine Corps Gazette*, 36 (1952) 17–23.

Homans, George C. "The Small Warship" *American Sociological Review*, 11 (1946) 294–300.

Janowitz, Morris; ed. *The New Military: Changing Patterns of Organization*. New York: Russell Sage Foundation, 1964.

Janowitz, Morris and Little, Roger, Lt. Col. *Sociology and the Military Establishment*. Rev. ed. New York: Russell Sage Foundation, 1965.

Joffee, Ellis. *Party and Army: Professionalism and Political Control in the Chinese Officer Corps, 1949–1964*. Cambridge, Mass.: Harvard East Asian Monographs, No. 19, 1965.

Kolkowicz, Roman. *The Soviet Military and the Communist Party.* Princeton, N.J.: Princeton University Press, 1967.

Lammers, Cornelius Jacobus. *Het Koninklijk Instituut voor de Marine* (with a summary in English). (Translated title: *The Royal Institute of the Navy: A Sociological Analysis of the Socialization of Candidate Officer Groups in the Royal Netherlands Navy.)* Amsterdam: Van Gorcum & Co., 1963.

Lang, Kurt. "Military Organizations" *Handbook of Organizations.* Edited by James G. March. Chicago, Rand McNally, 1965, lp. 838–878.

Leighton, Alexander. *Human Relations in a Changing World.* New York: Dutton & Co., 1949.

Little, Roger. "Buddy Relations and Combat Performance" *The New Military.* Edited by Morris Janowitz, New York: Russell Sage Foundation, 1964. pp. 195–223.

Mandelbaum, David G. *Soldier Groups and Negro Soldiers.* Berkeley, California: University of California Press, 1952.

Marlowe, David H. "The Basic Training Process" *The Symptom as Communication in Schizophrenia.* Edited by Kenneth L. Artiss. New York: Grune and Stratton, 1959. pp. 75–98.

Marshall, S.L.A. *Men Against Fire.* New York: William Morrow & Co. 1947.

Meyers, Samuel M. and Biderman, Albert D. eds., *Mass Behavior in Battle and Captivity: The Communist Soldier in the Korean War.* Chicago: University of Chicago Press, 1968.

Moskos, Charles. "Latent Ideology and American Combat Behavior in South Vietnam" Working Paper No. 98. Center for Social Organization Studies. University of Chicago, January 1968.

Nelson, Paul D., LCDR, MSC, USN, and CDR Berry, Newell H., MSC, USN. "Cohesion in Marine Recruit Platoons" *Journal of Psychology,* 68 (1968), 63–71.

Pike, Douglas. *Viet Cong.* Cambridge: M.I.T. Press, 1966.

Pipping, K. "The Social Life of a Machine Gun Company: *Acta Academiae Aboensis Humaniora,* 17 (1947). (English summary.)

Pye, Lucian W. *Guerrilla Communism in Malaya.* Princeton: Princeton University Press, 1956.

Roy, Jules. *The Battle of Dienbienphu.* New York: Harper & Row, 1965.

Seaton, Richard W. "Deterioration of Military Work Groups Under Deprivation Stress" *The New Military.* Edited by Morris Janowitz. New York: Russell Sage Foundation, 1964, pp. 225–249.

Shils, Edward A. "Primary Groups in the American Army" *Studies in the Scope and Method of "The American Soldier",* Edited by Robert K. Merton and Paul F. Lazarsfeld. New York: Free Press, 1950. pp. 16–39.

Shils, Edward A. and Janowitz, Morris "Cohesion and Disintegration in the Wehrmacht" *Public Opinion Quarterly,* 12 (1948), 280–315.

Speier, Hans. "The American Soldier and the Sociology of Military Organization" *Studies in the Scope and Method of "The American Soldier"* Edited by Robert K. Merton and Paul F. Lazarsfeld. New York, Free Press, 1950.

Stouffer, Samuel A. *et. al. The American Soldier.* 4 vols. Princeton, N.J.: Princeton University Press, 1949.

Zasloff, J.J. *Political Motivation of the Viet Cong: the Vietminh Regroupees.* Memorandum RM-4703/2-ISA/ARPA. Santa Monica: The RAND Corporation, May, 1968. (Original edition, August, 1966.)

Situational Determinants of
Leadership Structure*

by
David C. Korten

Leadership has long been a topic of considerable interest in the social sciences. Nearly every aspect of leadership has been the subject of some degree to study. The present paper is concerned with some of the situational factors which determine the form of leadership which will arise and be accepted in a group. Two basic questions will be considered:

1. Under what conditions will there be pressure toward centralized authoritarian leadership?

2. Under what conditions is a more participative democratic form of leadership likely to arise?

While this is certainly not a new topic, this paper attempts to develop a somewhat more systematic approach than has ordinarily been undertaken toward this subject. I feel that the "model" developed in this paper provides a framework or structure for further experimentation and theoretical development that has perhaps previously been lacking.

My initial interest in making such a study was stimulated by observation made last summer in Indonesia and Burma of a strong desire, particularly among certain high government officials, for centralized control. I observed this same trend beginning to develop in Malaya. Recent releases from Ghana suggest that this situation is not confined to Asia.

Particularly in Indonesia, which is the situation most familiar to me, there

---

*"Situational Determinants of Leadership Structure", by David C. Korten is reprinted from *The Journal of Conflict Resolution,* 1962, Vol. 6, No. 3 (Sept. 1962), pp. 222–235, by permission of the Publisher, Sage Publications, Inc.

was an original attempt at developing a free society and a free enterprise economy. In each of the countries mentioned there was no revolution in depth establishing the centralized control over more democratic institutions, nor has there been any other single totally disrupting occurrence which might account for the shift toward centralization. Though stress is certainly present, the overt crisis situation which is usually used to account for the rise of dictatorship is not entirely relevant. A more refined approach is needed.

Although each of these countries is unique in its own way, they all seem to have certain common elements in their situations which may be very important in exerting pressure for these centralizing trends. Mention of these seems helpful as a starting point for discussion.

1. Each of them is in a sense in a high drive state. There is great desire, at least among major elements of the population, for improvement and development.

2. In addition to the drive for development, there is a related but separate drive for national status to compensate for feelings of inferior status developed through years of colonial suppression.

3. A sense of crisis exists which is closely related to the high drive state and results in part from the self-imposed adverse results of many of the programs which have been attempted.

4. A reasonably definite goal structure is established which may be spelled out in great and specific detail as evidenced in the five-year plans, eight-year plans, etc., which establish production goals, and welfare measures to be attained at specific points in time.

5. All possess a low level of technical skill and an ill-developed understanding of the economic forces with which they must deal. The path to their goal is unclear and they are attempting to force clarity through control, although they lack the real understanding in many cases which is needed to accomplish effective control.

DEVELOPMENT OF A CONCEPTUAL MODEL

The first problem is one of developing a framework within which the important variables causing pressure for structural shifts can be studied and interrelated. From this framework, or model, it may then be possible to trace the forces leading a group or society from democratic to authoritarian forms of leadership and to compare these with the forces which lead the group in the opposite direction from an authoritarian to a democratic form.

This paper offers a very simplified proposal in order to facilitate initial study, even though simplification to the extent currently proposed may not be entirely realistic and certainly does not cover all possible cases. For example, no attempt has been made at this point to deal with laissez-faire forms of leadership.

We will, for the present, think in terms of a two-dimensional space represented by a four-cell matrix. The purpose is to represent discrete dimensions of authoritarian and democratic leadership against discrete dimensions of high goal structure and low goal structure. This is illustrated in Figure 1. The reasons for including the high and low goal structure dimensions should become clear later in the discussion.

	High Goal Structure	Low Goal Structure
Democratic		
*Authoritarian		

FIGURE 1
TWO DIMENSIONS OF LEADERSHIP

In the following discussion the attempt is made to characterize each of these dimensions. While it is realized that these dimensions in fact exist as continua, they are treated here as discrete for purposes of simplicity.

Goal Structure

Although I am not really satisfied with the terms *high* and *low goal structure* as being clearly descriptive of the concepts which I have in mind, I have not yet found a term which is substantially better in this respect. For this reason I suggest that preconceptions as to what the terms represent be avoided and their meaning instead be developed from the following discussion.

The consideration of goals came into the study at the very beginning in a comparative discussion of Russian communism with its presently authoritarian leadership and American democracy. In the United States approach we stress more *how* we want progress, rather than *where*, thus placing somewhat more emphasis on the method than on the outcome. Our goal is actually a continuing one and although we look for continual material and spiritual progress, we set no specific terminal goals and establish no time schedule. Our goals are to a large extent *non-operational*.[1]

On the other hand, the Russians seek to build a way of life not yet attained. Their stated orientation is toward future attainment and involves emphasis on change rather than on preservation. Their goals are fairly concrete or *operational* in such things as surpassing free world industrial output and communizing the world. Such terminal goals as these assume great importance and lead to the establishing of a definite timetable of accomplishment.

I feel these goal differences may have a great importance in helping to explain the differences in the forms of government adopted. It was consideration of these factors which led to adopting the term high and low goal structure which referred to the clarity of expression or structuring of future goals which the group was seeking to attain.

*Editor's note: Dr. Korten uses the terms authoritarian and autocratic synonymously. In this article he is referring to the willingness of the leader to share the decision-making process.

As the model developed further, this description broke down to some extent as it was found that the cognitive clarity was not so essential as the terminal quality. Still no alternative has been suggested which seems to be a real improvement. The original concept still fits very nicely into the final model, but the present model is not so limiting as the original concept.

High Goal Structure. In this situation we are concerned with groups which have rather specific goals which are of importance in the consensus of group opinion. The group is looked upon as a means of carrying out tasks or operations which will lead to these goals. It is not generally characterized by the desire to maintain the status quo, but rather by the desire to work toward a new situation or to attain something which the group has not presently attained. Group goals assume considerably more importance than individual goals. Individuals see the attainment of the group goal as prerequisite to the attainment of their own goals.

In some situations there may be a specific threat to the status quo which is introduced from a source external to the group. In this case the "new situation" would be the status quo with the threat removed. If a crisis has already occurred, the goal might be *reattainment* of the *old* status quo, but it would *not* be *maintainance* of the *present* status quo.

Low Goal Structure. The group in the low goal structure situation will have fewer or much less important shared achievement goals. Such goals as exist will more likely relate to maintaining routine functions necessary to maintaining the status quo or making slight readjustments in it. There will be less commonality of individual goals, and attraction to the group might be considered more social in nature. Emphasis will tend to be on individual rather than on group goals. To the extent that the person does identify with the group, the identification is likely to be based on personal attractiveness or on the means which the group offers for the facilitation of personal efforts to attain individual goals.

Descriptive Examples. A study carried out by Back (1) is very useful in describing or characterizing the interactions expected in the high and low goal structure situations. This study provides a discussion of differences in social interactions under different orientations toward group membership.

Two of the situations studied were cohesiveness based on the performance of a task and cohesiveness based on personal attraction.

It may be expected that interaction in the high goal structure group will be most closely characterized by that found in Back's task-oriented group where "group members wanted to complete the activity quickly and efficiently; they spent just the time necessary for the performance of the task, and they tried to use this time for the performance of the task only." There was an absolute minimum of social as opposed to task-oriented interaction.

The low goal structure situation would probably be more closely characterized by the group where cohesiveness was based on personal attraction and there was little emphasis on the group task. This group was essentially interested in enjoying the status quo. The activity of these groups tended toward "longish, pleasant conversation."

Sussman's study (12) of the "Calorie Collectors," an organization of women supposedly drawn together to participate in weight-losing activities, also provides a similar characterization of the two goal structure situations.

The members of this club could be divided into one of two classes. The first were those who were primarily interested in looking for social support and sympathy for their problem. These would be in the low goal structure situation. The other group was described as the serious dieters who were really interested in undertaking activities leading to the loss of weight. These would be in the high goal structure situation.[2]

A reasonably clear example could be described at the level of the local community. In the usual case, the function and orientation of this unit of organization will be toward providing the services upon which individuals are dependent for maintenance of their personal pursuits. Emphasis would be on such relatively routine functions as maintenance of the streets, law enforcement, fire protection, garbage collection, provision of utilities, and other common services. This would be an example of a low goal structure situation.

This same community might be considered in the high structure situation if the citizens were strongly intent upon making certain changes in their community. These might take the form of a massive community beautification campaign or an all-out effort to attract new industries, etc. Individual goals of having personal prosperity would be aroused and their attainment would be seen as dependent upon accomplishment of these group goals.

Leadership

In the discussion of democratic and authoritarian leadership. I have relied on the operational definitions developed by White and Lippitt (16, 26). Further elaboration will be made at a later stage concerning additional characteristics. For the present these operational definitions seem appropriate for either large or small groups. Since these are both well-known concepts, little further elaboration at this point seems necessary.

Authoritarian Leadership

1. All determination of policy by the leader.

2. Techniques and activity steps dictated by the leader, one at a time, so that future steps are always uncertain to a large degree.

3. The leader usually dictates the particular work task and work companion of each member.

4. The leader tends to be "personal" in his praise and criticism of the work of each member, but remains aloof from active group participation except when demonstrating.

Democratic Leadership

1. All policies a matter of group discussion and decision, encouraged and assisted by the leader.

2. Activity perspective gained during discussion period. General steps to group goal sketched, and where technical advice is needed the leader suggests two or more alternative procedures from which the choice can be made.

3. The members are free to work with whomever they choose, and the division of tasks is left up to the group.

4. The leader is "objective" or "fact-minded" in his praise and criticism, and tries to be a regular group member in its spirit without doing too much of the work.

THE DYNAMIC CHARACTERISTICS OF THE MODEL

So far we have been concerned only with the development of static definitional concepts. The real interest, however, is in the dynamic characteristics of the model—the forces causing shifts from one to another of the cells of the matrix.

The Influence of Stress

The term stress is used here to include actual stress, motivation, desire, etc., regardless of the source from which it might arise. The stress may have one of two origins. First would be from natural disaster or from some other form of externally imposed threat. The second would be motivation arising from increased level of expectation, changes in values, etc. In other words stress arising in the first case is essentially a threat to the status quo as in the cases of the crisis studies where a present equilibrium is threatened. In the second case stress results rather from an increase in the level of equilibrium along some dimension of desire.

The outcome seems much the same regardless of the source of the stress, but the two situations may appear somewhat different when they are experienced and may have later implications for refinements in the model. Probably the first will tend to be more severe in its effects.

Our attention will be directed first to movements along the goal structure continuum, or rather shifts between high and low goal structure cells while the leadership pattern remains constant. At this point the assertion will be tested that an increase in situational stress will cause an increase in goal structuring, while reduction in stress will lead to a reduction in goal structuring. This is diagramed in Figure 2.

Stress and Tolerance for Ambiguity. There have been a number of studies attempting to relate stress and tolerance of ambiguity. Wispe and Lloyd (17) did a study of 43 life insurance representatives in which they related sales productivity, preference for permissive or structured group organization, and

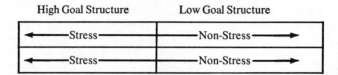

FIGURE 2
EFFECTS OF SITUATIONAL STRESS ON GOAL STRUCTURING

amount of threat perceived in the organizational environment. They find a significant tendency for persons who perceived little threat in their environment to prefer permissiveness in the group organization. Those with a higher threat orientation preferred the more highly structured group situation.

Smock (11) found that groups placed under stress showed a greater tendency to make an early attempt to recognize structure in an ambiguous situation. Furthermore, they tended to adhere more strongly to their prerecognition hypothesis in spite of increasing incongruity between their hypothesis and the stimuli.

Cohen (3) reports, from a study using an interview situation, that a highly significant relationship exists between lack of situational structure and the perception of threat in the power exercised by others. This experiment seems to suggest that a perception of threat and the anxiety or stress caused by such a perception can be reduced by seeking to increase situation structure.

Stress and Goal Clarity. Though specific empirical evidence has not been found, it might be suggested that in the absence of stress a group will tend to maintain less-structured goals or objectives. This is only to say that we tend to seek to maintain the status quo when our drives are satisfied and we feel secure.

The development of specific goals which might be difficult to attain develops the possibility of failure and creates anxiety or the pressure for attaining these goals. A less-structured goal situation is safer and less threatening.

When stress is introduced, the status quo is no longer satisfactory and change is sought to reduce the anxiety. The highly non-operational goal of anxiety reduction is introduced. If the cause of the stress is ambiguous, this in itself will further serve to increase the anxiety. It can be expected that the first efforts will be made to reduce the ambiguity by attempting to identify or give structure to the source of the anxiety.

Another source of ambiguity will be present when, even though the source of the stress is clear, it is not exactly clear what actions can be taken to remove the source of the stress.

Anxiety seems to serve as a motivation for three actions, which must logically be made in sequence. The completion of any one of these will serve to reduce a part of the anxiety.

1. Identify the source of the anxiety.
2. Identify the steps which must be taken to remove the anxiety.

3. Carry out the steps identified in 2.

The first two parts of the sequence are concerned primarily with reduction of ambiguity but are nearly essential to successful purposeful (as opposed to random) actions to reduce the anxiety. The ambiguity is a frustrating experience because it stands as a barrier to successful action. As Lewin (8, 255) points out, "An unstructured region has the same effect as an impassable obstacle. Being in unstructured surroundings leads to uncertainty of behavior because it is not clear whether a certain action will lead to or away from a goal."

Torrance (13), who studied a group of 200 Air Force personnel downed over enemy territory during World War II or Korea, relates the results of situations where the ambiguity is not reduced. He found that in this very stressful survival situation two types of structural unclarity were likely to be evident: (a) unclear structure of paths to survival and (b) unstablized relations among persons. He found that these were likely to lead to either random, trial-and-error behavior, or to development of a feeling of hopelessness which usually led to surrender to the enemy.

Studies have found that in stressful situations where goal and path clarity is not established, there will be a tendency to avoid the situation or to leave the group.

Gerard (4, 397) reported that low-status subjects whose group goals were unclear tended to withdraw from their group, become dissatisfied with their roles, and devaluate their own effectiveness.

Weitz (15) conducted a study of 474 life insurance salesmen who tend, as the nature of their occupation, to be under considerable competitive stress. A detailed book describing the work to be done was given to 226 of them. The other 248 were not given the book. There was a considerably higher rate of termination among those for whom the situation was not clearly defined.

It should be quite clear that once a goal is attained, it is no longer a goal. If the goal has been attained and the anxiety reduced, the group has almost automatically relocated itself in the low goal structure situation. Of course this is looking to a sort of "pure" case. Particularly in a larger organization it would be highly unlikely that all goals would be attained and all anxieties removed at any particular point in time. It seems at least conceptually possible, however, to think in terms of an overall index of anxiety and degree of goal structuring in order to place the group along the goal structure continuum.

Changes in Leadership

The shifts from one goal structure cell to another are merely incidental to a unified hypothesis regarding the development of pressures for shifts between democratic and authoritarian leadership.

The "Natural" Shifts in Leadership Patterns. While it is possible for these shifts between democratic and authoritarian leadership to take place at either the high or low goal structure levels, the hypothesis to be tested suggests that *unless outside pressure or force is exerted,* the direction of the shifts in the high goal structure situation will be only from democratic to authoritarian and in the low goal structure situation it will be only from authoritarian to democratic. This is represented very simply in Figure 3.

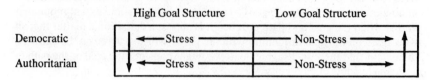

FIGURE 3
DIRECTION OF SHIFTS IN LEADERSHIP PATTERNS

High Stress Shift From Democratic to Authoritarian Leadership. We have already established that under stressful conditions there will be strong pressures exerted for the development of clear goals and clearly defined methods of attaining them. In going one step further, we may also expect that the more compelling and/or the more clearly structured the goal, the greater will be the desire to take a direct approach to the attainment of the goal. Pleasant socializing is replaced with more intense emphasis on achievement. This would suggest attempting to attain complete control over any ambiguities in the environment, especially those ambiguities which take the form of deviant individuals or subgroups. The greater the immediacy or urgency, the greater the demand that all available resources be channeled directly toward the attainment of this goal. This is sometimes difficult to do while still attempting to maintain truly democratic institutions.

Deviants loom as frustration-creating barriers to the goal attainment. The most direct way to remove the barrier is to control it and move it at will. There are two basic forms which this control may take. Of course, here again we must realize that we are in reality dealing with a continuum. The first is the control common to democratic institutions where certain limits are set on action, and control is carried out by the policing of exceptions. Actual attainment of goals is more likely to depend on conformity attained through perceived commonality of interest or through group social pressures. The second form of control is the authoritarian form which seeks to maintain absolute control over every action taking place within the organization. The greater the pressures for collective action and the greater the tendency for deviation within the group, the more likely it is that this form of control will have the greater appeal.

The assertion is explicit in the model that a democratic organization can maintain itself with a well-defined goal structure. It now remains to establish the conditions under which this is likely to be the case, as well as stating those conditions under which the appeal of authoritarianism will be more overpowering.

When is democracy retained?

We can see from the nature of the control methods available under democracy that the success of democracy in the face of crisis depends to large degree on the cohesiveness of the group and its ability to apply sanctions through social pressure. This is most assured if the goal is clear, the path to the goal is clear, and individuals identify their own objectives with group objectives and agree on the methods of attaining these. This means essentially a minimum of unresolved ambiguity. The statement is to some extent redundant in that when the goal and path are clear it is almost a definitional matter that all who agree on the goal or identify with the group will also agree on the path. To the extent that there is disagreement, we might consider the goal or the path to contain elements of ambiguity.[3]

When is there a shift to authoritarianism?

Stress reduction in itself does not provide a unifying group goal due to its rather extreme non-operational, ambiguous character. Cohesiveness under stress is dependent on some agreement as to the source of the stress, or on the goal, the attainment of which will reduce the stress. Further cohesiveness can be developed through agreement on the path to the attainment of the goal. Since the cohesiveness of the group becomes more and more task-oriented as the stress increases, the group will be evaluated in terms of its potential for providing a means of completing the task-stress reduction. Thus the less the agreement within the group with regard to how the objective may be attained, the less the individual who disagrees with the group view will be attracted to the group and the more he will attempt to take independent action, form opposition groups, etc.

This situation may be expected to lead to more overt action on the part of leaders to control these deviants in order to reduce the ambiguity which they face in their decision-making. Control over the deviants gives them greater control over their environment and removes impediments to what they consider to be effective action. The greater the stress, and the less the clarity and general agreement on goals and path, the greater the compulsion among the group members to give power to a central person who in essence promises to remove the ambiguity and reduce the stress. Hook (7, 13) points out that, ". . . insofar as alternatives of action are open, or even conceived to be open—a need will be felt for a hero to initiate, organize, and lead."

That there is a tendency toward reliance on a power figure in ambiguous situations may be demonstrated at even very low levels on the continuum, as is demonstrated in a study by Waring, Dwyer, and Junkin (14). They found that during meals on the first day of nursery school, children were more ready to acquiesce to the advice of the adult than later on when they felt themselves to be on better-known ground for resisting. In other words, during the period of initial ambiguity, they tended to submit to an authoritarian leader on whom they relied to help structure the situation.

Hamblin (5) found in laboratory groups subjected to apparent crisis in a problem-solving experience a tendency to replace the old leader with a new leader if the old leader did not have an obvious solution to the crisis problem. Hertzler (6) did an analysis of 35 historical dictatorships. Although his method was not as systematic and objectives as might be desired, his conclusion is consistent with the one reached here (6, 160).

"A befuddled and fearsome mass in time of crisis is nearly always ready, nay anxious, to give over control to anyone who gives evidence of ability to wield it efficiently. This situation, in turn, both demands and provides the opportunity for a leader or a cohesive minority group which offers a ready made formula of social procedure and which promises a dynamic attack upon the problems."

Other experiments have demonstrated increased suggestibility in situations of ambiguity which point up the increased possibility for an authoritarian leader to introduce distorting suggestions when ambiguity is present. Luchins and Luchins (9) presented subjects with a picture identification task. Subjects were influenced by an overheard judgment and by the experimenter's evaluation of the communication as right or wrong. Although there was more agreement with the true than with the false communications, the conformity with false communications, and failures to respond were higher for the ambiguous than for the clear-cut pictures.

Coffin (2) conducted a series of studies which are relevant to the present problem. In one case he used the Rorschach ink-blot tests as the ambiguous stimulus. Subjects were given a fictitious journal article stating that business and professional men would see the blots in one way while laborers would see them in another way. Using college students as subjects, the conclusion was reached that "subjects may be influenced by suggestion not only to accept or assent to a suggested statement, but actively to construct the imaginative situation in accordance with the suggestion given." From this not-very-surprising conclusion we see a laboratory demonstration of an often-used political technique to force judgments in unfavorable situations. "A good American will recognize that . . . etc."

Another experiment by Coffin (2) revealed low but consistent correlation between suggestibility and difficulty of a set of math problems. The degree of suggestibility declined with years of mathematical training. This may have particular relevance in the underdeveloped countries where the tasks are indeed difficult yet the level of training is very low. It is in these countries where there seems to be the greatest susceptibility to authoritarian leadership.[4]

Still another experiment conducted by Coffin (2) used sound stimuli and again found that suggestibility increased as the ambiguity of the assigned task increased.

Shifts From Authoritarian To Democratic Leadership Under Low Stress. In the low stress situation, it would seem difficult for authoritarian leadership to maintain itself. We can expect that the power held by the authoritarian figure will be reduced as was found in a study by Hamblin (5). He found that the person with highest influence in a group had the greatest influence (relative to other members of the group) during periods of crisis. This influence decreased as the goal was attained and the crisis was thereby reduced or removed.

Once major group goals have been attained, the cohesiveness of the group will once again come to depend more upon the socializing process. Greater importance will be placed on the attempt to satisfy individual needs which may have been either sacrificed or frustrated by the authoritarian leadership.

As in the case of the White and Lippitt study there will be decreased satisfaction with the authoritarian structure and the opportunity for greater individual participation and self-determination will be desired. In many cases the surface expressions of this discontent exhibited in the presence of the authoritarian leader are such as to probably go unnoticed, but at least in the White and Lippitt study these showed up clearly in careful analysis.

The following expressions of the discontent were noted (16, 74–76).

1. Four boys dropped out of the clubs during the experimental situation and all did so during periods of autocratic leadership.

2. Nineteen of twenty boys who made direct comparisons between the autocratic and democratic leaders stated preferences for the democratic leader.

3. The boys made significantly more discontented remarks to each other under autocratic than under democratic rule.

4. There were more expressions of discontent directed at the leader.

5. There was more ignoring of the leader's approaches.

Over a longer period of time as these resentments built up under the confining authority, we might expect that more overt signs of discontent would develop.

"Unnatural!" Shifts in Leadership Patterns. One can hardly imagine shifts between democratic and authoritarian leadership taking place in directions opposite to those just discussed *if* indeed the important variables are as they have been described. Cases can easily be found, however, of shifts counter to the direction indicated. It might be established that *these* shifts do not usually take place as a matter of group acceptance or from other internal pressures, but rather are forced upon the group through superior strength. A military dictator may arise in a time of indifference and establish military control; a department or office of a larger firm may be suddenly assigned a new administrator who introduces a more centralized control, etc. These shifts do take place, but they are of a somewhat artificial nature compared with the processes which we have been discussing.

A shift from authoritarian to democratic leadership in a situation of high stress would also seem to be very unlikely unless an outside force dedicated to democratic leadership overthrew or replaced the former leaders and then significantly reduced the source of the stress that had kept the authoritarian leader in power. Other special cases might be presented where an authoritarian leader apparently gave up his power voluntarily in time of high stress, but such occurrence is rare and such cases would have to be examined individually to determine their relationship to the present model.

The Equilibrium Cells

It should be clear that there are resistances to shifts in leadership patterns taking place. These are created by tradition and vested interest. There are thus important restraining factors involved to prevent the shifts previously indicated. The hypothesis we have developed establishes only the direction of the pressures which exist for change, but does not promise that the change will actually take place.

The direction of the pressures suggests that in the highly structured goal situation the equilibrium cell is one in which authoritarian leadership is exercised, while in the low goal structure situation, it is democratic leadership which exists in the equilibrium situation. In the low goal structure group, the emphasis will be on individual subgoals rather than super organization goals. In a sense this might be considered the characteristic nature of the democracy with its emphasis on the individual rather than the group. In this situation the group leadership will be sought which will serve the advancement of the individual. The autocrat will be hard put to maintain his position.

When a more all-consuming group goal is developed, the individual's role becomes subservient to the group and his only importance comes in his contribution to the group. This is the situation in the high goal structure condition and it is here that the autocracy will be in equilibrium. The democratic government will be in constant danger of running into new ambiguities and losing its consensus support.

Maintaining Authoritarian Equilibrium

It seems that authoritarian leaders have a particular appreciation of the equilibrium acting to maintain their power in the high stress, highly structured goal situation. Thus it can be seen that one of the most important activities of a dictatorship is that of stressing the threats created by both external and internal enemies in order to maintain the stress and produce the super goals which can be used to unite the populace. These must be constantly internalized by the people.

In Indonesia this is represented by the "struggle for West Irian" which is reiterated in nearly every public utterance by every public official. For the Communist countries, the "foe" is the menace of capitalism, represented by the United States in particular. The most extreme emphasis is placed on this in Communist China, where the internal problems are much more severe than in Russia, for example. Considerable dependence is placed on these central goals in directing the people's attention away from the frustrations experienced in satisfying their true personal goals.[5]

In Sussman's study (12, 354) we find a case where a group leader was attempting to maintain an essentially authoritarian leadership position; however, this leader made little pretense of establishing or working toward group goals. "Leadership as it existed in Calorie Collectors was one of attainment of personal influence and power by Mrs. Lott rather than achievement of group goals. The result was ultimate factionalism and disorganization." The group disintegrated and later reformed around another woman who was oriented more toward group objectives of planning programs to encourage weight reduction. This gives one example of loss of control by an authoritarian leader in a situation where the leader did not identify with group goals.

It is interesting to note further technique used by the authoritarian to maintain his leadership. This is mentioned in the operational definition by White and Lippitt (16, 26)—"Techniques and activity steps dictated by the authority, one at a time, so that future steps are always uncertain to a large degree."

This serves several functions. It provides reduction of immediate anxiety, but retains dependence on the authoritarian leader for further reduction of the ambiguity when the present step is completed. It also makes it difficult for failure to be evaluated, as it is not possible to determine the actual importance of any particular step that is taken. It is further not possible to certainly establish whether or not the current step is truly leading toward the *stated* goal. Considerable faith must be placed on the authoritarian. If his work is not accepted, the situation again becomes intolerably ambiguous.

Implications

It is difficult at this point to discuss specific applications of detailed knowledge of the influence of these situational pressures on leadership. However, it is possible to suggest where applications might be sought.

This study was undertaken from the point of view of an advocate of democratic or participative leadership. In order to insure the preservation of the democratic structure, it seems essential to understand the forces which cause pressure for a shift from democratic structure to more highly authoritarian structure.

Through greater understanding, possibly either the situations leading to the pressures may be avoided or effective countermeasures can be established to resist the pressures expected under certain circumstances. Not only does this have implication at the national and international political level and in particular in dealings with newly independent nations, but it might also prove of value in the implementation of the relatively new group-centered theories of management and organization. Systematic study and organization of the forces which resist the successful introduction and application of participative management are the first steps in finding suitable implementation techniques and in establishing the situation or environment in which such types of organization can persist in equilibrium.

More could be done at this point to discuss the problems of leadership in underdeveloped countries which served as the introduction of the paper. Most of the implications should, however, be reasonably clear and will for the present be left as they were presented—the initiating stimulus for undertaking the study. The important problem was to provide the model or "structure" which could then be adapted for application to these specific situational problems. The same statement could be made with regard to the applications to participative management.

END NOTES

1. March and Simon (10, 155) developed the concept of *operational* and *non-operational* goals. "When a means of testing actions is perceived to relate a particular goal or cri-

terion with possible courses of action, the criterion will be called operational. Otherwise the criterion will be non-operational."

2. It might be pointed out that a group can be in both of the goal structure situations at the same time as suggested by the Sussman observations. This is probably always true to some extent, but it also seems from the study that there were essentially two distinct groups within the "Calorie Collectors." When such a situation exists, the two subgroups may tend to work at cross purposes and the total effect may be very disruptive of group performance as was the case in this situation. This may account for the ineffective performance of many small informal organizations. While this would make a very interesting area for further study, it does not appear directly relevant to the present discussion.

3. Although this seems the situation most conducive to maintaining democratic leadership in time of stress or even crisis, it may be seen that there is also a danger in complete agreement, because in this case there may be too little concern with maintaining restrictions on the power of leaders. If those in power are opportunists, this provides their opportunity to establish authoritarian control. Thus even when the real crisis is passed, the people may find that now they are unable to regain the power which they originally passed to the central authority. "Where a democracy is wise, it will whole-heartedly cooperate with its leaders and at the same time be suspicious of the powers delegated to them—a difficult task but one which must be solved if democracy is not to become, as often in the past, a school for tyrants" (7, 14).

4. When Hook (7, 238) points out that "A successful democracy . . . may honor its statesmen: but it must honor its teachers more . . . " he is in a way suggesting that a democracy must be able to decrease situational ambiguity through increased knowledge of the situations likely to be encountered rather than relying upon a hero leader to provide this structure.

5. It will be noted that China is an especially complex case, as the "manufactured" crisis is used to structure the stress created by a real internal crisis. The attempt is to develop a structure more consistent with retaining the present government in power than would be the case if the structure were allowed to develop around the true source of the stress.

REFERENCES

1. Back, K.W. The exertion of influence through social communication. *Journal of Abnormal and Social Psychology,* 1951, 46, 9–24.

2. Coffin, T.E. Some conditions of suggestion and suggestibility: A study of some attitudinal and situational factors influencing the process of suggestion. *Psychological Monographs,* 1941, No. 241.

3. Cohen, A.R. Situation structure, self-esteem, and threat-oriented reactions to power. In D. Cartwright (Ed.), *Studies in social power.* Ann Arbor, Mich.: Institute for Social Research, 1959.

4. Gerard, H. Unpublished study reported in D. Cartwright and A. Zander, (Eds.) *Group dynamics research and theory.* Evanston, Ill.: Row, Peterson, 1960.

5. Hamblin, R.L. Leadership and crises. *Sociometry,* 1958, 21, 322–335.

6. Hertzler, J.O. Crises and dictatorship. *American Sociological Review,* 1940, 5, 157–169.

7. Hook, S. *The hero in history.* New York: John Day Co., 1943.

8. Lewin, K. *Field theory in social science.* New York: Harper, 1959.

9. Luchins, A.S., & Luchins, E.H. Previous experience with ambiguous stimulus under various social influences. *Journal of Social Psychological,* 1955, 42, 249–270.

10. March, J.G., & Simon, H.A. *Organizations.* New York: Wiley, 1958.

11. Smock, C.D. The influence of stress on the intolerance of ambiguity. *Journal of Abnormal and Social Psychology,* 1955, 50, 177–182.

12. Sussman, M.B. The calorie collectors: A study of spontaneous group formation, collapse, and reconstruction. *Social Forces,* 1956, 34, 351–356.

13. Torrance, E.P. The behavior of small groups under stress conditions of survival. *American Sociological Review,* 1954, 19, 751–755.

14. Waring, E.S., Dwyer, F.M., & Junkin, E. Guidance: The case of Ronald. *Cornell Bulletin for Homemakers,* 1939, 418, 1–112.

15. Weitz, J. Job expectancy and survival. *Journal of Applied Psychology.* 1956, 40, 245–247.

16. White, R.K., & Lippitt, R. *Autocracy and democracy: An experimental inquiry.* New York: Harper, 1960.

17. Wispe, L.G., & Lloyd, K.E. Some situation and psychological determinants of the desire for structured interpersonal relations. *Journal of Abnormal and Social Psychology,* 1955, 51, 57–60.

Vietnam: Why Men Fight*

by
Charles C. Moskos, Jr.

This study is based on my observations of American soldiers in combat made during two separate stays in South Vietnam. During the first field trip in 1965, I spent two weeks with a weapons squad in a rifle platoon of a paratrooper unit. The second field trip in 1967 included a six-day stay with an infantry rifle squad, and shorter periods with several other combat squads. Although identified as a university professor and sociologist, I had little difficulty gaining access to the troops because of my official status as an accredited correspondent. I entered combat units by simply requesting permission from the local headquarters to move into a squad. Once there, I experienced the same living conditions as the squad members. The novelty of my presence soon dissipated as I became a regular participant in the day-to-day activities of the squad.

The soldiers with whom I was staying were performing combat missions of a patrolling nature, the most typical type of combat operation in Vietnam. Patrols are normally small-unit operations involving squads (9-12 men) or platoons (30-40 men). Such small units made up patrols whose usual mission was to locate enemy forces which could then be subjected to ground, artillery or air attack. Patrols normally last one or several days and are manned by lower-ranking enlisted men, noncommissioned officers leading squads and lieutenants heading platoons.

In the vast majority of instances these patrols turn out to be a "walk in the

---

sun," meeting only sporadic or no enemy resistance. Even when enemy contact is not made, however, patrols suffer casualties from land mines and booby traps. But it is primarily on those occasions when enemy forces are encountered that casualty rates are extremely high. Upon return to the permanent base camp, members of the patrol are able to enjoy a modicum of physical comfort. They live in large tents, eat hot food, get their mail more or less regularly, see movies, and can purchase beer, cigarettes and toilet articles at field Post Exchanges. They spend the bulk of their time in camp on guard duty and maintaining equipment.

In both the 1965 and 1967 field trips, I collected data through informal observations and personal interviewing of combat soldiers. During the second field trip I also conducted 34 standardized interviews with the men of the particular squads with whom I was staying. Some of the information contained in these 34 interviews is amenable to tabular ordering. Yet even when given in tabular form the data are not to be conceived as self-contained, but rather as supportive of more broadly based observations.

The attitude expressed by the formally interviewed soldiers constantly reappeared in conversations I had with numerous other combat soldiers in both 1965 and 1967. Again and again, I was struck by the common reactions of soldiers to the combat experience and their participation in the war. By myself being in the combat situation, I could conduct lengthy interviews on an intimate basis. I assert with some confidence that the findings reflect a set of beliefs widely shared by American combat soldiers throughout Vietnam during the period of the field work.

A prefatory comment is needed on the social origins of the men I interviewed. The 34 soldiers had the following civilian background prior to entering the service: ten were high school dropouts, only two of whom were ever regularly employed; 21 were high-school graduates, six directly entering the service after finishing school; and three were college dropouts. None were college graduates. Eighteen of the 34 men had full-time employment before entering the service, 12 in blue-collar jobs and six in white-collar employment. About two-thirds of the soldiers were from working-class backgrounds with the remainder being from the lower-middle class.

As for other social background characteristics: eight were black; one was a Navajo; another was from Guam; the other 20 men were white including three Mexican-Americans and one Puerto Rican. Only seven of the squad members were married (three after entering the service). All the men, except two sergeants, were in their late teens and early twenties, the average age being 20 years. Again excepting the sergeants, all were on their initial enlistments. Twenty of the men were draftees and 14 were Regular Army volunteers. Importantly, except for occasional sardonic comments directed toward the Regulars by the draftees, the behavior and attitudes of the soldiers toward the war were very similar regardless of how they entered the service.

Few stories to come out of the Vietnam War are so poignant as the story of Company A of the 196th Light Infantry Brigade, Third Battalion. As told by Associated Press reporters Horst Fass and Peter Arnett in a cable dated

August 26, 1969, Company A had been pushing for five days through enemy-held territory in an effort to recover the bodies of eight Americans killed in a helicopter crash 31 miles south of Da Nang. Now, its strength halved to 60 men, its platoon leaders dead or wounded, Company A was ordered to move down a jungled rocky slope of Nuilon Mountain. They refused. Most of the men were 19 or 20 years old, draftees, and many of them had only a short time to go before being rotated back to the States. They were ordered to move out and they refused.

The rest of the story is unimportant; as far as the military command is concerned the whole story is unimportant. But for many Americans, Company A's refusal to fight that day must have raised terrible questions—perhaps, above all, questions about one's own personal courage, but questions too about how and why American soldiers continue to expose themselves to death and pain in a war that few civilians any longer believe in.

The most popular notion of how men are brought to kill and be killed in combat has to do with the presumed national character of the soldiers. Different national armies perform better or worse according to the putative martial spirit of their respective citizenries. Italians make "poor" soldiers, Germans "good" ones. Another view has it that combat performance is basically a consequence of the operation of the formal military organization—the strict discipline, military training, unit esprit de corps and so forth. This viewpoint is, naturally enough, found in traditional military thought, but the importance of military socialization is similarly emphasized—albeit from different premises— by antimilitarists concerned with the perversions that military life allegedly inflicts on men's minds. Another interpretation—often the hallmark of political rhetoric—holds that combat performance depends on the soldier's conscious allegiance to the stated purposes of the war. Whether motivated by patriotism or a belief that he is fighting for a just cause, the effective soldier is ultimately an ideologically inspired soldier.

Yet another explanation of combat motivation developed out of the social science studies of World War II. This interpretation deemphasizes cultural, formal socialization and ideological factors and focuses attention instead on the crucial role of face-to-face or "primary" groups. The motivation of the individual combat soldier rests on his solidarity and social intimacy with fellow soldiers at small-group levels. This viewpoint was characteristic of the studies that Samuel Stouffer and his associates reported in *The American Soldier,* as well as the analysis of the *Wehrmacht* by Edward Shils and Morris Janowitz. The rediscovery of the importance of primary groups by social scientists was parallelled in the accounts given by novelists and other writers about combat behavior such as Norman Mailer, James Jones, J. Glenn Gray and S.L.A. Marshall. In a few of the more extreme elaborations of this theory, primary relations among men in combat were viewed as so intense that they overrode not only preexisting civilian values and formal military goals, but even the individual's own sense of self-preservation.

My own research among American soldiers in Vietnam has led me to question the dominant influence of the primary group in combat motivation on at least two counts. First, the self-serving aspects of primary relations in combat units must be fully appreciated. War is a Hobbesian world and, in combat, life is truly short, nasty and brutish. But, to carry Hobbes a step farther, primary group processes in combat are a kind of rudimentary social contract, a contract that is entered into because of its advantages to oneself. Second, although the American soldier has a deep aversion to overt political symbols and patriotic appeals, this fact should not obscure his even deeper commitments to other values that serve to maintain the soldier under dangerous conditions. These values—misguided or not—must be taken into account in explaining the generally creditable combat performance American soldiers have given. Put most formally, I would argue that combat motivation arises out of the linkages between individual self-concern and the shared beliefs of soldiers as these are shaped by the immediate combat situation.

To convey the immediacy of the combat situation is hard enough for the novelist, not to say the sociologist. But to understand the fighting soldier's attitudes and behavior, it is vital to comprehend the extreme physical conditions under which he must try to live. It is only in the immediate context of battle that one can grasp the nature of the group processes developed in combat squads. For within the network of his relations with fellow squad members, the combat soldier is also fighting a very private war, a war he desperately hopes to leave alive and unscathed.

The concept of relative deprivation—interpreting an individual's evaluation of his situation by knowing the group he compares himself with—has been one of the most fruitful in social inquiry. We should not, however, forget that there are some conditions of life in which deprivation is absolute. In combat, a man's social horizon is narrowly determined by his immediate life chances in the most literal sense. The fighting soldier, as an absolutely deprived person, responds pragmatically to maximize any and all shortrun opportunities to improve his chances of survival. For the soldier the decisions of state that brought him into combat are irrelevant, meaningless.

Under fire, the soldier not only faces an imminent danger of his own death and wounding; he also witnesses the killing and suffering of his buddies. And always, there are the routine physical stresses of combat life—the weight of the pack, tasteless food, diarrhea, lack of water, leeches, mosquitos, rain, torrid heat, mud and loss of sleep. In an actual firefight with the enemy, the scene is generally one of terrible chaos and confusion. Deadening fear intermingles with acts of bravery and, strangely enough, even moments of exhilaration and comedy. If prisoners are taken, they may be subjected to atrocities in the rage of battle or its immediate aftermath. The soldier's distaste for endangering civilians is overcome by his fear that any Vietnamese, of any age or sex, could very well want him dead. Where the opportunity arises, he will often loot. War souvenirs are frequently collected, either to be kept or later sold to rear-echelon servicemen.

As Stendahl and Tolstoy noted long ago, once the fight is over, the soldier still has little idea of what has been accomplished in a strategic sense. His view of the war is limited to his own observations and subsequent talks with others in the same platoon or company. The often-noted reluctance of soldiers to discuss their war experiences when back home doesn't hold true in the field. They talk constantly, repetitiously, of the battles and skirmishes they have been through. They talk about them not just to talk, but more importantly to nail down tactics that may save their lives in future encounters with the enemy.

For the individual soldier, the paramount factor affecting combat motivation is the operation of the rotation system. Under current assignment policies Army personnel serve a 12-month tour of duty in Vietnam. Barring his being killed or severely wounded, then, every soldier knows exactly when he will leave Vietnam. His whole being centers on reaching his personal "DEROS" (Date Expected Return Overseas). It is impossible to overstate the soldier's constant concern with how much more time—down to the day—he must remain in Vietnam.

Within the combat unit, the rotation system has many consequences for social cohesion and individual motivation. The rapid·turnover of personnel hinders the development of primary group ties, even as it rotates out of the unit men who have attained fighting experience. It also, however, mitigates those strains (noted in World War II in *The American Soldier*) that occur when new replacements are confronted by seasonal combat veterans. Yet because of the tactical nature of patrols and the somewhat random likelihood of encountering the enemy, a new arrival may soon experience more actual combat than some of the men in the same company who are nearing the end of their tour in Vietnam. Whatever its effects on the long-term combat effectiveness of the American forces as a whole, however, the rotation system does largely account for the generally high morale of the combat soldier.

During his one-year stint in Vietnam, the fighting soldier finds his attitude undergoing definite changes. Although attitudes depend a good deal on individual personality and combat exposure, they usually follow a set course. Upon arrival at his unit and for several weeks thereafter, the soldier is excited to be in the war zone and looks forward to engaging the enemy. After the first serious encounter, however, he loses his enthusiasm for combat. He becomes highly respectful of the enemy's fighting abilities and begins to fear and scorn the South Vietnamese. He grows skeptical of victory statements from headquarters and of the official reports of enemy casualties. From about the third to the eighth month of his tour, the soldier operates on a kind of plateau of moderate commitment to his combat role.

Toward the ninth and tenth months, the soldier begins to regard himself as an "old soldier," and it is usually at this point that he is generally most effective in combat. As he approaches the end of his tour in Vietnam, however, he begins noticeably to withdraw his efficiency. He now becomes reluctant to engage in offensive combat operations; and increasingly, he hears and repeats stories of men killed the day they were to rotate back home.

It is significant, though, that "short-timer's fever" is implicitly recognized by the others, and demands on short-timers are informally reduced. The final disengagement period of the combat soldier is considered a kind of earned prerogative which those earlier in the rotation cycle hope eventually to enjoy.

Overall, the rotation system reinforces a perspective which is essentially private and self-concerned. Somewhat remarkably, for example, I found little difference in the attitudes of combat soldiers in Vietnam over a two-year interval. The consistency was largely due, I believe, to the fact that each soldier goes through a similar rotation experience. The end of the war is marked by the date a man leaves Vietnam, and not by its eventual outcomes—whether victory, defeat or stalemate. Even discussion of broader military strategy and the progress of the war—except when directly impinging on one's unit—appears irrelevant to the combat soldier: "My war is over when I go home."

When the soldier feels concern over the fate of others, it is for those he personally knows in his own outfit. His concern does not extend to those who have preceded him or will eventually replace him. Rather, the attitude is typically, "I've done my time; let the others do theirs." Or, as put in the soldier's vernacular, he is waiting to make the final entry on his "FIGMO chart"— "Fuck it, got my orders (to return to the United States)." Whatever incipient identification there might be with abstract comrades-in-arms, is flooded out by the private view of the war fostered by the rotation system.

Conventionally, the primary group is described as a network of interpersonal relationships in which the group's maintenance is valued for its own sake rather than as a mechanism that serves one's own interests. And, as has been noted, social science descriptions of combat motivation in World War II placed particular emphasis on the importance of groupings governed by intimate face-to-face relations. Roger Little's observations of a rifle company during the Korean War differed somewhat by pointing to the two-man or "buddy system" as the basic unit of cohesion rather than the squad or platoon.

My observations in Vietnam, however, indicate that the concept of primary groups has limitations in explaining combat motivation even beyond that suggested by Little. The fact is that if the individual soldier is realistically to improve his survival chances, he must necessarily develop and take part in primary relationships. Under the grim conditions of ground warfare, an individual's survival is directly dependent upon the support—moral, physical and technical—he can expect from his fellow soldiers.

He gets such support to the degree that he reciprocates to the others in his unit. In other words, primary relations are at their core mutually pragmatic efforts to minimize personal risk.

Interpreting the solidarity of combat squads as an outcome of individual self-interest can be corroborated by two illustrations. The first deals with the behavior of the man on "point" in a patrolling operation. The point man is usually placed well in front of the main body, in the most exposed position. Soldiers naturally dread this dangerous assignment, but a good point man is a safeguard for the entire patrol. What happens, as often as not, is that men on point behave in a noticeable careless manner in order to avoid being regularly assigned to the job. At the same time, of course, the point man tries not to be so incautious as to put himself completely at the mercy of an encountered enemy force. In plain language, soldiers do not typically perform at their best when on point; personal safety overrides group interest.

The paramountcy of individual self-interest in combat units is also indicated by the letters soldiers write. Squad members who have returned to the United States seldom write to those remaining behind. In most cases, nothing more is heard from a soldier after he leaves the unit. Perhaps even more revealing, those still in the combat area seldom write their former buddies. Despite protestations of life-long friendship during the shared combat period, the rupture of communication is entirely mutual, once a soldier is out of danger. The soldier writes almost exclusively to those he expects to see when he leaves the service: his family and relatives, girl friends, and civilian male friends.

Do these contrasting interpretations of the network of social relations in combat units—the primary groups of World War II, the two-man relationships of the Korean War, and the essentially individualistic soldier in Vietnam described here—result from conceptual differences on the part of the commentators, or do they reflect substantive differences in the social cohesion of the American soldiers being described? If substantive differences do obtain, particularly between World War II and the wars in Korea and Vietnam, much of this variation could be accounted for by the disruptive effects on unit solidarity caused by the introduction of the rotation system in the latter two wars.

Even if we could decide whether combat primary groups are essentially entities *sui generis* or outcomes of pragmatic self-interest, there remain other difficulties in understanding the part they play in maintaining organizational effectiveness. For it has been amply demonstrated in many contexts that primary groups can hinder as well as serve to attain the formal goals of the larger organization.

Thus, to describe effective combat motivation principally in terms of primary group ties leaves unanswered the question of why various armies—independent of training and equipment—perform differently in time of war. Indeed, because of the very ubiquity of primary groups in military organizations, we must look for supplementary factors to explain variations in combat motivation.

I propose that primary groups maintain the soldier in his combat role only when he has an underlying commitment to the worth of the larger social system for which he is fighting. This commitment need not be formally articulated, nor even perhaps consciously recognized. But the soldier must at some level accept, if not the specific purposes of the war, then at least the broader rectitude of the society of which he is a member. Although American combat soldiers do not espouse overtly ideological sentiments and are extremely reluctant to voice patriotic rhetoric, this should not obscure the existence of more latent beliefs in the legitimacy, and even superiority, of the American way of life. I have used the term "latent ideology" to describe the social and cultural sources of those beliefs about the war held by American soldiers. Latent ideology, in this context, refers to those widely shared sentiments of soldiers which though not overtly political, nor even necessarily substantively political, nevertheless have concrete consequences for combat motivation.

Students of political behavior have too often been uninterested in answers that do not measure up to their own standards of expressiveness. When a person responds in a way that seems either ideologically confused or apathetic, he is considered to have no political ideology. But since any individual's involvement in any policy is usually peripheral, it is quite likely that his political attitudes will be organized quite differently from those of ideologists or political theorists. Yet when one focuses on underlying value orientations, we find a set of attitudes having a definite coherence—especially within the context of that individual's life situation.

Quite consistently, the American combat soldier displays a profound skepticism of political and ideological appeals. Somewhat paradoxically then, anti-ideology itself is a recurrent and integral part of the soldier's belief system. They dismiss patriotic slogans or exhortation to defend democracy with "What a crock," "Be serious, man" or "Who's kidding who?" In particular, they have little belief that they are protecting an outpost of democracy in South Vietnam. United States Command Information pronouncements stressing defense of South Vietnam as an outpost of the "Free World" are almost as dubiously received as those of Radio Hanoi which accuse Americans of imperialist aggression. As one soldier put it, "Maybe we're supposed to be here and maybe not. But you don't have time to think about things like that. You worry about getting zapped and dry socks tomorrow. The other stuff is a joke."

In this same vein, when the soldier responds to the question of why he is in Vietnam, his answers are couched in a quite individualistic frame of reference. He sees little connection between his presence in Vietnam and the national policies that brought him there. Twenty-seven of the 34 combat soldiers I interviewed defined their presence in the war in terms of personal misfortune. Typical responses were: "My outfit was sent over here and me with it," "My tough luck in getting drafted," "I happened to be at the wrong place at the wrong time," "I was fool enough to join this man's army," and "My own stupidity for listening to the recruiting sergeant." Only five soldiers mentioned broader policy implications—to stop Communist aggression. Two soldiers stated they requested assignment to Vietnam because they wanted to be "where the action is."

Because of the combat soldier's overwhelming propensity to see the war in private and personal terms, I had to ask them specifically what they thought the United States was doing in Vietnam. When the question was phrased in this manner, the soldiers most often said they were in Vietnam "to stop Communism." This was about the only ideological slogan these American combat soldiers could be brought to utter; 19 of the 34 interviewed soldiers saw stopping Communism as the purpose of the war. But when they expressed this view it was almost always in terms of defending the United States, not the "Free World" in general and certainly not South Vietnam. They said: "The only way we'll keep them out of the States is to kill them here," "Let's get it over now, before they're too strong to stop," "They have to be stopped somewhere," "Better to zap this country than let them do the same to us."

Fifteen of the soldiers gave responses other than stopping Communism. Three gave frankly cynical explanations of the war by stating that domestic prosperity in the United States depended on a war economy. Two soldiers held that the American intervention was a serious mistake initially; but that it was now too late to back out because of America's reputation. One man even gave a Malthusian interpretation, arguing that war was needed to limit population growth. Nine of the soldiers could give no reason for the war even after extensive discussion. Within this group, one heard responses such as: "I only wish I knew" "Maybe Johnson knows, but I sure don't" and "I've been wondering about that ever since I got here."

I asked each of the 19 soldiers who mentioned stopping Communism as the purpose of the war what was so bad about Communism that it must be stopped at the risk of his own life. The first reaction to such a question was usually perplexity or rueful shrugging. After thinking about it, and with some prodding, 12 of the men expressed their distaste for communism by stressing its authoritarian aspects in social relations. They saw Communism as a system of excessive social regimentation which allows the individual no autonomy in the pursuit of his own happiness.

Typical descriptions of Communism were: "That's when you can't do what you want to do," "Somebody's always telling you what to do," or "You're told where you work, what you eat, and when you shit." As one man wryly put it, "Communism is something like the army."

While the most frequently mentioned features of Communism concerned individual liberty, other descriptions were also given. Three soldiers mentioned the atheistic and anti-church apsects of Communism; two specifically talked of the absence of political parties and democratic political institutions; and one man said Communism was good in theory, but could never work in practice because human beings were "too selfish." Only one soldier mentioned the issues of public versus private ownership.

I should stress once again that the soldiers managed to offer reasons for the war or descriptions of Communism only after extended discussion and questioning. When left to themselves, they rarely discussed the goals of America's military intervention in Vietnam, the nature of Communist systems, or other political issues.

To say that the American soldier is not overtly ideological is not to deny the existence of salient values that do contribute to his motivation in combat. Despite the soldier's lack of ideological concern and his pronounced embarrassment in the face of patriotic rhetoric, he nevertheless displays an elemental American nationalism in the belief that the United States is the best country in the world. Even though he hates being in the war, the combat soldier typically believes—with a kind of joyless patriotism—that he is fighting for his American homeland. When the soldier does articulate the purposes of the war, the view is expressed that if Communist aggression is not stopped in Southeast Asia, it will be only a matter of time before the United States itself is in jeopardy. The so-called domino theory is just as persuasive among combat soldiers as it is among the general public back home.

The soldier definitely does not see himself fighting for South Vietnam. Quite the contrary, he thinks South Vietnam is a worthless country, and its people contemptible. The low regard in which the Vietnamese—"slopes" or "gooks"—are held is constantly present in the derogatory comments on the avarice of those who pander to GIs, the treachery of all Vietnamese, and the numbers of Vietnamese young men in the cities who are not in the armed forces. Anti-Vietnamese sentiment is most glaringly apparent in the hostility toward the ARVN (Army of the Republic of Vietnam, pronounced "Arvin") who are their supposed military allies. Disparaging remarks about "Arvin's" fighting qualities are endemic.

A variety of factors underlie the soldier's fundamental pro-Americanism, not the least of them being his immediate reliance on fellow Americans for mutual support in a country where virtually all indigenous people are seen as actual or potential threats to his physical safety. He also has deep concern for his family and loved ones back home. These considerations, however, are true of any army fighting in a foreign land. It is on another level, then, that I tried to uncover those aspects of American society that were most relevant and important to the combat soldier.

To obtain such a general picture of the soldier's conception of his homeland I asked the following question, "Tell me in your own words, what makes America different from other countries?" The overriding feature in the soldier's perception of America is the creature comforts that American life can offer. Twenty-two of the soldiers described the United States by its high-paying jobs, automobiles, consumer goods and leisure activities. No other description of America came close to being mentioned as often as the high—and apparently uniquely American—material standard of living. Thus, only four of the soldiers emphasized America's democratic political institutions; three mentioned religious and spiritual values; two spoke of the general characteristics of the American people; and one said America was where the individual advanced on his own worth; another talked of America's natural and physical beauties; and one black soldier described America as racist. Put in another way, it is the materialistic—and I do not use the word pejoratively—aspects of life in America that are most salient to combat soldiers.

The soldier's belief in the superiority of the American way of life is further reinforced by the contrast with the Vietnamese standard of living. The combat soldier cannot help making invidious comparisons between the life he led in the United States—even if he is working class—and what he sees in Vietnam. Although it is more pronounced in the Orient, it must be remembered that Americans abroad—whether military or civilian—usually find themselves in locales that compare unfavorably with the material affluence of the United States. Indeed, should American soldiers ever be stationed in a country with a markedly higher standard of living than that of the United States, I believe they would be severely shaken in their belief in the merits of American society.

Moreover, the fighting soldier, by the very fact of being in combat, leads an existence that is not only more dangerous than civilian life, but more primitive and physically harsh. The soldier's somewhat romanticized view of life back home is buttressed by his direct observation of the Vietnamese scene, but also by his own immediate lower standard of living. It has often been noted that front-line soldiers bitterly contrast their plight with the physical amenities enjoyed by their fellow countrymen, both rear-echelon soldiers as well as civilians back home. While this is superficially true, the attitudes of American combat soldiers toward their compatriots are actually somewhat more ambivalent. For at the same time the soldier is begrudging the civilian his physical comforts, it is these very comforts for which he fights. Similarly, they envy rather than disapprove of those rear-echelon personnel who engage in sub rosa profiteering.

The materialistic ethic is reflected in another characteristic of American servicemen. Even among front-line combat soldiers, one sees an extraordinary amount of valuable paraphenalia. Transistor radios are practically *de rigueur*. Cameras and other photographic accessories are widely evident and used. Even the traditional letter-writing home is becoming displaced by tape recordings. It seems more than coincidental that American soldiers commonly refer to the United States as "The Land of the Big PX."

Another factor that plays a part in combat motivation is the notion of masculinity and physical toughness that pervades the soldier's outlook toward warfare. Being a combat soldier is a man's job. Front-line soldiers often cast aspersions on the virility of rear-echelon personnel ("titless WAC's"). A soldier who has not experienced combat is called a "cherry" (i.e. virgin). Likewise, paratroopers express disdain for "legs," as nonairborne soldiers are called. This he-man attitude is also found in the countless joking references to the movie roles of John Wayne and Lee Marvin. These definitions of masculinity are, of course, general in America and the military organization seeks to capitalize on them with such perennial recruiting slogans as "The Marine Corps Builds Men" and "Join the Army and Be a Man."

Needless to say, however, the exaggerated masculine ethic is much less evident among soldiers after their units have been bloodied. As the realities of combat are faced, more prosaic definitions of manly honor emerge. (Also, there is more frequent expression of the male role in manifestly sexual rather than combative terms, for example, the repeatedly heard "I'm a lover not a fighter.") That is, notions of masculinity serve to create initial motivation to enter combat, but recede once the life-and-death facts of warfare are confronted. Moreover, once the unit is tempered by combat, definitions of manly honor are not seen to encompass individual heroics. Quite the opposite, the very word "hero" is used to describe negatively any soldier who recklessly jeopardizes the unit's welfare. Men try to avoid going out on patrols with individuals who are overly anxious to make contact with the enemy. Much like the slacker at the other end of the spectrum, the "hero" is also seen as one who endangers the safety of others. As is the case with virtually all combat behavior, the ultimate standard rests on keeping alive.

On both of my trips to Vietnam I repeatedly heard combat soldiers—almost to a man—vehemently denounce peace demonstrators back in the United States. At first glance such an attitude might be surprising. After all, peaceniks and soldiers both fervently want the troops brought home. In fact, however, the troops I interviewed expressed overt political sentiments only when the antiwar demonstrations came up in the talk. Significantly, the soldier perceived the peace demonstrations as being directed against himself personally and not against the war. "Did I vote to come here? Why blame the GI?" There was also a widespread feeling that if peace demonstrators were in Vietnam they would change their minds. As one man stated: "How can they know what's happening if they're sitting on their asses in the States. Bring them here and we'd shape them up quick enough." Or as one of the more philosophically inclined put it, "I'd feel the same way if I were back home. But once you're here and your buddies are getting zapped, you have to see things different."

Much of the soldier's dislike of peace demonstrators is an outcome of class hostility. To many combat soldiers—themselves largely working class—peace demonstrators are socially privileged college students. I heard many remarks such as the following: "I'm fighting for those candy-asses just because I don't have an old man to support me." "I'm stuck here and those rich draft dodgers are having a ball raising hell." "You'd think they'd have more sense with all that smart education."

The peace demonstrators, moreover, were seen as undercutting and demeaning the losses and hardships already suffered by American soldiers. Something of this sort undoubtedly contributed to the noticeable hawklike sentiments of combat soldiers. "If we get out now, then every GI dies for nothing. Is this why I've been putting my ass on the line?" Here we seem to have an illustration of a more general social phenomenon: the tendency in human beings to justify to themselves sacrifices they have already made.

Sacrifice itself can create legitimacy for an organization over a short period of time. It is only after some point when sacrifices suddenly seem too much, that the whole enterprise comes under critical reevaluation. But sharp questioning of past and future sacrifices does not generally occur among combat soldiers in Vietnam. I believe this is because the 12-month rotation system removes the soldier from the combat theater while his personal stake remains high and before he might begin to question the whole operation. The rotation system, in other words, not only maintains individual morale but also fosters a collective commitment to justify American sacrifices.

Part III

The Individual As Leader

by
*Louis S. Csoka**

Man has been described previously as a social animal whose behavior is motivated by unsatisfied needs. He normally learns that many of his needs can best be satisfied by joining some type of informal or formal group or organization. However, as discussed in Part II, the consequences of belonging to a group serve not only to expand, but also to limit the capabilities and satisfactions of members. As members they must sacrifice some of their individuality in order to gain the need satisfaction made possible by membership. The individual will generally remain a part of the group only as long as his benefits as a member, whether they be from group goal achievement or interpersonal relationships, outweigh his membership costs.

Two important conclusions were evident in the previous study of groups:

1. Groups tend to have a dichotomous function—the accomplishment of some purposeful task and the maintenance of the group as an integral system through need satisfaction of individual members.

2. Individual members of the group emerge or are appointed to fulfill certain roles essential to the fulfillment of both of the above goals.

One of the primary roles identified is that of the leader. Obviously, if a leader is to be successful in influencing the actions of the group, he or she must, as a minimum, insure that task-related and group maintenance functions are fulfilled.

---

*Louis S. Csoka, (Major, U.S. Army) is on the faculty of the Office of Military Leadership at the United States Military Academy, West Point, New York. He received his B.S. from the United States Military Academy (1965) and his M.S. and PhD in Social Psychology from the University of Washington (1972).

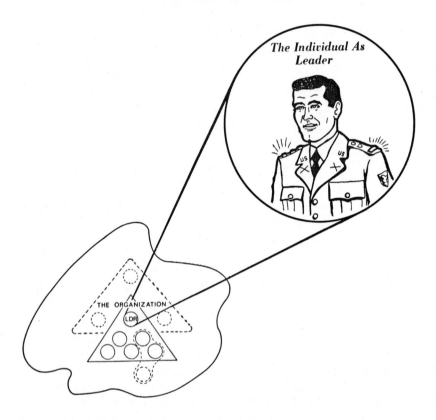

The introductory article to this text questioned the traditional view of the leader as some unique person endowed with certain characteristics which set him apart from his followers in all situations. A more accurate and realistic assessment of the leader would describe him as an individual about whom certain expectations have been formed as a result of his specific role. Earlier discussions have focused on the various psychological and social processes that influence an individual's personality and behavior. It is doubtful that these basic personality characteristics will change solely because one assumes the role of leader.

The purpose of this part of the text is to analyze the leader in an organizational setting emphasizing individual and situational factors which influence the manner in which the role expectations of leader can be met. The first article by Wheeler and Csoka traces the evolution of a behavioral approach to understanding leadership from the identification of important behavioral dimensions, through a universal model of leadership, to contingency models of leader behavior which attempt to account for the impact of situational variables on leader behavior. Such situational variables as stress and follower maturity are discussed in some detail. Research efforts continually have attempted to determine which behavior, or combination of behaviors, produce the most effective results in the leadership process. The findings have been somewhat contradictory, and it will become apparent that the situation is an essential moderating influence in linking leader behavior and organizational effectiveness.

Although most researchers have qualified their conclusions regarding the findings on leader behavior, Blake and Mouton have popularized a prescriptive behavioral approach in the Managerial Grid. In their universal approach, they have proposed a "best" combination of leader behavior for leadership effectiveness. Other researchers, unsatisfied with what they considered to be an over-simplified approach to leadership, have attempted to account for the effects of situational variables on leader behavior and effectiveness.

Korten (see also Part II, A Study of Organizational Leadership) has proposed a stress model of leadership which considers the stress or urgency of the task inherent in a situation, while Hersey and Blanchard in their Life Cycle Model consider the impact of subordinate maturity and competence on leader behavior.

The Wheeler and Csoka article concludes that no complete theory exists which relates leader behavior and organizational effectiveness. Therefore, absolute prescriptions or applications which cover all possible combinations of situations become difficult, if not impossible. Nevertheless, an effective technique for measuring leader behaviors has resulted from the social studies conducted. The Leader Behavior Description Questionnaire (LBDQ)[1] has been found to be most useful in describing the behavior of leaders and has received wide application. It will be discussed in greater detail in a following article. One of the largest studies to use this measuring technique is called: *Leadership for the 1970's*, conducted in 1971 by the U.S. Army War College. In this study, perceptions of leader behavior were measured from three different perspectives: subordinates, peers, and superiors. The article by Grunstad discusses the use of the Ohio State LBDQ in this study. He traces the assumptions about the principles of leadership, discusses the implications of the study and recommends how the perceptions of a leader's actions can be improved.

The next two readings are by McGregor. Here the reader will find a new term—leader style—which may cause some confusion. Unfortunately, various authors have used the terms *leader behavior* and *leader style* differently, and, in some cases, synonymously. To place into proper perspective the difference between the two terms, consider that many leader behaviors are included in a leader's style. The style of a leader results from his basic personality make-up (i.e., assumptions, beliefs, values, etc.). Leader style, therefore, simply defines the *range* of behaviors that are available to a leader given his personality characteristics and the situation which confronts him. Leader style might best be remembered as a description of what a leader does because of what he is. Inconsistent behaviors, of course, are quite possible. However, a person would feel very uncomfortable and less confident using them since they would not represent learned actions from past experience and would not conform to his basic personality make-up.

The McGregor articles are a modern version of one of the oldest debates in human history: "Is man inherently bad or inherently good?" McGregor gives two opposing lists of assumptions one might have about human nature— Theory X and Theory Y. The analogy is not perfect, but Theory X assumptions might be held by one who subscribes to the "bad" side of human nature, and Theory Y, the the "good" side. The assumptions or combination of assumptions one holds about human nature will affect one's style, and therefore, one's behavior. These assumptions are derived from Maslow's Need Hierarchy (see Part I). Theories X and Y are also quite popular in current management and will be considered again in Part V on Formal Organizations.

The reading by Fiedler is a discussion of his Contingency Model of Leadership Effectiveness. This article has brought together some of the most recent information available on the contingency model. Up to this point, numerous variables have been considered as important in the leadership process: personality characteristics, leader behavior and style, and situational factors. Unfortunately most research prior to Fiedler has dealt with these variables from a rather simplistic view. As explained in his article, Fiedler has attempted to look at the complexities by viewing leadership effectiveness as being contingent upon the interaction of personality characteristics, leader behavior, and situational factors to include leader-follower relations, power processes, and the nature of the task. The Contingency Model is complex and will require careful reading. However, it is presently one of the most publicized models in the leadership literature. Fiedler has attempted to synthesize diverse findings in an approach that aims at a more universal theory. The Model contains some interesting prescriptions on how to increase a leader's effectiveness. Non-obvious and rather surprising conclusions regarding the effects of leadership training, rotation and succession also can be derived from the model. It represents a very up-to-date example of how the complexities in the leadership process can be synthesized into a more universal theory of leadership.

The final reading by Caine discusses the leadership process which incorporates the dyadic relationship between the leader and his followers through the role-making/sending process. Leaders cannot and do not act in an identical manner towards each subordinate. Rather, they develop a unique "informal contract" with their subordinates which leads to interdependent behavioral expectations and relationship norms called *vertical dyad linkages.* Leader-member relations will change depending on the nature of the linkage being considered and the identification of the in-group, out-group, and mid-group relationship. Personal variables (see Hersey and Blanchard) and structural variables (goal-path clarity and task structure) are related to the formation and effects of dyadic linkages. Understanding subordinate differentiation and vertical dyadic linkages can assist a leader in optimizing unit effectiveness through their direct effect on leader-member relations.

Terms you should be able to discuss when you finish this part:

Leader Behavior
Leader Style
Consideration
Initiating Structure
Follower Maturity
Role Conflict
Performance Shortfall
Perception Shortfall
Opportunity Sensitivity
Dyadic Relationship

Informal Contract
Leadership Climate
Tri-Focal View of Leadership
Theory X
Theory Y
Relationship-Oriented
Task-Oriented
Situation Favorableness
Least Preferred Coworker (LPC)

END NOTE

1. In order to better understand how leader behavior descriptions are obtained, the reader will find it useful to complete the "Leadership Opinion Questionnaire" located at the end of this introductory section. Although this is a self-rating scale, it does indicate the manner in which the leader behavior dimensions are measured.

LEADERSHIP OPINION QUESTIONNAIRE*

Listed below are a number of different things that a leader of a group might do. For each statement, indicate *HOW IMPORTANT* you feel it is that a leader do that particular thing in order to be an effective officer. *DO NOT* consider what you might actually do in any given situation, but only how important you feel each item is for successful military leadership.

In case you feel that an item is actually *UNDESIRABLE* for effective leadership indicate this by marking an "X" through the "O" under the last column for that item. Use the following scale for your answers:

Absolutely Essential	Very Important	Moderately Important	Of Some Importance	Not Important at all	Undesirable
5	4	3	2	1	0

	5	4	3	2	1	0
1. permit compromise on a point	5	4	3	2	1	0
2. rule with an iron hand	5	4	3	2	1	0
3. do personal favors for the men in your unit	5	4	3	2	1	0
4. criticize poor performance	5	4	3	2	1	0
5. help your men with their personal problems	5	4	3	2	1	0
6. assign men in the unit to specific tasks	5	4	3	2	1	0
7. explain reasons for your orders	5	4	3	2	1	0
8. ask for sacrifices from your men for the good of the unit	5	4	3	2	1	0
9. back your men up in what they do	5	4	3	2	1	0
10. ask that your men follow to the letter standard routines handed down to you	5	4	3	2	1	0
11. criticize a specific act rather than a particular member of the group	5	4	3	2	1	0
12. put the welfare of your unit above the welfare of any man in it	5	4	3	2	1	0
13. be willing to make changes	5	4	3	2	1	0
14. stress being ahead of competing units	5	4	3	2	1	0
15. speak in a manner which invites questions	5	4	3	2	1	0
16. put suggestions made by your men into operation	5	4	3	2	1	0
17. "needle" men in your unit for greater effort	5	4	3	2	1	0
18. see to it that your men are working up to capacity	5	4	3	2	1	0

*This questionnaire contains items extracted from the "Leadership Opinion Questionnaire" by E. A. Fleishman in *Leader Behavior, It's Description and Measurement*, R. M. Stogdill and A. E. Coons, eds. Columbus, Ohio: College of Administrative Science, The Ohio State University, 1957, p. 122. Some words have been changed to suit the military environment.

Leader Behavior—Theory and Study

by
Wayne R. Wheeler*
and
Louis S. Csoka*

BACKGROUND

The initial theories in the field of leadership tended to focus on the "Great Man" and "Trait" approaches to leadership. Basically, these approaches viewed a leader as someone who possessed unique traits or superior characteristics which distinguished him from followers. Several researchers in the 1940s thoroughly reviewed the studies on the trait approach to leadership (Bird, 1940; Jenkins, 1947; Stogdill, 1948). Their conclusions are best summarized in Stogdill's most recent work:[1]

> . . . (1) that little success had been attained in attempts to select leaders in terms of traits, (2) that numerous traits differentiated leaders from followers, (3) that traits demanded in a leader varied from one situation to another, and (4) that the trait approach ignored the interaction between the leader and his group (Stogdill, 1974, p. 128).

Since the trait approach to the understanding of leadership had been unproductive, in the early 1950s a group of researchers from Ohio State University (OSU) began to study the influence process from a behavioral

---

*The authors are both on the faculty of the Office of Military Leadership at the United States Military Academy, West Point, New York. Wayne R. Wheeler (Major, US Army), received his BS from the United States Military Academy (1964) and his MA and PhD in Organizational Behavior from The Ohio State University (1972). Louis S. Csoka (Major, US Army), received his BS from the United States Military Academy (1965) and his MS and PhD in Social Psychology from the University of Washington (1972).

rather than a personality approach. After conducting several research studies, two main dimensions of leader behavior were identified—*Consideration and Initiating Structure.* These dimensions of leader behavior are defined in the following manner:

> CONSIDERATION reflects the extent to which an individual is likely to have job relationships characterized by mutual trust, respect for subordinates' ideas, and consideration of their feelings.
> INITIATING STRUCTURE reflects the extent to which an individual is likely to define his role and those of his subordinates toward goal attainment (Fleishman & Peters, 1962, pp. 43–44).

Based on the results of their studies, the researchers developed a survey instrument entitled the Leader Behavior Description Questionnaire (LBDQ) to measure these dimensions of behavior. This questionnaire is completed by subordinates who normally are asked to describe the behavior of their most immediate supervisor. Examples of some of the items contained in the LBDQ are shown below (Halpin, 1957a).

Consideration	*Initiating Structure*
He does little things to make it pleasant to be a member of the group.	He assigns group members to tasks. He maintains definite standards of performance.
He finds time to listen to group members.	He asks that group members follow standard rules and regulations.
He backs up the members in their actions.	
He is willing to make changes.	

Generally, Consideration and Initiating Structure are considered to be dichotomous, independent variables. Being independent variables a leader's rating on one variable does not affect his rating on the other. Figure 1 depicts these relationships more clearly.

In Figure 1 it can be seen that a leader may be described as being high on Structure and Consideration (Quadrant 2), low on Structure and Consideration (Quadrant 4), or any other combination of the two variables (Quadrants 1 and 3).

Literally hundreds of research studies in military, industrial and educational settings have been conducted using the LBDQ. Findings from these studies have been used by various individuals to support their own "mini-theories" of the leadership process. The remainder of this article will be devoted to tracing the evolution of a few of the more well-known model derivatives and pointing out the direction in which future research appears to be headed.

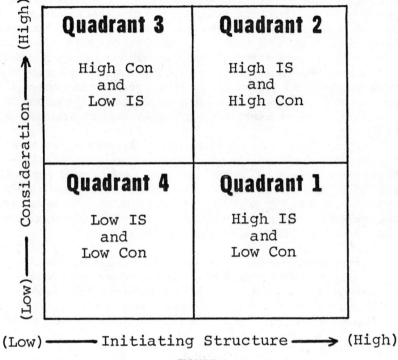

FIGURE 1
DIAGRAM OF LEADER BEHAVIOR DIMENSIONS

EARLY STUDIES ON LEADER BEHAVIOR

In the 1950s, several studies were conducted on air force bomber commanders in both training and combat settings. In training, commanders who were described by subordinates as being high on Structure and low on Consideration (Quadrant 1) generally received high efficiency ratings from superiors (Halpin & Winer, 1952). High crew-member satisfaction in training, however, was generally associated with the commander's being described as high on Consideration and low on Structure (Quadrant 3) (Halpin & Winer, 1952; Halpin, 1954, 1957). In combat, superiors again gave the highest ratings to those leaders described as high on Structure and low on Consideration (Quadrant 1); however, high crew member satisfaction was associated with leaders who were high on Consideration and high on Structure (Quadrant 2) (Halpin, 1954, 1957). Rush (1957) reported that high group harmony was associated with high Consideration in both combat and training crews. High group harmony (cohesiveness) was positively related to high Initiating Structure under conditions of combat, but uncorrelated in training situations.

Another study reports results on samples of ROTC cadets and industrial production foremen (Fleishman, 1957). High peer ratings of cadet leaders were positively associated with both high Consideration and Structure. Superiors' ratings of these cadets did not correlate with either dimension of leader behavior. In the industrial setting, high supervisory ratings were given to foremen who were rated by subordinates as high in Structure and low in Consideration (Note that these findings are similar to those reported on the bomber crew commanders). High turnover and high grievance rates among subordinates were also positively associated with high Structure, but did not correlate with Consideration.

The above studies seem to indicate that superiors generally tend to value more highly a subordinate leader who is high on Initiating Structure and low on Consideration (Quadrant 1), while subordinates, under routine conditions, generally are more satisfied with a leader who is high on Consideration and low on Structure (Quadrant 3). Stogdill (1974) in an exhaustive review of the literature across several research settings, recently put forth the following qualified conclusions about Consideration and Initiating Structure:

> Group productivity is *somewhat more* highly related to structure than to consideration. Member satisfaction, on the other hand, is *somewhat more* highly related to consideration than to structure. Group cohesiveness is related about equally often to consideration and structure. . . . The most effective leaders tend to be described high on both scales (pp. 395, 396). (emphasis added)

While Stogdill qualifies his conclusions regarding the findings of the OSU leadership studies, Blake and Mouton (1969) are more absolute in their application. Basically, they emphatically state that the most effective leader is one who is high on both dimensions. Let us now consider in more detail their popular, prescriptive approach to leadership.

THE MANAGERIAL GRID

Blake and Mouton (1964, 1969) have formulated a model commonly referred to as the Managerial or Leadership Grid. This model can be viewed as an extension of the two-dimensional diagram presented in Figure 1. However, instead of dichotomizing the two dimensions, Blake and Mouton (1969) have placed each on a continuum from "1" (low) to "9" (high). Additionally, they have associated different names with the leader dimensions: Consideration is termed "concern for people", and Initiating Structure is replaced by "concern for mission performance." Five major points are identified on their model as representing primary approaches to leadership:

1. Low concern for mission performance and people (Quadrant 4) is labeled "impoverished" leadership.

2. Low concern for people and high concern for mission performance (Quadrant 1) is referred to as "task" leadership.

3. Low concern for mission performance and high concern for people (Quadrant 3) is termed "country club" leadership.

4. Moderate concern for people and mission performance (intersection of all four quadrants) is called "middle of the road" leadership.

5. High concern for people and mission performance (Quadrant 2) is called "team" leadership.

The prescription that is suggested by these authors is that a "team" (Quadrant 2) approach to leadership will optimize task accomplishment and subordinate welfare. The least desirable leadership behavior is "impoverished" (Quadrant 4), since the leader is orienting neither his behavior nor his efforts in an organizationally functional direction.

The Leadership Grid has the advantages of being intuitively appealing and of simplifying one's cognitive approach to leadership. The inherent assumption and universal prescription in the model is that a leader *can* and *should* show high consideration and initiate high structure concomitantly, regardless of the situation and duration of the task.

Two simple examples can demonstrate the difficulty one might have in applying this basic principle across all situations. First, consider a platoon leader who is in the process of leading his platoon in breaching a minefield in combat. During the short period of time required to accomplish this task, can the platoon leader realistically be highly considerate and structuring at the same time? In which type of behavior are his subordinates more interested? Over a long period of time in combat, his subordinates undoubtedly would be more satisfied if he were highly considerate *and* structuring in his behavior (recall the previous studies on bomber crews in combat). Assuming this is the first time that the platoon has been tasked to clear a minefield in combat and the consequences are of life or death magnitude, platoon members will probably demand structure and be much less concerned with considerate behaviors, at least during the few hours required to complete the mission.

As a second example, consider the behavior of a platoon leader at a platoon party which he has oganized. The purpose of the party, presumably, is to enhance subordinate satisfaction and morale. To what extent would this be accomplished if the leader's behavior were highly structuring (e.g., "SGT Jones, don't drip your beer"; "PVT Smith, two drinks is enough for you"; etc)? Although these examples may seem facetious, they do demonstrate that the universal approach proposed by Blake and Mouton has obvious limitations.

A related shortcoming is that the Leadership Grid does not explain satisfactorily the relationships between member satisfaction and Initiating Structure as described earlier in the studies on air crew commanders. Recall that in these studies, high subordinate satisfaction was associated with *low* leader Structure in "everyday" training situations. However, during combat, high satisfaction was correlated with *high* Structure. Blake and Mouton's model would not have predicted the former outcome. Apparently, therefore, situational variables must be considered in determining appropriate leader behavior.

SITUATIONAL VARIABLES

Stress

Korten[2] (1962), a social scientist, provides an explanation of the effect of stress on leader behavior. He postulates that subordinates *demand* different behaviors from their leaders as situational stress changes.

Korten hypothesizes that as stress, or task urgency, increases, the consensus of group opinion will increase regarding the importance of specific goals. He refers to a high consensus as a desire for "high goal structure." Under high stress, the group will be willing to sacrifice some of its autonomy in order to attain the desired goal (which simply may be stress reduction), or to return to a status quo. Thus, conditions in a high stress situation may be ideal for an autocratic leader (i.e., one who is high on Initiating Structure). When the group goal is attained, however, and the status quo is reestablished, Korten predicts that the group will have less consensus regarding the importance of specific goals (i.e., the group will desire low goal structure), and will seek a democratic leader (i.e., one who is low in Initiating Structure).

The studies on air crew commanders which were reviewed earlier tend to support this formulation (Halpin & Winer, 1952; Halpin, 1954, 1957). Under combat conditions, stress evidently results in a desire for high goal structure among crew members (i.e., high consensus regarding survival and the reduction of uncertainty), and the desire for the leader to provide Initiating Structure (i.e., to be autocratic). In the training situation, the degree of stress is much less, as is the consensus regarding the group's goals. Thus, since the subordinates sought a more considerate, less structuring leader, training leaders who were high on Initiating Structure had dissatisfied subordinates.

Subordinate Maturity

A second variable, task competency of subordinates, has been identified as being another important situational determinant of leader behavior not considered in Blake and Mouton's Leadership Grid.

Consider an example wherein a new second lieutenant is assigned to a platoon in which the platoon sergeant and squad leaders are mature, competent and experienced noncommissioned officers. His company's mission during the initial period of his assignment is post support which includes sending a group of soldiers under the supervision of a squad leader to cut grass, rake leaves, move bleachers, and pick up litter. The platoon leader outlines specific detailed instructions and assignments for the platoon sergeant to follow, then corrects him for making a routine decision on his own. When inspecting the squad leaders and their detail members, he issues additional instructions, continually emphasizes the need to meet the deadline (the work is already progressing ahead of schedule), and continually "looks over their shoulders" to insure strict adherence to his specific policies. The result of his over-supervision and highly structuring behavior is sure to be dissatisfaction among his sergeants.

This example suggests that in determining appropriate leader behavior (degree of supervision), the complexity of the task vis-a-vis the maturity (task competency) of subordinates must be considered. Dessler (1972) has shown that when the task is complex, high subordinate satisfaction is associated with high Initiating Structure. House (1971) reports that when subordinates have a high degree of autonomy (and presumably more ambiguous task demands), high satisfaction is associated with high leader Structure and Consideration.

Hersey and Blanchard, (1969) proposed The Life-Cycle Theory of Leadership in an attempt to describe better the interrelationships among subordinate maturity and leader behavior

Their choice of subordinate maturity as the key element of the situation is well justified. The interaction between the leader and his followers has a strong impact on the accomplishment of assigned tasks as well as on subordinate satisfaction, absence rates, and turnover. As a group, the subordinates determine the actual personal power that the leader will have. The way in which the power is wielded is determined by the specific actions taken by the leader vis-a-vis his subordinates. Therefore, the leader behaviors exhibited in any given situation should be those which maximize the effectiveness of the group. This means that behaviors must be oriented toward the needs and requirements of the group members. The Life Cycle Theory is an attempt to identify the appropriate mix of leader behaviors as they relate to the maturity of subordinates.

The behaviors described in the Life Cycle Theory are basically the same two primary dimensions of leader behavior found in the Ohio State studies— Consideration and Initiating Structure. Hersey and Blanchard have labeled these dimensions *"Relationship"* and *"Task"* behaviors, respectively. Task behaviors are oriented on task accomplishment and include the leader's specifying what each subordinate is to do, as well as how, when, and where it is to be done. Relationship behaviors are best described as actions that the leader takes which indicate emotional support, communication, facilitation, and interpersonal relations. The group's *Maturity* is defined by (1) its capacity to set high but attainable goals, (2) its willingness and ability to take responsibility, and (3) its education and/or experience level. (Hersey and Blanchard, 1974).

As indicated in Figure 2, the Life Cycle Theory hypothesizes that a curvilinear relationship exists between leader behavior and follower maturity. As the level of subordinate maturity increases, the leader should adjust his task and relationship behaviors accordingly. In other words, when the followers are immature (e.g., they do not possess the capacity to set high goals, cannot assume responsibility, or do not have the experience required for the job), they will seek structure and direction and be less concerned about interpersonal relationships. In order to meet the needs of these subordinates, the leader should concentrate on task behaviors by structuring the job, organizing his people, and directing how the work is to be done. The time he spends on showing consideration to his subordinates should be minimal compared to the time

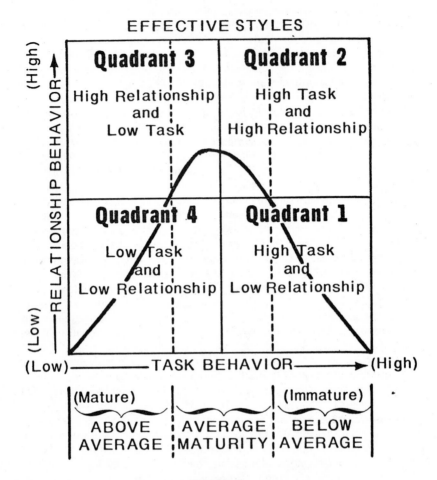

FIGURE 2
LIFE CYCLE THEORY OF LEADERSHIP

he spends on task-oriented behavior. His leadership approach is described best as high task and low relationship (Quadrant 1). One example of a group with which this approach might be appropriate is a newly formed platoon of recently enlisted basic trainees.

As subordinates gain experience and an appreciation for the established goals (i.e., increase in maturity), the leader will be more successful by providing emotional support, open communications, and an awareness of the interpersonal needs of group members in addition to maintaining task direction

(Quadrant 2). Enlisted trainees after several weeks of basic training may exemplify this level of maturity.

Eventually, subordinates may approach a level of maturity requiring minimal job direction by the leader, although their consideration needs may still be high (Quadrant 3). A well-trained infantry platoon conducting field training exercises may be an example of this level of maturity. In a few cases, subordinates may reach full maturity at which time the leader, according to Life-Cycle Theory, should decrease both relationship and task behaviors to a minimum level (Quadrant 4). An example of a group which might reach such a level of maturity is the Physical Education (PE) Committee at an Airborne School. Essentially, such committees operate independently.

While some examples can be given of a highly mature group, one must note that relatively few platoons ever reach this level of maturity. Limited formal education and job knowledge combined with personnel turnover normally limit the amount of common experience that a group can achieve. A platoon leader will probably find the maturity of the majority of his subordinates vacillating between Quadrants 1 and 2. In technical units, wherein subordinates tend to possess a higher degree of technical competence and formal education, subordinates may even approach Quadrant 3.

The reader might conclude that the leader becomes unnecessary when the subordinates approach full maturity since the requirement for leader task and relationship behaviors is minimal in Quadrant 4. However, this is not the case. One must remember that the situation is continually changing. As followers come and go, task requirements change, and interpersonal problems arise, the leader will be required to intercede with the appropriate behaviors. A few examples may help to clarify the dynamic aspects of the situation.

The PE Committee at the Airborne School has been considered as being capable of full group maturity. One must remember that the assumption is made that the group's assigned task is conducting physical training in preparation for airborne qualification. If the group were to assume the responsibility for the physical education at the Ranger School, most likely it would continue to possess a high degree of maturity since the task basically would be the same. If, however, the group were to assume responsibility for patrolling at a Ranger Camp, its maturity would probably decrease due to the difference in the assigned tasks. Thus, different behaviors by the leader might be required. Similar analyses could be made with a group at any level of maturity. The important point to remember is that maturity is task specific. When the task changes, the leader may have to change his behavior even though the same subordinates are involved.

Hersey and Blanchard (1974) also argue that when a leader finds himself in a situation where his subordinates have attained a high level of maturity, requiring minimal task and relationship behaviors on his part, the leader can serve a most useful and important function as a "linking pin" between his followers and his own superior (Likert, 1961). Under this concept, the leader becomes a representative for his group in the next level of the organizational hierarchy and serves to mediate between the organization and the group.

Instead of acting only as a supervisor, the leader's role becomes one of long-range planning, inter-unit coordination, and acquisition of resources that will help increase the performance of the group.

Implied in the above discussion is the notion that a leader becomes a "linking pin" only when his subordinates have achieved full maturity. The authors take exception to this idea. A leader in an organizational setting is *always* a "middle-man" or linking pin, even when his subordinates demonstrate relative immaturity. A leader always must serve as the point of contact between his superiors and his subordinates. In preparation for training, for example, a leader must plan the activities ahead of time, coordinate with the necessary agencies to arrange transportation and reserve training areas, and insure that the required resources (rations, ammunition, etc.) will be on hand. At the platoon level, such planning and coordination may be required, only with the company training officer or battalion staff—nevertheless, this "linking" function is continuous. The key point that Hersey and Blanchard seem to be emphasizing is that when one's subordinates are highly mature, the leader has *more* time to devote to his role as a "linking pin." He may be able to engage in longer-range planning and coordination (e.g., adventure training in the Rocky Mountains), be available for membership on post committees and councils, serve as counsel on courts-martial, or participate in various other additional duties which directly or indirectly link his platoon with higher or adjacent units.

In summary, the Life Cycle Theory of Leadership is an attempt to demonstrate the appropriate relationship between the leader's behavior and another aspect of the situation—subordinate maturity. According to the model, the leader must remain sensitive to his subordinates' level of maturity. As personal problems arise, new tasks are assigned, or the degree of stress inherent in the situation changes, subordinates may act less maturely. The model prescribes that the leader should adjust his behavior accordingly. Thus, the Life Cycle Theory assumes a dynamic situation where the maturity of the subordinates does change and where the leader's behavior must change appropriately in order to maintain effectiveness.

Two final comments regarding this model are in order. First, one must keep in mind that within any group, the individual members may have achieved different degrees of maturity. For example, in an infantry platoon, one would expect the senior noncommissioned officers to act more maturely when confronted with infantry-related tasks than the remainder of the platoon members. This suggests that the leader should provide different degrees of Structure and Consideration to the senior NCO's than he does to the privates.

Secondly, the situational dimension is much more complex than that described by Hersey and Blanchard, and many questions remain unanswered. For example, group maturity is defined as a multi-dimensional concept. The authors are unclear regarding how the three variables which comprise "maturity" (i.e., goal setting, accepting responsibility, and experience) are to be ordered and determined. Are any of the maturity factors more important than the others? Is maturity to be determined by the leader's perception of it or by some objective measurement? Good performance could easily be interpreted by the leader as an increase in subordinate maturity when, in fact, it might be a function of other factors. Until some of these questions are resolved, the Life Cycle Theory may be difficult to apply in real-life situations.

FUTURE TRENDS

Although a complete understanding of leader behavior does not exist currently, work is continuing in an effort to develop a more thorough contingency theory of leadership. Kerr and his associates at Ohio State recently have reviewed numerous research studies and proposed several hypotheses designed to explain contradictory findings in the literature (Kerr, Schriesheim, Murphy and Stogdill, 1974). These researchers have identified several variables which have been shown to moderate relationships between leader behavior and subordinate performance and satisfaction. Two of these variables were discussed earlier in this article: (1) task pressure (e.g., task urgency or situational stress); and (2) the informational needs of subordinates (e.g., subordinate competence and maturity). Other important variables cited by these researchers include: (1) intrinsic job satisfaction; (2) subordinate expectations of appropriate leader behavior; (3) the leader behavior of higher level management; and (4) the upward influence of the leader. Obviously, even this list of situational factors is not all-inclusive. However, it does provide an important foundation for future research which, in turn, will enhance further our understanding of the influence process.

CONCLUSIONS

This article has reviewed briefly some of the major research findings and models in the study of leader behavior. From the early Ohio State studies through the Life Cycle Theory of Leadership, one theme has prevailed: leadership is such a complex process that there is no simple prescription which will insure success. As yet, no overall theory of leadership behavior exists which satisfactorily incorporates all of the complexities of the leader, his subordinates, and the situation.

Implicit in the entire discussion of leader behavior has been the role conflict experienced by a leader as he finds himself both a superior and a subordinate. Prescriptions of appropriate leader behavior differ depending on whether these behaviors are derived from the subordinates or the superiors of the leader. These conflicting role expectations result from the overlapping memberships of leaders which are common in formal organizations. The Model of Organizational Leadership, presented in the beginning of this text, depicts the leader in two such groups—*his own formal work group* and the *next senior level*. Of course, he is in several others such as informal, off-duty social groups, a family grouping, and perhaps the junior officer's council, all of which could feasibly add to the role conflict being experienced by the leader.

Research by Stouffer and his associates (1949) clearly illustrates conflicting role expectations of mid-level leaders in a military setting. This study surveyed American soldiers during World War II. The researchers found that enlisted men were more favorably disposed toward sergeants whose characteristic behaviors centered around Consideration for subordinate welfare. Officers, on the other hand, were more inclined to prefer Initiating Structure from the sergeants. These findings are generally consistent with those described earlier in this article and reveal a basic dilemma: an intermediate level leader not only must accept the norms and values of the organization and serve as its agent, but also must gain the willing followership of his subordinates. As many studies have indicated, both Consideration and Initiating Structure are essential leader behaviors in order for a group to be successful. The problem arises in determining what combination of leader behaviors is best in what situation and as perceived by whom—the superiors or the subordinates.

END NOTES

1. Stogdill (1974) has modified the above conclusions based on a recent review of 163 studies on the trait approach to leadership conducted between 1947–1974. These revised conclusions are discussed in the first article of this text entitled "A Model of Organizational Leadership."

2. Korten's original article, "Situational Determinants of Leadership Structure," is contained in Part II of this text.

REFERENCES

Bird, C. *Social psychology*. New York: Appleton-Century, 1940.

Blake, R.R. and Mouton, J.H. *The Managerial Grid*. Houston: Gulf Publishing Co., 1964.

Blake, R.R. and Mouton, J.H. Military leadership in the post-70's. In *Leadership in the post-70's*. West Point: The United States Military Academy, 1969.

Fleishman, E.A. A leader behavior description for industry. In R.M. Stogdill and A.E. Coons (Eds.), *Leader behavior: its description and measurement*. Columbus: Ohio State University Press, 1957, 103–119.

Fleishman, E.A. and Peters, D.R. Interpersonal values, leadership attitudes, and managerial success. *Personnel. Psychology,* 1962, 15, 127–143.

Halpin, A.W. and Winer, B.J. *The leadership behavior of the airplane commander*. Columbus: O.S.U. Research Foundation, 1952.

Halpin, A.W. The leadership behavior and combat performance of airplane commanders., *Journal of Applied Social Psychology,* 1954, 49, 19–22.

Halpin, A.W. The leader behavior and effectiveness of aircraft commanders. In R.M. Stogdill and A.E. Coons (Eds.), *Leader behavior: its description and measurement*. Columbus: Ohio State University, Bureau of Business Research, 1957.

Halpin, A.W. *Manual for the leader behavior description questionnaire*. Columbus: O.S.U. Business of Bureau Research, 1957a.

Hersey, P. and Blanchard, K.H. Changing patterns of leadership: 3-D leader effectiveness theory. In *Leadership in the post-70's*. West Point: The United States Military Academy, 1969.

Hersey, Paul and Kenneth H. Blanchard. What's missing in MBO? *Management Review,* 1974, 63, No. 10, 25–32.

House, R.J. A path goal theory of leader effectiveness. *Administrative Science Quarterly,* 1971, 16, 321–338.

Jenkins, W.O. A review of leadership studies with particular reference to military problems. *Psychological Bulletin,* 1947, 44, 54–79.

Kerr, S., Schriesheim, C.A., Murphy, C.J., and Stogdill, R.M. Toward a contingency theory of leadership based upon the consideration and initiating structure literature. *Organizational Behavior and Human Performance,* 1974, 1, 62–82.

Korman, A.K. Consideration, initiating structure, and organizational criteria—A Review. *Personnel Psychology: A Journal of Applied Research,* 1966, Vol. 19, No. 4, pp. 349–361.

Korten, D.C. Situational determinants of leadership structure. *Journal of Conflict Resolution,* 1962, 6, 222–235.

Likert, Rensis. *New Patterns of Management,* New York: McGraw-Hill Book Co, Inc; 1961.

Rush, C.H. Leader behavior and group characteristics. In R.M. Stogdill and A.E. Coons (Eds.), *Leader behavior: its description and measurement.* Columbus: Ohio State University, Bureau of Business Research, 1957.

Stogdill, R.M. Personal factors associated with leadership: A survey of the literature. *Journal of Psychology,* 1948, 25, 35–71.

Stogdill, R.M. *Handbook of Leadership:* New York: The Free Press, 1974.

Stouffer, S.A. et al. *The American Soldier.* Vol. 1 Princeton: Princeton University Press, 1949.

Overview, USAWC Study of Leadership for the 1970's

by
*Norman L. Grunstad**

In January of 1971, the volunteer army was still in the experimental stage. One of the major concerns of then Chief of Staff, General Westmoreland, was whether the time honored "Principles of Leadership" would still be valid for this new army. To determine this, he asked the War College to conduct a broad-based and comprehensive study of army leadership which would produce useful answers to the following questions:

    1. To what extent will the existing principles meet the requirements of the volunteer army?

    2. If these principles are inappropriate, what principles or behaviors will meet the requirements?

    These are very important questions for the army. Answering them was a difficult and complex process which will be discussed only briefly in this article. For more details, refer to the references listed at the end of this article.

THE CENTRAL CONCEPTS

    The first concept is the *informal contract* which addresses the relationship between the army and the soldier—what each expects from the other. It is an unwritten contract of perceived "fairness" in the issues of reciprocity or exchange between the two parties. This concept is often discussed under another name—social exchange.

*Norman L. Grunstad (Major, US Army), is on the faculty of the Office of Military Leadership at the United States Military Academy, West Point, New York. He received his BS from the United States Military Academy (1964), and his MA and PhD in Organizational Behavior from the Ohio State University (1972).

The fact that the contract is informal in no way decreases its importance. It is very real in the eyes of both parties. The fulfillment of this contract (whether expectations are met or unmet) is critical to the general satisfaction of the parties with each other. To get a clearer picture of this issue, we might look at two elements of the contract which have been in heated negotiation lately— the post exchange and the commissary. Both of these institutions have received intense scrutiny by the congress with the added pressure, naturally enough, of the business community. Most members of the military consider these institutions to be "part of the package" when they join. True, the army does have a responsibility to provide adequate facilities for food, clothing, and other necessities where circumstances such as war or simple isolation dictate. That was the original intent, coupled with the fact that military pay has historically been far below that of our civilian compatriots. Without intending to take a position on this, the above circumstances are now the exception rather than the rule. However, what began as a needed service and a privilege has become a "right" in many minds. Recently, legislation was introduced which directed the army to make the commissaries self-supporting (as the post exchange has been for years). The resounding outcry that arose within the military community is a vivid example of a perceived "breach of contract." The fact that it is the breach of an *informal* contract is irrelevant to most members of the military. To add to the complexity of the problem, each soldier perceives the contract differently; each has his own unique expectations. This points out the need for upward communications.

Basically, there is a need for both parties to participate in stating and meeting the terms of the contract. One of the primary jobs of a leader is to articulate and mediate these terms by representing both parties, balancing individual and organizational needs. This "linking or mediating" role of the leader is mentioned several times in the original study and by many other students of leadership behavior.

The second concept is *leadership climate*. This is the totality of leadership as it is perceived by the organization's members. It is the medium, or environment, in which the informal contract is negotiated. Some authors would say it is the organization's "personality." The climate is composed of many elements which can be identified and measured. Because of normal reward and advancement systems, you could predict that the climate at any level will reflect the leadership above that level. Quite simply, this is because we do what the boss wants done. In order to change the climate, then, it would seem necessary to start at the top. The study finds this to be true and recommends a deeper look at the attitudes and values of officers in the grade of colonel and above. This same problem has been discovered in all organizations so the army is not unique in this respect.

Out of these two central concepts it was possible to develop a statement of the primary research objective:

The leadership most appropriate for the 1970's is that which produces a total leadership climate characterized by recognition and fulfillment of the informal contract in order to insure mission accomplishment over the long term.

DESIGN AND PERSPECTIVE

One of the first steps in the examination of the principles of leadership was to find an objective way to measure them. The War College chose to state the principles in terms of observable leader behaviors—things leaders do and can be seen doing. The behaviors chosen were those which were prepared and researched by the Ohio State leadership study group. Since the 1950's, this group has formulated and tested approximately 150 items of human activity which represent leader behavior. The War College chose 43 of the 150 behaviors used by the Ohio State group. These 43 behaviors (some slightly modified for military purposes) were chosen because they stated the principles of leadership in behavioral terms. To give you a better idea of the kinds of behaviors used in the study, ten of the 43 behaviors are listed below. These behaviors happen to be the ten most "powerful" in terms of the opportunity they offer for increasing both senior and subordinate satisfaction with leadership for all grades. Later in the article, we will discuss these under the title of "high opportunity sensitivity behaviors." You should also notice the similarity between these measurable behaviors and the principles of leadership.

1. He was technically competent to perform his duties.
2. He was easy to understand.
3. He communicated effectively with his subordinates.
4. He knew his men and their capabilities.
5. He approached each task in a positive manner.
6. He backed up his subordinates in their actions.
7. He set the example for his men on and off duty.
8. He set high standards of performance.
9. He was approachable.
10. He kept me informed of the true situation, good and bad, under all circumstances.

At this point, it became quite apparent that a new approach to measuring leader behaviors was needed. Normally, if we want to know how a certain lieutenant is doing, we ask his boss. We would probably get a reasonable estimate of the lieutenant's worth that way. This has been the army's way for years. However, if we asked the lieutenant himself, or other lieutenants, we might get an entirely different appraisal. Finally, if we asked the platoon sergeant, we would be very likely to get a completely different evaluation. Which one is accurate? Before that question can be answered, if indeed it can, we need to examine the two inherent features of our concept of leadership and the problem of selective perception.

In the simplest terms, leadership involves the accomplishment of the mission and the welfare of the men. The importance of and emphasis upon either or both of these factors is quite different depending on who you are and what the situation is. The "proper" mix might be defined quite differently by each of the three parties above. For the leader being observed, it is very important that he see himself as others see him so that he can adjust his behavior "realistically" to the situation. In short, to get an accurate picture of a leader, we should look at all three perceptions of that leader—superior, subordinate, and self. If we wish to look at the average behavior at some particular leadership level (say, for all second lieutenants), the same basic approach is used—superiors, subordinates, and peers. This is called the "Tri-focal" view of leadership and is shown in the figure below. There is no feasible way to study the terms of the informal contract unless all parties to the contract are heard.

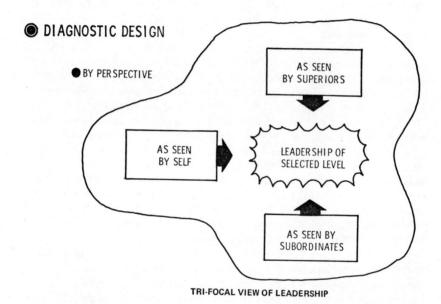

TRI-FOCAL VIEW OF LEADERSHIP

With this design, it was possible to start collecting data for analysis. Based on the tri-focal view, the subjects to be questioned were divided into three groups. The soldiers in one group rated their immediate subordinate, those in another rated themselves, and those in the third group rated their immediate superior on each of the 43 behaviors. There were three questions about each of these behaviors: how often the ratee engaged in that behavior, how often he should have engaged in it, and how important this behavior is. Each of these were answered on a scale from 1 to 7. This provided numerical data which could be analyzed statistically. Subjective data were also gathered in follow-up group interviews to see if the questionnaire was producing valid and reliable results. This approach provides a great deal of information about what one grade group expects from another and what it is actually getting. We will look at the analysis of that data next.

THE DATA

Although there were many possible ways to use the available data, it was decided to look at group data by grade level. This approach provides average data about all the members of each rank as seen by themselves (i.e., the peer group) and those immediately above and below.

Recall the discussion of the three questions asked about each behavior. If the score of the question "How much did he . . ." is subtracted from the score of the question "How much should he . . ." in the case of a platoon sergeant rating a lieutenant, we can get an indication of how much (or little) the lieutenant is meeting the sergeant's expectations. It is a measure of how well the informal contract is being fulfilled. This difference is called *"Performance Shortfall"* for obvious reasons. Since some behaviors are more important than others, performance shortfall is multiplied by the "Importance" score to get *"Weighted Performance Shortfall"*. This allows scores to be compared between behaviors. To find out how all lieutenants fared in some behavior, we can simply add their average shortfall on some behavior as seen by captains *and* by platoon sergeants to the average score of lieutenants rating themselves. This gives a more accurate picture than the perceptions of any one group.

"Perception Shortfall" is calculated by using the same figures. In its simplest terms, perception shortfall is the difference between the perceptions of a particular grade level and the perceptions of the superiors and subordinates of that grade level. It says nothing at all about performance. It merely says there is a difference between the way some group sees itself and the way others see it. Realistically enough, this is also called the *"coefficient of self-delusion"* because the larger the difference between how one group sees itself and the way others see it, the more the members are fooling themselves about how they are doing. This could be quite serious.

The final measure developed from the data was one called *"Opportunity Sensitivity."* This measure describes and predicts how much of an impact any specific behavior has on perceived overall performance. Briefly, some behaviors have a very great effect on how one is perceived as a leader. Others have little or no effect. If, for whatever reason, you find it necessary to set priorities on where to put your effort toward improvement, those behaviors with a high impact on your perceived performance would be the ones to work on. On the surface, this is a complicated measure so you should check the references for a more detailed explanation. You will find it simpler than you thought.

GENERAL FINDINGS

The findings and conclusions of this study were wide-ranging and significant. They will be discussed in general terms in this article.

To deal with the questions on the first page of this article, the principles of leadership were found to be both valid and appropriate for the 1970's. The methodology of the study is a reliable device for measuring leadership effectiveness and diagnosing problems. It is an excellent example of the application of behavioral theory to the real world.

The tri-focal approach uncovered many problems and made possible some valuable suggestions for improvement. The most visable finding of this approach was the wide variation in perception between grade levels. Satisfaction with army leadership increased as rank increased. Junior NCOs were 63% satisfied and General Officers were 98% satisfied. There is a steady (almost linear) increase from Junior NCOs to General Officers. The impact of this, especially if you are trying to sell a new program or a needed change, is obvious.

Perceptions of the importance of various principles also varied widely between grades. Even more important, there was a wide variation in the standards by which General Officers measure the effectiveness of their subordinates. The impact here is on the organizational climate. The "tone" of this climate is set at the top and filters down. If the standards at the top are unknown, arbitrary, or inconsistent, the climate will be the same. This phenomenon will be multiplied by the differences in perception between grades all the way down the chain.

The final grade level finding we will discuss in this brief summary is defective application of the principles by grade level. This is another example of the inability to see ourselves as others see us. To examine these issues, we will look at an example of one behavior across all grades. The example we will use is communication behavior—the ability to communicate up and down. (Refer to example behavior number three listed under DESIGN AND PERSPECTIVE in this article.)

The grade level which had the most serious *performance shortfall* in this behavior was senior NCOs. Junior NCOs had the next most serious problem. All other grades also had communications problems (as judged by all three levels of the tri-focal view) but they were not nearly as serious as those of the NCOs. This is a very important finding because these are the people closest to the troops. Failure to communicate makes it impossible to mediate the informal contract. What is even more startling is that the NCOs also had the greatest *perception shortfall* in this behavior. In short, they were unaware that they were not communicating effectively. Other grades were at least aware that they had problems here which probably contributed to the lower problem level. This kind of information by grade level can be very helpful in setting training priorities.

One interesting finding that the study pointed out was the high quality senior company grade (1LT and CPT) officers we had in 1970 and 1971. This group had the lowest performance and perceptual shortfalls across all behaviors and all ranks. There are many possible explanations for this finding. One of the most logical was alluded to earlier in the article—we do what the boss wants done. Over time (presumably after company grade) the socialization process creates problems where few existed. Another possible explanation is that the army happened to get a good group of senior company grade officers in the press of the Vietnam War. If this is true, then the leadership climate of the future should improve as these officers advance in rank.

RECOMMENDATIONS

Eight recommendations were made as a result of the study. All have either been implemented or are in the process of being worked into the system. A few examples should give the flavor of these recommendations.

It was recommended that an extensive and progressive program of academic and technical education be set up for career NCOs. This was done through the Noncommissioned Officer Education System (NCOES) and other means. It was recommended that more officers trained in the scientific study of leadership be provided to army staff sections and schools. This is being done. In conjunction with this last point, it was recommended that army leadership instruction concepts be revised to insure that contemporary scientific approaches to the subject were exploited. A new agency with proponency for leadership doctrine was set up at Fort Benjamin Harrison for this purpose. As this article is written, their leadership doctrine and implementation instructions are in the final approval stages before being sent to the field.

IMPLICATIONS

There are far more implications in this study than can be discussed or even summarized here. A few representative ones will be mentioned.

Many implications are contained in the findings and solution concepts (recommendations). The knowledge that satisfaction with leadership, perception and application of the principles, and high opportunity sensitivity behaviors all vary by grade level should be helpful in explaining why other people do things differently. The summary data tables can also be very helpful to you. They can assist you in being a better second lieutenant, help you prepare to be a good captain, and help you understand field grade officers. The Senior NCO, Junior Company Grade, and Senior Company Grade Tables are enclosed at the end of this article. These tables list the top five behaviors by grade in each of the categories discussed in the DATA section. The Junior Company Grade Table tells you what behaviors for second lieutenants have high impact on perceived overall performance and which ones do not, where second lieutenants do well or poorly, where they fool themselves and where they do not. By comparing this table to the one for senior company grade officers, you can see which behaviors are different. For example, by simply checking the "high opportunity sensitivity behaviors" for junior and senior company grade officers, you can see that there is an overlap of only one behavior out of the five with highest impact. You should notice similar differences in other categories of behaviors. Another example is shown in the behaviors where these two grades are unaware of their shortfalls (high self-delusion). Only one area of self-delusion is the same in the top five behaviors listed in that category. In short, you can see how the expectations change for captains. This illustrates the need for growth; captains cannot behave like lieutenants. Finally, by looking at the NCO tables, you should get some idea of how you might be able to use these tables to assist your NCOs. However, you should keep one important point in mind as you read over these tables. The data presented are *average* data. The information is about groups of people. A *particular* commander or a *particular* unit may require quite different behaviors. Still, as a guideline—a place to start—these tables can be a valuable tool. You should be able to find many more implications as you read through one of the studies referenced.

THE FUTURE

Since the publication of the original War College Study, six monographs were designed to provide more practical and detailed information in specific areas to school faculty members, individual officers, and students of leadership concepts and methods. The data base of the original study was 1800 soldiers. The data base for the monographs is now over 30,000 soldiers. Plans are to continue to update this study periodically as an on-going operation.

The first five monographs have been consolidated into a single publication by the US Army Administration Center. The sixth monograph is still a separate document. The monographs cover the areas indicated by their titles which are listed below:

Monograph 1   Demographic Characteristics of US Army Leaders
Monograph 2   Satisfaction with US Army leadership
Monograph 3   Junior NCO Leadership
Monograph 4   Senior NCO Leadership
Monograph 5   Company Grade Officer Leadership
Monograph 6   Field Grade Officer Leadership

Inquiries about the War College Study or these monographs should be addressed to:

U.S. Army Administration Center
ATTN: PACDA-HRD
Fort Benjamin Harrison, Indiana 46216
Autovon 699-3525

We can expect that this study and others like it have had, and will continue to have, a major impact on future leadership study and practice.

REFERENCES

1. Jacobs, T.O. *Leadership and Exchange in Formal Organizations.* Alexandria, Virginia: HumRRO, 1971.

2. Tagiuri, R. and G.H. Litwin (Eds.), *Organizational Climate; Explorations of a Concept.* Harvard University, Boston, 1968.

3. U.S. Department of the Army. U.S. Army War College. *Leadership for the 1970's: USAWC Study of Leadership for the Professional Soldier (Abbreviated Report),* Carlisle Barracks, Pennsylvania, 1 July 1971.

4. U.S. Department of the Army. U.S. Army War College. *Leadership for the 1970's: USAWC Study of Leadership for the Professional Soldier (Comprehensive Report)*, Carlisle Barracks, Pennsylvania, 20 October 1971.

5. U.S. Department of the Army. U.S. Military Academy. *Extract, USAWC Study of Leaaership for the Professional Soldier*, Office of Military Leadership, AY 1973–74.

TABLE 1

SENIOR NCO LEVEL

ITEMS WITH MAXIMUM OPPORTUNITY SENSITIVITY FOR IMPROVING OVERALL
PERCEPTION OF QUALITY OF LEADERSHIP
BY CHANGE IN LEVEL OF PERFORMANCE OF LEADERSHIP BEHAVIOR

He Communicated Effectively With His Subordinates.
He Was Technically Competent To Perform His Duties.
He Approached Each Task In A Positive Manner.
He Was Approachable.
He Was Easy To Understand.

ITEMS OF LOW OPPORTUNITY SENSITIVITY

He Stifled The Initiative Of His Subordinates.
He Resisted Changes In Ways Of Doing Things.
He Drew A Definite Line Between Himself And His Subordinates.
He Criticized A Specific Act Rather Than An Individual.
He Ruled With An Iron Hand.

LEADERSHIP BEHAVIORS WITH ESPECIALLY HIGH PERFORMANCE
SHORTFALL (DESIRED PERFORMANCE-OBSERVED PERFORMANCE) WEIGHTED BY IMPORTANCE

He Was Aware Of The State Of His Unit's Morale And Did All He Could
To Make It High.
He Set The Example For His Men On And Off Duty.
He Saw To It That People Under Him Worked Up To Their Capabilities.
He Approached Each Task In A Positive Manner.
He Knew His Men And Their Capabilities.

LEADERSHIP BEHAVIORS WITH EXCEPTIONALLY HIGH AGREEMENT
BETWEEN DESIRED AND OBSERVED PERFORMANCE

He Demanded Results On Time Without Considering The Capabilities
And Welfare Of His Unit.
He Assigned Immediate Subordinates To Specific Tasks.
He Refused To Explain His Actions To His Subordinates.
He Fought The Problem.
He Ruled With An Iron Hand.

LEADERSHIP BEHAVIORS WITH ESPECIALLY HIGH PERCEPTUAL SHORTFALL (SELF-DELUSION)

He Counseled, Trained, and Developed His Subordinates.
He Constructively Criticized Poor Performance.
He Kept Me Informed Of The True Situation, Good And Bad, Under All
Circumstances.
He Was Aware Of The State Of His Unit's Morale And Did All He Could
To Make It High.
He Saw To It That People Under Him Worked Up To Their Capabilities.

LEADERSHIP BEHAVIORS WITH EXCEPTIONALLY LOW SELF-DELUSION

He Was Selfish.
He Was Overly Ambitious At The Expense Of His Subordinates And His Unit.
He Fought The Problem.
He Ruled With An Iron Hand.
He Was Easy To Understand.

TABLE 2

JUNIOR COMPANY GRADE LEVEL

ITEMS WITH MAXIMUM OPPORTUNITY SENSITIVITY FOR IMPROVING OVERALL
PERCEPTION OF QUALITY OF LEADERSHIP
BY CHANGE IN LEVEL OF PERFORMANCE OF LEADERSHIP BEHAVIOR

He Knew His Men And Their Capabilities.
He Backed Up Subordinates In Their Actions.
He Distorted Reports To Make His Unit Look Better.
He Set The Example For His Men On And Off Duty.
He Was Selfish.

ITEMS OF LOW OPPORTUNITY SENSITIVITY

He Drew A Definite Line Between Himself And His Subordinates.
He Saw That Subordinates Had The Materials They Needed To Work With.
He Expressed Appreciation When A Subordinate Did A Good Job.
He Criticized A Specific Act Rather Than An Individual.
He Ruled With An Iron Hand.

LEADERSHIP BEHAVIORS WITH ESPECIALLY HIGH PERFORMANCE
SHORTFALL (DESIRED PERFORMANCE-OBSERVED PERFORMANCE) WEIGHTED BY IMPORTANCE

He Was Aware Of The State Of His Unit's Morale And Did All He Could
To Make It High.
He Saw To It That People Under Him Worked Up To Their Capabilities.
He Knew His Men And Their Capabilities.
He Set The Example For His Men On And Off Duty.
He Was Easy To Understand.

LEADERSHIP BEHAVIORS WITH EXCEPTIONALLY HIGH AGREEMENT
BETWEEN DESIRED AND OBSERVED PERFORMANCE

He Resisted Changes In Ways Of Doing Things.
He Fought The Problem.
He Drew A Definite Line Between Himself And His Subordinates.
He Refused To Explain His Actions To His Subordinates.
He Let Subordinates Share In Decisionmaking.

LEADERSHIP BEHAVIORS WITH ESPECIALLY HIGH PERCEPTUAL SHORTFALL (SELF-DELUSION)

He Kept Me Informed Of The True Situation, Good And Bad, Under All
Circumstances.
He Counseled, Trained, And Developed His Subordinates.
He Failed To Show An Appreciation For Priorities Of Work.
He Set High Standards Of Performance.
He Criticized Subordinates In Front Of Others.

LEADERSHIP BEHAVIORS WITH EXCEPTIONALLY LOW SELF-DELUSION

He Communicated Effectively With His Subordinates.
He Was Overly Ambitious At The Expense Of His Subordinates And His Unit.
He Approached Each Task In A Positive Manner.
He Assigned Immediate Subordinates To Specific Tasks.
He Let The Members Of His Unit Know What Was Expected Of Them.

TABLE 3

SENIOR COMPANY GRADE LEVEL

ITEMS WITH MAXIMUM OPPORTUNITY SENSITIVITY FOR IMPROVING OVERALL
PERCEPTION OF QUALITY OF LEADERSHIP
BY CHANGE IN LEVEL OF PERFORMANCE OF LEADERSHIP BEHAVIOR

He Communicated Effectively With His Subordinates.
He Was Easy To Understand.
He Saw To It That People Under Him Worked Up To Their Capabilities.
He Approached Each Task In A Positive Manner.
He Knew His Men And Their Capabilities.

ITEMS OF LOW OPPORTUNITY SENSITIVITY

He Let Subordinates Share In Decisionmaking.
He Ruled With An Iron Hand.
He Drew A Definite Line Between Himself And His Subordinates.
He Gave Detailed Instructions On How The Job Should Be Done.
He Criticized A Specific Act Rather Than An Individual.

LEADERSHIP BEHAVIORS WITH ESPECIALLY HIGH PERFORMANCE
SHORTFALL (DESIRED PERFORMANCE-OBSERVED PERFORMANCE) WEIGHTED BY IMPORTANCE

He Saw To It That People Under Him Worked Up To Their Capabilities.
He Was Easy To Understand.
He Let The Members Of His Unit Know What Was Expected Of Them.
He Constructively Criticized Poor Performance.
He Knew His Men And Their Capabilities.

LEADERSHIP BEHAVIORS WITH EXCEPTIONALLY HIGH AGREEMENT
BETWEEN DESIRED AND OBSERVED PERFORMANCE

He Drew A Definite Line Between Himself And His Subordinates.
He Resisted Changes In Ways Of Doing Things.
He Refused To Explain His Actions To His Subordinates.
He Let Subordinates Share In Decisionmaking.
He Ruled With An Iron Hand.

LEADERSHIP BEHAVIORS WITH ESPECIALLY HIGH PERCEPTUAL SHORTFALL (SELF-DELUSION)

He Kept Me Informed Of The True Situation, Good And Bad, Under All
Circumstances.
He Constructively Criticized Poor Performance.
He Treated People In An Impersonal Manner--Like Cogs In A Machine.
He Was Approachable.
He Expressed Appreciation When A Subordinate Did A Good Job.

LEADERSHIP BEHAVIORS WITH EXCEPTIONALLY LOW SELF-DELUSION

He Sought Additional And More Important Responsibilities.
He Approached Each Task In A Positive Manner.
He Fought The Problem.
He Ruled With An Iron Hand.
He Was Overly Ambitious At The Expense Of His Subordinates And His Unit

Theory X: The Traditional View of Direction and Control*

by
Douglas McGregor

Behind every managerial decision or action are assumptions about human nature and human behavior. A few of these are remarkably pervasive. They are implicit in most of the literature of organization and in much current managerial policy and practice:

1. *The average human being has an inherent dislike of work and will avoid it if he can.* This assumption has deep roots. The punishment of Adam and Eve for eating the fruit of the Tree of Knowledge was to be banished from Eden into a world where they had to work for a living. The stress that management places on productivity, on the concept of "a fair day's work," on the evils of feather-bedding and restriction of output, on rewards for performance—while it has a logic in terms of the objectives of enterprise—reflects an underlying belief that management must counteract an inherent human tendency to avoid work. The evidence for the correctness of this assumption would seem to most managers to be incontrovertible.

2. *Because of this human characteristic of dislike of work, most people must be coerced, controlled, directed, threatened with punishment to get them to put forth adequate effort toward the achievement of organizational objectives.* The dislike of work is so strong that even the promise of rewards is not generally enough to overcome it. People will accept the rewards and demand continually higher ones, but these alone will not produce the necessary effort. Only the threat of punishment will do the trick.

---

*From *The Human Side of Enterprise* by Douglas McGregor. © Copyright 1960 by McGraw-Hill Book Company, Inc., New York, Chap. 3. Reprinted by permission of McGraw-Hill Book Co.

The current wave of criticism of "human relations," the derogatory comments about "permissiveness" and "democracy" in industry, the trends in some companies toward recentralization after the postwar wave of decentralization—all these are assertions of the underlying assumption that people will only work under external coercion and control. The recession of 1957–1958 ended a decade of experimentation with the "soft" managerial approach, and this assumption (which never really was abandoned) is being openly espoused once more.

3. *The average human being prefers to be directed, wishes to avoid responsibility, has relatively little ambition, wants security above all.* This assumption of the "mediocrity of the masses" is rarely expressed so bluntly. In fact, a good deal of lip service is given to the ideal of the worth of the average human being. Our political and social values demand such public expressions. Nevertheless, a great many managers will give private support to this assumption, and it is easy to see it reflected in policy and practice. Paternalism has become a nasty word, but it is by no means a defunct managerial philosophy.

I have suggested elsewhere the name Theory X for this set of assumptions. . . . Theory X is not a straw man for purposes of demolition, but is in fact a theory which materially influences managerial strategy in a wide sector of American industry today. Moreover, the principles of organization which comprise the bulk of the literature of management *could only have been derived from assumptions such as those of Theory X.* Other beliefs about human nature would have led inevitably to quite different organizational principles.

Theory X provides an explanation of some human behavior in industry. These assumptions would not have persisted if there were not a considerable body of evidence to support them. Nevertheless, there are many readily observable phenomena in industry and elsewhere which are not consistent with this view of human nature.

Such a state of affairs is not uncommon. The history of science provides many examples of theoretical explanations which persist over long periods despite the fact that they are only partially adequate. Newton's laws of motion are a case in point. It was not until the development of the theory of relativity during the present century that important inconsistencies and inadequacies in Newtonian theory could be understood and corrected.

The growth of knowledge in the social sciences during the past quarter-century has made it possible to reformulate some assumptions about human nature and human behavior in the organizational setting which resolve certain of the inconsistencies inherent in Theory X. While this reformulation is, of course, tentative, it provides an improved basis for prediction and control of human behavior in industry.

SOME ASSUMPTIONS ABOUT MOTIVATION

At the core of any theory of the management of human resources are assumptions about human motivation. This has been a confusing subject because there have been so many conflicting points of view even among social scientists. In recent years, however, there has been a convergence of research findings and a growing acceptance of a few rather basic ideas about motivation. These ideas appear to have considerable power. They help to explain the inadequacies of Theory X as well as the limited sense in which it is correct. In addition, they provide the basis for an entirely different theory of management.

The following generalizations about motivation are somewhat oversimplified. If all of the qualifications which would be required by a truly adequate treatment were introduced, the gross essentials which are particularly significant for management would be obscured. These generalizations do not misrepresent the facts, but they do ignore some complexities of human behavior which are relatively unimportant for our purposes.

Man is a wanting animal—as soon as one of his needs is satisfied, another appears in its place. This process is unending. It continues from birth to death. Man continuously puts forth effort—works, if you please—to satisfy his needs.

Human needs are organized in a series of levels—a hierarchy of importance. At the lowest level, but preeminent in importance when they are thwarted, are the physiological needs. Man lives by bread alone, when there is no bread. Unless the circumstances are unusual, his needs for love, for status, for recognition are inoperative when his stomach has been empty for a while. But when he eats regularly and adequately, hunger ceases to be an important need. The sated man has hunger only in the sense that a full bottle has emptiness. The same is true of the other physiological needs of man—for rest, exercise, shelter, protection from the elements.

A satisfied need is not a motivator of behavior! This is a fact of profound significance. It is a fact which is unrecognized in Theory X and is, therefore, ignored in the conventional approach to the management of people. I shall return to it later. For the moment, an example will make the point. Consider your own need for air. Except as you are deprived of it, it has no appreciable motivating effect upon your behavior.

When the physiological needs are reasonably satisfied, needs at the next higher level begin to dominate man's behavior—to motivate him. These are the safety needs, for protection against danger, threat, deprivation. Some people mistakenly refer to these as needs for security. However, unless man is in a dependent relationship where he fears arbitrary deprivation, he does not demand security. The need is for the "fairest possible break." When he is confident of this, he is more than willing to take risks. But when he feels threatened or dependent, his greatest need is for protection, for security.

The fact needs little emphasis that since every industrial employee is in at least a partially dependent relationship, safety needs may assume considerable importance. Arbitrary management actions, behavior which arouses uncertainty with respect to continued employment or which reflects favoritism or discrimination, unpredictable administration of policy—these can be powerful motivators of the safety needs in the employment relationship at every level from worker to vice president. In addition, the safety needs of managers are often aroused by their dependence downward or laterally. This is a major reason for emphasis on management prerogatives and clear assignments of authority.

When man's physiological needs are satisfied and he is no longer fearful about his physical welfare, his social needs become important motivators of his behavior. These are such needs as those for belonging, for association, for acceptance by one's fellows, for giving and receiving friendship and love.

Management knows today of the existence of these needs, but it is often assumed quite wrongly that they represent a threat to the organization. Many studies have demonstrated that the tightly knit, cohesive work group may, under proper conditions, be far more effective than an equal number of separate individuals in achieving organizational goals. Yet management, fearing group hostility to its own objectives, often goes to considerable lengths to control and direct human efforts in ways that are inimical to the natural "groupiness" of human beings. When man's social needs—and perhaps his safety needs, too—are thus thwarted, he behaves in ways which tend to defeat organizational objectives. He becomes resistant, antagonistic, uncooperative. But this behavior is a consequence, not a cause.

Above the social needs—in the sense that they do not usually become motivators until lower needs are reasonably satisfied—are the needs of greatest significance to management and to man himself. They are the egoistic needs, and they are of two kinds:

1. Those that relate to one's self-esteem: needs for self-respect and self-confidence, for autonomy, for achievement, for competence, for knowledge

2. Those that relate to one's reputation: needs for status, for recognition, for appreciation, for the deserved respect of one's fellows

Unlike the lower needs, these are rarely satisfied; man seeks indefinitely for more satisfaction of these needs once they have become important to him. However, they do not usually appear in any significant way until physiological, safety, and social needs are reasonably satisfied. Exceptions to this generalization are to be observed, particularly under circumstances where, in addition to severe deprivation of physiological needs, human dignity is trampled upon. Political revolutions often grow out of thwarted social and ego, as well as physiological, needs.

The typical industrial organization offers only limited opportunities for the satisfaction of egoistic needs to people at lower levels in the hierarchy. The conventional methods of organizing work, particularly in mass production industries, give little heed to these aspects of human motivation. If the practices of "scientific management" were deliberately calculated to thwart these needs—which, of course, they are not—they could hardly accomplish this purpose better than they do.

Finally—a capstone, as it were, on the hierarchy—here are the needs for self-fulfillment. These are the needs for realizing one's own potentialities, for continued self-development, for being creative in the broadest sense of that term.

The conditions of modern industrial life give only limited opportunity for these relatively dormant human needs to find expression. The deprivation most people experience with respect to other lower-level needs diverts their energies into the struggle to satisfy *those* needs, and the needs for self-fulfillment remain below the level of consciousness.

Now, briefly, a few general comments about motivation:

We recognize readily enough that a man suffering from a severe dietary deficiency is sick. The deprivation of physiological needs has behavioral consequences. The same is true, although less well recognized, of the deprivation of higher-level needs. The man whose needs for safety, association, independence, or status are thwarted is sick, just as surely as is he who has rickets. And his sickness will have behavioral consequences. We will be mistaken if we attribute his resultant passivity, or his hostility, or his refusal to accept responsibility to his inherent "human nature." These forms of behavior are *symptoms* of illness—of deprivation of his social and egoistic needs.

The man whose lower-level needs are satisfied is not motivated to satisfy those needs. For practical purposes they exist no longer. (Remember my point about your need for air.) Management often asks, "Why aren't people more productive? We pay good wages, provide good working conditions, have excellent fringe benefits and steady employment. Yet people do not seem to be willing to put forth more than minimum effort." It is unnecessary to look far for the reasons.

Consideration of the rewards typically provided the worker for satisfying his needs through his employment leads to the interesting conclusion that most of these rewards can be used for satisfying his needs *only when he leaves the job.* Wages, for example, cannot be spent at work. The only contribution they can make to his satisfaction on the job is in terms of status differences resulting from wage differentials. (This, incidentally, is one of the reasons why small and apparently unimportant differences in wage rates can be the subject of so much heated dispute. The issue is not the pennies involved, but the fact that the status differences which they reflect are one of the few ways in which wages can result in need satisfaction in the job situation itself.)

Most fringe benefits—overtime pay, shift differentials, vacations, health and medical benefits, annuities, and the proceeds from stock purchase plans or profit-sharing plans—yield needed satisfaction only when the individual leaves the job. Yet these, along with wages, are among the major rewards provided by management for effort. It is not surprising, therefore, that for many wage earners *work is perceived as a form of punishment* which is the price to be paid for various kinds of satisfaction away from the job. To the extent that this is their perception, we would hardly expect them to undergo more of this punishment than is necessary.

Under today's conditions management has provided relatively well for the satisfaction of physiological and safety needs. The standard of living in our country is high; people do not suffer major deprivation of their physiological needs except during periods of severe unemployment. Even then, social legislation developed since the thirties cushions the shock.

But the fact that management has provided for these physiological and safety needs has shifted the motivational emphasis to the social and the egoistic needs. Unless there are opportunites *at work* to satisfy these higher-level needs, people will be deprived; and their behavior will reflect this deprivation. Under such conditions, if management continues to focus its attention on physiological needs, the mere provision of rewards is bound to be ineffective, and reliance on the threat of punishment will be inevitable. Thus one of the assumptions of Theory X will appear to be validated, but only because we have mistaken effects for causes.

People *will* make insistent demands for more money under these conditions. It becomes more important than ever to buy the material goods and services which can provide limited satisfaction of the thwarted needs. Although money has only limited value in satisfying many higher-level needs, it can become the focus of interest if it is the only means available.

The "carrot and stick" theory of motivation which goes along with Theory X works reasonably well under certain circumstances. The *means* for satisfying man's physiological and (within limits) safety needs can be provided or withheld by management. Employment itself is such a means, and so are wages, working conditions, and benefits. By these means the individual can be controlled so long as he is struggling for subsistence. Man tends to live for bread alone when there is little bread.

But the "carrot and stick" theory does not work at all once man has reached an adequate subsistence level and is motivated primarily by higher needs. Management cannot provide a man with self-respect, or with the respect of his fellows, or with the satisfaction of needs for self-fulfillment. We can create conditions such that he is encouraged and enabled to seek such satisfactions for himself, or we can thwart him by failing to create those conditions.

But this creation of conditions is not "control" in the usual sense; it does not seem to be a particularly good device for directing behavior. And so management finds itself in an odd position. The high standard of living created by our modern technological know-how provides quite adequately for the satisfaction of physiological and safety needs. The only significant exception is where management practices have not created confidence in a "fair break"— and thus where safety needs are thwarted. But by making possible the satisfaction of lower-level needs, management has deprived itself of the ability to use the control devices on which the conventional assumptions of Theory X has taught it to rely: rewards, promises, incentives, or threats and other coercive devices.

The philosophy of management by direction and control—regardless of whether it is hard or soft—is inadequate to motivate because the human needs on which this approach relies are relatively unimportant motivators of behavior in our society today. Direction and control are of limited value in motivating people whose important needs are social and egoistic.

People, deprived of opportunities to satisfy at work the needs which are now important to them, behave exactly as we might predict—with indolence, passivity, unwillingness to accept responsibility, resistance to change, willingness to follow the demagogue, unreasonable demands for economic benefits. It would seem that we may be caught in a web of our own weaving.

Theory X explains the *consequences* of a particular managerial strategy; it neither explains nor describes human nature although it purports to. Because its assumptions are so unnecessarily limiting, it prevents our seeing the possibilities inherent in other managerial strategies. What sometimes appear to be new strategies—decentralization, management by objectives, consultative supervision, "democratic" leadership—are usually but old wine in new bottles because the procedures developed to implement them are derived from the same inadequate assumptions about human nature. Management is constantly becoming disillusioned with widely touted and expertly merchandised "new approaches" to the human side of enterprise. The real difficulty is that these new approaches are no more than different tactics—programs, procedures, gadgets—within an unchanged strategy based on Theory X.

In child rearing, it is recognized that parental strategies of control must be progressively modified to adapt to the changed capabilities and characteristics of the human individual as he develops from infancy to adulthood. To some extent industrial management recognizes that the human *adult* possesses capabilities for continued learning and growth. Witness the many current activities in the fields of training and management development. In its *basic* conceptions of managing human resources, however, management appears to have concluded that the average human being is permanently arrested in his development in early adolescence. Theory X is built on the least common human denominator: the factory "hand" of the past. As Chris Argyris has shown dramatically in his *Personality and Organization,* conventional managerial strategies for the organization, direction, and control of the human resources of enterprise are admirably suited to the capacities and characteristics of the child rather than the adult.

In one limited area—that of research administration—there has been some recent recognition of the need for selective adaptation in managerial strategy. This, however, has been perceived as a unique problem and its broader implications have not been recognized. As pointed out in this and the previous chapter (of *The Human Side of Enterprise*), changes in the population at large—in educational level, attitudes and values, motivation, degree of dependence—have created both the opportunity and the need for other forms of selective adaptation. However, so long as the assumptions of Theory X continue to influence managerial strategy, we will fail to discover, let alone utilize, the potentialities of the average human being.

Theory Y: The Integration of Individual and Organizational Goals*

by
Douglas McGregor

To some, the preceding analysis will appear unduly harsh. Have we not made major modifications in the management of the human resources of industry during the past quarter-century? Have we not recognized the importance of people and made vitally significant changes in managerial strategy as a consequence? Do the developments since the twenties in personnel administration and labor relations add up to nothing?

There is no question that important progress has been made in the past two or three decades. During this period the human side of enterprise has become a major preoccupation of management. A tremendous number of policies, programs, and practices which were virtually unknown thirty years ago, have become commonplace. The lot of the industrial employee—be he worker, professional, or executive—has improved to a degree which could hardly have been imagined by his counterpart of the nineteen twenties. Management has adopted generally a far more humanitarian set of values; it has successfully striven to give more equitable and more generous treatment to its employees. It has significantly reduced economic hardships, eliminated the more extreme forms of industrial warfare, provided a generally safe and pleasant working environment, but it has done all these things without changing its fundamental theory of management. There are no exceptions here and there, and they are important; nevertheless, the assumptions of Theory X remain predominant throughout our economy.

---

*From *The Human Side of Enterprise* by Douglas McGregor. Copyright © 1960 by McGraw-Hill Book Company, Inc., New York, Chap. 4. Reprinted by permission of McGraw-Hill Book Co.

Management was subjected to severe pressures during the Great Depression of the thirties. The wave of public antagonism, the open warfare accompanying the unionization of the mass production industries, the general reaction against authoritarianism, the legislation of the New Deal produced a wide "pendulum swing." However, the changes in policy and practice which took place during that and the next decade were primarily adjustments to the increased power of organized labor and to the pressures of public opinion.

Some of the movement was away from "hard" and toward "soft" management, but it was short-lived, and for good reasons. It has become clear that many of the initial strategic interpretations accompanying the "human relations approach" were as naive as those which characterized the early stages of progressive education. We have now discovered that there is no answer in the simple removal of control—that abdication is not a workable alternative to authoritarianism. We have learned that there is no direct correlation between employee satisfaction and productivity. We recognize today that "industrial democracy" cannot consist in permitting everyone to decide everything, that industrial health does not flow automatically from the elimination of dissatisfaction, disagreement, or even open conflict. Peace is not synonymous with organizational health; socially responsible management is not coextensive with permissive management.

Now that management has regained its earlier prestige and power, it has become obvious that the trend toward "soft" management was a temporary and relatively superficial reaction rather than a general modification of fundamental assumptions or basic strategy. Moreover, while the progress we have made in the past quarter-century is substantial, it has reached the point of diminishing returns. The tactical possibilities within conventional managerial strategies have been pretty completely exploited, and significant new developments will be unlikely without major modifications in theory.

THE ASSUMPTIONS OF THEORY Y

There have been few dramatic break-throughs in social science theory like those which have occurred in the physical sciences during the past half-century. Nevertheless, the accumulation of knowledge about human behavior in many specialized fields has made possible the formulation of a number of generalizations which provide a modest beginning for new theory with respect to the management of human resources. Some of these assumptions were outlined in the discussion of motivation. Some others, which will hereafter be referred to as Theory Y, are as follows:

1. The expenditure of physical and mental effort in work is as natural as play or rest. The average human being does not inherently dislike work. Depending upon controllable conditions, work may be a source of satisfaction (and will be voluntarily performed) or a source of punishment (and will be avoided if possible).

2. External control and the threat of punishment are not the only means for bringing about effort toward organizational objectives. Man will exercise

self-direction and self-control in the service of objectives to which he is committed.

3. Commitment to objectives is a function of the rewards associated with their achievement. The most significant of such rewards, e.g., the satisfaction of ego and self-actualization needs, can be direct products of effort directed toward organizational objectives.

4. The average human being learns, under proper conditions, not only to accept but to seek responsibility. Avoidance of responsibility, lack of ambition, and emphasis on security are generally consequences of experience, not inherent human characteristics.

5. The capacity to exercise a relatively high degree of imagination, ingenuity, and creativity in the solution of organizational problems is widely, not narrowly, distributed in the population.

6. Under the conditions of modern industrial life, the intellectual potentialities of the average human being are only partially utilized.

These assumptions involve sharply different implications for managerial strategy than do those of Theory X. They are dynamic rather than static: They indicate the possibility of human growth and development; they stress the necessity for selective adaptation rather than for a single absolute form of control. They are not framed in terms of the least common denominator of the factory hand, but in terms of a resource which has substantial potentialities.

Above all, the assumptions of Theory Y point up the fact that the limits on human collaboration in the organizational setting are not limits of human nature but of management's ingenuity if discovering how to realize the potential represented by its human resources. Theory X offers management an easy rationalization for ineffective organizational performance: It is due to the nature of the human resources with which we must work. Theory Y, on the other hand, places the problems squarely in the lap of management. If employees are lazy, indifferent, unwilling to take responsibility, intransigent, uncreative, uncooperative, Theory Y implies that the causes lie in management's methods of organization and control.

The assumptions of Theory Y are not finally validated. Nevertheless, they are far more consistent with existing knowledge in the social sciences than are the assumptions of Theory X. They will undoubtedly be refined, elaborated, modified as further research accumulates, but they are unlikely to be completely contradicted.

On the surface, these assumptions may not seem particularly difficult to accept. Carrying their implications into practice, however, is not easy. They challenge a number of deeply ingrained managerial habits of thought and action.

THE PRINCIPLE OF INTEGRATION

The central principle of organization which derives from Theory X is that of direction and control through the exercise of authority—what has been called "the scalar principle." The central principle which derives from Theory

Y is that of integration: the creation of conditions such that the members of the organization can achieve their own goals best by directing their efforts toward the success of the enterprise. These two principles have profoundly different implications with respect to the task of managing human resources, but the scalar principle is so firmly built into managerial attitudes that the implications of the principle of integration are not easy to perceive.

Someone once said that fish discover water last. The "psychological environment" of industrial management—like water for fish—is so much a part of organizational life that we are unaware of it. Certain characteristics of our society, and of organizational life within it, are so completely established, so pervasive, that we cannot conceive of their being otherwise. As a result, a great many policies and practices and decisions and relationships could only be—it seems—what they are.

Among these pervasive characteristics of organizational life in the United States today is a managerial attitude (stemming from Theory X) toward membership in the industrial organization. It is assumed without question that organizational requirements take precedence over the needs of individual members. Basically, the employment agreement is that in return for the rewards which are offered, the individual will accept external direction and control. The very idea of integration and self-control is foreign to our way of thinking about the employment relationship. The tendency, therefore, is either to reject it out of hand (as socialistic, or anarchistic, or inconsistent with human nature) or to twist it unconsciously until it fits existing conceptions.

The concept of integration and self-control carries the implication that the organization will be more effective in achieving its economic objectives if adjustments are made, in significant ways, to the needs and goals of its members.

A district manager in a large, geographically decentralized company is notified that he is being promoted to a policy level position at headquarters. It is a big promotion with a large salary increase. His role in the organization will be a much more powerful one, and he will be associated with the major executives of the firm.

The headquarters group who selected him for this position have carefully considered a number of possible candidates. This man stands out among them in a way which makes him the natural choice. His performance has been under observation for some time, and there is little question that he possesses the necessary qualifications not only for this opening but for an even higher position. There is genuine satisfaction that such an outstanding candidate is available.

The man is appalled. He doesn't want the job. His goal, as he expresses it, is to be the "best damned district manager in the company." He enjoys his direct associations with operating people in the field, and he doesn't want a policy level job. He and his wife enjoy the kind of life they have created in a small city, and they dislike actively both the living conditions and the social obligations of the headquarters city.

He expresses his feelings as strongly as he can, but his objections are brushed aside. The organization's needs are such that his refusal to accept the promotion would be unthinkable. His superiors say to themselves that of course when he has settled in to the new job, he will recognize that it was the right thing. And so he makes the move.

Two years later he is in an even higher position in the company's headquarters organization, and there is talk that he will probably be the executive vice-president before long. Privately he expresses considerable unhappiness and dissatisfaction. He (and his wife) would "give anything" to be back in the situation he left two years ago.

Within the context of the pervasive assumptions of Theory X, promotions and transfers in large numbers are made by unilateral decision. The requirements of the organization are given priority automatically and almost without question. If the individual's personal goals are considered at all, it is assumed that the rewards of salary and position will satisfy him. Should an individual actually refuse such a move without a compelling reason, such as health or a severe family crisis, he would be considered to have jeopardized his future because of this "selfish" attitude. It is rare indeed for management to give the individual the opportunity to be a genuine and active partner in such a decision, even though it may affect his most important personal goals. Yet the implications following from Theory Y are that the organization is likely to suffer if it ignores these personal needs and goals. In making unilateral decisions with respect to promotion, management is failing to utilize its human resources in the most effective way.

The principle of integration demands that both the organization's and the individual's needs be recognized. Of course, when there is a sincere joint effort to find it, an integrative solution which meets the needs of the individual and the organization is a frequent outcome. But not always—and this is the point at which Theory Y begins to appear unrealistic. It collides head-on with pervasive attitudes associated with management by direction and control.

The assumptions of Theory Y imply that unless integration is achieved the organization will suffer. The objectives of the organization are not achieved best by the unilateral administration of promotions, because this form of management by direction and control will not create the commitment which would make available the full resources of those affected. The lesser motivation, the lesser resulting degree of self-direction and self-control are costs which when added up for many instances over time, will more than offset the gains obtained by unilateral decisions "for the good of the organization."

One other example will perhaps clarify further the sharply different implications of Theory X and Theory Y.

It could be argued that management is already giving a great deal of attention to the principle of integration through its efforts in the field of economic education. Many millions of dollars and much ingenuity have been expended in attempts to persuade employees that their welfare is intimately connected with the success of the free enterprise system and of their own companies. The idea that they can achieve their own goals best by directing their effort toward the objectives of the organization has been explored and developed and communicated in every possible way. Is this not evidence that management is already committed to the principle of integration?

The answer is a definite no. These managerial efforts, with rare exceptions, reflect clearly the influence of the assumptions of Theory X. The central message is an exhortation to the industrial employee to work hard and follow orders in order to protect his job and his standard of living. Much has been achieved, it says, by our established way of running industry, and much more could be achieved if employees would adapt themselves to management's definition of what is required. Behind these exhortations lies the expectation that of course the requirements of the organization and its economic success must have priority over the needs of the individual.

Naturally, integration means working together for the success of the enterprise so we all may share in the resulting rewards. But management's implicit assumption is that working together means adjusting to the requirements of the organization as management perceives them. In terms of existing views, it seems inconceivable that individuals, seeking their own goals, would further the ends of the enterprise. On the contrary, this would lead to anarchy, chaos, irreconcilable conflicts of self-interest, lack of responsibility, inability to make decisions, and failure to carry out those that were made.

All these consequences, and other worse ones, would be inevitable unless conditions could be created such that the members of the organization perceived that they could achieve their own goals best by directing their efforts toward the success of the enterprise. If the assumptions of Theory Y are valid, the practical question is whether, and to what extent, such conditions can be created. To that question the balance of this volume is addressed.

THE APPLICATION OF THEORY Y

In the physical sciences there are many theoretical phenomena which cannot be achieved in practice. Absolute zero and a perfect vacuum are examples. Others, such as nuclear power, jet aircraft, and human space flight, are recognized theoretically to be possible long before they become feasible. This fact does not make theory less useful. If it were not for our theoretical convictions, we would not even be attempting to develop the means for human flight into space today. In fact, were it not for the development of physical science theory during the past century and a half, we would still be depending upon the horse and buggy and the sailing vessel for transportation. Virtually all significant technological developments wait on the formulation of relevant theory.

Similarly, in the management of the human resources of industry, the assumptions and theories about human nature at any given time limit innovation. Possibilities are not recognized, innovating efforts are not undertaken, until theoretical conceptions lay a groundwork for them. Assumptions like those of Theory X permit us to conceive of certain possible ways of organizing and directing human effort, but not others. Assumptions like those of Theory Y open up a range of possibilities for new managerial policies and practices. As in the case of the development of new physical science theory, some of these possibilities are not immediately feasible, and others may forever remain unattainable. They may be too costly, or it may be that we simply cannot discover how to create the necessary "hardware."

There is substantial evidence for the statement that the potentialities of the average human being are far above those which we typically realize in industry today. If our assumptions are like those of Theory X, we will not even recognize the existence of these potentialities and there will be no reason to devote time, effort, or money to discovering how to realize them. If, however, we accept assumptions like those of Theory Y, we will be challenged to innovate, to discover new ways of organizing and directing human effort, even though we recognize that the perfect organization, like the perfect vacuum, is practically out of reach.

We need not be overwhelmed by the dimensions of the managerial task implied by Theory Y. To be sure, a large mass production operation in which the workers have been organized by a militant and hostile union faces management with problems which appear at present to be insurmountable with respect to the application of the principle of integration. It may be decades before sufficient knowledge will have accumulated to make such an application feasible. Applications of Theory Y will have to be tested initially in more limited ways and under more favorable circumstances. However, a number of applications of theory in managing managers and professional people are possible today. Within the managerial hierarchy, the assumptions can be tested and refined, techniques can be invented and skill acquired in their use. As knowledge accumulates, some of the problems of application at the worker level in large organizations may appear less baffling than they do at present.

Perfect integration of organizational requirements and individual goals and needs is, of course, not a realistic objective. In adopting this principle, we seek that degree of integration in which the individual can achieve his goals best by directing his efforts toward the success of the organization. "Best" means that this alternative will be more attractive than the many others available to him: indifference, irresponsibility, minimal compliance, hostility, sabotage. It means that he will continuously be encouraged to develop and utilize voluntarily his capacities, his knowledge, his skill, his ingenuity in ways which contribute to the success of the enterprise.[1]

Acceptance of Theory Y does not imply abdication, or "soft" management, or "permissiveness." As was indicated above, such notions stem from the acceptance of authority as the single means of managerial control, and from attempts to minimize its negative consequences. Theory Y assumes that people will exercise self-direction and self-control in the achievement of organizational objectives to the degree that they are committed to those objectives. If that commitment is small, only a slight degree of self-direction and self-control will be likely, and a substantial amount of external influence will be necessary. If it is large, many conventional external controls will be relatively superfluous, and to some extent self-defeating. Managerial policies and practices materially affect this degree of commitment.

Authority is an inappropriate means for obtaining commitment to objectives. Other forms of influence—help in achieving integration, for example—are required for this purpose. Theory Y points to the possibility of lessening the emphasis on external forms of control to the degree that commitment to organizational objectives can be achieved. Its underlying assumptions emphasize the capacity of human beings for self-control, and the consequent possibility of greater managerial reliance on other means of influence. Nevertheless, it is clear that authority is an appropriate means for control under certain circumstances—particularly where genuine commitment to objectives cannot be achieved. The assumptions of Theory Y do not deny the appropriateness of authority, but they do deny that it is appropriate for all purposes and under all circumstances.

Many statements have been made to the effect that we have acquired today the know-how to cope with virtually any technological problems which may arise, and that the major industrial advances of the next half century will occur on the human side of enterprise. Such advances, however, are improbable so long as management continues to organize and direct and control its human resources on the basis of assumptions—tacit or explicit—like those of Theory X. Genuine innovation, in contrast to a refurbishing and patching of present managerial strategies, requires first the acceptance of less limiting assumptions about the nature of human resources we seek to control, and second the readiness to adapt selectively to the implications contained in those new assumptions. Theory Y is an invitation to innovation.

END NOTE

1. A recent, highly significant study of the sources of job satisfaction and dissatisfaction among managerial and professional people suggests that these opportunities for "self-actualization" are the essential requirements of both job satisfaction and high performance. The researchers find that "the wants of employees divide into two groups. One group revolves around the need to develop in one's occupation as a source of personal growth. The second group operates as an essential base to the first and is associated with fair treatment in compensation, supervision, working conditions, and administrative practices. The fulfillment of the needs of the second group does not motivate the individual to high levels of job satisfaction and . . . to extra performance on the job. All we can expect from satisfying (this second group of needs) is the prevention of dissatisfaction and poor job performance." Frederick Herzberg, Bernard Mausner, and Barbara Bloch Snyderman, *The Motivation to Work.* New York: John Wiley & Sons, Inc., 1959, pp. 114–115.

Applications

The Contingency Model: New Directions for Leadership Utilization*

by
Fred E. Fiedler

Leadership research has come a long way from the simple concepts of earlier years which centered on the search for the magic leadership trait. We have had to replace the old cherished notion that "leaders are born and not made." These increasingly complex formulations postulate that some types of leaders will behave and perform differently in a given situation than other types. The Contingency Model is one of the earliest and most articulated of these theories;[1] taking into account the personality of the leader as well as aspects of the situation which affect the leader's behavior and performance. This model has given rise to well over one-hundred empirical studies. This article briefly reviews the current status of the Contingency Model and then discusses several new developments which promise to have considerable impact on our thinking about leadership as well as on the management of executive manpower.

THE CONTINGENCY MODEL

The theory holds that the effectiveness of a task group or of an organization depends on two main factors: the personality of the leader and the degree

*This paper is based on research performed under ARPA Order 454, Contract N00014-67-A-0103-0013 with the Advanced Research Projects Agency, United States Navy (Fred E. Fiedler, Principal Investigator) and Contract NR 177-472, N00014-67-A-0103-0012 with the Office of Naval Research, Department of the Navy (Fred E. Fiedler, Principal Investigator).
Reprinted by permission of the publisher from *Journal of Contemporary Business*, Autumn 1974, pp. 65–79.

to which the situation gives the leader power, control and influence over the situation or, conversely, the degree to which the situation confronts the leader with uncertainty.[2]

Leader Personality

The first of these factors distinguishes leader personality in terms of two different motivational systems, i.e., the basic or primary goals as well as the secondary goals which people pursue once their more pressing needs are satisfied. One type of person, whom we shall call "relationship-motivated," primarily seeks to maintain good interpersonal relationships with coworkers. These basic goals become very apparent in uncertain and anxiety-provoking situations in which we try to make sure that the important needs are secured. Under these conditions the relationship-motivated individual will seek out others and solicit their support; however, under conditions in which he or she feels quite secure and relaxed—because this individual has achieved the major goals of having close relations with subordinates—he or she will seek the esteem and admiration of others. In a leadership situation where task performance results in esteem and admiration from superiors, this leader will tend to concentrate on behaving in a task-relevant manner, sometimes to the detriment of relations with immediate subordinates.

The relationship-motivated leader's counterpart has as a major goal the accomplishment of some tangible evidence of his or her worth. This person gets satisfaction from the task itself and from knowing that he or she has done well. In a leadership situation which is uncertain and anxiety-provoking, this person will, therefore, put primary emphasis on completing the task. However, when this individual has considerable control and influence and knows, therefore, the task will get done, he or she will relax and be concerned with subordinates' feelings and satisfactions. In other words, business before pleasure, but business with pleasure whenever possible.

Of course, these two thumbnail sketches are oversimplified, but they do give a picture which tells us, first, that we are dealing with different types of people and, second, that they differ in their primary and secondary goals and, consequently, in the way they behave under various conditions. Both the relationship-motivated and the task-motivated persons may be pleasant and considerate toward their members. However, the task-motivated leader will be considerate in situations in which he or she is secure, i.e., in which the individual's power and influence are high; the relationship-motivated leader will be considerate when his or her control and influence are less assured, when some uncertainty is present.

These motivational systems are measured by the Least Preferred Coworker score (LPC) which is obtained by first asking an individual to think of all people with whom he or she has ever worked, and then to describe the one person with whom this individual has been able to work least well. The description of the least preferred coworker is made in a short, bipolar, eight-point scale, from 16 to 22 item-scale of the semantic differential format. The LPC score is the sum of the item scores; e.g.:

Friendly	:_:_:_:_:_:_:_:	Unfriendly
	1 2 3 4 5 6 7 8	
Cooperative	:_:_:_:_:_:_:_:	Uncooperative
	1 2 3 4 5 6 7 8	

High-LPC persons, i.e., individuals who describe their LPC in relatively positive terms, seem primarily relationship-motivated, Low-LPC persons, those who describe their least preferred coworker in very unfavorable terms, are basically task-motivated. Therefore, as can be seen, the LPC score is not a description of leader behavior because the behavior of high- and low-LPC people changes with different situations.

Relationship-motivated people seem more open, more approachable and more like McGregor's "Theory Y" managers, while the task-motivated leaders tend to be more controlled and more controlling persons, even though they may be as likeable and pleasant as their relationship-motivated colleagues.[3]

Current evidence suggests that the LPC scores and the personality attributes they reflect are almost as stable as most other personality measures. (For example, test-retest reliabilities for military leaders have been .72 over an 8-month period[4] and .67 over a 2-year period for faculty members.[5]) Changes do occur, but in the absence of major upsets in the individual's life, they tend to be gradual and relatively small.

The Leadership Situation

The second variable, "situational favorableness,"[6] indicates the degree to which the situation gives the leader control and influence and the ability to predict the consequences of his or her behavior.[7] A situation in which the leader cannot predict the consequences of the decision tends to be stressful and anxiety arousing.

One rough but useful method for defining situational favorableness is based on three subscales. These are the degree to which (a) the leader is, or feels, accepted and supported by his or her members (leader-member relations); (b) the task is clear-cut, programmed and structured as to goals, procedures and measurable progress and success (task structure); and (c) the leader's position provides power to reward and punish and, thus, to obtain compliance from subordinates (position power).

Groups then can be categorized as being high or low on each of these three dimensions by dividing them at the median or, on the basis of normative scores, into those with good and poor leader-member relations, task structure and position power. This leads to an eight-celled classification shown on the horizontal axis of Figure I. The eight cells or "octants" are scaled from "most favorable" (octant I) to the left of the graph to "least favorable" (octant VIII) to the right. A leader obviously will have the most control and influence in groups that fall into octant I; i.e., in which this leader is accepted, has high position power and structured task. The leader will have somewhat less control

(continued, p. 354)

<u>LEADERSHIP STYLE QUESTIONNAIRE</u>

People differ in the ways they think about those with whom they work. This may be important in working with others. Please give your immediate, first reaction to the items on the following two pages.

Below are pairs of words which are opposite in meaning, such as "Very neat" and "Not neat." You are asked to describe someone with whom you have worked by placing an "X" in one of the eight spaces on the line between the two words.

Each space represents how well the adjective fits the person you are describing, as if it were written:

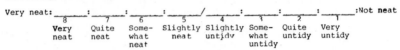

FOR EXAMPLE: If you were to describe the person with whom you are able to work least well, and you ordinarily think of him as being quite neat, you would put and "X" in the second space from the words Very Neat, like this:

Very neat: ___:__X__:___:___:__/__:___:___:___:___:Not neat

If you ordinarily think of the person with whom you can work least well as being only slightly neat, you would put your "X" as follows:

Very neat: ___:___:___:__X__/__:___:___:___:___:Not neat

If you would think of him as being very untidy, you would use the space nearest the words Not Neat.

Very neat: ___:___:___:___/__:___:___:__X__:___:Not neat

Look at the words at both ends of the line before you put in your "X". Please remember that there are no right or wrong answers. Work rapidly; your first answer is likely to be the best. Please do not omit any items, and mark each item only once.

LPC

Think of the person with whom you can work least well. He may be someone you work with now, or he may be someone you knew in the past.

He does not have to be the person you like least well, but should be the person with whom you had the most difficulty in getting a job done. Describe this person as he appears to you.

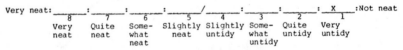

Pleasant	:__:__:__:__/__:__:__:__:	Unpleasant
	8 7 6 5 4 3 2 1	

Friendly	:__:__:__:__/__:__:__:__:	Unfriendly
	8 7 6 5 4 3 2 1	

Rejecting	:__:__:__:__/__:__:__:__:	Accepting
	1 2 3 4 5 6 7 8	

| Helpful | :__:__:__:__/__:__:__:__: | Frustrating |
| | 8 7 6 5 4 3 2 1 | |

| Unenthusiastic | :__:__:__:__/__:__:__:__: | Enthusiastic |
| | 1 2 3 4 5 6 7 8 | |

| Tense | :__:__:__:__/__:__:__:__: | Relaxed |
| | 1 2 3 4 5 6 7 8 | |

| Distant | :__:__:__:__/__:__:__:__: | Close |
| | 1 2 3 4 5 6 7 8 | |

| Cold | :__:__:__:__/__:__:__:__: | Warm |
| | 1 2 3 4 5 6 7 8 | |

| Cooperative | :__:__:__:__/__:__:__:__: | Uncooperative |
| | 8 7 6 5 4 3 2 1 | |

| Supportive | :__:__:__:__/__:__:__:__: | Hostile |
| | 8 7 6 5 4 3 2 1 | |

| Boring | :__:__:__:__/__:__:__:__: | Interesting |
| | 1 2 3 4 5 6 7 8 | |

| Quarrelsome | :__:__:__:__/__:__:__:__: | Harmonious |
| | 1 2 3 4 5 6 7 8 | |

| Self-assured | :__:__:__:__/__:__:__:__: | Hesitant |
| | 8 7 6 5 4 3 2 1 | |

| Efficient | :__:__:__:__/__:__:__:__: | Inefficient |
| | 8 7 6 5 4 3 2 1 | |

| Gloomy | :__:__:__:__/__:__:__:__: | Cheerful |
| | 1 2 3 4 5 6 7 8 | |

| Open | :__:__:__:__/__:__:__:__: | Guarded |
| | 8 7 6 5 4 3 2 1 | |

Fred E. Fiedler, *A Theory of Leadership Effectiveness* (New York: McGraw-Hill Book Company, 1967) pages 267–269.

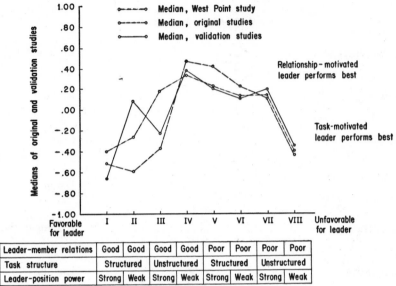

Figure I

and influence in octant II, where he or she is accepted and has a structured task, but little position power, and so on to groups in octant VIII, where control and influence will be relatively small because the leader is not accepted by his or her group, has a vague, unstructured task and little position power. Situational favorableness and LPC are, of course, neither empirically nor logically related to each other.

The Personality-Situation Interaction

The basic findings of the Contingency Model are that task-motivated leaders perform generally best in very "favorable" situations, i.e., either under conditions in which their power, control, and influence are very high (or, conversely, where uncertainty is very low) or where the situation is unfavorable, where they have low power, control, and influence. Relationship-motivated leaders tend to perform best in situations in which they have moderate power, control, and influence. The findings are summarized in Figure I. The horizontal axis indicates the eight cells of the situational favorableness dimension, with the most favorable end on the left side of the graph's axis. The vertical axis indicates the correlation coefficients between the leader's LPC score and the group's performance. A high correlation in the positive direction, indicated by a point above the midline of the graph, shows that the relationship-motivated leaders performed better than the task-motivated leaders. A negative correlation, shown by a point which falls below the midline of the graph, indicates that the task-motivated leaders performed better than relationship-motivated leaders, i.e., the higher the LPC score, the lower the group's performance.

The solid curve connects the median correlations within each of the octants obtained in the original studies (before 1963) on which the model was based. The broken line connects the median correlations obtained in various validation studies from 1964–1971.[8] As can be seen, the two curves are very similar, and the points on the curves correlate .76 (p<.01). Only in octant 2 is there a major discrepancy. However, it should be pointed out that there are very few groups in real life which have a highly structured task while the leader has low position power, e.g., in high school basketball teams and student surveying parties. Most of the validation evidence for octant 2 comes from laboratory studies in which this type of situation may be difficult to reproduce. However, the field study results for this octant are in the negative direction, just as the model predicts.

The most convincing validation evidence comes from a well-controlled experiment conducted by Chemers and Skrzypek at the U.S. Military Academy at West Point.[9] LPC scores as well as sociometric performance ratings to predict leader-member relations were obtained several weeks prior to the study, and groups then were assembled in advance, based on having the leader's LPC score and the expressed positive or negative feelings of group members about one another. The results of the Chemers and Skrzypek study are shown in the figure as a dotted line and give nearly a point-for-point replication of the original model with a correlation of .86 (p<.01). A subsequent re-analysis of the Chemers and Skrzpek data by Shiflett showed that the Contingency Model accounted for no less than 28 percent of the variance in group performance.[10] This is a very high degree of prediction, especially in a study in which variables such as the group members' intelligence, the leader's ability, the motivational factors of participants and similar effects were uncontrolled. Of course, it is inconceivable that data of this nature could be obtained by pure chance.

A different and somewhat clearer description of the Contingency Model is presented schematically in Figure II. As before, the situational favorableness dimension is indicated on the horizontal axis, extending from the most favorable situation on the left to the relatively least favorable situation on the right. However, here the vertical axis indicates the group or organizational performance; the solid line on the graph is the schematic performance curve of relationship-motivated (high-LPC) leaders, while the dashed line indicates the performance of task-motivated (low-LPC) leaders.

These curves show, first of all, that both the relationship and the task-motivated leaders perform well under some situations but not under others. Therefore, it is not accurate to speak of a "good" or a "poor" leader, rather, a leader may perform well in one type of situation but not in another. Outstanding directors of research teams do not necessarily make good production foremen or military leaders, and outstanding battle field commanders, like General Patton, do not necessarily make good chiefs of staff or good chairmen of volunteer school picnic committees.

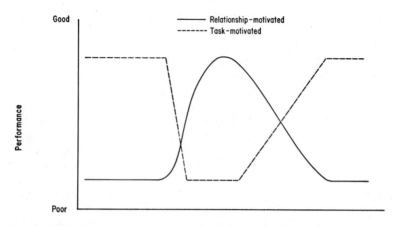

Leader-member relations	Good	Good	Good	Good	Poor	Poor	Poor	Poor
Task structure	High	High	Low	Low	High	High	Low	Low
Leader position power	Strong	Weak	Strong	Weak	Strong	Weak	Strong	Weak
	Favorable				Moderate			Unfavorable

Figure II The Performance of Relationship- and Task-motivated Leaders in Different Situational-Favorableness Conditions.

The second major implication of Figure II is that a leader's performance depends as much on the situation to which the organization assigns him (her) as on his or her own personality. Hence, organizational improvement can be achieved either by changing the leader's personality and motivational system— which is at best a very difficult and uncertain process—or by modifying the degree to which the situation provides the leader with power and influence. It should be obvious from the graph that certain leaders perform better with less rather than more power, i.e., some leaders let the power "go to their heads," they become cocky and arrogant, while others need security to function well.

EXTENSIONS OF THE CONTINGENCY MODEL

Two important tests of any theory are the degree to which it allows us to understand phenomena which do not follow common-sense expectations and, second, the extent to which it predicts non-obvious findings. In both of these respects, the Contingency Model has demonstrated its usefulness. We present here several important findings from recent studies, and then discuss some implications for management.

Effects of Experience and Training

One of the major research efforts in the area of leadership and management has been the attempt to develop training methods which will improve organizational performance. However, until now the various training programs have failed to live up to their expectations. Stogdill concluded that:

> "The research on leadership training is generally inadequate in both design and execution. It has failed to address itself to the most crucial problem of leadership—. . . [the] effects of leadership on group performance and member satisfaction." [11]

The Contingency Model would predict that training should increase the performance of some leaders and also decrease the performance of others. However, it raises the question of whether any current method of training logically can result in an across-the-board increase in organizational leadership performance. [12]

As pointed out before, a group's performance depends on the leader's personality as well as the degree to which the situation provides him or her with control, power, and influence. If the leader's power and influence are increased by experience and training, the "match" between leader personality and situational favorableness would change. However, increasing the leader's power and influence is exactly the goal of most leadership training. For example, technical training increases the leader's expert power; coaching and orthodox training programs which use the case study and lecture method are designed to increase the structure of the task by providing the leader with methods for dealing with problems which, otherwise, would require him or her to think of new solutions. Human relations training is designed to develop better relations with group members, thus enabling the leader to exert more personal influence or "referent power."

For example, let us take a newly-promoted supervisor of a production department in which he has not worked before. As he begins his new job, some of the tasks may seem unfamiliar and he will be unsure of his exact duties and responsibilities. He also may be uncertain of the power his position provides—how, for example, will the group react if he tries to dock an old, experienced worker who had come in late? Is this type of disciplinary measure acceptable to the group even though it may be allowed by the union contract? He may wonder how he should handle a problem with a fellow supervisor in the plant on whom he has to depend for parts and supplies. Should he file a formal complaint or should he talk to him personally.

After several years on the job, our supervisor will have learned the ropes; he will know how far he can go in disciplining his workers, how to troubleshoot various machines and how to deal with other managers in the organization. Thus, for the experienced supervisor the job is structured, his position power is high, and his relations with his group are probably good. In other words, his leadership situation is very favorable.

When he first started on the job, his leadership situation probably was only moderately favorable. If you will recall, relationship-motivated leaders tend to perform best in moderately favorable situations, while task-motivated leaders perform better in very favorable situations. Therefore, a relationship-motivated leader will perform well at first before gaining experience (e.g., by using the resources of group members and inviting their participation); a task-motivated leader will perform well after becoming experienced. In other words, the relationship-motivated leader actually should perform less well after gaining experience, while the task-motivated leader's performance should increase with greater experience.

A substantial number of studies now support this prediction.[13] A good example comes from a longitudinal study of infantry squad leaders who were assigned to newly organized units.[14] Their performance was evaluated by the same judges shortly after they joined their squads and, again, approximately 5 months later after their squad had passed the combat readiness test. As Figure III shows, the data are exactly as predicted by the Contingency Model. Similar results have been obtained in studies on the effects of training and experience of post office managers, managers of consumer cooperatives, police patrol supervisors, and leaders of various military units.

The effect of leadership training on performance also was demonstrated by a very ingenious experiment conducted at the University of Utah.[15] ROTC cadets and students were assembled a priori into four-man teams with high- and low-LPC leaders. One-half of the team leaders were given training in decoding cryptographic messages, i.e., they were shown how to decode simple

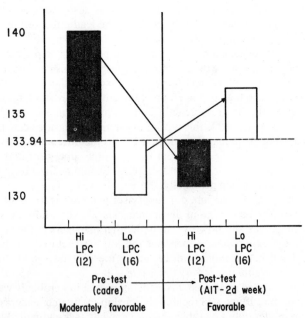

Figure III   Performance of High- and Low-LPC Leaders as a Function of Increased Experience and More Structured Task Assignment over Five Months.

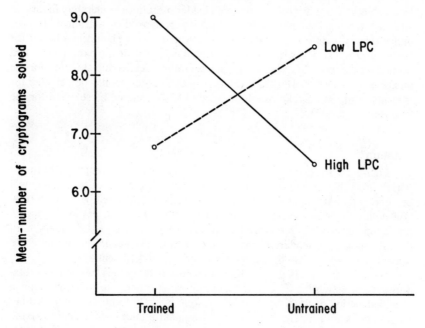

Figure IV Interaction of Training and LPC on Group Productivity.

messages easily by first counting all the letters in the message and considering the most frequent letter an "e." A three-letter word, ending with the supposed "e" is then likely to be a "the," etc. The other half of the leaders were given no training of this type. All teams operated under a fairly high degree of tension, as indicated by subsequent ratings of the group atmosphere. Because the task is by definition unstructured, the situation was moderately favorable for the trained leaders but unfavorable for the untrained leaders. Therefore, we would expect that the relationship-motivated leaders would perform better with training, while the task-motivated leaders would perform more effectively in the unfavorable situation, i.e., without the benefit of training. As can be seen in Figure IV, the findings support the predictions of the model.

FURTHER IMPLICATIONS
Selection

It seems highly likely from these and similar findings that we need to reconsider our management selection strategies. Obviously, the old adage calling for "the right man for the right job" is not as simple as it once appeared. The right person for a particular job today may be the wrong person in 6 months or in 1 or 2 years. As we have seen, the job which presents a very favorable leadership situation for the experienced leader presents a moderately favorable situation for the leader who is new and inexperienced or untrained. Hence, under these conditions a relationship-motivated leader should be chosen for the long run. The job which is moderately favorable for the experienced and trained leader is likely to represent an unfavorable leadership situation for the inexperienced leader. Hence, a task-motivated leader should be selected for the short run, and a relationship-motivated leader should be selected for the long run.

Rotation

Figure IV suggests that certain types of leaders will reach a "burn-out point" after they have stayed on the job for a given length of time. They will become bored, stable, disinterested and no longer challenged. A rational rotation policy obviously must be designed to rotate these leaders at the appropriate time to new and more challenging jobs. The other types of leaders, e.g., the task-motivated leaders represented in Figure IV, should be permitted to remain on the job so that they can become maximally efficient.

Most organizations and, in particular, the military services, have a rotation system which (at least in theory) moves all officers to new jobs after a specified period of time. Such a rigid system is likely to be dysfunctional because it does not properly allow for individual differences which determine the time required by different types of people to reach their best performance. Recent research by Bons also has shown that the behavior and performance of leaders is influenced by such other organizational changes as the transfer of a leader from one unit to a similar unit and by a reorganization which involves the reassignment of the leader's superiors.[16]

The Contingency Model clearly is a very complex formulation of the leadership problem. Whether it is more complex than is necessary, as some of its critics have claimed, or whether it is still not sufficiently complex, as others have averred, remains an open question. It is clear at this point that the theory not only predicts leadership performance in field studies and laboratory experiments, but also that it serves as a very important and fruitful source of new hypotheses in the area of leadership.

REFERENCES

1. F.E. Fiedler, "A Contingency Model of Leadership Effectiveness," in L. Berkowitz, ed., *Advances in Experimental Social Psychology* (Academic Press, 1964); Fiedler, F., *A Theory of Leadership Effectiveness* (New York: McGraw-Hill, 1967); Fiedler, F. and M.M. Chemers, *Leadership and Effective Management* (Glenview, Ill.: Scott, Foresman & Co., 1974).

2. D. Nebeker, "Situational Favorability and Environmental Uncertainty: An Integrative Study," *Administrative Science Quarterly,* Vol. 20, No. 2, June, 1975.

3. L.K. Michaelsen, "Leader Orientation, Leader Behavior, Group Effectiveness and Situational Favorability: An Empirical Extension of the Contingency Model," *Organizational Behavior and Human Performance,* 9 (1973), pp. 226–245.

4. P.M. Bons, "The Effect of Changes in Leadership Environment on the Behavior of Relationship- and Task-Motivated Leaders" (PhD. diss., University of Washington, 1974).

5. Joyce Prothero, "Personality and Situational Effects on the Job-Related Behavior of Faculty Members", (Honors thesis, University of Washington, 1974).

6. F.E. Fiedler, *Leadership Effectiveness*.

7. D. Nebeker, "Situational Favorability."

8. F.E. Fiedler, "Validation and Extension of the Contingency Model of Leadership Effectiveness: A Review of Empirical Findings," *Psychological Bulletin*, 76 (1971), pp. 128–148.

9. M.M. Chemers and G.J. Skrzypek, "Experimental Test of the Contingency Model of Leadership Effectiveness," *Journal of Personality and Social Psychology*, 24 (1972), pp. 172–177.

10. S.C. Shiflett, "The Contingency Model of Leadership Effectiveness: Some Implications of Its Statistical and Methodological Properties," *Behavioral Science*, 18 (1973), pp. 429–441.

11. R.M. Stogdill, *Handbook of Leadership: A Survey of Theory and Research* (New York: Free Press, 1974).

12. F.E. Fiedler, "The Effects of Leadership Training and Experience: A Contingency Model Interpretation," *Administrative Science Quarterly*, 17 (1972), pp. 453–470.

13. Ibid.

14. F.E. Fiedler, P.M. Bons and L.L. Hastings, "New Strategies for Leadership Utilization," in W.T. Singleton and P. Spurgeon, eds., *Measurement of Human Resources*, New York; Halsted Press, 1975, pp. 233–244.

15. M.M. Chemers et al., "Leader LPC, Training and Effectiveness: An Experimental Examination," *Journal of Personality and Social Psychology*, Vol. 31, No. 3, 1975.

16. P.M. Bons, "Changes in Leadership."

Role Making and the Assumption of Leadership

by
Bruce T. Caine*

Assuming the leadership role in a group or organization is a challenge to even the most experienced officers and executives. Never are the many variables influencing the leadership process less under the leader's control than in the early stages of his/her association with a group. The initial impressions that a leader makes on the members of the group, and that they make on the leader in return, can have long range effects on subsequent interactions. Yet (outside of the psychological laboratory) there has been limited systematic analysis of the process of assuming leadership.

Classic leadership theories, based on traits and principles, assume that possession of the former and adherence to the latter will foster acceptance of the individual as "leader" and enhance his/her effectiveness. Contemporary situational theories, in contrast, concentrate on environmental variables and social forces. Conceptually, as the situational forces vary, "required" or "appropriate" leader behavior also varies. Situational theories (i.e., Korten, 1962; Hershey and Blanchard, 1969) propose interactions between certain situational factors, leader behavior and "group" performance. More complete interactionist models, (i.e., Fiedler, 1967, 1972), combine the consideration of situational variability with the recognition of leader variability.

The problem with all of these models, is that follower variability, when

---

*Bruce T. Caine (Captain, U.S. Army) is on the faculty of the Office of Military Leadership at the United States Military Academy, West Point, New York. He received his BS from the College of William and Mary (1966), his MA in Social Psychology from the University of Florida (1975) and is a PhD candidate in Social Psychology at the University of Florida.

considered at all, is measured as a *group average* response or level of performance. In fact, implicit in most discussions of leadership in organizations is the assumption that the leader influences the group and the group as a distinct entity unto itself, responds. But such an assumption disregards both the individuality of group members and the logic that *people* behave, not groups! While people may act in concert to achieve goals that none could realize alone, their in-group behavior is still individual. Given this, the leader or manager who, following some esoteric principle of egalitarianism, believes he can and must act toward each subordinate in an identical way and that this consistent performance will somehow produce uniform reactions from each subordinate, is denying the realities of human behavior.

In a very real sense, a unique interactional relationship develops between the leader and each member of his group. This relationship derives its form and content from the individuality of the participants and from the environmental constraints within which the group operates.

Dr. George Graen and his associates at the University of Illinois have investigated these leader-follower associations and proposed the "vertical dyad approach" to the study of leadership in formal organizations. This approach, unlike most classic and contemporary theories of leadership, considers the *evolution* of the leader-follower relationship as well as the outcomes of that developmental process. It is the intent of this paper to review the vertical dyad approach and to analyze its usefulness as a tool for those aspiring to assume a leadership role in a formal organization.

THE LEADERSHIP ROLE

Most simply defined, the process of leadership centers on the effective exercise of influence. This ability to influence others is dependent on a variety of situational and personal variables. In 1950 Dexter wrote "The most important instrument with which the leader has to work is himself—his own personality and the impressions which he creates on other people" (p. 592). He further proposed that "the innovator or leader must study, to achieve maximum effectiveness, what role he ought to play and, within the limits of possibility, adapt himself to that role, realizing always that changing situations may call for a change in roles" (p. 593). One way to insure the best possible match between the demands of a social position and one's own abilities is to define the specific expectations associated with that position. To this end Goffman (1959) proposes:

> Regardless of the particular objective which the individual has in mind and of his motive for having this objective, it will be in his interest to control the conduct of the others, especially their responsive treatment of him. *This control is achieved largely by influencing the definition of the situation which the others come to formulate, and he can influence this definition by expressing himself in such a way to give them the kind of im-*

pression that will *lead them to act voluntarily* in accordance with his own plan. (p. 3–4) (Emphasis added)

The vertical dyad approach assumes that both the titular leader and his/her followers will attempt to influence the definition of the roles they play. These attempts have been labeled "role sending" and are part of an activity called "role making." Graen (1975) defines "role making" as a set of processes by which two functionally interdependent individuals work through how each will behave in certain situations and agree upon the structural characteristics of their relationship. This process occurs against the background of the society, the culture, and the formal or informal organization to which these individuals belong.

As adopted from sociology, classical role theory assumes that in the course of human interaction, certain behaviors will come to be associated with each position in a social group. These behavioral patterns or roles are traditionally seen as independent of the individual occupying the position. While generalized social role expectations do appear to exist in the normative structure of long-term groups, the vertical dyad approach assumes that each incumbent can influence the specific actions and qualities perceived by his associate as appropriate to the role each is enacting. Role making, therefore, is a significant factor in the dynamic social exchange system operating in groups. It is through this two-way negotiation process that members formulate the details of their "informal contract" or "working consensus." Among the more important agreements to be reached by the dyad in the formation of their linkage are (1) the degree of dominance each will have, (2) the level of intimacy that will exist and (3) the degree of emotionality and involvement that will be expected and tolerated.

Given the efficacy of individuation and the variety within even a small formal or informal group, vertical dyad theorists suggest that researchers and leaders abandon the search for the "group" response and concentrate on investigating the vertical dyad linkages that form *within* groups. By analyzing how and why these individual linkages form, we may be able to better answer the question: "What is the best way to assume the leadership in an organization?"

The main contribution of the vertical dyad approach to an understanding of leadership assumption is its emphasis on a consideration of human variability and the direct application of social exchange theory to the study of organizational leadership. An awareness of vertical dyad theory should help the leader design his behavior to match the initial and subsequent expectations of his subordinates and superior. As the leader becomes less concerned with presenting consistent leader behavior to all his subordinates and concentrates his/her efforts on establishing the optimum mixture of vertical dyad linkages to insure effective unit performance, the assumption of leadership becomes a more understandable process.

DIFFERENTIATION AND THE VERTICAL DYAD APPROACH

The vertical dyad linkage (VDL) concept is easily incorporated into the interactionist model of leadership in organizations (Bons, 1976). Within the formal group, the newly assigned, institutionally recognized leader establishes over time a dyadic relationship of varying design and complexity with each of his subordinates. Empirical evidence from a number of studies conducted by Graen and his co-workers indicates that managers/administrators tend to differentiate their subordinates into an in-group, an out-group and a middle group (Cashman and Graen, 1976). The key variables used to identify the members of each subgroup were (1) the degree of negotiating latitude permitted the subordinate in defining his own role, the role of the leader, and the dyad's informal contract of behavioral and relationship norms; and (2) the subsequent latitude the subordinate was given in the execution of assigned duties.

With the select sub-set of *in-group* members, the leader develops a pattern of what Graen and Cashman (1975) call "leadership linkages." These are characterized by open, two-way communication, mutual trust and respect, and the exercise of influence without resort to threat or coercion. With out-group individuals, a "supervisory linkage" is formed. This relationship is based on the formal authority of the leader and one-way downward communication. In the open exchange atmosphere of a "leadership" relationship, as compared to a supervisory one, the leader is more likely to be acceded what French and Raven (1959) refer to as "referrent power." This is seen as a direct result of the leader's concern and consideration for the in-group member coupled with the higher level of personal confidence in that member's ability and self-control. Such sensitivity will foster strong interpersonal attachments between the members of the dyad and the subordinate will come to value this relationship for its own sake rather than for some organizationally imposed sanction. Graen and Cashman (1975) found that in "leadership" or in-group dyads, subordinates and leaders reported the predominant use of expert and referrent power and only limited use of coercive power. "Supervisory" (out-group) exchanges, in contrast, are based on the terms of the formal employment contract in that they involve frequent use of coercive power and reflect more rigidly maintained status differences.

Followers in "leadership" dyads report greater satisfaction with both their work and with their superior. Leaders appear to provide members with greater opportunity for achievement and growth, more recognition, and increased responsibility, in exchange for higher quality and quantity work. In contrast, followers with whom the leader has established a "supervisory" relationship report being less satisfied with both their work and their boss. They have more job related problems and tend to base their exchange relationships with the leader on formal contractural items such as pay, security, working conditions, administrative policies and procedures. Therefore, unlike other models of leader-group interaction, Graen and Cashman propose that both democratic (leadership) and authoritarian (supervisory) behaviors may be reported to be representative of a given leader by different members of his/her task group (a

FIGURE ONE—VARIABLE VERTICAL DYAD LINKAGES WITHIN A FORMAL GROUP

phenomenon usually ignored by other researchers). Of course, the leader's mixture of task and consideration behaviors will vary depending on the type of vertical dyad linkage formed with each subordinate. As a result, while one subordinate may report his boss as being very "hard nosed" another might see him as a very pleasant person. According to VDL theory, this is not inconsistent.

Middle group subordinates can best be viewed as occupying an intermediate point with regards to role building and social exchange. These members either have "contracts" still undergoing development, or, by virtue of their individuality, prefer or merit moderation in their social interaction with the leader. It is assumed that a member joining an established group with a legitimized leader, will logically begin his "contract negotiations" from middle group status (for convenience, established middle group dyadic relationships will be called "stewardship linkages" in this paper). As shown in Figure 1, all of these relations may exist within the same unit at the same time. Accordingly, the leader must learn to recognize and deal with them to insure maximum effectiveness.

ASSUMING LEADERSHIP (BUILDING DYADIC LINKAGES)

The construction of a vertical dyad linkage begins with the first impression made by each member of the dyad. Initial observations and assessments are matched against those cultural expectations each of us has for those occupying a certain position. Physical appearance, bearing, speech patterns, symbols of status and past achievements, and other immediately identifiable pieces of information are perceived and evaluated. Thereafter, leaders and followers enter into a period of "feeling each other out." Graen calls this the "Sampling Phase" of the role-making process.

From the leader's viewpoint, his/her objective in this phase is to discover the relevant talents, abilities, interests and motivations of each primary subordinate. While some information is gained by simple observation, a more efficient method is to initiate a systematic sampling of the subordinate's responses to tasks of varying degrees of challenge and complexity. If the subordinate is successful in the given assignments, the leader will probably begin to reduce the degree of structure provided or increase the complexity of the task. If the subordinate fails to meet the leader's expectations, the leader will probably increase the task structure and degree of supervision. This successive approximation will continue until the leader finds the level of structure he and the subordinate are "comfortable with" and that is effective in producing the desired results on a given task. (Graen and Schiemann, 1976)

Concurrent with the sampling of follower responses to tasks, the leader must also investigate the degree of interpersonal consideration that the subordinate expects. Graen and Cashman (1975) call this process the "development of relationship norms." They see it as intimately related to the establishment of mutual trust and respect. In particular, tactful but candid, two-way communication of expectations and evaluations is essential to this process. Followers also test the new leader during this phase by observing generally how the leader handles assignments from above and reacts to feedback from below. The subordinate's attempts to define his/her role will require the leader to respond and these responses will also be evaluated.

The Sampling Phase provides the leader with information upon which to initiate the "Bargaining Phase" of role development. Subordinates who, on the basis of initial dyadic interactions, are perceived as trustworthy, reliable, and task competent (or in some cases simply "likable") are offered the opportunity to negotiate a leadership exchange agreement or informal contract. Operationally, these subordinates are permitted broader latitude in negotiating their contract with the leader, in defining the parameters of their role, and in sending expectations to the leader. These expectations may include the type and degree of guidance and supervision (task structure), the degree of interpersonal formality preferred (consideration), and reflect the subordinate's estimation of the leader. In offering to establish a leadership dyad, the leader is expressing his willingness to both share his/her positional resources and to protect his/her subordinate if that individual fails on a task. In exchange for this, the leader expects greater self-motivation and initiative on the part of the subordinate as well as a willingness to assume greater responsibility.

The subordinate may refuse the offer of a leadership relationship either as a result of distrust of the leader or due to a personal preference for a less demanding, more structured, and less binding relationship. Distrust might result from perceived task incompetence, abuse of positional powers and privileges, inter-personal unreliability, or immaturity on the part of the leader. A leader whose key subordinates have reached this conclusion after the sampling phase will be hard pressed to produce an effective organization. Without some referrent or expert power the leader must rely heavily on coercion to supplement legitimate power. At best this is a stressful situation for the leader and one that will become increasingly "expensive" for him/her in terms of time spent in observation, instruction, supervision and correction.

Certain subordinates will not be readily perceived by the leader as a potential in-group or out-group member. With these middle-group members, the Sampling Phase continues until each has acquired enough information to begin negotiations on an informal contact. It is not necessary for a middle group member to move to either extreme. Given their expertise or intrinsic interest in certain tasks, they may be treated as in-group members, issued mission type orders, and permitted to determine their own course of action and set their own pace. On other tasks, however, middle group members may expect the leader to exercise increased supervision.

Once the bargaining phase has produced an informal contact either by explicit or, more likely, implicit agreement, the "Commitment Phase" begins. Leaders and followers continue to interact and, based on their contract and subsequent performance, formulate behavioral and relationship norms that reflect the degree of trust, support and sensitivity that has now come to characterize their established dyaic interaction. Minor adjustment may continue to be made especially within the stewardship dyads, but commitments have been made and the relationship is no longer "new."

CAUTIONS REQUIRED WITH VERTICAL DYADS

Within the limitations imposed by the "maturity" of key subordinates and organizational policies and procedures, it would appear to be desirable for the leader to strive to establish "leadership" linkages whenever possible. However, as might be expected, there are dangers inherent in the differentiation of subordinates into an in-group, an out-group, and a middle-group if the proper criteria for these relationships is not made clear to the subordinates. There is a very real possibility of the in-group developing feelings of solidarity and cohesion to the exclusion of the remainder of the unit. Such insularity may prevent the effective coordination of efforts between peers, may cut off informal communication links, reduce overall feelings of unit cohesion, and further restrict the interpersonal relations of out-group members. In addition, competition among middle group members to achieve in-group status may become dysfunctional for the organization. This is especially likely if in-group status is not based on job performance but rather on ingratiation efforts directed at the leader. Care must be exercised to insure that differentiation is achieved to maximize the *contributions* of each member *to the group's tasks* rather than to satisfy the leader's need for self-aggrandizement.

It is particularly crucial for the leader to not "damn forever" a subordinate to out-group status. Subordinates who develop their task and/or interpersonal skills, establish their reliability and credibility, and demonstrate a willingness and capability for greater responsibility should be allowed to renegotiate his/her informal contract. The leader must remain open and perceptive to change and not allow a poor initial impression to overshadow later performance gains. Needless to say, in-group and middle-group members should also receive appropriate scrutiny.

VERTICAL DYAD LINKAGES AND THE LINKING PIN CONCEPT

Likert (1967) proposes that the unit leader serves as the Linking Pin between his/her subordinates and the next higher level in the hierarchy. This is based on the assumption that the unit leader mediates the exchange processes between his/her unit and the higher organization. Graen, et. al. (1976) contend that organizations can increase the effectiveness of junior leaders as "linking pins" by providing them greater resources (more information, more reward power and greater influence on decisions that impact on their group). With greater resources and influence, leaders should be in a better position to foster intergroup trust and cooperation while reducing pressures towards dysfunctional competition and antagonism within their unit.

Perhaps the most influencial factor in determining the eventual leadership climate that a leader will foster in his group is the dyadic relationship he establishes with his own immediate superior. One of the keys to effective leadership may well be the leader's ability to develop a leadership linkage as opposed to a supervisory relationship with his own boss. Such a leader will be more effective as a "linking pin" between his subordinates and the hierarchy as a result of his increased communication and resource agreements. Such "in-leaders" generally are able to *make things happen* outside their own group that will benefit their subordinates (Graen, Cashman, Ginsburgh, and Schiemann, 1976).

Through the mediation of individual and organizational needs, the leader/linking pin can increase the commitment of members to both their unit and the organization. There is clear evidence, both from controlled research in organizations as well as anecdotal reports, that the type of relationship a leader has with his/her boss will affect his own relationships with his subordinates. The type of dyadic relationship that is established by a new leader with his boss will influence the "quality of working life" (Graen, et. al., 1976) experienced by unit members and, over time, will affect the degree of involvement and dedication they feel to the organization.

For example, a platoon leader's relationship with his/her company commander will affect the leadership climate within which the platoon sergeant and squad leaders must operate. A platoon leader with a *leadership* dyad linkage with the company commander will get more "inside" information, can often "cut red tape," will have more influence on decisions the commander makes, and gain greater support for the decision he makes than will the lieutenant who is relegated to a *supervisory* relationship. The leadership linkage provides greater opportunity for change initiated from below to be recognized and acted upon favorably by those higher in the chain of command.

The lieutenant in a supervisory dyad with his commander, however, is not forced to establish only supervisory relationships with his/her subordinates. Through extra effort, the leader can gain essential information, increase his referent power and acknowledged expertise, contribute to the organization, and transmit to his superior the contributions and aspirations of his subordinates. If the leader's present status is the result of a "personality conflict" rather than performance deficiency, he can work to overcome these interpersonal communications difficulties, learn to operate effectively within the supervisory dyad, or seek a change of unit. Since almost every leader will himself be in each type of dyad at one time or another in his career, learning to cope with the demands and pressures unique to each is essential to long-range success. Each *can be* an effective social exchange agreement, beneficial to both the organization and the individual involved.

At this point the question may well be asked "How does a person achieve a leadership relationship with a superior?" An answer could read like a listing of leadership traits and principles, or, it might simply be better to say "that depends on the situation and the people involved." There are, however, certain cues that indicate, to the perceptive subordinate, that he/she has reached a stage of maturity in the eyes of his/her boss that merits an offer of a leadership relationship. These include: increased two-way communication, with the senior doing more of the listening; the senior's use of mission-type orders rather than explicit guidance when making assignments; an increase in the level of decision freedom permitted on what, when, and how tasks are accomplished; delegation of increasingly responsible duties by the senior; and an increase in the leader's own feeling of expert and referent power as reflected in the reactions and performance of his own subordinates.

CONCLUSION

Clearly, there are circumstances in which the leader must act in a uniform manner toward his subordinates. For the military leader probably the clearest cases are drill and ceremonies and the issuance of guidance or instruction to the group as a whole (although it must be recognized that the perception and evaluation of this singular performance will vary from member to member).

More frequently, however, leaders will interact with subordinates on an individual, face to face basis and it is during these encounters that the specific elements of their working consensus become fully operational. Even in the presence of others, subtle differences will be evident. Only by understanding that these differences do exist can the leader begin to optimize the effectiveness of each subordinate (and hence the entire unit).

Yet like most things involving humans, vertical dyad linkages are not static. When a member changes, the dyadic relationship changes. In a group, the most radical change, however, is the departure of the leader. When a leader departs, all unit-related vertical dyad linkages dissolve. Although some dyadic relationships may persist as friendships or professional associations, within the unit itself the role-making process must begin again with the arrival of the *new* leader and his/her assumption of leadership.

For the leader of a military, industrial or governmental organization, the reduction of impediments to effectiveness is of paramount importance. Tasked with the responsibility of directing the group's activities, and accountable for the group's performance on its assigned tasks, the leader must utilize every tool available to most effectively influence the behavior of others. Skillfully orchestrated role-making preceded by a systematic analysis of the situation will permit the leader to develop, to the maximum extent, leadership relationships both up and down.

REFERENCES

1. Bons, P.M. An Organizational Approach to the Study of Leadership. (See first article, this volume.)

2. Cashman, J. and Graen, G. The Nature of Leadership in the Vertical Dyad: The Team Building Process. Unpublished manuscript, University of Illinois, Champaign-Urbana, Ill., 1976.

3. Dexter, L. Some Strategic Considerations of Innovating Leadership. In A. Gouldner (Ed), *Studies in Leadership*. New York: Harper & Brothers, 1950, 592–604.

4. Fiedler, F. *A Theory of Leadership Effectiveness*. New York: McGraw-Hill, 1967.

5. Fiedler, F. Leadership experience and leadership training. Some new answers to an old problem. Seattle, Washington. University of Washington Technical Report 72-36, 1972.

6. French, J. and Raven, B. The basis of social power. In D. Cartwright (Ed.), *Studies in Social Power*. Ann Arbor, Michigan, University of Michigan, 1959.

7. Goffman, E. *The Presentation of Self in Everyday Life*. Garden City, New York: Doubleday, 1959.

8. Graen, G. and Cashman, J. A Role Making Model of Leadership in Formal Organizations: A Developmental Approach. In James G. Hunt and Lars L. Larson (Eds.) *Leadership Frontiers*. Kent, Ohio: Kent State University Press, 1975.

9. Graen, G., Cashman, J., Ginsburg, S. and Schiemann, W. Effects of Linking-pin quality upon the quality of working life of lower participants: A longitudinal investigation of the managerial understructure. Unpublished manuscript, University of Illinois, Urbana-Champaign, Illinois, 1976.

10. Graen, G. and Schiemann, W. Assessing the structure and functioning state of the leader-member exchange: A vertical dyad linkage approach, unpublished manuscript, University of Illinois, Champaign-Urbana, Illinois, 1976.

11. Hershey, P. and Blanchard, K. Changing patterns of leadership: 3-D leader effectiveness theory. *In Leadership in the Post-70's.* West Point, New York: USMA, 1969.

12. Korten, D. Situational Determinants of Leadership Structure. *The Journal of Conflict Resolution,* Vol 6, 1962, 222–235.

13. Likert, R. *The Human Organization: Its Management and Value.* New York: McGraw-Hill, 1967.

Part IV

Transactions

by
*Charles R. Scott**

All of the other parts of this book have directly or indirectly dealt with the notion of interactions, or, as this part is titled, TRANSACTIONS. Concepts such as attitude formation and change, group dynamics, social power and exchange, and leadership as an influence process are viable through the medium of some form of communication or transaction. As emphasized in the introductory article, the Model of Organizational Leadership appears to be a static model of individuals, groups and organizations surrounding the leader. The model suddenly becomes dynamic when transactions are superimposed on it between its various elements.

Part IV will now examine the area of interpersonal communications as a primary form of transaction between these elements. Organizations as an element of the model will be the focus in Part V, however, it will be necessary in this part to analyze some of the organizational constraints on the communication process.

To facilitate study, two major divisions are made in the area of transactions: the communication process and subordinate counseling by the leader. The Gibson, Ivancevich and Donnelly article, "The Communication Process," will examine communications in an organizational context. In addition to a discussion of the effects of organizational hierarchies and communication networks on the communication process, the authors present an overview of

---

*Charles R. Scott (Major, U.S. Army) is on the faculty of the Office of Military Leadership at the United States Military Academy, West Point, New York. He received his B.S. from the University of Illinois (1964) and his M.S. in Industrial Relations from Purdue University (1974).

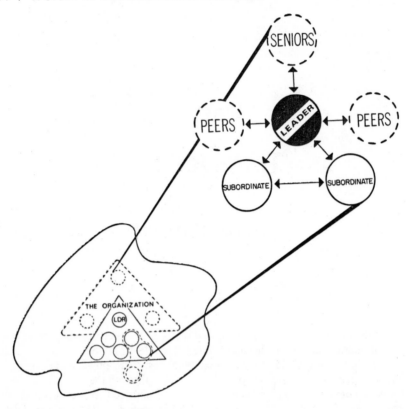

interpersonal communications, common barriers to effective interpersonal communications, and techniques for improving communications. In the second article, "Defensive Communications" by Gibb, the perception of threat, or defensiveness, is argued as a barrier to communications. Gibb discusses six pairs of behavior characteristics leading to defensive or supportive climates, and suggests that a supportive climate should be sought in order to create an atmosphere for more effective communications. Mehrabian in his article, "Communication Without Words," emphasizes the importance of nonverbal behavior in interpersonal communications. Experimentally, it has been shown that the words we use may convey only a small portion of our total message. Nonverbal behavior accounts for more than half of the total impact of our communication.

The concluding articles will examine a very specific area of transactions for the leader, that of appraisal/performance counseling and personal problem counseling. As a basic tool or function of the effective leader, counseling is defined in the Timmerman article as: "*A systematic communication process that is designed to foster meaningful choices and promote adjustment that will result in the subordinate's progressive development.*"

Reflecting back to the definition of leadership discussed in the first chapter of this text, it can be seen that much of the influence process is expressed in the counseling function. Recognized good performance tends to reinforce desired behaviors in subordinates, while criticism or indentification of poor performance hopefully will influence the subordinate to alter his behavior toward something more desirable to the leader, the organization, and himself. Maier, in his article, "The Appraisal Interview and Its Objectives," describes three specific methods of appraisal interviews for performance counseling. He labels these "Tell and Sell," "Tell and Listen," and "Problem Solving" (Self-Development), and analyzes the interviewer skill requirements, interviewee's reactions, motivational factors, and philosophy of each method. Turning more toward the area of personal problem counseling, Timmerman in his article, "The Unit Leader as a Counselor," deals with the unique aspects of the dual and frequently conflicting roles of superior and counselor that a leader faces. The author examines three approaches to counseling, directive, non-directive, and eclectic, with general guidance as to their situational applicability, and concludes with a list of DOs and DON'Ts for the leader counselor.

Attempting to perform the functions of both superior and counselor may pose some special ethical questions for the military leader. As a counselor the leader must be sincere to the degree that the counselee/subordinate recognizes and accepts this sincerity. The counselor must be able to portray a genuine desire to help the counselee. To be effective in this regard, information gained during counseling must be kept confidential by the counselor. However, in most situations, military leaders do not have the rights of privileged communication held by other counselors such as lawyers or chaplains. Thus the information gained during confidential counseling sessions may become an ethical dilemma between the use of information as a military leader with organizational loyalties and as a counselor concerned over the rights and desires of the counselee.

As an additional source of material on counseling for the military leader or potential military leader see FM 22-101 (June 1974) titled *Leadership Counseling*. Particular attention should be given to the first four parts of the manual; part one, the development of basic counseling skills; part two, reactions and pitfalls; part three, personal counseling; and part four, performance counseling.

Terms you should be able to discuss when you finish this part:

Channel	Tell and Listen
Feedback	Problem Solving (Self-Development)
Communication Barriers	Nonverbal Behavior
Grapevine	Active Listening
Defensive Climate	Reflective Summary
Supportive Climate	Directive Approach
Empathy	Non-Directive Approach
Tell and Sell	Eclectic Approach

Communications—Organizational and Interpersonal

The Communication Process*

by

*James L. Gibson, John M. Ivancevich,
and James H. Donnelly, Jr.*

INTRODUCTION

The manager in any organization must have accurate information that he communicates if the most effective decisions are to be made. The communication processes engaged in by the manager serve as the vital links between the manager, his subordinates, his peers, and the external environment. A careful analysis of these linkages points up the fact that communication involves decision-making, organizational structure, motivation, group dynamics, leadership, organizational climate, organizational development, and some other subcategories. The analysis further identifies that these behaviorally-laden categories occur only in a context of interaction between people.

In this chapter we will explore the interaction that occurs within the typical organizational setting. Specifically we will examine communication networks, the cybernetic system concept, and selected organizational factors such as division of labor and hierarchical position and how they influence communication flows. It is also our intention to discuss in some detail some of the procedures available to managers for improving communications within their organization.

The Doing Activity Of Managers

A major task of any manager is "to do" what is necessary to accomplish stated organizational goals. The manager of a unit or a department is appraised

---

*From Gibson, Ivancevich, and Donnelly, Jr., *Organizations: Structure, Processes, Behavior.* Copyright 1973 Business Publications, Inc. Reprinted by permission of Business Publications Inc., Dallas, Texas.

by superiors and if he meets various effectiveness expectations he is rewarded. A review of the tasks a manager must accomplish to be considered effective shows that he must determine a course of action. That is, the manager must decide what to do, as well as when, where, and how to do it.[1] For example, if a manager is appraised on the customer goodwill that his unit generates it would be in his best interest to keep customer complaints at a low-frequency level. If customer complaints were low the manager could be considered effective in the goodwill area of his job. In order to be effective in this aspect of his job he must carefully decide what course of action to follow.

If the manager in an organization is to be considered an effective doer he must utilize information that is made available to him from various sources—superiors, subordinates, peers, customers, and/or clients. Thus, the doing activity of managing is distinguished from the deciding activity. These two essential activities are interrelated and are certainly dependent upon the information processed within the organization. In this chapter we are primarily concerned with how the communication process allows managers to *do* their job as well as *decide* what is the best action to achieve organizational goals.

THE ORGANIZATION AS A COMMUNICATION NETWORK

Suppose that a manager is conducting a weekly meeting with five subordinates. Even a brief observation of this meeting would immediately reveal what is meant by a communication network shaping the structure of individual relationships. In a business organization that adheres to bureaucratic organizational design a number of characteristics would quickly surface from the meeting. Some of these would be:

1. The superior, or member that is highest in the managerial hierarchy, would generally initiate most of the discussion.

2. The superior would talk directly and most specifically to his immediate subordinates.

3. The subordinates, from all levels, would generally show their agreement with the superior by nodding and other gestures.

4. The flow of communications would typically be from the top down.

These characteristics are graphically summarized in Figure 1. The illustration used is that of a manufacturing operation. The dashed lines indicate that on three occasions the plant manager initiated discussions with two immediate subordinates (Divisions A and Public Relations) and one sub-subordinate (Chief of Product Design). On one occasion the Division B manager initiated communication in the upward direction.

Figure 1 clearly indicates that communication in an organizational context involves interactions between people. It also shows that the flow of communications serves as a necessary ingredient for coordination and the plant manager is in a hierarchical position to receive a great amount of information.[2] Simply stated the "boss" initiates most of the discussion and because of his authority position receives a large amount of information. This certainly is not to be taken as a statement that all or even most of the information received by an au-

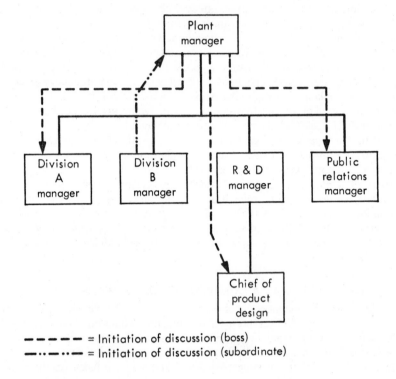

— — — — — = Initiation of discussion (boss)
— ·· — ··· — = Initiation of discussion (subordinate)

FIGURE 1
THE ORGANIZATION NETWORK (MEETING)

thority figure is accurate. In many cases the authority figure is given false or ambiguous information by those around him.

Definition Of Communication

The term *communication* implies *information* and it is difficult to distinguish between the two terms. Both terms are part of the same concept. Communication can be defined as: the use of words, letters, symbols or similar means to achieve common or shared information about an object or occurrence.[3]

Three aspects of communication are stressed in this definition. First, it emphasizes that some person is using words, letters, or symbols when interacting with others. Second, there is an objective in that achievement of common or shared information is essential. Third, communication involves two or more people.

By further dissecting the definition it becomes apparent that communication is a broad concept. Because of its broad range a number of technical terms are generally used to improve the clarity of the definition. The *semantics* of communication refers to the meaning of words and symbols. The *syntax* of communication designates the relationships that exist between the symbols used. For example, the relationships among words in a sentence is the syntax. A third aspect of communications is concerned with *pragmatics*.[4] This designates the effectiveness and efficiency of communications in achieving its objective. In a practical sense the manager is concerned with acquiring communications so that outcomes of decisions are both effective and efficient. Converting communication into action is basically the pragmatics of communication and is the core of decision-making.

CYBERNETICS

The contemporary approach to communication has been greatly influenced by the development of cybernetics. This term was coined by Wiener in 1947 to describe the study of communication and control in organizations.[5] The thrust of Wiener's theme is that man can control and modify his environment only through information, and this information is transmitted via messages. He also introduces the idea of monitoring a system via a feedback mechanism that signals deviations from the objectives of the system. Wiener believes that the flow and feedback of information has a significant effect on human behavior. For example, he contends that the permitted degree of feedback will increase with a manager's uncertainty about handling the problem. In other words the manager that is faced with a problem that is difficult and one in which he is uncertain about resolving will permit a significant amount of feedback between him and his subordinates.

A common cybernetic system is the thermostat arrangement that regulates the temperature of many homes. The furnace unit produces heat that is measured by the thermostat, which, in turn, controls the furnace. Basically the thermostat feeds back to the furnace instructions based upon the heat generated and the temperature setting. The idea of monitoring the feedback signal in terms of deviation between the actual heat and setting is the core of cybernetic theory.

The manager usually employs a system that is similar to the cybernetic thermostat arrangement. Figure 2 shows the manager transmitting criteria to subordinates, monitoring the output of subordinate actions, and making corrections; it illustrates that the feedback process is an important phase of communication and decision-making. Without adequate feedback any communicator is literally operating without knowing the effects of his actions.

A MODEL OF COMMUNICATION

The word communication is dervied from the Latin *communis,* meaning common. The sender (manager) seeks to establish a "commonness" with someone (a subordinate, a superior, a peer). He seeks to share information, an

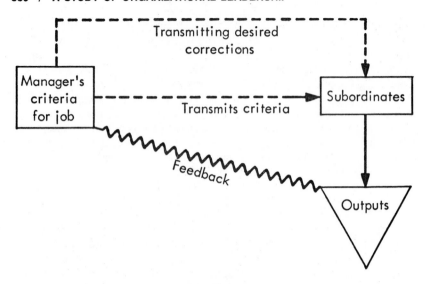

FIGURE 2
A MANAGERIAL CYBERNETIC APPROACH

attitude, or an idea. The concern with communication has produced several attempts to develop models of the process. The most widely used contemporary model has evolved mainly from the work of Shannon and Weaver, and Schramm.[6] Today the basic ingredients of the model include a source, an encoder, a message, a decoder, a receiver, feedback, and noise. There are numerous other models of the communication process which are quite similar to the one discussed here.[7] Mainly they differ in terminology, in the addition or subtraction of one or two elements, and in the point of view of the disciplines from which they emerged. However, each has contributed in some way to the basic model and to what we will consider to be "the" communications model as it is understood today. This evolved model has been diagrammed in Figure 3. Each of the elements in the process of communication will be explored in the following section.

The Elements Of Communication

Source. All communication requires at least three elements—the source, the message, and the receiver. In an organizational framework, the source is usually a member with ideas, intentions, information, and a purpose for communicating.

Encoding. As was noted previously, the source attempts to build up "commonness" with his intended receiver. Given the source, an encoding process must take place which translates the source's ideas into a systematic set of symbols—into a language expressing the source's purpose. The function

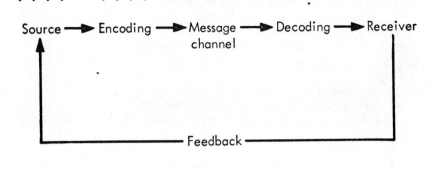

FIGURE 3
A COMMUNICATION MODEL

of encoding then is to provide a form in which ideas and purposes can be expressed as a message.

Message. The message has been defined as "the actual physical product of the source-encoder."[8] The purpose of the source is expressed in the form of the message. This is what he hopes to communicate effectively to the intended receiver and the form it takes depends to a great extent on the channel used. Decisions relating to the two are inseparable.

Channel. Channels refer to the carriers of messages from the source to the receiver. In the organizational environment this could be face to face, written, telephone, word of mouth, informal communication, group meetings, or numerous others.

Decoder-receiver. In order for the process of communication to be completed, the message must be decoded in terms of relevance to the receiver. Each receiver interprets (decodes) the message in light of his own previous experiences and frame of reference. The closer the decoded message is to the intent desired by the sender, the more effective is the communication.

Feedback. A source hopes that his message will have a high degree of "message fidelity."[9] Since message fidelity is rarely perfect, the provision for feedback in the communication process is desirable.[10] A feedback loop provides a channel for receiver response which enables the source to determine whether the message has been received and has produced the intended response.

Noise. A breakdown, interference, or distraction can occur anywhere within the communication process. Shannon and Weaver were perhaps the first to identify this concept as noise.[11] Although working for the Bell Telephone Laboratory and simply describing electronic communication, they developed a model which behavioral scientists have found useful in describing human communication. They defined noise as being those factors that distort the quality of the signal. In the behavioral science context, noise includes those factors in each of the elements of communication that can reduce message fidelity. In an organizational environment this can result from numerous factors. For example:

1. Distractions

2. Misinterpretations by receivers and/or senders.

3. Different meanings assigned to the same words by different people (semantic problems).

4. Time pressures.

5. Status difference between superiors and subordinates perceptions of organizational distance that consequently widen the communication gap between him and his superior.

6. Value judgments on the part of the receiver. This is assigning an overall worth to a message prior to receiving the entire communication. They may be based upon the receiver's evaluation of the sender, his previous experiences with him, or the messages anticipated meaning. Whatever the case, value judgments usually result in the receiver hearing only that part of the messages he wishes to hear.

The ingredients discussed in this section are essential to communication. They should not be viewed as separate things or entities or people. They are, rather, descriptive of the acts which have to be performed for communication to occur. The communication may be in terms of superior-subordinate (downward), subordinate-superior (upward), peer-peer (horizontal), or may involve one superior and a large group of subordinates, but the functions labeled as source, encoder, decoder, and receiver have to be present. Messages are always involved and, furthermore, must exist in some channel.

Some Determinants Of Effect

For the business manager, the hospital administrator, the college dean, or the governmental administrator, each of the elements in the communication process are necessary for effective communication. For example, it is easy to see that properly encoding a message is extremely important. However, according to many practitioners and theorists, the form that the communication takes should depend largely on what is known about the receiver(s). This requires the manager to figuratively place himself in the receiver's (superior, subordinate, peer) shoes for the purpose of anticipating how his messages are likely to be received. In other words, the manager should be receiver-oriented rather than source-oriented. As the source, the manager must make certain not only to speak the "same language" as the receiver but must also make certain that he does not conflict with the way the receiver sees and "catalogs" the world. Thus, it is vital that a manager understands and appreciates the process of decoding—receiving and the importance of feedback. Let us briefly examine each of these in more detail.

Decoding and receiving. Communication specialists agree that the most important factor that breaks down the "commonness" in communications between the source and the receiver is the variation that takes place in encoding and decoding. When the encoding and decoding processes are homogeneous, communication is most effective. When they become heterogeneous, communication tends to break down. Weiner refers to this problem as "entropy", or the tendency for human processes to break down rather than come together.[12] This is because, as a society advances, environments, experience, vocabulary, knowledge, interests, attitudes, values, personalities, and goals of individuals vary increasingly. This results in barriers to effective communication which reflect themselves in an inexact mesh between encoding and decoding. In an organizational environment this can be attributed to a failure of the encoder (superior) to realize that the decoder (subordinate) perceives situations differently than he does and consequently he (superior) does not attempt to learn more about the decoder. This problem has been depicted in Figure 4.[13]

The circles in the diagram represent the accumulated experiences of the two participants in the communication process. If the circles share a large area in common, communication effectiveness is facilitated. If the circles do not share any area in common—if there has been no common experience—then communication becomes impossible or at best highly distorted. Schramm makes the point that the ". . . source can encode, and the destination can decode, only in terms of the experience each has had."[14] Thus, the manager must keep in mind that his communications are decoded based on the receiver's perception of that particular message. How effectively he communicates is influenced by the receiver's perception of his message. The importance of perception as a determinant of effective communication must be noted. The manager should be aware that:

1. Information out of accord with a receiver's (e.g., superior, subordinate, peer) field of experience will be perceived less readily than that in accord with the field.

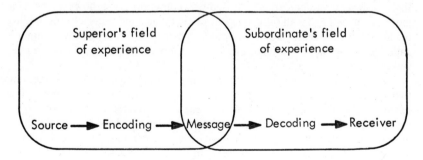

FIGURE 4
OVERLAPPING FIELDS OF EXPERIENCE

2. In a new situation, an individual will almost automatically choose a part of his own past experience that relates to the current experience and is helpful to him in forming conclusions and judgments.

3. Communications are perceived and evaluated in terms of the individual's own needs, personality, and field of experience.

4. The most objective information involves subjective perceptions.

5. Incongruencies in encoding and decoding result from the varying fields of experience and frames of reference of the source and receiver.

6. Language alone does not resolve incongruencies in encoding and decoding.

The importance of feedback. As was noted previously, provisions for feedback in the communication process are desirable. Hopefully, feedback will enable the manager to determine how "effectively" he is communicating and provide him with an opportunity to improve the "message fidelity" of future communications. The importance of feedback to the administrator is made apparent in an experiment conducted by Leavitt and Mueller.[15] In the experiment, an individual was asked to describe with words certain graphical patterns composed of connecting rectangles. From this description a group or a single listener was then required to draw a diagram of the rectangles. The description of the rectangles was given under two conditons:

1. The listener(s) could not ask any questions or see the sender. In effect this is a form of one-way communications.

2. The sender was placed in a setting where he could observe his audience and they could ask any questions. All of the communicating was done in spoken words. This is a form of two-way communications.

A number of experimentally related factors were measured:

1. The amount of time it took for the description to be made.

2. The degree of accuracy in the figures drawn by the respondents in the one-way and two-way communication groups.

3. The degree of confidence the senders and receivers had in the accuracy of the message sent and the figures drawn.

Figure 5 is an example of the patterns that were used in the experiment. The results of the experiment showed that one-way communication was faster than two-way communication. The two-way communication, however, was far more accurate in that the receivers drew rectangles more closely resembling the actual figures described by the source. The receivers in two-way communication also had more confidence in the accuracy of their figures than the one-way receivers.

This experiment points out the difficulty inherent in describing something that involves shapes and relationships that are out of the ordinary. For example, the manner in which the rectangles are related to each other (rectangle 2 touching rectangle 3) is out of the ordinary. There is a tendency in groups completing this experiment via two-way communications to develop a system to help clarify the relationships. In some instances a code is developed that aids the source and the receivers in understanding how the rectangles are touching. Through feedback, the sender is able to adjust his communication so

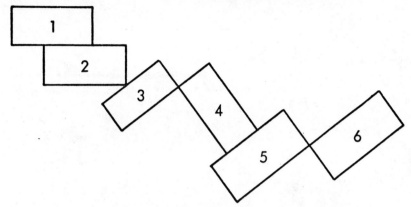

Source: Reproduced from Harold J. Leavitt, *Managerial Psychology*
(Chicago: University of Chicago Press, 1972), p. 116.

FIGURE 5
PATTERNS IN COMMUNICATION EXPERIMENT

that the descriptions of the rectangles are better understood by the receivers who must have accurate information to complete their drawing task.

In an organizational setting, feedback may come in many ways. In face-to-face communication the administrator may be able to obtain *direct* feedback through verbal exchanges with the receiver(s) or by more subtle means such as facial expression of discontent or misunderstanding. Otherwise, he will have to rely more on *indirect* means of feedback. For example, a decline in efficiency, increased absences and turnover, or poor coordination between units may indicate that communication has broken down. The effective manager attempts to keep aware of his effectiveness as a communicator and realizes the importance of communication in achieving the goals of the organization.

Communication Networks

There are many different types of communication network arrangements for sending and receiving messages. Some networks are more conducive to a particular factor such as quality or quantity of information. A series of studies by Leavitt investigated different networks and their ability to transmit information.[16]

Leavitt evaluated the effectiveness of various communication networks in one of his studies. Figure 6 illustrates four of the networks. Some visual imagination and slight alternation converts some of the networks into typical organizational arrangements. For example, the wheel resembles a typical organizational hierarchy in which four subordinates A, B, D, and E report to their superior C. The "Y" can be interpreted as two departmental managers reporting to their superiors according to their level in the organization, C, D, and then E. Similarly, the chain is representative of the chain of command.

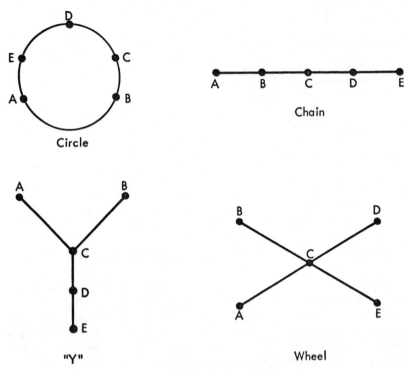

FIGURE 6
NETWORKS LEAVITT TESTED

The groups in this experiment were given a task to complete. Each group member was given a card containing five symbols: circles, stars, triangles, squares, and plus signs. Only one of the symbols was on the card of every group member. The task was to decide which was the common symbol on all five cards. The groups repeated these types of tasks 15 times with data collected on such factors as whether their decisions were correct, the attitudes of group members, and the length of time it took to reach a group decision.

The Results

Leavitt found that the time spent per trial to complete each of the 15 tasks followed a similar pattern. The mean time per trial for each of the four networks decreased with each additional trial, gradually leveling off around the 11th task. There was a much greater difference in the number of messages in the circle network and a relatively low number of messages sent in the wheel network.

The wheel had the fastest single correct trial for all repetitions in the experiment and the circle the longest. Speed is only one aspect of communicat-

TABLE 1
ACCURACY AS MEASURED BY ERRORS

Pattern	Total errors (15 trials)		Total errors last 8 trials		Final errors		Mean number of trials with at least one final error
	Mean	Range	Mean	Range	Mean	Range	
Circle	16.6	9–33	7.6	1–18	6.4	2–14	3.4
Chain	9.8	3–19	2.8	0–11	6.2	1–19	1.8
"Y"	2.6	1–18	0	0	1.6	0–5	0.8
Wheel	9.8	0–34	0.6	0–2	2.2	0–7	1.2

Source: Harold J. Leavitt, "Some Effects of Certain Communication Patterns," *Journal of Abnormal and Social Psychology*, vol. 46 (January 1951), p. 43.

ing, however, accuracy is just as important if not more so. The accuracy of the four networks is summarized in Table 1.

The experimenter did not designate a leader, but the participants were asked whether a leader emerged. The 23 participants that had formed various wheel groups agreed that the leader was the person occupying position C. The circle groups consisted of 25 people and 13 indicated that a leader existed. The choice of the leader was distributed among all the positions in the circle. The chain and the "Y" participants were not asked to identify leaders.

The satisfaction of group members was assessed by asking how they liked their job in the group in completing the 15 tasks. The circle group members reported the highest degree of satisfaction. The next most satisfied group was the chain, then the "Y", and finally the wheel.

Leavitt aptly summarizes the results in the following way:

"We may grossly characterize the kinds of differences that occur in this way: The circle, one extreme is active, leaderless, unorganized, erratic, and yet it is enjoyed by its members. The wheel, on the other extreme, is less active, has a distinct leader, is well and stably organized, is less erratic, and yet is unsatisfying to most of its members."[17]

The important points to note from this interesting experiment are the following:

1. The structure of the communication network affects accuracy of messages.

2. The structure of the communication network affects the task performance of the groups.

3. The structure of the communication network affects the satisfaction of group members.

This type of knowledge could aid the manager in developing accurate and task-oriented communication networks that influence positively the job satisfaction of employees.

Thus, the structure of the network is a potentially important component in the interaction patterns that exist within organizations. The important question is whether the structure of the network is as critical when the task becomes more complex than when identifying a common symbol.

In the more complex task experiments the group members were given five marbles and asked to find the common color. When the marbles were of varying colors and patterns the group was faced with a difficult task completion problem. In this more difficult experiment the circle network tended to show the best performance. The wheel groups had a more difficult time adapting to the more difficult situation.

Another study of groups and their structure has added further evidence to the proposition that networks have a direct influence on task performance. Guetzkow and Simon illustrated that the structure of the group was a factor in the groups ability to direct their efforts toward task completion.[18] It was found that the existence or absence of structure influenced overall performance. In this study the wheel structure was the easiest to organize for participants. After only a few trials, the organization that the wheel structure imposed on participants emerged and the group members adopted it. In the circle arrangements some groups became efficient and others did not. Those that became efficient spent considerable time deciding which form of organization was best suited for them and their task.

In these laboratory experiments the complexity of communications and how communications is influenced by organization and structure become readily apparent. The formal and informal communication networks that actually exist in real-world organizations take on many of the characteristics discovered and analyzed by Shannon, Weaver, Leavitt, Mueller, Guetzkow, and Simon.

THE REAL WORLD AND COMMUNICATIONS

It is virtually impossible, in this chapter, to identify each and every organizational factor that can positively or negatively influence communication. Only a selected few of these factors will be discussed. However, the factors chosen for discussion were selected because of their crucial importance in most organizational settings.

Hierarchical Position

The position of an individual in the formal organization is related to communications. In most organizations the major flow of communications is from the top down or from a superior to a subordinate. Davis illustrated in a study that people higher in the hierarchy tended to communicate more.[19]

Many organizations perpetuate the theme that communications in general and initiation of communication in particular is a vertical top-down activity. However, there are three dimensions of hierarchy that should be considered when discussing communications. These three dimensions are graphically

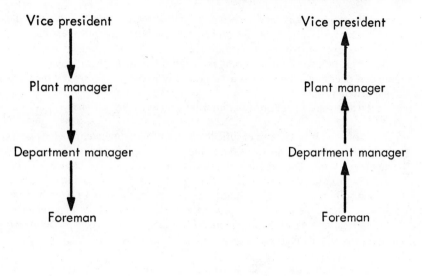

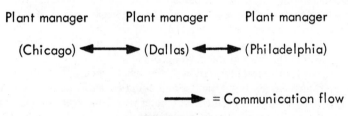

━━━▶ = Communication flow

FIGURE 7
HIERARCHICAL DIMENSIONS

presented in Figure 7. This figure shows a top-down, bottom-up, and a lateral flow. In most organizations these three flows are occurring together or at different times throughout the work day.

Two dimensions that receive relatively little managerial attention are the lateral and upward flows of communications. The easiest way to think about communication is to view orders, instructions, and policies flowing from the vice-president to the foreman and work-related information and required reports flowing from the foreman to the vice-president. This simplistic and incomplete view of communication in organizations neglects communication among peers and communication originating from subordinates.

Blau and Scott have studied communication among peers in a federal law enforcement agency and this insightful study sheds much light on lateral communication.[20] The job of the agents was to investigate business firms to determine if they were complying with federal laws. The agents had to work within operating procedures of the agency, but they had considerable decision-making discretion. In a sense the agents' performance was based upon the "results achieved" rather than the procedures used to accomplish results.

In situations where agents had difficulties they would consult peers. Officially the agents were forbidden to ask each other for advice. However, the practice of peer consultation was used primarily because it improved the decisions reached by agents.

In the analysis of peer consultation Blau and Scott argue that:

> . . . obstacles to the use of official channels of communication led agents to satisfy their needs for advice and social support by consulting one another. While the practice of turning to colleagues for advice was officially prohibited, it was tolerated, inasmuch as such operating rules were not strictly enforced. Consultation among peers appears to have had important consequences for the organization. . . Besides, the experience of being regularly asked by others for advice increased an agent's confidence in his own decision.[21]

Blau and Scott further discovered that the most technically competent agents were most often consulted. However, people tended to form dyads for peer consultation. That is, if a person frequently asks advice and the person giving the advice never consults or asks advice back the person asking for advice bestows superior status on the consultor.

In a sense the Blau and Scott study and the official restriction of lateral consultation in the law enforcement agency displays some of the obstacles for free-flowing lateral communication. Sole dependence upon superiors for information and advice is restrictive and could be avoided in most instances. Thus, it appears that it is in the best interest of managers to foster and encourage flows in all three directions—down, up and across. Any broad sweeping generalization that communication flows down, up, or across is too narrow in scope. Communication in each of these three directions is occurring simultaneously. It should also be remembered that the quantity of communications in each of these directions is a factor to consider.

Personality and Perception

The perceptions of members of an organization are determined partly by many organizational and personal factors. A change in a person's understanding may be introduced by changing the information received or by changing the person's work environment. A person's perceptions are also influenced by his previous experience and personality factors.

In an ongoing organization the orders of a top manager are basically filtered and then perceived. The filtration process is presented in Figure 8. The stimulus portion of Figure 8 can be construed as the top manager issuing an order to improve the quality of output of the reports he receives from subordinates. The person receiving this request is influenced by his perception of the nature of the information. The person may reject, alter, or embellish the information received and this is certainly a personal phenomenon.

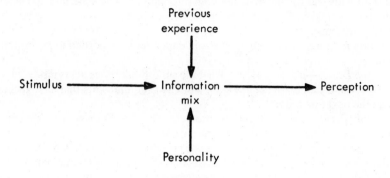

FIGURE 8
FILTRATION PROCESS

Leadership

Many people assume that superior-subordinate communication is a two-way information system that permits a free flow of information in both the downward and upward directions. This certainly is not the case when a superior is sending information relevant to task completion, about the use of new equipment, or how the new computer center can be used. The superior in a formal system or the leader in an informal setting influences directly the communication flow.

The leader or superior because of his position influences the direction and flow of information. Because of the high probability of noise distorting a message, the leader may establish rules that dictate that task-related or personal messages must flow in a particular direction and follow a specific sequence. If the group values the leader's insight and wisdom it will probably follow this leader-imposed constraint.

Some students of communication assume that democratic or permissive leadership permits a group to interact in a manner of their own choosing.[22] Research, however, discounts this assumption. It has been found that where groups are instructed to develop a solution to a problem, the successful group is the one whose democratic leader is involved in controlling communications. That is, he sees that all members participate, that no one member controls the communication for an extended time period, and that those reluctant to communicate are encouraged to enter into the flow of communications.[23] In order to exercise this degree of control the leader must be an influential individual as perceived by the group members.

The importance of understanding between superiors and subordinates cannot be underestimated. An American Management Association research project dramatically highlights communication difficulties between superiors and subordinates. Fifty-eight superior-subordinate combinations from the upper-management levels of five different companies were selected as a study group. Information concerning the understanding between the superior-subordinate dyads was obtained via in-depth interviews.[24] The superiors and subordinates were asked questions pertaining to the subordinates job concerning the following items:

Job Requirements—what skills and experience are needed to perform the job.

Job Duties—a description of what the subordinate does in his job.

Future Changes—changes in job duties or requirements that are expected over the next few years.

Job Performance Obstacles—problems that interfere with task-completion as seen by the subordinate and the superior.

A summary of the study results are presented in Table 2. A review of the table shows that 85 percent of the dyads interviewed agree on one-half or more of the subordinates' job duties. In the job performance obstacle area, however, 68.2 percent showed either no agreement or agreement on less than half of the obstacles.

The data displayed in Table 2 clearly indicate that there is a large amount of disagreement and misunderstanding among the superiors and subordinates included in this study. Whether the communication barriers arose from semantic problems, status, value judgments, or some other factor was not decided in this study. The fact of the matter, however, is that one or more communication barriers had affected the accuracy of messages and beliefs at the top levels of management in these five organizations.

Division of Labor

The division of labor on a micro or macro level facilitates communication between individuals within an organization. This facilitation is brought about because of a number of reasons such as:

1. The job is understood by the individuals and they share in this understanding thus making communication easier.

TABLE 2
AGREEMENT BETWEEN SUPERIOR—SUBORDINATE
DYADS ON SUBORDINATE'S JOB

Job factors	0 Almost no agreement	1 Agreement on less than half	2 Agreement on about half	3 Agreement on more than half	4 Agreement on all or almost all
Job duties	3.4%	11.6%	39.1%	37.8%	8.1%
Job requirements	7.0	29.3	40.9	20.5	2.3
Future changes	35.4	14.3	18.3	16.3	18.7
Job performance obstacles	38.4	29.8	23.6	6.4	1.7

Source: Norman R.F. Maier, L. Richard Hoffman, John J. Hoover, and William H. Reed, *Superior-Subordinate Communication in Management* (New York: American Management Association, 1961), AMA Research Study 52, p. 10.

2. The goals of a department or division are common and this leads to better communication.

3. The physical distance is usually shorter in a division of work layout and this encouraged communication.

Thus, common understanding of the job requirements, clear goals, and limited physical distance are associated with improved communication. These factors exist among bricklayers, mechanical engineers, academic deans, neurologists, and other specialized jobs. They are also inherently interwoven in functional arrangements in organizations such as accounting departments, production departments, colleges of education, and the billing departments of a hospital.

Dynamic Conditions

In a dynamic organizational environment we have to consider thoroughly the flow and accuracy of communication. In a stable organization in which little technological and personnel change occurs it is possible to develop a communication system that because of the routineness of message transmission and content can efficiently lead to understanding among the interacting parties. This relative ease of developing a communication network is, however, not the case in a dynamic organization.

A dynamic organization is one in which nonroutine information must be transmitted in order to obtain organizational objectives of profit, service, or conveying knowledge (the university). In a business firm a new product with unique engineering characteristics may necessitate new communication channels to develop, manufacture, and market the product. The channel may have to convey highly technical information during the development phase. Thus, the uniqueness of the product requires an alteration of the communication network that is not necessary in a stable organizational environment.

Information Exchange Within Organizations

A series of interesting studies reported by Allen analyze the process of information flow in research and development organizations.[25] He investigated the influence of the organization's formal structure and its informal structures on the network through which research and development type technical information flowed. Scientists in two laboratories were asked to:

1. Name the people within the laboratory whom they most frequently meet with on social occasions.

2. Name the people whom they consider as members of their work group.

3. Name the people whom they discuss technical matters with.

4. Name the person whom they contact to express ideas on a new research project.

Scientists in both laboratories tended to discuss technical matters with the individuals with whom they met socially. Allen further found that the formal organization influenced communication even more strongly than the informal network.

In the two laboratories it was found that status networks also influenced communication flows. The Ph.D.'s formed a cohesive group and communicated quite freely among themselves but seldom met socially or discussed technical matters with the non-Ph.D.'s. In fact the non-Ph.D's failed to even interact among themselves. The lack of information exchange can influence the quality of decisions made within the organization. Sharing knowledge and communicating is not only a problem in the research and development laboratory but also in the bank, hospital, university, and steel mill.

Grapevine

Management certainly is aware of the fact that informal communication networks exist throughout all organizations; and in many instances, the informal network is more accurate and efficient than the formal system. The *grapevine* is the major informal communication network. As such it is basically a network that serves as a bypassing mechanism. It bypasses the formal chain of command structure. It is entwined throughout the entire organization and bypasses the downward, upward, and lateral formal channels.

The grapevine has been described in the following manner:

Being flexible and personal it spreads information faster than most management communication systems operate. With the rapidity of a burning train, it filters out of the woodwork, past the manager's office, through the locker room, and along the corridors.[26]

This description points up a number of facts about the grapevine. First, it is a rapid form of communication. Second, all types of information are transmitted via the grapevine. Third, the flow of information follows no distinct pattern. Finally, the grapevine is notorious for distorting information. Since the grapevine is an informal network, there are no formal lines of responsibility or accountability. Consequently, a person in the grapevine chain can alter messages at his own discretion and this leads to a fragmentation of the facts.

The type of information that is especially attractive to grapevine users includes salary data, promotion details, personal data such as marriage gossip, and job-related factors. The point to recognize is that based on the characteristics of the grapevine vastly distorted messages can be developed.

IMPROVING COMMUNICATIONS WITHIN THE ORGANIZATION

There is no "cookbook" approach that can be applied to all organizations to bring about effective communications. The "How to do it better" book is usually platitudinous and frequently projects the impression that the answers have been found to communication problems and barriers. The theory and research cited above should indicate that these kinds of universal platitudes should be rejected. Presently, there is too little research work done on communication in everyday organizations. Thus, a number of *guidelines* to better communications will be presented.

Assessment Procedures

For the purpose of assessing communication in organizations it is best to consider the barriers that are generally associated with organizational message sending and receiving. Some of the more critical barriers are depicted in Figure 9.[27]

Understanding these distortion forces will aid all parties in the communication network. Failure to consider them mentally leads to slower, more cumbersome, and garbled, if not completely erroneous, messages. When these distortion factors are known and considered, the assessment exercise could then be concerned with the following:

Communicators. What are their positions in the hierarchy? Where are they in the status arrangements of the organization?

Channel. What form should be used? How much communication can the channel hold?

Message. How should it be coded? What type of language should be used? What is the purpose of the message?

After considering the distortion forces in general and the communicators, channel, and message specifically, different techniques can then be considered for communicating accurate messages. Some of the techniques are displayed in Figure 10.

The techniques displayed in Figure 10 indicate that communicating accurately and clearly involves much more than simply saying or writing something and then conveying it to a receiver. The manager must resort to a number of the techniques shown in Figure 10 and many others not shown, to facilitate the transmission of understanding between himself and his superiors, subordinates, and peers.

If there is a sound principle of communication that applies to most organizations it is that the manager should consider the total physical and human setting. This principle stresses the important point that many factors influence the overall impact of information, and the manager should be sensitive to these different factors. The communicator should consider each of the items discussed in this chapter such as the communication network, his hierarchical position, his receiver's personality and perceptions, the dynamic nature of the organizational environment, and the pervasiveness of the grapevine. By being constantly aware of the total setting in which he is communicating the manager can develop, alter, and implement communication systems that aid in overall decision-making.

SUMMARY

The communication process includes almost every form of human behavior found in an organizational setting. There can be no interaction among

Initiation of communication

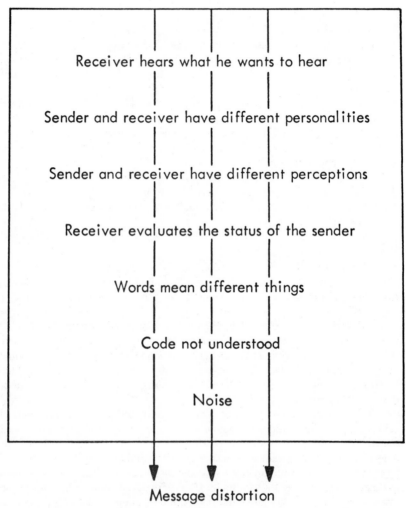

Receiver hears what he wants to hear

Sender and receiver have different personalities

Sender and receiver have different perceptions

Receiver evaluates the status of the sender

Words mean different things

Code not understood

Noise

Message distortion

FIGURE 9
SELECTED BARRIERS OF COMMUNICATION

people without communication occurring. A system for improving the understanding of the communication process was presented.

A communication model and elements of communication were discussed. The model and the elements served as a starting point for understanding real-world communication situations. The real-world discussion illustrated that

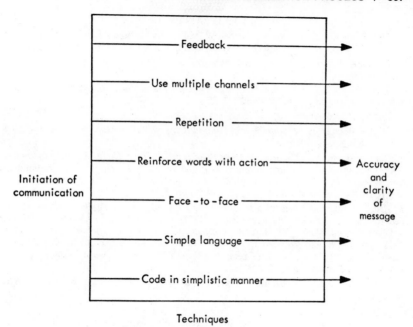

Techniques

FIGURE 10
TECHNIQUES FOR IMPROVING MESSAGE
ACCURACY AND CLARITY

nearly every aspect of superior-subordinate contact involves communication. Thus, since communicating is so prevalent in and vital to organizations a number of guidelines were developed. The recommended guidelines presented included feedback, use of multiple channels, and utilizing simple language.

DISCUSSION AND REVIEW QUESTIONS

1. Does the organizational structure or macro design affect information flow in an organization? How?

2. What type of communication skills must a decision-maker possess?

3. Is the grapevine an inevitable informal communication network? Why?

4. Why is the lateral flow of communication in an organization often distorted and limited?

5. Discuss the various behavioral factors that significantly influence communications.

6. How can excessive information hinder the perceptions of a manager?

7. Do you believe that in general organizations militate against upward communication? Why?

8. Discuss the concept of feedback and how it has influenced you in your study of organizational behavior.

END NOTES

1. This distinction is also made by David W. Miller and Martin K. Starr, *Executive Decisions and Operations Research* (Englewood Cliffs, N.J.: Prentice-Hall, 1969), p. 90.

2. Joseph A. Litterer, *The Analysis of Organizations* (New York: John Wiley & Sons, 1965), p. 256.

3. This concept is discussed in Colin Cherry, *On Human Communications* (New York: Science Editors, 1961), pp. 2–16 and 217–55.

4. Ibid., pp. 2–16.

5. Norbet Wiener, *The Human Use of Human Beings* (Garden City, N.Y.: Doubleday & Co., Anchor Books, 1954).

6. Claude Shannon and Warren Weaver, *The Mathematical Theory of Communication* (Urbana: University of Illinois Press, 1948); and Wilbur Schramm, "How Communication Works," in Wilbur Schramm (ed.), *The Process and Effects of Mass Communication* (Urbana: University of Illinois Press, 1953) pp. 3–26.

7. Bruce Westley and Malcolm MacLean, Jr., "A Conceptual Model for Communication Research," *Journalism Quarterly* (Fall 1957), pp. 31–38; Franklin Fearing, "Toward a Psychological Theory of Human Communication," *Journal of Personality* (Spring 1953), pp. 71–78; and Wendell Johnson, "The Fateful Process of Mister A Talking to Mister B," in "How Successful Executives Handle People," *Harvard Business Review*, vol. 31 (January-February 1953), p. 50.

8. David K. Berlo, *The Process of Communication* (New York: Holt, Rinehart & Winston, 1960), p. 54.

9. Ibid., p. 40.

10. The use of the term "feedback" in the social sciences has been credited to Norbert Weiner, *The Human Use of Human Beings*.

11. Shannon and Weaver, *The Mathematical Theory of Communication*, p. 5.

12. Norbet Weiner, *Cybernetics, On Control and Communication in the Animal and the Machine* (New York: John Wiley & Sons, 1948).

13. Adopted for the purpose of this text from Schramm, "How Communication Works," p. 6.

14. Ibid., p. 6

15. Harold J. Leavitt and R.A.H. Mueller, "Some Effects of Feedback on Communications," *Human Relations*, vol. 4 (1951), pp. 401–10.

16. Harold J. Leavitt, "Some Effects of Certain Communication Patterns on Group Performance," *Journal of Abnormal and Social Psychology*, vol. 46 (January 1951), pp. 38–50.

17. Leavitt, "Some Effects of Certain Communication Patterns," p. 46.

18. Harold Guetzkow and Herbert A. Simon, "The Impact of Certain Communication Nets upon Organization and Performance in Task Oriented Groups," *Management Science*, vol. 1 (1955), pp. 233–50.

19. Keith Davis, "Management Communication and the Grapevine," *Harvard Business Review*, vol. 31 (September-October 1953), pp. 43–49.

20. P. Blau and W.R. Scott, *Formal Organization* (San Francisco: Chandler Publishing Co., 1963).

21. Ibid., p. 130.

22. Litterer, *The Analysis of Organizations*, p. 279.

23. A. Paul Hare, "Small Discussions with Participating and Supervised Leadership," *Journal of Abnormal and Social Psychology*, vol. 48 (April 1953), pp. 273–75.

24. Norman R.F. Maier, L. Richard Hoffman, John J. Hoover, and William H. Reed, *Superior-Subordinate Communication in Management* (New York: American Management Association, 1961), AMA Research Study 52.

25. Thomas J. Allen, "Communications in the Research and Development Laboratory," *Technology Review*, vol. 70 (October-November 1967), pp. 31–37.

26. Keith Davis, *Human Relations in Business* (New York: McGraw-Hill Book Co., 1957), p. 244.

27. The idea for presenting Figures 9 and 10 was stimulated by Leonard R. Sayles and George Strauss, *Human Behavior in Organizations* (Englewood Cliffs, N.J.: Prentice-Hall, 1966), pp. 256–57.

ADDITIONAL REFERENCES

Allen, T.J., and Cohen, S.I. "Information Flow in Research and Development Laboratories," *Administrative Science Quarterly*, 14 (1969), 12–19.

Dewhirst, H.D. "Influence of Perceived Information-Sharing Utilization," *Academy of Management Journal*, 14 (1971), 305–15.

Ericson, R.F. "Organizational Cybernetics and Human Values," *Academy of Management Journal*, 13 (1970), 49–66.

Kahn, H., and Wiener, A.H. *The Year 2000: A Framework for Speculation on the Next Thirty-Five Years*, New York: Macmillan, 1967.

Klir, J., and Valach, M. *Cybernetic Modelling*. Princeton, N.J.: D. Van Nostrand Co., 1967.

Schmidt, W.H. *Organizational Frontiers and Human Values*. Belmont, Calif.: Wadsworth Publishing Co., 1970.

Simon, H.A. *Sciences of the Artificial*. Cambridge, Mass.: The M.I.T. Press, 1969.

Wicksburg, A.K. "Communications Networks in the Business Organization Structure," *Academy of Management Journal*, 11 (1968), 253–62.

Defensive Communication*

by
Jack R. Gibb

One way to understand communication is to view it as a people process rather than a language process. If one is to make fundamental improvement in communication, he must make changes in interpersonal relationships. One possible type of alteration—and the one with which this paper is concerned—is that of reducing the degree of defensiveness.

DEFINITION AND SIGNIFICANCE

Defensive behavior is defined as that behavior which occurs when an individual perceives threat or anticipates threat in the group. The person who behaves defensively, even though he also gives some attention to the common task, devotes an appreciable portion of his energy to defending himself. Besides talking about the topic, he thinks about how he appears to others, how he may be seen more favorably, how he may win, dominate, impress, or escape punishment, and/or how he may avoid or mitigate a perceived or an anticipated attack.

Such inner feelings and outward acts tend to create similarly defensive postures in others; and, if unchecked, the ensuing circular response becomes increasingly destructive. Defensive behavior, in short, engenders defensive listening, and this in turn produces postural, facial, and verbal cues which raise the defense level of the original communicator.

*Reprinted from the *Journal of Communication,* Sept. 1961, Vol. 2, No. 3, pp. 141–148 by permission of International Communication Association.

Defense arousal prevents the listener from concentrating upon the message. Not only do defensive communicators send off multiple value, motive, and affect cues, but also defensive recipients distort what they receive. As a person becomes more and more defensive, he becomes less and less able to perceive accurately the motives, the values, and the emotions of the sender. The writer's analyses of tape recorded discussions revealed that increases in defensive behavior were correlated positively with losses in efficiency in communication.[1] Specifically, distortions became greater when defensive states existed in the groups.

The converse, moreover, also is true. The more "supportive" or defense reductive the climate the less the receiver reads into the communication distorted loadings which arise from the projections of his own anxieties, motives, and concerns. As defenses are reduced, the receivers become better able to concentrate upon the structure, the content, and the cognitive meanings of the message.

CATEGORIES OF DEFENSIVE AND SUPPORTIVE COMMUNICATION

In working over an eight-year period with recordings of discussions occurring in varied settings, the writer developed the six pairs of defensive and supportive categories presented in Table 1. Behavior which a listener perceives as possessing any of the characteristics listed in the left-hand column arouses defensiveness, whereas that which he interprets as having any of the qualities designated as supportive reduces defensive feelings. The degree to which these reactions occur depends upon the personal level of defensiveness and upon the general climate in the group at the time.[2]

EVALUATION AND DESCRIPTION

Speech or other behavior which appears evaluative increases defensiveness. If by expression, manner of speech, tone of voice, or verbal content the sender seems to be evaluating or judging the listener, then the receiver goes on guard. Of course, other factors may inhibit the reaction. If the listener thought that the speaker regarded him as an equal and was being open and spontaneous, for example, the evaluativeness in a message would be neutralized and perhaps not even perceived. This same principle applies equally to the other five categories of potentially defense-producing climates. The six sets are interactive.

Because our attitudes toward other persons are frequently, and often necessarily, evaluative, expressions which the defensive person will regard as nonjudgmental are hard to frame. Even the simplest question usually conveys the answer that the sender wishes or implies the response that would fit into his value system. A mother, for example, immediately following an earth tremor that shook the house, sought for her small son with the question: "Bobby, where are you?" The timid and plaintive "Mommy, I didn't do it" indicated how Bobby's chronic mild defensiveness predisposed him to react with a pro-

TABLE 1

Categories of Behavior Characteristic of Supportive and
Defensive Climates in Small Groups

Defensive Climates	Supportive Climates
1. Evaluation	1. Description
2. Control	2. Problem orientation
3. Strategy	3. Spontaneity
4. Neutrality	4. Empathy
5. Superiority	5. Equality
6. Certainty	6. Provisionalism

jection of his own guilt and in the context of his chronic assumption that questions are full of accusation.

Anyone who has attempted to train professionals to use information-seeking speech with neutral affect appreciates how difficult it is to teach a person to say even the simple "who did that?" without being seen as accusing. Speech is so frequently judgmental that there is a reality base for the defensive interpretations which are so common.

When insecure, group members are particularly likely to place blame, to see others as fitting into categories of good or bad, to make moral judgments of their colleagues, and to question the value, motive, and affect loadings of the speech which they hear. Since value loadings imply a judgment of others, a belief that the standards of the speaker differ from his own causes the listener to become defensive.

Descriptive speech, in contrast to that which is evaluative, tends to arouse a minimum of uneasiness. Speech acts which the listener perceives as genuine requests for information or as material with neutral loadings is descriptive. Specifically, presentations of feelings, events, perceptions, or processes which do not ask or imply that the receiver change behavior or attitude are minimally defense producing. The difficulty in avoiding overtone is illustrated by the problems of news reporters in writing stories about unions, communists, Negroes, and religious activities without tipping off the "party" line of the newspaper. One can often tell from the opening words in a news article which side the newspaper's editorial policy favors.

CONTROL AND PROBLEM ORIENTATION

Speech which is used to control the listener evokes resistance. In most of our social intercourse someone is trying to do something to someone else—to change an attitude, to influence behavior, or to restrict the field of activity. The degree to which attempts to control produce defensiveness depends upon the openness of the effort, for a suspicion that hidden motives exist heightens resistance. For this reason attempts of nondirective therapists and progressive educators to refrain from imposing a set of values, a point of view, or a problem solution upon the receivers meet with many barriers. Since the norm is control, noncontrollers must earn the perceptions that their efforts have no hidden motives. A bombardment of persuasive "messages" in the fields of politics, education, special causes, advertising, religion, medicine, industrial relations, and guidance has bred cynical and paranoidal responses in listeners.

Implicit in all attempts to alter another person is the assumption by the change agent that the person to be altered is inadequate. That the speaker secretly views the listener as ignorant, unable to make his own decisions, uninformed, immature, unwise, or possessed of wrong or inadequate attitudes is a subconscious perception which gives the latter a valid base for defensive reactions.

Methods of control are many and varied. Legalistic insistence on detail, restrictive regulations and policies, conformity norms, and all laws are among the methods. Gestures, facial expressions, other forms of nonverbal communication, and even such simple acts as holding a door open in a particular manner are means of imposing one's will upon another and hence are potential sources of resistance.

Problem orientation, on the other hand, is the antithesis of persuasion. When the sender communicates a desire to collaborate in defining a mutual problem and in seeking its solution, he tends to create the same problem orientation in the listener; and, of greater importance, he implies that he has no predetermined solution, attitude, or method to impose. Such behavior is permissive in that it allows the receiver to set his own goals, make his own decisions, and evaluate his own progress—or to share with the sender in doing so. The exact methods of attaining permissiveness are not known, but they must involve a constellation of cues and they certainly go beyond mere verbal assurances that the communicator has no hidden desires to exercise control.

STRATEGY AND SPONTANEITY

When the sender is perceived as engaged in a stratagem involving ambiguous and multiple motivations, the receiver becomes defensive. No one wishes to be a guinea pig, a role player, or an impressed actor, and no one likes to be the victim of some hidden motivation. That which is concealed, also, may appear larger than it really is with the degree of defensiveness of the listener determining the perceived size of the suppressed element. The intense reaction of the reading audience to the material in the *Hidden Persuaders* indicates the prevalence of defensive reactions to multiple motivations behind strategy. Group members who are seen as "taking a role," as feigning emotion, as toying with their colleagues, as withholding information, or as having special sources of data are especially resented. One participant once complained that another was "using a listening technique" on him!

A large part of the adverse reaction to much of the so-called human relations training is a feeling against what are perceived as gimmicks and tricks to fool or to "involve" people, to make a person think he is making his own decision, or to make the listener feel that the sender is genuinely interested in him as a person. Particularly violent reactions occur when it appears that someone is trying to make a strategem appear spontaneous. One person has reported a boss who incurred resentment by habitually using the gimmick of "spontaneously" looking at his watch and saying, "My gosh, look at the time—I must run to an appointment." The belief was that the boss would create less irritation by honestly asking to be excused.

Similarly, the deliberate assumption of guilelessness and natural simplicity is especially resented. Monitoring the tapes of feedback and evaluation sessions in training groups indicates the surprising extent to which members perceive the strategies of their colleagues. This perceptual clarity may be quite shocking to the strategist, who usually feels that he has cleverly hidden the motivational aura around the "gimmick."

This aversion to deceit may account for one's resistance to politicians who are suspected of behind-the-scenes planning to get his vote, to psychologists whose listening apparently is motivated by more than the manifest or content-level interest in his behavior, or to the sophisticated, smooth, or clever person whose "oneupmanship" is marked with guile. In training groups the role-flexible person frequently is resented because his changes in behavior are perceived as strategic maneuvers.

In contrast, behavior which appears to be spontaneous and free of deception is defense reductive. If the communicator is seen as having a clean id, as having uncomplicated motivations, as being straightforward and honest, and as behaving spontaneously in response to the situation, he is likely to arouse minimal defense.

NEUTRALITY AND EMPATHY

When neutrality in speech appears to the listener to indicate a lack of concern for his welfare, he becomes defensive. Group members usually desire to be perceived as valued persons, as individuals of special worth, and as objects of concern and affection. The clinical, detached, person-is-an-object-of-study attitude on the part of many psychologist-trainers is resented by group members. Speech with low affect that communicates little warmth or caring is in such contrast with the affect-laden speech in social situations that it sometimes communicates rejection.

Communication that conveys empathy for the feelings and respect for the worth of the listener, however, is particularly supportive and defense reductive. Reassurance results when a message indicates that the speaker identified himself with the listener's problems, shares his feelings, and accepts his emotional reactions at face value. Abortive efforts to deny the legitimacy of the receiver's emotions by assuring the receiver that he need not feel bad, that he should not feel rejected, or that he is overly anxious, though often intended as support giving, may impress the listener as lack of acceptance. The combination of understanding and empathizing with the other person's emotions with no accompanying effort to change him apparently is supportive at a high level.

The importance of gestural behavioral cues in communicating empathy should be mentioned. Apparently spontaneous facial and bodily evidences of concern are often interpreted as especially valid evidence of deep-level acceptance.

SUPERIORITY AND EQUALITY

When a person communicates to another that he feels superior in position, power, wealth, intellectual ability, physical characteristics, or other ways, he arouses defensiveness. Here, as with the other sources of disturbance, whatever arouses feelings of inadequacy causes the listener to center upon the affect loading of the statement rather than upon the cognitive elements. The receiver then reacts by not hearing the message, by forgetting it, by competing with the sender, or by becoming jealous of him.

The person who is perceived as feeling superior communicates that he is not willing to enter into a shared problem-solving relationship, that he probably does not desire feedback, that he does not require help, and/or that he will be likely to try to reduce the power, the status, or the worth of the receiver.

Many ways exist for creating the atmosphere that the sender feels himself equal to the listener. Defenses are reduced when one perceives the sender as being willing to enter into participative planning with mutual trust and respect. Differences in talent, ability, worth, appearance, status, and power often exist, but the low defense communicator seems to attach little importance to these distinctions.

CERTAINTY AND PROVISIONALISM

The effects of dogmatism in producing defensiveness are well known. Those who seem to know the answers, to require no additional data, and to regard themselves as teachers rather than as co-workers tend to put others on guard. Moreover, in the writer's experiment, listeners often perceived manifest expressions of certainty as connoting inward feelings of inferiority. They saw the dogmatic individual as needing to be right, as wanting to win an argument rather than solve a problem, and as seeing his ideas as truths to be defended. This kind of behavior often was associated with acts which others regarded as attempts to exercise control. People who were right seemed to have low tolerance for members who were "wrong"—i.e., who did not agree with the sender.

One reduces the defensiveness of the listener when he communicates that he is willing to experiment with his own behavior, attitudes, and ideas. The person who appears to be taking provisional attitudes, to be investigating issues rather than taking sides on them, to be problem-solving rather than debating, and to be willing to experiment and explore tends to communicate that the listener may have some control over the shared quest or the investigation of the ideas. If a person is genuinely searching for information and data, he does not resent help or company along the way.

CONCLUSION

The implications of the above material for the parent, the teacher, the manager, the administrator, or the therapist are fairly obvious. Arousing defensiveness interferes with communication and thus makes it difficult—and sometimes impossible—for anyone to convey ideas clearly and to move effectively toward the solution of therapeutic, educational, or managerial problems.

END NOTES

1. J.R. Gibb, "Defense Level and Influence Potential in Small Groups," in L. Petrullo and B.M. Bass (eds.), *Leadership and Interpersonal Behavior* (New York: Holt, Rinehart and Winston, Inc., 1961), pp. 66–81.

2. J.R. Gibb, "Sociopsychological Processes of Group Instruction," In N.B. Henry (ed.), *The Dynamics of Instructional Groups* (Fifty-ninth Yearbook of the National Society for the Study of Education, Part II, 1960), pp. 115–135.

Communication Without Words*

by
Albert Mehrabian

Suppose you are sitting in my office listening to me describe some research I have done on communication. I tell you that feelings are communicated less by the words a person uses than by certain nonverbal means—that, for example, the verbal part of a spoken message has considerably less effect on whether a listener feels liked or disliked than a speaker's facial expression or tone of voice.

So far so good. But suppose I add, "In fact, we've worked out a formula that shows exactly how much each of these components contributes to the effect of the message as a whole. It goes like this: Total Impact = .07 verbal + .38 vocal + .55 facial."

What would you say to that? Perhaps you would smile good-naturedly and say, with some feeling, "Baloney!" Or perhaps you would frown and remark acidly, "Isn't science grand." My own response to the first answer would probably be to smile back: the facial part of your message, at least, was positive (55 percent of the total). The second answer might make me uncomfortable: only the verbal part was positive (seven percent).

The point here is not only that my reactions would lend credence to the formula but that most listeners would have mixed feelings about my statement. People like to see science march on, but they tend to resent its intrusion into an "art" like the communication of feelings, just as they find analytical and quantitative approaches to the study of personality cold, mechanistic and unacceptable.

The psychologist himself is sometimes plagued by the feeling that he is trying to put a rainbow into a bottle. Fascinated by a complicated and emotionally rich human situation, he begins to study it, only to find in the course of his research that he has destroyed part of the mystique that originally intrigued and involved him. But despite a certain nostalgia for earlier, more intuitive approaches, one must acknowledge that concrete experimental data have added a great deal to our understanding of how feelings are communicated. In fact, as I hope to show, analytical and intuitive findings do not so much conflict as complement each other.

It is indeed difficult to know what another person really feels. He says one thing and does another; he seems to mean something but we have an uneasy feeling it isn't true. The early psychoanalysts, facing this problem of inconsistencies and ambiguities in a person's communications, attempted to resolve it through the concepts of the conscious and the unconscious. They assumed that contradictory messages meant a conflict between superficial, deceitful, or erroneous feelings on the one hand and true attitudes and feelings on the other. Their role, then, was to help the client separate the wheat from the chaff.

The question was, how could this be done? Some analysts insisted that inferring the client's unconscious wishes was a completely intuitive process. Others thought that some nonverbal behavior, such as posture, position and movement, could be used in a more objective way to discover the client's feelings. A favorite technique of Frieda Fromm-Reichmann, for example, was to imitate a client's posture herself in order to obtain some feeling for what he was experiencing.

Thus began the gradual shift away from the idea that communication is primarily verbal, and that the verbal messages includes distortions or ambiguities due to unobservable motives that only experts can discover.

Language, though, can be used to communicate almost anything. By comparison, nonverbal behavior is very limited in range. Usually, it is used to communicate feelings, likings and preferences, and it customarily reinforces or contradicts the feelings that are communicated verbally. Less often, it adds a new dimension of sorts to a verbal message, as when a salesman describes his product to a client and simultaneously conveys, nonverbally, the impression that he likes the client.

A great many forms of nonverbal behavior can communicate feelings: touching, facial expression, tone of voice, spatial distance from the addressee, relaxation of posture, rate of speech, number of errors in speech. Some of these are generally recognized as informative. Untrained adults and children easily infer that they are liked or disliked from certain facial expressions, from whether (and how) someone touches them, and from a speaker's tone of voice. Other behavior, such as posture, has a more subtle effect. A listener may sense how someone feels about him from the way the person sits while talking to him, but he may have trouble identifying precisely what his impression comes from.

Correct intuitive judgments of the feelings or attitudes of others are especially difficult when different degrees of feeling, or contradictory kinds of feelings, are expressed simultaneously through different forms of behavior. As I have pointed out, there is a distinction between verbal and vocal information (vocal information being what is lost when speech is written down—intonation, tone, stress, length and frequency of pauses, and so on), and the two kinds of information do not always communicate the same feeling. This distinction, which has been recognized for some time, has shed new light on certain types of communication. Sarcasm, for example, can be defined as a message in which the information transmitted vocally contradicts the information transmitted verbally. Usually the verbal information is positive and the vocal is negative, as in "Isn't science grand."

Through the use of an electronic filter, it is possible to measure the degree of liking communicated vocally. What the filter does is eliminate the higher frequencies of recorded speech, so that words are unintelligible but most vocal qualities remain. (For women's speech, we eliminate frequencies higher than about 200 cycles per second; for men, frequencies over about 100 cycles per second.) When people are asked to judge the degree of liking conveyed by the filtered speech, they perform the task rather easily and with a significant amount of agreement.

This method allows us to find out, in a given message, just how inconsistent the information communicated in words and the information communicated vocally really are. We ask one group to judge the amount of liking conveyed by a transcription of what was said, the verbal part of the message. A second group judges the vocal component, and a third group judges the impact of the complete recorded message. In one study of this sort we found that, when the verbal and vocal components of a message agree (both positive or both negative), the message as a whole is judged a little more positive or a little more negative than either component by itself. But when vocal information contradicts verbal, vocal wins out. If someone calls you "honey" in a nasty tone of voice, you are likely to feel disliked; it is also possible to say "I hate you" in a way that conveys exactly the opposite feeling.

Besides the verbal and vocal characteristics of speech, there are other, more subtle, signals of meaning in a spoken message. For example, everyone makes mistakes when he talks—unnecessary repetitions, stutterings, the omission of parts of words, incomplete sentences, "ums" and "ahs." In a number of studies of speech errors, George Mahl of Yale University has found that errors become more frequent as the speaker's discomfort or anxiety increases. It might be interesting to apply this index in an attempt to detect deceit (though on some occasions it might be risky: confidence men are notoriously smooth talkers).

Timing is also highly informative. How long does a speaker allow silent periods to last, and how long does he wait before he answers his partner? How long do his utterances tend to be? How often does he interrupt his partner, or wait an inappropriately long time before speaking? Joseph Matarazzo and his colleagues at the University of Oregon have found that each of these speech habits is stable from person to person, and each tells something about the speaker's personality and about his feelings toward and status in relation to his partner.

Utterance duration, for example, is a very stable quality in a person's speech; about 30 seconds long on the average. But when someone talks to a partner whose status is higher than his own, the more the high-status person nods his head the longer the speaker's utterances become. If the high-status person changes his own customary speech pattern toward longer or shorter utterances, the lower-status person will change his own speech in the same direction. If the high-status person often interrupts the speaker, or creates long silences, the speaker is likely to become quite uncomfortable. These are things that can be observed outside the laboratory as well as under experimental conditions. If you have an employee who makes you uneasy and seems not to respect you, watch him the next time you talk to him—perhaps he is failing to follow the customary low-status pattern.

Immediacy or directness is another good source of information about feelings. We use more distant forms of communication when the act of communicating is undesirable or uncomfortable. For example, some people would rather transmit discontent with an employee's work through a third party than do it themselves, and some find it easier to communicate negative feelings in writing than by telephone or face to face.

Distance can show a negative attitude toward the message, itself, as well as toward the act of delivering it. Certain forms of speech are more distant than others, and they show fewer positive feelings for the subject referred to. A speaker might say "Those people need help," which is more distant than "These people need help," which is in turn even more distant than "These people need our help." Or he might say "Sam and I have been having dinner," which has less immediacy than "Sam and I are having dinner."

Facial expression, touching, gestures, self-manipulation (such as scratching), changes in body position, and head movements—all these express a person's positive and negative attitudes, both at the moment and in general, and many reflect status relationships as well. Movements of the limbs and head, for example, not only indicate one's attitude toward a specific set of circumstances but relate to how dominant and how anxious one generally tends to be in social situations. Gross changes in body positions, such as shifting in the chair, may show negative feelings toward the person one is talking to. They may also be cues: "It's your turn to talk," or "I'm about to get out of here, so finish what you're saying."

Posture is used to indicate both liking and status. The more a person leans toward his addressee, the more positively he feels about him. Relaxation of posture is a good indicator of both attitude and status, and one that we have been able to measure quite precisely. Three categories have been established for relaxation as indicated by muscular tension in the hands and rigidity of posture; moderate relaxation is indicated by a forward lean of about 20 degrees and a sideways lean of less than 10 degrees, a curved back, and, for women, an open arm position; and extreme relaxation is indicated by a reclining angle greater than 20 degrees and a sideways lean greater than 10 degrees.

Our findings suggest that a speaker relaxes either very little or a great deal when he dislikes the person he is talking to, and to a moderate degree when he likes his companion. It seems that extreme tension occurs with threatening addressees, and extreme relaxation with nonthreatening, disliked addressees. In particular, men tend to become tense when talking to other men whom they dislike; on the other hand, women talking to women show dislike through extreme relaxation. As for status, people relax most with a low-status addressee, second-most with a peer, and least with someone of higher status than their own. Body orientation also shows status: in both sexes, it is least direct toward women with low status and most direct toward disliked men of high status. In part, body orientation seems to be determined by whether one regards one's partner as threatening.

The more you like a person, the more time you are likely to spend looking into his eyes as you talk to him. Standing close to your partner and facing him directly (which makes eye contact easier) also indicate positive feelings. And you are likely to stand or sit closer to your peers than you do to addressees whose status is either lower or higher than yours.

What I have said so far has been based on research studies performed, for the most part, with college students from the middle and upper-middle classes. One interesting question about communication, however, concerns young children from lower socioeconomic levels. Are these children, as some have suggested, more responsive to implicit channels of communication than middle-and upper-class children are?

Morton Weiner and his colleagues at Clark University had a group of middle-and lower-class children play learning games in which the reward for learning was praise. The child's responsiveness to the verbal and vocal parts of the praise-reward was measured by how much he learned. Praise came in two forms: the objective words "right" and "correct," and the more affective or evaluative words, "good" and "fine." All four words were spoken sometimes in a positive tone of voice and sometimes neutrally.

Positive intonation proved to have a dramatic effect on the learning rate of the lower-class group. They learned much faster when the vocal part of the message was positive than when it was neutral. Positive intonation affected the middle-class group as well, but not nearly as much.

If children of lower socioeconomic groups are more responsive to facial expression, posture and touch as well as to vocal communication, that fact could have interesting applications to elementary education. For example, teachers could be explicitly trained to be aware of, and to use, the forms of praise (nonverbal or verbal) that would be likely to have the greatest effect on their particular students.

Another application of experimental data on communication is to the interpretation and treatment of schizophrenia. The literature on schizophrenia has for some time emphasized that parents of schizophrenic children give off contradictory signals simultaneously. Perhaps the parent tells the child in words that he loves him, but his posture conveys a negative attitude. According to the "double-bind" theory of schizophrenia, the child who perceives simultaneous contradictory feelings in his parent does not know how to react: should he respond to the positive part of the message, or to the negative? If he is frequently placed in this paralyzing situation, he may learn to respond with contradictory communications of his own. The boy who sends a birthday card to his mother and signs it "Napoleon" says that he likes his mother and yet denies that he is the one who likes her.

In an attempt to determine whether parents of disturbed children really do emit more inconsistent messages about their feelings than other parents do, my colleagues and I have compared what these parents communicate verbally and vocally with what they show through posture. We interviewed parents of moderately and quite severely disturbed children, in the presence of the child, about the child's problem. The interview was video-recorded without the parents' knowledge, so that we could analyze their behavior later on. Our measurements supplied both the amount of inconsistency between the parents' verbal-vocal and postural communications, and the total amount of liking that the parents communicated.

According to the double-bind theory, the parents of the more disturbed children should have behaved more inconsistently than the parents of the less disturbed children. This was not confirmed: there was no significant difference between the two groups. However, the total amount of positive feeling communicated by parents of the more disturbed children was less than that communicated by the other group.

This suggests that (1) negative communications toward disturbed children occur because the child is a problem and therefore elicits them, or (2) the negative attitude precedes the child's disturbance. It may also be that both factors operate together, in a vicious circle.

If so, one way to break the cycle is for the therapist to create situations in which the parent can have better feelings toward the child. A more positive attitude from the parent may make the child more responsive to his directives, and the spiral may begin to move up instead of down. In our own work with disturbed children, this kind of procedure has been used to good effect.

If one puts one's mind to it, one can think of a great many other applications for the findings I have described, though not all of them concern serious problems. Politicians, for example, are careful to maintain eye contact with the television camera when they speak, but they are not always careful about how they sit when they debate another candidate of, presumably, equal status.

Public relations men might find a use for some of the subtler signals of feelings. So might Don Juans. And so might ordinary people, who could try watching other people's signals and changing their own, for fun at a party or in a spirit of experimentation at home. I trust that does not strike you as a cold, manipulative suggestion, indicating dislike for the human race. I assure you that, if you had more than a transcription of words to judge from (seven percent of total message), it would not.

Counseling—Performance and Personal Problem

The Appraisal Interview and Its Objectives*

by
Norman R.F. Maier

One of the most common executive development procedures is for the supervisor to appraise an employee's performance and interview the employee in connection with the appraisal. This procedure may be set up in various ways, but it is always adapted to the line organization and requires interviews.

SOME POSSIBLE PROBLEM AREAS

The Need For Skill

Unless skillfully conducted, the interview may be an unpleasant experience for supervisor and employee, and the person interviewed may lose the motivation to improve. The skill of the interviewer is an important factor in the success of an interview because interviews are conducted by supervisors at all levels, interviewing skill is a general managerial requisite. Fortunately, an interview that is satisfactory to the interviewer is likely to satisfy the one interviewed and can be a constructive experience for both.

The Need For Accuracy

One way to increase the success of appraisal programs is to improve the accuracy of the appraisal, assuming that a person will accept criticism that is

---

*Reprinted from Norman R.F. Maier, *The Appraisal Interview: Three Basic Approaches.* La Jolla, Calif.; University Associate, 1976. Used with permission.

constructive and true. To achieve greater accuracy, committee appraisals, standardized rating procedures, and training programs for raters have been developed. These modifications make ratings more objective and less dependent on individual differences. Unfortunately, the desire to avoid unpleasantness in interviews actually introduces one of the major sources of error: the appraiser makes an evaluation generous to avoid hurt feelings and resistance in the interview. Thus, inaccuracy rather than accuracy may be encouraged by the interview, which, incidentally, is an unpleasant experience whenever a subordinate questions the appraisal. (See Chapter 12 for more complete treatment of the need for accuracy in appraisal.)

The tendency to be generous, particularly among supervisors who are human relations oriented, means that appraisals have little value for decision making for promotions and transfers. Proponents of appraisal plans regret that evaluations so painstakingly made are not more widely used by higher management, but they do not realize that value judgments made with the coming interview in mind are bound to be quite different from those made with a promotion in mind.

Method vs. Skills

If a successful interview can not be achieved by improving the evaluation and appraisal procedures, it may be that the answer lies in the *type* of interview that is conducted or in the interviewer's skills. Two skilled interviewers may practice quite *different methods*. It may be that each method has its own specific skills and it follows that more can be accomplished with whatever method is superior, even when skills are equal.

Once an interviewer differentiates between skill and method, the problem of developing skills is greatly simplified. No longer is it necessary to attempt to reconcile apparently contradictory skills, and the goals or objectives that the skills are intended to accomplish are also clarified. The problem of developing skills in any activity is simplified when the objective is made clear. For example, if the objective when driving a golf ball is direction rather than distance, the orientation of the body while swinging, rather than the force of the stroke, takes on meaning as a skill.

Conflicting Objectives

Management supervisors conduct appraisal interviews with subordinates to: (a) let them know where they stand; (b) recognize good work; (c) communicate directions for improvement; (d) develop employees on their present jobs; (e) develop and train them for higher jobs; (f) let them know how they may make progress within the company; (g) serve as a record for assessment of the department or unit as a whole, showing where each person fits into the larger picture; and (h) warn certain employees that they must improve. It is frequently supposed that several or all of these objectives may be achieved by a single interview plan, but this is not true.

The differences among these objectives are slight in some cases, but even minor differences may affect the course of the interview. For example, "letting an employee know where he stands" suggests that a rather complete report should be given, but "recognizing an employee for good work" suggests that the interview should be favorable and more selective in content.

Another factor that sometimes affects the outcome is a discrepancy between the goals of the interviewer and those of the subordinate who is being evaluated. For example, a very superior employee has many virtues and few faults. The interviewer may make a minor criticism or pass off something as "satisfactory" in light of the praise given, forgetting that the superior person may see even the "satisfactory" category as a criticism and may feel crushed by any suggestion for improvement.

A very weak subordinate may be treated rather carefully by a supervisor because the latter does not wish to hurt the employee's feelings. The supervisor may call the employee's best point "quite satisfactory" although it is about average and then spend time praising the person for trying. Such an employee may emerge from the interview greatly relieved and perhaps more secure than he is entitled to feel.

When an appraisal interview is to serve as a warning that an employee has failed to improve, it is necessary to keep a record of the interview. Borderline employees frequently say, "No one has ever told me that I was doing an unsatisfactory job." As evidence that the employee has been warned, some companies require the employee to sign the appraisal. If a signature is required, an objective inconsistent with those of most of the other appraisal interviews has been injected into the plan.

THREE METHODS WITH SPECIFIC OBJECTIVES

The three interview methods used in this book have specific and slightly different objectives. The differences are highly important to determine the skills required by an interviewer, and to a great extent the methods need different skills from the interviewer's repertoire, as a very unique interaction sequence characterizes each of the methods. This qualitative difference makes the skill requirements for each interview specific to the method. The three appraisal interview methods described and demonstrated in this book are Tell and Sell, Tell and Listen, and Problem-Solving.

THE TELL AND SELL METHOD

Objectives

The initial objective of the Tell and Sell method is to communicate the employee's evaluation as accurately as possible. The accuracy and fairness of the evaluation are assumed. The supervisor must (a) let the employee know how he is doing; (b) gain the employee's acceptance of the evaluation; and (c) have the employee agree to follow a plan for improvement. The three objectives seem, at first glance, to be consistent with each other and attainable through a single method.

If it is also assumed that a person has a desire to correct his faults, that the judgment of the superior is acceptable to the subordinate, and that the subordinate has the ability to change in the direction specified, it is reasonable to suppose that the desired objectives can be achieved. However, it is not uncommon for subordinates to think that supervisors' expectations are unreasonable and their criticisms are unjustified or to think that the methods of work suggested are inefficient. It may not be reasonable, either, to expect a person to improve just because he wishes he could. Abilities to make wise decisions, to be patient, to get along with people, to conduct conferences, and to stand up under strain may be sought, but may not be subject to voluntary control, although abilities such as getting to work on time, turning in honest expense accounts, and doing more work are usually considered to be matters of volition. However, even some of these may require more than the desire to change them, and frequently they are as much a problem of emotional adjustment as of motivation. Emotional maladjustment may require therapy, and improper attempts on the part of an employer to make improvements may aggravate rather than correct the condition.

For purposes of discussion, we will assume that extreme and difficult cases are exceptions and that the interviewer has to deal with management personnel who probably are above average in their ability to take criticism.

Skill Requirements

The skills required for success in the Tell and Sell interview are considerable. They include the ability to persuade the person to change in the prescribed manner (and this may require the development of new needs in the person), as well as an ability to make use of the kinds of incentives that motivate each particular individual. The salesperson must know a client in order to influence him, and selling an evaluation makes the same demands on a supervisor who attempts to upgrade an employee.

The method is especially difficult if the supervisor encounters resistance. Because the interviewing supervisor sees himself as doing something for the good of the employee, failure on the part of the latter to appreciate this gesture places the supervisor on the defensive, and from this point on, the situation becomes strained or deteriorates into obvious hostility. This result, of course, is not part of the interviewing plan, and yet it sometimes happens despite anything the interviewer can do.

Usually, however, the employee senses the supervisor's increased aggression before actual hostility is apparent and refrains from questioning the evaluation. The passive resistance and verbal agreement that follow are often seen by the interviewer as acceptance of the evaluation. A failure to allow the subordinate to discuss the evaluation introduces a different difficulty. When the subordinate ceases to talk, the supervisor feels more obligated to talk and, consequently, lectures or preaches. This is something the supervisor does not plan to do during the session, and yet he may find himself dominating the discussion and unable to stop.

Potential Reactions

Defensive Feelings. Whether expressed through docility or overt behavior, defensive feelings are a natural reaction to the Tell and Sell interview situation, because the supervisor is cast in the role of a judge who has the diagnosis and the remedy. However, the person who is being judged is motivated to make as good a showing as possible. The employee would like to conceal any weaknesses and, if he feels the criticism is severe or the praise faint, is inclined to protest. If the criticism appears unjust (and this is bound to happen because the judge never knows all the circumstances and provocations) defensive responses are impossible to repress.

Face Saving. Once the subordinate questions the superior's evaluation, a face-saving situation is created and, unless the interviewer is very patient or something happens to break the chain of events that naturally comes from this type of conflict, the relationship continues to deteriorate. Without unusual interviewing skill or a salvaging event, someone must lose face. Because the superior usually has some degree of power, it is the subordinate who invariably learns to give in. Actually, subordinates often can develop a degree of insensitivity and not become unduly disturbed by criticism on these occasions. The employee's viewpoint can be expressed as "everybody gets criticized during appraisal interviews, so you just take it with a grain of salt." Some interviewers attempt to comfort their subordinates by saying that they themselves are also evaluated and criticized.

Motivational Factors

Although an appraisal interview of the Tell and Sell type may be unpleasant for both parties, this does not mean that it lacks merit. It may be that correction is necessarily unpleasant. Most of us can recall ways in which we have discarded faults because of criticisms that once were painful. There is no question but that faulty behavior can be inhibited or replaced when someone points out a better way. The crucial issue is to find the most effective way or the most dependable approach. Both training and motivation are essential to any change.

When an employee lacks the ability to do a job in the way a superior desires, the problem is whether to train or transfer. If the person is worthy of being developed on the present job, then the interviewer needs to clarify the job demands so that the subordinate knows what is expected. He also must indicate where and how the subordinate can acquire the desired knowledge or skills.

Because people usually want to do a job in an effective way and behave in the proper fashion, there is motivation to adopt correct methods and habits. Even approval from the boss may be an important source of motivation.

Sometimes, however, employees have their own views about a job or are inclined to continue as they have previously because they do not wish to show a lack of ability to change. If employees have "bad habits" or are negligent in certain respects, they may resist the change because the undesirable behavior is attractive to them. Whenever one kind of behavior is more attractive to an employee than another, motivational conditions must change to produce a modification. One way to make the old behavior unattractive is to use punishment and threats of discharge. This is similar to removing an undesirable growth through surgery. The *operative* approach is unpleasant for the employee, who must either do without the desired behavior or suffer undesirable consequences.

A second method is to make another behavior attractive by rewarding it or promising a better future for the person if a given change is made. This is the *substitution* approach and it is usually more pleasant and effective than the *operative* approach, not only because the threat of punishment is unnecessary, but also because an alternative is supplied. For example, a child's emotional disturbance will be reduced if a toy that has been removed is replaced by another, and a smoker will find it somewhat easier to give up cigarettes by substituting gum. However, something pleasant (a reward) must be added to the alternative to make the choice attractive and voluntary.

Both approaches require that an external motivating factor be added to one of the alternatives; a negative incentive (punishment) must be connected with the undesirable behavior, or a positive incentive (reward) must be connected with the acceptable alternative. This form of motivation is *extrinsic*, or external to the activity itself, in contrast to *intrinsic* motivation, where the activity itself is satisfying and is chosen for its own sake, e.g., the motivation for walking to reach a restaurant is extrinsic; the motivation for walking for pleasure is intrinsic. When extrinsic motivation is used to correct behavior, the new way is not accepted for its own sake, but for the products of the activity. Undoubtedly, if an employer knows an employee's needs, he can find highly effective incentives, but such an approach can only lead to extrinsic forms of motivation.

Because of the limited motivation and the defensive attitudes that are aroused, the Tell and Sell method lacks effectiveness. A selling situation permits two possibilities: either the product is bought or it is not, although the produce may be accepted with limited enthusiasm. Frequently, the subordinate buys the evaluation, or says he does, in order to get out of the interview situation. Regardless of the degree of acceptance a subordinate has for a supervisor's judgment or plan, a selling situation permits only two possibilities: continue as before or change to the superior's plan. However, plans for improving a work situation and ways of dealing with a behavior problem can seldom be reduced to two possibilities.

When To Use Tell And Sell

Favorable Conditions. No plan can be expected to be satisfactory in all situations, and an approach that is effective in one situation may fail in another.

The Tell and Sell method has its greatest potential with young and/or new employees, who may be inexperienced and insecure and want the advice and assurance of an authority figure. The superior is likely to be respected, not only because of position, but also because knowledge and experience are so obviously greater. To a considerable degree, this same favorable condition prevails when the employee is new on an assignment; mutually recognized inexperience with a given assignment of any kind tends to assure a favorable reaction to the Tell and Sell method.

Individual differences also play a part in reactions to the Tell and Sell method. Persons who are easygoing, uncritical, and somewhat unimaginative and who accept authoritarian leadership should be most able to profit from the method.

From a company's point of view, it is an efficient method, providing it works. It takes less time to present an evaluation than to discuss one and, if the person interviewed accepts the presentation, a fairly complete evaluation can be covered in fifteen minutes. However, if the subordinate resists the appraisal, the time required may be considerable if any potential gains are to be achieved.

Unfavorable Conditions. Although the Tell and Sell method may produce positive results under favorable conditions, it also may be harmful. The method becomes undesirable if the harmful effects exceed the gains. For this reason, an interviewer must examine the possible gains in light of the price that must be paid for them.

When subordinates perceive appraisals as unfair, they may feel unappreciated and think that their interests and those of the company are no longer the same. Loyalty depends on *mutual interests* and both supervisors and the company may lose employees' loyalties in the process of conducting appraisal interviews.

If the exchange becomes personal, face-saving problems come up; these may extend beyond an interview and strain the day-to-day relationship between superior and subordinate. If each finds the relationship unpleasant and stressful, these feelings depress job satisfaction for both.

The greatest risk, particularly where appraisals include middle and top management, occurs when the subordinate accepts the judgment of the superior and tries to please him rather than give his own best thinking to the job. Every language has a word for a "yes man" and no superior wishes to develop one, yet the Tell and Sell method is bound to encourage this kind of reaction. Using the method, the superior assumes that he knows best; he is the parental figure and the dispenser of rewards and punishments. An executive who relies on Tell and Sell expects employees to want to please him, and they soon learn to know what is expected of them. Often, they compete with each other to gain favors. Although the boss may ask subordinates to make independent judgments and take the initiative, the fact that the boss appraises and recommends motivates the weaker among them to find out what the boss wants and then do it his way. Even adopting the boss's manners and dress can forestall criticism, because no executive can criticize a person for following in his footsteps. Dependent and docile behavior is likely to be developed in those with whom the method works best; individualistic and rebellious behavior may be produced in those who are least able to profit. Neither extreme is desirable.

Underlying Organizational Philosophy. Organizations vary in the extent to which they are conservative at one extreme and receptive to new methods, fads, and ideas at the other. When decisions are made from the top down, it is difficult for anything new to enter the organization, except at the top. New values can enter the organization if top personnel are recruited from outside, but this requires overcoming resistance to change down the line. Because the Tell and Sell interview is a form of downward communication that makes no provision for upward communication, the perpetuation of existing values is one of its pronounced effects. Although changes can occur effectively when initiated from the top or when approved by the proper superiors, methods for stimulating and discovering new ideas are not built into the plan. The Tell and Sell method of developing employees promotes conservatism rather than change, and insofar as conservatism has merit, the Tell and Sell method is effective in assuring it.

THE TELL AND LISTEN METHOD

Objectives

The Tell and Listen method is somewhat unnatural for an interviewer and he often views it with skepticism because he must be a bit ambiguous about authority to use it. The general idea of the Tell and Listen interview is to communicate the evaluation to the employee and then wait for a response. This means that the interviewer covers the strong and weak points of a subordinate's job performance during the first part of the interview and avoids interruption and controversy by postponing any points of disagreement for later consideration. The second part of the interview is devoted to thoroughly exploring the subordinate's feelings about the evaluation. The superior is still in the role of a judge, but he always listens to disagreement and defensive behavior without attempting to refute any statements. Actually, the interviewer encourages the employee to disagree and to express feelings, because he sees the objective as not only to communicate an appraisal, but also to allow the release of feelings aroused by the evaluation. The value of catharsis, that the verbal expression or release of frustrated feelings tends to reduce or remove them, is assumed.

Skill Requirements

Accepting Defensive Reactions. Initially, reactions to the Tell and Listen method are similar to those for the Tell and Sell method because both begin with the presentation of the evaluation. However, they differ radically in the way disagreement and resistance are handled. Instead of dominating the discussion to clarify his views, the interviewer encourages the subordinate to disagree with the evaluation, and to relate his own feelings. Thus, the interviewer is a nondirective counselor (Rogers, 1942) during the second part of the interview.

The skills of the Tell and Listen approach are (a) *active listening*—to refrain from talking, and to accept and try to understand the employee's attitudes and feelings; (b) effective *use of pauses*—to wait patiently and avoid embarrassment, knowing that a pause will cause the other person to talk; (c) *reflection of feelings*—to respond to feelings to show understanding; and (d) *summarizing of feelings*—to indicate progress, to show understanding, and to point up aspects of the problem, as well as to wrap up the interview. None of these skills requires that the interviewer either agree or disagree with what is said. Rather, he strives to communicate that he understands the subordinate's position; he entertains the possibility that the evaluation may be unjust and even incorrect; and he reveals that he wants the employee to take from the appraisal only ideas that may be helpful.

Potential Reactions

Face Saving Reduced. Because it is assumed at the outset that there are two sides to the appraisal, face-saving issues are not aggravated and the superior is not caught in a situation where he feels the need to defend his evaluation. He does not expect the subordinate to agree and is not disappointed when the employee resists. The unpleasant aspects of the appraisal interview are reduced when the superior has a method for dealing with defensive responses and when he is in a better position to understand and respect feelings. For this reason, the manager who is able to practice the Tell and Listen method is less inclined to avoid appraisal interviews than is the Tell and Sell interviewer, who may be overanxious and overprepared to fend off signs of resistance.

Motivational Factors

The motivational factors in the Tell and Listen interview are complex. Fears of reprisal and of displeasing the superior are reduced, so most motivational factors associated with fear of displeasing the superior are weakened, if not lost. Unadaptive defensive behavior fanned in part by these same fears is also reduced. Thus, *resistance to change* is overcome or reduced by the counseling process, and the desire to change to avoid displeasing the boss is sacrificed. Which of these two opposed motivations is of greater value undoubtedly varies from one individual to another.

The positive motivation that is created by having a pleasant experience with the boss is undoubtedly greater for the Tell and Listen type of interview than for the Tell and Sell type, because the former reduces any hostility that may have been engendered. In addition, it makes the subordinate feel accepted and even important. This is conducive to the formation of a constructive attitude—so essential to growth. A subordinate is more likely to want to please a supervisor he likes than one he fears. When fear is the dominant motive, a person, at best, shies away from the wrongdoing but does not extend himself to perform beyond the call of duty.

Up to this point, the motivational factors discussed have been *extrinsic*—that is, the incentives lie outside the job activity but the task or work itself has not been made more interesting, although some increase in job satisfaction may come about. Interest in a job depends on the work itself and on the social climate in which it is performed. An employee who likes the boss will find the job more satisfying than an employee who fears or dislikes the boss. Other employees also influence job interest, and a supervisor who respects and knows how to deal with feelings is able to reduce strains in interpersonal relationships and create a relaxed and friendly social climate. Any change in job interest represents a form of *intrinsic motivation*.

A more important intrinsic motivation is present if the interview results in (a) solving some job problems; (b) clarifying certain misunderstandings between supervisor and subordinate; or (c) solving a personal problem. The motivational possibilities vary from individual to individual and are greater when an employee's performance shows deficiencies that can be corrected.

If the superior listens and learns from the interview, additional intrinsic motivational gains are possible. The superior can modify job assignments and expectations; alter his evaluation; perceive the subordinate's job differently; and discover his own negligence in training and assisting. These gains tend to depend upon an exceptional interviewer, however, because the appraisal has been made prior to the interview and a previous commitment reduces the interviewer's ability to see inaccuracies or injustices in the appraisal (Maier, 1973a).

When To Use Tell And Listen

Favorable and Unfavorable Results. The result that the Tell and Listen interview is most likely to produce is a good relationship between superior and subordinate during the interview. The employee is likely to leave with a positive feeling and with a favorable attitude toward the supervisor. He is likely to regard the interview as worthwhile and feel important to the company as an individual. The superior can profit from what he learns about the employee's needs and aspirations and should not be misled by a defensive attitude or feelings expressed emotionally.

There is a risk, however, that the interview may not achieve its first objective, letting the employee know where he stands. Although the employee may change, depending on new insights, he is not likely to discover ways to improve the job. An employee may leave the interview with satisfaction, but not necessarily with a program for developing on the job.

Underlying Organizational Philosophy. The values promoted by the Tell and Listen interview are tolerance and respect for the dignity of the individual. Any supervisor who tries to understand a subordinate's viewpoint experiences an increased respect for the employee, so the method tends to make management personnel employee minded rather than production minded. Because supervisors who are employee centered tend, in general, to stimulate higher moral than others (Katz, Maccoby, & Morse, 1950) this influence may be a constructive one. However, simply because high morale and higher productivity frequently are related, it does not mean that there may not be variations in productivity among groups that have equally high morale.

The fact that the interviewer may profit from the appraisal interview is one of the greatest potential values of the Tell and Listen method. Change initiated from below can occur because a subordinate is able to influence a superior's views on how the job may be improved by changes in (a) supervision; (b) work methods; (c) job assignments; and (d) job expectations. Very often the people who supervise the work of others once performed the jobs of those they now supervise. This causes them to expect the job to be performed much as they themselves did it (Read, 1962). Because individuals differ, and times as well as jobs change, this expectation may be unreasonable, impractical, or biased—yet it is most understandable. The expectations of a superior, under the best circumstances, tend to restrict freedom, stifle initiative, and inhibit improvements that have their origin with subordinates. Although some of the loss in new ideas from below may be recaptured by suggestion boxes, it is important not to stifle new ideas through an appraisal program that was designed to develop employees. A supervisor who listens and learns may encourage upward communication in deed as well as in word; the belief that constructive forces for change can come from below may be an important part of organizational philosophy.

THE PROBLEM-SOLVING METHOD

Objectives

The Problem-Solving approach to an appraisal interview is a product of the author's research on problem solving and his studies of executive development. Of the three methods presented in this book, it deviates the most from commonly held management views. It is the only method that takes the interviewer out of the role of a judge and makes him a helper. Although the interviewer may always wish to be a helper to a subordinate, he can not escape retaining the role of a judge in the other two types of interview because the process of appraising is inconsistent with helping. Because an appraisal, by its nature, is an evaluation or judgment, it may appear that the purpose of the interview has been lost if the evaluation is not directly communicated to the subordinate. However, the development of the employee's performance often is the primary reason for conducting an appraisal interview and this objective may be lost in the process of communicating the evaluation directly.

Although the two methods discussed in the preceding sections communicate the appraisal to the subordinate, they do not assume his understanding and acceptance. The Problem-Solving approach, in contrast, has no provision for communicating the appraisal, and indeed it may not be essential to do so. If the appraisal is required for other purposes, it may be desirable to delay making it until after the interview.

The soundness of having the development of the employee's performance serve as the objective of the interview is apparent; this establishes a *mutual interest* between the interviewer and his subordinate. Both would like the employee to improve on the job and both would agree that the boss could assist in this improvement. When the subordinate accepts the supervisor as a helper, he is more willing to describe the nature of his difficulties. When the boss passes judgment on job performance, however, the interests conflict. The employee wants to impress his boss favorably and is motivated to cover up any weaknesses. The interviewer, on the other hand, would like to avoid being deceived and is inclined to discuss weaknesses that have come to his attention. The mutual interest factor in the traditional appraisal interview, therefore, is present only as long as the employee's merits are extolled and ends when the interviewer indicates that he is not satisfied.

Because job performance can also be improved by changes in the job itself, problem solving places attention on the situation, not on the individual. Subordinates are not on the defensive when discussing how their jobs can be made more satisfying and efficient. "Changing the job" explores an entirely different dimension of job performance and avoids the implication that individuals must change, which invariably leads to defensiveness.

Another way to improve job performance is to change the nature of the supervision. Superiors have great influence on the productivity of their subordinates, but subordinates are reluctant to be critical of their superior's style of supervision. Discussion of job-related factors can reveal problems in this area.

The Problem-Solving approach may show four ways in which the performance of subordinates can improve: (1) changing the subordinate's behavior; (2) changing the job duties or the job procedure; (3) changing jobs; and (4) changing the pattern of supervision. The Tell and Sell and the Tell and Listen approaches tend to limit improvement to the first of these four changes and this change is often the least acceptable to the subordinate.

Essential Attitudes

Although the objective of the Problem-Solving approach is improved job performance, the interviewer can not specify the area in which this development should take place because this constitutes diagnosis and judgment. The interviewer must limit his influence to stimulating thinking, rather than supplying remedies or solutions. He must be willing to accept for consideration all ideas on job improvement that the employee brings up. It is his function to discover the subordinate's interests so that he can respond to them and cause the employee to examine himself and his job duties. To accomplish these things, the interviewer must forget his own viewpoint and try to see the job as the employee sees it. If the employee's ideas seem impractical, the interviewer should explore the views expressed more thoroughly, using questions to learn more specifically what the employee has in mind. Often the ideas that are difficult to accept are ones that are misunderstood or viewed with a different mental set. Each person speaks from his own frame of reference, but each listener has a different frame of reference. Communication is faulty until the backgrounds, attitudes, and experiences of each are mutually understood.

When the interviewer finds that a subordinate's thinking is naïve and in need of upgrading, he must be willing to assume that a problem-solving discussion is the best way to stimulate growth and sophistication. If an employee can grow in this way, it is never necessary that he know he has had weaknesses and faults. The process may be analogous to the training of children; to learn to be graceful and skilled, they never need to know that they once were gawky and uncoordinated. As a matter of fact, they might improve more if left to themselves and not exposed to too much faultfinding. These assumptions are not easily converted to practice, largely because discriminating adults are so concerned with the faults they observe that it is difficult for them to suppress comments and advice. Wisdom and experience can be a handicap to an individual who directs the work of others, unless he knows how to share them in an acceptable manner.

Problem-solving behavior is characterized by the exploration and evaluation of a variety of solutions. It is inhibited whenever one person feels threatened by an evaluation, because this directs attention to the person rather than the situation. When people are placed in the spotlight, they are motivated to hide defects and alerted to protect themselves. Defensive behaviors are attempts to justify old behaviors, and as long as people defend their past actions they are not searching for new or better ways to perform. If an evaluation is very threatening it may induce frustration, which not only arouses hostile and childish behavior, but also promotes stubbornness. These behavior characteristics also delay problem solving because they are in direct opposition to rational thinking.

Skill Requirements

The skills associated with the Problem-Solving approach are consistent with the nondirective procedures discussed in connection with the Tell and Listen method: listening, accepting, and responding to feelings. The interviewer needs to be especially alert and notice any expression of concern during the introductory period. A remark such as, "Well, this is the day we get overhauled, I suppose," should be answered with a statement such as, "You consider these interviews somewhat rough on people in some ways, I suppose."

However, the objective of the Problem-Solving interview is to go beyond an interest in the subordinate's feelings. As soon as he is ready to discuss the job situation (and this may be at the very outset if the employee is not anxious about the interview), the interviewer can ask questions about the job. Such questions are directive in order to channel the subject of conversation, but nondirective about feelings that an employee can express.

In some situations, the employee's job description should be explored and its importance discussed. The interviewer may find differences in perceptions of what the job is that may account for some of the unfavorable points in the evaluation. For example, the interviewer may be surprised to learn that the subordinate sees the job as "getting an assignment finished on time, regardless of the feelings of others" and that he has this mistaken emphasis because of a previous reprimand. These differences should be passed over and should serve to enlighten the interviewer about misunderstandings and the need for better job descriptions, training, or communication.

In the typical appraisal interview with an employee of long standing, the job analysis may be omitted because it can be assumed that this understanding has been accomplished with previous interviews. The employee can be asked to review the year's progress and discuss the problems, needs, innovations, satisfactions, and dissatisfactions he has encountered. The idea is to make this interview the employee's opportunity to get the boss's ear.

To help a subordinate talk freely, it is desirable for the superior to consider all problems the employee wishes to raise. Restating ideas in somewhat different words is an effective way for the interviewer to test his understanding, and it demonstrates that the superior is interested in considering changes that are important to the subordinate. An interviewer need not agree or disagree with ideas to accept them. Understanding or accepting ideas is an important neutral position between agreeing and disagreeing.

When the employee's ideas are numerous, it may be wise for a supervisor to jot them down so they can be referred to later. Making a record of ideas is an act of accepting and considering without taking a stand for or against. Later, these same ideas can be evaluated to pick out the best ones.

Skillful questioning is an effective way for an interviewer to stimulate a subordinate to evaluate his own ideas. Questions should not be used to put an employee on the spot or indicate the weakness of a plan, but should indicate that the listener wants to hear the complete story. The following examples illustrate stimulating exploratory questions:

Can this plan of yours deal with an emergency situation, in case one arose?

Would you have other people at your level participate in the plan?

Could your own employees be induced to go along with the change?

What kinds of problems do you anticipate with a changing market?

Have you examined the plan from the point of view of quality control?

Nonthreatening exploratory questions are effective for drawing an employee out and making him think more clearly; in addition, they may serve to direct attention to areas that have been overlooked. The last two questions above are examples of broad questions, and the first three stimulate more detailed examination of a delineated area.

Skillful summarizing serves a variety of purposes, and opportunities for useful summaries usually occur several times during an appraisal interview. Effective summaries may be used to accomplish the following:

1. To restate the points already covered in a broader sense;

2. To demonstrate that the interviewer understands the ideas expressed up to the point at which the summary occurs;

3. To facilitate communication by creating opportunities to check and refine ideas; and

4. To separate what has been covered from the problems that remain unexplored.

The effective *use of pauses* is one of the most subtle skills and is useful in connection with the Problem-Solving method, as well as the Tell and Listen method. Ideas require thought, and if the interviewer interrupts the employee he disturbs a train of thought. By waiting patiently he gives the subordinate time to explore and evaluate. This is in contrast to the cross-examination some interviewers practice.

Motivational Factors

Problems offer opportunities to explore the unknown, and their solutions lead to new experiences. The statement of a problem can cause a group to engage in a lively problem-solving discussion. Curiosity is a strong drive and, as long as fear is not aroused, it leads to exploratory behavior. Children, for example, have a strong motivation to explore their surroundings when they are in a free and secure environment, but the exploration ceases when danger or threats of punishment are introduced. If a subordinate is free to analyze the job and expects to have an influence on any improvements that are made, he is immediately motivated to think constructively, rather than defensively. Some *extrinsic* motivational factors, such as gaining approval or avoiding failure, may be present, but essentially the problem-solving activity itself has interest value and is a form of *intrinsic* motivation. Intrinsic motivation is present in many of the things we like to do and is an important aspect of play. If intrinsic motivation could be made a larger part of the job, then work would become more like play and the problem of gaining acceptance of any changes would be nonexistent because employees would be carrying out their own solutions.

Sources of Job Satisfaction. An examination and a re-evaluation of the job description are bound to suggest some changes, because there always are aspects of the job that give more satisfaction (or less dissatisfaction) than others. Usually, how to maximize the best features and how to minimize the poorer ones are topics of mutual interest for the interviewer and the subordinate.

When the job itself is a topic for consideration, it is apparent that there are four distinctly different ways in which job satisfaction may be improved. These are (a) the job itself may be reorganized, enlarged, subdivided, or rescheduled; (b) the subordinate's perception of the job and the meanings of its various aspects may be changed; (c) the superior's understanding of the job problems may be increased so that he will relate differently to his subordinates, supply assistance in the form that is needed, or improve communications; and (d) the opportunity may be created for solving problems that are of a group nature, involving all of the subordinates who report to the interviewer.

When To Use Problem Solving

Favorable and Unfavorable Results. Since problem solving can lead to so many different approaches to job satisfaction, improvement seems possible for every employee. If no acceptable solutions come under discussion, the interviewer can ask questions to explore various possibilities and a selection can be made in terms of practicality and interest. If the goal of the interview is to experiment and to improve the job situation in line with the employee's wishes, then problem solving gives good assurance that a change in the desired direction will occur.

If the subordinate recommends changes that conflict with the goals of the company or the superior, the superior may respond by asking how the change can take place without being unfair to other employees or without violating company objectives. Invariably, such questions lead to further clarification. Superiors often turn down suggestions prematurely because they see obstacles in the path of the change, but if an obstacle is discussed, ways to avoid it may be discovered or the subordinate may realize that he has overlooked certain consequences of a new plan. Ideas that seem impractical can be tabled for future consideration and the exploration can be directed to other topics. An interview can give considerable satisfaction, even if only one of many new ideas can be implemented.

If a subordinate has no ideas and fails to respond to the Problem-Solving approach, it may be assumed that this method has failed, but this does not preclude use of one of the other two methods.

Underlying Organizational Philosophy. One of the unique advantages of the Problem-Solving approach is that it affords both participants a highly favorable opportunity to learn and communicate. Usually, training and developing others is a one-way process: the superior gives knowledge and know-how, and the subordinate receives them. The Problem-Solving approach, like the Tell and Listen method, offers the interviewer an opportunity to learn because it stimulates upward communication. Unlike Tell and Listen, Problem-Solving also creates a climate for high-quality decisions and changes because it pools the thinking of those most likely to have supplementary experiences. The Problem-Solving approach allows an interviewer not only to remove sources of frustration through *listening* skills, but to activate or stimulate change through discussion of a problem.

The interviewer is most likely to have the proper attitude for effective problem solving if he understands that effective plans, decisions, and ideas must be not only factually sound, but also acceptable to the persons who must implement them. This attitude encourages an interviewer to respect the problem-solving ability of each subordinate and to place mutual interests above personal interests. A favorable opportunity to explore a problem with an experienced and understanding superior can stimulate a subordinate's thinking and lead to increased job interest, as well as to a better utilization of a subordinate's talents.

The Problem-Solving method cuts across barriers created by rank and places the attention on mutual interests, rather than on prerogatives, status, and personality clashes. To use the method an interviewer assumes that change is an essential part of an organization and that participation in change is essential to healthy growth.

Figure 1 outlines the three types of appraisal interviews described on previous pages and compares them on ten different variables. Because the psychological assumptions vary considerably from one method to another, quite different outcomes may result from their use, as discussed previously.

REFERENCES

1. C.R. Rogers, *Counseling and Psychotherapy*. Boston: Houghton Mifflin, 1942.
2. D. Katz, N. Maccoby, and N.C. Morse, *Productivity, Supervision and Morale in an Office Situation*. Ann Arbor, University of Michigan: Institute for Social Research, 1950.

Method	Tell and Sell	Tell and Listen	Problem Solving (Self-Development)
Role of Interviewer	Judge	Judge	Helper
Objective	To communicate evaluation. To persuade Interviewee to improve	To communicate evaluation. To release defensive feelings	To stimulate growth and development in Interviewee
Assumptions	Interviewee desires to correct weaknesses if he knows them. Any person can improve if he so chooses. A superior is qualified to evaluate a subordinate	People will change if defensive feelings are removed	Growth can occur without correcting faults. Discussing job problems leads to improved performance
Reactions	Defensive behavior suppressed. Attempts to cover hostility	Defensive behavior expressed. Person feels accepted	Problem-solving behavior
Skills	Salesmanship. Patience	Listening and reflecting feelings. Summarizing	Listening and reflecting feelings. Using exploratory questions. Summarizing
Attitude	People profit from criticism and appreciate help	One can respect the feelings of others if one understands them	Discussion develops new ideas and mutual interests
Motivation	Use of positive or negative incentives or both (Extrinsic in that motivation is added to the job itself)	Resistance to change reduced. Positive incentives (Extrinsic and some intrinsic motivation)	Increased freedom. Increased responsibility (Intrinsic motivation in that interest is inherent in task)
Gains	Success most probably when Interviewee respects Interviewer	Develops favorable attitude toward superior which increases probability of success	Almost assured improvement in some respect
Risks	Loss of loyalty. Inhibition of independent judgement. Face-saving problems created	Need for change may not be developed	Interviewee may lack ideas. Change may be other than what superior had in mind
Values	Perpetuates existing practices and values	Interviewer can change his views based on Interviewee's responses. Some upward communication	Both learn since experience and views are pooled. Change is facilitated

FIGURE 1

CAUSE AND EFFECT RELATIONS IN THREE TYPES OF APPRAISAL INTERVIEWS

The Unit Leader as a Counselor

by
Frederick W. Timmerman Jr.*

Perhaps, the most difficult yet important task that faces any unit leader is the responsibility to counsel his men and assist them with their adjustment difficulties. It is a difficult task because effective counseling involves effective communication. Moreover, counseling is important because, through the process, the subordinate will become aware of whether or not the leader is really concerned about the subordinate as a person. Meaningful counseling by a leader can do much to engender a sense of loyalty, responsiveness, security, and adjustment in subordinates. In contrast, an indifferent or closed attitude toward subordinate problems may exacerbate small problems to the point that they endanger unit efficiency.

Does this mean that the unit leader is expected to be a professionally trained, competent psychotherapist? Certainly not, but he must be able to give assistance to his men even if it involves nothing more than referring them to an appropriate professional agency and then insuring that they receive prompt assistance. The Army, although it is seen as a structured organization, is still composed of people, and people have problems.

Problems themselves may range from such concerns as dissatisfaction with one's job to emotional, family, or financial difficulties. Further, many times problems will arise from the very structure of the Army itself. As an or-

* Frederick W. Timmerman, Jr. (Major, US Army), a former member of the Office of Military Leadership at the United States Military Academy, West Point, NewYork, he received his Bachelor of Science from the United States Military Academy (1965), his MED in Counseling and Guidance from Duke University (1972) and PhD in Counseling Psychology from Duke University (1974).

431

ganization, the Army can foster impressions of impersonality in relations between seniors and subordinates as well as feelings in the subordinate that he is powerless to deal effectively with the organization. As a consequence, the subordinate might: (1) see himself as operating in a somewhat stressful environment; (2) magnify personal problems unreasonably; (3) feel he cannot communicate, making him especially vulnerable to anxiety producing situations; or (4) close himself to formal communications.

Since the leader is primarily an agent of the organization, one might be inclined to conclude that there is a great potential for role conflict when he acts as a counselor. This certainly can be the case if the leader approaches the matter of counseling from the common perception that it involves simply personal advice giving and does not imply a systematic process. Fortunately, effective counseling does not connote this type of interpersonal exchange. *For the effective leader, counseling can be defined as: A systematic communication process that is designed to foster meaningful choices and promote adjustment that will result in the subordinate's progressive development.*[1]

As a systematic process, counseling has certain characteristics which act to insure that potential role conflicts will be minimized and the process will be effective. *First,* the process of counseling is only undertaken with a specific objective in mind. The counselee has a concern and the leader-counselor works with him to provide a framework for the solution of the problem. Here, it is important for the leader to remember throughout the counseling process that the counselee must maintain responsibility for his own actions if the process is to be a success. *Second,* the leader-counselor must demonstrate a genuine, sincere interest in the counselee as he appears at the moment of counseling. The power of counseling lies in interpersonal relationships that are open, sincere, and dependable but are not close in the ordinary sense of the word (Tyler, 1969, p. 15). *Third,* the counselee is usually in a distressed state whereas the leader-counselor is not. Therefore, the leader can act as a stabilizing influence. *Fourth,* the counseling environment is limited to promote development. All counseling sessions are structured to promote counselee movement toward the solution of personal difficulties. Time limits for interaction between counselor and counselee are set—usually fifty minutes or less. Moreover, discussion during the session is specifically limited to the problem being discussed and is not allowed to digress to topics that are not related to difficulties being experienced or to subjects that do not promote counselee adjustment. *Fifth,* insofar as the situation will allow, all matters discussed are treated in a confidential, non-evaluative fashion by the counselor. If the counselee is going to be open with the leader-counselor he must be able to trust him. If information discussed in the counseling session is transmitted to other members of the unit or used against the counselee, the leader's effectiveness as a counselor may end. *Finally,* and most importantly, the leader-counselor employs a specific counseling approach. Since counseling in the Army is not limited to the office environment, but may take place almost anywhere, it is important that a leader-counselor adopt a counseling approach that is consistent with his leadership style. Failure to do this will raise the possibility that the leader might be seen as being inconsistent by his subordinates.

While there are many specific counseling methods based on different theoretical schools of thought, all can be generally classified as adhering to one of three approaches to counseling—*directive* (counselor centered), *non-directive* (client centered), or *eclectic*. The major differences between these approaches lie in techniques and philosophies about people rather than overall counseling objectives, which are very similar. As a leader-counselor, it is most important that one begin with an approach that is most comfortable for him. As one gains experience in counseling he will find that he tends to use the techniques of a variety of approaches and that theoretical differences will become blurred.

The directive approach to counseling is a rational approach in which the leader-counselor acts as a teacher and problems are solved in a "one-to-one" teaching environment. The term "directive" could be misunderstood, for the counselor does not direct a solution, assume an authoritarian, judgmental attitude, nor does he dictate actions which will lead to solutions. Rather, this approach presupposes considerable skill on the part of the counselor acquired through education and experience. This, in turn, allows the counselor to assume the role of a specialist equipped with the skills to separate the relevant from the irrelevant and to offer courses of action leading to problem solutions. The counselor will leave the decisions to the subordinate being counseled, but he will be direct in his guidance, making it a short-cut or economical approach to problem-solving.

Directive counseling is normally the approach that is used in industry and public schools. It is accomplished by interested dedicated individuals, but also by individuals who, in many cases, lack the professional training or qualifications to carry out directive counseling as it is conceived by the true professionals in the field. Nevertheless, the directive approach to counseling still retains much of its effectiveness as an approach even though it most often:

1. is concerned more with immediate rather than long range problems;
2. does very little to attempt any major personality reorganization, but is concerned more with the immediate adjustment to frustrating situations;
3. is considered more problem-centered than being concerned with the totality of the person;
4. concerns itself with changing specific aspects of a person's behavior such as social behavior, attitudes, and task behavior patterns.

In contrast to the directive approach to counseling, the *nondirective* or *client-centered approach* implies that the leader-counselor adopts the frame of reference of the subordinate. This approach to counseling appears to have a surface simplicity about it. However, unlike the directive approach to counseling, the client-centered approach sees the counselee as the important agent in the change process. The basic counseling objective is change or growth in the counselee. The counselor is a vital instrument in the process of change, not as an intellectual resource, but as a human being who can fully be the kind of person he really is and can accept the counselee for what he is. This approach assumes that only the counselee can really deal with his problem and any change must come from within himself, not from any kind of direction or guidance from an external source. The basic hypothesis of the non-directive approach is, therefore, that every individual has the capacity to understand himself, determine the source of his problem, and reorganize himself in a direction that will be ultimately adjustive. Using this approach, the counselor's task is to:

1. establish an atmosphere and a relationship with the counselee so that the counselee can start to understand and reorganize himself;
2. totally accept the counselee, his behavior, and his values;
3. refrain from guiding, directing, or advising the counselee;
4. act to clarify the counselee's feelings, empathize with the counselee, and establish a relationship of acceptance and confidence.

The task of the non-directive counselor is not an easy one. There is the danger that the beginning leader-counselor will interpret the client centered approach as meaning that he must establish a friendship relation with the counselee, thereby creating role conflict and defeating the purpose of counseling. Further, it is a time-consuming operation. The counselor must not only be able to see the world through the eyes of the counselee, but must be able to accept his feelings and behaviors without value judgment. The non-directive counselor certainly does not deny that he will have an influence on the counselee, but the counselor avoids forcing his own values on the counselee and avoids criticism of the counselee's values. A non-directive counselor does provide information to the counselee if he desires this information in order to make a choice.[2]

The eclectic approach to counseling is one in which the leader-counselor does not adhere to any single theoretical approach. Rather, he focuses on a given subordinate's problem and then selects an approach or combination of approaches that he feels will lead to the best solution. He may find it advantageous to use a directive approach in one case and a non-directive approach in another. This should not be confused with trial and error counseling. A real eclectic counselor must have as much or more training than one who adheres to one approach. He merely strives to select what he finds best in the various approaches and then applies them based on his experiences.

What should a leader look for when trying to determine which of the three approaches to use? Generally the characteristics of the particular organizational setting will guide him in his search. Here, such variables as the time available, relationship with the counselee, setting of the interview, and the counselor's personality and desires will govern the choice. There is one other variable, however, that is also important: the degree of discomfort felt by the counselee as he approaches his problem—is he being emotional or rational? When a counselee is rational and logical in his thinking, the counselor is able, typically, to be more directive since the counselee is able to accept the counselor's guidance and make a rational choice. In contrast, when the counselee is approaching his problem emotionally, a non-directive approach is indicated. This affords the counselee the opportunity to talk out his feelings to a point where he can assume a more rational stance.

While the counseling process has been defined, the characteristics of the process explained, and the general approaches to counseling discussed, the matter of the characteristics of the leader-counselor have been omitted to this point so they might be addressed as a separate vital topic. Primarily, the leader must be a good communicator to be a successful counselor and he must avoid entering counseling with preconceived ideas about what will transpire. Further, he must communicate three essential qualities about himself to the counselee. *First*, he must demonstrate and communicate acceptance of the counselee. This involves a personal willingness on the part of the counselor to allow counselees to differ from one another and a realization that the ongoing experience of each counselee is a complex pattern of striving, thinking, and feeling. *Second*, the counselor must communicate understanding to the counselee. This is the quality of being able to feel what the counselee is feeling and communicating this fact to him in an empathic fashion. *Finally*, the counselor must communicate a sense of sincerity or genuineness to the counselee. The counselor must not see counseling as a menial task, rather he must be himself and be involved. While seemingly simple to accomplish, the idea of sincerity is the most difficult quality to project, especially when administrative requirements are pending, the counselee's problem seems rather insignificant, or the leader-counselor has other concerns on his mind.[3]

In conclusion, there are some do's and don'ts that can be helpful to the leader-counselor as he goes about his very important task:

DON'T—
1. Go beyond your capability as a counselor—when in doubt refer the counselee to an expert.
2. Jump to conclusions in counseling.
3. Set preconditions on the counselee for counseling.
4. Get sidetracked into expressions of opinion about what the counselee says or does.
5. Use emotionally loaded words in counseling.
6. Talk about similar cases with the counselee.
7. Remove the decision-making process from the counselee's hands.
8. Talk about counseling sessions outside the counseling environment.
9. Use psychological jargon.

DO—
1. Know what resources are available to assist you in the counseling process.
2. Understand your position and limit the counseling process to promote growth.
3. Prepare for your counseling sessions.
4. Facilitate verbalization, feeling, and development of the problem by the counselee.
5. Use the counselee's side of an issue under discussion rather than someone else's position.
6. Be able to handle periods of silence.

7. Listen for themes in the counselee's discussions.
8. Insure that you grasp the essential structure of what the counselee is saying.
9. Be a good listener and be responsive to the counselee.
10. Think before replying to the counselee's comments to insure you understand all ramifications of the communication.

END NOTES

1. Leona E. Tyler, in the book *The Work of the Counselor* (Appleton-Century-Crofts, NY: 1969) deals with the matter of counseling in a clearly written fashion. Especially good is the discussion of the components of the counseling process.

2. Carl Roger's book *On Becoming a Person* (Houghton Mifflin Company, Boston: 1970) is strongly recommended if the reader desires a more complete treatment of client-centered counseling.

3. C.G. Kemp discusses the matter of personal characteristics needed by the counselor in a fine book entitled *Intangibles in Counseling* (Houghton Mifflin Company, Boston: 1967).

REFERENCES

Guidelines for Counseling. West Point, NY: Office of Military Leadership, 1969.

Kemp, C.G. *Intangibles in Counseling*. Boston: Houghton Mifflin Company, 1961.

Rogers, C.R. *On Becoming a Person*. Boston: Houghton Mifflin Company, 1970.

Timmerman, F.W. Jr. Prediction of Enlisted Soldier Discipline Problems in Line Combat Units of the United States Army. Unpublished doctoral dissertation, Duke University, 1973.

Timmerman, F.W. Jr. Unit Counselor as a Member of the Team. *Army Magazine*, 1971, 23 (12), 48–50.

Tyler, Leona E. *The Work of the Counselor*. New York: Appleton-Century-Crofts, 1969.

Weitz, Henry. *Behavior Change Through Guidance*. New York: John Wiley and Sons, Inc., 1964.

Part V

The Organization

by
David H. Ohle*

In the preceding four Parts the main elements and processes of the Model of Organizational Leadership that influence the structure, functioning, and morale of the organization have been examined. In this Part the ORGANIZATION itself will be considered.

An organization has been defined in many ways by organizational theorists. March and Simon in their book *Organizations* do not attempt to define the term at all. Instead they claim, "it is easier, and probably more useful, to give examples of formal organizations than to define the term." (March and Simon, 1958, p. 1) This appears to be sound guidance. Therefore, rather than define an organization in the words of any particular theorist, we will identify the main characteristics of an organization and use these characteristics as the definition of an organization.

Based upon Porter, Lawler, and Hackman's list of the five distinguishing characteristics, organizations are:

1. social compositions of individuals and groups,
2. goal oriented,
3. differentiated by functions,
4. intended to be rationally coordinated and directed, and
5. perpetual in nature. (Porter et al., 1975, p. 99)

---

*David H. Ohle (Captain, U.S. Army) is on the faculty of the Office of Military Leadership at the United States Military Academy, West Point, New York. He received his B.S. from the United States Military Academy (1968) and his M.A. in Organizational Behavior and Social Psychology from the Ohio State University (1974). He is currently a doctoral candidate in Organizational Behavior and Social Psychology at the Ohio State University.

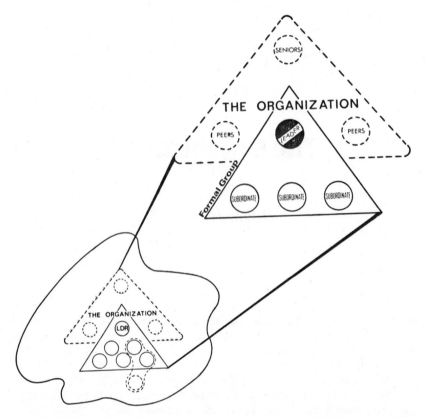

The first area to be considered is that of formal organizational theory. This section includes a discussion from the book *Bureaucracy in Modern Society* by Blau and Meyer entitled "Theory and Development of Bureaucracy." The authors outline the characteristics of a bureaucracy as defined by Max Weber, a German economist and social scientist who lived from 1864–1920. Weber's characteristics define an "ideal type" or "model" bureaucracy—an organization he felt would maximize efficiency. These characteristics are quite useful for both analysis and comparison of organizations. One of the central concepts of Weber's work was that of "legitimate authority." This feeling of "ought-ness" is the glue which holds the organization together. Simon, in a section of his classic work *Administrative Behavior*, continues the discussion of this very important subject of authority in an organizational setting. These two articles should provide some insight into the rationale behind many things you have already observed in organizations such as the Army.

The hierarchical structure and the channels of authority typical of most organizations determine, to a great extent, the goals and functions of those organizations. Frequently, however, these goals do not coincide with those of the individual employees. To the extent that they do not, there is organizational conflict. Argyris (1974) in his article "Personality vs. Organization" describes this basic conflict situation. Part III discussed the expectations that individuals have of the organization and the expectations the organization has of the individuals. In the *War College Study,* this was called the "informal contract." As discussed in the introductory article of this book, the mediator of this contract is the leader. The leader is the "linking pin" between the individual and the organization. One of the principal duties of the leader is to reduce the discrepancies in expectations between the two parties of the contract and to fulfill the expectations of both parties to the greatest extent possible.

These two sets of expectations are shown clearly in the figure entitled The Systems Approach and the Linking Elements Concept. (Didactic Systems, Inc.) This figure also depicts very clearly the meeting point of each of the two sets of expectations. This is the area in which the leader must bring the parties together by providing the linking elements, thereby reducing the inherent conflict and satisfying the terms of the "informal contract." Each of the linking elements has been discussed previously in an earlier part of the text. The student should examine the model and note how the issues discussed in the text thus far have been integrated in it. It will be beneficial to refer to this figure often as you read the articles in this Part.

Individual motivation in an organizational setting is another area of potential conflict. Hunt and Hill in their article, "The New Look in Motivational Theory for Organizational Research," identify three motivation theories as possible solutions to the conflict. The authors ultimately conclude that Vroom's expectancy theory of motivation provides the best framework through which organizational motivation conflict can be reduced.

Most organizations, to include the United States Army, have recognized the potential problems of organizational conflict and change and have instituted programs called "Organizational Development" or "Organizational Effectiveness" to assist their managers and leaders in handling human problems and increasing the effectiveness of their organization. The final article in this section, "Organizational Development" by Shaler, discusses the history and development of Organizational Development and its current applications in the U.S. Army.

These are terms you should be able to discuss after reading the articles in Part V.

Authority	Motivation Factors
Bureaucracy	Organization
Conflict	Organizational Development
Dysfunctional	Personality and Organization
Influence	Theory
Hygiene Factors	Process Consultation
Job Enlargement	Survey Feedback
Job Enrichment	Team Building
Job Loading	Zone of Acceptance
Linking Elements	Zone of Indifference
Motivation	

THE SYSTEMS APPROACH AND THE LINKING ELEMENTS CONCEPT

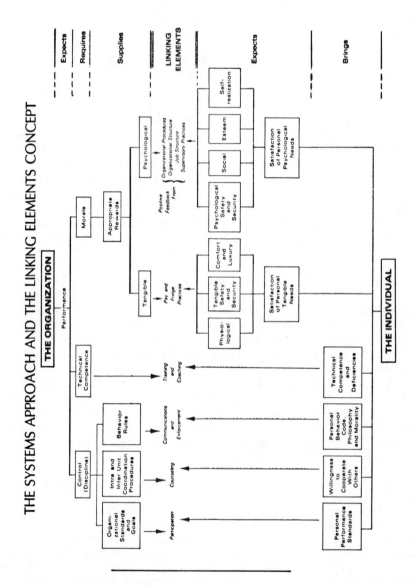

Organization Theory and Authority

Theory and Development of Bureaucracy*

by
Peter M. Blau and Marshall W. Meyer

Advancement in any science depends on developments in both theory and empirical research and on a close connection between them. The objectives of science are to improve the accuracy and scope of explanations of phenomena as a basis for better predictability and control. A system of interrelated explanatory propositions is a scientific theory. Not every insight, however, is a scientific proposition; this term refers only to those that have empirical implications that can be confirmed in systematic research, which is not the case for all explanations. Arnold Toynbee's interpretation of history in terms of challenge and response, for instance, although it may provide new insights into the course of history, cannot be empirically tested, since there is no conceivable factual evidence that would clearly disprove it. An important methodological principle of science holds that only those propositions can be empirically corroborated that indicate precisely the evidence necessary for disproving them.

If undisciplined speculating does not further the advancement of science, neither does random data-collecting. A large number of miscellaneous facts contribute as little to the building of systematic theory as a large number of odd stones contribute to the building of a house. To be sure, unsophisticated fact-finding has its uses, and so does undisciplined imagination, but for empirical research and theoretical insights to serve science, they must be integrated. This

---

*From *Bureaucracy in Modern Society,* Second Edition, by Peter M. Blau and Marshall W. Meyer. Copyright © 1956, 1971 by Random House, Inc. Reprinted by permission of the publisher.

requires that theory be precise enough to direct research, and that research be oriented toward establishing theoretical generalizations.

The lesson to be learned from these considerations is that the study of bureaucracy should be governed by a theoretical orientation and should focus upon the investigation of empirical cases. These empirical studies of bureaucracies, in turn, will help to clarify and refine our theoretical understanding of this social structure and its functioning. Following this procedure, we shall start with Max Weber's famous theory of bureaucracy.

THE CONCEPT OF BUREAUCRACY

The main characteristics of a bureaucratic structure (in the "ideal-typical" case[1]), according to Weber, are the following:

1. "The regular activities required for the purposes of the organization are distributed in a fixed way as official duties."[2] The clear-cut division of labor makes it possible to employ only specialized experts in each particular position and to make every one of them responsible for the effective performance of his duties. This high degree of specialization has become so much part of our socioeconomic life that we tend to forget that it did not prevail in former eras but is a relatively recent bureaucratic innovation.

2. "The organization of offices follows the principle of hierarchy; that is, each lower office is under the control and supervision of a higher one."[3] Every official in this administrative hierarchy is accountable to his superior for his subordinates' decisions and actions as well as his own. To be able to discharge his responsibility for the work of subordinates, he has authority over them, which means that he has the right to issue directives and they have the duty to obey them. This authority is strictly circumscribed and confined to those directives that are relevant for official operations. The use of status prerogatives to extend the power of control over subordinates beyond these limits does not constitute the legitimate exercise of bureaucratic authority.

3. Operations are governed "by a consistent system of abstract rules . . . [and] consist of the application of these rules to particular cases."[4] This system of standards is designed to assure uniformity in the performance of every task, regardless of the number of persons engaged in it, and the coordination of different tasks. Explicit rules and regulations define the responsibility of each member of the organization and the relationships among them. This does not imply that bureaucratic duties are necessarily simple and routine. It must be remembered that strict adherence to general standards in deciding specific cases characterizes not only the job of the file clerk but also that of the Supreme Court justice. For the former, it may involve merely filing alphabetically; for the latter, it involves interpreting the law of the land in order to settle the most complicated legal issues. Bureaucratic duties range in complexity from one of these extremes to the other.

4. "The ideal official conducts his office . . . [in] a spirit of formalistic impersonality, 'Sine ira et studio,' without hatred or passion, and hence

without affection or enthusiasm."[5] For rational standards to govern operations without interference from personal considerations, a detached approach must prevail within the organization and especially toward clients. If an official develops strong feelings about some subordinates or clients, he can hardly help letting those feelings influence his official decisions. As a result, and often without being aware of it himself, he might be particularly lenient in evaluating the work of one of his subordinates or might discriminate against some clients and in favor of others. The exclusion of personal considerations from official business is a prerequisite for impartiality as well as for efficiency. The very factors that make a government bureaucrat unpopular with his clients, an aloof attitude and a lack of genuine concern with them as human beings, actually benefit these clients. Disinterestedness and lack of personal interest go together. The official who does not maintain social distance and becomes personally interested in the cases of his clients tends to be partial in his treatment of them, favoring those he likes over others. Impersonal detachment engenders equitable treatment of all persons and thus equal justice in administration.

5. Employment in the bureaucratic organization is based on technical qualifications and is protected against arbitrary dismissal. "It constitutes a career. There is a system of 'promotions' according to seniority or to achievement, or both."[6] These personnel policies, which are found not only in civil service but also in many private companies, encourage the development of loyalty to the organization and esprit de corps among its members. The consequent identification of employees with the organization motivates them to exert greater efforts in advancing its interests. It may also give rise to a tendency to think of themselves as a class apart from and superior to the rest of the society. Among civil servants, this tendency has been more pronounced in Europe, notably in Germany and France, than in the United States, but among military officers, it may be found here too.

6. "Experience tends universally to show that the purely bureaucratic type of administrative organization . . . is, from a purely technical point of view, capable of attaining the highest degree of efficiency."[7] "The fully developed bureaucratic mechanism compares with other organizations exactly as does the machine with nonmechanical modes of production."[8] Bureaucracy solves the distinctive organizational problem of maximizing organizational efficiency, not merely that of individuals.

The superior administrative efficiency of bureaucracy is the expected result of its various characteristics as outlined by Weber. For an individual to work efficiently, he must have the necessary skills and apply them rationally and energetically; but for an organization to operate efficiently, more is required. Every one of its members must have the expert skills needed for the performance of his tasks. This is the purpose of specialization and of employment on the basis of technical qualifications, often ascertained by objective tests. Even experts, however, may be prevented by personal bias from making rational decisions. The emphasis on impersonal detachment is intended to eliminate this source of irrational action. But individual rationality is not enough. As noted above, if the members of the organization were to make rational decisions independently, their work would not be coordinated and the efficiency of the organization would suffer. Hence there is need for discipline to limit the scope of rational discretion, which is met by the system of rules and regulations and the hierarchy of supervision. Moreover, personnel policies that permit employees to feel secure in their jobs and to anticipate advancements for faithful performance of duties discourage attempts to impress superiors by introducing clever innovations, which may endanger coordination. Lest this stress on disciplined obedience to rules and rulings undermine the employee's motivation to devote his energies to his job, incentives for exerting effort must be furnished. Personnel policies that cultivate organizational loyalty and that provide for promotion on the basis of merit serve this function. In other words, the combined effect of bureaucracy's characteristics is to create social conditions which constrain each member of the organization to act in ways that, whether they appear rational or otherwise from his individual standpoint, further the rational pursuit of organizational objectives.

Without explicitly stating so, Weber supplies a *functional* analysis of bureaucracy. In this type of analysis, a social structure is explained by showing how each of its elements contributes to its persistence and effective operations. Concern with discovering all these contributions, however, entails the danger that the scientist may neglect to investigate the disturbances that various elements produce in the structure. As a result, his presentation may make the social structure appear to function more smoothly than it actually does, since he neglects the disruptions that do in fact exist. To protect ourselves against this danger, it is essential to extend the analysis beyond the mere consideration of functions, as Robert K. Merton points out.[9] Of particular importance for avoiding false implications of stability and for explaining social change is the study of *dysfunctions,* those consequences that interfere with adjustment and create problems in the structure.[10]

A reexamination of the foregoing discussion of bureaucratic features in the light of the concept of dysfunction reveals inconsistencies and conflicting tendencies. If reserved detachment characterizes the attitudes of the members of the organization toward one another, it is unlikely that high esprit de corps will develop among them. The strict exercise of authority in the interest of discipline induces subordinates, anxious to be highly thought of by their superiors, to conceal defects in operations from superiors, and this obstruction of the flow of information upward in the hierarchy impedes effective management. Insistence on conformity also tends to engender rigidities in official conduct and to inhibit the rational exercise of judgment needed for the efficient performance of tasks. If promotions are based on merit, many employees will not experience advancements in their careers. If they are based primarily on seniority so as to give employees this experience and thereby to encourage them to become identified with the organization, the promotion system will not furnish strong incentives for exerting efforts and excellent performance. These illustrations suffice to indicate that the same factor that enhances efficiency in one respect often threatens it in another; it may have *both* functional and dysfunctional consequences.

Weber was well aware of such contradictory tendencies in the bureaucratic structure. But since he treats dysfunctions only incidentally, his discussion leaves the impression that administrative efficiency in bureaucracies is more stable and less problematical than it actually is. In part, it was his intention to present an idealized image of bureaucratic structure, and he used the conceptual tool appropriate for this purpose. Let us critically examine this conceptual tool.

IMPLICATIONS OF THE IDEAL-TYPE CONSTRUCT

Weber dealt with bureaucracy as what he termed an "ideal type." This methodological concept does not represent an average of the attributes of all existing bureaucracies (or other social structures), but a pure type, derived by abstracting the most characteristic bureaucratic aspects of all known organizations. Since perfect bureaucratization is never fully realized, no empirical organization corresponds exactly to this scientific construct.

The criticism has been made that Weber's analysis of an imaginary ideal type does not provide understanding of concrete bureaucratic structures. But this criticism obscures the fact that the ideal-type construct is intended as a guide in empirical research, not as a substitute for it. By indicating the characteristics of bureaucracy in its pure form, it directs the researcher to those aspects of organizations that he must examine in order to determine the extent of their bureaucratization. This is the function of all conceptual schemes: to specify the factors that must be taken into consideration in investigations and to define them clearly.

The ideal typical model of bureaucracy, however, is not simply a conceptual scheme. It includes not only definitions of concepts but also implicit generalizations about the relationships among them, and specifically the hypothesis that the diverse bureaucratic characteristics increase administrative efficiency. If certain attributes (for example, specialization, hierarchy, rules, and impersonality) are distinctive of bureaucracy compared to other forms of administration, and if bureaucracy is the most efficient form of administration, then at least some of the attributes of bureaucracy must be conducive to efficient operations. Whereas conceptual definitions are presupposed in research and not subject to verification by research findings, hypotheses concerning relationships among factors are subject to such verification. Whether strict hierarchical authority, for example, indeed furthers efficiency is a question of empirical fact and not one of definition. But as the scientific construct Weber intended it to be, the ideal type cannot be refuted by empirical evidence. If a study of several organizations were to find that strict hierarchical authority is not related to efficiency, this would not prove that no such relationship exists in the ideal-type bureaucracy; it would show only that these organizations are not fully bureaucratized. Since generalizations about idealized states defy testing in systematic research, they have no place in science. On the other hand, if empirical evidence is taken into consideration and generalizations are modified accordingly, we deal with prevailing tendencies in bureaucratic structures and no longer with a pure type.

Two misleading implications of the ideal-type conception of bureaucracy deserve special mention. The student of social organization is concerned with the patterns of activities and interactions that reveal how social conduct is organized, and not with exceptional deviations from these patterns. The fact that one official becomes excited and shouts at his colleague, or that another arrives late at the office, is unimportant in understanding the organization, except that the rare occurrence of such events indicates that they are idiosyncratic, differing from the prevailing patterns. Weber's decision to treat only the purely formal organization of bureaucracy implies that all deviations from these formal requirements are idiosyncratic and of no interest for the student of organization. Later empirical studies have shown this approach to be misleading. Informal relations and unofficial practices develop among the members of bureaucracies and assume an organized form without being officially sanctioned. Chester I. Barnard, one of the first to call attention to this phenomenon, held that these "informal organizations are necessary to the operations of formal organizations."[11] These informal patterns, in contrast to exceptional occurrences, are a regular part of bureaucratic organizations and therefore must be taken into account in their analysis.

Weber's approach also implies that any deviation from the formal structure is detrimental to administrative efficiency. Since the ideal type is conceived as the perfectly efficient organization, all differences from it must necessarily interfere with efficiency. There is considerable evidence that suggests the opposite conclusion; informal relations and unofficial practices often contribute to efficient operations. In any case, the significance of these unofficial patterns for operations cannot be determined in advance on theoretical grounds but only on the basis of empirical investigations. Before examining such case studies of bureaucracies we shall explore the conditions that give rise to bureaucratization.

CONDITIONS THAT GIVE RISE TO BUREAUCRATIZATION

To say that there is a historical trend toward bureaucracy is to state that many organizations change from less to more bureaucratic forms of administration. Yet the historical trend itself and the changes in any specific organization are different phenomena. Both are expressions of the process of bureaucratization, but since different conditions account for them, they will be discussed separately.

Historical Conditions

One of the historical conditions that favors the development of bureaucracy is a money economy. This is not an absolute prerequisite. Bureaucracies based on compensation in kind existed, for example, in Egypt, Rome, and China. Generally, however, a money economy permits the payment of regular salaries, which, in turn, creates the combination of dependence and independence that is most conducive to the faithful performance of bureaucratic duties. Unpaid volunteers are too independent of the organization to submit unfailingly to its discipline. Slaves, on the other hand, are too dependent on their masters to have the incentive to assume responsibilities and carry them out on their own initiative. The economic dependence of the salaried employee on his job and his freedom to advance himself in his career engender the orientation toward work required for disciplined *and* responsible conduct. Consequently, there were few bureaucracies prior to the development of a monetary system and the abolition of slavery.

It has already been mentioned that sheer size encourages the development of bureaucracies, since they are mechanisms for executing large-scale administrative tasks. The large modern nation, business, or union is more likely to be bureaucratized than was its smaller counterpart in the past. More important than size as such, however, is the emergence of special administrative problems. Thus in ancient Egypt the complex job of constructing and regulating waterways throughout the country gave rise to the first known large-scale bureaucracy in history. In other countries, notably those with long frontiers requiring defense, bureaucratic methods were introduced to solve the problem of organizing an effective army and the related one of raising taxes for this purpose. England, without land frontiers, maintained only a small army in earlier centuries, which may in part account for the fact that the trend toward bureaucratization was less pronounced there than in continental nations, which had to support large armies. Weber cites the victory of the Puritans under the leadership of Cromwell over the Cavaliers, who fought more heroically but with less discipline, as an illustration of the superior effectiveness of a bureaucratized army.[12]

The capitalistic system also has furthered the advance of bureaucracy. The rational estimation of economic risks, which is presupposed in capitalism, requires that the regular processes of the competitive market not be interrupted by external forces in unpredictable ways. Arbitrary actions of political tyrants interfere with the rational calculation of gain or loss, and so do banditry, piracy, and social upheavals. The interest of capitalism demands, therefore, not only the overthrow of tyrannical rulers but also the establishment of governments strong enough to maintain order and stability. Note that after the American Revolution such representatives of the capitalists as Alexander Hamilton advocated a strong federal government, while representatives of farmers, in the manner of Jefferson, favored a weak central government.

Capitalism then promotes effective and extensive operations of the government. It also leads to bureaucratization in other spheres. The expansion of business firms and the consequent removal of most employees from activities directly governed by the profit principle make it increasingly necessary to introduce bureaucratic methods of administration for the sake of efficiency. These giant corporations, in turn, constrain workers, who no longer can bargain individually with an employer they know personally, to organize into large unions with complex administrative machineries. Strange as it may seem, the free-enterprise system fosters the development of bureaucracy in the government, in private companies, and in unions.

These historical conditions were not causes of bureaucracy in the usual sense of the term. Evidently, a large and effective army did not cause bureaucracy; on the contrary, bureaucratic methods of operation produced an effective large army. The need for these methods, however, arose in the course of trying to build such an army without them and helped bring about a bureaucratic form of organization. The qualifying word "helped" is essential. If needs inevitably created ways of meeting them, human society would be paradise. In this world, wishes are not horses, and beggars do not ride. Social needs, just as individual ones, often persist without being met. Knowledge of the conditions that engendered a need for bureaucracy does not answer the question: what made its development actually possible under some circumstances and not under others? The Cavaliers were in need of a better fighting force, as their defeat demonstrates. Why was it not they but the Puritans who organized a disciplined army?

In *The Protestant Ethic and the Spirit of Capitalism*, Weber indirectly answers this question. He shows that the Reformation—especially Calvinism, the religious doctrine of the Puritans—apart from its spiritual significance, had the social consequence of giving rise to this-worldly asceticism, a disciplined devotion to hard work in the pursuit of one's vocation. The Protestant has no Pope or priest to furnish spiritual guidance and absolve him for his sins, but must ultimately rely on his own conscience and faith; this encourages the emergence of self-imposed discipline. The strong condemnation of pleasure and emotions, exemplified by the Puritan "blue laws," generates the sobriety and detachment conducive to rational conduct. Moreover, in contrast to Catholicism and even Lutheranism, Calvinism does not emphasize that the existing order is God's creation but that it has been corrupted by man's sinfulness. Man's religious duty is not to adapt to this wicked world, nor to withdraw from it into a monastery, but to help transform it *in majorem gloriam Dei* through methodical efforts in his everyday life and regular work. The anxieties aroused by the doctrine of double predestination, according to which man cannot affect his predestined fate or even know whether he will be saved or damned, reinforced the Calvinist's tendency to adopt a rigorous discipline and immerse himself in his work as a way of relieving his anxieties.

Protestantism, therefore, has transplanted the ascetic devotion to disciplined hard work (which must be distinguished from the exertion of effort as a means for reaching specific ends) from monastic life, to which it was largely confined earlier, to the mundane affairs of economic life. Although the explicit purposes of the Reformation were other-worldly and not this-worldly, the psychological orientation it created had the unanticipated consequence of helping to revolutionize the secular world. For without this orientation toward ceaseless effort and rational conduct as intrinsic moral values, Weber argues convincingly, modern capitalism could not have emerged when it did, and neither, it should be added, could full-blown bureaucracy have developed, because it too depends on rational discipline.[13]

Structural Conditions

The historical conditions that led to the pervasiveness of bureaucracy today do not, of course, explain why some organizations in contemporary society are highly bureaucratized and others are not. These variations raise the problem of the conditions within a given social structure that give rise to its bureaucratization. A recent empirical study is concerned with this problem.

Alvin W. Gouldner investigated the process of bureaucratization in a gypsum plant.[14] After the death of the old manager, the company that owned the plant appointed a man who had been in charge of one of its smaller factories as his successor. The new manager, anxious to prove himself worthy of the promotion by improving productivity, was faced with special difficulties. He was not familiar with the ways of working that had become customary in this plant, had not established informal relations with his subordinates, and did not command the allegiance of workers, who still felt loyal to his predecessor. To marshal the willing support of workers and induce them to identify with his managerial objectives, he attempted to cultivate informal relations with them; but this could not be done overnight. In the meantime, he found it necessary to discharge his managerial responsibilities by resorting to formal procedures. In the absence of informal channels of communication to keep him informed about the work situation, the new manager instituted a system of regular operational reports for this purpose. Since he did not know the workers well enough to trust them, he closely checked on their operations and ordered his lieutenants to establish strict discipline. When some of these lieutenants, used to the more lenient ways of the former manager, failed to adopt rigorous methods of close supervision, he replaced them by outsiders who were more sympathetic with his disciplinarian approach. These innovations alienated workers and deepened the gulf between them and the manager, with the result that he had to rely increasingly on formal bureaucratic methods of administration.

> The role of the successor . . . confronted Peele with distinctive problems. He had to solve these problems if he wished to hold his job as manager. In the process of solving them, the successor was compelled to use bureaucratic methods. Peele intensified bureaucracy not merely because he wanted to, not necessarily because he liked bureaucracy, nor because he valued it above other techniques, but also because he was constrained to do so by the tensions of his succession.[15]

In the interest of his objective of gaining control over the operations in the plant, it was necessary for the successor to introduce bureaucratic procedures. At the same time, for workers to realize their objective of maintaining some independent control over their own work, it was necessary for them to oppose the introduction of disciplinarian measures. As noted above, the existence of a need does not explain why it is met. In this case, two conflicting needs existed side by side, with the "victor" determined by the power structure in the organization. The powerful position of the manager was responsible for his ability to meet his need by bureaucratizing operations, as indicated by the following comparison with a situation where he was not similarly successful.

This plant consisted of a gypsum mine and a wallboard factory, but the process of bureaucratic formalization was largely confined to the factory. Stronger informal ties and more pronounced group solidarity prevailed among miners than among factory workers, partly as a consequence of the common danger to which they were exposed in the mine. Miners were highly motivated to work hard, and they had developed their own unofficial system of assigning tasks among themselves; for instance, new miners had to do the dirty jobs. Hence there was less need in the mine for formal discipline and rules prescribing exact duties.

Nevertheless, Peele attempted to formalize operating procedures there, too. The strength of their informal organization, however, made it possible for miners, in contrast to factory workers, effectively to resist their attempts. The process of bureaucratic formalization generated by succession in management is not inevitable; collective resistance can arrest it.

The miners, so to speak, had evolved an unofficial bureaucratic apparatus of their own. Their effective informal organization, by regulating their work, took the place of a more formal system of control and simultaneously gave them sufficient power to defeat endeavors to impose a formal system of discipline upon them against their will. Did efficiency suffer? Gouldner implies it did not, although he does not specifically deal with this question. In any case, the conduct of the miners calls attention, once more, to the importance of informal relations and unofficial practices in bureaucratic structures.

Time Of Origin

The historical period in which organizations were established affects their characteristics. Armies, which originated many centuries ago, still have today a more authoritarian structure than factories, which are of more recent origin. For bureaucratic structures are characterized by a great deal of inertia, and they often resist innovations, even those that would improve efficiency. When an organization is founded, its structure usually reflects the latest in both technology and administrative practices. Once it has been founded, however, its structure tends to remain intact for some time, little affected by new technologies and often insensitive to changes in operating procedures that would enable it to perform better.

A study by Arthur Stinchcombe classified major industries according to their age and certain characteristics of the work force which were reported in the 1950 census.[16] The analysis focused on four variables: the proportion of unpaid family workers in an industry, the proportion of managerial posts occupied by the owner's family, the number of clerical employees, and the proportion of administrators with professional qualifications. The oldest industries—agriculture, wholesale and retail trades, water transportation, and the like—had in 1950 relatively many unpaid family employees and family members acting as managers, whereas the numbers of clerks and of professionals were relatively low. Industries formed later, in the early nineteenth century, by contrast, had nearly no unpaid family members in 1950 (though relatives remained as managers), and clerical component was substantial—about half of administrative employees were clerks. The woodworking, apparel, textile, and banking industries were included in this group. Late nineteenth-century organizations—railroads, mining, and metals firms—clearly separated ownership from managerial responsibility; that is, the proportion of family members acting as managers was very small. Again, the clerical component was quite large in these industries. Finally, industries established in this century are similar to their nineteenth-century counterparts except that they employ many professionals. With only one exception (automobile repairs), industries in this category require professional qualifications of more than half of their managers.

Stinchcombe's data would seem to lend credence to the notion that bureaucracies develop in stages. First, cash salaries replace unpaid work by family members. Then, a clerical component is added, and owners are separated from management. Finally, managers are expected to have professional qualifications. The data suggest that newer industries are most bureaucratized, in the sense of having large administrative machineries and of selecting managers on the basis of impersonal rational criteria. Many organizations founded in the nineteenth century have not altered their original structures, perhaps because they have no need to do so, but more likely because they have resisted change. One has only to consult the business pages to find that older industries are generally less profitable than newer ones, which suggests that their efficiency has suffered from lack of innovation. We must conclude, therefore, that the conditions conducive to rationalization or bureaucratization do not necessarily give rise to it in already established organizations.

Resistance to change in organizations has many sources. Change often endangers careers and disturbs vested interest, generating resistance against it. It seems to require a crisis or a change of management to precipitate reorganization, at least in large industries. The historian Alfred Chandler shows in case studies of four corporations—DuPont, General Motors, Sears Roebuck, and Standard Oil of New Jersey—that this is the situation. All four suffered considerable declines in business before they considered reorganization and adopted a modern decentralized structure.[17] Finally, an unpublished study by Jacques Gellard shows that recently appointed managers are considerably more likely than old-timers to institute change in American government finance departments.[18] To overcome bureaucratic inertia seems to require new organizations or new managers, unencumbered by traditions and personal loyalties, and not already enmeshed in the social processes that characterize the interpersonal relations in the organization.

END NOTES

1. The "ideal type" is discussed later in this chapter.
2. H.H. Gerth and C. Wright Mills (eds.), *From Max Weber: Essays in Sociology* (New York: Oxford University Press, 1946), p. 196. By permission.

3. Max Weber, *The Theory of Social and Economic Organization,* translated by A.M. Henderson and Talcott Parsons (New York: Oxford University Press, 1947), p. 331.

4. *Ibid.,* p. 330.

5. *Ibid.,* p. 340.

6. *Ibid.,* p. 334.

7. *Ibid.,* p. 337.

8. Gerth and Mills, *op. cit.,* p. 214.

9. Robert K. Merton, *Social Theory and Social Structure,* 3rd ed. (New York: Free Press, 1968), pp. 73–138.

10. For a general discussion of functional analysis, see Ely Chinoy, *Sociological Perspective* (New York: Random House, 1968), Chap. 5.

11. Chester I. Barnard, *The Functions of the Executive* (Cambridge: Harvard University Press, 1948), p. 123.

12. Gerth and Mills, *op. cit.,* pp. 256–257. The advanced student will have recognized the indebtedness of the foregoing discussion to Weber's (pp. 204–216). It goes without saying that Weber's fund of historical knowledge and his profound theoretical insights about bureaucracy can be acknowledged as outstanding contributions in the field, even if one rejects his use of the ideal-type construct.

13. For a fuller discussion of the unintended effects of Protestantism, see Elizabeth K. Nottingham, *Religion: A Sociological Review* (New York: Random House, 1971).

14. Alvin W. Gouldner, *Patterns of Industrial Bureaucracy* (Glencoe, Ill.: Free Press, 1954).

15. *Ibid.,* pp. 97–98.

16. Arthur Stinchcombe, "Social Structure and Organizations," in James March (ed.), *Handbook of Organizations* (Chicago: Rand McNally, 1965), pp. 155–160.

17. Alfred Chandler, *Strategy and Structure* (Cambridge: MIT Press, 1962).

18. Jacques Gellard, "Determinants and Consequences of Executive Succession in Government Finance Agencies" (unpublished M.A. thesis, University of Chicago, 1967).

Authority*

by
Herbert A. Simon

Even the very simple illustrations that have been presented of organized behavior exhibit, in embryo at least, the phenomenon of authority. *Authority* may
be defined as the power to make decisions which guide the actions of another.
It is a relationship between two individuals, one "superior," the other "subordinate." The superior frames and transmits decisions with the expectation that
they will be accepted by the subordinate. The subordinate expects such decisions, and his conduct is determined by them.[1]

The relationship of authority can be defined, therefore, in purely objective
and behavioristic terms. It involves behaviors on the part of both superior and
subordinate. When, and only when, these behaviors occur does a relation of
authority exist between the two persons involved. When the behaviors do not
occur there is not authority, whatever may be the "paper" theory of organization.

The behavior pattern of the superior involves a command—an imperative
statement concerning the choice of a behavior alternative by the other—and an
expectation that the command will be accepted by the other as a criterion of
choice.[2]

The behavior pattern of the subordinate is governed by a single inde-
terminate decision, or criterion for decision, to "follow that behavior alternative which is selected for me by the superior." That is, he holds in abeyance his

own critical faculties for choosing between alternatives and uses the formal criterion of the receipt of a command or signal as his basis for choice.[3]

Now since the relation of authority involves a particular criterion of choice as the basis for the subordinate's behavior, it is clear that the two persons may stand in a relation of authority at one moment and not at the next. For the subordinate's behavior may be governed at the first moment by a command, and not at the next. Nor does it follow that when two persons recognize each other as "superior" and "subordinate" respectively, all the verbalizations of the first which affect the behaviors of the second are "commands." The willingness of the subordinate to accept a command, *if given,* does not imply that all, or even most, of his behavior choices are governed by commands.

It is necessary to distinguish, therefore, between specific behaviors which are momentary instances of the exercise of authority and the roles played by two persons over a period of time which involve an *expectation of obedience* by the one and a *willingness to obey* by the other.

DISTINCTION BETWEEN INFLUENCE AND AUTHORITY

The relation of authority by no means comprehends all situations where the verbalizations of one person influence the behavior of another. The verbs "persuade," "suggest," etc., describe several kinds of influence which do not necessarily involve any relationship of authority. The characteristic which distinguishes authority from other kinds of influence is one already mentioned above, namely, that a subordinate holds in abeyance his own critical faculties for choosing between alternatives and uses the formal criterion of the receipt of a command or signal as his basis for choice. On the other hand, a person who receives a suggestion accepts it as only one of the evidential bases for making his choice—but the choice he will make depends upon conviction. Persuasion, too, centers around the reasons for or against a course of action. Persuasion and suggestion result in a change in the evidential environment of choice which may, but need not, lead to conviction. Obedience, on the other hand, is an abdication of choice.

Confusion among these terms results from the fact that all three phenomena—persuasion, suggestion, and command—are frequently present in a single situation. Even when a behavior can be secured by the exercise of authority, a superior often and perhaps usually prefers to employ suggestion or persuasion. Some reasons for this will be discussed presently. But confusion will be avoided if it is remembered—as has been pointed out already—that the mere fact that two persons accept the roles of superior and subordinate does not imply that all, or even most, of their behaviors will be instances of the exercise of authority.

The line of demarcation between suggestion and command is perhaps not so clear as would be suggested by this discussion, however. Certain subtleties are concealed in the term "conviction," which was used as the distinguishing criterion.

A conviction, as used in this connection, is a belief in a factual or value premise which is relevant to a particular decision. Belief in a factual proposition may be induced in a number of ways, one of which is *proof*.

But we are convinced of a great number of things which never have been proved to us logically or empirically. Most persons in this country would agree that the atom bomb has been invented, though they would be hard put to demonstrate this either by pure logic or by the evidence of the senses. Likewise, few persons before taking prescribed medicines ask their physicians for a demonstration of the curative properties of the prescription.

In other words, conviction often results from the social transmission of factual statements, even in the absence of proof. So, a secretary who has been instructed by her employer to investigate a particular question of office procedure may report: "I have looked into the problem, and suggest that you act in this manner." This suggestion may be accepted without any review of its evidential basis by the employer, merely on the strength of his confidence in the secretary. Here is evident the same relaxation of critical faculties that we have said was characteristic of the relation of authority.

Statements, then, may convince without proving by virtue of the status or position of the person making the statement. An individual who does not have a recognized status, or who is not recognized by his associates as expert with respect to a certain kind of knowledge, will have a more difficult time convincing his listeners that a recommendation is sound than one who possesses the credentials of "expertness." Recommendations are judged partly on the merits of the persons making the recommendations. This is true both because the individuals acting upon the recommendations often do not have the expertise needed to judge them, and because pressure of time requires them to accept the recommendations of those whom they trust. This is an important reason for the resistance that is usually experienced in any organization to suggestions that are made outside the line of duty, or that are volunteered through other than the usual lines of communications.

It should not be implied that this resistance to "irregular" suggestions is entirely a weakness of organization. The specialization of decision-making functions, and the fixing of responsibility for particular kinds of expertness upon particular individuals are an important source of organizational efficiency that must be balanced against the potential loss of independent ideas which results.

At the expense of a possible abuse of the term, we shall use "authority" broadly, and comprehend under it all situations where suggestions are accepted without any critical review or consideration. If this definition is accepted, it follows that when A is superior to B at one moment, B may act as superior to A at the next moment. What is meant, then, when A is described as *the* superior of B?

AUTHORITY AND THE "LAST WORD"

In the situations that have been discussed, a subordinate accepts commands in the absense of a determinate choice of his own. But a subordinate may also accept commands in opposition to a determinate choice of his own. In such a case, the element of authority in the behavior pattern is unequivocal. When there is a disagreement between two persons, and when the disagreement is not resolved by discussion, persuasion, or other means of conviction, then it must be decided by the authority of one or the other participant. It is this "right to the last word" which is usually meant in speaking of "lines of authority" in an administrative organization. Too often, however, the element of disagreement in obedience is overemphasized at the expense of the other elements of the situation. The term "authority" would be too narrowly employed if it were restricted to such instances of disagreement.

A final complication must be added to the notion of authority. If authority were evidenced entirely in the acceptance of explicit commands, or in the resolution of disagreements, its presence or absence in any relationship could be sought in the presence or absence of these tangible concomitants. But it is equally possible for obedience to anticipate commands. The subordinate may, and is expected to, ask himself "How would my superior wish me to behave under these circumstances?" Under such circumstances, authority is implemented by a subsequent review of completed actions, rather than a prior command. Further, the more obedient the subordinate, the less tangible will be the evidences of authority. For authority will need to be exercised only to reverse an incorrect decision.

This phenomenon has been pointed out by Friedrich,[4] who calls it a "rule of anticipated reactions." It affords a striking example of the manner in which expectations and anticipations govern human behavior, and the difficulties which result from this for the analysis of human institutions. The difficulty in determining authority relations because of the operation of the rule of anticipated reactions is common to all "power" situations. Any study, for instance, of a governor's veto power must take into consideration what bills failed of passage in the legislature because of the anticipation of veto, and what bills were passed for the very same reason.[5]

Any study of power relations which confines itself to instances where the sanctions of power were invoked misses the essential fact of the situation. To avoid this fallacy, authority has been defined in this study not in terms of the sanctions of the superior but in terms of the behavior of the subordinate.

THE SANCTIONS OF AUTHORITY

Having decided, tentatively at least, what authority is, we must examine the circumstances surrounding its exercise. Why and to what extent will a subordinate accept the decision of another as governing his own conduct?

The superior-subordinate relationship is one of many possible examples of the role-taking which characterizes broad areas of human conduct. Perhaps the most important basis for such role-taking is custom. That is, a great deal of conduct requires no further explanation than that, under the circumstances, it is the socially "expected" conduct. For the reasons why particular conduct is dictated by custom it would be necessary to study the social history of the society in question.

The "institutions" of society may be regarded as rules specifying the roles that particular persons will assume in relation to one another under certain circumstances. The range of possible roles and possible behaviors is as broad as the ingenuity of man for dramatic invention.

One of the socially determined roles in many societies is that of "employee." The particular content of the role—the degree of obedience expected—will vary with the social situation. The American workingman today, for example, probably has a somewhat narrower zone of acceptance, so far as the employer's instructions are concerned, than his father had. In part this may be due to his stronger bargaining position, or conversely, the weaker sanctions of the employer; but there is probably also present here a more fundamental change in social attitudes as to what it is "proper" for an employer to ask an employee to do. This changed attitude is reflected also in social legislation limiting the terms of the employment contract.

There are wide differences, too, among different types of employees in their expectations of the authority relations in their positions. Professional men and skilled workmen are apt to have relatively narrow zones of acceptance, particularly in the areas of their professional competences or skills.

No attempt will be made here to explain the genesis of these social attitudes that establish an expectation of obedience in certain situations, nor their dependence upon and relation to other attitude clusters in the society. There has been much speculation that the central attitudes of a society must be reflected in administrative organization, so that administration in a democracy will be in some sense "democratic" while administration in a totalitarian system will be "authoritarian." Thus far, the thesis has been expounded, but by no means demonstrated.

There are a number of other, more specific, factors which induce acceptance of authority in organization. In a broad sense they might be called "sanctions," although that word is usually confined to stimuli which act through punishment, while some of the factors listed below are more properly classified as rewards.

(1) The social sanctions are the first to be noted, and perhaps the most important. Not only does society set up in the individual expectations of obedience in certain social situations, but the individual who fails to accept his role will feel, in one way or another, the social disapprobation of his fellows. Insubordination can be as embarrassing, under these circumstances, as failure to wear a necktie to church.

On the other hand, in so far as fellow employees may receive vicarious satisfaction when an individual "tells off" the boss, social sanctions may operate to decrease the effectiveness of authority. The extent to which group attitudes of acceptance or resistance will condition the individual's reactions to authority has been much emphasized in the Hawthorne studies.[6]

(2) Psychological differences between individuals may play an important part in enforcing such relations. Though the study of leadership is in a very primitive stage, there are some indications that there may be certain personality types that lead, and others that follow.[7]

(3) Purpose has been stressed by students of administration as a sanction of prime importance . . . In voluntary organizations efforts are contributed largely because the contributor is sympathetic to the purpose of the organization. He is willing to obey commands because he realizes that the coordination secured thereby is useful to the attainment of the joint purpose.[8]

Several conditions must be satisfied if purpose is to be an effective sanction of authority. The subordinate must have confidence that the command is issued in furtherance of a purpose with which he is in sympathy. Second, he must have confidence that the command will be effective in achieving this purpose. This confidence may be based less on his own knowledge of the correctness of the command (as a matter of fact, such acceptance would fall outside our definition of authority) than on his faith in the ability of those who issue the command, his recognition that they have information he does not have, and his realization that his efforts and those of fellow workers will be ineffective in reaching the desired objective without some coordination from above. Within limits, he will even accept commands he knows to be incorrect because he does not wish to challenge or unsettle a system of authority that he believes to be beneficial to his aims in the long run.

(4) More formal sanctions in our society are based on the relation between the "job" and economic security and status. Thus, obedience may be the price of retaining the position, securing a higher salary, or other advantages. The facts that most organizations will tolerate large quantities of insubordination—particularly if it is not verbalized—without dismissal, and that many organization members are not desirous of promotion, diminish the importance of these sanctions as a means for securing acceptance of authority in the day-to-day work of an organization.

(5) Particularly in the case of individuals not much affected by influences in the third and fourth categories, simple unwillingness or disinclination to accept responsibility may be a major reason for the acceptance of decisions made by others. If the assigned task is not unduly unpleasant, many individuals would prefer being told what to do to being forced to make the decisions themselves. As a matter of fact, this is probably characteristic of most individuals when the decision in question lies outside the area of their experience and competence. The psychological roots of this lie deeper than a mere fear of the consequences which may be forthcoming in case of an incorrect decision, and there is great variability among individuals in this characteristic.

THE LIMITS OF AUTHORITY

The most striking characteristic of the "subordinate" role is that it establishes an area of acceptance[9] in behavior within which the subordinate is willing to accept the decisions made for him by his superior. His choice is then determined, always within the area of acceptance, by his superior, and the relation of superior-subordinate holds only within this area. Acceptance may be due to any of the influences discussed in the previous section, and may take place when the subordinate does not care which alternative is slected, or when the sanctions are sufficiently strong to induce him to carry out an undesired alternative.

The magnitude of the area is influenced by a large number of circumstances. A voluntary organization with poorly defined objectives has perhaps the narrowest range of acceptance. An army, where the sanctions as well as the customs are of extreme severity, has the broadest area of acceptance.[10]

Restraint of the superior is as important as obedience of the subordinate in maintaining the relationship. Modern writers on administration have emphasized the need for restraint by recommending the use when possible of other means of influence, leading to conviction, rather than authority, leading often to nothing more than acquiescence.

The corresponding limitations of political authority have been discussed by Professor Charles E. Merriam.[11] Theoreticians of history have often questioned the extent to which "leaders" really lead. How broad is the area of indifference within which a group will continue to follow its leadership? In a very real sense, the leader, or the superior, is merely a bus driver whose passengers will leave him unless he takes them in the direction they wish to go. They leave him only minor discretion as to the road to be followed.

END NOTES

1. For other descriptions of authority see L.D. White, *Introduction to the Study of Public Administration* (New York: The MacMillan Company, 1939), pp. 44–46, and C.I. Barnard, *The Functions of the Executive*, p. 163.

2. This idea was central to the utilitarian concept of the state. See, for example, Jeremy Bentham, *A Fragment on Government* (Oxford: Clarendon Press).

3. Cf. Ordway Tead, *Human Nature and Management* (New York: McGraw-Hill Book Co., Inc., 1929), p. 149; and E.O. Stene, "An Approach to a Science of Administration," *American Political Science Review*, 34:1131 (Dec., 1940).

4. C.J. Friedrich, *Constitutional Government and Politics* (New York: Harper & Bros., 1937), p. 16. Cf. Bentham's very interesting definition: "A tacit *expression of will* is that which is conveyed by any other signs than words whatsoever; among which none are so efficacious as acts of punishment annexed in times past, to the nonperformance of acts of the same sort with those that are the objects of the will that is in question." (*A Fragment on Government*, p. 138).

5. Leslie Lipson, *The American Governor: From Figurehead to Executive* (Chicago: University of Chicago Press, 1939), pp. 210–212.

6. See, for example, F.J. Roethlisberger and W.J. Dickson, *Management and the Worker* (Cambridge: Harvard University Press, 1939).

7. Charles E. Merriam, *Political Power* (New York: McGraw-Hill Book Co., Inc., 1934), pp. 24–26; and Harold D. Lasswell, *Psychopathology and Politics*, pp. 38–64, 78–152.

8. C.I. Barnard, *op. cit.*, pp. 165–166; and Luther Gulick, "Notes on the Theory of Organization," in Luther Gulick and L. Urwick, eds., *Papers on the Science of Administration* (New York: Institute of Public Administration, 1937), pp. 37–38.

9. This concept is adopted from Barnard (*op cit.*, pp. 168–169), who, however, does not develop to any great extent the positive significance of what he calls the "zone of indifference."

10. Military literature shows a clear recognition of the importance of the area of acceptance as a fundamental element in tactics. Cf. Col. J.F.C. Fuller's graphic description of the psychology of battle in *The Foundations of the Science of War* (London: Hutchinson & Co., 1925), pp. 140–141.

11. See the chapter "The Poverty of Power" in his *Political Power* (pp. 156-183).

Organizational Conflict

Personality Vs. Organization*

by
Chris Argyris†

Approximately every seven years we develop the itch to review the relevant literature and research in personality and organization theory, to compare our own evolving theory and research with those of our peers—an exercise salutary, we trust, in confirmation and also confrontation. We're particularly concerned to measure our own explicit model of man with the complementary or conflicting models advanced by other thinkers. Without an explicit normative model, personality and organization theory (P. and O. theory) tends to settle for a generalized description of behavior as it is observed in existing institutions—at best, a process that embalms the status quo; at worst, a process that exalts it. Current behavior becomes the prescription for future actions.

By contrast, I contend that behavioral science research should be normative, that it is the mission of the behavioral scientist to intervene selectively in the organization whenever there seems a reasonable chance of improving the quality of life within the organization without imperiling its viability. Before

---

*Reprinted by permission of the publisher from *Managerial Review*, October, 1974, copyright © 1974 by AMACOM, a division of American Management Associations.
†Chris Argyris has been conducting research on understanding organizational illness and health for more than two decades. His major thesis began with *Personality and Organization* (Harper and Row, 1957), and continued with *Integrating the Individual and the Organization* (John Wiley and Sons, 1964), *Organization and Innovation* (Richard D. Irwin, 1965), *Intervention Theory and Method* (Addison Wesley, 1970), culminating in his most recent study of one of our country's leading newspapers entitled *Behind the Front Page* (Jossey-Bass, 1974). With Professor Donald Schon he has also written a book that presents a new theory of action as well as new suggestions on the redesign of professional education (*Theory in Practice*, Jossey-Bass, 1974).

surveying the P. and O. landscape, however, let's review the basic models of man and formal organization.

FUNDAMENTALS OF MAN AND ORGANIZATION

The following steps indicate how the worlds of man and formal organization have developed:

(1) Organizations emerge when the goals they seek to achieve are too complex for any one man. The actions necessary to achieve the goals are divided into units manageable by individuals—the more complex the goals, other things being equal, the more people are required to meet them.

(2) Individuals themselves are complex organizations with diverse needs. They contribute constructively to the organization only if *on balance,* the organization fulfills these needs and their sense of what is just.

(3) What are the needs that individuals seek to fulfill? Each expert has his own list and no two lists duplicate priorities. We have tried to bypass this intellectual morass by focusing on some relatively reliable predispositions that remain valid irrespective of the situation. Under any circumstances individuals seek time, their exact nature, potency, and the degree to which they must be fulfilled are influenced by the organizational context—for example, the nature of the job. In their attempt to live, to grow in competence, and to achieve self-acceptance, men and women tend to program themselves along the lines of the continua depicted in Figure 1.

Figure 1
Developmental Continua

Infants begin as	Adults strive toward
(1) being dependent and submissive to parents (or other significant adult)	(1) relative independence, autonomy, relative control over their immediate world
(2) having few abilities	(2) developing many abilities
(3) having skin-surfaced or shallow abilities	(3) developing a few abilities in depth
(4) having a short time perspective	(4) developing a longer time perspective

Together, these continua represent a developmental logic that people ignore or suppress with difficulty, the degree of difficulty depending on the culture and the context, as well as the individual's interactions with the key figures in his or her life. The model assumes that the thrust of this developmental program is from left to right, but nothing is assumed about the location of any given individuals along these continua.

A central theme of P. and O. theory has been the range of differences between individuals and how it is both necessary and possible to arrange a match between the particular set of needs an individual brings to the job situation and the requirements—technical and psychological—of the job itself, as well as the overall organizational climate.

We have written four studies that highlighted an individual's interrelationship with the work context. In each study, a separate analysis was made of each participant that included (1) the predispositions that he or she desired to express, (2) the potency of each predisposition, (3) the inferred probability that each would be expressed, and (4) a final score that indicated the degree to which the individual was able to express his or her predispositions.

A personal expression score enabled us to make specific predictions as to how individuals would react to the organization. We had expected individuals with low scores, for example, to state that they were frustrated and to have poorer attendance records and a higher quit rate—expectations that also showed how individual differences in predispositions were differentially rewarded in different types of department. Bank employees with a need to distrust and control others, for example, instinctively opted for positions in the internal audit department of the bank.

So much for the model of man. Now to organizations, which have a life of their own, in the sense that they have goals that unfortunately may be independent of or antagonistic to individual needs. The next step was to determine if there was a genetic logic according to which organizations were programmed.

Observation and reading combined to suggest that most organizations had pyramided structures of different sizes. The logic behind each of these pyramids—great or small—was first, to centralize information and power at the upper levels of the structure; second, to specialize work. According to this logic, enunciated most clearly by Frederick Winslow Taylor and Max Weber, management should be high on the six organizational activities summarized in Figure 2.

Figure 2
Continua of Organizational Activities

1.   Designing specialized and fractionalized work

low	high

2.   Designing production rates and controlling speed of work

low	high

3.   Giving orders

low	high

4.   Evaluating performance

low	high

5.   Rewarding and punishing

low	high

6.   Perpetuating membership

low	high

This model assumed that the closer an organization approached the right ends of the continua, the closer it approached the ideal of formal organization. The model assumed nothing, however, about where any given organization would be pointed along these continua.

PERSONALITY VS. ORGANIZATION

Given the dimensions of the two models, the possibilities of interaction are inevitable and varied; so is the likelihood of conflict between the needs of individuals and the structured configuration of the formal organization. The nature of the interaction between the individual and the organization and the probability of conflict vary according to the conditions depicted in Figure 3.

Figure 3
Conditions of Interaction

If the individual aspired toward	And the organization (through its jobs, technology, controls, leadership, and so forth) required that the individual aspire toward
(1) adulthood dimensions	(1) infancy dimensions
(2) infancy dimensions	(2) adulthood dimensions
(3) adulthood dimensions	(3) adulthood dimensions
(4) infancy dimensions	(4) infancy dimensions

From this model, we can hypothesize that the more the organization approaches the model of the formal organization, the more individuals will be forced to behave at the infant ends of the continua. What if—still operating at the level of an intellectual exercise—the individuals aspired toward the adult end of the continua? What would the consequences be? Wherever there is an incongruence between the needs of individuals and the requirements of a formal organization, individuals will tend to experience frustration, psychological failure, short-time perspective, and conflict.

What factors determine the extent of the incongruence? The chief factors are: first, the lower the employee is positioned in the hierarchy, the less control he has over his working conditions and the less he is able to employ his abilities; second, the more directive the leadership, the more unilateral the managerial controls, the more dependent the employee will feel.

We have said that individuals find these needs difficult to ignore or suppress, and if they are suppressed, frustration and conflict result. These feelings, in turn, are experienced in several ways:

• The employee fights the organization and tries to gain more control—for example, he may join a union.
• The employee leaves the organization, temporarily or permanently.
• The employee leaves it psychologically, becoming a half-worker, uninvolved, apathetic, indifferent.

• The employee downgrades the intrinsic importance of work and substitutes higher pay as the reward for meaningless work. Barnard observed almost 40 years ago that organizations emphasized financial satisfactions because they were the easiest to provide. He had a point—then and now.

We want to emphasize several aspects about these propositions. The personality model provides the base for predictions as to the impact of any organizational variable upon the individual, such as organizational structure, job content, leadership style, group norms, and so on. The literature has concentrated on employee frustration expressed in fighting the organization, because it's the commonest form of response, but we shouldn't ignore the other three responses.

In a study of two organizations in which technology, job content, leadership, and managerial controls confined lower-skilled employees to the infancy end of the continua, their response was condition three—no union, almost no turnover or absenteeism, but also apathy and indifference.

Last, we believe that the model holds regardless of differences in culture and political ideology. The fundamental relationships between individuals and organizations are the same in the United States, England, Sweden, Yugoslavia, Russia, or Cuba—a drastic statement but, we think, a true one.

RESEARCH THAT TESTS THE MODEL

Several studies in the past six years designed specifically to test the validity of the model all bore it out, to a greater or lesser extent. One study involved a questionnaire that measured self-expression as designed by our model. In a random sample of 332 U.S. salaried managers, hourly-paid workers, and self-employed businessmen, it was found that the lower the self-actualization, the more likely employees were to exhibit the following behavior: to day-dream, to have aggressive feelings toward their superiors, to have aggressive feelings toward their co-workers, to restrict output or make avoidable errors, to postpone difficult tasks or decisions, to emphasize money as the reward for service, and to be dissatisfied with their current jobs and think about another job.

A study in a different culture—Brazil—dealt with 189 employees in 13 banks. It revealed that 86 percent of the employees registered a discrepancy between their own felt needs and the formal goals of the organization. All agreed that the organizational goals were important, but only the top managers felt an absence of conflict between their own needs and the goals of the organization.

A second U.S. study involving 329 respondents—104 businessmen, 105 managers, 120 workers—confirmed the model, but not in most cases to a degree that was statistically significant. On balance, however, the respondents supported the proposition that employees who perceive their work situations as highly bureaucratic feel more isolated, alienated, and powerless.

RESEARCH THAT SUPPORTS THE MODEL

Additional studies with no formal relationship to the model nevertheless tend to underwrite it. A national sample of 1,533 employees in 1972, for example, showed that among all age groups interesting work was more important than money in providing job satisfaction.

Bertil Gardell, a Swedish psychologist, examined four plants in mass-production and process industries, seeking to relate production technology to alienation and mental health. Among his feelings were these:

• The more skilled the task and the more control the individual feels over how he performs it, the more independence and the less stress he experiences.

• There is a big discrepancy between people as to which jobs they deem interesting; some employees, for example, describe jobs with low discretion as interesting—this is a contradiction of our model, but they account for only 8 percent of the employees surveyed.

• Income is not a factor in determining alienation. A high-income employee with little control over his job feels just as alienated as the man laboring for a pittance.

Gardell concluded:

Severe restrictions in worker freedom and control and in skill level required are found to be related to increased work alienation and lowered level of mental health even after control is made for age, sex, income, type of leadership, and satisfaction with pay. The relation between task organization and mental health is valid, however, only after allowance is made for work alienation. In both industries certain people regard jobs of low discretion and skill level as interesting and free from constraint, but these groups amount to only 8 percent in each industry and are strongly over-represented as to workers above 50 years of age.

Within the mass-production industry, restrictions in discretion and skill level are found to go together with increased feelings of psychological stress and social isolation. People working under piece rate systems—compared with hourly paid workers—find their work more monotonous, constrained, and socially isolating, as well as having lower social status . . .

High self-determination and job involvement are found to be related to high demands for increased worker influence on work and company decisions in the process industries, while in the mass production industries demand for increased worker influence is greatest among those who feel their work to be monotonous and constrained. Perceptions of strong worker influence by collective arrangements are accompanied by influenced demands for individual decision-power as well as increased job satisfaction and decreased alienation.

A batch of studies reaffirmed the relationship between job specialization and feelings of powerlessness on the job and of frustration and alienation. One that compared craftsmen, monitors, and assemblers found that job satisfaction varied dramatically according to the degree of specialization: Job satisfaction was lowest among the assemblers—14 percent; next were the monitors—52 percent; and last were the craftsmen—87 percent. The same study found a strong relationship between job specialization and powerlessness on the job. Thus, 93 percent of the assemblers and 57 percent of the monitors, but only 19 percent of the craftsmen, experienced a lack of freedom and control.

Still other studies related job levels to the degree of dissatisfaction with the jobs. A comparison of 15 managers with 26 supervisors and 44 workers showed that the degree of satisfaction paralleled their position in the hierarchy, with managers the most satisfied and workers the least satisfied.

Frederick Herzberg reported a study of 2,665 Leningrad workers under 30 that again correlated job level with job satisfaction. Researchers who have concentrated on the higher levels of the organization typically have found a systematic tendency—the higher the positions held by the individuals in the organization, the more positive their attitudes tended to be.

An unusual study by Allam Wicker compared undermanned situations in which participants assumed more responsibility and performed larger tasks with overmanned situations in which the tasks were small and the responsibilities minute. Not surprisingly, in the overmanned situations employees reported less meaningful tasks and less sense of responsibility.

Can we reduce powerlessness at work, a factor closely linked to job alienation? One suggestive article points up three possibilities: Employees should allocate their own tasks; crews should be allowed to select themselves through sociometric procedures; the members of the group should select the group leaders.

Finally, research throws light on the question of whether time is the great reconciler. How long do dissatisfaction and frustration with the job persist? The answer appears to be—indefinitely. An interesting comparison of an old and a new assembly plant found that after 14 years the presumably acclimated employees were more dissatisfied and less involved with the product and the company than the new employees. Familiarity breeds frustration, alienation, and contempt.

RESEARCH RESULTS EXPLAINED BY THE MODEL

If employees are predisposed toward greater autonomy and formal organizations are designed to minimize autonomy, at least at the lower levels, we would expect to find a significant correlation between job status and job satisfaction—the lower the job, the less the job satisfaction. This has been found in a number of studies. Harold Wilensky, for example, reported in one of his studies the proportion of satisfied employess ranged from 90 percent for professors and mathematicians to 16 percent for unskilled auto workers. Furthermore, he found that the percentage of people who would go into similar work if they could start over again varied systematically with the degree of autonomy, control, and the chance to use their abilities that they experienced in their current jobs.

Several studies focused on the relationship between control and job satisfaction. An analysis of 200 geographically separate systems that were parts of larger organizations—for example, automotive dealers, clerical operations, manufacturing plants, and power plants in the same company—revealed that the greatest discrepancy between actual and ideal control occurred at the level of the rank-and-file employee. Ninety-nine percent of the work groups wanted more control over their immediate work area. Still another study found that employees became more dissatisfied after moving to a new, more efficient plant because of the reduction of their control over work. These studies were in the United States. Similar research in Yugoslavia and Norway further buttressed the point that employees want to enlarge the degree of their control over their immediate work world.

What about the impact of control upon turnover? The logic of the model leads us to predict that employees would be more likely to quit an organization when they experienced too much control by the organization or its representatives. Once again, research supports the hypothesis. One study found that the authoritarian foreman was a major factor in labor turnover; a second showed that there was a close relationship between the supervisor's inequitable treatment—he could not be influenced, did not support his subordinates, and did not attempt to redress employee grievances—and the turnover rate. Employees, in short, fled from unfair treatment.

One assemblage of studies would appear at first glance to contradict the model. We refer to those studies that show that lower-skilled workers appear to be more interested in how much money they make than they are in how interesting their jobs are. As John Goldthorpe and others demonstrate, however, they are merely being realists. Goldthorpe, in particular, points out repeatedly and documents in detail the fact that workers do desire intrinsically satisfying jobs, but find such aspirations to be unrealistic. In the long run, however great the reluctance and the pain, they adapt.

His research dealt with British workers but a number of studies in the United States replicate his findings. As you move up the job hierarchy, employees consistently assign a higher value to job characteristics that potentially fulfill growth needs. Medium and high-status white-collar workers, for example, placed primary emphasis on work-content factors as a source of job satisfaction, while low-status white-collar workers and blue-collar workers tended to play them down. As our model would predict, employees seek out job satisfactions they feel are second rate, because higher-level satisfactions are unattainable—certainly in their current jobs.

In summary, this research demonstrates first, that the overall impact of the formal organization on the individual is to decrease his control over his immediate work area, decrease his chance to use his abilities, and increase his dependence and submissiveness; second, that to the extent to which the individual seeks to be autonomous and function as an adult, he adapts by reactions ranging from withdrawal and noninterest, to agggression, or perhaps to the substitution of instrumental money rewards for intrinsic rewards. The weight of the deprivations and the degree of adaption increase as we descend the hierarchy. Formal organization, alas, is unintentionally designed to discourage the autonomous and involved worker.

JOB ENLARGEMENT OR ENRICHMENT

Job enlargement in the true sense, not the multiplication of meaningless tasks, but quite literally the enrichment of the job either by adding tasks that provide intrinsic satisfactions or increasing the worker's control over the tasks he already performs, obviously conforms to our models. And we would expect that employees whose jobs were enriched would be more satisfied with their jobs and less likely to manifest their dissatisfaction in ways that undermine the organization. Looking at the other side of the coin, we also would expect that more positive attitudes would be accompanied by increased productivity.

And we would not be disappointed. No fewer than eight studies testify that designing jobs that permit more self-regulation, self-evaluation, self-adjustment, and participation in goal-setting both improved attitudes and increased productivity.

Of particular importance is a study by Hackman and Lawler that correlated the core dimensions of jobs—variety, autonomy, task identity, and feedback—with motivation, satisfaction, performance, and attendance. The principle findings of their study are these:

• The higher the jobs are on core dimensions, the higher the employees are rated by their supervisors as doing better quality work and being more effective performers.

• When jobs rank high on the core dimensions, employees report feeling more intrinsically motivated to perform well.

• Core dimensions are strongly and positively related to job satisfaction and involvement.

• The job satisfaction items that strongly correlate with the job core dimension are related to control over one's own work, feeling of worthwhile accomplishment, and self-esteem.

• The strength of the relationships described above increases with those employees who seek to meet higher-order needs. This finding is significant because research seldom examines individual differences in this way.

Hackman and Lawler differentiate between horizontal enlargement—increasing the number of things an employee does—and vertical enlargment—increasing the degree to which an employee is responsible for making most major decisions about his work. They would argue and we would concur that a combination of both types of enlargement—what we have earlier called role enlargement—is optimal.

What about practice? The concept of job enrichment isn't new. A study of

IBM published in 1948 included an assessment of job enrichment and its benefits.

We would expect a concept so fulfilling, so helpful in meeting the goals of both the employee and the organization, to be widely adopted. And we would be disappointed. A recent survey of 300 of the top 1,000 *Fortune* industrials showed that only 4 percent had made any formal, systematic attempt to enrich jobs. And even they had enriched only a very small percentage of their total jobs.

What accounts for the lag in adopting job enrichment? Two factors seem to be at work and to reinforce each other. First, most managements are convinced that job enrichment doesn't pay off economically. This belief, in turn, leads them to exhibit signs of the ostrich syndrome—they ignore the accumulating body of evidence as to the substantial psychic dividends that employees derive from job enrichment.

Let me quote from just two of the voluminous research studies that demonstrate the efficiency of job enrichment. The first is the ambitious and significant attempt by the Gaines dog food division of General Foods to design an entire plant using horizontal and vertical enlargement of work. The key features of the design are the following:

(1) Autonomous work groups that develop their own production schedules, manage production problems, screen and select new members, maintain self-policing activities, and decide questions such as who gets time off and who fills which work station.

(2) Integrated support functions. Each work team performs its own maintenance, quality control, and industrial engineering functions—plus challenging job assignments.

(3) Job mobility and rewards for learning. People are paid not on the basis of the job they are doing, but on the basis of the number of jobs that they are prepared to do.

(4) Self-government for the plant community.

The transition from a work environment on the infant ends of our continua to the adult ends was not easy for the people involved. Drastic change never is, even when the participants benefit from the change. The results to date, however, are impressive. A similar plant, organized along traditional lines, would require 110 employees; this one was manned by 70. The plant has met or exceeded production goals. Employees reported greater opportunities for learning and self-actualization. And team leaders and plant managers were more involved in community affairs than foremen and managers of comparable plants.

A second significant experiment in job enlargement is taking place at Volvo's new auto assembly plant in Kalmar, Sweden, Volvo faced serious problems—wildcat strikes, absenteeism, and turnover that were getting out of hand. Turnover in the old car assembly plant was over 40 percent annually. Absenteeism was running 20 to 25 percent. Now, assembly has been divided among teams of 15 to 25 workers, who will decide how to distribute the job of car assembly among themselves. Each team determines its own work pace, subject to meeting production standards that are set for them. Each team selects its own boss, and deselects him if it's unhappy with him.

The new plant cost approximately 10 percent more than it would have if it had been constructed along traditional lines. Will the benefits justify the extra expense? Time alone will tell—the plant has been on stream for only a matter of months—but Pehr Gyllenhammar, the managing director of Volvo, hopes that it will realize both his economic and social objectives: "A way must be found to create a workplace that meets the needs of the modern working man for a sense of purpose and satisfaction in his daily work. A way must be found of attaining this goal without an adverse effect on production."

THE MODEL OF MAN AND THE DESIGN OF ORGANIZATION

Organizations depend on people. Thus, many organizational variables are designed around an explicit or implicit model of man. Taylor's molecularized jobs, for example, took a one-dimensional view of man and assumed that one could hire a hand; by contrast, the champions of vertical and horizontal job enrichment assume that one hires a whole human being.

Then there are the theorists who take the sociological viewpoint and impoverish their theories by ignoring the psychological element and treating man as a black box.

In each case the complexity of organizational reality leads them into contradictions, the significance of which they either play down or ignore altogether. Crozier, for example, although lacking an explicit model of man, also concluded that his data did not confirm the inhumanity of organizations toward individuals—but how can one define inhumanity without a concept of man? Nevertheless, in the same work he stated that monotonous and repetitive work produces nervous tension in workers, that apathy and social isolation are great, and that work loads produce pressure.

Charles Perrow is a technological determinist who argues that the structure of organization depends on the requirements of the technology. An electronics plant making components should have a different structure from one making inertial guidance system components because of differences in the kind of research required by their technology, unanalyzable versus analyzable, or the number of exceptions it requires—few or many. Perrow's insight, valid but partial, is an inadequate concept to explain the total relationship between man and organization, an inadequacy that Perrow himself is coming to recognize. He concedes that "personality factors can have a great deal of influence upon the relations between coordination and subordinate power," that Robert McNamara, for example, was the key factor in changes in the Defense Department.

To elevate any one as *the* defining characteristic of organizations as Perrow did with technology and make all other characteristics dependent variables only leads to poor theory and inadequate and incomplete explanations of behavior in organizations. An error of equal magnitude is to ignore either the sociological or the psychological view in studying organizations.

We need a synthesis of the sociological and psychological views in studying man and a recognition that there are no fewer than four sets of independent but interacting characteristics that determine the behavior of any organization—structure and technology, leadership and interpersonal relations, administrative controls and regulations, and human controls. The strength of each of the four will vary from organization to organization, vary within different parts of the same organization, and vary over time within the same parts of each organization. However, any major change in an organization's structure is doomed to failure unless major changes take place in all four characteristics.

RATIONAL MAN DECISION THEORISTS

In addition to those with no explicit model of man we have the rational man decision theorists such as Simon, Cyert, and March, whose partial view of man focuses on the concept of man as a finite information processing system striving to be rational and to "satisfice" in his decision making. What this model neglects are the issues stressed by P. and O. theory, such as dependence, submissiveness, the need for psychological success, confirmation, and feelings of essentiality. As we have written elsewhere, "Simon saw management's task as designing organizational structures and mechanisms of organization influence which ingrained into the nervous system of every member what the organization required him to do. Intendedly, rational man was expected to follow authority, but he was also given appropriate and indirect inducements to produce."

Cyert and March retain the basic perspectives of the pyramidal structure—specialization of tasks and centralization of power and information—but they add elements of reality and sophistication. By cranking into their models the concepts of people as members of coalitions politicking against each other for scarce resources and settling for the quasi-reduction of conflicts between them, they were able to predict more accurately how the organization was going to behave, for example, in setting prices.

That the rational man thinkers have indeed helped managers to make more effective decisions in some situations—those in which the factors involved corresponded to their model—shouldn't lead us to ignore the more frequent situations in which the rational man theories were either a poor predictive tool or acted themselves to exacerbate the situation. Recent research suggests that managers may resist the management information systems designed by the rational man theorists precisely because they work well—for example, accomplish the desired objective or reducing uncertainty. What accounts for the apparent paradox? Man is not primariiy rational, or rather he reacts in response to what we like to call the rationality of feelings. He dislikes being dependent and submissive toward others; he recognizes the increased probability that when management information systems work best he will tend to experience psychological failure. The organization's goals are being met at the expense of his own. Management information systems, in consequence, have become to managers at many levels what time-study people were to the rank and file years ago—an object of fear commingled with hatred and aggression.

Another trend that totally escapes the rational man theorists is the increasing hostility of an increasing number of young people toward the idea that organizations should be able to buy off people to be primarily rational, to submit to the mechanisms of organizational influence, and to suppress their feelings.

A third trend flows from the combined impact of the first two. Given the inability to predict the relationship of emotionality versus rationality in any particular context, and the reaction against rational man and organizational mechanisms of influence, add to these elements the largely unintended support of the status quo, and the use of "satisficing" to rationalize incompetence, and we end up with an interaction of forces that makes change in organizations seem almost impossible.

Hard to follow or accept? The line of argument is as follows:

(1) To the degree that man accepts inducements to behave rationally, he acts passively in relation to the way power, information, and work are designed in the organization.

(2) Over time, such individuals sterilize their self-actualizing tendencies by any one or a combination of approaches: They suppress them, deny them, or destroy them. Eventually, they come to see their legitimate role in the organization—at least, as it bears on the design of power, information, and tasks—as pawns rather than as initiators.

(3) A little further down the road, individuals come to view being passive and controlled as good, natural, and necessary. Eventually, they may define responsibility and maturity in these terms.

(4) Individuals soon create managerial cultures—some have already done so—in which the discussion of self-actualizing possibilities is viewed as inappropriate.

(5) The youth who because of the very success of the system are able to focus more on the self-actualizing needs will attempt to change things. They will come up, however, against facts one to four and end up terribly frustrated.

(6) The frustration will tend to lead to regression, with two probably polarized consequences—withdrawal into communes or militancy.

(7) Because we know very little about how to integrate self-actualizing activities with rational activities, older people will resent the hostility of youth or look upon their withdrawal as a cop-out.

The last and most important point is that the rational man theory, unlike P. and O. theory, could not predict the single most important trend about public and private organizations—their increasing internal deterioration and lack of effectiveness in producing services or products. As citizen, consumer, and presumably an organization man, you either feel it or you don't. We do feel strongly on this score. And we cite that while 25 years ago 75 percent of the respondents in a national survey felt that public and private organizations performed well, only 25 percent had the same opinion in 1972. How many believe that the percentage would be higher today?

THE CASE FOR NORMATIVE RESEARCH

Most of the research that we have reviewed has been descriptive research that contents itself with describing, understanding, and predicting human behavior within organizations. In our research the emphasis is normative and based upon the potentialities of man. We're interested in studying man in terms of what he is capable of, not merely how he currently behaves within organizations.

Looked at from this normative viewpoint, the most striking fact about most organizations is the limited opportunities they afford most employees to fulfill their potential. We can show empirically that the interpersonal world of most people in ongoing organizations is characterized by much more distrust, conformity, and closedness than trust, individuality, and openness. This world—we call it Pattern A—fits with, if indeed it isn't derived from, the values about effective human behavior endemic in the pyramidal structure or in what Simon calls the mechanisms of organizational influence. Thus, findings based on descriptive research will tend to opt for the status quo.

Moreover, unless we conduct research on new worlds, scholars will tend to use data obtained in the present world as evidence that people do not want to change. Many of them are doing so already. What they forget is how human beings can desire or even contemplate worlds that they have learned from experience to view as unrealistic.

Take a recent publication by Ernest Gross in which he suggests that concepts like individual dignity and self-development probably reflect academic values instead of employee desires, because employees rarely report the need to express such values. The question still remains whether this state of affairs implies that people should accept them and should be trained to adapt to them. Gross appears to think so. He stated that there is little one can do by way of providing opportunities for self-actualization and, if it were possible, providing them would frighten some people. Furthermore, he noted that assembly-line jobs didn't require a worker to demonstrate initiative or to desire variety. "One wants him (the worker) simply to work according to an established pace. Creativity, then, is not always desirable."

Note the logic. Gross starts by asserting that the P. and O. theorists cannot state that one *should* (his italics) provide workers with more challenge or autonomy in accordance with their values because to do so would be to rest their case not on a scientific theory, but on a program for organizations. Then he suggests that no one has proved how harmful dissatisfaction, anxiety, dependency, and conformity are to the individual—which is probably correct. He goes on to argue that these conditions are, to a degree, both unavoidable and helpful, although offering no empirical data to support his assertion. Then he concludes that employees should be educated to live within this world:

Perhaps the most general conclusion we can draw is that since organizations appear to be inevitable . . . a major type of socialization of the young ought to include methods for dealing with the organization. . . . [For example] an important consideration in the preparation of individuals for work should include training for the handling of or adjustment to authority.

At this point Gross has taken a normative position, but one with which I vigorously dissent.

I am very concerned about those who hold that job enrichment may not be necessary because workers in an automobile factory have about the same attitude toward their jobs as do workers in jobs with greater freedom and job variety. But what is the meaning of the response to a question such as "How satisfied would you say you are with your present job?" if the man is working under conditions of relative deprivation? We think that what it means is that workers recognize that they are boxed in, that few opportunities are available to them for better-paid or more interesting work; in consequence, they become satisfied with the jobs they have because the jobs they want are unobtainable. It is frequently observed that the greatest dissatisfaction on a routine job occurs during the first years. After three to five years, the individual adapts to the job and feels satisfied. On the other hand, Neil Herrick in a recent book with the catchy title *Where Have All the Robots Gone?* reported that for the first time, there was a major drop in the number of Americans expressing job satisfaction.

That most jobs as currently designed are routine and provide few opportunities for self-actualization, that the social norms and the political actions that support these norms tend to produce mostly individuals who simultaneously value and fear growth and who strive for security and safety, tell only part of the unfortunate tale of the present industrial conditions. Employees perceive— and the perception is accurate—that few men at the top want to increase their opportunities for self-actualization; even fewer men at the top are competent to do the job.

Make no mistake—employees are conservative on this issue. They have no interest in seeing their physiological and security needs frustrated or denied because their organization collapsed while trying to increase their chances for self-actualization. And the possibility of such a collapse is a real one. Our own experience and the published research combine to suggest that there now does not exist a top-management group so competent in meeting the requirements of the new ethic that they do not lose their competence under stress. With expert help and heavy emphasis on top-management education, one such group was still encountering great difficulties after five years of attempting to raise the quality of life within its organization.

If the ethic, as employees themselves recognize, is so difficult to realize in practice, is the effort worthwhile? Is a game with so many incompetent players worth the playing?

On two counts we feel strongly that it is: First, on normative grounds we feel that social science research has an obligation to help design a better world. Secondly, we feel that the game is worth the playing because eventually some people and some organizations can be helped to play it effectively. Take the case of job enrichment. Let us assume that all jobs can be enriched. The assumption is probably unrealistic; many jobs in fact, can never be enriched. If we opt for the world that is psychologically richer, however, we will induce employees at every level into developing whatever opportunities for enrichment exist in each job situation.

I believe with Maslow in taking the behavior that characterizes rare peak experiences and making it the behavior toward which all employees should aspire. The skeptic argues that such behavior is so rare that it is useless to try to achieve it. I agree that the behavior is rare, but go on to plead for systematic research that will tell us how the behavior may be made more frequent. Twenty years ago no one had pole-vaulted higher than 16 feet. Yet no one took this as a given. Today the 16-foot mark is broken continually because people refused to view the status quo as the last word and focused on enhancing the potentiality of man. Over time, a similar focus on enhancing the potentiality of man-on-the-job should produce similar breakthroughs.

Organizational Motivation

The New Look in Motivation Theory for Organizational Research*

by
J.G. Hunt
J.W. Hill

During the last few years the treatment of motivation with respect to industrial and other formal organizations has more often than not been in terms of models by Maslow or Herzberg.[1] Where theories are apparently so thoroughly accepted, one naturally assumes a fairly substantial amount of data leading to empirical verification. However, as we shall show, there is relatively little empirical evidence concerning Maslow's theory; and while there are many studies bearing on Herzberg's theory, it remains controversial. After comparing these two approaches and reviewing their present status, we will describe a newer motivation theory developed by Vroom, which is similar to those developed by Atkinson et al. and Edwards in experimental psychology, and Peak, Rosenberg and Fishbein in social psychology.[2] It is our contention, on both theoretical and empirical grounds, that Vroom's theory, more than Maslow's or Herzberg's, is in line with the thinking of contemporary psychologists and industrial sociologists and is the best yet developed for organizational use.

THE MASLOW MODEL

Maslow's theory hypothesizes five broad classes of needs arranged in hierarchical levels of prepotency so that when one need level is satisfied, the next level is activated. The levels are: (1) physiological needs; (2) security or safety needs; (3) social, belonging, or membership needs; (4) Esteem needs

---

*Reproduced by permission of the Society for Applied Anthropology from *Human Organization* 28(2), 1969.

further subdivided into esteem of others and self-esteem including autonomy; and (5) self-actualization or self-fulfillment needs.

The original papers present very little empirical evidence in support of the theory and no research at all that tests the model in its entirety. Indeed, Maslow argues that the theory is primarily a framework for future research. He also discusses at length some of the limitations of the model and readily admits that these needs may be unconscious rather than conscious. While Maslow discusses his model and its limitations in detail, a widely publicized paper by McGregor gives the impression that the Model can be accepted without question and also that it is fairly easy to apply.[3] In truth, the model is difficult to test, which is probably why there are so few empirical studies to either prove or refute the theory.

Porter provides the most empirical data concerning the model.[4] At the conscious level he measures all except the physiological needs. His samples are based only on managers, but they cover different managerial levels in a wide range of business organizations in the United States and thirteen other countries. Porter's studies have a number of interesting findings, but here we are primarily concerned with two: (1) in the United States and Britain (but not in the other twelve countries) there tends to be a hierarchical satisfaction of needs as Maslow hypothesizes; and (2) regardless of country or managerial level there is a tendency for those needs which managers feel are most important to be least satisfied.

A study by Beer of female clerks provides additional data concerning the model.[5] He examines the relationship between participative and considerate or human relations oriented supervisory leadership styles and satisfaction of needs. He also goes one step further and argues that need satisfaction, as such, does not necessarily lead to motivation. Rather, motivation results only from need satisfaction which occurs in the process of task oriented work. He reasons that a participative leadership style should meet this condition since it presumably allows for the satisfaction of the higher order needs (self-actualization, autonomy, and esteem). Beer found that workers forced to arrange needs in a hierarchy (as required by his ranking method) tend to arrange them as predicted by Maslow. He also found that self-actualization, autonomy, and social needs were most important, while esteem and security needs were least important, although his method (unlike Porter's) did not allow a consideration of the relationship between importance and need satisfaction. Interestingly enough, there was no significant relationship between need satisfaction and Beer's measure of motivation nor between any of the leadership style dimensions and motivation. There were, however, significant relationships between leadership style dimensions and need satisfaction. Beer concludes that the model has questionable usefulness for a theory of industrial motivation although it may provide a fairly reliable measurement of the a priori needs of industrial workers.

We have found only three studies that systematically consider the Maslow theory in terms of performance.[6]

The first of these, by Clark, attempts to fit a number of empirical studies conducted for different purposes into a framework which provides for progressive activation and satisfaction of needs at each of the hierarchical levels. The findings are used to make predictions concerning productivity, absenteeism, and turnover as each need level is activated and then satisfied. While the article does not explicitly test the Maslow model, it is highly suggestive in terms of hypotheses for future research that might relate the theory to work group performance.

A second study, by Lawler and Porter, correlates satisfaction of managers' needs (except physiological) with rankings of their performance by superiors and peers. All correlations are significant but low, ranging from 0.16 to 0.30. Lawler and Porter conclude that satisfaction of higher order needs is more closely related to performance than satisfaction of lower order needs. However, the differences are not very great and they are not tested for significance. For example, correlations of superior ratings for the lower order security and social needs are 0.21 and 0.23, while for the higher order esteem, autonomy, and self-actualization needs they are 0.24, 0.18, and 0.30. Peer correlations are similar. Thus, unlike Lawler and Porter, we conclude that in this study the correlations for lower order needs are about the same as for higher order needs.

A more recent Porter and Lawler investigation seems to provide additional support for their earlier findings by showing that higher order needs accounted for more relationships significant at the 0.01 level than lower order needs. However, they do not report correlations between these needs and performance and so we cannot evaluate their conclusion as we did for their earlier study.

THE HERZBERG MODEL

A second frequently mentioned motivational model is that proposed by Herzberg and his associates in 1959.[7] They used a semi-structured interview technique to get respondents to recall events experienced at work which resulted in a marked improvement or a marked reduction in their job satisfaction. Interviewees were also asked, among other things, how their feelings of satisfaction or dissatisfaction affected their work performance, personal relationships, and well-being. Content analysis of the interviews suggested that certain job characteristics led to job satisfaction, while different job characteristics led to job dissatisfaction. For instance, job achievement was related to satisfaction while working conditions were related to dissatisfaction. Poor conditions led to dissatisfaction, but good conditions did not necessarily lead to satisfaction. Thus, satisfaction and dissatisfaction are not simple opposites. Hence a two-factor theory of satisfaction is needed.

The job content characteristics which produced satisfaction were called "motivators" by Herzberg and his associates because they satisfied the individual's need for self-actualization at work. The job environment characteristics which led to satisfaction were called "hygienes" because they were work-supporting or contextual rather than task-determined and hence were analogous to the "preventative" or "environmental" factors recognized in medicine. According to this dichotomy, motivators include achievement, recognition, advancement, possibility of growth, responsibility, and work itself. Hygienes, on the other hand, include salary; interpersonal relations with superiors, subordinates, and peers; technical supervision; company policy and administration; personal life; working conditions; status; and job security.

There is considerable empirical evidence for this theory. Herzberg himself, in a summary of research through early 1966, includes ten studies of seventeen populations which used essentially the same method as his original study.[8] In addition, he reviews twenty more studies which used a variety of methodologies to test the two-factor theory. Of the studies included in his review, those using his critical incident method generally confirm the theory. Those using other methods give less clear results, which Herzberg acknowledges but attempts to dismiss for methodological reasons. At least nine other studies, most of which have appeared since Herzberg's 1966 review, raise even more doubts about the theory.[9]

While it is beyond the scope of the present article to consider these studies in detail, they raise serious questions as to whether the factors leading to satisfaction and dissatisfaction are really different from each other. A number of the studies show that certain job dimensions appear to be more important for both satisfaction and dissatisfaction. Dunnette, Campbell, and Hakel, for example, conclude from these and also from their own studies that Herzberg is shackled to his method and that achievement, recognition, and responsibility seem important for both satisfaction and dissatisfaction, while such dimensions as security, salary, and working conditions are less important.[10] They also raise by implication an issue concerning Herzberg's methodology which deserves further comment. That is, if data are analyzed in terms of percentage differences between groups, one result is obtained; if they are analyzed in terms of ranks within groups, another result occurs. The first type of analysis is appropriate for identifying factors which account for differences between events (as Herzberg did in his original hypothesis). The second type of analysis is appropriate if we want to know the most important factors within the event categories (which is what Herzberg claims he was doing). Analyzing the findings of Dunnette and his colleagues by the first method, we confirm Herzberg's theory; but if we rank the findings within categories, as Dunnette et al. also did, we find no confirmation. If we want to know whether "achievement" is important in job satisfaction we must look at its relative rank among other factors mentioned in the events leading to satisfaction, not whether it is mentioned a greater percentage of the time in satisfying events than in dissatisfying events. This distinction in analytical methods was discussed several years ago by Viteles and even earlier by Kornhauser.[11]

We conclude that any meaningful discussion of Herzberg's theory must recognize negative evidence even though the model seems to make a great deal of intuitive sense. Much the same can be said of Maslow's theory.

FURTHER CONSIDERATIONS IN USING THE MASLOW AND HERZBERG THEORIES

Putting aside for the moment the empirical considerations presented by the two models, it is instructive to compare them at the conceptual level suggested in Figure 1. While the figure shows obvious similarities between the Maslow and Herzberg models, there are important differences as well. Where Maslow assumes that any need can be a motivator if it is relatively unsatisfied, Herzberg argues that only the higher order needs serve as motivators and that a worker can have unsatisfied needs in both the hygiene and motivator areas simultaneously. One might argue that the reason higher order needs are motivators is that lower order needs have essentially been satisfied. However, Herzberg presents some evidence that even in relatively low level blue collar and service jobs, where presumably lower order needs are less well-satisfied, the higher order needs are still the only ones seen by the workers as motivators.[12]

FIGURE 1

Maslow's Need-Priority Model Compared with Herzberg's
Motivation-Hygiene Model°

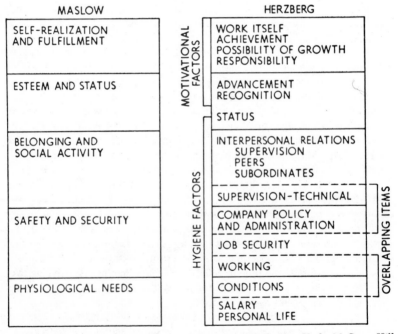

° Adapted from K. Davis, *Human Relations at Work.* New York: McGraw-Hill, 1967, p. 37.

Another important consideration is the relationship of these models to the accomplishment of organizational objectives. Even if there were unequivocal empirical support for the theories, there is need to translate the findings into usable incentives for promoting such objectives as superior performance, lower turnover, lower absenteeism, etc. If not, they are of little use to industrial organizations. As indicated earlier, there is relatively little evidence empirically relating Maslow's model to performance, or even to psychological well-being. Furthermore, the one Lawler and Porter study seems to show that satisfaction of higher and lower order needs are about equally related to performance, although their later investigation suggests that the former are more strongly related to performance than the latter. But we cannot tell for sure because correlations and differences between correlations are not reported.

Similarly, although Herzberg asked his respondents for effects of job events on their performance, he reports only two studies which attempt to measure performance independent of the respondent's estimate. These seem to show the performance is favorably influenced as more "motivators" are provided in the job.[13] However, insufficient data are presented to permit evaluation of the adequacy of the experimental design and performance measures. A study of Friedlander and Walton that considered employee turnover used a modification of Herzberg's technique and found that employees' reasons for staying on the job were different from their reasons for leaving.[14] The reasons for staying would be called "motivators" while those for leaving were "hygiene" factors.

We conclude that Herzberg's two-factor theory may be related to turnover and performance; but present studies are subject to serious criticisms. And we could find only two empirical investigations which related Maslow's model to any of these outputs.

In addition, it should be noted that neither model adequately handles the theoretical problem of some kind of linkage by which individual need satisfaction is related to the achievement of organizational objectives. Given the present formulation, it is entirely possible that there can be need satisfaction which is not necessarily directed toward the accomplishment of organizational goals. For example, an important organizational objective might be increased production, but workers might conceivably receive more need satisfaction from turning out a higher quality product at a sacrifice in quantity. They might also be meeting their needs through identification with a work group with strong sanctions against "rate busting."

Finally, neither of these theories as they stand can really handle the problem of individual differences in motivation. Maslow, for example, explains that his model may not hold for persons with particular experiences. His theory is therefore nonpredictive because data that do not support it can be interpreted in terms of individual differences in previous need gratification leading to greater or lesser prepotency of a given need category.[15] Herzberg, in similar fashion, describes seven types of people differentiated by the extent to which they are motivator or hygiene seekers, or some combination of the two, although he never relates these differences empirically to actual job performance. We turn then to a model which explicitly recognizes these issues and appears to offer great potential for understanding motivation in organizations.

THE VROOM MODEL

Brayfield and Crockett as long ago as 1955 suggested an explicit theoretical linkage between satisfaction, motivation, and the organizational goal of productivity. They said:

> It makes sense to us to assume that individuals are motivated to achieve certain environmental goals and that the achievement of these goals results in satisfaction. Productivity is seldom a goal in itself but is more commonly a means to goal attainment. Therefore, . . . we might expect high satisfaction and high productivity to occur together when productivity is perceived as a path to certain important goals and when these goals are achieved.[16]

Georgopoulas, Mahoney, and Jones provide some early empirical support for this notion in their test of the "path-goal hypothesis."[17] Essentially, they argue that an individual's motivation to produce at a given level depends upon his particular needs as reflected in the goals toward which he is moving and his perception of the relative usefulness of productivity behavior as a path to attainment of these goals. They qualify this, however, by saying that the need must be sufficiently high, no other economical paths must be available to the individual, and there must be a lack of restraining practices.

More recently, Vroom has developed a motivational model which extends the above concepts and is also related to earlier work of experimental and social psychologists.[18] He defines motivation as a "process governing choices, made by persons or lower organisms, among alternative forms of voluntary activity."[19] The concept is incorporated in Figure 2, which depicts Vroom's model graphically. Here, the individual is shown as a role occupant faced with a set of alternative "first-level outcomes." His preference choice among these first-level outcomes is determined by their expected relationship to possible "second-level outcomes."

Two concepts are introduced to explain the precise method of determining preferences for these first-level outcomes. These concepts are valence and instrumentality. Valence refers to the strength of an individual's desire for a particular outcome. Instrumentality indicates an individual's perception of the relationship between a first-level outcome and a second-level outcome or, in other words, the extent to which a first-level outcome is seen as leading to the accomplishment of a second-level outcome.

Valence is measured by instructing workers to rank important individual goals in order of their desirability, or they may rate goals on Likert-types scales. Instrumentality can be measured by rating scales which involve perceived differences in the direction and strength of relationships between various first- and second-level outcomes. Important goals of industrial workers

FIGURE 2

Vroom's Motivational Model[°]

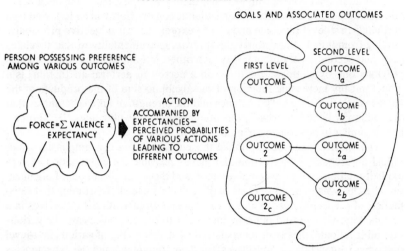

* Adapted from M. D. Dunnette, "The Motives of Industrial Managers," *Organizational Behavior and Human Performance*, Vol. 2, 1967, p. 178. (Copyright, Academic Press, Inc.)

often cited in the empirical behavioral science literature are promotion, pay, pleasant working conditions, and job security. The goals can be ranked by individual workers in terms of their desirability. The resulting scores are measures of valence. In addition, each individual can be instructed to indicate on an appropriate scale the likelihood that a certain job behavior, e.g., high productivity, will lead to each of the four goals described. This score is the instrumental relationship between productivity and a specified goal. Obviously there are alternative methods of measurement available for the concepts; we will leave these for a more detailed discussion later.

Vroom expresses the valence of a first-level outcome to a person "as a monotonically increasing function of an algebraic sum of the products of the valences of all [second-level] outcomes and his conceptions of its instrumentality for the attainment of the [second-level] outcomes."[20]

For example, assume that an individual desires promotion and feels that superior performance is a very strong factor in achieving that goal. His first-level outcomes are then superior, average, or poor performance. His second-level outcome is promotion. The first-level outcome of high performance thus acquires a positive valence by virtue of its expected relationship to the preferred second-level outcome of promotion. Assuming no negative second-level outcomes associated with high performance and no other first-level outcomes that contribute to promotion, we expect motivation toward superior performance because promotion is important and superior performance is seen as instrumental in its accomplishment. Or, to put it in Vroom's terms, performance varies directly with the product of the valence of the reward (promotion) and the perceived instrumentality of performance for the attainment of the reward.

An additional concept in Vroom's theory is expectancy. This is a belief concerning the likelihood that a particular action or effort will be followed by a particular first-level outcome and can be expressed as a subjective probability ranging from 0 to 1. Expectancy differs from instrumentality in that it relates first- and second-level outcomes to each other. Vroom ties this concept to his previous one by stating, "the force on a person to perform an [action] is a monotonically increasing function of the algebraic sum of the products of the valences of all [first-level] outcomes and the strength of his expectancies that the [action] will be followed by the attainment of these outcomes."[21] "Force" here is similar to our concept of motivation.

This motivational model, unlike those discussed earlier, emphasizes individual differences in motivation and makes possible the examination of very explicit relationships between motivation and the accomplishment of organizational goals, whatever these goals may be. Thus instead of assuming that satisfaction of a specific need is likely to influence organizational objectives in a certain way, we can find out how important to the employees are the various second-level outcomes (worker goals), the instrumentality of various first-level outcomes (organizational objectives) for their attainment, and the expectancies that are held with respect to the employees' ability to influence the first-level outcomes.

EMPIRICAL TESTS OF VROOM'S MODEL

Vroom has already shown how his model can integrate many of the empirical findings in the literature on motivation in organizations.[22] However, because it is a relatively recent development, empirical tests of the model itself are just beginning to appear. Here we shall consider four such investigations.

In the first study, Vroom is concerned with predicting the organizational choices of graduating college students on the basis of their instrumentality-goal index scores.[23] These scores reflect the extent to which membership in an organization was perceived by the student as being related to the acquisition of desired goals. According to the theory, the chosen organization should be the one with the highest instrumentality-goal index. Ratings were used to obtain preferences for fifteen different goals and the extent to which these goals could be attained through membership in three different organizations. These two ratings were thus measures of the valences of second-level outcomes and the instrumentality of organizational membership for attainment of these outcomes, respectively. The instrumentality-goal index was the correlation between these two measures. But Vroom's theory also involves consideration of expectancy, i.e., how probable it is that the student can become a member of a particular organization. The choice is not his alone but depends upon whether he is acceptable to the organization. A rough measure of expectancy in this study was whether or not the student had received an offer by the organization. If he had received an offer, expectancy would be high; if not, it would be low.

The results show that, considering only organizations from which offers of employment were actually received, 76 percent of the students chose the organization with the highest instrumentality-goal index score. The evidence thus strongly supports Vroom's theory.

The next study, by Galbraith and Cummings, utilizes the model to predict the productivity of operative workers.[24] Graphic rating scales were used to measure the instrumentality of performance for five goals—money, fringe benefits, promotion, supervisor's support, and group acceptance. Similar ratings were used for measuring the desirability of each of the goals for the worker. The authors anticipated that a worker's expectation that he could produce at a high level would have a probability of one because the jobs were independent and productivity was a function of the worker's own effort independent of other human or machine pacing. Figure 3 outlines the research design.

Multiple regression analysis showed that productivity was significantly related positively to the instrumentality-goal interactions for supervisor support and money, and there was an almost significant (p<0.10) relationship with group acceptance. The other factors did not approach significance and the authors explain this lack of significance in terms of the situational context. That is, fringe benefits were dependent not so much on productivity as on a union/management contact, and promotion was based primarily on seniority. Thus the instrumentality of productivity for the attainment of these goals was

FIGURE 3

Individual Goals and Productivity as Measured by Vroom's
Model in One Industrial Plant°

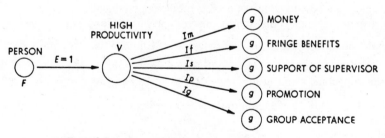

g = Desirability of a particular outcome (rating).
I = Instrumentality of production for particular outcomes (rating of relationship).
E = Expectancy (=1 here because worker sets own pace and is assumed to be capable of high productivity).
V = (Valence) the sum of the cross products of instrumentality and g.
F = (Force) expectency times the valence of productivity.
Productivity = Objective measures of amount of production in relation to the production standard.

low and the model would predict no relationship. The Galbraith and Cummings study thus supports Vroom's contention that motivation is related to productivity in those situations where the acquisition of desired goals is dependent upon the individual's production and not when desired outcomes are contingent on other factors.

A third study is that of Hill relating a model similar to Vroom's to behavior in a utility company.[25] Hill's model is based upon Edwards' subjective expected utility maximization theory of decision making.[26] Here one given a choice between alternatives A and/or B will select that alternative which maximizes his subjective expected utility or expected value. If the outcomes associated with action A are more desirable than those associated with B, and their probability of occurrence is greater than or equal to those associated with B, then an individual will choose behavior A over behavior B. The basic concepts are subjective expectation and subjective utility or valence. Expectation and utility are multiplicatively related and can be measured by the same techniques used to test Vroom's theory. Where a relationship is found between Subjective Expected Utility (SEU) and overt behavior, it can be interpreted by support for Vroom.

The behavior considered in Hill's study is that of job bidding. This behavior is encountered in organizations that post descriptions of job openings on employee bulletin boards and encourage qualified employees to "bid" (apply) for them. Here records were kept of the number of bids made over a three-year period by groups of semiskilled electrical repairmen matched in learning ability, seniority in grade, and age. The men were asked about the consequences of bidding and not bidding on the next higher grade job, and rated the consequence on a seven-point scale of desirability and a similar scale of probability of occurrence. Bidders were those who had bid three or more times during that time.

Fourteen different SEU indices were computed from interview data to determine the relative validity of each in predicting bidding behavior. Typical of these indices were: (1) the sums of the cross products of expectation and utility for the positive consequences of bidding ($\Sigma \overset{+}{SEU}$); (2) the same score for the negative consequences of bidding ($\Sigma \overset{-}{SEU}$); and (3) the cross products of the mean expectation and utility scores for positive and negative consequences $\left(\dfrac{\Sigma \overset{+}{SEU}}{N}, \dfrac{\Sigma \overset{-}{SEU}}{N} \right)$. In addition to these SEU indices, two traditional attitudinal and motivational measures were used. Semantic differential scales measured each subject's respective evaluation of bidding and the next higher grade job and each subject's need for achievement was obtained.[27]

It was hypothesized that: (1) there would be a positive correlation betweem the SEU indices and bidding; and (2) the SEU indices would be more highly related to bidding behavior than the traditional measures.

We do not discuss relationships for all of the indices here but do consider results for one of the more comprehensive indices and those from multiple regression analysis. This index is the algebraic sum of the cross products of the positive and negative consequences of bidding minus the same score for not bidding for each individual. The correlation of this index with bidding was 0.26, $p < 0.05$ for a one-tailed test. The correlations between the two semantic differential scales and bidding were -0.09 and -0.25, respectively. Neither of these is significant for a one-tailed test predicting a positive correlation. The correlation between need for achievement and bidding was a nonsignificant 0.17. A multiple regression analysis determined the relative contribution of the SEU indices to the prediction of bidding. A variable was selected for analysis on the basis of its relationship to the criterion and its intercorrelation with the other predictors. The multiple correlation for bidding and seven selected variables was 0.61, $p < 0.05$. This correlation included four SEU indices, all of which had higher beta weights than the semantic differentials or need for achievement. Thus these variables accounted for more variance in the criterion than did the traditional attitudinal and motivational measures. Both hypotheses were therefore confirmed. This study adds support to the usefulness of this type of model in the study of motivation.

Finally, Lawler and Porter report a study that attempts to relate managerial attitudes to job performance rankings by superiors and peers.[28] In it, 145 managers from five different organizations completed questionnaires concerning seven kinds of rewards, and their expectations that different kinds of behavior would lead to these rewards. The expectations and the ratings of the importance of instrumentality and valence, respectively, were combined multiplicatively to yield multiple correlations which were significantly related to supervisor and peer rankings of the manager's effort to perform his job well. The correlations were higher with effort to perform the job than with the rankings of job performance. Lawler and Porter predicted this result because they reasoned that job performance is influenced by variables other than motivation, e.g., by ability and role perceptions. Of course, Vroom's model is not a behavioral theory but one of motivation only. Motivation is not going to improve performance if ability is low or role perceptions are inaccurate. Vroom's model explains how goals influence effort and that is exactly the relationship found by Lawler and Porter.

CONCLUSION

Taken together, the four studies discussed in the previous section seem to show that Vroom's model holds great promise for predicting behavior in organizations. There still remain some unanswered questions. We do not know all of the goals that have positive valence in a work situation. We do not know how much of a difference in force is necessary before one kind of outcome is chosen over another. Nor do we know what combination of measures yields the best prediction in a given situation. The answers to these and other questions await further research.

One more point should perhaps be made concerning the four studies and their measurement of Vroom's concepts. While it is true that all of them used subjective measures, the model can in fact be tested with more objective devices. Instrumentality can be inferred from organization practices, expectations can be manipulated by instructions, and goals can be inferred from observed approach and avoidance behaviors. Of course, all of these techniques require assumptions concerning their relationship to the worker's subjective perceptions of the situation; but the model is certainly not bound to the methods of measurement used so far. In fact, Vroom specifies in considerable detail the different kinds of techniques that might be used to test his model.[29]

More work must be done before we can make any statements concerning the overall validity of Vroom's model. But the rigor of his formulation, the relative ease of making the concepts operational, and the model's emphasis on individual differences show considerable promise. We are also encouraged by the results of relatively sophisticated studies testing the theory. We believe it is time for those interested in organizational behavior to take a more thoroughly scientific look at this very complex subject of industrial motivation, and Vroom's model seems a big step in that direction.

END NOTES

1. A.H. Maslow, *Motivation and Personality,* New York: Harper and Row, 1954; "A Theory of Human Motivation," *Psychological Review,* Vol. 50, 1943, pp. 370–396; and *Eupsychian Management,* Homewood, Illinois: Irwin-Dorsey, 1965; F. Herzberg, B. Mausner, and B.B. Snyderman, *The Motivation to Work.* New York: Wiley, 1959; and F. Herzberg, *Work and the Nature of Man.* Cleveland, Ohio: World Publishing Co., 1966, pp. 130–131. V.H. Vroom, *Work and Motivation.* New York: Wiley, 1964.

2. J.W. Atkinson, J.R. Bastian, R.W. Earl, and G.H. Litwin, "The Achievement Motive, Goal Setting, and Probability Preferences," *Journal of Abnormal and Social Psychology,* Vol. 60, 1960, pp. 27–36; W. Edwards, "Behavioral Decision Theory," *Annual Review of Psychology.* Palo Alto, California: Annual Reviews Inc., 1961, pp. 473–499; H. Peak, "Attitude and Motivation," *Nebraska Symposium on Motivation.* Lincoln, Nebraska: University of Nebraska Press, 1955, pp. 148–184. M. Rosenberg, "Cognitive Structure and Attitudinal Affect," *Journal of Abnormal and Social Psychology,* Vol. 53, 1956, pp. 367–372; M. Fishbein, "An Operational Definition of Belief and Attitude," *Human Relations,* Vol. 15, 1962, pp. 35–43.

3. D. McGregor, "Adventure in Thought and Action," *Proceedings of the Fifth Anniversary Convocation of the School of Industrial Management, Massachusetts Institute of Technology.* Cambridge, Massachusetts: Massachusetts Institute of Technology, 1957, pp. 23–30.

4. L.W. Porter, *Organizational Patterns of Managerial Job Attitudes.* New York: American Foundation for Management Research, 1964. See also M. Haire, E. Ghiselli and L.W. Porter, *Managerial Thinking: An International Study.* New York: Wiley, 1966, especially chapters 4 and 5.

5. M. Beer, *Leadership, Employee Needs, and Motivation.* Columbus, Ohio: Bureau of Business Research, Ohio State University, 1966.

6. J.V. Clark, "Motivation in Work Groups: A Tentative View," *Human Organization,* Vol. 19, 1960, pp. 199–208. E.E. Lawler and L.W. Porter, "The Effect of Performance on Job Satisfaction," *Industrial Relations,* Vol. 7, No. 1, 1967, pp. 20–28. L.W. Porter and E.E. Lawler, *Managerial Attitudes and Performance.* Homewood, Illinois: Irwin-Dorsey, 1968, pp. 148, 150.

7. Herzberg, Mausner and Snyderman, *op. cit.*

8. Herzberg, *op. cit.,* chapters 7, 8. See also K. Davis, *Human Relations at Work* (third

edition). New York: McGraw-Hill, 1967, pp. 32–36; and R.J. Burke, "Are Herzberg's Motivators and Hygienes Undimensional?" *Journal of Applied Psychology*, Vol. 50, 1966, pp. 217–321.

9. For a review of six of these studies as well as a report on their own similar findings see M.D. Dunnette, J.P. Campbell, and M.D. Hakel, "Factors Contributing to Job Satisfaction and Job Dissatisfaction in Six Occupational Groups," *Organizational Behavior and Human Performance*, Vol. 2, 1967, pp. 143–174. See also C.L. Hulin and P.A. Smith, "An Empirical Investigation of Two Implications of the Two-Factor Theory of Job Satisfaction," *Journal of Applied Psychology*, Vol. 51, 1967, pp. 396–402; C.A. Lindsay, E. Marks, and L. Gorlow, "The Herzberg Theory: A Critique and Reformulation," *Journal of Applied Psychology*, Vol. 51, 1967, pp. 330–339. This latter study and one by J.R. Hinrichs and L.A. Mischkind, "Empirical and Theoretical Limitations of the Two-Factor Hypothesis of Job Satisfaction," *Journal of Applied Psychology*, Vol. 51, 1967, pp. 191–200, are especially useful for suggesting possible reformulations and extensions of the theory which may help overcome some the objections voiced in the studies mentioned above.

10. Dunnette, Campbell and Hakel, *op. cit.*, pp. 169–173.

11. M.S. Viteles, *Motivation and Morale in Industry*, New York: Norton, 1953, chapter 14: A. Kornhauser, "Psychological Studies of Employee Attitudes," *Journal of Consulting Psychology*, Vol. 8, 1944, pp. 127–143.

12. Herzberg, *op. cit.*, chapters 7–9.

13. Herzberg, *op. cit.*, chapter 8.

14. F. Friedlander and E. Walton, "Positive and Negative Motivations Toward Work," *Administrative Science Quarterly*, Vol. 9, 1964, pp. 194–207.

15. It should be noted that the Porter and Lawler research reported above extends the Maslow model by providing an explicit linkage between need satisfaction and performance and also implicitly recognizes individual motivational differences. To do these things, their research makes use of Vroomian concepts discussed in the next section.

16. A.H. Brayfield and W.H. Crockett, "Employee Attitudes and Employee Performance," *Psychological Bulletin*, Vol. 52, 1955, p. 416.

17. B.S. Georgopoulas, G.M. Mahoney, and N.W. Jones, "A Path-Goal Approach to Productivity," *Journal of Applied Psychology*, Vol. 41, 1957, pp. 345–353.

18. This section is based especially on discussions in Vroom, *op. cit.*, Chapters 2 and 7. See also J. Galbraith and L.L. Cummings, "An Empirical Investigation of the Motivational Determinants of Task Performance: Interactive Effects between Instrumentality-Valence and Motivation-Ability," *Organizational Behavior and Human Performance*, Vol. 2, 1967, pp. 237–257.

19. Vroom, *op. cit.*, p. 6.

20. Vroom, *op. cit.*, p. 17.

21. Vroom, *op. cit.*, p. 18.

22. Vroom, *op. cit.*

23. V.H. Vroom, "Organizational Choice: A Study of Pre- and Postdecision Processes," *Organizational Behavior and Human Performance*, Vol. 1, 1966, pp. 212–225.

24. Galbraith and Cummings, *op. cit.*, pp. 237–257.

25. J.W. Hill, "An Application of Decision Theory to Complex Industrial Behavior," unpublished dissertation, Wayne State University, Detroit, Michigan, 1965.

26. Edwards, *op. cit.*, pp. 473–499.

27. For discussions of these measures see C. Osgood, G. Suci, and P. Tannenbaum, *The Measurement of Meaning*, Urbana, Ill.: University of Illinois Press, 1957; A.L. Edwards, *Personal Preference Schedule Manual*. New York: Psychological Corporation, 1959.

28. E.E. Lawler and L.W. Porter, "Antecedent Attitudes of Effective Managerial Performance," *Organizational Behavior and Human Performance*, Vol. 2, 1967, pp. 122–142.

29. Vroom, *Work and Motivation*, chapter 2.

Applications

Organization Development

by
Michael D. Shaler*

As man entered the twentieth century, he found himself confronted by an environment that differed markedly from that encountered by his forebears. No longer was the environment placid and predictable, rather it was turbulent, rapidly changing and heavily influenced by the explosive growth in science and technology. In response to this environment, the search for adjustment and improvement induced twentieth century man to seek more efficient methods to accomplish the tasks at hand. In the organizational context, this led to exploration of ways to produce a product or render a service more effectively and at lower cost while simultaneously improving the quality of the services or good produced.

In pursuit of the better way, more and more demands have been placed on the people in the organization. Demands for increased productivity, the development of new, more complex skills, and the requirement for increased mobility have resulted in counter demands for higher wages, salaries, and fringe benefits. The net effect is a rapid appreciation in the worth of the human side of the organization. People are a valuable and increasingly expensive resource. If an organization is to survive and prosper, maximum performance from its people is essential to ensure its long term viability.

The twentieth century also has witnessed an extensive increase in the

*Michael D. Shaler, (Major, U.S. Army) is on the faculty of the Office of Military Leadership at the United States Military Academy, West Point, New York. He received his B.A. in Psychology from Gonzaga University (1962) and his Master of Business Administration (MBA) from the Wharton School, University of Pennsylvania (1972).

understanding of human behavior. Behavioral scientists have reached a significant and ever-increasing level of reliability as they predict human response under certain situations. Organization development is the application in the workplace of that knowledge of human behavior acquired through behavioral research and experimentation. It is a collaborative relationship between leaders and managers on the one hand and behavioral scientists on the other—the objective of which is to improve performance and increase efficiency in the organization.

The practice of organization development (OD) is relatively new, the first efforts being initiated about twenty-five years ago. The roots of OD, however, may be traced to the efforts at improved performance which were begun by Frederick W. Taylor around the turn of the century.

CHRONOLOGY

In 1910 Taylor, who later became known as the Father of Scientific Management, undertook a series of industrial experiments designed to maximize the efficiency of the worker. Taylor's work measurement studies and programming of labor had a heavy impact as worker efficiency became an end unto itself. Taylor changed the organization, the people, and the manner in which jobs were accomplished. Scientific Management flourished in an era of rapid industrial growth and expansion, and Henry Ford's automobile assembly line became the epitome of Taylorism.

Taylor's efforts were supported by work in related disciplines. For example, psychology was anxious to be treated as a science and had entered the industrial sector. Psychology at the time was physiologically oriented and measurement happy and the finger dexterity tests of the psychologists meshed neatly with Taylor's work in time and motion studies.

Due in large part to his theoretical tendency to treat workers as readily interchangeable parts in the industrial machine, Taylor was subsequently attacked for being inhuman. This dispute pointed out the heightening conflict between technology and humanity.

Scientific Management laid the foundation for the operations research and information processing fields, which sought to develop technical methods for solving problems in the workplace, and on the other hand led to intensified efforts by behavioral scientists to resolve the issues raised by Taylor through investigation and further definition of the dimensions of human behavior. One of the earliest such studies was undertaken by Western Electric Company.

HAWTHORNE

In an attempt to increase the productivity of its work force, a team of researchers at the Hawthorne plant of the Western Electric Company sought to determine the relationship between certain physical changes in working conditions and employee output. These experiments began in 1924 in the Hawthorne plant near Chicago, where worker morale was high and working conditions were satisfactory. The initial experiments were designed to vary the quality and quantity of illumination in the Relay Assembly Room and to isolate this change from the effect of other variables in the work environment. The effect of these changes was to be determined by measuring changes in the rate of output. Subsequent tests varied working hours and the spacing of break periods, using again rate of output as the measure.

Prior to the experiments, the test and control groups were informed that management was interested in studying the effect of certain changes in working conditions and that under no circumstances were they to make a "production race" out of the test. Both supervisors and researchers took great care to convince the workers that the purpose of the test was not to determine maximum output but to determine those factors which contribute to improved efficiency.

As the tests progressed, experimenters found that productivity in fact increased in both test and control groups in almost equal magnitude. Greater efficiency and productivity resulted, but were not dependent on the hypothesized key variables in the physical surroundings. Something happened in the Hawthorne plant which could not be explained by the experimentally controlled conditions of work. It appeared that the employees selected for the test were reacting to the experiment in the way in which they assumed that they were expected to react. The workers apparently received signals which conveyed to them a very clear message: the experimenters *were* interested in increased output. The tested group knew that the eyes of the company were upon them and they had thus committed themselves to increasing production regardless of fluctuations in the physical environment.

This increased commitment on the part of the workers was based on the treatment received from the experimenters which was almost perfectly, albeit unconsciously, designed to increase the worker's feelings of self-worth. In their attempts to create an optimal climate for objective research, the researchers influenced those very factors most likely to facilitate change. Initially tense and unsure in their new and unfamiliar experimental situation, the workers became subjects of genuine concern by the research team. The person introducing the changes was held in high regard; the workers perceived that increased production was the specific objective of the tests based on the subtle signals emitted by the supervisors and researchers; the workers formed new groups and adopted new attitudes built around the experimental activities; and the overall nature of the test conditions gave the workers an increased sense of self-worth and esteem.

Thus was born the "Hawthorne effect"—in essence the first documented recognition that social factors in the work group contribute significantly to the performance of individual workers. The findings were later interpreted to substantiate the point that the effect of group membership is one of the major determinants of productivity and worker satisfaction.

EXPLORATION OF GROUP DYNAMICS

The forces of the group, which were initially revealed as a result of the Hawthorne experiments, intrigued a number of behavioral scientists who began to explore methods to utilize these group forces to achieve desired change. Kurt Lewin in the early 1940's proposed that as man attempts to solve human problems a certain re-education must occur—this being a normative change as well as cognitive and perceptual change. Lewin (1947) emphasized the point that man must participate in his own re-education if he is to be re-educated at all; it is an active involvement rather than a passive process.

The organization of the National Training Laboratories (NTL) near Bethel, Maine in 1947 (Bennis, Benne, & Chinn, 1969) was a milestone in the development of normative-re-educative approaches to changing as suggested by Lewin. NTL developed their program around the "Laboratory education" concept wherein people in a group create their own laboratory in which to learn about their behavior and to experiment with new behaviors. Of the various approaches to laboratory education, the T-Group (Training Group) was most widely utilized. The T-Group is designed to provide maximum possible opportunity for individuals to expose their behavior, give and receive feedback, experiment with new behaviors in a safe surrounding, and develop long-term awareness and acceptance of self and others.

The T-Group members are given the opportunity to learn the nature of effective group functioning and to develop a group that could achieve specific goals with minimum possible human cost. In the T-Group some learning comes from the facilitator, trainer or educator, but most of the learning results from the experience of the individual group members interacting with one another. Beginning with little or no structure, the T-Group develops its own learning agenda, selects leaders or decides on the leadership process it will follow and adopts the norms which will govern group operation. The group gradually develops its own unique social system, which evolves from a situation that is fraught with anxiety at the outset. It then may address the need on the part of the members to either appoint a leader or chairman or to rely on functional leadership whereby the group delegates leadership to those who are most competent in the subject being addressed or in satisfying the group need operant at the time.

A T-Group is a process of deep personal involvement and value change. The emphasis is upon the ongoing (referred to as the "here and now") processes and events which are occurring in the group situation at hand, rather than upon past experiences of the members. The goals of the T-Group have been variously stated and include the development of:

- Self-insight
- Sensitivity to conditions which inhibit or facilitate interpersonal functioning
- Skills in diagnosing individual and group behavior
- Increase in role flexibility
- Understanding of the dynamics of the communication process within and between groups
- Increase in skills in solving problems which involve the human element
- Stronger motivation to try to improve one's own performance or the performance of one's group

T-Group composition is itself a key issue. "Stranger" groups are composed of individuals who are organizational strangers who gather only for the duration of the T-Group session. The emphasis is on individual growth and the individual is relied upon to perform a "seeding" function as he returns to his work unit. Difficulty may arise when he returns and attempts to use his new behavioral skills in the old setting where he may receive little social support for these new, and in the minds of work group members, alien behaviors.

"Cousin" groups are conducted for persons of similar rank and occupational responsibilities within the organization but from different functional groups. "Diagonal slices" may be composed of persons of different rank but not in the same work group or in direct supervisory relationships. "Family" groups consist of integral functional units of the organization and include the manager/leader and his key subordinates. The more the composition of the T-Group approaches the "family" group the more the total organization is affected. The risk of on-the-job repercussion, however, probably increases in direct proportion and must be considered. If the possibility for change in the host organization is slim, then T-Group training in "cousin" and "stranger" groups is at least questionable and the focus should be directed toward a "family" experience with expectations for change realistically outlined.

The early work of NTL was based primarily on "stranger" groups where emphasis was placed on individual growth and development and the training was conducted at a site well removed from the work environment. Individual change as self-reported by the participants was impressive and received a wide coverage and T-Groups increased in popularity. Indeed, by 1968 NTL alone had conducted T-Group sessions for more than 14,000 persons. The reported positive change in interpersonal competence by participants, however, was not reflected by increased performance by the work group except in isolated examples. The common problem was that people would attend one of the NTL or similar T-Group sessions, return to their organizational setting and receive little support for their changed and "refrozen" values and behaviors. The only organizational component that had changed were some small number of the people; the other component variables had remained unchanged.

THE ORGANIZATION AS A SYSTEM

The laboratory education approach pioneered by NTL appeared to be effective in bringing about desired changes in individuals and groups and had some utility in dealing with organizational dysfunctions. On the whole, the evidence relating individual and group change to an increase in organizational effectiveness was equivocal, due in the most part to the isolated treatment of only one variable of the total organization—the people.

Leavitt (1970) views an organization as a multivariate system in which at least four key variables interact. These variables are highly interdependent and a change in any one will usually result in a compensatory or retaliatory change in the others.

The variable of technology involves the technical tools associated with the accomplishment of organizational functions. The clearest example are those

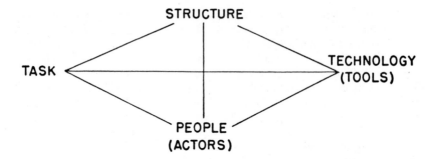

FIG. I

problem-solving and work reduction devices such as computers and their associated programs. The task includes the production of goods or services and the mission of the organization including the large number of different but operationally meaningful subtasks that may exist in complex organizations. Included in the people variable are all the organizational actors who bring with them individual human needs for growth and fulfillment. Structure is comprised of the system of authority, the flow of work, communication systems and such varied issues as centralization/decentralization, standardization, formalization and the overall size of the organization to include the physical layout of its sub-elements.

Although Leavitt differentiates structure from people and technology from task, his differentiation is in points of origin, conceptual approach and relative emphasis, not in the exclusion of the other variables. Regardless of the point of origin, efforts to effect organizational change must eventually address all the interrelated variables. Those who advocate organizational intervention through the people variable, such as the patrons of laboratory training, must invent or alter technical devices for implementing their ideas and must address alternative structures that are supportive of the desired change in human behavior. Structuralists must address the human element and seek to induce the kinds of human interaction that are supportive of their position and be prepared to deal with that which threatens to undermine it.

STRUCTURE AND PROCESS

Advancing one step further, the interrelationship of these variables in the organization has been described by Friedlander and Brown (1974) in their study of OD. The component variables defined by Leavitt are depicted as interacting in techno-structural and human-processual systems which converge at the interface of the organizational process and structure.

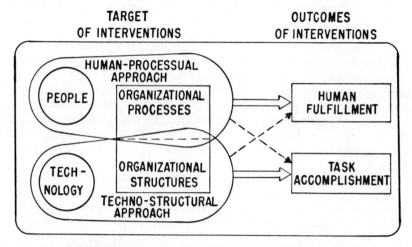

FIG.2 APPROACHES TO ORGANIZATION DEVELOPMENT

Friedlander and Brown state that both process and structure are concerned with authority, communication, decision making, goal setting and conflict resolution. Process, however, implies the implementation of these as dynamic behavioral events and interactions, whereas structure describes them as ongoing sets of durable roles and relationships. Attitudes and behavior are clearly affected by both structure and process.

In viewing the organization as a system, since process and structure are so embedded in each other, it is impossible to create lasting change in one without clearly addressing the other. Most OD interventions in the organization originate with either the techno-structural or the human-processual approach.

Techno-structural interventions are intended to affect the job content and method of work and the sets of relationships among workers. Broad examples of this type intervention are the approaches to job design, job enlargement and Frederick Herzberg's job enrichment (1968), all of which focus upon both the technical aspects of the job and the social structures which support it. In Herzberg's interventions, for example, there is an attempt to increase job satisfaction and performance by building in greater variety, discretion, feedback, identity, and responsibility for completion of a whole task. Herzberg's theory stresses that man's needs at work are met essentially by the nature of his work, so the initial target of change becomes job content, not the employee. This type of intervention seeks to provide the employee a task which offers greater challenge; he will then become intrinsically more motivated with a concomitant increase in efficiency. However, by providing the worker greater responsibility and recognition for his efforts while engaging in a meaningful task, approaches such as job enrichment become deeply involved in altering and modifying the human processual systems in the organization.

Human-processual interventions focus on the people of the organization and the processes of communication, problem solving and decision making. It is through these processes that the actors in the organization seek to achieve their individual goals while accomplishing the organization's goals. The advocates of change through process intervention generally tend to place a high value on human fulfillment and to project improved organizational performance as a result of improved human functioning within the processes mentioned earlier. Three general areas of process intervention that are widely practiced are survey feedback, group development and intergroup development activities.

Survey feedback is an OD technology whereby data is gathered from the members of the organization, usually by means of questionnaires or interviews, and fed back to selected individuals in the organization. The design of the questionnaires or interview format ideally should involve both outside consultants and organization members. Summarization, analysis, interpretation and presentation of the data by a joint inside-outside team has proven to be more effective than either outside consultants or current organization members alone. The assumption underlying the survey feedback approach is that as discrepancies between organizational ideals and conditions as reported in the surveys are made known a general motivation for change will provide the climate necessary for movement toward the ideal condition. There is little evidence, however, that survey feedback alone leads to changes in individual behavior, or improved organizational performance. Survey feedback can be an effective bridge between the diagnostic activities of questionnaire administration and interviewing and active intervention. The action steps and subsequent follow-ups identified and instigated by a satisfactory survey feedback intervention produce the longer term change necessary for improved functioning of the organization.

Group development interventions are widely reported as the most important single type of OD intervention and are frequently identified as one of the action steps necessary to assist the organization in moving in the direction identified during the survey feedback process. The technology of "team-building" as a group development activity involves the establishment of clear goals for the work groups, improvement of the quality of interaction among team members, increased clarity concerning the role and responsibilities of each team member, and development of skills involved in managing conflict. The goals of "team-building" reflect the goals of the T-Group form of laboratory training discussed earlier and "family" T-Groups are frequently utilized as the vehicle for team-building interventions.

Of primary concern to OD practitioners are problems which arise at the interface between different functional groups within an organization and are frequently described during survey feedback activities. Intergroup problems often revolve around such issues as overlapping responsibilities, confused lines of authority, or unhealthy competitiveness. Conflicts may exist between different departments, different functional groups (e.g., sales and engineering), between headquarters and field teams, or between union and management representatives. Intergroup development interventions, designed to improve relationships and manage conflict, are based on information sharing, confrontation of differences, and working together to form new understandings. A popular design for intergroup development requires groups to develop lists of their perceptions of themselves, the other group, and their views of the other group's perception of them. These lists are then used as inputs to develop better understanding on the part of each group, develop a shared conception of problems, and to create future action plans to manage the intergroup conflict. Positive changes in individual behavior and improved organizational performance resulting from intergroup development interventions have been widely reported in a variety of case studies, but further systematic research is needed to determine the long-term effectiveness of such interventions.

A SUCCESSFUL OD EFFORT DEFINED

A number of applications of the various OD strategies have been documented and a survey of these case studies reveals a common set of characteristics present in the successful OD efforts.

1. *The OD effort should be directly related to the purpose of the organization.* The OD process does not seek to improve effectiveness in the abstract. It is an effort aimed specifically at creating conditions which will improve the organization's ability to achieve its primary purpose.

2. *The OD process should be a long-term effort.* Time required for change to take effect and be maintained is dependent on a wide range of variables to include the size of the organization, the operational environment, organizational climate, and the resources available to support the process. Most practitioners stipulate that at least one year is required to observe any noticeable change and satisfactory results may require three to five years.

3. *The OD process, and the subordinate programs and projects, should be action-oriented.* The individual OD activities in which organization members participate are aimed at changing some aspect of the organization or its members within the organizational setting. OD activities differ from many other training efforts where the activity itself, such as a management development workshop or individual training course, is designed to produce increased knowledge, skill, or understanding on the part of the individual member. The trained individual is then supposed to transfer this newly acquired knowledge to the operating situation. In OD activities, the group builds in the connections from learning to action and establishes follow-up activities that are aimed at implementing and measuring the action programs agreed upon. The action programs are directly related to the organization's purpose or mission.

4. *The OD process should involve the whole system.* The whole system approach is essential in OD because the process promotes planning and implementation of changes to one of the component variables of the system (task,

structure, people, or technology), and a change in any of these variables results in a change in one or more of the others.

5. *Top management and top leadership must be committed to the OD process and should support the methods used to achieve the goals.* Top management of the organization has a personal investment in the OD process and its outcomes. Their formal participation in all the programs and projects is not required, but their knowledge of and commitment to the goals of the overall OD effort are essential.

6. *OD works primarily with groups.* One of the underlying assumptions of the OD process is that groups and teams are the basic units of the organization to be changed or modified as the organization moves toward improved effectiveness. Individual learning and personal growth occur to a large extent through the OD process, but the primary purpose is to improve the organization.

7. *OD usually relies on some form of experience-based learning activity.* Most OD strategies incorporate one of the approaches to experience-based learning since change of attitude, behavior and performance of people are necessary to accomplish the goals of the OD process. The precise form of experience-based training activity utilized varies widely in content and depth of exploration, but the T-Group training discussed earlier is one of the more popular forms.

A CRITIQUE OF OD

To date, no definitive appraisal of the long-term effectiveness of OD has been made utilizing objective data. Most of the documented work consists of case studies, frequently authored by those involved in the change efforts. This provides little opportunity to control variables which may be as important as the outcome of the OD process itself. A frequent charge is that reported OD successes are little more than "Hawthorne effects" in action—a charge that is difficult to refute given the lack of scientific proof. Even the more carefully designed longitudinal studies of OD have difficulty in establishing cause-effect relationships because of the complexity, diversity, and dynamic nature of the human side of the organization. This lack of scientific proof that OD efforts lead to improved organizational performance does not require that we conclude the converse—that OD efforts do not lead to improved performance. What is required is for OD practitioners to improve their strategies and technologies and for researchers to focus on the key variables and mechanisms in the OD process while refining their approaches for gathering and analyzing empirical data.

In addition to the issue of evaluation and validation of the OD process, the ethical considerations of OD have stirred a good deal of concern. There is an inherent requirement to maintain a high degree of voluntarism regarding the nature and extent of an individual's participation in the deeper OD technologies such as T-Groups. When an individual participant in one of these deeper change strategies is coerced by economic or bureaucratic pressures, then the ethics of intervention clearly run counter to the values of a democratic society. OD as a field is continually faced with decisions about the balance it can and will strike between the often conflicting goals of changing organizations to increase human fulfillment and changing people to promote organizational efficiency

OD IN THE U.S. ARMY

The Chief of Staff, US Army appointed a study group in 1971 to investigate the application within the Army of the knowledge and techniques of the behavioral sciences. This study group recommended that the Army conduct a two year pilot program to test the feasibility and desirability of instituting OD on an Army-wide basis. A test directorate was established in 1972 at Fort Ord, California and for two years the techniques of OD were applied to a variety of Army organizations.

The Army OD test program was conducted using a four-step process: assessment, planning, implementation and followup. During the first step, surveys and interviews are used to diagnose the current state of the organization and identify appropriate areas for intervention in a manner similar to the survey feedback technology discussed earlier. This diagnostic information is returned to the unit commander and is used jointly by the OD consultant and the commander to develop a plan to improve the functioning of the organization and to enhance mission accomplishment. The various change strategies selected, such as team building and intergroup development activities, are then implemented. Followup action reinforces the changes sought and may lead to a re-assessment and, if warranted, the initiation of another cycle.

At the conclusion of the two-year test period, the OD program was evaluated as a valuable process for improving the organizational effectiveness of Army units and the decision was made to undertake OD in the Army on a widespread basis. The OD program, redesignated the Organizational Effectiveness (OE) program to more accurately portray the Army's efforts, has proliferated and is currently underway in a number of combat units and a variety of administrative headquarters. Additionally, using as a nucleus the trained personnel at Fort Ord who had conducted the pilot program, a school was established to train OE staff officers. These officers will act as OE consultants to commanders of Army units as the program continues to expand.

The Army's OE program possesses the same basic strengths and faces the same limitations described earlier for the OD process in general. Some additional Army-specific problems also arise and must be considered and dealt with.

Difficulty in Measuring Results

The problem of measuring results, or even determining what results to measure presents a significant challenge to the OE effort. Most Army organizations do not produce a "product" as such, and those that produce a "service," for example, the defense of our air corridors, produce something that is indeed difficult to measure. Added to this is an Army penchant for measurable, quantifiable results, and the requirement to justify programs for budgetary consideration on an annual basis in the never-ending competition for scarce fiscal resources.

Transient Nature of Military Organizations

Although current policy of the Department of the Army is moving toward stabilizing tours of duty for key individuals, sufficient personnel turbulence will exist to require a substantive training program for personnel newly assigned to a unit involved in an OE program. New arrivals may find the situation in the new organization very unfamiliar, and departing personnel may find their subsequent units of assignment unreceptive to any efforts to transfer newly acquired skills and habits.

SUMMARY

Organization development is the utilization of the knowledge and techniques of the applied behavioral sciences to improve the effectiveness and efficiency of an organization. OD seeks to improve organizational functioning through planned, systematic, long range efforts at changing both the processes and structures of the organizational system. OD addresses such areas as the development of leadership, group processes, organizational roles, intergroup relationships and structures while attempting to integrate individual goals with organizational goals.

REFERENCES

Bennis, Warren G.; Kenneth D. Benne; and Robert Chin (eds.) *The Planning of Change.* (New York: Holt, Rinehart, and Winston, Inc.) 1969.

Friedlander, Frank and L. Dave Brown. "Organization Development," in M. Rosenzweig and L. Porter (eds.) *Annual Review of Psychology 1974.* (Palo Alto, California: Annual Reviews, Inc.) 1974.

Herzberg, Frederick. "One More Time: How Do You Motivate Employees?" in *Harvard Business Review,* Vol. 46 (Jan-Feb), pp. 53–62, 1968.

Leavitt, Harold J. "Applied Organizational Change in Industry: Structural, Technical and Human Approaches," in G. Dalton and P. Lawrence (eds.) *Organizational Change and Development.* (Homewood, Illinois: Irwin, Inc.) 1970.

Lewin, Kurt. "Group Decision and Social Change", in T. Newcomb and E. Hartley (eds.) *Readings in Social Psychology.* (New York: Holt, Rinehart and Winston, Inc.) 1947.

Part VI

Interface With Society

by
Allan J. Futernick
and
*Peter M. Elson**

SOCIETY may be defined as "a group of human beings cooperating in the pursuit of several of their major interests, invariably including self-maintenance and self-perpetuation." (Fairchild, 1966, p. 200) The irregular boundary delimiting society in our leadership model represents the state of flux in which American society has always been. It was noted in the introductory chapter that these changes were often rapid and present two major sources of conflict for the leader. First, the view of society concerning the military organization affects policy, control, goals, and morale. Second, input to the military organization at all levels is composed of members of this society, thus resulting in possible conflict if as a result of prior socialization, the values of these entrants are different from the traditional organizational values.

The individual, the group, the leader, and the organization as elements in the dynamic process of leadership have already been examined. Conflicts between individual and group goals were examined at the micro level with em-

*The authors are both on the faculty of the Office of Military Leadership at the United States Military Academy, West Point, New York. Allan J. Futernick (Major, US Army) received his B.A. from the City College of New York (1964), and his M.A. (1973) and Ph.D. (1976) from the University of Alabama. Peter M. Elson (Major, US Army) received his B.S. from the United States Military Academy (1964) and his M.S. in Industrial Relations from Purdue University (1973).

phasis on a social psychological perspective. This part concentrates on the interface between the organization and the perspective of the impact of society on the military profession and its leadership.

Three specific areas of interest are addressed in order to better understand the two areas of potential conflict mentioned above. The first area deals with CIVIL-MILITARY RELATIONS and seeks to establish the relationship between the military organization and the larger civilian society. The major variable in this area is the degree of control the civilian sector exerts over the military sector. Huntington's article "Civilian Control of the Military: A Theoretical Statement" suggests "subjective control" and "objective control" (see Fig. 1) as two types of control which are clearly distinguishable and evident at the following three levels of civil-military relations: (1) between the military order as a whole and society as a whole; (2) between the officer corps and other elite groups; and (3) between the highest military commanders and the civilian governmental leadership.

Janowitz's article "Civilian Control" notes a slowing of the trend in civilianization of the military. He sees the possible divergence of the military and civilian sectors with the current all-volunteer force. This, he fears, will

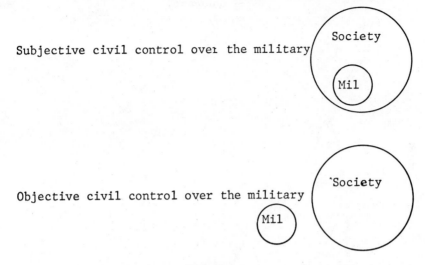

Subjective civil control over the military

Objective civil control over the military

FIGURE 1
TWO MODELS OF CIVIL-MILITARY RELATIONS

lead to increased isolation of the military sector and along with this the inherent dangers of such a trend.

The second major area to be addressed is that of THE MILITARY AS A PROFESSION. The objective is to examine the military as a professional organization in society and to confront the inherent problems. Many of these problems stem from the fact that the military possesses characteristics of a bureaucracy, a governmental organization, and a profession, as shown in Figure 2 next.

The first two articles address this problem directly. Huntington's "Officership as a Profession" analyzes the modern officer corps in light of the following characteristics of a profession: (1) *expertise,* which he views as the "management of violence"; (2) responsibility, which is to the "state" and which is guided by a code of ethics; and (3) its bureaucratic nature. Bradford and Brown in their article "A Pluralistic Profession" criticize Huntington for attempting to define military professionalism within the framework of the other professions. They claim that the military's status as a profession can only be understood in terms of its unique obligation to serve the state. They also see different motivation for different types of professionals within the military, making for a "pluralistic" profession. Finally, they make recommendations for putting the concept of a pluralistic profession into practice, emphasizing the need for individual initiative. Hauser's article "Professionalism" brings us up to date with an incisive examination of how the Army has responded to external pressures on issues concerning professionalism. Specifically, incidents in the areas of war crimes, corruption, and careerism during the

THE MILITARY: A PROFESSIONAL ORGANIZATION

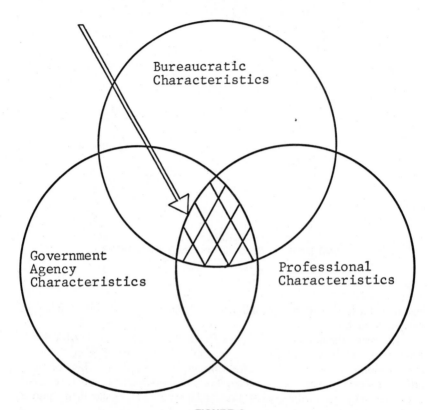

FIGURE 2
THE MILITARY: A BUREAUCRACY, A PROFESSION,
AND A GOVERNMENT AGENCY

Vietnam era are addressed. Hauser looks at the Army and its relationship to society in an attempt to unravel the antecedents of these incidents.*

Finally, the third area deals with ETHICS. Since the professional officer corps stands or falls on its code of ethics, the importance of this chapter to the military leader cannot be overemphasized. A general examination of the concept is presented in each of the articles along with some of the problems the professional officer may face. Johns' article "Ethical Conduct" approaches the seeming dilemma posed by the absolute versus the situational ethic as a guide to behavior. Emphasis is placed on the inherent problems faced if one

---

*Editor's Note: This article is a single chapter from Hauser's book *America's Army in Crisis*. The reader is cautioned against a possible misunderstanding of Hauser's overall position on the military profession without having read the entire book.

adopts and pursues the latter to its extreme. The question is "Where does one draw the line?" It is noted that this issue is of particular concern to those who are about to be commissioned since they will become future standard bearers of the Officer Corps. Similarly, Hays and Thomas in their article "Moral Aspects of Leadership" establish the basis for the military code and apply it to the concepts of Duty, Honor, Country. When reading about the areas of possible difficulty each officer may face in ethical decision making, recall the discussion in the Johns article. Finally, Chaplain Johnson's article "Ethical Issues of Military Leadership" presents the military leader with four ethical issues to consider and the dangers posed by each. The issues of *ethical relativism*, the *loyalty syndrome, image,* and the *drive for success* can be found in the situational problems posed by Hays and Thomas, as well as the areas in which Hauser found the Army to be deficient professionally. Johnson's appeal for the building of an ethical environment can be found to be interwoven throughout each of the articles.

Terms you should be able to discuss when you finish this part:

Absolute Ethic	Military Industrial Complex
Careerism	Objective Control
Core Values	Pluralistic Profession
Corporateness	Profession
Ethical Code	Professional
Ethics	Professionalism
Expertise	Situational Ethics
Managers of Violence	Subjective Control

Civil-Military Relations

Civilian Control of the Military:
A Theoretical Statement*

by
Samuel P. Huntington

IN WESTERN SOCIETY, civilian control has suffered the fate of consensus. No one, civil or military, is ever against civilian control. Consequently, it has achieved acceptability at the price of becoming meaningless. Everyone believes in civilian control, but in all the vast literature on civil-military relations, no one has satisfactorily defined it. This essay is an attempt to remedy this deficiency and to define civilian control in terms which will make it a useful analytical tool for social scientists.[1]

Presumably, civilian control has something to do with the relative power of civilian and military groups. Presumably, also, civilian control is achieved to the extent to which the power of civilian groups is enhanced and that of military groups is reduced. But, presumably, too, civilian control does not require that all civilian groups have more power than all military groups. What is essential is the relation between the power of military groups and the power of the civilian governmental leadership. Civilian control of the military is governmental control of the military. Consequently, the criterion of civilian control is the extent to which military leadership groups, and through them, the armed forces as a whole, respond to the direction of the civilian leaders of the government.

This goal may be achieved through two quite different and mutually contradictory means which we will label "subjective civilian control" and "ob-

*Reprinted with permission of the Free Press from *Political Behavior: A Reader in Theory and Research,* ed. by Heinz Eulau, Samuel J. Eldersveld, and Morris Janowitz. Copyright 1956 by the Free Press.

jective civilian control."[2] The civil-military relations of any actual society will combine elements of both types. In theory, however, the two types are clearly distinguishable, and their differences are manifest at three levels of civil-military relations: (1) between the military order as a whole and society as a whole; (2) between the officer corps and other elite groups; and (3) between the highest military commanders and the civilian governmental leadership.

THE SUBJECTIVE CONTROL MODEL

The essence of subjective civilian control is the absence of any clear line between military and civilian groups or between military and civilian values. The military forces are an integral part of society, reflecting and embodying the dominant social forces and political ideologies of that society. The military order tends to become coextensive with society. Every citizen has an equal responsibility to contribute to national defense, just as he has an equal responsibility to pay taxes, obey the laws, and, if the society is democratic, to participate in the choice of political leaders.

Historically, this philosophy of the "nation in arms" has been embraced by such diverse political types as Jefferson, Jaures, and Ludendorff. Subjective control also does not permit the officer corps to be a specialized, isolated group living apart from society. Its members typically have many social roles in addition to that of officership. They may also be the social, political, or even economic leaders of society. Numerous and close affiliations exist between the officer corps and other elite groups, and the corps itself is highly permeable: individuals move in and out of it at a variety of points. At the highest levels of the military structure and of the government no sharp difference exists between civilian and military leadership. The ranking military officers think in political terms and play political roles. The civilian leaders of the government do not hesitate to participate in the direction of more strictly military matters. High military officers assume posts of political leadership having little connection with military affairs.

In brief, in subjective civilian control, the military are at one with society. Civilian control, consequently, is the product of the identity of thought and outlook between civilian and military groups. The military officer does not differ from other members of society and shares in its dominant values. The military leadership responds to the direction of the government because it participates actively in the government. It obeys orders because it agrees with the orders. If the society goes to war, the military leaders, the officer corps, and the rank and file respond and fight because they believe in the value of the political aims for which the war is fought.

THE OBJECTIVE CONTROL MODEL

Objective civilian control presupposes a sharp line between the military and society. The military forces, the officer corps, and the military leaders have their own peculiar roles, functions, and values which distinguish them from the nonmilitary portions of society. At the broadest level of the relation of the military order to society, the military function is presumed to be a highly specialized one. The members of society do not have an equal responsibility for the defense of society. This function is assigned to a distinct group, just as the functions of fire-fighting or the maintenance of domestic law and order are assigned to distinct groups. The military group consists in part of a small number of individuals who undertake military responsibilities over a long period of time (careerists) and in part of a large number of persons who assume military responsibilities for a short period of time (conscripts). But in each case the military role is sharply separated from other roles: the career group is normally isolated socially and physically from other elements in the social structure; the active service of the conscript is isolated from his prior and subsequent roles and interests in civilian life. Similarly, the officer corps has few contacts with other elite groups.

Entrance into the Corps is normally possible only at the lowest levels and the members of the corps usually spend their entire working lives in its ranks. The vocation of officership absorbs all their energies and furnishes them with all their occupational satisfactions. Officership, in short, is an exclusive role, incompatible with any other significant social or political roles. Its members recruited at an early age, the officer corps tends to be isolated and divorced from society. At the highest level of government, a clear distinction in role and function exists between military and civilian leaders.

The military leaders are professional expert advisers to the civilian political leaders who make the decisions. The functions of the military leaders are: (1) to represent within the governmental structure society's needs for military security; (2) to advise the governmental leaders from a "strictly military viewpoint" as to the military implications of proposed policies; and (3) to execute in the military sphere the decisions of the government. Civilian control is thus achieved not because the military groups share in the social values and political ideologies of society, but because they are indifferent to such values and ideologies. The military leaders obey the government not because they agree with its policies but simply because it is their duty to obey. If society goes to war, the military fight not because they believe in the goals of the war, but because it is their function to fight, and to fight successfully, for whatever ends the government wishes to pursue.

Subjective and objective control are thus directly opposed to each other. Subjective control requires the military to be the mirror of society; objective control requires the military to be the tool of society. Subjective control achieves its end by civilizing the military, objective control by militarizing them. Subjective control demands the blending of civilian and military interests; objective control demands their sharp delimitation. Subjective control presupposes military participation in politics; objective control is based on the recognition of such a sphere. Subjective control minimizes military power by rendering it indistinguishable from civilian power; objective control minimizes military power by confining it to a restricted sphere and rendering it politically sterile and neutral on all issues outside that sphere. Subjective control depends on agreement between military leaders and civilian leaders; objective control presupposes disagreement and depends on the obedience of military leaders to political leaders.

The essence of subjective control is reflected in von Schleicher's injunction that: "The Army must always be in tune with the spirit of the times." The essence of objective control is reflected in the declaration by Schleicher's associate and rival, Wilhelm Groener, that: "It is altogether mistaken to ask where the Army stands. The Army does what it is ordered to do, and that's all there is to it!" Subjective control views military institutions as the product of society, and hence assumes that they must assume different forms in different societies: the military institutions of a democratic society will differ fundamentally from those of a totalitarian society. Objective control views military institutions as reflecting universal, permanent, functional imperatives, and consequently assumes that equal levels of military knowledge in two societies will tend to produce similar military institutions.

THE PLURA ORMS OF SUBJECTIVE CONTROL

Subjective civilian control thus exists in a plurality of forms reflecting the conflicting interests of different civilian groups. Objective control exists in only a single form reflecting the demands for autonomy by the military group. Under subjective control the divisions within society are reflected in the military order. Hence each civilian group attempts to expand its influence within the military sphere by identifying its interests with civilian control. Civilian control has a different meaning for each civilian group, and thus it inevitably involves the power relations among civilian groups. It thus becomes an instrumental slogan like "states' rights" rather than an end in itself. Just as the banner of states' rights is normally raised by economic groups which have more power at the state than at the national level in struggles with other groups which have more power in the national government, so the slogan of civilian control is utilized by groups which lack power over the military forces in struggles with other civilian groups which have such power.

Like states' rights, civilian control may cover a variety of sins. It is always necessary to ask which civilians are to do the controlling. Except very recently in western society, civilian control has existed only in the subjective sense. Subjective civilian control is, indeed, the only form of civilian control possible in the absence of a professional officer corps. In its various historical manifestations, subjective civilian control has been identified with the maximization of the power of particular governmental institutions, particular social classes, and particular constitutional forms.

THE CONFLICT OF GOVERNMENTAL INSTITUTIONS

In the seventeenth and eighteenth centuries in England and America and in the nineteenth century in Germany the military forces were generally under the control of the Crown and the slogan "civilian control" was adopted by the parliamentary groups as a means of increasing their power vis-à-vis the Crown. Since the king, however, was just as civilian as they were, what they actually wanted was to maximize parliamentary control over the armed forces rather than civilian control in general. And parliamentary control was sought not as a means of reducing the power of the military but as a way of curtailing the power of the king. At the present time in the United States Congress and the President engage in a comparable struggle. The Chief Executive identifies civilian control with presidential control; Congress is too large and poorly organized to control the military forces effectively. Congress, on the other hand, identifies civilian control with congressional control. Congress is closer to the people than the President, who is likely to become the prisoner of his military advisers. But both Congress and President are fundamentally concerned with the distribution of power between executive and legislative rather than between civilian and military.

THE CONFLICT OF SOCIAL CLASSES

In the eighteenth and nineteenth centuries the European aristocracy and bourgeoisie struggled for control of society, government, and the armed forces. Each class had its own distinctive military manifestation. The standing army was an essentially aristocratic institution; the enlisted men recruited from the dregs of society by bribery or coercion had little contact with the civilian world, but the officers held military rank by virtue of their social or financial position. Except in the artillery and engineers, the bourgeoisie were excluded from military officership. In opposing the aristocracy politically, the bourgeoisie also advanced their own form of military organization: the citizen militia which reflected liberal, democratic principles and in which the distinctions between officers and enlisted men were minimized. Since the aristocratic standing army was the prevailing military form in the eighteenth century, the bourgeoisie groups made the greatest use of the slogan of civilian control and identified aristocratic control with military control. But, again, the real issue was not whether the military should control the civilians or the civilians the military. It was whether the aristocrats or the bourgeoisie was to control the armed forces.

THE CONFLICT OF CONSTITUTIONAL FORMS

A broader application of this subjective identification of civilian control with a particular civilian interest occurs when the claim is made that only a specific constitutional form—usually democracy—can insure civilian control. Civilian control is identified with democratic government, military control with absolute or totalitarian government. In democratic countries, it is argued, policy is determined by persuasion and compromise; in absolutist countries it is determined by force and coercion (or at least the implied threat of force or coercion). Hence, the military, who control the most powerful instrument of violence, can be more powerful in totalitarian countries than democratic ones.

Actually, however, this argument is not necessarily true. In a democratic country, the military may undermine civilian control and acquire great political power through the legitimate processes and institutions of democratic government and politics (e.g., the United States in World War II). In a totalitarian regime, on the other hand, the power of the military may be reduced by breaking the officer corps into competing units, establishing party armies and special military forces (Waffen-SS and MVD), infiltrating the military hierarchy with independent chains of command (political commissars), and similar techniques. Terror, conspiracy, surveillance, and force are the methods of government in a totalitarian state; terror, conspiracy, surveillance, and force are the means by which civilians in such a state control their armed forces. If employed sufficiently ruthlessly, these means may virtually eliminate military political power (e.g., Germany in World War II).

Thus, the claim of each civilian group that it alone could insure civilian control has never been historically valid. Civilian control was dependent not upon the ascendancy of any particular group, but upon the reflection within the armed forces of both the agreement and the tensions of civilian society. The identification by each civilian group of civilian control with its own particular interests, however, explains the otherwise peculiar historical fact that although civilian control was regularly invoked in politics and frequently written about in the eighteenth and nineteenth centuries, it was, nonetheless, never satisfactorily defined. Behind the façade of civilian agreement upon civilian control lay the reality of conflicting civilian interests.

THE UNITY OF OBJECTIVE CONTROL

The historical condition necessary for objective civilian control is the existence of an autonomous military profession recognized as having a special responsibility for the military security of society. This condition has been met only very recently in world history and even then, only in a very few of the more advanced nations of western civilization. The military profession, and hence objective control, were a product of the nineteenth century.[3] "Interchangeability between the statesman and the soldier," as Field Marshal Wavell has written, "passed forever, I fear, in the last century. The Germans professionalized the trade of war; and modern inventions, by increasing its technicalities, have specialized it. It is much the same with politics, professionalized by democracy. No longer can one man hope to exercise both callings, though both are branches of the same craft, the governance of men and the ordering of human affairs."[4]

In virtually all the nations of Latin America, the Middle East, and Southeast Asia, however, the military role has yet to be differentiated from other social roles and no autonomous military profession exists. Consequently subjective civilian control necessarily prevails, and in a country like Egypt the army becomes the vehicle of social reform. Even in a more advanced country like Japan, subjective control predominated down through World War II with military commanders playing an active and decisive role in the direction of the government.[5] Objective control has thus only been achieved to any real degree in Europe, the British Commonwealth, and the United States. As Mosca and Mannheim suggest, the existence of large military institutions within society which passively acquiesce to governmental direction and control may well be one of the distinguishing characteristics of western civilization.[6] Other, less perceptive writers have tended either to view military affairs from the perspective of a single civilian group or have become infatuated with the older forms of military organization. Consequently they have failed to recognize the emergence of objective civilian control.[7]

The various forms of subjective control reflected the conflicting demands of different civilian groups. The demand for objective control reflects the interests of the military group. Subjective control means the maximizing of the power of some particular civilian group or groups in military affairs. Objective control, contrariwise, means the maximizing of military professionalism, that is, the distribution of political power between military and civilian groups which is most conducive to the emergence of professional attitudes and behavior among the members of the officer corps. This produces the lowest possible reduction of military political power with respect to all civilian groups. At the same time it preserves that essential element of power which is necessary for the existence of a military profession. A highly professional officer corps stands ready to carry out the wishes of any civilian group which secures legitimate authority within the state.

In effect, this sets definite limits to military political power without reference to the distribution of political power among the various civilian groups. Any further reduction of military power beyond the point where professionalism is maximized only rebounds to the benefit of some particular civilian group and only serves to enhance the power of that group in its struggles with other civilian groups. The distribution of political power which most facilitates military professionalism is thus also the lowest point to which military power can be reduced without playing favorites among civilian groups. Because of this, the objective definition of civilian control furnishes a single concrete standard of civilian control which is politically neutral and which all social groups can recognize. It elevates civilian control from a political slogan masking group interests to a scientific concept independent of group perspectives.

Subjective civilian control presupposes a conflict between civilian control and the needs of military security. Sustained and intense threats to the security of society give rise to strong functional military imperatives which conflict with the interests of civilian groups. The continued assertion of the particular forms of subjective control requires that these imperatives either be transformed or be denied. If this can not be done, subjective control becomes impossible. This fact has been generally recognized by the adherents of subjective control, who gloomily prophesy that continued military insecurity will destroy civilian control.[8] On the other hand, the enhancement of civilian control in the subjective sense may undermine military security. Because they do not, for instance, recognize the existence of a separate military profession with its own outlook on national policy, civilian groups frequently assume that the reduction of military power is necessary to preserve peace. This decrease in the power of the military, however, often results in increased power for much more belli-cose civilian groups. Consequently, those civilian groups which try to mini-mize the risks of war by reducing the power of the military frequently en-courage exactly what they were attempting to avoid.

It is hardly coincidental that the years immediately prior to World War II saw the systematic reduction of the political power of the military in all the fu-ture belligerents except Japan (where an extreme form of subjective control had long prevailed), or that the temperature of the Cold War seems to vary in-versely with the political power of the generals in the Soviet Union. If civilian control is defined in the objective sense, however, no conflict exists between it and the goal of military security. Indeed, just the reverse is true. Objective ci-vilian control not only reduces the power of the military to the lowest possible level vis-à-vis all civilian groups, it also maximizes the likelihood of achieving military security.

OBJECTIVE VS. SUBJECTIVE CONTROL IN THE UNITED STATES

Only modern western society has achieved any high degree of objective ci-vilian control. And yet, even within the nations of the West, the demands of particular civilian groups for subjective control have remained strong. The extent to which a society achieves objective control depends upon the level of its military science, the extent to which there is agreement to remove the military order from politics, the character of the constitutional and govern-mental system of the society, and the nature and intensity of the threats to the military security of society. In the nineteenth century, for instance, their com-parative geographical security caused both Britain and the United States to lag behind the countries of continental Europe in developing the institutions of ob-jective control. The emergence of objective control in the United States, moreover, was further hampered by the American constitutional system which reflected the devotion of its framers to subjective control and dispersed au-thority over the military among a variety of civilian institutions.[9]

The conflicts between the functional military imperatives making for ob-jective control and the social, economic, and political imperatives making for subjective control, moreover, continues to be a real one in the United States today, and manifests itself in varied forms at each of the three levels of civil-military relations. For instance, at the most basic level of the general relation-ship of the military order to society, the efforts of the Doolittle Board im-mediately after World War II to introduce liberal, democratic values into the military services were a clear manifestation of subjective civilian control. Into the same category fall the attempts to incorporate into the military services much of the vaunted civilian American standard of living. Opposed to these subjective currents are the military views that a fighting organization must place a high value upon discipline, rank differentiations, and respect for authority, on the one hand, and physical toughness, privation, and Spartan leanness upon the other. Similarly, civilians believing in subjective control criticize the officer corps for being aloof and apart from the rest of society. Others, however, reflecting the objective viewpoint, condemn the officers for assuming nonmilitary roles and positions in government and business. At the highest level of civil-military relations, the controversy has revolved about the roles and functions of the Joint Chiefs of Staff. Should the Joint Chiefs function purely as narrow-gauged military experts and make their recommendations to the government solely from "the military viewpoint"? Will the pressures of American politics and of the constitutional separation of powers permit them to assume this role? Or should the Chiefs act as broad-gauged military statesmen and do their own political and economic thinking?

National security in a prolonged Cold War may depend in large part upon how these questions are answered. The implications and the importance of these questions, however, have been obscured by the failure to distinguish between objective and subjective civilian control. Recognition of this distinction will aid statesmen and political theorists in clarifying the relative merits of these two patterns of civil-military relations. It also will permit the social scientists to analyze the extent to which any particular institution or proposal tends to enhance or to obstruct the achievement of the desired form of civilian control.

END NOTES

1. For brilliant and suggestive theoretical analyses of civil-military relations which, however, do not focus primarily upon the concept of civilian control, see Alexis DeTocqueville, *Democracy in America,* vol. II, chaps. 22–26; Gaetano Mosca, *The Ruling Class* (New York; 1939), chap. 9; Karl Mannheim, *Freedom, Power, and Democratic Planning* (New York, 1950), pp. 127–31; Stanislaw Andrzejewski, *Military Organization and Society* (London, 1954); Morris Janowitz, "The Professional Soldier and Political Power: A Theoretical Orientation and Selected Hypotheses" (Bureau of Government, Institute of Public Administration, Univ. of Michigan, 1953, mimeo.); Burton Sapin, Richard C. Snyder, and H.W. Bruck, *An Appropriate Role for the Military in American Foreign Policy-Making: A Research Note (Foreign Policy Analysis Series No. 4,* Organizational Behavior Section, Princeton Univ., 1954).

2. These concepts owe much to Friedrich's general distinction between objective functional responsibility and subjective political responsibility in the public service. See Carl J. Friedrich, et al., *Problems of the American Public Service* (New York, 1935), pp. 36–37.

3. For analysis of the characteristics of the military profession and its evolution in the 18th and 19th centuries, see this author's volume, *The Soldier and the State: A Study in the Theory and Practice of Civil-Military Relations* (Cambridge, Mass., 1960) chaps. 1, 2.

4. *The Good Soldier* (London, 1948), pp. 27–28.

5. See *The Soldier and the State,* chap. 5, for analysis of the contrast between Japanese political militarism and German professional militarism.

6. See *supra,* note 1.

7. See, e.g., Silas Bent McKinley, *Democracy and Military Power* (New York, 1941); Katherine Chorley, *Armies and the Art of Revolution* (London, 1943).

8. For recent statements of the incompatibility of continued military insecurity with continued civilian control, see Louis Smith, *American Democracy and Military Power* (Chicago, 1951), and the various writings of Harold Lasswell in which he expounds his "garrison state" concept.

9. For a detailed description of the ways in which the American Constitution frustrates objective control, see *The Soldier and the State*, chap. 7.

Civilian Control*

by
Morris Janowitz

The imagery and the realities of civilian control condition the military pattern of strategic planning. The term *military-industrial complex* has activated the professional officer's defensiveness. It reminds him of the important percentage of national resources which has been placed at the disposal of the military. And it implies that military weaponry was not procured as a result of careful calculation in the public interest, but rather as the result of fierce political struggles in which profits are an essential component. For the military man the term is replete with ambiguities, since he is prone to believe that basic decisions are made by civilians for civilian "political considerations."

The professional officer does not realize that the term military-industrial complex, as employed in the work of C. Wright Mills, the independent "radical" sociologist, and Malcolm Moss, liberal political scientist and presidential speech writer, has become dated. In academic circles, it is generally recognized that the original decisions to intervene in Vietnam and the decisions to deescalate and to start negotiations rested in civilian hands and were under presidential initiative. The military remained prepared to accept a firm decision to terminate hostilities by political arrangements, regardless of any officer's personal views. At most, the military were junior partners in formulating United States foreign policy. Such an orientation could be found in the writings of radical critics of American foreign policy, for example, Gabriel Kolko.[1]

In the 1960's, the formulations of the military as a pressure group, as set forth in *The Professional Soldier*, came into sharper focus. The military is a unique pressure group because of the immense resources under its control and the gravity of its functions. In particular, research highlighted the well-known imbalance in the resources and effectiveness of the Department of Defense in contrast to the Department of State in managing both the day-to-day operations and the longer-term patterns of United States foreign policy.[2] The effectiveness of the military as a pressure group is enhanced by its unified training and educational system, especially its higher schools, which develop a strong sense of corporate identity among its members.

Relations between the armed forces and the Central Intelligence Agency, on the other hand, are vague and under a screen of secrecy. It seems probable, however, that the Central Intelligence Agency often exercises the greater initiative and influence.[3] Paul Blackstock's comprehensive historical study of covert foreign relations in a variety of nations underlines the inherent three-way struggle between the officials responsible for foreign affairs (the Department of State), the professional intelligence services (Central Intelligence Agency) and the covert operational personnel of the armed forces.[4] There is no reason to believe that these issues will become less acute in the decade of the 1970's.

Economic pressures have undermined any oversimplified notions of the military-industrial complex. In a period of continuous inflation, the business community has produced powerful sources of opposition to existing United States military policy, although it may be difficult to translate business opposition into political policy. Reduction in defense spending, a wide range of economists believed, would not reduce overall levels of economic activity in the United States. However, a small number of industrial concentrations with substantial vested interests in military spending would suffer more than other industries would gain. Stanley Lieberson's analysis has identified the states that would suffer from cuts in defense spending.[5] It is striking that senators from those states dominate the Senate Armed Services Committee, a base from which they are able to act as powerful agents on behalf of defense and defense-related industries. This coalition must compete with the other major "interests," and they have been able to do this with considerable success, since outside the Soviet bloc the United States spends a larger share of its gross national product and government budget on its military than any other nation except Israel. In evaluating past and future trends, however, it needs to be recorded that the proportion of the federal budget spent on military affairs was higher for long periods in the nineteenth century, that a large fraction of the expenditures in the second half of 1960–70 were used to support the war in Vietnam, that conventional forces consume a larger share of the budget than do nuclear forces (to the extent to which the distinction can be made), and that even with the expansion of the military budget for the fiscal years 1968 and 1969, the military expenditures as a proportion of the gross national product declined.

In 1960–70, the military establishment was given vast resources to impose on Southeast Asia, by force, a logic of containment first applied to western Europe. This military effort during a period of domestic social and political tension produced the most violent antimilitarism in modern United States history and profoundly exacerbated the cleavages in the American political system. The military, in turn, developed a defensiveness and a deep sense of strain. However, in summary, the impact of Vietnam on the military profession must be seen in the context of the military's gradual transformation since the end of World War II. After a half-century of increased interpenetration of the military and the civilian sectors, the trend toward "civilianization" has been slowed and may even have reached its limits in many of its aspects. Technology and the changed role of the military in international relations, either actual or desired, mean the decline of mass armed forces.

The outcome is not predetermined, but in the 1970's the end of the traditional format of selective service is in sight. An all-volunteer system will result in a marked reduction in the size of the military force, and this in turn will have a profound impact on international relations. In the first instance, the issue is conceptual, professional, and political; that is, a clearer understanding is required by both the military profession and political leadership of the potentials and limits within which force, especially United States force, has come to operate, and the political consequences of every military act or intent. Mechanical thinking about force levels and logistics must give way to realistic analysis of the manner in which the United States military projects and represents its political intentions and political aspirations.

The mechanics of civilian control and the structure of military forces designed more and more for specific purposes leave little room for a pool of resources and men to be used in unexpected contingencies. For example, military planners have resisted the notion that future military forces could be effective and their morale maintained if they have secondary functions. One such secondary, stand-by function is as an emergency force for natural and man-made disasters, including power failures, pollution emergencies, and the like. By 1970, the nation could not engage in emergency overseas relief programs (as in Jordan and Pakistan), clean beaches after oil mishaps, search continuously for lost survivors at sea, or engage in a great variety of related tasks without the support of the armed services. However, military leaders preferred not to make these activities explicit in planning for the future.

Likewise, the military has effectively resisted efforts to use its facilities in educational and remedial programs. It felt that such efforts would divert it from its basic task, lower the quality of its manpower, and reduce its prestige. In a democratic society, funds cannot be allocated to the military which legitimately belong to civilian educational institutions. However, the military has traditionally served as a second chance institution in its routine training functions and without extra cost. The military has failed to understand that in this role it is not expected to solve the unsolved problems of civilian society, but rather, to operate a small-scale demonstration effort—a by-product of its ongoing activities. Therefore, the success of Project 100,000, a small-scale program of inducting men with limited educational achievement, should demonstrate to civilian institutions the modifications they must at least consider. The armed forces have been able to function as a remedial educational institution because they deemphasize the social background and the prior failures of their recruits, make use of labor intensive techniques, avoid excessive professionalization, and build on the social cohesion and self-esteem that military life affords their lower-status recruits.

The prospect of an all volunteer force implies that the profession will be smaller and more self-contained and that there will be a new pattern of civil-military relations. Although some dimensions of military life, such as its internal authority, will continue to converge with civilian society, its skill structure, its patterns of recruitment, its style of garrison life, and its search to maintain its heroic image will continue to differentiate it in important ways from civilian society.

Domestically, the all-volunteer armed forces entails potentials of greater social isolation and new political imbalances and tensions. The danger rests in highly selective linkages with civilian society. These include a possible officer and enlisted body markedly unrepresentative of civilian society, excessive emphasis on in-service education, and narrow and uniform career experiences for top leaders. It rests in the possibility of an inbred force which would hold deep resentments toward the civilian society and accordingly develop a strongly conservative, "extremist" political ideology, which in turn would influence professional judgments.

But in the summer of 1970, the prospect of an all-volunteer force began to release new critical and innovative energies in the military. There are many mechanisms by which the undesirable features of an all-volunteer armed force could be reduced. These include approaches such as one year in a civilian university for all academy cadets, a stronger emphasis on officer candidate schools, the development of five- and ten-year career officers, lateral entry into the military profession at middle-level ranks, an improved system of military justice, and more effective grievance procedures. The personnel problems of the military profession in the 1970's will be complex because of the declining career prospects and problems of transition to a second civilian career. In particular, intellectual isolation from the main current of American university life may be one of the main trends that needs to be avoided. Much of the initiative to offset such intellectual isolation will have to be taken by civilian universities, if they are to remain centers of vigorous intellectual investigation and discourse.

There are civilian scholars who believe that the mechanics of the marketplace will correct the problems and difficulties of the military profession. They underestimate the issues of self-esteem and self-conceptions. The military think of themselves as civil servants in national service, and that is an essential ingredient of civil control. To be paid adequately is essential for one's prestige; but the military resist the idea that civilian society should assume that they are in the military merely or primarily because of considerations of the marketplace. Such a definition leads them to feel that they are mercenaries and not professionals subject to internal and external control. A volunteer armed force will be much less likely to think of itself as mercenary if military service is seen as part of a broader system of community and national service, itself based on voluntary participation.

END NOTES

1. Kolko, Gabriel, *The Roots of American Foreign Policy*. Boston: Beacon Press, 1969.

2. For example, see Adam Yarmolinsky, "Bureaucratic Structure and Political Outcomes," *Journal of International Affairs*, No. 2, 1969, pp. 225–235.

3. Ransom, Harry Howe, *The Intelligence Establishment*. Cambridge: Harvard University Press, 1970.

4. Blackstock, Paul, *The Strategy of Subversion: Manipulating the Politics of Other Nations*. Chicago: Quadrangle Books, 1964.

5. Lieberson, Stanley, "An Empirical Study of Military-Industrial Linkages," *American Journal of Sociology*, January 1970, pp. 562–584.

The Military:
A Professional Organization

Officership as a Profession*

by
Samuel P. Huntington

PROFESSIONALISM AND THE MILITARY

The modern officer corps is a professional body and the modern military officer a professional man. This is, perhaps, the most fundamental thesis of this book. A profession is a peculiar type of functional group with highly specialized characteristics. Sculptors, stenographers, entrepreneurs, and advertising copywriters all have distinct functions but no one of these functions is professional in nature. Professionalism, however, is characteristic of the modern officer in the same sense in which it is characteristic of the physician or lawyer. Professionalism distinguishes the military officer of today from the warriors of previous ages. The existence of the officer corps as a professional body gives a unique cast to the modern problem of civil-military relations.

The nature and history of other professions have been thoroughly discussed. Yet the professional character of the modern officer corps has been neglected. In our society, the businessman may command more income; the politician may command more power; but the professional man commands more respect. Yet the public, as well as the scholar, hardly conceives of the officer in the same way that it does the lawyer or doctor, and it certainly does not accord to the officer the deference which it gives to the civilian professionals. Even the military themselves are influenced by their image in the public mind

---

*Reprinted by permission of the publishers from pp. 7–18 *The Soldier and the State* by Samuel P. Huntington, Cambridge, Mass.: The Belknap Press of Harvard University Press, © 1960 by the President and Fellows of Harvard College.

and at times have refused to accept the implications of their own professional status. When the term "professional" has been used in connection with the military, it normally has been in the sense of "professional" as contrasted with "amateur" rather than in the sense of "profession" as contrasted with "trade" or "craft." The phrases "professional army" and "professional soldier" have obscured the difference between the career enlisted man who is professional in the sense of one who works for monetary gain and the career officer who is professional in the very different sense of one who pursues a "higher calling" in the service of society.

THE CONCEPT OF PROFESSION

The first step in analyzing the professional character of the modern officer corps is to define professionalism. The distinguished characteristics of a profession as a special type of vocation are its expertise, responsibility, and corporateness.[1]

Expertise

The professional man is an expert with specialized knowledge and skill in a significant field of human endeavor. His expertise is acquired only by prolonged education and experience. It is the basis of objective standards of professional competence for separating the profession from laymen and measuring the relative competence of members of the profession. Such standards are universal. They inhere in the knowledge and skill and are capable of general application irrespective of time and place. The ordinary skill or craft exists only in the present and is mastered by learning an existing technique without reference to what has gone before. Professional knowledge, however, is intellectual in nature and capable of preservation in writing. Professional knowledge has a history, and some knowledge of that history is essential to professional competence. Institutions of research and education are required for the extension and transmission of professional knowledge and skill. Contact is maintained between the academic and practical sides of a profession through journals, conferences, and the circulation of personnel between practice and teaching.

Professional expertise also has a dimension in breadth which is lacking in the normal trade. It is a segment of the total cultural tradition of society. The professional man can successfully apply his skill only when he is aware of this broader tradition of which he is a part. Learned professions are "learned" simply because they are an integral part of the total body of learning of society. Consequently professional education consists of two phases: the first imparting a broad, liberal, cultural background, and the second imparting the specialized skills and knowledge of the profession. The liberal education of the professional man is normally handled by the general educational institutions of society devoted to this purpose. The second or technical phase of professional education, on the other hand, is given in special institutions operated by or affiliated with the profession itself.

Responsibility

The professional man is a practicing expert, working in a social context, and performing a service, such as the promotion of health, education, or justice, which is essential to the functioning of society. The client of every profession is society, individually or collectively. A research chemist, for instance, is not a professional man because the service he renders, while beneficial to society, is not essential to its immediate existence and functioning: only Du Pont and the Bureau of Standards have a direct and immediate interest in what he has to offer. The essential and general character of his service and his monopoly of his skill impose upon the professional man the responsibility to perform the service when required by society. This social responsibility distinguishes the professional man from other experts with only intellectual skills. The research chemist, for instance, is still a research chemist if he uses his skills in a manner harmful to society. But the professional man can no longer practice if he refuses to accept his social responsibility: a physician ceases to be a physician if he uses his skills for antisocial purposes. The responsibility to serve and devotion to his skill furnish the professional motive. Financial remuneration cannot be the primary aim of the professional man *qua* professional man. Consequently, professional compensation normally is only partly determined by bargaining on the open market and is regulated by professional custom and law.

The performance of an essential service not regulated by the normal expectation of financial rewards requires some statement governing the relations of the profession to the rest of society. Conflicts between the professional man and his clients, or among members of the profession, normally furnish the immediate impetus to the formulation of such a statement. The profession thus becomes a moral unit positing certain values and ideals which guide its members in their dealings with laymen. This guide may be a set of unwritten norms transmitted through the professional educational system or it may be codified into written canons of professional ethics.

Corporateness

The members of a profession share a sense of organic unity and consciousness of themselves as a group apart from laymen. This collective sense has its origins in the lengthy discipline and training necessary for professional competence, the common bond of work, and the sharing of a unique social responsibility. The sense of unity manifests itself in a professional organization which formalizes and applies the standards of professional competence and establishes and enforces the standards of professional responsibility. Membership in the professional organization, along with the possession of special expertise and the acceptance of special responsibility, thus becomes a criterion of professional status, publicly distinguishing the professional man from the layman. The interest of the profession requires it to bar its members from capitalizing upon professional competence in areas where that competence has no relevance and likewise to protect itself against outsiders who would claim professional competence because of achievements or attributes in other fields.

Professional organizations are generally either associations or bureaucracies. In the associational professions such as medicine and law, the practitioner typically functions independently and has a direct personal relationship with his client. The bureaucratic professions, such as the diplomatic services, possess a high degree of specialization of labor and responsibilities within the profession, and the profession as a whole renders a collective service to society as a whole. These two categories are not mutually exclusive: bureaucratic elements exist in most associational professions, and associations frequently supplement the formal structure of bureaucratic professions. The associational professions usually possess written codes of ethics since each practitioner is individually confronted with the problem of proper conduct toward clients and colleagues. The bureaucratic professions, on the other hand, tend to develop a more general sense of collective professional responsibility and the proper role of the profession in society.

THE MILITARY PROFESSION

The vocation of officership meets the principal criteria of professionalism. In practice, no vocation, not even medicine or law, has all the characteristics of the ideal professional type. Officership probably falls somewhat further short of the ideal than either of these. Yet its fundamental character as a profession is undeniable. In practice, officership is strongest and most effective when it most closely approaches the professional ideal; it is weakest and most defective when it falls short of that ideal.

The Expertise of Officership

What is the specialized expertise of the military officer? Is there any skill common to all military officers and yet not shared with any civilian groups? At first glance this hardly seems to be the case. The officer corps appears to contain many varieties of specialists, including large numbers which have their counterparts in civilian life. Engineers, doctors, pilots, ordnance experts, personnel experts, intelligence experts, communications experts—all these are found both within and without the modern officer corps. Even ignoring these technical specialists, each absorbed in his own branch of knowledge, just the broad division of the corps into land, sea, and air officers appears to create vast differences in the functions performed and the skills required. The captain of a cruiser and the commander of an infantry division appear to be faced with highly different problems requiring highly different abilities.

Yet a distinct sphere of military competence does exist which is common to all, or almost all, officers and which distinguishes them from all, or almost all, civilians. This central skill is perhaps best summed up in Harold Lasswell's phrase "the management of violence." The function of a military force is successful armed combat. The duties of the military officer include: (1) the organizing, equipping, and training of this force; (2) the planning of its activities; and (3) the direction of its operation in and out of combat. The direction, operation, and control of a human organization whose primary function is the application of violence is the peculiar skill of the officer. It is common to the activities of the air, land, and sea officers. It distinguishes the military officer *qua* military officer from the other specialists which exist in the modern armed services. The skills of these experts may be necessary to the achievement of the objectives of the military force. But they are basically auxiliary vocations, having the same relation to the expertise of the officer as the skills of the nurse, chemist, laboratory technician, dietician, pharmacist, and X-ray technician have to the expertise of the doctor. None of the auxiliary specialists contained within or serving the military profession is capable of the "management of violence," just as none of the specialists aiding the medical profession is capable of the diagnosis and treatment of illness. The essence of officership is embodied in the traditional admonition to Annapolis men that their duty will be to "fight the fleet." Individuals, such as doctors, who are not competent to manage violence but who are members of the officer corps are normally distinguished by special titles and insignia and are excluded from positions of military command. They belong to the officer corps in its capacity as an administrative organization of the state, but not in its capacity as a professional body.

Within the profession itself there are specialists in the management of violence on sea, on land, and in the air, just as there are heart, stomach, and eye specialists within medicine. A military specialist is an officer who is peculiarly expert at directing the application of violence under certain prescribed conditions. The variety of conditions under which violence may be employed and the different forms in which it may be applied form the basis for subprofessional specialization. They also form the basis for evaluating relative technical competence. The larger and more complex the organizations of violence which an officer is capable of directing, and the greater the number of situations and conditions under which he can be employed, the higher is his professional competence. A man who is capable of directing only the activities of an infantry squad has such a low level of professional ability as to be almost on the border line. A man who can manage the operations of an airborne division or a carrier task force is a highly competent professional. The officer who can direct the complex activities of a combined operation involving large-scale sea, air, and land forces is at the top of his vocation.

It is readily apparent that the military function requires a high order of expertise. No individual, whatever his inherent intellectual ability and qualities of character and leadership, could perform these functions efficiently without considerable training and experience. In emergencies an untrained civilian may be capable of acting as a military officer at a low level for a brief period of time, just as in emergencies the intelligent layman may fill in until the doctor arrives. Before the management of violence became the extremely complex task that it is in modern civilization, it was possible for someone without specialized training to practice officership. Now, however, only the person who completely devotes his working hours to this task can hope to develop a reasonable level of professional competence. The skill of the officer is neither a craft (which is primarily mechanic) nor an art (which requires unique and nontransferable talent). It is instead an extraordinarily complex intellectual skill requiring comprehensive study and training. It must be remembered that the peculiar skill of the officer is the management of violence, not the act of violence itself. Firing a rifle, for instance, is basically a mechanical craft; directing the operations of a rifle company requires an entirely different type of ability which may in part be learned from books and in part from practice and experience. The intellectual content of the military profession requires the modern officer to devote about one-third of his professional life to formal schooling, probably a higher ratio of educational time to practice time than in any other profession. In part this reflects the limited opportunities of the officer to acquire practical experience at the most important elements of his vocation. But to a large degree it also reflects the extreme complexity of the military expertise.

The peculiar skill of the military officer is universal in the sense that its essence is not affected by changes in time or location. Just as the qualifications of a good surgeon are the same in Zurich as they are in New York, the same standards of professional military competence apply in Russia as in America and in the nineteenth century as in the twentieth. The possession of a common professional skill is a bond among military officers cutting across other differences. The vocation of the officer also possesses a history. The management of violence is not a skill which can be mastered simply by learning existing techniques. It is in a continuous process of development, and it is necessary for the officer to understand this development and to be aware of its main tendencies and trends. Only if he is aware of the historical development of the techniques of organizing and directing military forces can the officer expect to stay on top of his profession. The importance of the history of war and military affairs receives sustained emphasis throughout military writings and military education.

The military skill requires a broad background of general culture for its mastery. The methods of organizing and applying violence at any one stage in history are intimately related to the entire cultural pattern of society. Just as law at its borders merges into history, politics, economics, sociology, and psychology, so also does the military skill. Even more, military knowledge also has frontiers on the natural sciences of chemistry, physics, and biology. To understand his trade properly, the officer must have some idea of its relation to these other fields and the ways in which these other areas of knowledge may contribute to his own purposes. In addition, he cannot really develop his analytical skill, insight, imagination, and judgment if he is trained simply in vocational duties. The abilities and habits of mind which he requires within his professional field can in large part be acquired only through the broader avenues of learning outside his profession. The fact that, like the lawyer and the physician, he is continuously dealing with human beings requires him to have the deeper understanding of human attitudes, motivations, and behavior which a liberal education stimulates. Just as a general education has become the prerequisite for entry into the professions of law and medicine, it is now also almost universally recognized as a desirable qualification for the professional officer.

The Responsibility of Officership

The expertise of the officer imposes upon him a special social responsibility. The employment of his expertise promiscuously for his own advantage would wreck the fabric of society. As with the practice of medicine, society insists that the management of violence be utilized only for socially approved purposes. Society has a direct, continuing, and general interest in the employment of this skill for the enhancement of its own military security. While all professions are to some extent regulated by the state, the military profession is monopolized by the state. The skill of the physician is diagnosis and treatment; his responsibility is the health of his clients. The skill of the officer is the management of violence; his responsibility is the military security of his client, society. The discharge of the responsibility requires mastery of the skill; mastery of the skill entails acceptance of the responsibility. Both responsibility and skill distinguish the officer from other social types. All members of society have an interest in its security; the state has a direct concern for the achievement of this along with other social values; but the officer corps alone is responsible for military security to the exclusion of all other ends.

Does the officer have a professional motivation? Clearly he does not act primarily from economic incentives. In western society the vocation of officership is not well rewarded monetarily. Nor is his behavior within his profession governed by economic rewards and punishments. The officer is not a mercenary who transfers his services wherever they are best rewarded, nor is he the temporary citizen-soldier inspired by intense momentary patriotism and duty but with no steadying and permanent desire to perfect himself in the management of violence. The motivations of the officer are a technical love for his craft and the sense of social obligation to utilize this craft for the benefit of society. The combination of these drives constitutes professional motivation. Society, on the other hand, can only assure this motivation if it offers its officers confinuing and sufficient pay both while on active duty and when retired.

The officer possesses intellectualized skill, mastery of which requires intense study. But like the lawyer and doctor he is not primarily a man of the closet; he deals continuously with people. The test of his professional ability is the application of technical knowledge in a human context. Since this application is not regulated by economic means, however, the officer requires positive guides spelling out his responsibilities to his fellow officers, his subordinates, his superiors, and the state which he serves. His behavior within the military structure is governed by a complex mass of regulations, customs, and traditions. His behavior in relation to society is guided by an awareness that his skill can only be utilized for purposes approved by society through its political agent, the state. While the primary responsibility of the physician is to his patient, and the lawyer to his client, the principal responsibility of the military officer is to the state. His responsibility to the state is the responsibility of the expert adviser. Like the lawyer and physician, he is concerned with only one segment of the activities of his client. Consequently, he cannot impose decisions upon his client which have implications beyond his field of special competence. He can only explain to his client his needs in this area, advise him as to how to meet these needs, and then, when the client has made his decisions, aid him in implementing them. To some extent the officer's behavior towards the state is guided by an explicit code expressed in law and comparable to the canons of professional ethics of the physician and lawyer. To a larger extent, the officer's code is expressed in custom, tradition, and the continuing spirit of the profession.

The Corporate Character of Officership

Officership is a public bureaucratized profession. The legal right to practice the profession is limited to members of a carefully defined body. His commission is to the officer what his license is to a doctor. Organically, however, the officer corps is much more than simply a creature of the state. The functional imperatives of security give rise to complex vocational institutions which mold the officer corps into an autonomous social unit. Entrance into this unit is restricted to those with the requisite education and training and is usually permitted only at the lowest level of professional competence. The corporate structure of the officer corps includes not just the official bureaucracy but also societies, associations, schools, journals, customs, and traditions. The professional world of the officer tends to encompass an unusually high proportion of his activities. He normally lives and works apart from the rest of society; physically and socially he probably has fewer nonprofessional contacts than most other professional men. The line between him and the layman or civilian is publicly symbolized by uniforms and insignia of rank.

The officer corps is both a bureaucratic profession and a bureaucratic organization. Within the profession, levels of competence are distinguished by a hierarchy of ranks; within the organization, duties are distinguished by a hierarchy of office. Rank inheres in the individual and reflects his professional achievement measured in terms of experience, seniority, education, and ability. Appointments to rank are normally made by the officer corps itself applying general principles established by the state. Assignments to office are normally somewhat more subject to outside influence. In all bureaucracies authority derives from office; in a professional bureaucracy eligibility for office derives from rank. An officer is permitted to perform certain types of duties and functions by virtue of his rank; he does not receive rank because he has been assigned to an office. Although in practice there are exceptions to this principle, the professional character of the officer corps rests upon the priority of the hierarchy of rank over the hierarchy of office.

The officer corps normally includes a number of nonprofessional "reservists." This is due to the fluctuating need for officers and the impossibility of the state maintaining continuously an officer corps of the size required in emergencies. The reservists are a temporary supplement to the officer corps and qualify for military rank by education and training. While members of the corps, they normally possess all the prerogatives and responsibilities of the professional in the same rank. The legal distinction between them and the professional is preserved, however, and entrance into the permanent corps of officers is much more restricted than entrance into the reserve corps. The reservists seldom achieve the level of professional skill open to the career officers; consequently, the bulk of the reservists are in the lower ranks of the professional bureaucracy while the higher ranks are monopolized by the career professionals. The latter, as the continuing element in the military structure and because of their superior professional competence as a body, are normally charged with the education and indoctrination of the reservists in the skills and the traditions of the vocation. The reservist only temporarily assumes professional responsibility. His principal functions in society lie elsewhere. As a result, his motivations, values, and behavior frequently differ greatly from those of the career professional.

The enlisted men subordinate to the officer corps are a part of the organizational bureaucracy but not of the professional bureaucracy. The enlisted personnel have neither the intellectual skills nor the professional responsibility of the officer. They are specialists in the application of violence not the management of violence. Their vocation is a trade not a profession. This fundamental difference between the officer corps and the enlisted corps is reflected in the sharp line which is universally drawn between the two in all the military forces of the world. If there were not this cleavage, there could be a single military hierarchy extending from the lowest enlisted man to the highest officer. But the differing character of the two vocations makes the organizational hierarchy discontinuous. The ranks which exist in the enlisted corps do not constitute a professional hierarchy. They reflect varying aptitudes, abilities, and offices within the trade of soldier, and movement up and down them is much more fluid than in the officer corps. The difference between the officer and enlisted vocations precludes any general progression from one to the other. Individual enlisted men do become officers but this is the exception rather than the rule. The education and training necessary for officership are normally incompatible with prolonged service as an enlisted man.

END NOTE

1. This author has discovered only one volume in English which analyzes officership as a profession: Michael Lewis, *England's Sea Officers: The Story of the Naval Profession* (London, 1939). More typical is the standard history of the professions in Great Britain which omits mention of the military "because the service which soldiers are trained to render is one which it is hoped they will never be called upon to perform." A.M. Carr-Saunders and P.A. Wilson, *The Professions* (Oxford, 1933), p. 3. Sociological studies, following Max Weber, have usually analyzed the military as a bureaucratic structure. See H.H. Gerth and C. Wright Mills (eds.), *From Max Weber* (New York, 1946), pp. 221–223; C.D. Spindler, "The Military—A Systematic Analysis," *Social Forces,* XXVII (October 1948), 83–88; C.H. Page, "Bureaucracy's Other Face," *Social Forces,* XXV (October 1946), 88–94; H. Brotz and E.K. Wilson, "Characteristics of Military Society," *Amer. Jour. of Sociology,* LI (March 1946), 371–375. While bureaucracy is characteristic of the officer corps, it is, however, a secondary, not an essential, characteristic. Other writers have followed the liberal tendency to identify the military with the enemies of liberalism and have stressed the federal-aristocratic elements in militarism. See Alfred Vagts, *A History of Militarism* (New York, 1937), and Arnold Rose, "The Social Structure of the Army," *Amer. Jour. of Sociology,* LI (March 1946), 361–364. For definitions

of professionalism, see Carr-Saunders and Wilson, *The Professions*, pp. 284–285, 298, 303, 365, 372; A.M. Carr-Saunders, *Professions: Their Organization and Place in Society* (Oxford, 1928), p. 5; Talcott Parsons, "A Sociologist Looks at the Legal Profession," *Essays in Sociological Theory* (Glencoe, Ill., rev. ed., 1954), p. 372, and *The Social System* (Glencoe, Ill., 1951), p. 454; Abraham Flexner, "Is Social Work a Profession?" *Proceedings,* National Conference of Charities and Correction (1915), pp. 578–581; Carl F. Taeusch, *Professional and Business Ethics* (New York, 1926), pp. 13–18; Roy Lewis and Angus Maude, *Professional People* (London, 1952), pp. 55–56, 64–69, 210; Roscoe Pound, *The Lawyer from Antiquity to Modern Times* (St. Paul, 1953), pp. 4–10; R.H. Tawney, *The Acquisitive Society* (New York, 1920), p. 92; Graham Wallas, *Our Social Heritage* (New Haven, 1921), pp. 122–157; M.L. Cogan, "The Problem of Defining a Profession," *Annals* of the American Academy, CCXCVII (January 1955), 105–111. Professional education is discussed in T. Parsons, "Remarks on Education and the Professions," *Intntl. Jour. of Ethics,* XLVII (April 1937), 366–367, and Robert M. Hutchins, *The Higher Learning in America* (New Haven, 1936), pp. 51–57. The ups and downs of the legal profession in the United States may be traced in terms of the liberal education requirement. See Pound, *Lawyer from Antiquity to Modern Times,* p. 229; M. Louise Rutherford, *The Influence of the American Bar Association on Public Opinion and Legislation* (Philadelphia, 1937). pp. 46ff. On professional ethics, see Tacusch, *Professional and Business Ethics;* Benson Y. Landis, *Professional Codes* (New York, 1927); R.D. Kohn, "The Significance of the Professional Ideal: Professional Ethics and the Public Interest," *Annals* of the American Academy, CI (May 1922), 1–5; R.M. MacIver, "The Social Significance of Professional Ethics," *ibid.,* pp. 6–7; Oliver Garceau, *The Political Life of the American Medical Association* (Cambridge, 1941), pp. 5–11; James H. Means, *Doctors, People, and Government* (Boston, 1953), pp. 36–40; George Sharswood, *An Essay on Professional Ethics* (Philadelphia, 5th ed., 1907, first published 1854); Samuel Warren, *The Moral, Social, and Professional Duties of Attornies and Solicitors* (Edinburgh and London, 1848); Henry S. Drinker, *Legal Ethics* (New York, 1953); "Ethical Standards and Professional Conduct," *Annals* of the Amer. Academy, CCXCVII (January 1955), 37–45. For the origins of occupational values in general, see E.C. Hughes, "Personality Types and the Division of Labor," *Amer, Jour of Sociology,* XXXIII (March 1928), 762.

A Pluralistic Profession*

by
Zeb B. Bradford, Jr., and Frederick J. Brown

THE NEED FOR NEW CONCEPTS

In previous chapters we have touched upon several areas which have an impact upon the nature of the military profession and upon the basic philosophy which motivates and gives a sense of identity and purpose to the career commissioned and non-commissioned officers of the Army. Attention was first focused upon the Army in terms of forces—as a combat structure. We argued that a greater degree of specialization was required within the active structure to provide for greater flexibility and better use of high-cost manpower and equipment. A better balance between support and combat structure was suggested to improve readiness without mobilization. These changes would accelerate the importance of numerous non-combat specialists within the active ranks.

We then dealt with the Army as an institution adapting to change and proposed the concept of a pluralistic Army to accommodate the diversity which is required in the active force and which parallels much of society.

If they are to endure these new prospectives must be compatible with the concepts of professionalism with which the career personnel identify. At the present time, this is not the case. The traditional view is one of a substantially unitary professionalism subordinating nearly all functional activities, regardless of how vital to the organization, to a model of the combat leader—to the "manager of violence" as described by Samuel Huntington. While this ethic is essential to the combat elements of the force, it can inhibit appropriate development of new attitudes necessary for the Army to diversify and to accommodate change. In this chapter we will therefore question the theoretical underpinnings of the profession as they have generally been accepted and offer some alternate views. (*Author's Note:* The discussion in the section concerning professional expertise is based in part on Z.B. Bradford and J.N. Murphy, "A New Look at the Military Profession," *Army* [1969].) We will then examine policy initiatives which could translate a more pluralistic concept of professionalism into career patterns for the officer corps.

PROFESSIONAL EXPERTISE

To deal with the military as a profession, we may start with the definition by Samuel P. Huntington in *The Soldier and the State*—perhaps the best known, most widely accepted, and certainly the most methodically developed conceptualization.

Huntington states that the military is a profession because it possesses three characteristics common to all generally acknowledged professions and essential to professional status: expertise, responsibility, and corporateness. For the unique expertise of the military, he adopts from Harold Lasswell the concept of "management of violence." This is distinct from mere application of violence, such as physically firing weapons, for this ability gives only technical competence or tradesman status. All activities conducted within the military establishment, Huntington says, are related to this unique expertise: management of violence. This peculiar expertise is the hallmark of the profession as a whole and distinguishes the professional officer. Furthermore, the military holds a monopoly on this particular expertise. No one else may both possess and apply it.

The second characteristic Huntington cites is social responsibility. The nature of military expertise imposes an obligation upon the military to execute its function not for selfish ends but only in the service of society. The military profession does not exist for self-interest, profit, or personal motives.

Corporateness, the final characteristic, means that there is a shared sense of organic unity and group consciousness which manifests itself in a particular professional organization. The organization formalizes, applies, and enforces the standards of professional competence. For the individual, membership in the organization is a criterion of professional status; laymen are excluded. In the case of the military, Huntington designates the officer corps as the professional organization. Not all officers are considered professionals in his view, however, since some lack functional competence in the peculiar military expertise of management of violence. Those only temporarily serving, with no thought of a military career, are only amateurs. Enlisted men, as a group, are considered tradesmen and are outside the professional corps, although many career soldiers may qualify for the higher status—most frequently those in the upper non-commissioned ranks.

Huntington's model is attractive in its consistency and logic, and it is true that the military does share in some measure characteristics of other professional groups such as law and medicine. But the analogy is insufficient to describe the military as a profession, or as an adequate basis for progress. The error is due to the attempt to find characteristics in the military which allow it to fall within a conventional definition of profession better fitted to other recognized groups. Rather than defining the military by its own distinguishing characteristics, it is interpreted in accordance with a socially standardized definition. This approach leads to the search for a particular expertise upon which the military can peg its professional status.

There are two basic objections to this approach. First, "management of violence" (or similar formulations for the same thing such as "the ordered application of force to the resolution of a social problem") is insufficient to describe what is actually required of the American military establishment in our contemporary global security commitments. Second, the military profession cannot be defined sufficiently in terms of any single functional expertise.

Military expertise is not a constant; it is contingent and relative. Military expertise will vary according to whatever is required of the profession to support the policies of the state. The range of possibilities includes a broad variety of skills and tasks encompassing not only the traditional tasks related to leadership in combat but many technical and managerial ones as well.

Within our defense establishment, the past decades have seen a great transformation in the skills required of the military. The widespread use of systems analysis and our mushrooming technology have created whole new dimensions of military expertise necessary for national security. Quite obviously, any attempt to decide who is a professional, based only upon the relationship of his occupational skill to management of violence or combat role, is arbitrary and too restricted. It also can be self-denying, in terms of doing what is required by the country, if the military does not comprehend a broader role and develop the necessary skills as part of professional expertise. Combat expertise, of course, is the single most vital skill of the soldier, and one uniquely his to develop and use. Certainly it is both basic and essential to the value and effectiveness of the combat arms, and for the entire combat Army as described in Chapter 11. Hopefully, however, this would not lead to the exclusion of all other essential skills needed by the military, particularly in the support Army. . . . a more sustainable, specialized, and capital-intensive Army will put a premium on a range of professional skills. Societal changes toward greater diversity reinforce the need to recognize greater diversity within the professional ranks. As Morris Janowitz points out in *The Professional Soldier,* there is a narrowing skill differential between military and civilian elites. The task now is to make appropriate adjustment in our thinking about the profession to take this into account.

The other two characteristics which Hungtington cites—responsibility and corporateness—are indeed features of the military profession, although they are of importance independent of any combat-related expertise.

Huntington's model has been discussed at some length because it has come to dominate much of the thinking about the profession and illustrates the tendency toward narrowness, an urge to define the profession as unitary in origin rather than pluralistic. The effects of this can be unfortunate.

This has been at least a part of the reason for the tremendous pressures to reduce the length of the command tour. With relatively few commands available in comparison with the number of professional officers who "march to the sound of the guns," the competition becomes intense—as the Vietnam experience amply demonstrated. A broader concept of professionalism and a corresponding program of career development would avoid this.

A MORE PLURALISTIC PROFESSION

We must construct a concept of professionalism for the military on a different basis than for other groups such as lawyers and doctors. The term itself has to mean something different in the military case.

The military profession can be properly defined only in terms of both its purpose and the conditions placed upon the fulfillment of that purpose. The military exists only for the service of the state, regardless of the skills required or functions performed. As a profession the military does not condition this commitment, for in the words of Lt. Gen. Sir John Hackett, a distinguished British soldier-scholar, the contract for service includes an "unlimited liability clause," cited in Chapter 11, as vital to the combat Army as a whole.

The military's obligation of unconditional service to the lawful authority of the state is unique. There are, from time to time, changes in the nature of expertise required for this service. There may even be changes in the meaning of national security itself when viewed in terms of policies and programs. But these do not alter the basic character of the military profession. Many people outside the profession may have a self-imposed commitment to unconditional service to the state, but only the military possesses the obligation *collectively* as a defining characteristic. Certainly, in this respect, it is far different from any other profession.

The military's status as a profession, therefore, can be defined only in terms of its unique, unconditional obligation to serve the lawful authority of the state. It will develop whatever expertise is required to fulfill its unlimited contract for public service.

Obviously there is room here for all variety of dedicated individuals who possess needed skills. The profession does not have to be unitary. There is a hard core which must serve as common denominator, however.

The officer cannot be a member of his profession without subscribing to the operating norms of his professional community as a whole. These norms are in fact a necessity for the success of the group in fulfilling its tasks. Without a collective sense of duty the military could not function and certainly could not be trusted. Military professionals must share a sense of duty to the nation. The professional officer must be an unconditional servant of state policy; he must have a deep normative sense of duty to do this. The rigorous demands made upon the profession by this sense of duty, and the tasks required of it, explain the premium placed upon other "soldierly" qualities. One cannot do his duty unless he has courage, selflessness, and integrity. The military profession must have these group values as a functional necessity.

A sense of duty is necessary, but not sufficient, for professional status. The person must have competence to perform the service required to fulfill his obligations as well. . . . this may require one or more of a number of skills. Finally, he must be a member of the armed forces for an extended period of time. By joining the officer corps he makes his professional commitment and adopts the values of the military community as his own.

Professionalism is more than simply belonging to the officer corps. It is a status determined jointly by the officer and his government. Neither the state nor the officer corps will grant professional standing to the man who lacks the necessary competence or who will not agree to make an unconditional commitment to duty if he is in the combat Army. The unconditional quality of this commitment is signified by the career length and life of selfless sacrifice, ranging from Melville Goodwin's "genteel poverty" to the Gettysburg "last full measure of devotion."

Professionalism thus has both objective and subjective content. It is objective in that professional status is granted by the state if certain performance criteria are met by the officer. It is subjective in that the officer must feel a sense of duty to serve the lawful government "for the full distance," even at the risk of his life. Mentally, he does not condition this obligation.

Some may feel the denial of a single professional expertise akin to that of law or medicine is a self-inflicted wound. We would argue, on the contrary, that the acceptance of our broader concept of professionalism is essential to enable the Army to respond to new conditions and to accept a more demanding role in national security policy. *As a profession of unlimited service, no skill which is necessary for the Army to fulfill its military obligation to the nation conflicts with the professional status of the officer.*

This concept of professionalism clearly applies to the military as we have come to view it in today's Army, and would likewise be sufficient without difficulty for the combat portion of a pluralistic Army. But the nature of a support Army would require a somewhat different manifestation of professionalism. Obviously the officer who provides a non-combat specialty will probably never have to face up to "going the full distance" as may the infantry officer. And based upon the functional requirements of the Army, his service may not even be required on a continuous basis. What then defines his professionalism? To answer this we must go back to the basic purpose of the military itself. The military exists only to perform a service to the state of which it is a creature. No elements of it, combat or support, can be in business independently. Therefore, all members of the organization must be required to place some value upon the higher goals of the military if they are to be accorded professional status. Within the support Army, subordination to a higher goal would be represented by a choice between monetary compensation in return for limited obligated service, on the one hand, and professional compensation to include career benefits in return for longer term commitment, largely on the government's terms, on the other hand.

Educational development might serve to illustrate the distinction. The "professional" member of the support Army might leave the uniformed service to attend graduate civil schooling. But he would do so at the expense of the government and with a commitment to repay the government in service at a later time. Retirement benefits would eventually compensate his obligation. The non-professional specialist, on the other hand, could also leave active service to receive graduate education, but would do so without obligation to return to service and without financial assistance. But during his stay on active service he might well be paid somewhat more than his professional counterpart to compensate for the absence of tenure.

Essentially we accept that the core professional attribute for both combat and support Army personnel is commitment to the service of the state through the military institution. Simultaneously we acknowledge that the attribute of service can carry different forms in a diverse pluralistic Army.

Ethos of Service—The Meaning of Duty

A more pluralistic profession raises the question of diversity with regard to motivations of different type professionals within a single professional organization. As discussed earlier, all must share a commitment of duty. But widely varying conditions of service, career patterns, educational backgrounds, and even life styles mean that in everyday affairs the meaning of duty will and must inevitably take appropriately different forms.

We are familiar with the traditional forms usually measured against the absolute norm of combat and "putting our life on the line." This will continue as an important ethical model. As in the past the combat officers of the Army will be given constant reminders of this standard both in their educational development and as they undergo rigorous and demanding field training which keeps the organization attuned to a battlefield psychology.

Support Army officers will also be exposed to this concept of duty in their professional education; however, we must develop an outlook which is more relevant to their everyday concern. The professional within the support Army will be distinguished from his peers by his approach to his responsibilities. In contrast to the non-professional, he will have an abiding "proprietary interest" in the enhancement of the organization as opposed to advancement of his own particular interests.

An analogy to business might be appropriate here. A "member of the firm" is concerned with the long-term interests of the organization and will make short-term personal sacrifices to advance these interests. He interprets rules and regulations from the standpoint of how they contribute to the well-being of the organization as a whole rather than an arbitrary set of rules laid down to inhibit individual behavior. This latter approach might well characterize the attitude of an "in-and-outer" in a business firm. The professional officer in the support Army will in his outlook be a "member of the firm." The Army will have first claim on his interests. He will share the goals of the Army in fulfilling the spirit of the regulations.

This ethos must be fostered by initially exposing the officer to the overall goals and purposes of the organization and his place in it—as is now done generally by focusing on the combat Army, assuming that the model is suitable for the Army as a whole. But the sense of duty of the professional in the support Army will require continued reinforcement as he progresses in responsibility. In contrast to the non-professional, he must be given recognition that he is a "member of the firm" by preferential assignments and opportunities for broadening experiences.

Enhancing Individualism

The profession requires constructive initiative. There is a perennial dilemma in attempting to foster innovative thought and encourage individuals to stand on principle, even if it is unpopular or at odds with established opinion. On the one hand, large organizations ossify if individualism is stifled. But on the other hand, individualism can be destructive of an organization if taken to an extreme.

Therefore, in asking for individual strength of conviction and willingness to "stand up and be counted," we condition this with several caveats. First we seek a balance—order and diversity in harmony. We do not seek initiative at the price of the destruction of essential discipline. Secondly, we seek initiative not in order to fulfill individual psychic needs for recognition but to serve the broader interests of the organization. This leads to a third and final condition: we wish to foster initiative from those whose values and abilities complement and support the longer term interests of the Army.

This last point may very well mean that in effect true freedom to dissent is legitimate only for a minority grouping within the organization which by some means has been identified as constructive and basically loyal, even if at times disconcerting. The distinction is the difference between a professional who will risk his own career for the betterment of the organization and one who, while perhaps attempting to appear to be similarly motivated, in fact either does not value the organization's survival or would subordinate it to his own ends or psychic needs.

Within these three important constraints, the Army must carefully insure that it fosters a forthright and independent-minded core of professionals. It is not that the officer corps consists of conformists; it does not. But the profession must constantly attempt to provide incentives to demonstrate distinctive excellence and to do more than that which the system has identified as adequate. Any tendency to maintain a convenient myth of professionalism which shies from paying the price of enforcing the rigorous standards of competition which would make professional status truly meaningful must be avoided at all costs.

To take but one aspect of this issue—our schooling system. The low percentage of failure at our Army officer schools may imply that the system is not designed to stimulate sufficiently productive competition among professionals. And one of the implications of this is that there may be little or no overt incentive for accepting responsibility for making critical judgments about officer standards. To flunk out an officer is painful and difficult. It is much easier to accept a minimum standard and permit all to stay than it is to acknowledge difference in ability and motivation.

A profession whose stock in trade is the ability to make hard life-and-death decisions in situations of great stress must not shy from hard decisions concerning professional education. We think that the profession would benefit from enforcement of more rigorous professional standards. This is the means by which we would attempt to improve the conditions for encouraging responsible individualism within the ranks of the career officer corps.

Much of our concern about stimulating greater individual initiative expressed above could also be described as the case against equity—a common concern of large organizations, that all receive equal treatment. Let there be no mistake. All should be treated *fairly;* but not all can or should be treated *equally.* We believe that individual distinctive excellence should be more explicitly encouraged by the Army.

FROM THEORY INTO PRACTICE: NEW DIRECTIONS

Translating a concept of pluralistic professionalism into practice requires substantial initiatives in several key areas. These are officer career management (which is now being addressed by the Army); officer education; and officer recruitment and retention policy.

Officer Career Patterns

At the present time, the Army is grappling with the need to move toward more pluralistic and specialized patterns of career development for officers which will serve the needs of the service for diverse contribution and the needs of the individual for a meaningful career.

This is the purpose behind the recently publicized Officer Personnel Management System (OPMS). OPMS proposes a substantial modification in officer career management, primarily through heavier emphasis on specialization. In other words, the Army is re-examining the essence of military professionalism.

Now being seriously considered, the new system would do three things. It requires every officer to develop both a primary and secondary specialty early in his career; it makes command a "specialty" open only to a few officers, thereby sharply limiting those in competition for command positions; and it provides far greater opportunities for advancement to the rank of general officer via a variety of non-command specialty (support Army) routes. Full implementation will of course take several years to accomplish.

This would be a substantial departure from the current system, which has reflected the self-image of a unitary "management of violence" career force. In order to maintain this image, while yet encompassing a broad array of different functions within the professional officer corps, the career system has traditionally defined "specialist" as very narrow indeed, including distinctly "non-military" functions such as medicine and religion. All other skills related to "management of violence" were included under the umbrella of "generalist." In other words, the contributions of the great majority of officers have been considered to be sufficiently similar to allow for a common career pattern for all but a few. OPMS would not just tolerate but rather reward the development of individual skills.

We consider the goals of OPMS highly desirable for evolution to the professional officer corps we consider necessary for the future. We support its rapid implementation.

Officer Education

As we have discussed above, the Army's educational system—a crucial aspect of military professionalism—will require substantial revision to support a more specialized officer corps and a more pluralistic Army. First and most basic, the Army should encourage competition within the Army school system by a combination of curriculum and faculty reform. The curriculum must both educate (requires exercise of logic) rather than train (requires assimilation of doctrine and proven technique) and it must explicitly measure achievement in the academic environment to include dismissing those not meeting minimum standards.

Second, the educational system should be changed to develop distinct patterns for the combat Army, on the one hand, as compared to the support Army, on the other. The thrust of the change would have the command specialist generally operate within the combat Army system, while most other specialists would follow the educational pattern within the support Army.

The educational system within the combat Army would change little. The combat arms employment schools, Command and General Staff College and War College, would be maintained with modest changes to improve understanding of current social problems and to increase the professional content. Civilian graduate education should be retained as much for the integrative effects of exposure to civilian elite groups as for the academic discipline. It should be possible, however, to focus on those disciplines which are most relevant to the combat Army.

The support Army would rely heavily on educational and training techniques developed by civilian industry. Technical service schools and an Administrative/Logistics College equivalent to the Command and General Staff College should provide sufficient professional content. These should be complemented with extensive graduate schooling in technical areas for officers and use of civilian skill improvement centers for NCOs. All officers would expect continuing upgrading of their technical skills throughout their term of service.

Officer Recruitment and Retention

Once the concept of a more pluralistic profession is accepted, it should be possible also to initiate more diversified patterns of officer recruitment and retention.

Recruitment of officers for the combat Army would generally follow currently established patterns. Entry would be at the lowest rank, with a required minimum age which is quite young. Leadership potential, character, and general intelligence would be basic criteria. For the support Army, more weight would be given to the particular skills of the officers. For a range of specialties, entry into commissioned service might be much later in life and at a higher grade than would be the case for combat arms officers. The background required of the officer upon entry would be that necessary for his specialty rather than for an increasingly responsible role in leading others.

Promotion and retention policies would also vary. Promotion policy would favor the combat officers both as an incentive to service and due to the physical demands of leadership of combat forces. Combat Army leaders would face accelerated promotion and force out. The system should permit most officers to command companies from about age 25 to 30, battalions from 30 to 35, and brigades from 35 to 40. General officers should be required to retire at age 50 unless selected for promotion to lieutenant general by that age.

The support Army would have very liberal promotion policies permitting captains or majors at age 40 to 45. Colonels would be permitted to remain on active service until age 60. More rapid promotion would be possible but exceptional. The basic attraction of service in the support Army is the satisfaction of public service through continued improvement in technical competence in a stable, financially secure environment.

Professionalism*

by
Colonel William L. Hauser†

Military professionalism is a concept difficult to define. Harold Lasswell and Abraham Kaplan explain it in simple terms, as "specializing in instruments of violence."[1] Thus defined, it is not the expertise itself but its subject matter which is unique. Zeb B. Bradford and James R. Murphy, career officers, take a different view. What distinguishes military professionalism from other varieties of a "collective sense of duty," they say, is being "the *unconditional* servant of lawful state authority."[2] Their words echo the insights of Charles Burton Marshall:

> The specialty of the [military] profession inheres not in technical matters only, but in a basic moral requirement relevant to command and obedience. . . . A carpenter ordered to work on wood that will ruin his tools can say no. A tenor called on to attempt consecutive high Cs in such numbers as to crack his tone thereafter can properly decline. A sergeant told to turn out his men for a patrol that will probably be the last duty for most or all of them must comply.[3]

---

†Editor's Note: The author's views do not necessarily represent the views of the U.S. Army or the United States Military Academy. The Office of Military Leadership does support internal critique as one of the key characteristics of a profession. This is one example of such a critique by an Army officer currently on active duty in good standing.

This chapter does not attempt to redefine or cast new light on military professionalism itself. Instead, as in previous chapters, the focus will be on how the Army has responded to external pressures on issues concerning professionalism.

War crimes will be taken up first, in particular the My Lai incident and the actions taken by various echelons of the Army in the aftermath of that tragedy. Second is the matter of corruption, as seen in the scandals involving military clubs, messes, and post exchanges. Finally, there is the difficult question of "careerism," the charge that professional ethics are being sacrificed on the altar of ambition. In each of these three seemingly disparate areas, the Army has suffered extreme embarrassment in recent years and has been accused of having somehow lost or betrayed its professional creed of "Duty, Honor, Country."

The problems discussed in the previous chapters—race and dissent, discipline and justice, and drugs—are to a significant degree "spill-overs" from the larger society. Recruitment also occurs at the interface of the Army and society and illustrates, in a tangible manner, the extent to which the society is willing to support its army and the conditions on which it will give or withhold that support. Military professionalism, on the other hand, is the core value system of the armed services, particularly of the officer corps. It is deliberately set apart from the civilian culture, for reasons which seem obvious and proper to career soldiers.

Some scholars of civil-military relations, such as Morris Janowitz and Kurt Lang, urge the U.S. Army to follow the current German example of maximum cultural integration with society.[4] Others, notably Samuel Huntington, appear to favor a solution not unlike that of the French Army—a major reform of the profession conducted in semi-isolation from society. The problem, which will be examined here in the context of war crimes, corruption, and careerism, is perhaps the crucial one facing the Army, as was forecast by Huntington in 1957, even before the terrible stresses of the Vietnam war:

> The leadership produced by the American officer corps has so far been extraordinary. Only a small handful of the hundreds of general and flag officers have proved incapable in battle, and the top commanders in all three twentieth century wars have been men of exceptional ability. This success, however, was to a large extent the product of the old pattern of civil-military relations. Since 1940, the American people have been coasting on the quality of the past. Unless a new balance is created, the continued disruption of American civil-military relations cannot help but impair the caliber of military professionalism in the future.[5]

WAR CRIMES

Charges leveled against the Army in the My Lai case were for sins of omission as well as commission. Retired Brigadier General Telford Taylor, who was chief prosecution counsel at Nuremberg, stated that the U.S. Army in

Vietnam had countenanced widespread violations of the Geneva Convention. Official policy may have been to adhere to the Convention, he said, but the fact that many war crimes were known to have been committed but were not punished meant that the implicit policy was other than that stated.[6]

In reply to such accusations, the Army stated in June, 1971 that war crimes allegations were always investigated. The Vietnam war had thus far produced 168 such cases, of which 59 had been dropped for lack of evidence and 54 referred to commanders for trial and appropriate punishment. The remaining 55 cases were still under investigation. A slightly different set of figures showed that 58 soldiers had actually been tried for war crimes, of which 32 had been convicted.[7] Allegations of other specific offenses, in many cases made by members of dissident veterans' groups, generally proved to lack substantiation. One of many such was the charge of a former member of the brigade involved at My Lai that his squad had murdered civilians and gone unpunished on another occasion. When Army investigators asked for his assistance in following up the case, he refused.

A celebrated case in 1971 was that of Brigadier General John W. Donaldson, who commanded the 11th Brigade of the American Division in the year after the My Lai incident. According to his accusers, Donaldson had wantonly fired on "innocent civilians" from his command helicopter. The Department of the Army ordered a formal investigation of these charges in June. Donaldson was quoted as acknowledging that his helicopter had fired on nonuniformed persons who took "evasive action" under "suspicious circumstances." He was cleared, after a lengthy investigation, in December. Some critics charged that his absolution represented official acquiescence in callous use of aerial firepower; others, that his career had been ruined "to score points among hostile segments of national opinion."[8]

Whatever the case in the past, the Army was—however belatedly—taking steps to minimize such occurrences in the future. Surveys were taken among soldiers returning from Vietnam to determine the truth of allegations that they had been insufficiently instructed in the Geneva Convention; the results were disappointingly affirmative. It was also suspected that many soldiers believed in the "mere gook rule," that the lives of the Vietnamese were cheap and not protected by the laws of war. To counter such leanings, the Army revamped its course of instruction on the Geneva Convention, doubling its length and including a film which admitted U.S. atrocities in the Indian wars and the Philippine insurrection and even depicted an officer in Vietnam ordering the killing of prisoners to raise the "body count." In contrast to earlier days, when, it was charged, instructors distinguished between "Theory" and "real situations," military students and trainees were now being taught that both the letter and the spirit of the law were absolute.[9]

The series of investigations and trials which arose out of the My Lai incident raised two fundamental questions: (1) how responsible is a low-ranking soldier who obeys an "unlawful order" to commit a war crime, or, approached from another direction, at what rank does a soldier become liable to prosecution for having obeyed such an order? (2) how direct must be the degree of supervision, or what is the limit to the number of echelons of command involved, before a commander can be judged guilty for the actions of his subordinates?

Regarding the first of these questions, Sergeant James Hutto was acquitted of all charges in a trial by court-martial, on the grounds that he was following orders. All other enlisted men formerly of the platoon commanded by Lieutenant William Calley were also cleared by investigation or acquitted by court-martial, either because of insufficient evidence or through a defense similar to Hutto's; those who had been discharged were considered no longer subject to military jurisdiction. The implication was thus that enlisted men were not "responsible." This assumption was borne out in a poll by two Harvard psychologists, who reported that 67 percent of a sample of nine hundred civilians believed that most people would follow orders to shoot civilians, 61 percent believed the actions at My Lai to have been justified, and 51 percent reported that they would have done the same themselves.[10]

At the upper end of the ladder of command, General Abrams was cleared by Secretary of the Army Stanley Resor of charges that he had been present during an interrogation allegedly involving torture. General Westmoreland, Abrams' predecessor and in command at the time of the My Lai incident, told a Houston news conference in April, "any time there are atrocities it is the result of bad leadership," but he termed the insinuation that there had been such leadership failure at his level "an absurd allegation." Lawyers at the trial of Colonel Oran K. Henderson, who had commanded the 11th Brigade of the American Division at the time, hinted that Westmoreland may have known about the My Lai atrocity shortly after its occurrence, but they never raised this charge publicly. Major General Kenneth Hodson, Judge Advocate General of the Army, replied to questions on this point that high-level leaders could not be held responsible for isolated atrocities committed by their subordinates, for, unlike General Yamashita in the Philippines in World War II, each had taken "reasonable action to control his troops."[11]

Charges were also dismissed against Major General Samuel Koster and Brigadier General George Young, the commander and assistant commander, respectively, of the American Division, and against a number of other officers who had been in the division or had been advisors to the Vietnamese in its geographical area. However, many of these officers subsequently received letters of censure, were stripped of certain decorations, or were subjected to other seemingly punitive measures, and it was generally believed that their military careers were finished. General Young, referring to the action in his case, commented acidly, "The new modern Army has developed a technique that obviates troublesome details like a trial."[12] Colonel Henderson was tried for his alleged coverup of the war crime and was acquitted. Three months earlier, Captain Ernest L. Medina, Calley's company commander, had been acquitted of taking part in or being responsible for the atrocity.

So in the end it was Lieutenant Calley who alone stood condemned—in a legal sense—for the entire tragedy. James M. Gavin, a retired lieutenant general known for his criticism of the war, called the verdict "devastating in its implications for the morale of the Army. Junior officers are bound to feel that they're carrying the terrible burden of the war, that the buck stops with them."[13] Reports from elsewhere in the Army did indeed indicate widespread resentment, both toward the Department of the Army for supposedly making Calley a scapegoat and toward the media for portraying My Lai as typical of the behavior of American troops in Vietnam.

Was Calley a scapegoat? Congressman Samuel S. Stratton believed so, and suggested darkly that cases important to military justice might well be taken out of the hands of the military courts. President Nixon did in fact elevate the Calley case to his own office, with the result that even more controversy was raised, at least temporarily. At the same time, the Army published a White Paper explaining that, unfortunate as it might appear, the evidence against others was inconclusive while that against Calley was "overwhelming." A long-time British observer of the American political scene attributed Calley's isolation not to any conscious act (much less a conspiracy) but to another "spill-over" from American society, to which both Calley and the Army fell victim: "Leadership is precisely the quality that is left to chance in American society. Democratic thought simply assumes that it will emerge when needed . . . . Although Lieutenant Calley was in the dock, he was symbolic of the common man whose century this was supposed to be, symbolic of a social and political system that is today paying the price of having turned leadership into a dirty word."[14]

From the day of the My Lai incident until the present, there have been persistent accusations of a systematic coverup of the atrocity. As noted earlier, it was for this sort of offense that the two generals and several other officers were investigated, for which Colonel Henderson was tried, and for which many officers received administrative penalties which were tantamount to punishment. The most disturbing aspect of the case to many thoughtful observers was that, to whatever extent there was concealment, it appeared to have been total, not only in the American Division but in other Army organizations operating in the same area of Vietnam.

There was apparently a lot to conceal. Brigadier General Andy A. Lipscomb testified at the Henderson trial that the 11th Infantry Brigade was unready for combat when he took it to Vietnam. Interviews of various witnesses at trials and investigations by reporters revealed a widespread belief that units of the American Division, especially its 11th Brigade, were unprepared for combat, relatively unschooled in the laws of war, and consistently negligent in reporting civilian casualties. The brigade had been a typically understrength and undertrained stateside unit until it was hurriedly filled, shipped to Vietnam and incorporated into the hastily organized American Division. Such a unit might reasonably be expected to suffer from the sorts of disciplinary problems discussed in Chapter 7. After the incident Colonel Henderson ordered a sweep of the hamlet "to ascertain the number of civilians who might have been hurt and what was the cause of it," but he was overruled by Major General Koster.[15] Later, said Captain Medina in his testimony at Colonel Henderson's trial, he had lied to Colonel Henderson about what had happened.

Whether Colonel Henderson was negligent in conducting his subsequent investigation or was deceived by Captain Medina and did the best he could in light of his other duties was never determined. The failure of certain individuals, however, is not nearly so damaging to the Army as the suspicion that a cross-section of the entire officer corps had agreed, at least tacitly, not to follow up rumors that there had been, as General Peers termed it, "a tragedy of major proportions." Moreover, as Seymour Hersh's analysis of the Peers Commission report showed,[16] the Americal Division staff seemed to be continuing to conceal the My Lai incident, and the inadequacy of the original investigation, even a year later, after every officer who had been directly involved had left the division.[17] A special House subcommittee commented that "the disappearance of so many documents from the files of so many different U.S. units can hardly be attributed to coincidence." The reason for the completeness of the coverup may well have been that a cross-section of the officer corps—not just a few individuals—was profoundly ashamed of what the tragedy revealed about the profession. An unnamed "senior general" was quoted as saying, "My Lai is a blot on the military that will never be erased in our lifetime."[18]

CORRUPTION

Whatever offenses professional soldiers may have committed in the aftermath of My Lai, and whether their motives were protection of the profession's good name or of their own career prospects, the goal was not material gain. In the cases to be discussed here, however, Army officers and NCOs, some very highly placed, were accused of committing acts which were just plain crooked. Particularly heinous was the general context of the corruption—that the system of clubs, messes, and post exchanges organized to ease the soldier's lot in a combat theater had been used to swindle him.

In the fall of 1970 the Senate Permanent Investigations Subcommittee, which had been looking for more than a year into the subject of kickbacks from suppliers to club managers, began checking into alleged irregularities in the slot machine business. Slot machine contracts were under the supervision of local commanders, as was the club system in general, and brought in around $27.5 million each year. It was a lucrative business which, unless closely supervised, almost invited corruption and scandal. A particular target of the investigation was Colonel (formerly Brigadier General) Earl Cole, who had been Deputy Chief of Staff for Personnel and Administration of the Army in Vietnam during the period when the alleged offenses occurred.

At the same time, the Justice Department was investigating five Army sergeants. Sergeant Major William O. Wooldridge had been Sergeant Major of the Army, a post at the pinnacle of the enlisted ranks, and Master Sergeant William W. Higdon had been manager of one of the largest club systems in Vietnam. They and three other non-commissioned officers since retired were accused of having systematically swindled clubs and messes in various parts of the Army over a span of several years. Their cases were linked with that of retired Major General Carl C. Turner, former Provost Marshal General of the Army, who was alleged to have covered up the scandal in its early stages. Turner was himself indicted by a federal grand jury in January 1971 for obtaining firearms from the Chicago Police Department under false pretenses.

The Senate investigation discovered an incredibly tangled skein of names, places, and events. The former general manager of the firm which supplied slot machines to Vietnam testified that General Cole had been paid a thousand dollars a month to provide free storage for illegally imported air conditioners, refrigerators, and similar equipment. A former lieutenant echoed this report with a story of having been ordered to accept large quantities of unordered equipment for transport to another area of Long Binh Post, and of being told by a sergeant that the equipment was for "some civilian . . . it's some deal General Cole made." A warrant officer told of being ordered to keep quiet by the lieutenant colonel who headed the post exchange system in Vietnam, a retired colonel described his adventures in preventing a steam bath from becoming a brothel, and Senate staff investigators reported that the post exchange system in Vietnam did more than $1 million in diamond sales each month, an operation said to be a cover for smuggling large amounts of currency out of the country.

Two episodes were particularly disturbing. The former Staff Judge Advocate of American forces in Vietnam testified that he had accepted favors from a concessionaire in Hong Kong, but that he had thought it all right because the man was General Cole's "old Chinese friend whom he had helped escape from the Communists."[19] Finally, a major told of refusing a bribe offered by Master Sergeant Higdon, of being forced to buy expensive silver services to present to the visiting Army Chief of Staff, General Harold K. Johnson, and to Sergeant Major Wooldridge, and of being privately threatened with physical violence by Wooldridge.[20]

Testimony also indicated that General Cole, when reassigned to Europe, tried to get himself assigned instead to Dallas, as head of the Army-Air Force Exchange Service. Failing that, he urged the incumbent to purchase more beer from a company which was later shown to be involved in bribery and kickbacks in Vietnam. Brigadier General Harley L. Moore, the Provost Marshal General of the Army in Europe, said that Cole went AWOL from his post in Europe at the time when his name first came up in the Senate and that he told Moore upon his return that he had been offered a fifty-thousand-dollar bribe to keep quiet. All of the charges were "unprecedented, unproved, untrue, and scandalous," said Cole. He had merely gone to Munich to get privacy to call Hong Kong so that he could obtain a receipt for a jade figurine he had given a senior general's wife some years earlier.[21]

In November 1971 the Senate subcommittee published its report, "Fraud and Corruption in the Management of Military Club Systems." The report condemned those individuals who had committed illegal acts and castigated both military and civilian hierarchies for incompetent and negligent supervision. The report also found almost incredible the vast plethora of clubs, slot machines, steambaths, luxury purchases, and other non-essentials which were flourishing in a war zone.

While the Senate investigation was still going on, a number of corrective steps were being taken. Defense Secretary Laird directed the Secretary of the Army in the Spring of 1971 "to develop a C.I.D. [criminal investigation division] agency which has vertical control of all C.I.D.'s worldwide."[22] In the fall Colonel Henry H. Tufts, who had been castigated by the Senate subcommittee for helping the Army "whitewash" Cole but who had not himself been accused of any wrongdoing, was appointed head of the new Army-wide command. Brigadier General Moore commented that the Army had been "abysmally negligent" in trying to "ease Cole out" without embarrassment, a charge hardly borne out by Cole's unavoidably newsworthy reduction to colonel. Major General Turner was sentenced by a civilian court to three years in prison, and Sergeant Higdon received a dishonorable discharge and a $25,000 fine. Sergeant Major Wooldridge was allowed to retire after he had been indicted by a federal grand jury. Slot machines were banned from Army clubs, and the post exchange system, like the C.I.D. Agency, was subjected to more highly centralized control.[23]

The Army, like civilian society, is subject to corruption in low and in high places. The uniqueness of the military situation lies in the vast sums—and therefore vast temptations—afforded by the monopoly status of military clubs and post exchanges overseas. These temptations were reinforced in Vietnam by the relative freedom from civil authority of "carpet-bagging" commercial agents. It would therefore appear that the centralizing of criminal investigation, post exchange management, and club system supervision demonstrated the Army's determination that it would never again get into such a moral quagmire.

CAREERISM

In his annual statement in *Army*, the journal of the Association of the United States Army, Chief of Staff William C. Westmoreland admitted candidly that the "root causes of some of the Army's problems undoubtedly lie in our own self-imposed personnel policies." There had grown up, he said, far too much emphasis on short-term objectives and statistical indicators (e.g., numbers of court-martial cases, AWOL rates, inspection scores, charity drive participation, training test scores). As a result, officers tended to manipulate such indicators to show themselves to best advantage, with too little regard for the long-term adverse effects of such emphasis on their subordinates and on the Army's ultimate mission. To correct this situation, the Army was addressing those attributes of the personnel system which impelled officers toward undesired behavior—too short command tours and overly varied assignments. Lengthened command tours would allow commanders to become truly competent and would encourage them to emphasize long-term improvement of their units; a more highly specialized career pattern would also aid officers to develop more competence and therefore more intellectual honesty at their jobs. They would be less "jack-of-all-trades and master of none."[24]

The most notorious of the statistical indicators was the "body count." This indicator, imposed by the Defense establishment early in the Vietnam war to force tactical commanders to be "honest," instead resulted in charges of widespread, even commonplace, dishonesty. The combat leader, often unwilling or unable to force his men back over a booby-trapped battlefield (often still under fire) for the dreary task of counting enemy dead, was forced to estimate, but to call the estimate a "body count." From this sort of "little white lie" sprang the temptation of officers, difficult to resist, to accept without question the inflated estimates of their emotionally keyed-up subordinates or even knowingly to inflate the overall estimate.

The issue had been debated in professional military circles since the beginning of the war.[25] By the fall of 1970, there was a consensus that the "body count" was not only an invalid indicator but also an extremely deleterious influence on professional ethics. Winston Churchill expressed this lesson in his writings on World War I, and his comments go far to explain the decline in the Army's public image:

> There is required for the composition of a great commander . . . an element of legerdemain . . . which leaves the enemy puzzled as well as beaten. It is because military leaders are credited with gifts of this order . . . that their profession is held in such high honour. For if their art was nothing more than a weary process of exchanging lives, and counting heads at the end, they would rank much lower in the scale of human esteem.[26]

Another indicator which appeared to have been abused in the Vietnam war was that of decorations. Critics charged that awards for valor were distributed disproportionately to officers of high rank and that there were unwritten policies that certain "packets" of medals went almost automatically to commanders of combat units.

The most notorious example of this alleged practice was that of Brigadier General Eugene P. Forrester, assistant commander of the 1st Cavalry Division, who was presented with a Silver Star in a ceremony honoring his departure from the unit. Shortly thereafter, three enlisted men, clerks in the division's awards office, wrote to a congressman telling of being ordered by a major, the Assistant Adjutant General of the division, to fabricate an award citation for the medal. They did so, the General's aide-de-camp and copilot then attested to the imaginary events, and the division Chief of Staff authorized the award. The Chief of Staff later took upon himself the blame for the fabrication, having earlier cited as justification the General's overall reputation for bravery. The clerks who wrote the congressman, he said, were "sanctimonious."

General Forrester was cleared of any wrongdoing in this particular case (he had apparently accepted the Silver Star in good faith, having performed acts essentially similar to those cited but on other occasions), but the suspicions that medals had been handed out too lavishly persisted. Statistics revealed that 1,273,987 awards for bravery (about 800,000 of them Air Medals, unsurprising in the first "airmobile" war) had been given by the Army in Vietnam, an average of almost one per man who had served there—this compared with 1,766,546 such medals in all of World War II and only 50,258 in Korea.[27] The numbers increased as the Vietnam war waned: 416,693 awards of all types were given in 1968, when there were 14,592 Americans killed in action; in 1970 there were 522,905 awards but only 3,946 men killed.[28] Almost half of the generals who served in Vietnam received one or more medals for bravery.

In the burst of public interest which followed the Silver Star case described above, a number of persons rushed into print to tell their favorite anecdotes on the subject. Helicopter pilots told of Distinguished Flying Crosses and Air Medals being given to senior officers for acts which, if done by an ordinary working pilot, would not have rated such awards. One captain told of receiving a Bronze Star for meritorious achievement during the same period in which he received an unsatisfactory efficiency report. A colonel, he added, received a Silver Star for taking frozen Thanksgiving turkeys to a "besieged" Special Forces camp.

Official sources held that some degree of embellishment was often necessary because of lapsed memories, personnel transfers, and the tendency by high-level awards committees (and subsequent promotion boards) to give weight to flowery language. Whether that argument was valid or not, replied many critics, the net result was an inflation and consequent cheapening of military medals. The very number of medals awarded appeared to be *prima facie* evidence that the system had been abused. Charles de Gaulle commented in 1934 on this common foible of military professionals, saying that "the passion for rank and honours" was "only careerism."[29]

The officer corps of the Army was deeply troubled, not only by the bad image created by all of these events, but also by a sense that something was fundamentally amiss. General Matthew B. Ridgway, a former Army Chief of Staff and a hero of the Korean war and of World War II, told of being questioned by officer students at the Army War College. Could an officer still have a successful career even though he spoke his mind? Even though he refused to conform to unethical practices? Even though he refused to repeat the military "party line" to civilian officials? The answer, replied General Ridgway, is that he must do these things regardless of career considerations.[30] Author-philosopher Max Lerner saw in that same group of potential Army leaders great hope for coping with current problems. He was impressed, he said, with "their quality, their alertness to broad historical and social forces, and their open-mindedness to ideas. But they have not been politicized . . . [Instead they] see the broad picture steadily with a tough-minded liberalism."[31]

Others were not so sanguine. One reporter said that his interviews with officers all over the Army revealed them to be conservative, politically cautious, and isolated from urban America. They were hostile toward individuals who transgressed the military code of honor but were not convinced that there were fundamental defects in the system. Another frequent writer on military matters quoted a colonel as saying that unless it fundamentally reforms itself, "The Army will be substantially smaller . . . top-heavy in rank and low in capability . . . most capable officers will have left."[32]

The problem, said retired Lieutenant Colonel Edward L. King in testimony before the Senate Military Appropriations Subcommittee, was that the Army was already top-heavy. He cited the sergeant first class who ran the household goods office in Schwabisch Hall, Germany, the lieutenant colonel who was in charge of hunting and fishing in Europe, and the brigadier general who ran the European post exchange system. None of these, and many others like them, contributed a whit to national security. The U.S. Army, he said, was "a dragon with a huge tail and tiny teeth."[33]

Both the House and Senate held hearings on this subject in 1971. Senate Majority Leader Mike Mansfield, in his drive to reduce American forces in Europe, relied heavily on a study done by Lieutenant Colonel King. After demonstrating how he believed manpower might be significantly reduced with no appreciable loss of combat power, King concluded that the Army's failure to cut back was attributable to three factors: bureaucratic inertia, preference for "soft living" in Europe, and civilian abdication of control. The criticism brings to mind the saying attributed to the Confederate General Richard Ewell: "The path to glory cannot be followed with much baggage."

In House hearings on military manpower policy, Representative Otis Pike noted that although the services had 315,000 fewer men than they had had in 1946, they had 26,000 more captains, 21,000 more majors, 15,000 more lieutenant colonels, and 4,000 more colonels. Combat troops comprised only 14 percent of military manpower, compared with 24.1 percent in 1946.[34] Representative Teno Roncallo likened the services to a "top heavy balloon." The House Appropriations Committee also noted that the Armed Services had more three-star and four-star generals and admirals than at the height of World War II. The services were ordered to explain the apparent excess in middle-grade and senior officers and the large size of headquarters staffs and to outline the steps being taken to correct the situation before the 1973 budget was presented to the Congress.[35]

Two articulate critics of the officer corps rose from within the Army. Lieutenant Colonel Anthony B. Herbert charged that the Army had ruined his career because he had tried to expose a series of war crimes in his unit in Vietnam. Colonel David H. Hackworth, on the other hand, voluntarily retired from a highly successful career because of his disapproval of trends he observed in the Army.

Lieutenant Colonel Herbert, a much-decorated hero of the Korean war, initially gained the image of "the Dreyfus of the U.S. Army." In the winter-spring of 1969, he said, he was first the brigade inspector-general and then commander of a battalion in the 173d Airborne Infantry Brigade in Vietnam. He was relieved of his battalion command by the brigade commander, Brigadier General John W. Barnes, and the deputy commander, Colonel J. Ross Franklin, because he had pleaded with them to investigate war crimes which he had observed. Warned by various persons that raising the war crimes issue would prejudice his appeal of the damaging efficiency report which accompanied his relief from command, he kept silence for a year and a half. Meanwhile, his assignment to the Command and General Staff College had been canceled, he had been reassigned as a recruiting officer at Fort McPherson, Georgia, he had been passed over for promotion to "permanent" (Regular Army) major as a result of the bad report (which under the law meant mandatory retirement a year thereafter), and his appeal had been denied for the final time. Only then, he said, with the statute of limitations running out for the offense of dereliction of duty in not reporting war crimes, did he make the charges. In March 1971 he formally accused General Barnes and Colonel Franklin with covering up war crimes.[36]

The Army immediately sent Colonel Henry Tufts, commander of the Army's new CID, to Vietnam to investigate Herbert's charges. The records of officers named in the charges were "flagged," an action which presumably denied them any favorable personnel action until after the case was resolved. (When Brigadier General Barnes was promoted to major general despite this rule, the Army explained that he had not been formally named in Herbert's original complaint.) The Third Army Adjutant General recommended in September that Herbert's bad efficiency report be expunged; Secretary of the Army Froehlke then personally reviewed the case, and in October he ordered the report removed from the record. In November, a special board having selected Herbert for promotion to Regular Army major, the President sent the nomination to the Senate for confirmation. Herbert announced that he was glad to be vindicated but that he intended to retire anyway, in order to be better able to reform the Army "from the outside."[37]

It appeared that Herbert's judgment might be correct in this regard, for he was having a difficult time on the inside. He was removed in September from his job as Third Army reenlistment officer, for which he had recently won an award, and was assigned as assistant industrial operations officer of Fort McPherson, a position which he commented had hitherto been unfilled. A spokesman at Third Army headquarters explained the shift: "The role he has established for himself as an Army critic is not compatible with the job of persuading young men to stay in the Army."[38] There followed an appearance on a popular television talk show, during which Herbert recounted how the authorities at Fort McPherson had harassed him; the next week saw an on-again, off-again cliff-hanger as to whether he would be granted permission to make a second appearance. Herbert later told of a confrontation with the colonel who was his supervisor, in which the senior gave the junior some rather basic instruction in the proper way to salute and to address a superior officer.[39]

After Herbert had won his promotion and the smoke and dust of verbal battle had settled, the Army released three fact sheets. The first, dated November 5, 1971, pointed out that Herbert had not officially made any war crimes accusations until almost eighteen months after his relief from command. As soon as he had made his accusations official, they were investigated. The second fact sheet, dated November 17, was from Third Army headquarters. It denied that Herbert had been harassed, explaining that the Third Army had been extraordinarily patient with his neglect of assigned duties while he devoted his attention to his own personal problems. His application to retire on March 1, 1972, would be accepted. The last was, like the first, from the Department of the Army, and was a detailed, item-by-item explanation of how each alleged war crime had been handled. Some were unsubstantiated, others had been investigated and found legally unprovable, and the remainder had been investigated, indicted, tried, and in many cases, their perpetrators convicted and punished.[40]

As Herbert's star began to fade, other voices began to be heard. Major General Barnes replied to a press conference question that he had relieved Herbert because of a "gut feeling that he was a cold-blooded killer who would be disastrous in the coming pacification role." When told that Herbert had submitted to a lie-detector test, Barnes replied, "if you live a lie long enough, you can pass a lie test."[41] S.L.A. Marshall, the noted military historian, reported that three lieutenant colonels who had also served in the 173d Brigade had requested in vain to appear in rebuttal on the talk show with Herbert.[42] Finally, a former captain in Herbert's battalion, now a civilian in Milwaukee, wrote to a series of political leaders, including members of both congressional armed services committees. Herbert prided himself on his ability to manipulate the figures to advance his career, the captain said, and was both physically brutal in handling his men and dishonest in reporting body counts. He concluded: "LTC Herbert's open pride in his ability to manufacture untruth . . . left an indelible scar on my memory of what was otherwise a proud experience with men ordered to perform in battle."[43]

Colonel David H. Hackworth was, like Lieutenant Colonel Herbert, a highly decorated infantryman. He grew up on the wrong side of the tracks, joined the Army at an early age, and won a battlefield commission. He then made his way up the career ladder until, at the age of forty, he was one of the youngest colonels in the Army and a strong contender for the stars of a general. He had served several years in Vietnam with distinction, and had earned an awe-inspiring chestful of decorations.

In June 1971 Hackworth put in his retirement papers and held a press conference in Vietnam. He was leaving the Army, he said, because he was fed up with it. The Army was top-heavy, support-heavy, and soft. The officer corps was corrupt, with its lying about body counts, its "ticket-punching" careerism, and its unearned medals. In a column which appeared in the *Washington Post* about the same time, he wrote that the "Army's long obsession for training high-level military managers for 'automated warfare' and its failure to provide, as Mr. [Morris] Janowitz says, 'the traditions of the heroic leader' have rendered the Army incapable of dealing with Vietnam. . . . I hold that the war was winnable, and that ineffective Army leadership is the root reason why the Army is now crawling out of that war-wracked country with its tail between its legs."[44] The post-Korea Army, he said, had emphasized "ticket-punching" careers (the "tickets" being graduate degrees, high level staff duty, diversification of assignments, and a necessary but minimal amount of troop duty), which had the twin drawbacks of superficiality and overemphasis on statistical indicators: "One cannot blame the officer corps for this system, for they were just awash in the tide of the system; to fight it meant banishment to Fort Nowhere and the guaranteed end of a career."[45]

A long-time observer of military affairs reported that most career officers believed Hackworth to have violated professional taboos in speaking out as he did. Many officers essentially agreed, though, that the Army had two major ills: an overemphasis on short-term indicators and an equally great overemphasis on management rather than personal leadership.[46] S. L. A. Marshall dismissed his long-time friend Hackworth as "overlong in battle and emotionally imbalanced." A genuine hero, he concluded, but "beyond his depths."[47]

But in one particular, Colonel Hackworth's credentials were hard to dismiss. He had served as operations officer and commander of an infantry battalion in the Vietnamese Highlands, as a battalion commander in the Mekong Delta, and as an advisor to Vietnamese forces in both areas. When he said that the U.S. Army should have—and could have—fought the guerrilla with guerrilla tactics, his arguments were hard to ignore. The opposite stand was taken by Lieutenant Colonel Zeb B. Bradford, who wrote: "If our costly involvement in Vietnam is to be more than a painful memory, we must learn from it as we go about the task of building for the future. . . . Large scale counterguerrilla operations are poor options for our use in the future because of characteristics inherent in both insurgency warfare and in ourselves—no matter how much we would wish it otherwise."[48] Colonel Donald F. Bletz, a member of the Army War College faculty and a former deputy commander of the 173d Airborne Infantry Brigade in Vietnam, sided with neither Hackworth nor Bradford on the issue of American capabilities in guerrilla warfare. He did agree with Hackworth, however, that the Army's massive use of fire-power had been a mistake. Military expertise in the war had been "technical" rather than truly "professional": "Essentially the failure of American military professionalism in Vietnam centers on the fact that the techniques that were used to bring force to bear, well done though they were, were frequently inconsistent with the political objectives. The 'ordered application of force in resolution of a social problem was not all that 'ordered'.' "[49]

As it had with the issues of war crimes and corruption, the Army was working toward a solution here. General Westmoreland had recognized in his 1970 statement to the Association of the U.S. Army that lack of career specialization created officers who were "jack-of-all-trades and masters of none." The policy of variegated assignments, designed to produce well-rounded generalists whom the Army in theory might use with great flexibility, in practice had resulted in the "ticket-punching" described above. Many officers were rotated through a series of jobs (including command positions) so fast that they could seldom gain genuine expertise in any one. The shortness of each tour, combined with their inexperience, led many of them to overemphasize superficial indicators of success, which not only hurt the unit's long-term effectiveness and set a destructive example to junior officers but compounded the problem by hampering organizational communication. Victor Thompson, a student of organizational theory, has shed light on this common problem of modern organizations: "Not only are formal channels intolerably overloaded, . . these channels are notoriously unreliable because of opportunities and motives for suppression and censorship at each hierarchical communication station."[50]

In January 1971 Lieutenant General Walter T. Kerwin, the Deputy Chief of Staff for Personnel, announced that the Army was studying the "generalist-specialist problem." A proposed program of increased specialization of officer careers, he said, would enhance job satisfaction and result in higher retention rates. An unofficial news story published at the same time described the program in more detail. Officers would be encouraged to choose specialized career fields for which they were best suited or in which they had experience. A limited number would be chosen as "command specialists." The purpose of the program was to end "ticket-punching." It remained to be seen, however, how the officer corps was going to react to proposals for such radical change in the career system.[51]

There was good reason to fear a sharp reaction from many officers. Colonels Hackworth and Herbert may well represent one of the extremes to which Morris Janowitz referred when he said that the history of the modern military establishment could be described as "a struggle between leaders who embody traditionalism and glory, and military managers who are concerned with the scientific and rational conduct of war."[52] Two other military sociologists also foresaw conflict between the necessity for military officers to specialize in order to manage the complex bureaucracy of a modern armed force and the traditional desire to maintain the profession as a homogeneous corps of generalists.[53] In short, the proposal was a long way from implementation throughout the Army.

In his annual message in *Army* in October 1971, a year after he had first mentioned the subject, General Westmoreland discussed the proposed Officer Personnel Management System in general terms: "The system will be designed to recognize and support requirements for officers who are professionally qualified to assume assignments of high command and heavy managerial responsibility, officers who are professionally qualified to assume assignments requiring in-depth expertise in narrow specialty areas, as well as those officers whose professional qualifications may lie between these two extremes."[54] He went on to emphasize that the fundamental precepts of military professionalism would not be sacrificed. Leadership techniques were receiving renewed emphasis through special studies, traveling instructional teams, and additional in-service school hours devoted to ethics and personal communication. A program of career system reform was also being planned for NCOs. The officer corps would still be unified in its devotion to Duty, Honor, and Country but would diversify its talents, the better to respond to a diversity of challenges.[55]

The events described in this chapter paint a dismal picture. The Army's officer corps—or at least an apparently representative cross-section of it—seems to have tried to conceal a major war crime. Whether the motive was to protect the Army from anti-war critics or to protect individual careers, the act calls into question the fundamental honesty of the profession. In like manner, the misdeeds of certain highly placed officers and NCOs cast doubt on the professional health of the organization which raised them to their stations. Finally, widespread allegations of manipulation of statistical indicators, unseemly pursuit of rank and decorations, and "ticket-punching" careerism—even if some of the critics appear to have come into court with unclean hands—are too damning to be ignored.

Perhaps all of these bad things would not have occurred but for the Vietnam war's stresses and strains. Perhaps these incidents would have been regarded as isolated wrongs in an otherwise healthy profession had not public opposition to the war fastened upon the Army as the symbol of the conflict. But one is forced to surmise that, whatever outside pressures were placed on the Army, it cannot have been a totally sound organization to have so yielded to them. To assert, as many critics have, that American society is sick begs the question. The Army's mission is to protect the nation, and the military profession has an obligation to keep itself healthy to fulfill that task.

It seems almost simplistic to conclude that a disjuncture between the Army and society has brought about this long litany of troubles, but that is what the evidence suggests. The Army has been unable to isolate itself from society sufficiently to maintain its authoritarian discipline or to prevent the intrusion of such social ills as racial discord and drug abuse; it has, at the same time, created (or suffered) a widening gulf of suspicion and disbelief. It is scarcely able to attract a sufficient quantity and quality of voluntary manpower to fill its ranks and perform its functions; the end of recruitment through conscription threatens its effectiveness. Finally, its failure to develop the personnel management suitable to modern technology—specialized career patterns and advancement based on specialized competence (in combat operations as well as elsewhere)—may have engendered a wholesale pretense at adherence to an outdated generalist ideal.

END NOTES

1. *Power and Society* (New Haven, Conn.: Yale University Press, 1950), p. 195.

2. "A New Look at the Military Profession," *Army,* February 1969, p. 59.

3. "The Military Mind," *Army,* May 1965, p. 88.

4. Janowitz, *The Professional Soldier;* Lang, "Technology and Career Management in the Military Establishment."

5. *The Soldier and the State,* p. 464.

6. "Who's Really Guilty in My Lai Case: G.I. Defendants or Military System?" *Philadelphia Inquirer,* November 15, 1970.

7. "Army Is Still Studying 55 Atrocities Charges," *New York Times,* June 3, 1971, p. 5.

8. Robert D. Heinl, Jr., "Flagrant Charges by Army Demoralizing to Officers," *Norfolk Virginia-Pilot,* December 16, 1971.

9. Tom Bailey, "The Rules of Land Warfare," *Soldiers,* August, 1971, pp. 4–7.

10. S. L. A. Marshall, "Hasn't the Calley Case Taught Us Anything?" *Philadelphia Inquirer,* January 16, 1972.

11. Austin C. Wehrwein, "Army Argues Guilt Limits in My Lai Cases," *Washington Post,* June 19, 1971.

12. Paul Greenberg, "Get-the-Generals," *New York Times,* June 7, 1971, p. 33.

13. "Pentagon Won't Comment on Verdict," *New York Times,* March 30, 1971, p. 12.

14. Worsthorne, *The Socialist Myth,* p. 190.

15. Testimony of Major Charles C. Calhoun, former S-3 of the task force involved at My Lai, at the trial of Colonel Henderson, United Press International dispatch, September 2, 1971.

16. The Army refused to release the Peers Commission report on the grounds that it would be improper to do so while the Calley appeal was still pending ("Army Bars Release Now of Viet Data," *Washington Post,* December 23, 1971, p. 4).

17. Seymour M. Hersh, "Cover-Up," *New Yorker,* January 22, 1972, pp. 34–69, January 29, 1972, pp. 40–71. How Hersh got hold of a copy of the report remained a mystery, but two unnamed former members of the Commission were quoted as saying that his facts were obviously authentic ("My Lai Papers Called Authentic," *Washington Post,* January 20, 1972, p. 4).

18. George W. Ashworth, "Calley Found Guilty of Premeditated Murder," *Christian Science Monitor,* March 30, 1971.

19. Muriel Dobbin, "Colonel Denies Role in Kickback Scheme," *Baltimore Sun,* March 9, 1971, p. 7.

20. "Major Says Noncom Warned 'Snooping' Could Be Perilous," *Baltimore Sun,* March 4, 1971, p. 6.

21. David Hoffman, "Ex-General Denies Charges in PX Deal," *Washington Post,* March 11, 1971, p. 3.

22. "Laird Tightening Pentagon Control of Army Criminal Investigators," *New York Times,* April 8, 1971, p. 15.

23. "Pentagon PX Shifts Start in December," *New York Times,* November 30, 1971, p. 28.

24. William C. Westmoreland, "From Army of the '70s: A Flawless Performance," *Army,* October 1970, p. 11.

25. An excellent analysis of the impact of the "body count" was by Lt. Col. Richard W. Hobbs, "All the Answers Are Not in the Statistics," *Army,* March 1968, pp. 77–78.

26. *The World Crisis, 1911–1918* (London: Thornton Butterworth Ltd., 1931), pp. 297–98.

27. "Viet Medals Exceed 2 Million," *Washington Post,* February 14, 1971, p. E9.

28. Iver Peterson, "Medals System under Study by U.S.; Many Awarded Though War Wanes," *New York Times,* November 20, 1970, p. 10.

29. *The Army of the Future* (New York: J.B. Lippincott, 1941), p. 174.

30. "The Ordeal of the Army," *New York Times,* April 2, 1971.

31. "The Trouble in the Army," *Boston Herald-Tribune,* September 21, 1971.

32. George W. Ashworth, "U.S. Army's Challenge for '70s: An Improved Ethical Climate," *Christian Science Monitor,* July 14, 1971, p. 7.

33. United Press International dispatch, May 26, 1971.

34. Dick Seelmeyer, "Trouble with Our Military Brass Is There's Too Much of It," *Philadelphia Inquirer,* October 19, 1971, p. 29.

35. Orr Kelly, "Whittling Down the Pentagon Staff," *Washington Star,* November 16, 1971; Orr Kelly, "Military's Star Shine Is Legal, Pentagon Says," *Washington Star,* November 22, 1971, p. 21.

36. United Press International dispatch, March 16, 1971; George W. Ashworth, "Herbert vs Army," *Christian Science Monitor,* November 11, 1971.

37. Associated Press dispatch, October 19, 1971.

38. Phil Gailey, "Army-Officer Critic of Brass on Way Out," *Washington Post,* September 3, 1971, p. 8.

39. George C. Wilson, "Col. Herbert Charges Harassment; Army Denies It," *Washington Post,* November 5, 1971, p. 12.

40. "The Herbert Case and the Record," *Army,* February 1972, pp. 6–8.

41. "Living a Lie," *New York Times,* November 14, 1971.

42. "Hero With a Flaw? Some Closing Words on Lt. Col. Herbert," *Philadelphia Inquirer,* November 27, 1971.

43. S.L.A. Marshall, "Letter Paints a Different Picture," *Norfolk Virginian-Pilot,* January 9, 1972.

44. David H. Hackworth, "Army Leadership Is Ineffective," *Washington Post,* June 29, 1971.

45. Ibid.

46. George W. Ashworth, "Post Vietnam Role Worries Army," *Christian Science Monitor,* July 7, 1971, p. 1.

47. "A Real American Hero—Far Out of His Depth," *Los Angeles Times,* July 11, 1971.

48. "U.S. Tactics in Vietnam," p. 73.

49. *The Role of the Military Professional in U.S. Foreign Policy* (New York: Praeger, 1972), p. 279.

50. *Modern Organization* (New York: Alfred A. Knopf, 1961), p. 86.

51. George W. Ashworth, "Army Marches toward Change," *Christian Science Monitor,* January 18, 1971.

52. "Armed Forces and Society: A World Perspective," p. 23.

53. Coates and Pellegrin, *Military Sociology,* pp. 107–8.

54. William C. Westmoreland, "An Army Taking Stock in a Changing Society," *Army,* October 1971, p. 20.

55. Ibid. For a more detailed analysis of the proposed Officer Personnel Management System and its possible ramifications, see William L. Hauser and Zeb B. Bradford, Jr., "Officer Corps Reform Is Our Job," *Army,* November 1971, pp. 34–39. Similar concepts are found in Kurt Lang, "Military Career Structures: Emerging Patterns and Alternatives," paper presented to the Inter-University Seminar on Armed Forces and Society, Chicago, November 20, 1971.

The Professional Military Ethic: A Rationale

Ethical Conduct

by
*John H. Johns**

The U.S. military profession is currently undergoing a very critical examination by some segments of U.S. society. This is not the first, nor will it be the last time we have undergone such criticism. We believe that much of the current criticism is unfounded in the sense that it is based on factors beyond our control, e.g., ignorance of the military role in policy, emotions toward the Vietnam War, etc. In another area of criticism, however, one factor is very much subject to our control—the matter of moral conduct of military personnel. The publicity surrounding My Lai, club scandals, corruption in high places such as the Sergeant Major of the Army and Provost Marshal General, have left a blotch on our image.

Before we get into a detailed discussion, however, let us say at this point that we reject any implication of moral decadence in the Army. Rather, we believe:

1. The code of ethics of the Army officer corps, as epitomized by the United States Military Academy (USMA) motto, "Duty, Honor, Country," sets a standard of conduct as high as any professional code.

2. The vast majority of Army officers conform to the code as well or better than members of other professions conform to their code.

---

*Colonel Johns is a former member of the faculty of the Office of Military Leadership. He received a BA from the University of Alabama (1952), an MA (Psychology) from Vanderbilt (1960), an MS (International Affairs) from George Washington University (1974), and is a doctoral candidate (ABD in Sociology) at American University (1974). He is also a graduate of The Command and General Staff College (1964) and the National War College (1974).

3. But, we must always strive for improvement.

Briefly stated, a professional code of ethics is a systematic arrangement of principles, standards and rules of behavior set up by, and for, a professional group for the guidance of its members. Ethical codes vary in their scope and the degree to which they are explicitly defined. The Army officer's code would be difficult, if not impossible, to express in writing. While we can point to certain specific rules of conduct, we most often refer to the Graeco-Roman philosophy and Judeo-Christian ethical system as the basis of our code. A big problem with this is that these sources themselves are complex, vague, and ambiguous. Furthermore, their abstract principles require interpretation when applied to today's world. Where does this leave us then, in formulating our concept of the Army's Code? We have taken the position that the USMA motto of *Duty, Honor, Country* epitomizes our code. But again, these are abstract concepts that are subject to a wide variety of interpretations. As we know, even the concept of Honor differs among USMA cadets. Just what behavior is to be governed by the Honor Code and what responsibility does a cadet have to "police" his peers' conduct? The concept of Duty is subject to even more variation, particularly when it involves the responsibility to police classmates.

To have a common ground for discussion, we need to develop an "operational" definition of the ethical code, i.e., define it in terms of specific behavior to which it applies. For example, are all Army, USMA, and United States Corps of Cadets (USCC) rules and regulations part of the code? What about the federal, state, and local laws?

As the textbook quotes Kant, "Taken objectively, morality is in itself practical, being the totality of unconditionally mandatory laws according to which we ought to act." Stated another way: "A moral code is a collection of moral rules and principles relating what ought or ought not to be done—what is right or wrong. *An ethic includes both the moral code and all the ethical conceptions and argumentation which are associated with it.*" Note that Kant is not restricting the boundaries of ethics to only those rules concerning "moral" values in the usual sense of the term "moral."

Another view of ethics restricts the ethical code to include only "core values" of behavior. According to this view, violation of regulations and laws promulgated by officials is not "unethical" conduct unless the violation involves core values. For example, violation of regulations by cadets would not be judged "unethical" unless they are honor violations.

The argument for restricting the ethical code to the core values is apparently based on the belief that a code of ethics only deals with norms that are internalized as part of the value system of individual members. Violation of these norms is supposed to result in guilt feelings in the violator and moral indignation by other group members. Norms outside the ethical code are viewed as fair game "as long as one does not get caught." No particular guilt feelings are expected from violators and moral indignation is not used to censor the violator. He is expected to accept his punishment (impersonal, legal) and often loses no moral status in the group.

Part of the problem in defining the boundaries of the ethical code is due to confusion over the term "moral." While the dictionary definition of the word is a broad reference to "the standards of right and wrong conduct of a group," the word has come to be widely used to refer only to behavior governed by religious teachings. Hence, when ethics are equated to morality, the concept is rather narrow.

For our purposes, we will use "moral" in the broad sense, and will use it interchangeably with "ethical." *An ethical code refers to those rules or principles of conduct that are commonly understood and generally accepted by the members of a given social group, and subject to social sanctions of varying degrees of severity.* Translated into sociological terms used in PL 401, an ethical code consists of all group norms which define personal conduct. This gives the ethical code a functional value, that is, the rules of conduct are designed to make the group more effective as a group.

If indeed a code of ethics is to include all the norms designed to make the group work better, can one argue about Army Regulations? The fact that certain norms have been put in writing as regulations is *prima facie* evidence that such norms are deemed functional (by someone) for group performance. Other things being equal, violation of these written norms will ostensibly reduce the effectiveness of the Army. Whether a given rule is in fact functional is a different issue which we will take up later in the discussion of "situational ethics."

The argument to treat certain "core-value" norms differently than the overall norms of conduct appears to be valid. That certain norms (e.g., those concerning lying, cheating, stealing) are more vital to group survival and should be enforced more stringently is obvious. To extend the sanctions of guilt and moral indignation to other norms would clearly attenuate their efficacy with respect to the central-value norms. This does not mean, however, that the code of ethics has to be restricted to the limits of these norms. The norms outside the honor code need only be enforced with different sanctions. One should not expect a clear distinction, however, between norms concerning honor and other norms. Lying, for example, is an ambiguous term and can be by omission as well as commission. Is an officer dishonorable if he intentionally omits certain information from a report because it would make him look bad? Or, is it cheating when one parks in a restricted zone? The restriction was put there for the good of all and requires cooperation. Why should one person benefit at the expense of the others? So we see that it is not a simple matter.

In summary, then, I would argue that all norms concerning what officers should or should not do should be included in the code of ethics. The honor code, which consists of norms relating to core values of central importance, is included in the ethical code. In general, different sanctions are used to enforce the honor code, but this is often a matter of degree because of the vague line separating the two classes of norms. Ideally, we would like all norms to be internalized by group members and made a part of their conscience, but realistically, we know this will not happen in everyday life. To appeal too often to the conscience as a means of enforcing all norms would result in a weakening of the honor code. Consequently, what we do in practice is rely more on external sanctions to enforce ethical norms outside the honor code. This, of course, can also be carried to the extreme and have a deleterious effect if officers look at regulations as "fair game" for violation if they can get away with it. The net effect of all this is that we have something of a continuum running from "baldfaced lies" for personal gain to taking electrographic pencils from the classroom. As one moves from one end of the continuum, less guilt is involved and more reliance is put on external sanctions.

In essence, I am suggesting that we *ought* to feel guilty for any willing violation of a rule if we think it is a useful rule. In practice, many of us do *not* feel guilt in many instances, e.g., speeding in a school zone, even though we know there is a good reason for the rule. To be sure, there are some who seem to have a "moral callousness" toward all standards of conduct and for these people behavior is governed by a "don't-get-caught" attitude. Conscience has no role for these individuals ((the scientific term for such individuals is a psychopath or sociopath). The big question is to where to draw the line. I don't think I would like a person who feels guilty every single time he breaks a rule. On the other hand, I cannot trust a sociopath and don't want him around. So each of us will have to develop our own boundaries on this issue. One word of warning, however, one can start out by "little" violations such as "little white lies," but each transgression makes the next one (perhaps a more serious violation) easier. It is an easy road to "moral callousness" if one is not careful. The best defense is to jealously guard a strong conscience.

But, one might say, when we speak of "norms" we are speaking of "guides" for behavior and not rigid absolutes. In a sense, this is true, for as pointed out elsewhere, norms are flexible, with many of them stated in abstract, ambiguous terms so that they can be applied to a wide variety of situations. Therefore, does this necessarily mean that the "rightness" or "wrongness" of an act depends on the situation (situational ethics)?

Briefly, the concept of situational ethics (often referred to as the "new morality") is that each situation must be evaluated on its own merits and each person must decide for himself what is right or wrong behavior based on his evaluation of the specific situation. In essence, this view of morality rejects the existence of moral absolutes. As Paul Tillich has put it, "The truth of ethical relativism lies in the moral law's inability to give commandments which are unambiguous both in their general form and in their concrete applications." Every moral law is abstract in relation to the unique and totally concrete situation. This is true of what has been called "natural" law and of what has been called "revealed" law.

The proponent of situation ethics, then, rejects the idea that situational circumstances should always be subordinated to predetermined general "laws" of morality. He does not reject the use of principles as guides, but he believes the governing consideration is the situation, with all of its contingencies and exigencies. The situationist enters into every decision-making situation armed with principles, just as the absolute moralist does. But the all-important validity difference is that he considers the moral principles as "maxims" of general or frequent validity, *but their validity always depends on the situation.* He is prepared in any concrete case to suspend, ignore, or violate any principle if by doing so he can effect more good than by following it. For example, the situationist would not tell an ugly woman she is ugly just to adhere to the moral dictum, "thou shalt not lie" if in fact he considers more good would result if he told her otherwise.

What, then, should be our approach to ethical conduct? Should we insist that we conduct ourselves in accordance with predetermined absolute rules, or should we allow each officer to decide right or wrong based on his analysis of the situation? Is there some happy mixture? These are crucial questions that are not easy to answer. In addition to the philosophical issue, we have to take into account the "real world" in which the Army officer lives.

Not even the officers in The Office of Military Leadership agree completely on which approach is best for us to teach USMA cadets. We recognize that norms are general rules for conduct and that rigid adherence to every rule and regulation would be dysfunctional. On the other hand, the total endorsement of situational ethics would open Pandora's Box and possibly lead to anarchy. The following discussion, therefore, may appear indecisive.

Since we are talking about "norms" as standards of behavior it is useful to review some of the characteristics of norms before discussing the issue of approaches to morality.

Norms are practical rules (whether they be sacred or secular in origin is irrelevant) that guide behavior. They are designed to make a group function better.

Norms have varying degrees of flexibility, i.e., some deviation is permitted, depending on how important it is for the group to have them followed. Some norms are considered so important that they are designated as a special class (e.g., "honor" code) and are rigidly and severely enforced. Other norms (e.g., Public Demonstration of Affection, or PDA) tend to be loosely enforced. The same norm may be treated differently depending on the situation. For example, during a crisis, such as war, norms concerning group security are more rigidly enforced. Also, when violations of a particular norm get too widespread (e.g., crime) the group usually tightens up on enforcement and the degree of deviation permitted.

The group member tends to conform to norms to the extent he accords them legitimacy. Legitimacy can be granted because of respect for authority (sacred or secular) or because the norm is perceived as of practical use. Short haircuts, PDA, etc., are not likely to be internalized and may not be accorded legitimacy unless a clear rationale for them is given.

Norms that are common to several reference groups, e.g., the Army, age peers, family, etc., are more likely to be internalized as part of the value system of the individual member. Thus, lying, cheating, and stealing (of the more blatant type) are violation of norms that are readily accepted at USMA because the norms are core values of society at large.

Norms that are internalized will tend to be enforced by guilt feelings (conscience) and peers. Norms that are not internalized (PDA, short haircuts) will, generally speaking, have to be enforced by officially designated enforcers such as superiors and police forces.

Norms that are made by authorities (e.g., regulations) and are unpopular, will use up "legitimacy" credits. If such norms are not enforced, they undermine confidence in the legitimacy of other norms.

Now back to the discussion of approaches to morality. If the avowed purpose of an ethical code is to make a group function better, should the violation of a norm be considered unethical conduct even if adherence would be dysfunctional? Logic tells us that if, on balance, the good outweighs the bad, the behavior is ethical. Theoretically speaking, we agree with that conclusion, but there are some practical problems involved in applying the theory. How does one go about weighing the good and bad consequences of a given act? Long-term consequences are often intangible and cumulative over time so that it is difficult to evaluate a specific act in the overall context of group behavior during an extended period. The endorsement of situational ethics per se has undesirable consequences, since it undermines a person's ability to predict what his fellow man will do in a given situation.

Since every violation of the code has some undesirable consequences, each such violation represents, *prima facie,* unethical behavior. The burden of proof therefore shifts to the violator to justify his deviance from the norm. If such justification is shown, that is, the beneficial consequences of the act "justified" the violation of the norm, one could argue that the actor was not guilty of unethical conduct. On the other hand, one could argue that the conduct is still unethical, but justified under the circumstances. This is largely a question of semantics, but semantics can sometimes be important. If one holds to the absolutist view of morality, the conduct is unethical. If one favors the situational view, the conduct is ethical. How do you feel about it?

Clearly, if we were to insist on a rigid adherence to absolute rules of conduct regardless of special circumstances, our system could not work. Not even the groups who accept absolute morality are rigid or callous about sticking to the letter of the law in every situation, although they differ in the degree of latitude allowed.

On the other hand, if we openly condone individual freedom for determining right and wrong conduct, i.e., situational ethics, we open the door to possible anarchy. We see some signs of this danger in the behavior of the "new left" groups. Under the banner of "rational analysis" and "reason," some of these groups have repudiated tradition and society's norms and have taken it on themselves to decide right and wrong. The fact is that some moral dilemmas do not lend themselves to easy rational analysis.

We do not believe it is desirable to choose either the absolute or the situational approach to ethics; rather, we would like to have some mixture that would produce a responsible balance between the extremes of rigidity and anarchy. Admittedly, this is a difficult task. Should we put more stress on the morality issue in the religious sense or should we place more emphasis on providing officers with the knowledge to make sound rational judgments for each specific situation?

"Moralizing" in the religious sense does not appear to be very effective as a means for obtaining conformity to the ethical code in general, although it varies with individuals. Also, even for those who respond to religious teachings as a basis for ethical behavior, there is a tendency to compartmentalize norms and apply the religious standard differentially. In general, those norms that concern "honor" and sexual behavior are most often subject to internalized sanctions by those with a strong religious orientation, although here again, this varies with individuals and some people apply their religious teachings across the board to all rules and regulations.

Irrespective of whether one's conscience has a religious or secular orientation, he is likely to restrict the use of conscience as a guide to behavior and apply it only to his core values. In the case of those norms which are related to "honor," 99% of cadets and officers have had these as core values all their life. Consequently, we can expect that such norms have been deeply internalized. We can witness this in the operation of the honor code at USMA. To a somewhat lesser degree, we see it working Army-wide.

As mentioned before, however, the boundaries which define "honor codes" are vague. Explicit and blatant lying, cheating, and stealing are easily categorized, but what about false reports to superiors when such reports are common practice and in fact, one may be ordered to submit a readiness report that is not accurate? Cadets are aware of this problem from the standpoint of the question of what norms (regulations) are to fall under the jurisdiction of the USMA Honor Code, which is a codified extension of the core values of our society applied to a specific situation. While the Army has honorable conduct as a core value, it has no formal code and consequently, the boundaries are even more vague.

Even though the boundaries of "honor" are vague, it is important that we strive to develop a high sense of honor and recognize the consequences of loose interpretation of what is honorable. For example, where do the following fall with respect to honor:

Padding mess hall headcount?
Falsifying marksmanship scores?
Moonlight requisitions?
Personal use of office supplies?
Inflated deductions on income tax?

In the final analysis, our conscience must be our guide even though we recognize that each person's concept of right and wrong is different. Nevertheless, we hold the concept of honor as absolute.

When we move outside the boundaries of "honor," we encounter a different attitude toward conformity to norms. How many of us have guilt feelings when we violate a traffic regulation (and don't get caught)? When we don't shine our shoes? When we keep unauthorized lights? The fact is that guilt does not play the same role, suggesting that the norms have not been internalized as part of our own value system. Rather, we are constrained from misconduct more by external sanctions, e.g., the police, green-suiters, or else we conform because we see the practical function of the rule or regulations.

Whether we agree or disagree from a philosophical standpoint, in the real world situational ethics plays a large role in conformity to norms other than those related to honor. This has always been so, but is accentuated by the current rejection of authoritative norms and the deliberate fostering of a critical attitude by our educational system. If the situational approach to ethics is a fact of life, it is best that we know something about it.

Situational ethics is based on the assumption that each person is better equipped to judge right and wrong in a given situation based on the peculiar circumstances rather than rely on an absolute rule set down by authorities. Undoubtedly, this has some merit. In practice, however, there is a tendency to reject general rules of conduct unless the individual considers them legitimate and in turn, the legitimacy of the authority is dependent on the perceived legitimacy of the rules promulgated by the authority. The two are mutually interdependent.

While there *may* have been a time when rules and regulations were accepted as legitimate until proved otherwise, it is certainly not the case today. Ask yourself how cadets view USMA and USCC Regulations? The answer for many is that many of the regs are "stupid, outdated, the product of archaic thinking, etc." Ask a teenager about his parents' rules; ask a soldier about Army Regulations; ask anyone in a formal organization. The answer will be pretty much the same. Why? Is it because authorities tend to lose touch with the world of other group members, or is it because group members "don't understand the problem"? *Warning:* the answer is not simple.

How well is the average Army officer equipped to determine the ultimate consequences of his behavior? Assuming that no personal gains or losses are involved, how does one determine the overall consequences for society? In practice, long-term, intangible consequences are given little weight while immediate, concrete results are exaggerated. Under the guise of "pragmatism," the situationalist often ignores the subtle, long-term consequences of his act. Thus, one can see a disdain for symbolism, ritual, sexual fidelity and other practices that have been developed through generations of experience. Are some of the hallowed rituals outmoded? Yes! But which ones? In our haste to modernize, we may "throw the baby our with the bathwater."

What, then, can we conclude with respect to specific guidelines about ethical conduct of USMA graduates.

First, you are held as the standard by the Army. Like it or not, unethical conduct on your part is a more serious offense than for other officers. Being the standard, you are given extra respect, but you must pay the price by being in the spotlight.

Second, develop a high standard of honor and guard it jealously. You will gain recognition for such and be respected for your integrity.

Third, accord legitimacy to all laws and regulations and insist on conformity. If in your opinion, a regulation should be changed, strive to have it changed. Have the moral courage to speak up when you disagree. Until a rule is changed, however, follow it in your own personal conduct.

Fourth, accept the reality of situational ethics and understand it. If not kept in "reasonable" boundaries, it can lead to anarchy. A critical issue in this regard is the amount of deviation that should be allowed. This is a matter of judgment that you will have to determine for yourself depending on the situation. While in Rome, you do not have to do as the Romans do, but you have to have some degree of tolerance for their behavior (unless you are the Commander, of course). One way of looking at his problem is to view each person as having so many credits for deviation. Not all deviations use the same amount of credit, e.g., a single blatant honor violation may use all one's credits while at the other extreme using a single sheet of official stationery for personal use may use only a fraction of a credit. Each deviation from ethical conduct, however, contributes to the weakening of the code and hurts the image that EM and the public have of the officer corps.

It is incumbent on all of us in the officer corps to take a hard look at ourselves to see if our ethical behavior is what it should be. This is of particular concern to you, because as newly commissioned USMA graduates, you will become standard bearers.

Two good rules of thumb:

1. "If everyone did what I am about to do, what would be the consequences?"

2. "If all my respected colleagues knew what I am about to do, would I still do it?"

Moral Aspects of Leadership*

by
Samuel H. Hayes and William N. Thomas†

The exercise of leadership inevitably involves moral and ethical considerations, regardless of the organizational level or type of organization. The very act of assuming responsibility for guiding, directing, or controlling others presupposes a moral responsibility for goals, missions, and methods. Even the act of counseling implies the assumption by the counselor of moral responsibility for the soundness of the goals he suggests as well as for the results of following his guidance. These responsibilities are inherent in the leader's role. He cannot escape them. The mantle of leadership carries with it a set of expectations on the part of both superiors and subordinates. Not only do they expect him to carry out the functions of a leader, but also they expect him to perform them in a manner approved by society. His personal behavior, his value systems, and his moral decisions are an integral part of his role and are reflected in the expectations of those he serves.

In addition, the status of leadership confers inescapable moral responsibility for setting the example for the group. The example the leader sets goes far toward determining the actual attitude and behaviors of the group, further, in fact, than verbal or written instructions. Thus the ethical and moral prin-

---

*Reproduced from text *Taking Command,* Stackpole Co. 1967, pp. 45–59 by permission of publisher.
†The authors are former members of the Office of Military Leadership at the United States Military Academy, West Point, New York. Colonel Hays received his BS from the United States Military Academy (1942) and his M.A. in Political Science from Columbia University (1950). Colonel Thomas received his BS from the United States Military Academy (1951) and his M.A. in Industrial Relations from Purdue (1964).

ciples of the leaders are critical to the efficiency and effectiveness of an organization although their degree of importance and their impact on the structure may vary with the situation and the objectives sought.

MORAL CODES

Emmanuel Kant, in his Perpetual Peace, states, "Taken objectively, morality is in itself practical, being the totality of unconditionally mandatory laws according to which we ought to act" (as quoted in Ladd, 1957, p. 7). More recently an anthropologist, in studying the moral code of the Navahos, said that, "A moral code is a collection of moral rules and principles relating what ought or ought not to be done—what is right or wrong. An ethic includes both the moral code and all the ethical conceptions and argumentation which are associated with it." (Ladd, 1957, p. 9.) A moral code includes the fundamental rules of behavior necessary for that society's continued existence in its cultural environment. As Erich Fromm puts it, "The function of an ethical system in any given society is to sustain the life of that particular society." (Fromm, 1964, p. 241.) Moral codes establish a major portion of the framework and rationale in which leadership in a society is exercised.

Background. Ethical principles and moral codes have been in existence as long as man himself. The very existence of the societies in which men live is predicated upon the existence of established norms or rules of behavior. These ethical systems may gradually evolve within groups or cultures or be devised by a single law giver or philosopher. Some are attributed to and receive the sanction of Divine authority either as Natural Law or as the dogmas of specific religious faiths. Regardless of source, moral codes provide the basic foundations for common law as well as the rules by which a society conducts its business.

For centuries thinking men have been concerned with the whys and wherefores of moral codes. Traditionally these matters were considered to be the proper study of priests or theologians. This accounts for much of the aura of sanctity and divine inspiration with which they are frequently clothed. In addition to religious leaders, philosophers also have considered morals and ethics a proper field of study as their works from Plato and Aristotle to Josiah Royce and John Dewey testify. More recent scientific analyses verify that both primitive and modern societies face the same general questions of right and wrong. How should we behave? What are the rules?

For those of us raised in modern Western society, the historic Graeco-Roman philosophy and Judeo-Christian ethical system provide the basis for our moral code. Intertwined in the ethical history of Western man are concepts of virtuous behavior, the dignity of man, man's duty to man, and the concepts of freedom and equality. These have slowly evolved through the ages. As understood in the democratic society of today, they include the concepts of equal opportunity and social justice. These norms, and the ethical and moral concepts upon which they are based, provide the basic guideposts and limits for the conduct of the leaders of our society.

Military Code. Within the larger Western society many professional subgroups have ethical systems and moral rules that differ from those of the larger society by being more restrictive and more specific. A profession is an occupational field that, in general, requires specialized training in some abstract or practical body of knowledge. It accepts some degree of responsibility for the actions of its members and has sufficient corporate character to act as a body. Professions that wield extensive influence over the health or welfare of the members of society obviously require moral commandments in order to prevent the unscrupulous use of their power for the benefit of a few. Since the public is essentially at the mercy of the professional specialists, its primary protection lies in the professional's ethical code and the expectation that he will follow it.

The military, legal, educational, theological, and medical professions wield great influence over public welfare. Accordingly, they have developed the moral codes necessary to prescribe the ethical behavior of their members. The Hippocratic Oath of the medical profession has long guided the professional conduct of the doctor. The professional code of the warrior has an equally long history, extending from antiquity to modern times. Modern technology has greatly expanded the powers wielded by the professions. Therefore, far from reducing the requirement for these codes, the industrial conditions of modern society demand even stricter adherence to their rules.

Basis for Military Codes. The military profession differs somewhat from the other professions in that for at least the past three centuries, it has been an arm of the state. It is highly organized on a hierarchical basis and normally controls a near monopoly over those weapons, men, and organizations which comprise the nation's coercive power. In the sixteenth and seventeenth centuries, the conditions resulting from the employment of mercenary soldiery made it clear that the professional military required rules of conduct. They further needed a greater degree of subordination to the governing political authorities. By the time of the American Revolution, the development of ethical and moral codes for the military profession was well under way. Understood as well was the principle that the military institution is subordinate to the guidance and control of the nation's political authorities.

The Army under George Washington carefully followed these inherited rules, as it has ever since. Washington scrupulously obeyed the desires of the Congress, even when it meant subordinating his military plans to the strategic desires of that body, which was not always in those days noted for its military expertise. The loyalty he exhibited toward the Congress, and to which he held the officers of his army, set the example and established the pattern for all American leaders who were to follow.

The fact that the nation entrusts its safety, wealth, and sons to the professional group is an indication of the special trust and confidence both the political leaders and the public at large must have in the military profession. Since Washington's day the power of the military profession has increased rather than diminished. Weapons have become more complex, specialized, and costly, as have the techniques and tactics of their employment. Larger proportions of the nation's manpower can be brought into service. Greater social control can be exerted over both the members of the military service and the public at large. Rapid communications and mass-destruction weapons, coupled with the requirements of international leadership, have forced military professionals into national policy-making circles.

Formal control over the military organizations of the United States is effected by law and administrative regulation. These laws, however, represent only the outward manifestation of the underlying professional ethical system and moral code that supports them. Fundamentally, the Army is controlled and self-regulated by its own informal ethical code. The code envelops all who exercise authority and leadership. It is at once an indication of the public faith in the Army's ability to uphold proper standards of conduct and at the same time a measure of the general expectation of performance by military leaders. This internal professional code establishes the atmosphere of mutual faith, security, and solidarity necessary to an organization in which each member must depend on his fellows for his success and, in combat, frequently his life.

Professional Solidarity. The leader's professional code supports him in his performance of duty. In turn, he contributes to the strength of the officer or noncommissioned officer corps by supporting the code. Any act of commission or omission made by a member of the group reflects either for or against the entire profession. Each leader must bear in mind that his conduct is not just his own business. It is the business of every other member of the profession as well. When an officer is arrested for speeding, it is not just John Doe who is arrested; it is Lieutenant or Sergeant John Doe, a member of a specific unit of the U.S. Army. Each member owes a moral obligation to the military profession as well as to the nation to ensure that the actions of its leaders conform to the highest traditions of the service and to its professional ethics and moral code.

Indoctrination. The indoctrination into this professional code begins with the leader's entry into the profession of arms. The concepts of higher loyalty, duty, honor, and country embodied in the code are exemplified by those leaders who have preceded him. Much of the code is taught in noncommissioned officer academies, in ROTC, in OCS, or in the service academies. Honor systems that demand integrity help to inculcate in each future leader the basic fundamentals of the code. They assist him in developing the moral courage required to make the hard moral decisions that he must make as a leader. The fact that these standards of the profession are more exacting than those of the general society makes this indoctrination a critical element in the development of military leadership in the service.

It is difficult, if not impossible, to express in writing the complex of ideas, attitudes, and injunctions that make up an ethical system or moral code. It is so interwoven into the fabric of our spiritual heritage and culture that only with great difficulty can one separate specific elements for analysis. For these reasons ethics or moral codes are seldom completely expressed or defined in writing. Over the years they have been impressed on generations of soldiers through the examples of their predecessors, the customs of the service, and the traditions of the units in which they have served. Unit or organizational traditions are frequently exemplified in a motto or slogan which embellishes its crest, such as

No mission too difficult, no sacrifice too
    great; duty firsı.
Unity is strength.
I'll try, sir.
Duty, Honor, Country.

Usually such mottos express some facet of the professional code. Duty, Honor, Country, the motto of the Military Academy, provides the most comprehensive basis for an examination of the component elements of the military moral code of the U.S. Army and the rationale for its ethical system.

DUTY

The first element in the military code is the concept of duty. Duty is a dedication to the service, its obligations, expressed or implied, coupled with loyalty to designated military and civilian authorities. This duty is first expressed in the words of the oath of office that state:

> I will support and defend the Constitution of the United States against all enemies foreign and domestic. . . . I will well and faithfully discharge the duties of the office. . . .
>
> (U.S.C. S16, 1958.)

Duty, then, for the military professional is service; service to country. to superiors, and to subordinates. The fundamental code considers that the leader is not working for himself, to advance his own fortunes, reputation, social status, or safety. Rather he is dedicating himself to the welfare of his unit, the support of his commander, and the execution of the responsibilities of his office in behalf of his country. That this element of the code has the sanction of law was shown in the words of the Commanding General, Sixth U.S. Army, in a reprimand to an officer found guilty of misbehavior in Korea.

> You have held personal safety and comfort above duty, honor, and country, and in so doing have deliberately violated your oath . . . as an officer of the United States Army.
>
> (Hq., Sixth Army, 1956)

Thus, under the concept of duty in the professional code, the military contract demands an almost unconditional subordination of individual interest, friends, or family to the performance of his duty and in fulfilling his responsibilities should such be required (Hackett, 1963).

Responsibility. Implicit in the concept of duty is a sense of responsibility. The primary distinguishing characteristics of a commander's role stems from his assumption of responsibility for all that his unit does or fails to do. Many of the leader's responsibilities are prescribed in regulations, field manuals, and job descriptions. Some are required by Federal law. Others are issued as directives from various headquarters. The Code of Conduct is an example of an expression of the requirements of duty as they apply to prisoners of war. Over and above the detailed prescribed duties lies the leader's moral obligation to further the mission of his assigned organization and to cooperate with and assist others in accomplishing their missions. This is a part of his overall moral responsibility to take all possible actions to enhance the security of the country through the use of his own talents, skills, or special knowledge.

Example. One of the foremost responsibilities of a leader is to serve as the example or model for his followers in everything that he does or is. The motto of the Infantry School, "Follow Me," clearly expresses the leader's duty of setting the example. Actually, the leader always sets an example, whether for good or bad. If group performance is to be good, the example set by the leader must be good. This is a moral obligation imposed by subordinates. They look to him for a model of what they ought to be. Not that they always reach the standard set if it is a high one, but many will be sure to outdo that standard if it is a low one. Both in his adherence to the professional code and in his personal conduct the effective leader must have the respect of his subordinates. Deviations from the strictest ethical behavior by an officer or leader are not easily forgotten or forgiven. The effectiveness of the leader is diminished by the degree of esteem he loses in the eyes of his followers.

Courage. One of the most dramatic ways a leader can lose esteem is to exhibit a lack of courage. The military profession places a high premium on this quality; it is a self-evident aspect of a leader's concept of duty. To lead a platoon in the attack, to fight off the advancing enemy even though outnumbered, this is the stuff of citations and decorations. Even leading or commanding a group of men with one's reputation and future hanging on their performance requires courage. The implicit demands of duty that require an officer to place his responsibilities and mission above the call of self-interest or friendship frequently require the exercise of courage beyond that called for in combat. This little-advertised aspect of moral courage is no less required than the physical type. It requires moral courage to stand up for an unpopular course of action when some of those opposed are one's seniors. It requires moral courage to take an unpopular action against one's subordinates when it has to be done. Yet duty requires just such decisions and just such courage of one's convictions. No effective military organization could exist were such courage lacking in its leaders.

Obedience. No organization can function effectively without the obedience of its members to the direction and will of the leader. One of the principal aspects of military character has always been the trait of habitual obedience to properly constituted authority. To be effective, this obedience must be prompt and willing; however, the responsiveness expected of the military professional is intelligent and discriminating rather than blind and unreasoning. The fast-moving situations of today put increased emphasis on knowing the reason and purpose behind orders and instructions. As much damage can result from exact compliance with instructions in inappropriate situations as from failing to take action at all.

Initiative. It is quite clear that the code expects much more of a leader than unquestioning obedience to orders. Situations change; unpredicted factors crop up. A leader must be able to analyze his orders in terms of the overall mission, referring any question to his superiors, if possible, or making the decision himself, if not. The action taken must be a serious requirement, however, and must be what the individual believes would have been the action of his superior had he been present and known all the facts. The leader's proper performance of duty requires almost unlimited use of his initiative. Far from inhibiting individual initiative, the professional code establishes the expectation that a leader who sees that something must be done will take action, if necessary, on his own authority. The result of many a battle has hung on the thread of acceptance of individual responsibility and the exercise of initiative.

Loyalty to Man. Intelligent obedience requires steadfast loyalty to superiors, peers, and subordinates. The more critical the task of the unit, the more pressures that are brought to bear on decisions and performance, the more critical is the loyalty of the members of the team. Loyal support of a superior does not imply supine acquiescence in his every suggestion or proposal. The most effective loyalty is displayed by the officer who assists his superior in arriving at the best possible decision. He then accepts that decision as his own and loyally carries it out without passing the buck. Some have questioned whether this loyalty is to a man or to an office. In most instances it is to the man acting in his official capacity in the office. It is not just to the man himself or to the office by itself. Thus, loyalty is extended to the policies, attitudes, and desires of the man who is in the office rather than being limited to his official pronouncements. In turn, no leader achieves the wholehearted loyalty of his peers or subordinates without being loyal to them. In this instance, the demands of duty are that the leader protect the welfare and interests of his peers and subordinates to the same or even greater degree than he would his own— that is, to the extent that the mission and situation permit. Loyalty as an aspect of leadership is a three-way orientation. Ideally, it must exist mutually between superiors, subordinates, and peers.

HONOR

A fundamental component of the military professional code through the ages has been that of honor. A soldier without honor has always been a sad thing indeed, and in today's military profession he is nearly useless as well. Both the cohesion and the solidarity of the combat unit in battle and the reliable and effective performance of the staff or logistic organization in the rear rest heavily upon the honor of its leaders at all levels. Honor can be said to be made up of several components. The first of these is integrity.

Integrity. The quality of saying what one means and meaning what one says, of being upright, honest, and sincere is a vital component of honor in the military code. Soldiers throughout the centuries have depended upon others to support them as they risked their lives in combat. They have always had to depend upon the word of their subordinates and superiors, and the proud boast of an officer has long been that his word and signature are his bond. Lives, careers, battles, and the fate of nations have hung upon the ability of military leaders to state all the true facts to the best of their knowledge, regardless of what effect these facts might have on themselves or others. Today the battlefield requirements for integrity are still present. In addition, the complex requirements involved in the development and procurement of costly weapons systems and in the international political policy area make the demand for integrity as great as ever. Subordinates must be able to trust their leaders implicitly. Nothing can disrupt the morale and effectiveness of an organization more quickly than an untrustworthy, quibbling, or temporizing leader. Cheating, violating a trust, sacrificing others for selfish interest, gaining unfair advantage; these are the cancers in a military society that must be rooted out wherever found, if that society is to retain its vitality and life. Personal integrity is an essential component of a successful leader's reputation.

Reputation. The influence and hence the effectiveness of a leader is largely determined by his reputation which, in part, is a reflection of his honor. His reputation with his superiors is critical to his career and determines the types of positions and missions he is given. His reputation with his associates and subordinates determines to a large extent his ability to get the job done. Reputation is the reflected image of his character and the standard of performance that others expect of him. It can be damaged by malicious gossip, hearsay evidence, or the unwitting ill-considered actions of the individual himself. For this reason, the professional code has always expected the leader to cherish his reputation and to do nothing that would tarnish its luster. Likewise, members of the profession are expected to avoid saying or doing anything that would unjustly reflect against the reputation of others. Weakening or tearing down the reputation of military leaders reflects against the profession as a whole, destroys the esteem in which it is held, and reduces its effectiveness.

Authority. The power of authority has a unique ability to corrupt and destroy the reputation of its holders. The temptations of authority and power are many: the use of power for its own sake, for enhancing individual ego, for furthering one's self-interests, for personal advancement, or for personal spite. All such corruptions of authority damage the honor of the leader and seriously weaken the military structure. The measured and proper use of authority is an integral part of leadership, closely related to a leader's honor.

Justice. The extensive authority that a military leader has over his subordinates makes his application of justice critical to the morale and welfare of the organization. Subordinates in a military organization expect to be treated fairly and impartially. Any hint of favoritism or misuse of authority quickly creates a lack of confidence in the leader and reduces his influence and his effectiveness. Hence, both reward and punishment must be meted out without bias and with absolute impartiality.

COUNTRY

Every citizen is expected to be loyal to his country. By entering the profession of arms and taking the oath of allegiance, however, the military leader undertakes a special obligation. The military leader is not only a member of a profession specifically designated to guard and protect the state, he is also a member of an organization that could do his country and its citizens the greatest amount of damage. Either by failing to live up to the professional code, and thus not performing as expected, or by taking actual steps to destroy or threaten its institutions, the military profession could violate its trust and become the enemy of the common good.

Loyalty to Country. The concept of patriotism and loyalty is easy to grasp. Every school child would probably say he knew what it meant. When the officer swears that "I will support and defend the Constitution of the United States against all enemies, foreign and domestic; and I will bear true faith and allegiance to the same," (U.S.C. S16, 1958), he has clearly established his primary loyalty. Nevertheless, questions of divided loyalty sometimes arise. In the natural course of events, loyalties tend to be strongest at the small-group level. Each individual belongs to several groups or organizations, some with strong ties of loyalty. The Civil War brought a specific problem of divided loyalties to the Regular officers from the South. Many of these, including Robert E. Lee, found that their loyalties to their state or region were stronger than to the Federal government and the Constitution they had sworn to defend. They solved their problem through resignation. Yet, many people at the time considered them to be traitors, while other considered them heroes and honorable men.

Problems of divided loyalty may appear today in different forms. Domestic disturbances that take on regional character could again raise the issue of loyalty to state before loyalty to country. Officers assigned to international agencies find that the clash of loyalties generated by conflicting national and international interests can be troublesome. It is in our national interest that our officers be assigned to such agencies. Frequently, however, they have to ask themselves whether their highest loyalty is to their country or to the international agency to which they are assigned. This is a complicated problem for which there are few precedents and no general agreements. Louis B. Sohn, Professor of International Law at Harvard, has stated his opinion that:

> The officer who becomes a permanent employee of the United Nations owes basic allegiance to it rather than to his native country. This rule would not apply, of course, to contingents temporarily given to the United Nations for short-term tasks.
>
> (As quoted in Reese, 1964, p. 37.)

Faced with a conflict of interest between the international authority and his national loyalty, an officer usually can ask for instructions. This does not always solve the problem, however. As international agencies and international command structures become more numerous, this area of conflicting loyalties can be expected to become more prominent.

Conflicting loyalties could occur in still another area, such as between the Constitution and some program of a specific administration. This problem has occurred rarely in this country, although it did happen in Nazi Germany when

Hitler required his army to take an oath of allegiance to him rather than to the country or to the constitution. As we have seen, the military code requires loyalty to one's duly constituted authorities, while the oath of office requires that officers support and defend the Constitution and by implication the laws of the land. Were some future chief executive to give instructions to the Army that were in violation of law or the Constitution, a moral dilemma could arise. In such an instance, it would be the responsibility of the courts to establish the legality of the order. Pending that decision, the leader would remain obligated to obey the orders of his superior unless they clearly violated the Constitution or existing law.

Civil-Military Relationship. With support of the Constitution and its processes as a basis, the military professional must now work out his relationships with the civilian agencies of government. George Washington set the example and pattern for dealing with the legislative branch of the government. Subsequent military commanders have been equally careful in their loyal support of the civilian secretaries who represent the Administration in providing guidance for military policy. The principle of civilian control over the military establishment is so firmly established as to be unquestioned.

Taking a commission or warrant does not mean that a leader ceases to have a political point of view. The professional code prescribes that the leader in his official position, or in fact in any role which could affect his official position, should remain totally neutral with regard to political parties and issues. Privately, he should vote according to his beliefs and desires. Publicly, he has a moral obligation to the men he leads not to influence or sway them by word or deed to support one party or another. The authority and sanctions available to military leaders in the chain of command are too strong to permit their use to influence the political allegiance of their subordinates. Further, each military leader can expect to serve under a number of different administrations composed of members of different parties. As long as he remains in the military service, he must be as loyal to one as to another. The confidence in which the military organization is held by the members of the administration depends in good measure on its political neutrality.

While the professional military leader must be neutral toward political parties and issues and fully responsive to the policy guidance of civilian authority, he is not excused from having a complete knowledge of the principles and operation of our government, as well as of current public issues involved. If he is to support the Constitution intelligently, he must know in some detail just how our system of government operates. Secondly, the ideological struggle over the past half-century has made mandatory the education of all military personnel on our system of government and on the issues that it faces. As the reaction of our prisoners of war in Korea tended to show, only too often our men have been inadquately prepared to defend themselves against the propaganda and psychological stratagems of their captors. A leader has the moral obligation not only to prepare himself to understand and support our constitutional system, but also to train and prepare his men to do likewise.

Support of Policy. The military organization is a part of the executive branch of the government. As such, it is required to execute public policy as defined by the President and his policy representatives in the Department of Defense. Occasionally, some of these policies may be unpopular among some or all of the members of the military service. It is immaterial whether the individual leader likes or believes in the policy. So long as it is clearly not illegal or immoral, he is bound by the professional code and his oath of office to execute that policy to the best of his ability, and to support it wholeheartedly before his subordinates. As the servant of the nation, he must do the nation's bidding whether he likes the nation's bidding or not. Since the military leader represents himself not as an individual but as an official of the government, he may not publicly oppose or protest.

AREAS OF POSSIBLE DIFFICULTY

The preceding discussion of various elements of the professional code has touched upon a number of problem areas. Some specific problems of a moral nature that a leader must face repeatedly during a military career are examined more fully below.

Integrity. Reporting. Full and accurate presentation of all the facts in administrative or operational reports is essential in the military structure. Reports form the basis for individual administrative actions, for the procurement of personnel and equipment, for the formulation of public policy, and for the preparation of combat operational plans. Information on the status of individuals, on the status of equipment, on the location or actions of the enemy, on what occurred during a specific action or incident is reported from a variety of units. It is then consolidated, analyzed, and made the basis for high-level decisions involving millions of dollars and frequently thousands of lives. On some occasions, making an accurate report at a lower level might tend to cast the lower unit commander in an unfavorable light or suggest negligence or deficiency in accomplishing a mission expected of him. Many times it requires considerable moral courage to report facts which thus indicate poor performance by the maker of the report. It also requires considerable courage to report to a senior commander facts that he does not want to hear, even if they are true. Yet the issues are so critical that there must be no equivocating, quibbling, or evasion in the preparation of reports, verbal or written. Every inaccurate or untrue report weakens the military structure, damages its efficiency, and makes the system more susceptible to subsequent and even greater falsifications or inaccuracies.

Recommendations and Decisions. The necessity for making the best recommendations and decisions can challenge the moral courage of a leader. The military leader from corporal to general must make recommendations to his superiors on proposed actions or policies. Inevitably, moral issues arise. The leader faces the problem of weighing all of the considerations. Sometimes, the best recommendation may not be the most politic one. A practical and sound policy recommendation may be unpopular or contrary to his superior's stated preference. Occasionally, the leader faces the necessity of standing up for what he believes to be correct, even if it appears that he is bound to lose the decision and possibly the esteem of his superiors by doing so. Problems of this type become ever more critical as the leader increases in rank and responsibility. There is much pressure on the individual in this area and much rides on his decision. In the long run, the health of the military institution depends on each officer making his recommendations based on his own experience and professional knowledge. After carefully weighing the pros and cons, he should give his views objectively to his superiors, regardless of what he feels the views of others might be. If he is overruled, he should support the decision made. Until such a decision is made, he should support his own views as strongly as the merits of his particular position would indicate.

The superior's decision may still be unpopular. On these occasions the leader must avoid the easy way out by passing the buck of responsibility for the directive on the higher authority. The code prescribes that he should issue the directive and enforce it as if it were his own. This requirement is soundly based in practical necessity. If the men see their leader enthusiastically supporting the directive, their own response is likely to be much more positive.

Occasionally, the leader must take unpopular action on his own authority. Commanders at all levels frequently come face to face with the necessity for making a decision that is unpopular with some or all of their subordinates. Here again, he must have the moral courage to make the correct decision despite the fact that, by so doing, he might gain the temporary or even permanent disfavor of his subordinates.

Avoiding Blame. The leader frequently finds that some decision or action he took turns out poorly, often for reasons that he had not anticipated. In such cases, the natural instinct is to protect one's position or reputation by searching for some excuse or some way to transfer the blame to someone else. In fact, in some individuals this form of ego protection is almost automatic. For fairly obvious reasons, the military code expects a leader to assume full responsibility for his acts and decisions, even if they turn out to be mistaken or have undesirable results. Similarly, a commander is expected to assume responsibility for the failure of an individual or unit in his command, even though he himself was not directly involved in the act itself. The commander who shifts blame or censure on others for actions for which he is responsible will soon lose the respect of his subordinates and his effectiveness as a leader.

Expedience. Illegal or Immoral Orders. Adherence to the professional ethic by all officers normally protects subordinates in the chain of command from being faced with illegal or immoral orders. Problems of this nature tend to occur primarily in the higher levels of command where the issues are more ambiguous and the interpretation of applicable law or policy more uncertain. On rare occassions, a leader may receive instructions that he knows in fact to be illegal. Such an occasion might occur as the result of ignorance, indifference, or misinterpretation of law at a higher headquarters. Both the law and the code hold that a leader is responsible for his acts, as is the superior who gave him the orders. No leader, then, should execute an illegal order. By doing so, he becomes personally responsible for violating the law.

Orders that tend to violate public or international morality can raise more difficult questions, since these moral standards are not clearly defined and at times appear to be subject to considerable variation. The International Military Tribunal at Nuremberg tried accused Nazis for war crimes after World War II. It took the position that there was a recognized international morality and that a person could be found guilty of violating it, even though he was following the orders of constituted authority. Since that time, this concept has been expanded by efforts of the United Nations to codify these standards of international morality through international conventions, such as the one on Human Rights. The rapid expansion of weapons systems, particularly those involved in mass destruction, and the rise of revolutionary warfare and counterinsurgency raise problems revolving around the question of whether the ends justify the means. Faced with an enemy who employs torture, terrorism, blackmail, and subversion, there is a natural tendency to fight fire with fire and to employ similar methods to defeat him. It is all too easy to rationalize the situation by telling oneself that the end or objective is good; hence, one can be excused for unethical means in achieving it. The gaining of a short-run advantage, however, should not be allowed to compromise the long-run objective. The winning of a battle might mean the eventual loss of the peace. Unfortunately, in many cases, the moral outrage aroused by unethical behavior ends up by overshadowing or neutralizing any good there may have been in obtaining the objective. In other words, the ends sought cannot be separated from the means employed. The ends do not justify the means. Each action must stand on its own, regardless of how good the end result might be. Each leader issuing an order, or executing an order issued by a superior, is responsible for its morality as well as its legality, and should guide himself accordingly. If the action concerned is illegal, unethical, or immoral, it will stay that way even if the outcome sought might appear to be a positive gain for all. Countless years of experience shows that moral behavior produces the best results in the long run (Hazlitt, 1964, p. 354).

Situational Ethics. Today there is an increasing tendency, particularly on the part of youth, to belittle moral rules and to attempt to evaluate right and wrong based on the situation. Advocates of the so-called situational ethics claim that the inflexibility of existing moral rules tends to make them inapplicable and inappropriate in many cases. This situational approach has grave deficiencies when applied to the military ethic. The moral rules of the game create an expectation that members of the profession will behave in a specific way. Secondly, the moral acts of a military man have widespread implications. The individual who acts never knows how far these implications extend, how many people are affected, or what the end results might be. While these considerations apply to any moral code, they are particularly critical to the military profession with its extensive responsibilities.

Money Management. The military leader charged with money management responsibilities may not feel the code is realistically compatible with the business world of today. Occasionally, he may be tempted to renounce or modify the code for himself at the moment. The area of money management has always been fraught with great pressures and temptations. Where large sums of money are involved or business interests brought to bear, there is a possibility of conflict between the moral and ethical codes of the business world and those of the military profession. Club managers, officers in charge of various nonappropriated funds, and procurement officers are subject to these pressures and problems. All too often the unsuspecting officer finds himself in the position of being trapped into receiving favors from persons with whom he is doing business before he realizes that they fully expect something in return. What to them is a legitimate business expense in promoting the sale of their product, to the officer can be a concealed form of bribery that weakens his moral position of impartiality and objectivity in office. For this reason, the code, reinforced by law and regulation, protects the officer by requiring him not to place himself in the position of accepting personal favors from those with whom he is doing business or of allowing his personal interests to be involved or appear to be involved in these transactions. Frequently, the mere appearance of personal involvement can be as damaging to his position as actual involvement.

Concern for Property. The exigencies of the moment, both in combat and garrison, place many pressures and temptations on those in charge of the management of supplies and equipment. It is an easy matter for a leader to slight materiel management under the pressure of a crisis. Although the leader's primary problem is the influencing and managing of people, he also has a positive role in managing and using property. Moral issues arise even in materiel management. The professional leader, like the sentry on guard, takes charge of his post and all government property in view. In many cases he is actually charged with personal responsibility for it. There are many regulations and procedures prescribed for the care, safeguarding, procurement, and disposal of government property. These rules are established to provide for the most efficient use of the property, to enable it to be readily available when needed, and to be disposed of when not needed.

On some occasions the pressure to obtain results in an inspection or competition or to improve the welfare or efficiency of a unit tempts military personnel to violate prescribed procedures in procuring equipment or in disposing of it. Borrowing or expropriating the property of another unit, or hiding excess equipment in order to present an equipment status picture different from that which is actually the case are typical examples of violations. Such actions are more than mere violations of procedures; they are morally indefensible. First, they are dishonorable deceptions in that they tend to present a picture of good management and readiness that, in fact, is not the case. Secondly, such actions tend to enhance unjustly the reputation or effectiveness of one unit at the expense of another. In the third place, it is an improper and weak substitute for the proper supply action and will ultimately cause somebody else to pay for the poor administrative procedures of the unit in question.

Another problem area in this field is the conversion of government property to private or personal use. All government property, vehicles, tools, weapons, or bedding, were procured for specific purposes and are expected to be used for them. Some leaders are tempted to use this equipment for their own personal advantage. This temptation should be resisted. Succumbing to it in one instance tends to make future violations easier and to corrupt the integrity or the reputation of the leader.

There are many other situations in which moral or ethical questions arise in the conduct of the daily business of being a leader in the military service. In each case, adhering to the moral code, even though more difficult, will strengthen the position and enhance the reputation of the leader. Violating the professional code and succumbing to temptation will destroy his reputation, weaken his moral courage, and ultimately destroy his value as a leader.

SUMMARY

Institutional leadership reflects the moral foundations upon which the institution is built. The American military institutions are built primarily upon the moral concepts of Western society and its Judeo-Christian ethics, together with the modern democratic norms as expressed in the American Constitution. On this foundation, the professional moral code of the military service, because of the responsibility and critical nature of the profession, emphasizes certain aspects and demands higher standards than those of the general society. In addition to the moral commandments incumbent upon any individual, a man accepting a position of leadership in the Armed Forces is bound by the formal and informal codes of his profession. His oath of office and commission dictate that he meet specific ethical standards of conduct. These standards impose restrictions on the leader's behavior. By assuming the responsibility of leadership, the military leader assumes moral responsibility for the means used and the ends sought. In the process, he must face many moral problems concerned with these means and ends. By accepting the professional military ethic as his own, the leader not only finds it easier to cope with moral problems, but also supports and is supported by these professional standards. If the military profession of the United States is to retain its effectiveness and the public trust that it has so proudly held, each member must continue to hold these standards high.

REFERENCES

1. Duke, M.L., "The Lawful Order," *Proceedings*. U.S. Naval Institute, 92, July, 1966, pp. 82–90.

2. Hq., Sixth U.S. Army, General Court-Martial Order No. 14, 21 February 1956.

3. Janowitz, M., *The Professional Soldier*. Glencoe, Ill.: Free Press of Glencoe, 1960.

4. Ladd, J., *The Structure of a Moral Code*. Cambridge, Mass.: Harvard University Press. 1957.

5. Mackett, J.W., *The Profession of Arms*. London: Times Publishing Co., 1963.

6. Marshall, S.L.A., *The Officer as a Leader*. Harrisburg, Pa.: Stackpole Company, 1966.

7. Mazlitt, M., *The Foundations of Morality*. Princeton, N.J.: Van Nostrand, 1964.

8. Reese, T.H., "An Officer's Oath," Department of the Army Pamphlet 27-100-25, *Military Law Review*. Washington: U.S. Government Printing Office, July 1964.

9. Roskill, S.W., *The Art of Leadership*. Hamden, Conn.: Archor Books, 1965.

Ethical Issues of Military Leadership*

by
Kermit D. Johnson†

Earlier this year, I awoke at 0500 hours thinking about an ethics talk I was scheduled to give at the US Army War College Memorial Chapel. As I allowed my mind to wander in free association, I got more than I bargained for. I started out with a flashback of Vice-President Nixon's visit to the heavy mortar company I commanded on Okinawa in 1954.

It was pleasant to recall that my company had been selected for the Vice-President's visit because we consistently had the best mess on the island. However, this triggered a thought about my mess sergeant. For some unknown reason, he could come up with juicy steaks whenever they were needed, whether they were on the menu or not. I recalled that he had some contacts with the Air Force and apparently was involved in trading, but I never bothered to look into it.

My next thought was that trading in steaks really wasn't much different

---

*Reprinted from *Parameters,* Journal of the US Army War College, Vol. IV, No. 2, 1974, pp. 35–39, by permission of the Commandant, US Army War College, Carlisle Barracks, Pennsylvania.

†Colonel Kermit D. Johnson, Chaplain Corps, graduated from USMA in 1951 and was commissioned as a 2LT, Infantry. He first commanded an infantry platoon in the 82d Airborne Division, Ft. Bragg. He then saw combat in Korea with the 2d Infantry Division as a platoon leader and a company commander, and later commanded a heavy mortar company in the 29th Regimental Combat Team, Okinawa. COL Johnson received his Master of Divinity degree from Princeton Theological Seminary in 1960 and entered the Chaplain Corps. He has had Chaplain's assignments at Ft. Benning, West Point, in Germany and Vietnam. Currently he is the Post Chaplain at Carlisle Barracks.

from trading in bullet-proof vests. This brought to mind the supply sergeant of another company I commanded during the Korean War. He had no administrative ability whatever, but he always had a good supply of bullet-proof vests. The only thing that helped me out of Korea without supply shortages were those bullet-proof vests—valuable trading materials.

These uncomfortable thoughts, dredged from the semi-subconscious at five in the morning, formed the starting point for my thinking about the ethics of military leadership. But still another question forced itself upon me: "Is this the sort of thing which forms the substance of Watergate and mini-Watergates?"

With this as background, I can't pose as a flaming prophet or crusader in the ethical area. Maybe this is just as well. Perhaps in order to have an ethical consciousness we should be aware of our personal fallibility. In recent reading I've noticed this awareness in Abraham Lincoln's life. He was constantly at odds with puritanical moralists and idealists whom he could never please. Yet Lincoln knew very intimately what we are like as human beings. It came out in a comment he made about our judicial system as he quoted Thomas Jefferson, with approval: "Our judges are as honest as other men, and not more so. They have, with others, the same passions for party, for power, and the privilege of their corps."[1]

At the outset, I must admit that I am probably as silent, as tactful, as self-protective, and as non-risk taking and gutless as anyone else. Yes, I have been forced to take some clear-cut goal line stands—those Martin Luther deals where you say, "Here I stand. I can do no other," whether it's to the detriment of efficiency report, career, or whatever. However, this is exceptional.

On a day to day basis, the tightrope is a better metaphor. I believe that we walk a tightrope, constantly oscillating between the extremes of crusader and chameleon; both roles are difficult and we burn up a lot of energy attempting to walk the tightrope between these two positions. The crusader, to use a phrase of J.D. Salinger, seems to "give off the stink of piousness"[2] or self-righteousness. On the other hand, the chameleon is so non-principled that if you told him "A" was right one week and then that "non-A" was right the next week, he'd dutifully and loyally click his heels together and say "Yes, sir."

My own self-understanding, then, in discussing this matter of ethics is that of a tightrope walker caught alternately between the positions of crusader and chameleon—in one instance donning the uniform of a pure knight in shining armor and, at the other times, crawling into my chameleon skin of comfort and compromise. To the extent that others have felt this ethical tension, I hope this article will encourage fellow crusader-chameleons to surface those ethical issues with which we all struggle from day to day.

In the December 1973 issue of *Worldview*, Josiah Bunting, a former Army officer and a crusader type who wrote *The Lionheads*, refers to "the tyranny of the dull mind," which, he says, "one so often encounters in the military." But he's objective enough to speak also of "the tyranny of the gifted mind," and he says these types are more dangerous because they withhold their true judgments lest they jeopardize the hopes for success which their ambitions have carved out for them.

He quotes B.H. Liddell Hart, discussing British officers, at this point:

A different habit, with worse effect, was the way that ambitious officers, when they came in sight of promotion to the general's list, would decide that they would bottle up their thoughts and ideas, as a safety precaution, until they reached the top and could put these ideas into practice. Unfortunately, the usual result, after years of such self-repression for the sake of their ambition, was that when the bottle was eventually uncorked the contents had evaporated.[3]

What Hart is saying should not be limited to promotion to general. The process starts much earlier. I would have to agree that if we don't *now* expose the relevant ethical issues that affect our daily lives, when we become Chief of Staff or Chief of Chaplains and open up the bottle, we're going to find that there isn't any carbonation left, no zip. It will be gone. It simply can't be saved that long.

I would like to emphasize four pressing ethical issues for leaders in the military establishment to consider. The first is the danger posed by the acceptance of various forms of *ethical relativism,* or the blurring of right from wrong. It appears obvious that the erosion of a sense of right and wrong in the favor of a "no-fault" society poses a threat to sound ethical judgments.

A brilliant young major, now out of the Army, once told me that we can never say anything is right or wrong. He said very blatantly, "Everything is relative. There is no right or wrong." I then asked him if the killing of six million Jews in World War II was wrong and whether the actions of an Adolph Eichmann were wrong. He said, "Well, it depends on what was going on in Eichmann's mind." What basis does this man have for making ethical judgments with his belief that all is relative?

Less blatant but equally devastating to ethical judgments is a subtle and disguised form of ethical relativism practiced frequently in the military setting. It comes out of the tendency to have a functional or pragmatic attitude. I've heard Army officers say impatiently, "Hell, don't give me all that theory. I just want to know what works."[4] This, of course, *is* a theory—"what works is right." Such a hazardous ethical position is made worse by emphasis on getting the job done, no matter what. Performance of the mission is everything; therefore, the question of what is right often gets lost in the shuffle of practicality and necessity, if indeed ethical questions are even raised.

A second ethical issue every military leader should face is what I call the *loyalty syndrome.* This is the practice wherein questions of right and wrong are subordinated to the overriding value of loyalty to the boss. Loyalty, an admirable and necessary quality within limits, can become all-consuming. It also becomes dangerous when a genuine, wholesome loyalty to the boss degenerates into covering up for him, hiding things from him, or not differing with him when he is wrong.

General Shoup, former Marine Corps Commandant, once said something like this: "I don't want a 'yes' man on my staff, because all he can give back to me is what I believe already." Now for a leader to honestly say this and to attempt to carry it out, I would think he would have to be very secure. To turn it around, the less secure a leader is, the greater his need for pseudo-loyalty, that is, for fewer ideas that threaten his position. The simplest and quickest way he can get this type of loyalty is through fear. There is little doubt in my mind that fear is often a motivational factor in Army leadership, and also a major trouble spot in terms of ethical practice. This is confirmed in a study entitled *The United States Army's Philosophy of Management,* done by eight officers in the Army Comptrollership Program at Syracuse University. With reference to a survey of officers and civilians on managerial practices in the Army, the report said:

> From the statements concerning fear, one can conclude that the use of fear is perceived by a majority of respondents, especially the lower ranking respondents, to deeply pervade the Army's organization structure. Lower ranking respondents generally believe that managers are unwilling to admit errors and are encouraged to stretch the truth because of how fear operates within the system. They believe that fear itself and the life and death power of efficiency reports are the primary means used by their superiors to motivate subordinates' performance. When lower ranking officers are afraid to tell superiors about errors, embarrassing situations for the individual, the manager, and the organization can arise when the errors are finally disclosed. The persistence of fear as a stimulator of performance can have repercussions.[5]

This report says that "when lower ranking officers are afraid to tell superiors about errors" it is an "embarrassing situation." More than this, the use of fear to guarantee a sterile form of loyalty contributes to an environment where suppression of truth is guaranteed.

Concern about what might turn out to be an "embarrassing situation" leads into a third ethical trap on which we've been particularly hung-up for years in the Army, namely, the anxious worry over *image.* We frequently run scared; instead of acting upon what is right, we often hear: "You know, if we do this, it'll be embarrassing to the Army's image."

Whereas with the loyalty syndrome people are reluctant to tell the truth, with the image syndrome they aren't even interested in it. What becomes important is how things are perceived, rather than how things really are. Thus, a dream world of image is created which is often different from the world of reality.

Let's look at some quick examples:

- the former recruiting poster: not "Join the U.S. Army" but "The Army wants to join you." How true is it?

- A general at his new duty station who tells his information officer: "You're going to make me my next star."
- A unit commander who says: "This is the best unit in the U.S. Army," and yet refuses to seriously consider negative input.
- And what about our craze for "innovation"? How much of it is based on a desire for good publicity of catching our rater's eye with "dash and flash," and how much of it is based on the desire for quality and solid achievement in the unglamorous "bread and butter" items of our daily job?

As you read this, add examples from your own experience and you will probably arrive fairly close to my conclusion: at times, the obsession with image in the U.S. Army borders on institutional paranoia.

A fourth ethical trouble spot in our military experience involves *the drive for success.* This is the masochistic whip by which, sometimes, we punish ourselves and by which we sometimes are beaten sadistically by others.

In Vietnam, I escorted a speaker who was sponsored by the Department of Defense. I took him to see some of the best and the brightest of our leadership. On one occasion, I heard a high-ranking officer tell our visitor about a field grade officer who objected to the body count and to the wisdom of some current operations. The General to whom we were talking repeated gruffly what he told this field grade officer's superior: "Give 'em some candy and send 'em back up," In other words, you can buy off his ethical sensitivity—give him some medals and ribbons and send him back to his unit.

Compare this with a comment by one of the respondents in the section on "Integrity" from the *Study on Military Professionalism* done by the US Army War College in 1970: "One of the most violent reactions we got was from the body count, particularly from the young combat arms officers recently back from Vietnam . . . basically being given quotas, or if not given quotas, being told that their count wasn't adequate—go back and do it again."[6] "Give 'em some candy and send 'em back up." But at what price success or even survival?

The internally-generated drive for success which we all possess is compounded by the externally-demanded results which signal success. In one word this adds up to *pressure.* We have this in common with other professions. While reading a study of 1,700 executive readers entitled "How Ethical Are Businessmen?", conducted by *Harvard Business Review,* I found the following comments under the title "Pressure":

A controller resents "repeatedly having to act contrary to my sense of justice in order to 'please.' In upper middle management, apparently, one's own ethical will must be subordinated to that of interests 'at the top'—not only to advance, but even to be retained."

The sales manager of a very large corporation phrases his view most bluntly: "The constant everyday pressure from top management to obtain profitable business; unwritten, but well understood, is the phrase, 'at any cost.' To do this requires every conceivable dirty trick."

A young engineer testifies that he was "asked to present 'edited' results of a reliability study; I refused, and nearly got fired. I refused to defraud the customer, so they had others do it."[7]

It may be small comfort to realize that business leaders also experience pressures to buy off ethical sensitivity, through jeopardy of career advancement or retention. Yet one would hope for better standards in the military services where profit motive demands are absent, and where its members are dedicated to a lifetime of service to their country.

Interestingly enough, the *Harvard Business Review* study also indicated that there were pressures from bosses which helped employees to act ethically. The study concluded *if you want to act ethically, find an ethical boss.*[8]

Fortunately, there are a great many leaders in the Army who, by personal example, offer this ethical encouragement to others. However, while the Army neither compels its personnel to compromise their ethical principles nor condones unethical behavior, the importance of an institutional drive to push ethical leaders to the fore becomes significant since individuals cannot always choose their commanders. It also means building into the institutional structure and leadership training process such emphasis on ethics that leaders who use unethical methods will be exposed.

The task of building an ethical environment where leaders and all personnel are instructed, encouraged, and rewarded for ethical behavior is a matter of first importance. All decisions, practices, goals, and values of the entire institutional structure which make ethical behavior difficult should be examined, beginning with the following:

1. Blatant or subtle forms of *ethical relativism* which blur the issue of what is right or wrong, or which bury it as a subject of little or no importance.

2. The *exaggerated loyalty syndrome,* where people are afraid to tell the truth and are discouraged from it.

3. The obsession with *image,* where people are not even interested in the truth.

4. The *drive for success,* in which ethical sensitivity is bought off or sold because of the personal need to achieve.

Before being sentenced for his Watergate role, Jeb Stuart Magruder testified: "Somewhere between my ambition and my ideals I lost my ethical compass. I found myself on a path that had not been intended for me by my parents or my principles or by my own ethical instincts."[9] In the Army, we must insure that the ambition of the professional soldier can move him along the path of career advancement only as he makes frequent azimuth checks with his ethical compass.

END NOTES

1. Elton Trueblood, *Abraham Lincoln, Theologian of American Anguish* (New York· Harper and Row, 1973), p. 123.

2. J.D. Salinger, *Franny and Zooey* (Boston: Little, Brown, 1955), p. 159.

3. Josiah Bunting, "The Conscience of a Soldier," *Worldview* (December 1973), p. 7.

4. Scientific research by James W. Tyler in "A Study of the Personal Value Systems of U.S. Army Officers and a Comparison with American Managers," an unpublished University of Minnesota thesis in August 1969, has shown "first-order" values to be pragmatic ones such as high productivity, organizational efficiency, my boss, and achievement. "Second-order" values are ethical and moral values such as trust, honor, dignity, equality, etc. See US Army War College, *Study on Military Professionalism*, Carlisle Barracks, Pa., 30 June 1970, pp. B-6 and B-7.

5. Management Research Center Report, *The United States Army's Philosophy of Management*, Syracuse University, August 1972, p. 77.

6. US Army War College, *Study on Military Professionalism*, Carlisle Barracks, Pa., 30 June 1970, pp. B-1-10.

7. George A. Smith, Jr., *Business, Society, and the Individual* (Homewood, Ill.: Richard D. Irwin, 1962), pp. 59–60.

8 Ibid., p. 52.

9 *New York Times*, May 22, 1974, p. 37.

Index